CURVES

BC	Beginning of curve
	(PC) Point of curve
	(TC) Tangent to curve
BVC	Beginning of vertical curve
C	Chord
CS	Curve to spiral
D	Degree of curve
Δ (delta)	Deflection angle between tangents;
	also central angle of circular curve
E	External distance
EC	End of curve
	(PT) Point of tangency
	(CT) Curve to tangent
EVC	End of vertical curve
L	Length of curve
L_S	Length of spiral
M	Midordinate distance
PC	Point of curve
PCC	Point of compound curve
PI	Point of intersection
PRC	Point of reverse curve
PT	Point of tangency
PVI	Point of vertical intersection (grade-lines)
R	Radius
SC	Spiral to curve
ST	Spiral to tangent
T	Tangent
TC	Tangent to curve
TS	Tangent to spiral

CONSTRUCTION

Asph	Asphalt
BB	Batterboard
Bldg	Building
Blvd	Boulevard
CB	Catch basin
Chkd	Checked
Conc. culv.	Concrete culvert
Csp	Corrugated steel pipe
Dia	Diameter
Dwg	Drawing
Fdn	Foundation
Ftg	Footing
Hwy	Highway
Hyd	Hydrant
Inv	Invert
MH	Manhole (maintenance hole)
OG	Original ground
Rd	Road
San	Sanitary sewer
SS	Slope stake
Stm	Storm sewer
WM	Water main

ac	Acre
bbl	Barrel
cu ft	Cubic foot
cu in	Cubic inch
cu yd	Cubic yard
cwt	Hundred weight
ft	Foot or feet
fbm	Foot board measure
gal	Gallon(s)
in.	Inch(es)
lb	Pound
lf	Linear foot (feet)
mi	Mile(s)
mph	Miles per hour
psi	Pounds per square inch
sq ft	Square foot (feet)
sq in	Square inch(es)
sq yd	Square yard(s)
mf bm	Thousand foot board measure
m gal	Thousand gallons
yd	Yard(s)

METRIC UNITS

C	Celsius
cm	Centimeter
ha	Hectare
kg	Kilogram(s)
km	Kilometer(s)
kN	Kilonewton(s)
kPa	Kilopascal(s)
L	Liter(s)
m	Meter(s)
m^2	Square meter
m^3	Cubic meter
mm	Millimeter(s)
t	Tonne

SURVEYING
With Construction Applications

SURVEYING
With Construction Applications

Fourth Edition

Barry F. Kavanagh

Upper Saddle River, New Jersey
Columbus, Ohio

Library of Congress Cataloging-in-Publication Data

Kavanagh, Barry F.
    Surveying : with construction applications / Barry F. Kavanagh.—4th ed.
        p. cm.
    ISBN 0-13-027143-8
        1. Surveying. 2. Building sites. I. Title.
    TA625.K38 2001
    526.9—dc21

                                                              00-022294

Vice President and Publisher: Dave Garza
Editor in Chief: Stephen Helba
Executive Editor: Ed Francis
Production Editor: Christine M. Buckendahl
Production Coordination: Clarinda Publication Services
Design Coordinator: Robin G. Chukes
Cover Designer: Dean Barrett
Cover Photo: Index Stock
Insert Designer: Rod Harris
Production Manager: Pat Tonneman
Marketing Manager: Jamie Van Voorhis

This book was set in Times Roman by The Clarinda Company and was printed and bound by R. R. Donnelley & Sons Company. The cover was printed by Phoenix Color Corp.

10 9 8 7 6 5 4 3
ISBN: 0-13-027143-8

Preface

There have been many technological advances in surveying since *Surveying with Construction Applications* was first published. This fourth edition is up to date, with the latest in advances in instrumentation technology, field data capture, and data-processing techniques. Although surveying is becoming much more efficient and automated, the need for a clear understanding of the principles underlying all forms of survey measurement remains unchanged.

Accordingly, the general surveying principles and techniques used in all branches of surveying are presented in Chapters 1 to 9, while contemporary applications for the construction of most civil projects are covered in Chapters 10 to 16. In this way, not only is the text useful for the student, but also it can be used as ready reference for the graduate who may choose a career in civil design or construction. The glossary has been expanded to include new terminology.

Every effort has been made to remain on the leading edge of new developments in techniques and instrumentation, while maintaining complete coverage of traditional techniques and instrumentation. This edition features a completely revised and expanded chapter on Global Positioning System (GPS); this technology is rapidly replacing the more traditional techniques in positioning—affecting the way we perform control surveys, preliminary surveys, and especially construction layout surveys. New topics include point positioning and differential positioning using both code measurements and carrier phase measurements, continuously operating reference stations (CORS), real-time measurements, field techniques, and vertical positioning.

Although some of the older instruments (e.g., vernier transits, dumpy levels) are still in use in some college programs, they have been deemphasized in this edition—recognizing that technological advances have been so rapid that most new equipment now being purchased has been on the market for only a year or two.

The author, in addition to streamlining existing text matter, has included new material on electronic surveying in the areas of field coding, automatic target recognition, guide lights for the prism holder, typical field operations, and remote-controlled surveying. Chapter 7 covers the preelectronic surveying techniques for topographic surveying, whereas Chapter 5 covers the modern and more efficient field practices in electronic surveying.

With the conversion to metric practice now well underway in many U.S. federal and state projects, this text will be of particular value, as it continues to fully prepare surveying student for their careers in both imperial and metric practice.

In Appendix B, the reader will note a comprehensive list of Internet web sites for a wide variety of surveying activities.

Finally, in Appendix D, the author has included a broad selection of typical field projects designed to both complement and expand on the text presentation.

The surveying practioner now has to struggle to keep up with the amazing explosion of technology advances; it is the author's hope that students using this text will be completely up to date in this subject area as they continue with further education or as they seek employment in this rewarding field.

Acknowledgments

The author is grateful for the comments and suggestions offered by professors who have adopted the text for class use. Particular thanks are due to Professor Lynn Wallace of Brigham Young University, Utah; Mr. Henri B. Ayers, QLS, CLS, of Leica Canada; and Professor Carlos J. Lara of SIAST Saskatchewan for their assistance with the text and with the Solutions Manual. James L. Otter of Pittsburgh State University and David Zenk of Dunwoody Institue deserve a note of appreciation for reviewing this edition. Additionally thanks are due the faculty and staff of the Civil/Resources Department, Seneca College, for their generous assistance and support.

The following surveying, engineering, and equipment manufacturing companies provided generous assistance:

American Association of State Highway and Transportation Officials (AASHTO), Washington, D.C.
American Augers Inc., Wooster, Ohio
American Concrete Pipe Association, Vienna, Virginia
American Congress on Surveying and Mapping, Bethesda, Maryland
American Society of Civil Engineers, New York, New York
Barber-Greene Co., Aurora, Illinois
J. D. Barnes, Ltd., Surveyors, Markham, Ontario
Cansell Surveying Equipment Co., Toronto, Ontario
J. I. Case Co., Chicago, Illinois
Caterpillar Inc., Peoria, Illinois
Cooper Tool Group (Lufkin Tapes), Barrier, Ontario
Corrugated Steel Pipe Association, New York, New York
Corvallis MicroTechnology, Inc., Corvallis, Oregon
CST Corporation, Watseka, Illinois
John Deere, Ltd., Grimby, Ontario
David Evans and Assoicates, Inc. Portland, Oregon

Geodimeter of Canada, Toronto, Ontario
Geomatics Canada, Ottawa, Ontario
Laser Alignment Co., Grand Rapids, Michigan
Leica Canada Ltd., Toronto, Ontario
Leica Geosystems, Norcross, Georgia
Magellan Systems Corporation (Ashtec), San Dimas, California
Marathon Letourneau Co., Longview, Texas
Marshall, Macklin, Monoghan, Surveyors and Engineers, Markham, Ontario
M. F. Industrial, Manchester, England
Ministry of Transportation, Toronto, Ontario
National Geodetic Survey (NGS), Rockville, Maryland
National Swedish Institute for Building Research, Sweden
Nikon, Inc., Melville, New York
Pacific Crest Corporation, Santa Clara, California
Pentax Corporation, Englewood, Colorado
Position Inc., Calgary, Alberta
Puckett Brothers Manufacturing Co. Inc., Lithonia, Georgia
Roads and Transportation Association, Ottawa, Canada
The Robbins Co., Kent, Washington
Schreiber Instruments Inc., Denver, Colorado
Sokkia Canada, Markham, Ontario
Sokkia Corporation, Overland Park, Kansas
Spectra Physics, Dayton, Ohio
Topcon Instrument Corporation, Paramus, New Jersey
Toronto Department of Roads and Traffic, Toronto, Ontario
Trimble Navigation, Sunnyvale, California
Tripod Data Systems, Corvallis, Oregon
VME Americas, Inc., Cleveland, Ohio
David White Instruments, Germantown, Wisconsin
Wild Heerbruug, Heerbruug, Switzerland
Carl Zeiss, Oberkochen, Germany
Carl Zeiss, Inc., Thornwood, New York

Contents

PART II CONSTRUCTION APPLICATIONS   341

10 *Highway Curves*   *345*

Field Note Index

PART I
Surveying Principles

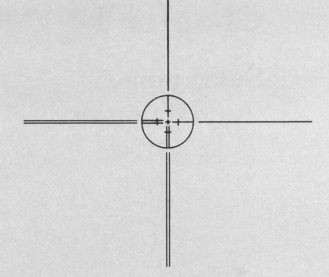

Part I introduces students to traditional and state-of-the-art techniques of data collection, layout, and presentation of field data. Chapter 1 provides an abbreviated historical perspective of surveying techniques and instrumentation.

Distance measurement is covered in the chapters on taping (Chapter 2), electronic surveying (Chapter 5), and stadia surveying (Chapter 7). Elevation determination is covered in the chapters on leveling (Chapter 3), electronic surveying (Chapter 5), stadia surveying (Chapter 7), and Global Positioning Systems (GPS) (Chapter 9). Data presentation is covered in survey drafting (Chapter 7) and digital plotting (Chapter 5). Angle measurements and geometric analysis of field measurements are covered in Chapter 4, Transits and Theodolites, and Chapter 6, Traverse Surveys.

Horizontal positioning, a relatively new concept, is covered in Chapter 9, Global Positioning Systems (GPS). Finally, control for both data-gathering surveys and layout surveys is covered in Chapter 8.

Although distance measurement has been largely dominated by electronic distance measurement (EDM) techniques, there are still many applications for steel taping on short-distance measurements, as are often found in construction layouts. Procedures such as stadia are almost obsolete (replaced by EDM), but are given complete coverage in the text because many colleges use a stadia project to introduce topographic surveys and to provide an opportunity for students to develop hands-on skills with transits and theodolites.

Chapter 1

Surveying Fundamentals

1-1 Surveying Defined

Surveying* is the art and science of making field measurements on or near the surface of the earth. Survey field measurements include horizontal and slope distances, vertical distances, and horizontal and vertical angles. In addition to taking measurements in the field, the surveyor can derive related distances and directions through geometric and trigonometric analysis.

Since the 1980s, the term **geomatics** has come into popular usage to describe the computerization and digitization of data collection, data processing, data analysis, and data output. Geomatics includes traditional surveying as its cornerstone, but also reflects the now-broadened scope of measurement science and information technology. Figure 5-37, computerized surveying data system, gives the reader a sense of the diversity of the integrated scientific activities now covered by the term *geomatics.*

The vast majority of engineering and construction projects are so limited in geographic size that the surface of the earth is considered to be a plane for all *X* (east) and *Y* (north) dimensions. *Z* dimensions (height) are referred to some datum, usually mean sea level. Surveys that ignore the curvature of the earth are called **plane surveys.** Surveys that cover a large geographic area—for example, state or provincial boundary surveys—must have corrections made to the field measurements so that these measurements will reflect the curved (ellipsoidal) shape of the earth; these surveys are called **geodetic surveys.** The *Z* dimensions (heights) in geodetic surveys are also referenced to a datum—usually mean sea level.

Traditional geodetic surveys were very precise surveys of great magnitude—for example, national boundaries, control networks. Modern surveys (data-gathering, control, and layout) utilizing Global Positioning Systems (GPS) (satellite surveying) are also based

***Boldface** is used in this text either to identify terms that are especially important or to give extra emphasis. *Italics* is used for regular emphasis.

on the geometric shape of the earth; such survey measurements must be mathematically translated to be of use in leveling and other local surveying projects.

Engineering or construction surveys that span long distances (e.g., highways, railroads) are treated as plane surveys, with corrections for curvature being applied at regular intervals (e.g., at 1-mile intervals or at township boundaries).

Engineering surveying* is defined as those activities involved in the planning and execution of surveys for the *location, design, construction,* maintenance, and operation of civil and other engineered projects. Such activities include

1. Preparation of surveying and related mapping specifications.
2. Execution of photogrammetric and field surveys for the collection of required data, including topographic and hydrographic data.
3. Calculation, reduction, and plotting (manual and computer-aided) of survey data for use in engineering design.
4. Design and provision of horizontal and vertical control survey networks.
5. Provision of **line and grade** and other layout work for construction and mining activities.
6. Execution and certification of quality control measurements during construction.
7. Monitoring of ground and structural stability, including alignment observations, settlement levels, and related reports and certifications.
8. Measurement of material and other quantities for inventory, economic assessment, and cost accounting purposes.
9. Execution of as-built surveys and preparation of related maps, plans, and profiles upon completion of the project.
10. Analysis of errors and tolerances associated with the measurement, field layout, and mapping or other plots of survey measurements required in support of engineered projects.

Engineering surveying **does not** include surveys for the retracement of existing land ownership boundaries or the creation of new boundaries; these activities are reserved for licensed property surveyors—also known as land surveyors or cadastral surveyors.

1-2 Surveying: General

Surveys are usually performed for one of two reasons. First, surveys are made to collect data, which can then be drawn to scale on a plan or map (preliminary surveys); second, surveys are made to lay out dimensions shown on a design plan in order to precisely define the field location for the proposed construction facility. The layouts of proposed property lines and corners as required in land division are called **layout surveys;** the layouts of proposed construction features are called **construction surveys. Preliminary** and **construction** surveys for the same area must have this one thing in common: Measurements for both surveys must be referenced to a common base for X, Y, and Z dimensions. The establishment of a base for horizontal and vertical measurements is known as a **control survey.**

*Definition adapted from the definition of engineering surveying as given by the American Society of Civil Engineers (ASCE) in their *Journal of Surveying Engineering* in 1987.

1-3   Control Surveys

Control surveys establish reference points and reference lines for preliminary and construction surveys. Vertical reference points, called **benchmarks,** are established using leveling surveys (Chapter 3). Horizontal control surveys can be tied into (1) state or provincial coordinate grid monuments, (2) property lines, (3) roadway centerlines, and (4) arbitrarily placed baselines or grids. These topics are discussed in some detail in Chapter 8.

1-4   Preliminary Surveys

Preliminary surveys (also known as preengineering surveys, location surveys, or data-gathering surveys) are used to collect measurements showing the location of natural features, such as trees, rivers, hills, valleys, and the like, and the location of man-made features, such as roads, structures, pipelines, and so forth. Measured tie-ins can be taken by any of the following techniques.

1-4-1   Rectangular Tie-Ins

The rectangular tie-in (also known as the right-angle offset tie) is one of the most widely used field location techniques. This technique, when used to locate point P [see Figure 1-1(a)] to baseline AB, requires distance AC (or BC), where C is on AB @ 90 degrees to point P, and it also requires measurement CP.

1-4-2   Polar Tie-Ins

Polar tie-ins (also known as the angle/distance technique) are now the most widely used location technique. Here, point P is located from point A on baseline AB by measuring angle θ and distance AP. See Figure 1-1(b) and Sections 7-5 to 7-8—stadia surveys.

1-4-3   Intersection Tie-Ins

This technique is useful in specialized location surveys. Point P [Figure 1-1(c)] is located to baseline AB either by measuring angles from A and B to P or by swinging out arc lengths AP and BP until they intersect. The angle intersection technique is useful for nearshore

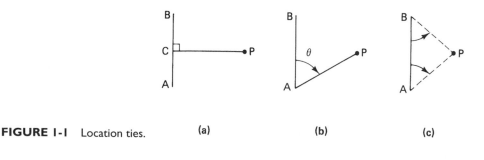

FIGURE 1-1   Location ties.   (a)   (b)   (c)

marine survey tie-ins; the distance arc intersection technique is a good method of replacing "lost" survey points from preestablished reference ties.

1-4-4   Positioning Tie-Ins

Topographic features can also be "tied in" using GPS survey techniques (see Chapter 9). Point *P* could be located by simply holding a pole-mounted GPS receiver/antenna directly on the point.

1-5   Construction Surveys

Construction surveys provide *line and grade* for a wide variety of construction projects —for example, highways, streets, pipelines, bridges, buildings, and site grading. The construction layout marks the horizontal location *(line)* as well as the vertical location or elevation *(grade)* for the proposed work. The contractor can measure from the surveyor's markers to the exact location of each component of the facility to be constructed. Layout markers can be wood stakes, steel bars, nails with washers, spikes, chiseled marks in concrete, and so forth.

When commencing a construction survey, it is important that the surveyor use the same control survey points as were used for the preliminary survey on which the construction design was based.

1-6   Distance Measurement

Distances between two points can be *horizontal, slope,* or *vertical* and are recorded in feet or meters. See Figures 1-2 and 1-3.

Horizontal and *slope* distances can be measured with a cloth or steel tape or with an electronic distance measuring device. In surveying, the horizontal distance is always required for plan-plotting purposes; a distance measured on slope can be trigonometrically converted to its horizontal equivalent by using either the slope angle or the difference in elevation (vertical distance) between the two points.

Vertical distances can be measured with a tape, as in construction work, or, as is more usually the case, with a surveyors' level and rod. See Figures 1-4 and 1-5.

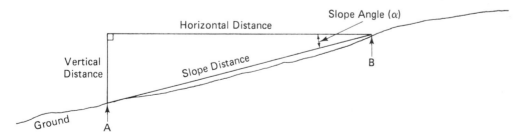

FIGURE 1-2   Distance measurement.

FIGURE 1-3 Preparing to measure to a stake tack, using a plumb bob and steel tape.

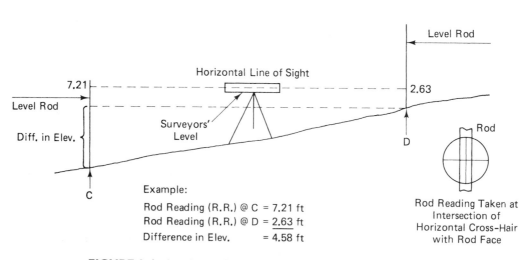

Example:

Rod Reading (R.R.) @ C = 7.21 ft
Rod Reading (R.R.) @ D = 2.63 ft
Difference in Elev.   = 4.58 ft

Rod Reading Taken at
Intersection of
Horizontal Cross-Hair
with Rod Face

FIGURE 1-4 Leveling technique.

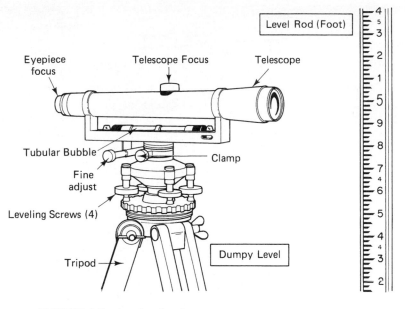

FIGURE 1-5   Level and rod.

1-7   Angle Measurement

Horizontal and vertical angles can be measured with a transit or theodolite. Engineers' transits typically measure to the closest minute or 30 seconds, whereas theodolites are manufactured to read angles to the closest minute, 20 seconds, 10 seconds, 6 seconds, or 1 second. Figure 1-6(a) shows a 1-minute transit together with a 20-second optical theodolite; Figure 1-6(b) shows a 20-second electronic theodolite.

Slope angles can also be measured with a clinometer (see Chapter 2); the precision of this instrument is typically 10 minutes.

1-8   Units of Measurement

Although the foot system of measurement has been in use in the United States from the early settler days until the present, the metric system has been making steady inroads. The Metric Conversion Act of 1975 made conversion to the metric system largely voluntary, but subsequent amendments and government actions have now made mandatory the use of the metric system for all federal agencies, as of September 1992. By January 1994, the metric system was required in the design of many federal facilities; additionally, many states' departments of transportation have already commenced the switch over to the metric system for fieldwork and highway design.

The complete changeover to the metric system will take many years—perhaps several generations. The impact of all of this on the American surveyor is that, from now on, most surveyors will have to be proficient in **both** the foot and the metric systems.

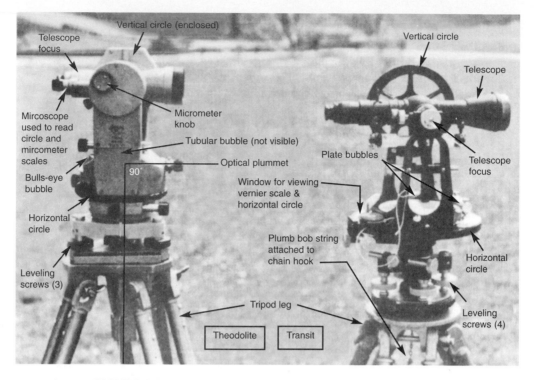

FIGURE 1-6(a) Optical theodolite and vernier transit.

Additional equipment costs in this dual system are mostly limited to measuring tapes and leveling rods.

System International (SI) units are a modernization (1960) of the long-used metric units. This modernization included a redefinition of the **meter** (international spelling: metre) and the addition of some new units (e.g., newton; see Table 2-1). With the United States committed to switching to metric units, all industrialized nations on earth are now using the metric system.

Table 1-1 describes and contrasts metric and foot units. Degrees, minutes, and seconds are used almost exclusively in both metric and foot systems; however, in some European countries, the circle has also been graduated into 400 gon (also called grad). Angles, in that system, are expressed to four decimals (e.g., a right angle = 100.0000 gon).

1-9 Stationing

In surveying, measurements are often taken along a baseline and at right angles to that baseline. Distances along a baseline are referred to as **stations** or **chainages,** and distances at right angles to the baseline (offset distances) are simple dimensions. The beginning of the survey baseline—the zero end—is denoted as 0 + 00; a point 100 ft (m) from the zero end is denoted as 1 + 00; a point 156.73 ft (m) from the zero end is 1 + 56.73; and so on.

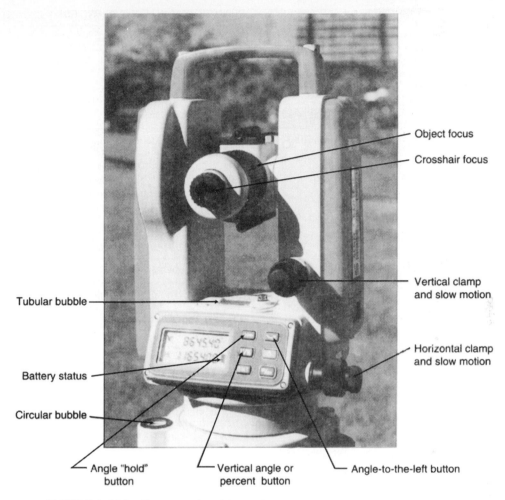

FIGURE 1-6(b)   Electronic theodolite.

In the preceding discussion, the *full stations* are at 100-ft (m) intervals, and the *half stations* are at even 50-ft (m) intervals. Twenty-meter intervals are often used as the key partial station in the metric system for preliminary and construction surveys.

With the ongoing changeover to metric units, most municipalities have kept the 100-unit station (i.e., $1 + 00 = 100$ meters), whereas highway agencies have adopted the 1000-unit station (i.e., $1 + 000 = 1000$ meters).

Figure 1-7 shows a building tied in to the centerline (₵) of Elm St. and shows the ₵ (baseline) distances as stations and the offset distances as simple dimensions.

1-10   Types of Construction Projects

The first part of this text covers the surveying techniques common to most surveying endeavors, including mapping surveys, property surveys, and the like. The second part of the

Table 1-1 MEASUREMENT DEFINITIONS AND EQUIVALENCIES

Linear Measurements	Foot Units
1 mile = 5280 feet	1 foot = 12 inches
= 1760 yards	1 yard = 3 feet
= 320 rods	1 rod = 16½ feet
= 80 chains	1 chain = 66 feet
1 acre = 43,560 ft² = 10 square chains	1 chain = 100 links

Linear Measurement		Metric (SI) Units
1 kilometer	=	1000 meters
1 meter	=	100 centimeters
1 centimeter	=	10 millimeters
1 decimeter	=	10 centimeters
1 hectare (ha)	=	10,000 m²
1 square kilometer	=	1,000,000 m²
	=	100 hectares

Foot to Metric Conversion

1 ft	=	0.3048 m (exactly)	1 inch = 25.4 mm (exactly)*
1 km	=	0.62137 mile	
1 hectare (ha)	=	2.471 acres	
1 km²		= 247.1 acres	

Angular Measurement

1 revolution = 360°		1 revolution = 400.0000 gon	
1 degree	= 60′ (minutes)	(used in some European countries)	
1 minute	= 60″ (seconds)		

*Prior to 1959, the United States used the relationship 1 m = 39.37 in. This resulted in a U.S. survey foot of 0.3048006 m.

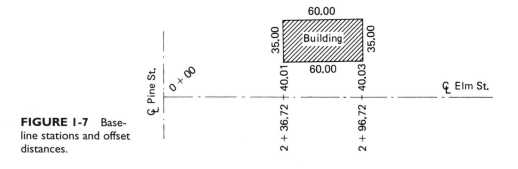

FIGURE 1-7 Baseline stations and offset distances.

text is devoted to construction surveying applications—an area that accounts for most surveying activity.

Listed below are the types of construction projects that depend a great deal on the construction surveyor or engineering surveyor for the successful completion of the project.

1. Streets and highways
2. Drainage ditches
3. Intersections and interchanges
4. Sidewalks
5. Buildings—high- and low-rise
6. Bridges and culverts
7. Dams and weirs
8. River channelization
9. Sanitary landfills
10. Mining—tunnels, shafts
11. Gravel pits, quarries
12. Storm and sanitary sewers
13. Water and fuel pipelines
14. Piers and docks
15. Canals
16. Railroads
17. Airports
18. Reservoirs
19. Site grading, landscaping
20. Parks, formal walkways
21. Heavy equipment locations
22. Electricity transmission lines

1-11   Errors—Random and Systematic

An error is the difference between a measured, or observed, value and the "true" value. Since no measurement can be performed *perfectly* (except for counting), it follows that every measurement must contain some error. Errors can be minimized to an acceptable level by the use of skilled techniques and appropriately precise equipment.

For the purposes of calculating errors, the "true" value of a dimension is determined statistically after repeated measurements have been taken.

Systematic errors are defined as being those errors for which the magnitude and the algebraic sign can be determined. The fact that these errors can be determined allows the surveyor to eliminate them from the measurements and thus further improve the accuracy. An example of a systematic error is the effect of temperature on a steel tape. If the temperature is quite warm, the steel will expand, causing the tape to be longer than normal—for example, at 83°F a 100-ft steel tape will expand to 100.01 ft, a systematic error of 0.01 ft. The surveyor knowing of this error can simply subtract 0.01 ft each time the tape is used at that temperature.

Random errors are associated with the skill and vigilance of the surveyor. Random errors (also known as accidental errors) are introduced into each measurement mainly because no human can perform perfectly.

Random errors can be illustrated by the following example: Say point *B* is to be located a distance of 109.55 ft from point *A*. Since the tape is only 100.00 ft long, an intermediate point must first be set at 100.00 ft, and then 9.55 ft must be measured from the intermediate point. Random errors will occur as the surveyor is marking out 100.00 ft. The actual mark may be off a bit—that is, the mark may actually be made at 99.99 or 99.98, and so on. When the final 9.55 ft are measured out, two more opportunities for error exist: The lead surveyor will have the same opportunity for error as existed at the 100.00 mark, and the rear surveyor may introduce a random error by inadvertently holding something other than 0.00 ft on the intermediate mark—for example, 0.01.

This example illustrates two important characteristics of random errors. First, the magnitude of the random error is unknown; second, since the surveyor is estimating too high (or too far right) on one occasion and probably too low (or too far left) on the next occasion, over the long run random errors will tend to cancel out.

A word of caution: Large random errors, possibly due to sloppy work, will also tend to cancel out, giving the appearance of accurate work to work that could be highly inaccurate.

1-12   Accuracy and Precision

Accuracy is the relationship between the value of a measurement and the "true" value of the dimension being measured; the greater the accuracy, the smaller the error.

Precision describes the degree of refinement with which the measurement is made; for example, a distance measured four times with a steel tape by skilled personnel will be more precise than the same distance measured twice by unskilled personnel using a cloth tape.

The **accuracy ratio** of a measurement or a series of measurements is the ratio of the error of closure to the distance measured. The error of closure is the difference between the measured location and its theoretically correct location.

Since relevant systematic errors and mistakes can and should be eliminated from all survey measurements, the error of closure will normally comprise random errors.

To illustrate, a distance is measured and found to be 196.33 ft. The distance was previously known to be 196.28 ft. The error is 0.05 ft in a distance of 196.28 ft.

$$\text{Accuracy ratio} = 0.05/196.28 = 1/3926 \approx 1/3900$$

The accuracy ratio is expressed as a fraction whose numerator is 1 and whose denominator is rounded to the closest 100 units. Many engineering surveys are specified at 1/3000 and 1/5000 levels of accuracy; property surveys are often specified at 1/5000 and 1/7500 levels of accuracy. With the trend to polar layouts from coordinated control surveys, control measurements can be specified at 1/10,000 or 1/15,000 levels of accuracy. See Chapter 8 for various survey specifications.

1-13   Mistakes

Mistakes are blunders made by survey personnel. Examples of mistakes are transposing figures (recording a value of 86 as 68), miscounting the number of full tape lengths in a long measurement, and measuring to or from the wrong point.

Students should be aware that mistakes will occur. Mistakes must be discovered and eliminated, preferably by the people who made them. *All survey measurements are suspect until they have been verified.* Verification may be as simple as repeating the measurement, or verification may result from geometric or trigonometric analysis of related measurements.

As a rule, all measurements are immediately checked or repeated. This immediate repetition enables the surveyor to eliminate most mistakes and at the same time to improve the precision of the measurement.

1-14 Field Notes

One of the most important aspects of surveying is the taking of neat, legible, and complete field notes. The notes will be used to plot scale drawings of the area surveyed and also will be used to provide a permanent record of the survey proceedings.

Modern surveys, employing electronic data collectors, automatically store point positioning angles and distances, which will later be transferred to the computer. Surveyors have discovered that reliable field notes are also invaluable for these modern surveys. See also Section 5.10.

An experienced surveyor's notes will be complete without redundancies, well arranged to aid in comprehension, and neat and legible to ensure that the correct information is conveyed. Sketches will be used to illustrate the survey and thus remove possible ambiguities.

The field notes are placed in bound field books or in loose-leaf binders. Loose-leaf notes are preferred for small projects, as they are easily filed alphabetically by project name or by number. Bound books are used to advantage on large projects, such as highway construction or other heavy construction operations, where the data can readily fill one or more field books.

COMMENTS: BOUND BOOKS

1. Name, address, and phone number should be in ink on the outside cover.
2. Pages are numbered throughout.
3. Space is reserved at the front of the field book for title, index, and diary.
4. Each project must show the date, title, surveyors' names, and instrument numbers.

COMMENTS: LOOSE-LEAF BOOKS

1. Name, address, and phone number should be in ink on the binder.
2. Each page must be titled and dated, with identification by project number, surveyors' names and instrument numbers.

COMMENTS: ALL FIELD NOTES

1. Entries are to be in pencil in the range of 2H to 4H lead (lead softer than 2H will cause unsightly smears on the notes).
2. All entries are neatly printed. Uppercase letters can be used throughout, or they can be reserved for emphasis.
3. All arithmetic computations are to be checked and signed.
4. Although sketches are not scale drawings, they are drawn roughly to scale to help order the inclusion of details.
5. North arrows are placed so that they are pointing upward on the page.
6. Sketches are not freehand; straightedges and curve templates are used for all line work.
7. Crowding information on the page is one of the chief causes of poor-looking field notes.
8. Mistakes in the entry of measured data are to be carefully lined out, not erased.

9. Mistakes in entries other than measured data (e.g., descriptions, sums or products of measured data) may be erased and reentered neatly.

10. If notes are copied, they must be clearly labeled as such so that they are not thought to be field notes.

11. Lettering on sketches is to be read from the bottom of the page or from the right side; any other position is upside down.

12. Note keepers verify all given data by repeating the data aloud as they enter the data in their notes; the surveyor who originally gave the data to the note keeper will listen and respond to the verification call out.

13. If the data on an entire page are to be voided, the word VOID, together with a diagonal line, is placed on the page. A reference page number is shown for the new location of the relevant data.

1-15 Evolution of Surveying

Surveying is a profession with a very long history. Since the beginning of property ownership, boundary markers have been required to differentiate one property from another. Historical records dating to almost 3000 B.C. show evidence of surveyors in China, India, Babylon, and Egypt. The Egyptian surveyor, called the **harpedonapata** (rope-stretcher), was in constant demand as the Nile River flooded more or less continuously, destroying boundary markers in those fertile farming lands. These surveyors used ropes with knots tied at set graduations to measure distances.

Ropes were also used to lay out right angles. The early surveyors discovered that the $3:4:5$ ratio provided right-angled triangles. To lay out XZ at 90 degrees to XY (see Figure 1-8), a 12-unit rope would have knots tied at unit positions 3 and 7, as shown in Figure 1-8. One surveyor held the three-unit knot at X, the second surveyor held the seven-unit knot at Y, and the third surveyor, holding both loose ends of the rope, stretched the rope tightly, resulting in the location of point Z. These early surveyors knew that multiples of $3:4:5$ (e.g., $30:40:50$) would produce more accurate positioning.

Another ancient surveying instrument (see Figure 1-9) consisted of three pieces of wood in the form of an isosceles triangle with the base extended in both directions. A plumb bob suspended from the apex of the frame would line up with a notch cut in the midpoint of the base only when the base was level. These "levels" came in various sizes, depending on the work being done.

It is presumed that the great pyramids were laid out with knotted ropes, levels as described here, and various forms of water-trough levels for the foundation layout. These Egyptian surveying techniques were empirical solutions that were field proven. It remained for the Greeks to provide the mathematical reasoning and proofs to explain why the field techniques worked. Pythagoras is one of many famous Greek mathematicians; he and his school (about 550 B.C.) developed theories regarding geometry and numbers. They were also among the first to deduce that the earth was spherical by noting the shape of the shadow of the earth that was cast on the moon. The term **geometry** is Greek for "earth measurement," clearly showing the relationship between mathematics and surveying. In fact, the history of surveying is closely related to the history of mathematics and astronomy.

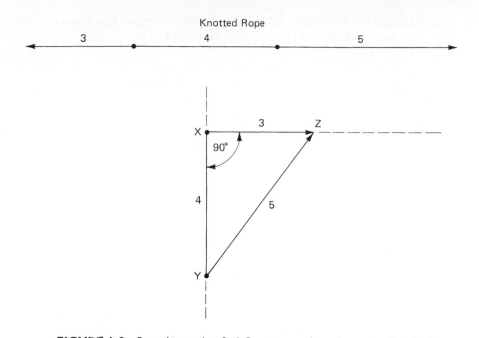

FIGURE 1-8 Rope knotted at 3:4:5 ratio—used to place point Z at 90 degrees to point X from line XY.

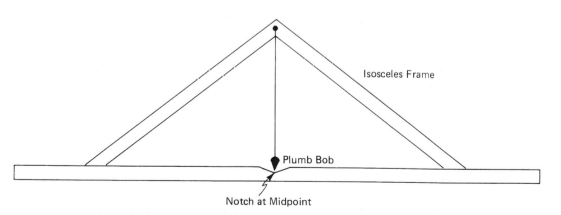

FIGURE 1-9 Early Egyptian level.

By 250 B.C., Archimedes recorded in a book known as the "Sand Reckoner" that the circumference of the earth was 30 myriads of stadia (i.e., 300,000 stadia). He had received some support for this value from his friend Eratosthenes, who was a mathematician and a librarian at the famous library of Alexandria in Egypt. According to some reports, Eratosthenes's technique was as follows: Eratosthenes knew that a town called Syene was 5000 stadia south of Alexandria. He also knew that at summer solstice (around June 21) the sun was directly over Syene at noon—there were no shadows. That condition was demonstrated by noting that the sun's reflection was exactly centered in the well water.

Eratosthenes assumed that at the summer solstice the sun, the towns of Syene and Alexandria, and the center of the earth all lay in the same plane (see Figure 1-10). At noon

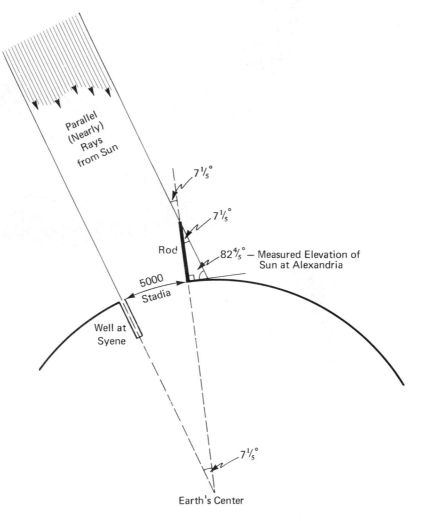

FIGURE 1-10 Illustration of Eratosthenes' technique for computing the earth's circumference.

on the day of the summer solstice, the elevation of the sun was measured at Alexandria as being 82 4/5 degrees. The angle from the top of the rod to the sun was then calculated as being 7 1/5 degrees. Since the sun is such a long distance from the earth, it can be assumed that the sun's rays are parallel as they reach the earth. With that assumption, it can be deduced that the angle from the top of the rod to the sun is the same as the angle at the earth's center—7 1/5 degrees. Since 7 1/5 degrees is 1/50th of 360 degrees, it follows that the circular arc subtending 7 1/5 degrees (the distance from Syene to Alexandria) is 1/50th of the circumference of the earth. The circumference of the earth is thus determined to be 250,000 stadia. If the stadia being used were 1/10 of a mile (different values for the stadium existed, but one value was roughly 1/10 of our mile), then it is possible that Eratosthenes had calculated the earth's circumference to be 25,000 miles. Using the Clarke Ellipsoid with a mean radius of 3960 miles, the circumference of the earth would actually be $C = 2 \times 3.1416 \times 3960 = 24,881$ miles.

After the Greeks, the Romans made good use of practical surveying techniques for many centuries to construct roadways, aqueducts, and military camps. Some Roman roads and aqueducts exist to this day. For leveling, the Romans used a **chorobate,** a 20-foot (approximate) wooden structure with plumbed end braces and a 5-foot (approximate) groove for a water trough; see Figure 1-11. Linear measurements were often made with wooden poles 10 to 17 feet long. With the fall of the Roman Empire, surveying and most other intellectual endeavors became lost arts in the Western world.

Renewed interest in intellectual pursuits may have been fostered by the explorers' need for navigational skills. The lodestone, a naturally magnetized rock (magnetite), was first used to locate magnetic north; later the compass would be used for navigation on both

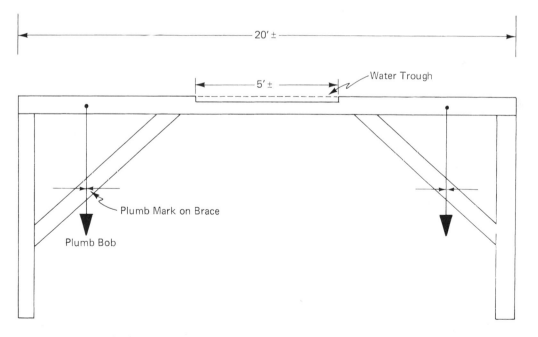

FIGURE 1-11 Roman level (chorobate).

land and water. In the mid-1500s, the surveyors' chain was first used in the Netherlands, and an Englishman, Thomas Digges, first used the term **theodolite** to describe an instrument that was graduated in 360 degrees and used to measure angles. By 1590, the **plane table** (a combined positioning and plotting device) was created by Jean Praetorius; it wasn't a great deal different from the plane tables used in the early 1900s. The telescope was invented in 1609 by Galileo (among others). The telescope, attached to a **quadrant** (angle-measuring device), permitted the technique of triangulation—a simpler method of determining long distances. Jean Picard (1620–1682) was apparently the first to use a spider-web crosshair in a telescope. He also used vernier scales to improve the precision of angular measurement. James Watt, inventor of the steam engine, is also credited with being the first to install stadia hairs in the survey telescope.

The first dumpy levels were created in the first half of the 1700s by combining a telescope with a bubble level. The repeating style of theodolite (see Section 4-5) was seen in Europe in the mid-1800s, but soon lost favor because scale imperfections caused large cumulative errors. Direction theodolites (see Section 4-6) were favored because high accuracy could be achieved by reading angles at different positions on the scales, thus eliminating the effect of scale imperfections. Refinements to theodolites continued over the years with better optics, micrometers, coincidence reading, lighter-weight materials, and so on. Heinrich Wild is credited with many significant improvements in the early 1900s that greatly affected the design of most European survey instruments produced by the Wild, Kern, and Zeiss companies.

Meanwhile, in the United States, William J. Young of Philadelphia is credited with being the first to create the transit [Figure 1-6(a)], in 1831. The transit differed from the early theodolites in that the telescope was shortened so that it could be revolved (transited) on its axis. This simple, but brilliant adaptation permitted the surveyor to produce straight lines accurately by simply sighting the backsight and transiting the telescope forward (see Section 4-10, Double Centering). When this technique was repeated—once with the telescope normal and once with the telescope inverted—many of the potential errors (e.g., scale graduation imperfections, crosshair misalignment, standards) in the instrument could be removed by averaging.

Also, when using a repeating instrument, angles could be quickly and accurately accumulated (see Section 4-4-6, Measuring Angles by Repetition). The transit proved to be superior for North American surveying needs. If the emphasis in European surveying was on precise control surveys, the emphasis in North America was on enormous projects in railroad and canal construction and vast projects in public land surveys, which were occasioned by the influx of large numbers of immigrants.

The American repeating transit was fast to use, practical, and accurate, and thus was a significant factor in the development of the North American continent. It wasn't until the 1950s and 1960s that the vernier transit received strong competition from European and Japanese repeating instruments characterized by micrometer or scale readouts (most with 10- or 20-second least count) and optical plummets. These optical instruments are now being replaced by electronic theodolites and total stations.

Electronic distance measurement (**EDM**) was first introduced by Geodimeter, Inc., in the 1950s and has largely replaced triangulation for control survey distance measurements and the steel tape for all but short distances in boundary and engineering surveys.

Aerial surveys became very popular after World War II. This technique is a very efficient method of performing large-scale topographic surveys and accounts for the majority of such surveys, although total station surveys are now competitive at lower levels of detail density.

In this text, reference is made to aerial photography in Chapter 10, Highway Curves; Chapter 11, Highway Construction Surveys; and Chapter 12, Municipal Construction Surveys. Aerial photography and the higher resolution satellite images can be manipulated to produce plans of very large geographic areas at a much reduced cost compared with field surveying techniques. See Kavanagh and Bird, *Surveying Principles and Applications,* 5th edition (Prentice Hall) for more on this topic.

The images captured on aerial photographs can be converted to scaled plans through the techniques of photogrammetry. The science of photogrammetry has undergone continuous advances. The latest techniques, called *digital* (or *softcopy*) *photogrammetry,* have greatly automated the photogrammetric process—scanning of aerial photos into the computer, aerotriangulation (for scale control), elevation mapping, digital terrain models (DTM) and digital elevation models (DEM), orthophoto products and mosaics, and planimetric features mapping. The need for the human element in photogrammetry has changed from the predominance of large numbers of highly skilled stereomachine operators to much fewer numbers of highly skilled data and process editors—an enormous improvement in efficiency. See Appendix F for illustrations of this emerging technology.

Satellite imagery has been used for many years to assess crop inventories, flood damages, and other large-scale geographic projects. As the resolution of satellite images is rapidly improving, remotely sensed data will be of use in many more applications, including civil engineering projects. An example of new developments occurred in early 2000 when the National Aeronautics and Space Administration (NASA) launched an *Endeavor* space shuttle whose mission was designed to map the earth using radar imagery.

In the late 1980s, the total station instrument was thought to be the ultimate in surveying instrumentation—electronic data collection of angles, distances, and descriptive data, with transfer to the computer and plans drawn by digital plotter, all on the same day. Now, with the wide use of **GPS** receivers and with the accompanying drop in costs, many more applications are being introduced (see Chapter 9). Perhaps in the future many large-scale control surveys and topographic surveys will be accomplished using these versatile positioning techniques.

Over the years, many different measuring units had been used, causing no end of confusion. An attempt to standardize weights and measures led to the creation of the metric system in the 1790s. To lessen ambiguity, it was agreed that the standard unit of length would be the meter (also spelled metre). The length of the meter was supposed to be one ten-millionth of the distance from the north pole to the equator. In 1866, the United States Congress made the use of metric weights and measures legal. The meter was equal to 39.37 inches, or 1 foot (U.S. survey foot) = 0.3048006 meter. In 1959, the United States officially adopted the international foot, where 1 foot = 0.3048 meter exactly. One U.S. survey foot = 1.000002 international feet. In 1960, the metric system was modernized and called the "System International d'Unites" (SI). (See Table 2-1 for selected unit comparisons.)

Chapter 2

Taping

2-1 Methods of Linear Measurement

Survey measurements can be acquired by using direct techniques, indirect techniques, or calculation. An example of a direct technique would be applying a graduated tape against the marks to be measured. An example of an indirect technique would be measuring the phase differences between the transmitted and reflected lightwaves used by the electronic distance measurement (EDM) instruments. An example of a calculated measurement would be when the desired measurement (perhaps over water) is one side of a triangle that has had the other sides and angles measured.

2-1-1 Pacing

Pacing is a very useful method of approximate measure. Surveyors can determine the length of pace that, for them, can be comfortably repeated. Pacing is particularly useful when one is looking for survey markers in the field; the plan distance from a found marker to another marker can be paced off to aid in locating that marker. Another important use for pacing is that of rough-checking all key points in a construction layout.

2-1-2 Odometer

Automobile odometer readings can be used to measure from one fence line to another as they intersect the road right-of-way. These readings are precise enough to differentiate rural fence lines and thus assist in identifying property lines. This information is useful when one is collecting information to begin a survey. Odometers are also used on measuring wheels that are simply rolled along the ground on the desired route; this approximate technique is employed where low-order precision is acceptable—for example, property frontages are often checked this way by surveyors from the assessor's office.

2-1-3   Stadia

Techniques that indirectly provide required measurements are called *tacheometry*. Stadia is a form of tacheometry that utilizes a telescopic crosshair configuration to assist in determining distances and elevations. Stadia is covered in detail in Chapter 7.

2-1-4   Electronic Distance Measurement (EDM) Instruments

EDM instruments function by sending a lightwave or microwave along the path to be measured and then measuring the phase difference between transmitted and received signals (microwaves), or measuring the phase difference required in returning the reflected lightwave to its source. EDM instruments and related tacheometric techniques are described in Chapter 5.

2-1-5   Subtense Bar

A subtense bar is a tripod-mounted bar having targets precisely 2.000 m apart. The targets are kept precisely 2.000 m apart by the use of invar wires under slight tension. The subtense bar (also a form of tacheometry) is positioned over the point and then positioned perpendicular to the survey line. A theodolite (1-second capability) is used to measure the angle between the targets—the longer the distance, the smaller the angle. This technique is accurate (1/5000) at short distances—that is, less than 500 ft. This instrument was used to obtain distances over difficult terrain—for example, across freeways, across water or steep slopes. See Figure 2-1. Field use of this instrument has declined with the advent and proliferation of EDM instruments. Subtense bars are now being used for calibrating baselines in electronic coordinate determination—a fairly recently developed technique of precise positioning using two or more electronic theodolites interfaced to a computer used, for example, to position robotic welding machines on automobile assembly lines.

2-2   Gunter's Chain

The measuring device in popular usage during the time of the settlement of North America (eighteenth and nineteenth centuries) was the Gunter's chain, which was 66 ft long and

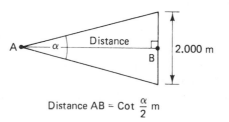

Distance AB = Cot $\frac{\alpha}{2}$ m

FIGURE 2-1   Subtense bar.

subdivided into 100 links. This chain, named after its inventor, was uniquely suited for work in English units:

$$80 \text{ chains} = 1 \text{ mile}$$
$$10 \text{ sq chain} = 1 \text{ acre } (10 \times 66^2 = 43{,}560 \text{ ft}^2)$$
$$4 \text{ rods} = 1 \text{ chain}$$

The original surveys for most of North America were performed by surveyors using Gunter's chains. Most of the continent's early legal plans and records contain dimensions in chains and links. Present-day surveyors occasionally must use these old plans and must make conversions to feet or meters.

■ EXAMPLE 2-1
An old plan shows a dimension of 5 chains, 32 links. Convert this value to (a) feet and (b) meters.

(a) $5.32 \times 66 = 351.12$ ft

(b) $5.32 \times 66 \times 0.3048 = 107.02$ m

2-3   Tapes

Woven tapes made of linen, Dacron, and the like can have fine copper strands interwoven to provide strength and to limit deformation due to long use and moisture. See Figure 2-2. Measurements taken near electric stations should be made by dry nonmetallic or fiberglass tapes. Fiberglass tapes have now come into widespread use.

All tapes come in various lengths, the 100-ft and 30-m tapes being the most popular, and are used for many types of measurements where high precision is not required. All woven tapes should be periodically checked (e.g., against a steel tape) to verify their precision.

Many tapes are now manufactured with foot units on one side and metric units on the reverse side. Foot unit tapes are graduated in feet, 0.10 ft, and 0.05 ft or in feet, inches, and 1/4-inches. Metric tapes are graduated in meters, centimeters (0.01 m), and 1/2-centimeters (0.005 m).

2-4   Steel Tapes

Steel tapes are manufactured in both foot and metric units and come in a variety of lengths, graduations, and unit weights (see Figure 2-3). Foot unit tapes commonly used are 100-, 200-, and 300-ft lengths, the 100-ft length being the most widely used.

Metric unit tapes commonly used are the 20-, 30-, 50-, and 100-m lengths; the 30-m length is the most widely used, as it closely resembles the 100-ft length in field characteristics.

Generally, lightweight tapes are graduated throughout and are used on the reel; heavier tapes are designed for use off the reel (drag tapes) and do not have continuous small-interval markings (see Figure 2-3). Drag tapes are popular in route surveys (high-

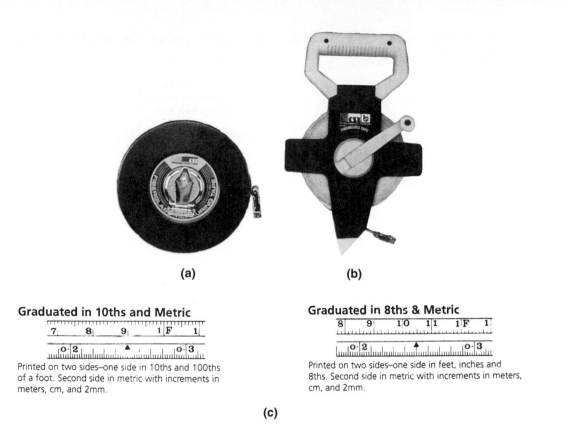

(a)   **(b)**

Graduated in 10ths and Metric

```
7       8       9       1 F     1
```
```
0·2              ▲         0·3
```

Printed on two sides—one side in 10ths and 100ths
of a foot. Second side in metric with increments in
meters, cm, and 2mm.

Graduated in 8ths & Metric

```
8     9     10     11     1 F    1
```
```
0·2                ▲         0·3
```

Printed on two sides—one side in feet, inches and
8ths. Second side in metric with increments in meters,
cm, and 2mm.

(c)

FIGURE 2-2   Fiberglass tapes. (a) Closed case. (b) Open reel. (c) Tape graduations. (Courtesy of CST Corporation, Illinois)

ways, railways, etc.), whereas lightweight tapes are more popular in structural and municipal work.

Invar tapes are composed of 35 percent nickel and 65 percent steel. This alloy has a very low coefficient of thermal expansion, making the tapes useful in precise linear measurement. Steel tapes are occasionally referred to as chains, a throwback to early surveying practice.

2-4-1   Types of Readouts

Steel tapes are normally graduated in one of three ways:

1. The tape is graduated throughout in feet and hundredths (0.01) of a foot or in meters and millimeters (see Figures 2-3 and 2-4).
2. The *cut* tape is marked throughout in feet, with the first and last foot graduated in tenths and hundredths of a foot [see Figure 2-3(b)]. The metric *cut* tape is marked throughout in meters and decimeters, with the first and last decimeters graduated in millimeters.

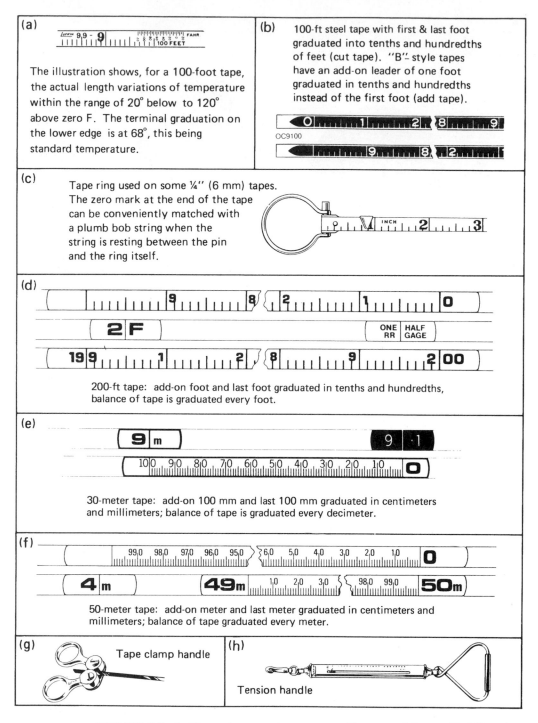

(a) The illustration shows, for a 100-foot tape, the actual length variations of temperature within the range of 20° below to 120° above zero F. The terminal graduation on the lower edge is at 68°, this being standard temperature.

(b) 100-ft steel tape with first & last foot graduated into tenths and hundredths of feet (cut tape). "B" style tapes have an add-on leader of one foot graduated in tenths and hundredths instead of the first foot (add tape).

OC9100

(c) Tape ring used on some ¼" (6 mm) tapes. The zero mark at the end of the tape can be conveniently matched with a plumb bob string when the string is resting between the pin and the ring itself.

(d) 200-ft tape: add-on foot and last foot graduated in tenths and hundredths, balance of tape is graduated every foot.

(e) 30-meter tape: add-on 100 mm and last 100 mm graduated in centimeters and millimeters; balance of tape is graduated every decimeter.

(f) 50-meter tape: add-on meter and last meter graduated in centimeters and millimeters; balance of tape graduated every meter.

(g) Tape clamp handle

(h) Tension handle

FIGURE 2-3 Lufkin steel tapes and accessories. (Courtesy of Cooper Tool Group)

Chap. 2   Taping

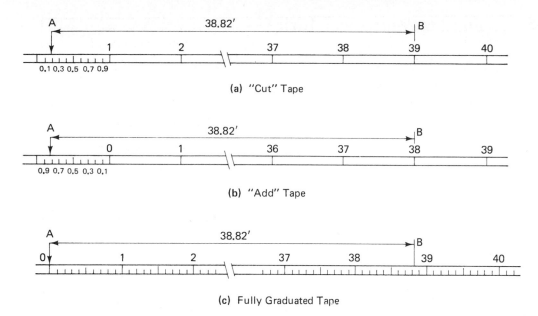

FIGURE 2-4 Various tape markings (hundredth marks not shown). (a) Cut tape. (b) Add tape. (c) Fully graduated tape.

A measurement is made with the *cut* tape by one surveyor holding an even foot (decimeter) mark, which will allow the other surveyor to read a distance on the first foot (decimeter), which is graduated in hundredths of a foot (millimeters). For example, the distance from *A* to *B* in Figure 2-4(a) is determined by holding 39 ft at *B* and reading 0.18 ft at *A*. Distance *AB* = 38.82 ft (i.e., 39 ft *cut* 0.18). Since each measurement involves this mental subtraction, care and attention are required from the surveyor to avoid unwelcome blunders.

3. The *add* tape is also marked throughout in feet, with the last foot graduated in hundredths of a foot. An additional foot, graduated in hundredths, is included prior to the zero mark [see Figure 2-3(d), (e), and (f)]. For metric tapes, it is the last decimeter and extra before-the-zero decimeter that are graduated in millimeters. The distance *AB* in Figure 2-4(b) is determined by holding 38 ft at *B* and reading 0.82 ft at *A*. Distance *AB* is 38.82 ft (i.e., 38 ft *add* 0.82).

As noted, the *cut* tapes have the disadvantage of creating opportunities for subtraction mistakes; the *add* tapes have the disadvantage of forcing the surveyor to adopt awkward measuring stances when measuring from the zero mark. The full meter *add* tape is most difficult to use correctly, as the surveyor must fully extend his or her left (right) arm (which is holding the end of the tape) in order to position the zero mark on the tape over the ground point.

The problems associated with both *add* and *cut* tapes can be eliminated if the surveyor uses tapes graduated throughout, which are available in both drag tapes and reel-type tapes.

2-5   Taping Accessories and Their Use

2-5-1   Plumb Bob

Plumb bobs are normally made of brass and weigh from 8 to 18 oz, with 10 and 12 oz being the most common. Plumb bobs are used in taping to transfer from tape to ground (or vice versa) when the tape is being held off the ground in order to maintain its horizontal alignment. See Figure 2-5.

2-5-2   Hand Level

The hand level (see Figure 2-6) can be used to keep the steel tape horizontal when one is measuring distances. The hand level is taken by the surveyor at the lower elevation, and a sight is taken back at the higher-elevation surveyor [see Figure 2-6(a) and 2-6(b)]. For example, if the surveyor with the hand level is sighting with the instrument crosshair horizontally on his or her partner's waist, and if both are roughly the same height, then the surveyor with the hand level is lower by the distance from eye to waist. The low end of the tape is held that distance off the ground (using a plumb bob), the high end of the tape being held on the mark.

Also shown is an Abney hand level *(clinometer).* See Figure 2-7(a). In addition to the level bubble and crosshair found on the standard hand level, the clinometer can take vertical angles (closest 10 minutes). The clinometer is used mainly to record vertical angles for slope distance reduction to horizontal or to determine heights of objects by setting the scale to 45° and then measuring the horizontal distance to the object. These two applications are illustrated in the following examples.

■ EXAMPLE 2-2

For height determination, a value of 45° is placed on the scale. The surveyor moves backward and forward until the point that is being measured is sighted [e.g., the top of the building shown in Figure 2-7(b)]. The distance from the observer to the surveyor at the base of the building is measured with a cloth tape. The partial height of the building (h_1) is equal to this measured distance (i.e., h_1/measured distance = tan 45° = 1). If the distance h_2 [eye height—see Figure 2-7(b)] is now added to the mea-

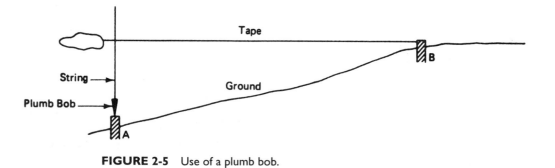

FIGURE 2-5   Use of a plumb bob.

Chap. 2   Taping

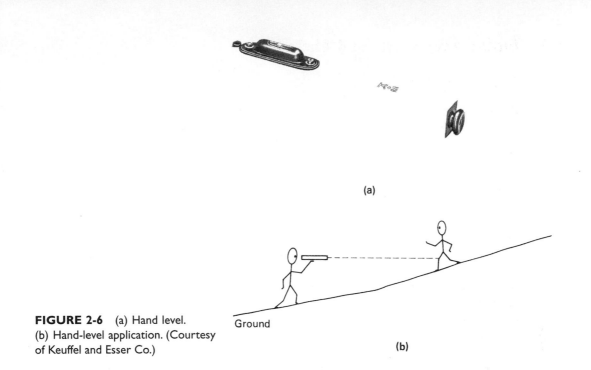

(a)

Ground

(b)

FIGURE 2-6   (a) Hand level.
(b) Hand-level application. (Courtesy
of Keuffel and Esser Co.)

sured distance, the height of the building (this example) is found. In addition to determining heights of buildings, this technique is particularly useful in determining heights of electric power lines for highway construction clearances. In this example [Figure 2-7(b)], if the measured distance to the second surveyor at the building is 63.75 ft and if the horizontal line of sight hits the building (the clinometer scale is set to zero for horizontal sights) at 5.55 ft (h_2), the height of the building is 63.75 + 5.55 = 69.30 ft.

■ EXAMPLE 2-3

The clinometer is useful when one is working on route surveys for which extended-length tapes (300 ft or 100 m) are being used. The long tape can be used in slope position under proper tension. (Since the tape will be touching the ground in many places, it will be mostly supported, and the tension required will not be too high.) The clinometer can be used to measure the slope angle for each tape measurement. These slope angles and related slope distances can later be used to compute the appropriate horizontal distances. The angles, measured distances, and computed distances for a field survey are summarized in Figure 2-7(c).

2-5-3   Additional Taping Accessories

The *clamp handle* [see Figure 2-3(g)] helps grip the tape at any intermediate point without bending or distorting the tape.

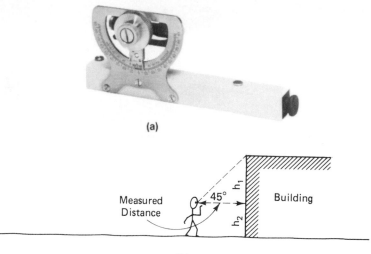

(a)

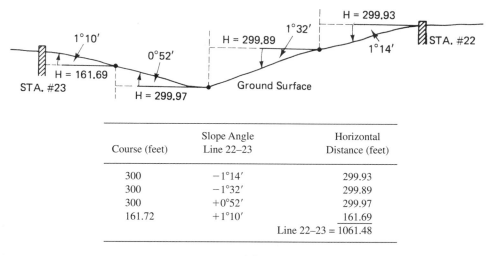

(b)

Course (feet)	Slope Angle Line 22–23	Horizontal Distance (feet)
300	−1°14′	299.93
300	−1°32′	299.89
300	+0°52′	299.97
161.72	+1°10′	161.69
	Line 22–23 =	1061.48

(c)

FIGURE 2-7   (a) Abney hand level: scale graduated in degrees with a vernier reading to 10 minutes. (Courtesy of Keuffel & Esser Co.). (b) Abney hand-level application in height determination. (c) Abney hand-level typical application in taping.

Tension handles [see Figure 2-3(h)] are used in precise work to ensure that the appropriate tension is being applied. They are graduated to 30 lb, in 1/2-lb graduations (50 N = 11.24 lb).

Chaining pins (marking arrows) come in sets of 11. They are painted alternately red and white and are 14 to 18 in. long. Chaining pins are used to mark intermediate points on the ground. In route surveying, the whole set of pins is used to mark out the centerline; the

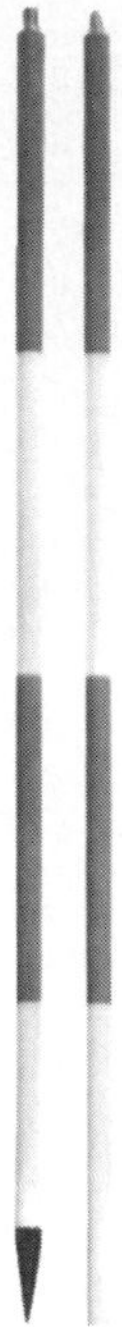

FIGURE 2-8   Two-section range pole.

rear surveyor is responsible for checking the number of whole tape lengths by keeping an accurate count of the pins collected. Eleven pins are used to measure out 1000 ft.

Tape repair kits are available so that broken tapes can be quickly put back into service. The repair kits come in three main varieties: (1) punch pliers and repair eyelets, (2) steel punch block and rivets, and (3) tape repair sleeves. The second technique (punch block) is the only method that will give lasting repair; although the technique is simple, great care must be exercised to ensure that the integrity of the tape is maintained.

Range poles are 6-ft wooden or aluminum poles with steel points. The poles are usually painted alternately red and white in 1-ft sections. Range poles are used in taping and transit work to provide alignment sights. See Figure 2-8.

Plumb bob targets are also used to provide alignment sights (see Figure 2-9). The plumb bob string is threaded through the upper and lower notches so that the target center-line is superimposed on the plumb bob string. The target, which can be adjusted up and down the string for optimal sightings, is preferred to the range pole due to its portability—it fits into the surveyor's pocket.

2-6   Taping Techniques

Taping is normally performed with the tape held horizontally. If the distance to be measured out is across smooth, level land, the tape can simply be laid on the ground and the end mark lined up against the initial survey marker; the tape is properly aligned and tensioned, and then the zero mark on the tape can be marked on the ground. If the distance between two marked points is to be measured, the tape is read as already described in Section 2-4-1.

FIGURE 2-9 Plumb bob cord target used to provide a transit sighting.

If the distance to be measured is across sloping or uneven land, then at least one end of the tape must be raised off the ground to keep the tape horizontal. The raised end of the tape is referenced back to the ground mark with the aid of a plumb bob (see Figure 2-10). Normally the only time that both ends of the tape are plumbed is when the ground—or other obstruction—rises between the marks being measured (see Figure 2-11).

2-6-1 Measuring Procedure

The measurement begins with the head surveyor carrying the zero end of the tape forward toward the final point. He or she continues walking until the tape has been unwound, at which time the rear surveyor calls "Tape" to alert the head surveyor to stop walking and to prepare for measuring. If a drag tape is being used, the tape is removed from the reel and a leather thong is attached to the reel end of the tape (the zero end already is equipped with a leather thong). If the tape is not designed to come off the reel, the winding handle is folded to the lock position so that the reel can be used to help hold the tape. The head surveyor is put on line by the rear surveyor, who is sighting a range pole or other target that has been erected at the final mark. In precise work, these intermediate marks can be aligned by theodolite.

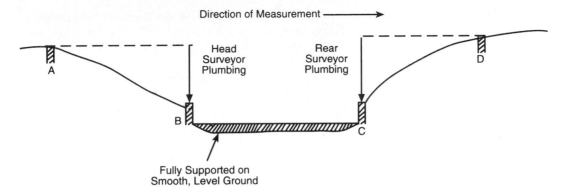

Direction of Measurement ⟶

Head Surveyor Plumbing

Rear Surveyor Plumbing

A

B

C

D

Fully Supported on Smooth, Level Ground

FIGURE 2-10 Horizontal taping; plumb bob used at one end.

The rear surveyor holds the appropriate graduation (e.g., 100.00 ft, or 30.000 m) against the mark from which the measurement is being taken. The head surveyor, ensuring that the tape is straight, slowly increases tension to the proper amount and then marks the ground with a chaining pin or other marker. Once the mark has been made, both surveyors repeat the measuring procedure to check the measurement. If necessary, corrections are made and the check procedure is repeated.

If the ground is not horizontal (determined by estimation or by use of a hand level), one or both surveyors must use a plumb bob. When one is plumbing, the tape is often held at waist height, although any height between the shoulders and the ground is common. Holding the tape above the shoulders creates more chance for error, as the surveyor must move his or her eyes up and down to include both the ground mark and the tape graduation in his or her field of view—when the surveyor's eyes are on the tape, the plumb bob may move off the mark, and when his or her eyes are on the ground mark, the plumb bob string may move off the correct tape graduation.

The plumb bob string is usually held on the tape with the left thumb (right-handed people); take care not to completely cover the graduation mark. The reason for this is that as the tension is increased, it is not unusual for the surveyor to take up some of the tension

Both Surveyors Plumbing

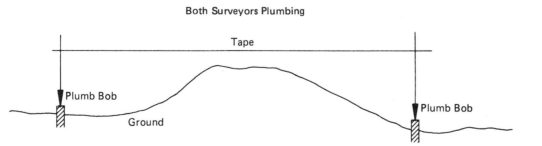

Tape

Plumb Bob

Plumb Bob

Ground

FIGURE 2-11 Horizontal taping; plumb bob used at both ends.

with the left thumb, causing it to slide along the tape. If the graduations have been completely covered with the left thumb, the surveyor is not aware that the thumb (and string) has moved, resulting in an erroneous measurement.

When one is plumbing, it is advisable to hold the tape close to the body in order to provide good leverage for applying or holding tension and to accurately transfer from tape to ground and vice versa.

If the rear surveyor is using a plumb bob, he or she shouts out "Tape" or some other word indicating that at that instant in time he or she was right over the mark. If the head surveyor is also using a plumb bob, he or she must wait until both his or her and the rear surveyor's plumb bobs are simultaneously over their respective marks.

The student will discover that plumbing and marking are difficult aspects of taping. The student will encounter difficulty in holding the plumb bob steady over the point and at the same time applying the appropriate tension. To help steady the plumb bob, the plumb bob is held only a short distance over the mark and is continually touched down to the point. This momentary touching down will dampen the plumb bob oscillations and generally steady the plumb bob. The student is cautioned against allowing the plumb bob to actually rest on the ground or other surface, as this will result in an erroneous measurement.

2-6-2   Breaking Tape

When one is measuring on a slope, it sometimes happens that the slope is too steep to permit an entire tape length to be held horizontal. When this occurs, shorter measurements are taken, each with the tape held horizontal; these shorter measurements are then totaled to provide the overall dimension. This technique, called *breaking tape,* must be done with greater care, as the extra marking and measuring operations will provide that many more opportunities for the occurrence of random errors—errors associated with marking and plumbing. There are two common methods of *breaking tape:* (1) The head surveyor takes the zero end forward one tape length and then walks back to a point where he or she can hold the tape horizontal with the rear surveyor; if working downhill, the tape can be held at shoulder height; using a plumb bob, the ground can be marked at an even foot or meter graduation (say, 80 ft or 25 m); the rear surveyor will then come forward and hold that same graduation on the ground mark while the head surveyor moves forward to the next graduation, which is also to be held at shoulder height (say, 30 ft or 10 m); this procedure is repeated until the head surveyor can hold the zero graduation and thus complete one full tape length. (2) Alternatively, the head surveyor can proceed forward only until his or her shoulders are horizontal with the rear surveyor and mark the zero end on the ground; the rear surveyor, who is probably holding an even foot or meter, calls out that value, which is then recorded. This process is repeated until the whole distance has been measured and all the intermediate measurements totalled for the final answer. See Figure 2-12.

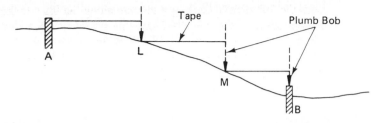

FIGURE 2-12 Breaking tape.

2-6-3 Taping Summary

REAR SURVEYOR

1. Aligns the head surveyor by sighting to a range pole or other target, which is placed at the forward station.
2. Holds the tape on the mark, either directly or with the aid of a plumb bob. Calls out "Tape" or some other word to signal that the tape graduation—or the plumb bob marking the tape graduation—is momentarily on the mark.
3. Calls out the station and tape reading for each measurement and listens for verification from the head surveyor.
4. Keeps a count of all full tape lengths included in each overall measurement.
5. Maintains the equipment (e.g., wipes the tape clean at the conclusion of the day's work or as conditions warrant).

HEAD SURVEYOR

1. Carries the tape forward, ensuring that the tape is free of loops that could lead to kinks and tape breakage.
2. Prepares the ground surface for the mark (e.g., clears away grass, leaves).
3. Applies proper tension after first ensuring that the tape is straight.
4. Places marks (e.g., chaining pins, wood stakes, iron bars, nails, rivets, cut crosses).
5. Takes and records measurements of distances and other factors (e.g., temperature).
6. Supervises the taping work.

2-7 Standard Conditions for the Use of Steel Tapes

Tape manufacturers, noting that steel tapes will behave differently in various temperature, tension, and support situations, specify the accuracy of their tapes under the following *standard conditions:*

Foot System	Metric System
1. Temperature = 68°F	1. Temperature = 20°C
2. Tape fully supported throughout	2. Tape fully supported throughout
3. Tape under a tension of 10 lb	3. Tape under a tension of 50 N (newtons)
	(1 lb force = 4.448 N)

Field conditions usually dictate that some or all of the above standard conditions cannot be met. The temperature is seldom exactly 68°F (20°C), and since many measurements are taken on slope, the condition of full support also is not regularly fulfilled. Errors introduced by temperature, tension, and sag are included in the next section, which deals with systematic error corrections.

2-8 Systematic Taping Errors and Corrections

The previous section outlined the standard conditions that must be accounted for if a steel tape is to give precise results. The standard conditions referred to a specific temperature and tension and to a condition of full support. In addition, the surveyor must be concerned with horizontal versus slope distances and with ensuring that the actual taping techniques are sufficiently precise to provide the desired accuracy.

2-8-1 Slope Corrections

Survey distances can be measured either horizontally or on a slope. Since survey measurements are usually shown on a plan, if they are taken on a slope, they must then be converted to horizontal distances before they can be plotted. To convert slope distances to their horizontal equivalents, the slope angle (θ), the zenith angle ($90 - \theta$), or the vertical distance (V) must also be known:

$$\frac{H \text{ (horizontal)}}{S \text{ (slope)}} = \cos \theta \qquad \text{or} \qquad H = S \cos \theta \tag{2-1}$$

$$\frac{H}{S} = \sin (90 - \theta) \qquad \text{or} \qquad H = S \sin (90 - \theta) \tag{2-1a}$$

where θ is the angle of inclination and ($90 - \theta$) is the zenith angle.

$$H = \sqrt{S^2 - V^2} \tag{2-2}$$

where V is the difference in elevation: see Example 2-4, part (c).

Slope can also be defined as *gradient,* or *rate of grade.* The gradient is expressed as a ratio of the vertical distance over the horizontal distance; this ratio is multiplied by 100 to give a percentage gradient. For example, if the ground rises 2 ft (m) in 100 ft (m), it is said to have a 2 percent gradient (i.e., 2/100 × 100 = 2); if the ground rises 2 ft (m) in 115 ft (m), it is said to have a 1.74 percent gradient (i.e., 2/115 × 100 = 1.739).

If the elevation of a point on a gradient is known, the elevation of any other point on that gradient can be calculated as follows:

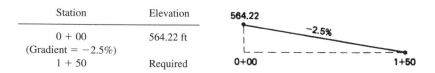

Station	Elevation
0 + 00	564.22 ft
(Gradient = −2.5%)	
1 + 50	Required

$$\text{Difference in elevation} = 150 \times (-2.5/100) = -3.75$$
$$\text{Elevation at } 1 + 50 = 564.22 - 3.75 = 560.47 \text{ ft}$$

If the elevations of two points are known, as well as the distance between them, the gradient between can be calculated as follows:

Station	Elevation
1 + 00	471.37
4 + 37.25	476.77

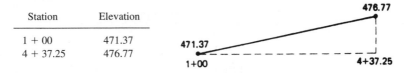

$$\text{Elevation difference} = 5.40$$
$$\text{Distance} = 337.25$$
$$\text{Gradient} = +5.40/337.25 \times 100 = +1.60\%$$

■ **EXAMPLE 2.4** *Slope Corrections*
(a) Given the slope distance (S) and slope angle θ:

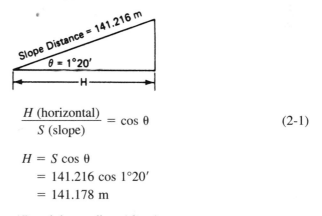

$$\frac{H \text{ (horizontal)}}{S \text{ (slope)}} = \cos \theta \qquad (2\text{-}1)$$

$$H = S \cos \theta$$
$$= 141.216 \cos 1°20'$$
$$= 141.178 \text{ m}$$

(b) Given the slope distance (S) and the gradient (slope):

$$\frac{1.50}{100} = \tan \theta$$
$$\theta = 0.85937°$$

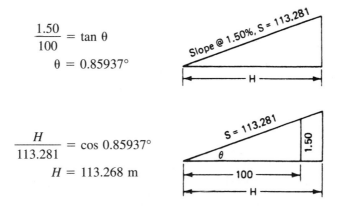

$$\frac{H}{113.281} = \cos 0.85937°$$
$$H = 113.268 \text{ m}$$

(c) Given the slope distance (S) and difference in elevation (V):

$$H^2 = S^2 - V^2$$
$$H = \sqrt{(S^2 - V^2)}$$
$$= \sqrt{(253.101^2 - 3.721^2)}$$
$$= 253.074 \text{ m}$$

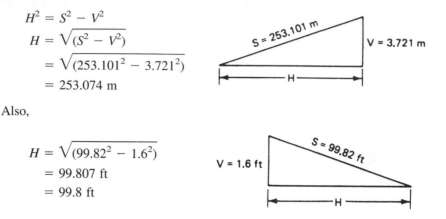

Also,

$$H = \sqrt{(99.82^2 - 1.6^2)}$$
$$= 99.807 \text{ ft}$$
$$= 99.8 \text{ ft}$$

In practice, most measurements are taken with the tape held horizontally. If the slope is too great to permit an entire tape length to be employed, then shorter increments will be measured until the required distance has been covered. This operation is known as *breaking tape*. Figure 2-12 shows the distance AB comprising increments AL, LM, and MB.

2-8-2 Erroneous Tape-Length Corrections

For all but precise work, new tapes as supplied by the manufacturer are considered to be correct under standard conditions. As a result of extensive use, tapes do become kinked, stretched, and repaired—perhaps imprecisely. The length can become something other than that specified. When this occurs, the tape must be corrected, or the measurements taken with the erroneous tape must be corrected.

■ **EXAMPLE 2-5**

A measurement is recorded as 171.278 m with a 30-m tape that is found to be only 29.996 m under standard conditions. What is the corrected measurement?

$$\text{Correction per tape length} = -0.004$$
$$\text{Number of tape lengths} = \frac{171.278}{30}$$
$$\text{Total correction} = -0.004 \times \frac{171.278}{30}$$
$$\text{Total correction} = -0.023 \text{ m}$$
$$\text{Corrected distance} = 171.278 - 0.023$$
$$= 171.255 \text{ m}$$

Or

$$\text{Corrected distance} = \frac{29.996}{30} \times 171.278 = 171.255$$

■ **EXAMPLE 2-6**

It is required to lay out the front corners of a building, a distance of 210.08 ft. The tape to be used is known to be 100.02 ft under standard conditions.

$$\text{Correction per tape length} = +0.02 \text{ ft}$$
$$\text{Number of tape lengths} = 2.1008$$
$$\text{Total correction} = 0.02 \times 2.1008 = +0.04 \text{ ft}$$

When the problem involves a **layout distance,** the algebraic sign of the correction must be reversed before being applied to the layout measurement. We must find the distance that, when corrected by +0.04, will give 210.08 ft:

$$\text{Layout distance} = 210.08 - 0.04 = 210.04 \text{ ft}$$

The student will discover that four variations of this problem are possible: correcting a measured distance using (1) a long tape or (2) a short tape and precorrecting a layout distance using (3) a long tape or (4) a short tape. To minimize confusion as to the sign of the correction, the student is urged to consider the problem with the distance reduced to that of only one tape length (100 ft or 30 m).

In Example 2-5, a recorded distance of 171.278 m was measured with a tape only 29.996 m long. The total correction was found to be 0.023 m. If doubt exists as to the sign of 0.023, ask yourself what the procedure would be for correcting only one tape length. In this example, after one tape length has been measured, it is recorded that 30 m (the nominal length of the tape) has been measured. If the tape is only 29.996 m long, then the field book entry of 30 m must be corrected by −0.004; if the correction for one tape length is minus, then the corrections for the total distance must also be minus.

The magnitude of a tape error can be precisely determined by having the tape compared with a tape that has been certified by the National Bureau of Standards in the United States or the National Research Council in Canada.

In field practice, if a tape is found to be incorrect, it is either precisely repaired or discarded.

2-8-3 Temperature Corrections

Most measurements taken with a steel tape occur at some temperature other than standard (68°F or 20°C). When the temperature is warmer or cooler than standard, the steel tape will expand or contract and thus introduce an error into the measurement.

The coefficient of thermal expansion and contraction of steel is 0.00000645 per unit length per degree Fahrenheit (°F) or 0.0000116 per unit length per degree Celsius (°C).

FOOT UNIT TEMPERATURE CORRECTIONS

$$C_t = 0.00000645(T - 68)L \tag{2-3}$$

where C_t is the correction, in feet, due to temperature
T is the temperature (°F) of the tape during measurement
L is the distance measured in feet

METRIC UNIT TEMPERATURE CORRECTIONS

$$C_t = 0.0000116(T - 20)L \qquad (2\text{-}4)$$

where C_t is the correction, in meters, due to temperature

T is the temperature (°C) of the tape during measurement

L is the distance measured in meters

■ EXAMPLE 2-7

A distance is recorded as being 471.37 ft at a temperature of 38°F. What is the corrected distance?

$$C_t = 0.00000645(38 - 68)471.37$$
$$= -0.09 \qquad (2\text{-}3)$$

Corrected distance is $471.37 - 0.09 = 471.28$ ft.

■ EXAMPLE 2-8

It is required to lay out two points in the field that will be exactly 100.000 m apart. Field conditions indicate that the temperature of the tape will be 27°C. What distance will be laid out?

$$C_t = 0.0000116(27 - 20)100.000$$
$$= +0.008 \text{ m} \qquad (2\text{-}4)$$

Since this is a layout (precorrection) problem, the correction sign must be reversed (i.e., we are looking for the distance that, when corrected by +0.008 m, will give us 100.000 m):

$$\text{Layout distance} = 100.000 - 0.008 = 99.992 \text{ m}$$

Accuracy demands for most surveys do not require high precision in determining the temperature of the tape. Usually it is sufficient to estimate the air temperature. However, for more precise work (say 1 : 10,000 and higher), care is required in determining the actual temperature of the tape—which can be significantly different from the temperature of the air.

INVAR STEEL TAPES

High-precision surveys may require the use of steel tapes that have a low coefficient of thermal expansion. The invar tape is a nickel-steel alloy that has a coefficient of thermal expansion of 0.0000002 to 0.00000055 per degree Fahrenheit.

In the past, invar tapes were used to measure baselines for triangulation control surveys; currently the baselines are measured more efficiently by EDM instruments. Invar tapes can, however, still be used to advantage in situations where high precision is required over short distances.

2-8-4 Tension and Sag Corrections

If a steel tape is fully supported and a tension other than standard (10 lb, foot system; 50 newtons, metric system) is applied, a *tension* (pull) error exists.

The tension correction formula is

$$C_P = \frac{(P - P_S)L}{AE}$$

(2-5)

If a tape has been standardized while fully supported and is being used without full support, an error called *sag* will occur.

The force of gravity pulls the center of the unsupported section downward in the shape of a caternary, thus creating an error $B'B$. The sag correction formula is

$$C_S = -\frac{w^2L^3}{24P^2} = -\frac{W^2L}{24P^2}$$

(2-6)

where $W^2 = w^2L^2$, W = weight of tape between supports, w = weight of tape per unit length, and L = length of the tape between supports.

Table 2-1 further defines the terms in these two formulas.

With reference to Table 2-1, 1 newton is the force required to accelerate a mass of 1 kg by 1 m/s^2.

$$\text{Force} = \text{mass} \times \text{acceleration}$$
$$\text{Weight} = \text{mass} \times \text{acceleration due to gravity } (g)$$
$$g = 32.2 \text{ ft/s}^2 = 9.807 \text{ m/s}^2$$

Table 2-1 CORRECTION FORMULA TERMS DEFINED (FOOT, METRIC, AND SI UNITS)

Unit	Description	Foot	Old Metric	Metric (SI)
C_P	Correction due to tension per tape length	ft	m	m
C_s	Correction due to sag per tape length	ft	m	m
L	Length of tape under consideration	ft	m	m
P_s	Standard tension	lb (force)	kg (force)	N (newtons)
	Typical standard tension	10 lb	4.5–5 kg	50 N
P	Applied tension	lb	kg	N
A	Cross-sectional area	in.^{2}	cm^2	m^2
E	Average modulus of elasticity of steel tapes	29×10^6 lb/in.^{2}	21×10^5 kg/cm^2	20×10^{10} N/m^2
E	Average modulus of elasticity in invar tapes	21×10^6 lb/in.^{2}	14.8×10^5 kg/cm^2	14.5×10^{10} N/m^2
w	Weight of tape per unit length	lb/ft	kg/m	N/m
W	Weight of tape	lb	kg	N

In SI units, a mass of 1 kg has a weight of $1 \times 9.807 = 9.807$ N (newtons). That is,

$$1 \text{ kg (force)} = 9.807 \text{ N}$$

Since some spring balances are graduated in kilograms and since standard tension is given in newtons by the tape manufacturers, surveyors must be prepared to work in both old metric and SI units.

Examples of Tension Corrections

■ EXAMPLE 2-9

Given a standard tension of a 10-lb force for a 100-ft steel tape that is being used with a 20-lb force pull, if the cross-sectional area of the tape is 0.003 in.^{2}, what is the tension error for each tape length used?

$$C_P = \frac{(20 - 10)100}{29000000 \times 0.003} = +0.011 \text{ ft} \tag{2-5}$$

If a distance of 421.22 ft has been recorded, the total correction is $4.2122 \times 0.011 = +0.05$ ft. The corrected distance is 421.27 ft.

■ EXAMPLE 2-10

Given a standard tension of 50 N for a 30-m steel tape that is being used with a 100-N force, if the cross-sectional area of the tape is 0.02 cm^2, what is the tension error per tape length?

$$C_P = \frac{(100 - 50)30}{0.02 \times 21 \times 10^5 \times 9.807} = +0.0036 \text{ m} \tag{2-5}$$

If a distance of 182.716 m has been measured under these conditions, the total correction is

$$\frac{182.716}{30} \times 0.0036 = +0.022 \text{ m}$$

The corrected distance is 182.738 m.

The cross-sectional area of a tape can be calculated from micrometer readings, taken from the manufacturer's specifications, or determined from the following expression:

Tape length × tape area × specific weight of tape steel = weight of tape

or

$$\text{Tape area} = \frac{\text{weight of tape}}{\text{length} \times \text{specific weight}} \tag{2-7}$$

■ EXAMPLE 2-11

A tape is weighed and found to weigh 1.95 lb. The overall length of the 100-ft steel tape (end to end) is 102 ft. The specific weight of steel is 490 lb/ft^2. What is the cross-sectional area of the tape?

$$\frac{102 \text{ ft} \times 12 \text{ in.} \times \text{area (in.}^2)}{1728 \text{ in.}^3} \times 490 \text{ lb/ft}^3 = 1.95 \text{ lb}$$

$$\text{Area} = \frac{1.95 \times 1728}{102 \times 12 \times 490} = 0.0056 \text{ in.}^2$$

Tension errors are usually quite small and as such have relevance only for very precise surveys. Even for precise surveys, it is seldom necessary to calculate tension corrections, as availability of a tension spring balance allows the surveyor to apply standard tension and thus eliminates the necessity of calculating a correction.

Examples of Sag Corrections

■ EXAMPLE 2-12

A 100-ft steel tape weighs 1.6 lb and is supported only at the ends with a force of 10 lb. What is the sag correction?

$$C_S = \frac{-1.6^2 \times 100}{24 \times 10^2} = -0.11 \text{ ft}$$

If the force is increased to 20 lb, the sag correction will be reduced to

$$C_S = \frac{-1.6^2 \times 100}{24 \times 20^2} = -0.03 \text{ ft}$$

■ EXAMPLE 2-13

Calculate the length between two supports if the recorded length is 42.071 m, the mass of this tape is 1.63 kg, and the applied tension is 100 N.

$$C_S = \frac{-(1.63 \times 9.807)^2 \times 42.071}{24 \times 100^2}$$

$$= -0.045 \text{ m}$$

Therefore, the length between supports is $42.071 - 0.045 \doteq 42.026$ m.

NORMAL TENSION

The error in measurement due to sag can sometimes be eliminated by increasing the applied tension.

Tension that will eliminate sag errors is known as *normal tension*. Normal tension ranges from about 19 lb (light 100-ft tapes) to 31 lb (heavy 100-ft tapes).

$$P_n = \frac{0.204W\sqrt{AE}}{\sqrt{P_n - P_S}} \tag{2-8}$$

This formula will give a value for P_n that will eliminate the error caused by sag. The formula is solved by making successive approximations for P_n until the equation is satisfied. This formula is not used often because of the difficulties in determining the individual tape characteristics.

Experiment to Determine Normal Tension. Normal tension can be determined experimentally for individual tapes, as shown in the following example.

■ **EXAMPLE 2-14** *Normal Tension for a 100-ft Steel Tape*

1. Lay out the tape flat on a horizontal surface; an indoor corridor is ideal.
2. Select (or mark) a well-defined point on the surface at which the 100-ft mark is held.
3. Attach a tension handle at the zero end of the tape. Apply standard tension—say, 10 lb—and mark the surface at 0.00 ft.
4. Repeat the process, switching personnel duties and ensuring that the two marks are, in fact, exactly 100.00 ft apart.
5. Raise the tape off the surface to a comfortable height (waist). While the surveyor at the 100-ft end holds a plumb bob over the point, the surveyor at the zero end slowly increases tension until his or her plumb bob is also over the mark. The tension read from the tension handle will be *normal tension* for that tape. The readings are repeated several times, and the average results are used for subsequent field work.

The most popular steel tapes (100 ft) now in use require a normal tension of about 24 lb. For most 30-m steel tapes now in use (lightweight), a normal tension of 90 N (20 lb) is appropriate. For structural and bridge surveys, very lightweight 200-ft tapes are available that can be used with a comfortable *normal tension*—in some cases, about 28 lb.

2-9 Random Taping Errors

Random errors occur because surveyors cannot measure perfectly. There is always a factor of estimation present in all measuring activity (except counting). In the previous section, systematic errors were discussed; in each area discussed, there was also the opportunity for random errors to occur. The temperature problems all require the determination of temperature—if the temperature used is the estimated air temperature, there could be a random error associated with the estimation; also, the temperature of the tape could be significantly different from that of the air. In the case of sag and tension, random errors could exist when one is estimating applied tension or even estimating between graduations on a spring balance. The higher the precision requirements are, the greater must be the care taken in determining these parameters.

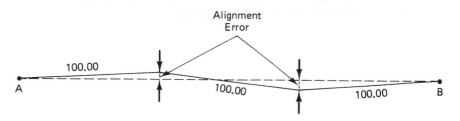

FIGURE 2-13 Alignment errors.

In addition to the above-mentioned random errors, there are perhaps more significant random errors associated with *alignment, plumbing and marking,* and *estimating horizontal positions.*

Alignment errors occur when the tape is inadvertently aligned off the true path (see Figure 2-13). Usually a rear surveyor can keep the head surveyor on line by sighting a range pole marking the terminal point. It would take an alignment error of about 1 1/2 ft to produce an error of 0.01 ft in 100 ft. Since it is not difficult to keep the tape aligned by eye to within a few tenths of a foot (0.2 to 0.3 ft), alignment is not normally a major concern. It should be noted that although most random errors are compensating, alignment errors are cumulative (misalignment can randomly occur on the left or on the right, but in both cases, the result of the misalignment is to make the measurement too long). Alignment errors can be virtually eliminated on precise surveys by using a transit to align all intermediate points.

Marking and *plumbing* errors are often the most significant of all random errors. Even experienced surveyors must exercise great care to accurately place a plumbed mark within 0.02 ft of true value—in a distance of 100 ft. Horizontal measurements, taken with the tape fully supported on the ground, can be more accurately determined than measurements taken on a slope requiring the use of plumb bobs; additionally, rugged terrain conditions that require many breaks in the taping process will cause marking and plumbing errors to multiply significantly.

Errors are also introduced when surveyors *estimate a horizontal position* for a plumbed measurement. The effect of this error is identical to that of the alignment error previously discussed, although the magnitude of these errors is often larger than alignment errors. Skilled surveyors usually can estimate a horizontal position within 1 ft (0.3 m) over a distance of 100 ft (30 m); however, even experienced surveyors can be seriously in error when measuring across sidehills, where one's perspective with respect to the horizon can be distorted. These errors can be largely eliminated by using a hand level.

2-10   Techniques for "Ordinary" Taping Precision

"Ordinary" taping is referred to as being at the level of 1/5000 accuracy. The techniques used for "ordinary" taping, once mastered, can easily be maintained. It is possible to achieve an accuracy level of 1/5000 with little more effort than is required to attain the 1/3000 level. Since the bulk of all taping measurements is at either the 1/3000 or the

Table 2-2 SPECIFICATIONS FOR 1/5000 ACCURACY

Source of Error	Maximum Effect on One Tape Length	
	100 ft	30 m
Temperature estimated to closest 7°F (4°C)	±0.005 ft	±0.0014 m
Care is taken to apply at least normal tension (lightweight tapes) and tension is known within 5 lb (20 N)	±0.006 ft	±0.0018 m
Slope errors are no larger than 1 ft/100 ft (0.30 m/30 m)	±0.005 ft	±0.0015 m
Alignment errors are no larger than 0.5 ft/100 ft (0.15 m/30 m)	±0.001 ft	±0.0004 m
Plumbing and marking errors are at a maximum of 0.015 ft/100 ft (0.0046 m/30 m)	±0.015 ft	±0.0046 m
Length of tape is known within ±0.005 ft (0.0015 m)	±0.005 ft	±0.0015 m

1/5000 level, experienced surveyors will often use 1/5000 techniques even for 1/3000 level work. This practice permits good measuring work habits to be continually reinforced without appreciably increasing surveying costs.

Because of the wide variety of field conditions that can be encountered, absolute specifications cannot be prescribed. The specifications in Table 2-2 can be considered typical for "ordinary" 1/5000 taping.

To determine the total random error in one tape length, take the square root of the sum of the squares of the individual maximum anticipated errors:

Feet	Meters
0.005^2	0.0014^2
0.006^2	0.0018^2
0.005^2	0.0015^2
0.001^2	0.0004^2
0.015^2	0.0046^2
0.005^2	0.0015^2
0.000337	0.000031

$$\text{Error} = \sqrt{(0.000337)} = 0.018 \text{ ft} \quad \text{or} \quad \text{Error} = \sqrt{(0.000031)} = 0.0056 \text{ m}$$

$$\text{Accuracy} = 0.018/100 = 1/5400 \quad \text{or} \quad \text{Accuracy} = 0.0056/30 = 1/5400$$

2-11 Mistakes in Taping

If errors can be associated with inexactness, mistakes must be thought of as being blunders. Whereas errors can be analyzed and to some degree predicted, mistakes are unpredictable. Since just one undetected mistake can nullify the results of an entire survey, it is essential to perform the work in a manner that will minimize the opportunity for mistakes to occur and also allow for verification of the results.

The opportunities for the occurrence of mistakes are minimized by setting up and then rigorously following a standard method of performing the measurement. The more standardized and routine the measurement manipulations are, the more likely it is that the surveyor will spot a mistake. The immediate double-checking of all measurement manipulations reduces the opportunities for mistakes to go undetected and at the same time increases the precision of the measurement. In addition to immediately checking all measurements, the surveyor is constantly looking for independent methods of verifying the survey results.

Gross mistakes can often be detected by comparing the survey results with distances scaled (or read) from existing plans. The simple check technique of pacing can be a valuable tool for rough verification of measured distances—especially construction layout distances. The possibilities for verification are limited only by the surveyor's diligence and imagination.

Common mistakes encountered in taping are the following:

1. Measuring to or from the wrong marker.
2. Reading the tape incorrectly or transposing figures (e.g., reading 56 instead of 65).
3. Losing proper count of the number of full tape lengths involved in a measurement.
4. Recording incorrectly the values in the notes. It sometimes happens that the note keeper will hear the rear surveyor's call out correctly, but then transpose the figures when they are entered into the notes. This mistake can be eliminated if the note keeper calls out each value as it is recorded. The rear surveyor listens for these call outs to ensure that the numbers called out are the same as the data originally given.
5. Calling out figures ambiguously. The rear surveyor can call out 20.27 as "twenty (pause) two seven." This might be interpreted as 22.7. To avoid mistakes, this should be called out as "twenty, decimal (point), two, seven."
6. Not identifying correctly the zero point of the tape when a cloth or fiberglass tape is used. This mistake can be avoided if the surveyor checks unfamiliar tapes before use. The tape itself can be used to verify the zero mark.
7. Making arithmetic mistakes in sums of dimensions and in error corrections (e.g., temperature). These mistakes can be identified and corrected if each member of the crew is responsible for checking (and initialing) all computations.

2-12   Field Notes for Taping

Section 1-14 introduced field notes and stressed the importance of neatness, legibility, completeness, and clear presentation. Sample field notes will be included in this text for all typical surveying operations. Figures 2-14 and 2-15 typify field notes representing taping surveys.

Figure 2-14 shows the taping notes for a traverse survey. The sides of the traverse have been measured forward and back, with the results being averaged (mean) if the

No. PROJECT # 3 TRAVERSE SURVEY — No. TEMP. = 14°C

SENECA TRAVERSE — Date OCT 26 2000 — Page 18

	COURSE DISTANCES		
COURSE	DIRECT	REVERSE	MEAN
AB	30.000	30.000	
	22.583	22.577	
	52.583	52.577	52.580
BC	~~28.970~~	28.940	
	28.950		28.945
CD	30.000	30.000	
	10.002	10.008	
	40.002	40.008	40.005
DE	30.000	30.000	
	8.505	8.520	
	38.505	38.520	38.513
EA	8.217	8.500	
	8.672	8.911	
	5.395	4.879	
	22.284	22.290	22.287
TOLERANCE BETWEEN DIRECT			
AND REVERSE =		0.015 m.	

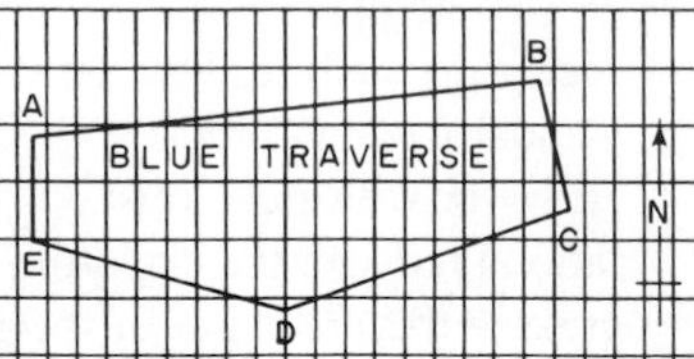

CREW: BARRY ARRINDELL – NOTES
JEFF AUCOIN – TAPE
BRIAN BAILEY – TAPE

CORRECTIONS: $C_T = 0.0000116\,(T-20)\,L_m$

COURSE	MEAS. DIST.	CORR. DIST.
AB	52.580	52.576
BC	28.945	28.943
CD	40.005	40.002
DE	38.513	38.510
EA	22.287	22.285

Checked: B Bailey
J Aucoin

FIGURE 2-14 Taping field notes for a closed traverse.

discrepancy is within acceptable limits (0.015 in this example). The reader will observe that the notes are clear and complete and generally satisfy the requirements in Section 1-14.

Figure 2-15 shows taping notes for a building dimension survey. In this example, the measurements are entered right on the sketch of the building. If the sketch has lines that are too short to directly show the appropriate measured distance, those distances can be neatly entered in an uncrowded portion of the sketch, with arrows joining the measurements to the correct lines on the sketch.

In this example, the required building walls have been measured, with the results entered on the sketch. Each wall is remeasured, and if the result is identical to the first measurement, a check mark is placed beside that measurement; if the result varies, the new measurement is also entered beside the original. If the two measurements do not agree within the specified tolerance (0.02 m), the wall is measured again until the tolerance has been met.

It is suggested that the reader also compare this page of field notes to the requirements of Section 1-14.

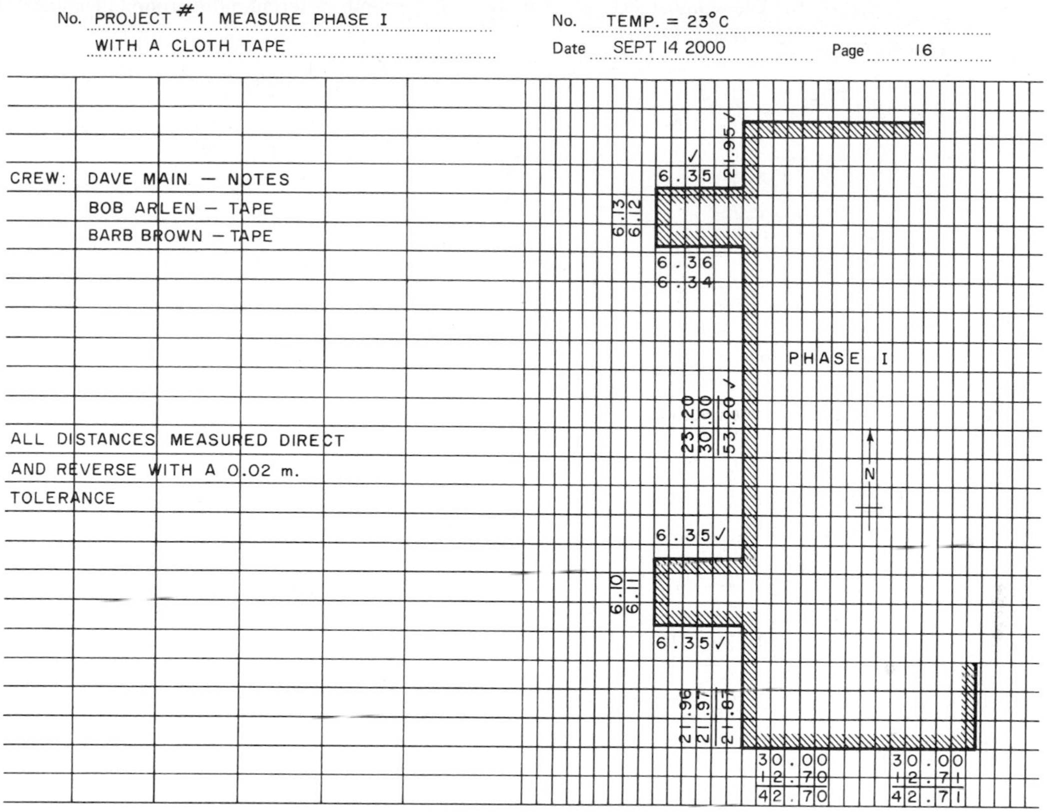

No. PROJECT # 1 MEASURE PHASE I
WITH A CLOTH TAPE
No. TEMP. = 23°C
Date SEPT 14 2000
Page 16
CREW: DAVE MAIN — NOTES
BOB ARLEN — TAPE
BARB BROWN — TAPE
ALL DISTANCES MEASURED DIRECT
AND REVERSE WITH A 0.02 m.
TOLERANCE
21.95 ✓
6.35 ✓
6.13
6.12
6.36
6.34
PHASE I
23.20
30.00
53.20 ✓
N
6.35 ✓
6.10
6.11
6.35 ✓
21.96
21.97
21.87
30.00
12.70
42.70
30.00
12.71
42.71

FIGURE 2-15 Taping field notes for building dimensions.

Problems

2-1. Give two examples of possible uses for each of the following field measurement techniques: **(a)** pacing, **(b)** odometer, **(c)** EDM, **(d)** stadia, **(e)** subtense bar, **(f)** woven tape, **(g)** steel tape.

2-2. The following measurements were taken from an early topographic survey where the measurements were made with a Gunter's chain. Convert each of these measurements to both feet and meters: **(a)** 40 chains, 11 links; **(b)** 17.52 chains; **(c)** 37 chains, 91 links; **(d)** 22 ch., 22 lk.

2-3. It is required to determine the ground clearance of an overhead electrical cable. Surveyor B is positioned directly under the cable (surveyor B's position can be checked by his sighting past the string of a plumb bob, held in his outstretched hand, to the cable); surveyor A sets her clinometer to 45° and then backs away from surveyor B until the overhead electrical cable is on the crosshair of the leveled clinometer. At this point, surveyors A and B determine the distance between them to be 52.3 ft. Surveyor A then sets the clinometer to 0° and sights surveyor B; this horizontal line of sight cuts surveyor B at the knees, a distance of 2.3 ft above the ground. Determine the ground clearance of the electrical cable.

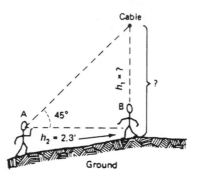

2-4. A 100-ft "cut" steel tape was used to check the layout of a building wall. The rear surveyor held 93 ft while the head surveyor "cut" 0.38 ft. What is the distance measured?

2-5. A 100-ft "add" steel tape was used to measure a partial baseline distance. The rear surveyor held 47 ft while the head surveyor held 0.59 ft. What is the distance measured?

2-6. The slope distance between two points is 56.883 m, and the slope angle is $1°22'$. Compute the horizontal distance.

2-7. The slope distance between two points is 77.48 ft, and the difference in elevation between them is 3.99 ft. Compute the horizontal distance.

2-8. A distance of 230.008 m was measured along a 2 percent slope. Compute the horizontal distance.

2-9. A 100-ft steel tape, known to be 100.02 ft (under standard conditions), was used to measure a distance that was recorded as 582.63 ft. What is this distance when corrected for erroneous tape length?

2-10. A 30-m steel tape, known to be only 29.992 m long (under standard conditions), was used to measure a distance recorded as 180.023 m. What is this distance when corrected for erroneous tape length?

2-11. It is required to lay out a rectangular commercial building 170.00 ft wide and 150.00 ft long. If the steel tape being used is 100.05 ft long (under standard conditions), what distances will be measured out?

2-12. A steel tape was used to measure a distance of 4621.52 ft when the field temperature was 83°F. What is this distance when corrected for temperature?

2-13. A steel tape was used to measure a distance of 347.233 m when the field temperature was 15°C. What is the distance corrected for temperature?

2-14. Station 10+21.78 must be marked in the field. If the steel tape to be used is only 99.98 (under standard conditions) and if the temperature will be 90°F at the time of the measurement, how far from the existing station mark at 8+73.26 will the surveyor have to measure to locate the new station?

2-15. The point of intersection of the centerline of Elm Rd. with the centerline of First St. was originally recorded as being at 28+98.761. How far from existing station mark 28+00 on First St. will a surveyor have to measure along the centerline to reestablish the intersection point under the following conditions?

Temperature to be -8°C, with a tape that is 29.996 under standard conditions.

2-16. through 2-20. Compute the corrected **horizontal** distance.

Problem	Temperature	Tape Length	Slope Data	Slope Measurement
2-16	57°F	100.00 ft	Slope angle = +1°30′	273.77 ft
2-17	0°C	30.000 m	Slope @ +2.30%	61.662 m
2-18	93°F	100.02 ft	Elev. diff. = 5.11 ft	813.73 ft
2-19	22°C	29.993 m	Slope angle = −4°30′	215.004 m
2-20	78°F	99.97 ft	Slope @ −1.2%	513.71 ft

2-21. through 2-25. Compute the distances to be laid out under the specified conditions.

Problem	Temperature	Tape Length	Required Horizontal Distance
2-21	26°C	30.009 m	176.296 m
2-22	58°F	100.04 ft	205.43 ft
2-23	−10°F	99.95 ft	176.76 ft
2-24	5°C	29.994 m	90.000 m
2-25	50°F	100.02 ft	510.11 ft

2-26. A 50-m tape is used to measure between two points. The average weight of the tape per meter is 0.320 N. If the measured distance is 48.888 m with the tape supported only at the ends and with a tension of 100 N, find the corrected distance.

2-27. A 30-m tape has a mass of 544 g and is supported only at the ends with a force of 80 newtons. What is the sag correction?

2-28. A 100-ft steel tape weighing 1.8 lb and supported only at the ends with a tension of 24 lb is used to measure a distance of 471.16 ft. What is the distance corrected for sag?

2-29. A distance of 72.55 ft is recorded; a steel tape supported only at the ends with a tension of 15 lb and weighing 0.016 lb per foot is used. Find the distance corrected for sag.

Chapter 3

Leveling

3-1 Definitions

Leveling is the procedure used when one is determining differences in elevation between points that are remote from each other. An *elevation* is a vertical distance above or below a reference datum. In surveying, the reference datum that is universally employed is that of *mean sea level* (MSL). In North America, 19 years of observations at tidal stations in 26 locations on the Atlantic, Pacific, and Gulf of Mexico shorelines were reduced and adjusted to provide the *national geodetic vertical datum* (NGVD) of 1929. This datum has been further refined to reflect gravimetric and other anomalies in the 1988 general control readjustment (North American vertical datum—NAVD 88). Although, strictly, the NAVD may not precisely agree with mean sea level at specific points on the earth's surface, the term *mean sea level* is generally used to describe the datum. MSL is assigned a vertical value (elevation) of 0.000 ft or 0.000 m. See Figure 3-1.

A *vertical line* is a line from the surface of the earth to the earth's center. It is also referred to as being a plumb line or a line of gravity.

A *level line* is a line in a level surface. A level surface is a curved surface parallel to the mean surface of the earth. A level surface is best visualized as being the surface of a large body of water at rest.

A *horizontal line* is a straight line perpendicular to a vertical line.

3-2 Theory of Differential Leveling

Differential leveling is used to determine differences in elevation between points that are some distance from each other by using a surveyors' level together with a graduated measuring rod. The surveyors' level consists of a crosshair-equipped telescope and an attached spirit level tube, all of which are mounted on a sturdy tripod.

The surveyor is able to sight through the telescope to a graduated (in feet or meters) rod and determine a measurement reading at the point where the crosshair intersects the rod.

With reference to Figure 3-2, if the rod reading at $A = 6.27$ ft and the rod reading at $B = 4.69$ ft the difference in elevation between A and B is $6.27 - 4.69 = 1.58$ ft. If the

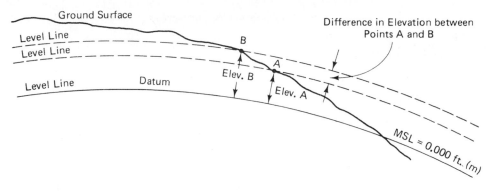

FIGURE 3-1 Leveling concepts.

elevation of A is 61.27 ft (above MSL), then the elevation of B is $61.27 + 1.58 = 62.85$ ft. That is,

61.27 (elev. A) + 6.27 (rod reading at A) − 4.69 (rod reading at B) = 62.85 (elev. B)

Referring to Figure 3-3, the student can visualize a potential problem. Whereas elevations are referenced to level lines (surfaces), the line of sight through the telescope of a surveyors' level is, in fact, almost a horizontal line. All rod readings taken with a surveyors' level will contain an error c over a distance d. The author has greatly exaggerated the curvature of the level lines shown in Figures 3-1 through 3-3 for illustrative purposes. In fact, the divergence between a level line and a horizontal line is quite small. For example, over a distance of 1000 ft, the divergence is 0.024 ft, and for a distance of 300 ft, the divergence is only 0.002 ft (0.0008 m in 100 m).

3-3 Curvature and Refraction

The previous section introduced the concept of curvature error—that is, the divergence between a level line and a horizontal line over a specified distance. When considering the divergence between level and horizontal lines, one must also account for the fact that all sight lines are refracted downward by the earth's atmosphere. Although the magnitude of the refraction error is dependent on atmospheric conditions, it is generally considered to be about one-seventh of the curvature error. It is seen in Figure 3-4 that the refraction error of AB compensates for part of the curvature error of AE, resulting in a net error due to curvature and refraction $(c + r)$ of BE.

From Figure 3-4, the curvature error can be computed as follows:

$$(R + C)^2 = R^2 + KA^2$$
$$R^2 + 2RC + C^2 = R^2 + KA^2$$
$$C(2R + C) = KA^2$$
$$C = \frac{KA^2}{2R + C} \approx \frac{KA^2}{2R} \tag{3.1}$$

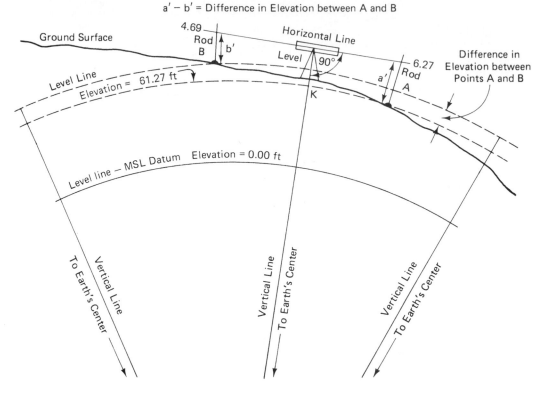

FIGURE 3-2 Leveling terms.

Take $R = 6370$ km:

$$C = \frac{KA^2 \times 10^3}{2 \times 6370} = 0.0785\, KA^2$$

Refraction is affected by atmospheric pressure, temperature, and geographic location, but, as noted earlier, it is usually expressed as being roughly equal to one-seventh of C.

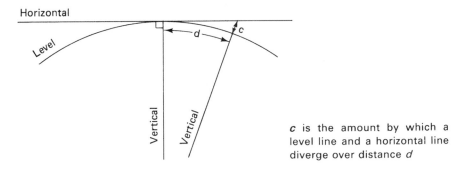

c is the amount by which a level line and a horizontal line diverge over distance d

FIGURE 3-3 Relationship between a horizontal line and a level line.

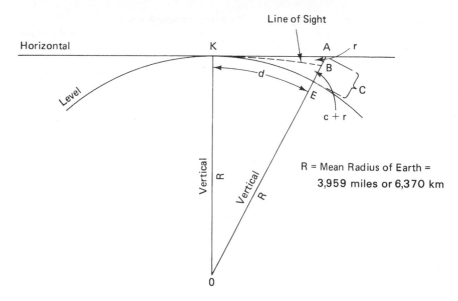

FIGURE 3-4 Effects of curvature and refraction.

$$\text{If } r = 0.14C$$
$$c + r = 0.0675K^2$$

where $K = KA$ (Figure 3-4) and is the length of sight in kilometers. The combined effects of curvature and refraction $(c + r)$ can be determined from the following formulas:

$$(c + r)_\text{m} = 0.0675K^2, \qquad (c + r)_\text{m} \text{ in meters;} \qquad K \text{ in kilometers} \qquad (3\text{-}2)$$

$$(c + r)_\text{ft} = 0.574K^2, \qquad (c + r)_\text{ft} \text{ in feet;} \qquad K \text{ in miles} \qquad (3\text{-}3)$$

$$(c + r)_\text{ft} = 0.0206M^2, \qquad (c + r)_\text{ft} \text{ in feet;} \qquad M \text{ in thousands of feet} \qquad (3\text{-}4)$$

■ EXAMPLE 3-1

Calculate the error due to curvature and refraction for the following distances:

(a) 2500 ft: $\quad c + r = 0.0206 \times 2.5^2 = 0.13$ ft

(b) 400 ft: $\quad c + r = 0.0206 \times 0.4^2 = 0.003$ ft

(c) 2.7 miles: $\quad c + r = 0.574 \times 2.7^2 = 4.18$ ft

(d) 1.8 km $\quad c + r = 0.0675 \times 1.8^2 = 0.219$ m

It can be seen from the figures in Table 3-1 that $(c + r)$ errors are relatively insignificant for differential leveling. Even for precise leveling, where distances of rod readings are seldom in excess of 200 ft (60 m), it would seem that this error is of only marginal importance. It will be shown in a later section that the field technique of balancing distances of rod readings effectively cancels out this type of error.

Table 3-1 SELECTED VALUES FOR $(c + r)$ AND DISTANCE

Distance (m)	30	60	100	120	150	300	1 km
$(c + r)_m$	0.0001	0.0002	0.0007	0.001	0.002	0.006	.068
Distance (ft)	100	200	300	400	500	1000	1 mile
$(c + r)_{ft}$	0.000	0.001	0.002	0.003	0.005	0.021	0.574

3-4 Types of Levels—Dumpy, Tilting, Automatic, and Digital

3-4-1 Dumpy Level

The dumpy level (Figure 3-5) was at one time used extensively on all engineering works. Although this simple instrument has, to a large degree, been replaced by more sophisticated instruments, it is shown here in some detail to aid in the introduction of the topic. For purposes of description, the level can be analyzed with respect to its three major components: telescope, level tube, and leveling head (Figure 3-6).

The telescope assembly is illustrated in Figure 3-6(b). Rays of light pass through the objective (1) and form an inverted image in the focal plane (4). The image thus formed is magnified by the eyepiece lenses (3) so that the image can be clearly seen. The eyepiece lenses also focus the crosshairs, which are located in the telescope in the principal focus plane. The focusing lens (negative lens) (2) can be adjusted so that images at varying distances can be brought into focus in the plane of the reticle (4). In most telescopes designed for use in North America, additional lenses (prisms) are included in the eyepiece assembly so that the inverted image can be viewed as an erect image. The minimum focusing distance for the object ranges from 1 to 2 m, depending on the instrument.

The line of collimation (line of sight) joins the center of the objective lens to the intersection of the crosshairs. The optical axis is the line taken through the center of the objective lens and perpendicular to the vertical lens axis. The focusing lens (negative lens)

FIGURE 3-5   Dumpy level. (Courtesy of Keuffel & Esser Co.)

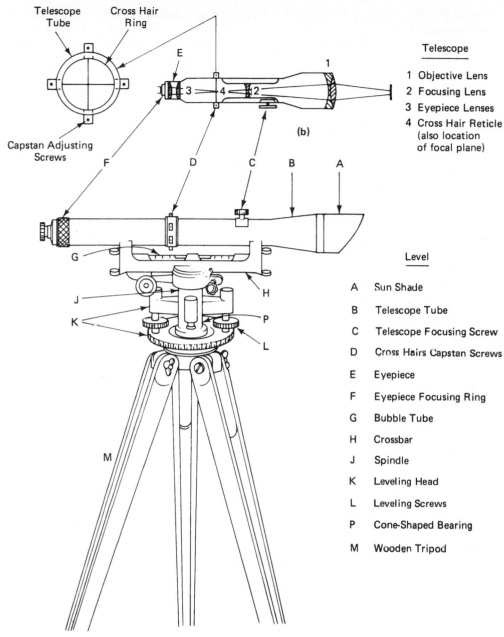

Telescope Tube

Cross Hair Ring

E

3   4   2

1

(b)

Telescope

1 Objective Lens

2 Focusing Lens

3 Eyepiece Lenses

4 Cross Hair Reticle
   (also location
   of focal plane)

Capstan Adjusting
Screws

F   D   C   B   A

G

J

K

M

H

P

L

Level

A   Sun Shade

B   Telescope Tube

C   Telescope Focusing Screw

D   Cross Hairs Capstan Screws

E   Eyepiece

F   Eyepiece Focusing Ring

G   Bubble Tube

H   Crossbar

J   Spindle

K   Leveling Head

L   Leveling Screws

P   Cone-Shaped Bearing

M   Wooden Tripod

(a)

FIGURE 3-6 (a) Dumpy level. (b) Telescope for a dumpy level. (Adapted from *Construction Manual*, Ministry of Transportation, Ontario)

moved by focusing screw C [Figure 3-6(a)] has its optical axis the same as the objective lens. See also Figure 4-19.

The crosshairs [Figure 3-6(b), no. 4] can be thin wires attached to a crosshair ring, or, as is more usually the case, crosshairs are lines etched on a circular glass plate that is enclosed by a crosshair ring. The crosshair ring, which has a slightly smaller diameter than does the telescope tube, is held in place by four adjustable capstan screws. The crosshair ring (and the crosshairs) can be adjusted left and right or up and down simply by loosening and then tightening the two appropriate opposing capstan screws.

The level tube [Figure 3-6(a), G] is a sealed glass tube mostly filled with alcohol or a similar substance. The upper (and sometimes lower) surface has been ground to form a circular arc. The degree of precision possessed by a surveyors' level is partly a function of the sensitivity of the level tube; the sensitivity of the level tube is directly related to the radius of curvature of the upper surface of the level tube. The larger the radius of curvature, the more sensitive the level tube.

Sensitivity is usually expressed as the central angle subtending one division (usually 2 mm) marked on the surface of the level tube. The sensitivity of many engineers' levels is 30″; that is, for a 2-mm arc, the central angle is 30″ ($R = 13.75$ m or 45 ft). See Figure 3-7.

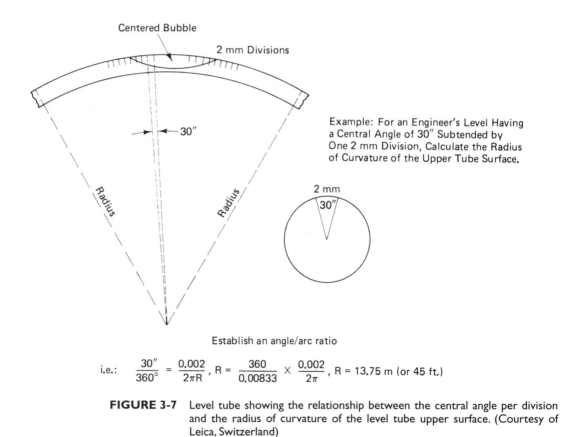

Centered Bubble

2 mm Divisions

30″

Radius

Radius

Example: For an Engineer's Level Having a Central Angle of 30″ Subtended by One 2 mm Division, Calculate the Radius of Curvature of the Upper Tube Surface.

2 mm

30″

Establish an angle/arc ratio

i.e.: $\dfrac{30''}{360°} = \dfrac{0.002}{2\pi R}$, $R = \dfrac{360}{0.00833} \times \dfrac{0.002}{2\pi}$, $R = 13.75$ m (or 45 ft.)

FIGURE 3-7 Level tube showing the relationship between the central angle per division and the radius of curvature of the level tube upper surface. (Courtesy of Leica, Switzerland)

The sensitivity of levels used for precise work is usually 10″; that is, $R = 41.25$ m or 135 ft.

Precise levels, in addition to possessing more sensitive level tubes, have improved optics, including a greater magnification power. The relationship between the quality of the optical system and the sensitivity of the level tube can be simply stated: For any observable movement of the bubble in the level tube, there should be an observable movement of the crosshair on the leveling rod.

In the case of the dumpy level, four leveling foot screws are utilized to set the telescope level. The four foot screws surround the center bearing of the instrument (Figure 3-6) and are used to tilt the level telescope using the center bearing as a pivot.

Figure 3-8 illustrates how the telescope is positioned during the leveling process. The telescope is first positioned directly over two opposite foot screws. The two screws are kept only snugly tightened (overtightening makes rotation difficult and could damage the threads) and rotated in opposite directions until the bubble is centered in the level tube. If the foot screws become loose, it is an indication that the rotations have not proceeded uniformly; at worst, the foot screw pad can rise above the plate, making the telescope wobble. The solution for this condition is to turn one screw until it again contacts the base plate and provides a snug friction when turned in opposition to its opposite screw.

The telescope is first aligned over two opposing screws; the screws are turned in opposite directions until the bubble is centered in the level tube. The telescope is then turned 90° to the second position, over the other pair of opposite foot screws, and the leveling

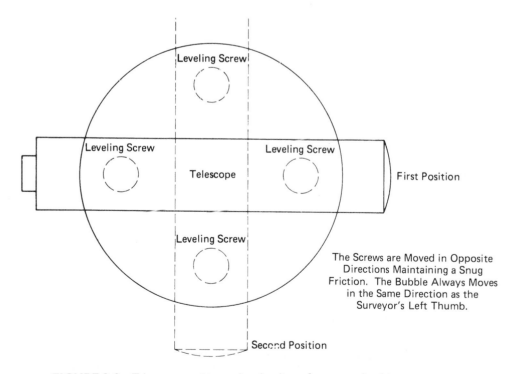

FIGURE 3-8   Telescope positions when leveling a four-screw level instrument.

procedure is repeated. This process is repeated until the bubble remains centered. When the bubble remains centered in these two positions, the telescope is then turned 180° to check the adjustment of the level tube.

If the bubble does not remain centered when the telescope is turned 180°, it indicates that the level tube is out of adjustment. However, the instrument can still be used by simply noting the number of divisions that the bubble is off center and by moving the bubble half the number of those divisions. For example, if upon turning the leveled telescope 180° it is noted that the bubble is four divisions off center, the instrument can be leveled by moving the bubble to a position of two divisions off center. It will be noted that the bubble will remain two divisions off center no matter which direction the telescope is pointed. It should be emphasized that the instrument is, in fact, level if the bubble remains in the same position when the telescope is revolved, regardless of whether or not that position is in the center of the level vial.

3-4-2 Tilting Level

The tilting level is roughly leveled by observing the bubble in the circular spirit level. Just before each rod reading is to be taken, and while the telescope is pointing at the rod, the telescope is precisely leveled by manipulating a tilting screw, which effectively raises or lowers the eyepiece end of the telescope. The level is equipped with a tube level, which is precisely leveled by operating the tilting screw. The bubble is viewed through a separate eyepiece or, as is the case shown in Figure 3-10, through the telescope. The image of the bubble is longitudinally split in two and viewed with the aid of prisms. One-half of each end of the bubble is seen (see Figure 3-10), and after adjustment, the two half-ends are brought to coincidence and appear as a continuous curve. When coincidence has been achieved, the telescope has been precisely leveled. It has been estimated (Leica Ltd.) that the accuracy of centering a level bubble with reference to the open tubular scale graduated at intervals at 2 mm is about one-fifth of a division, or 0.4 mm. With coincidence-type (split bubble) levels, however, this accuracy increases to about one-fortieth of a division, or 0.05 mm. As can be seen, these levels are useful where a relatively high degree of precision is required; however, if tilting levels are used on ordinary work (e.g., earthwork), the time (expense) involved in setting the split bubble to coincidence for each rod reading can scarcely be justified.

Most tilting levels (most new surveying instruments) come equipped with a three-screw leveling base. Whereas the support for a four-screw leveling base is the center bearing, the three-screw instruments are supported entirely by the foot screws themselves. This means that adjustment of the foot screws of a three-screw instrument effectively raises or lowers the height of the instrument line of sight. Adjustment of the foot screws of a four-screw instrument does not affect the height of the instrument line of sight, as the instrument is supported by the center bearing. Accordingly, the surveyor should be aware that adjustments made to a three-screw level in the midst of a setup operation will effectively change the elevation of the line of sight and could cause significant errors on very precise surveys (e.g., benchmark leveling or industrial surveying).

The bubble in the circular spirit level is centered by adjusting one or more of the three independent screws. Figure 3-9 shows the positions for a telescope equipped with a tube level when using three leveling foot screws. If this configuration is kept in mind when

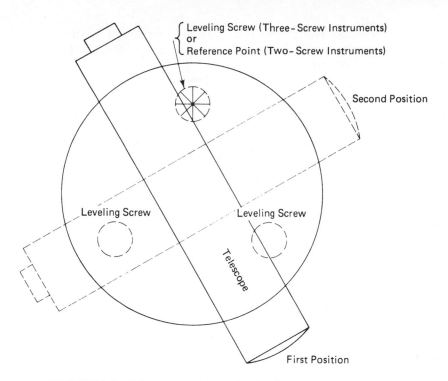

Leveling Screw (Three-Screw Instruments)
or
Reference Point (Two-Screw Instruments)

Second Position

Leveling Screw

Leveling Screw

Telescope

First Position

FIGURE 3-9 Telescope positions when leveling a three- or two-screw instrument.

one is leveling the circular spirit level, the movement of the bubble is easily predicted. Some manufacturers produce levels and transits equipped with only two leveling screws. Figure 3-9 shows that the telescope positions are identical for both two- and three-screw instruments.

The level shown in Figure 3-10 is a Swiss-made 18″/2-mm precision level. This level has the coincidence bubble display in the telescopic field of view, allowing the surveyor to verify coincidence at the instant the rod reading is taken. Both the dumpy level and the tilting level have now been largely replaced by automatic levels.

3-4-3   Automatic Level

The automatic level employs a gravity-referenced prism or mirror compensator to automatically orient the line of sight (line of collimation).

The instrument is quickly leveled when a circular spirit level is used; when the bubble has been centered (or nearly so), the compensator takes over and maintains a horizontal line of sight, even if the telescope is slightly tilted [see Figure 3-11(a)].

Automatic levels are extremely popular in present-day surveying operations and are available from most survey instrument manufacturers. They are quick to set up, are easy to use, and can be obtained for use at almost any required precision.

A word of caution: All automatic levels employ a compensator referenced by gravity. This operation normally entails freely moving prisms or mirrors, some of which are hung

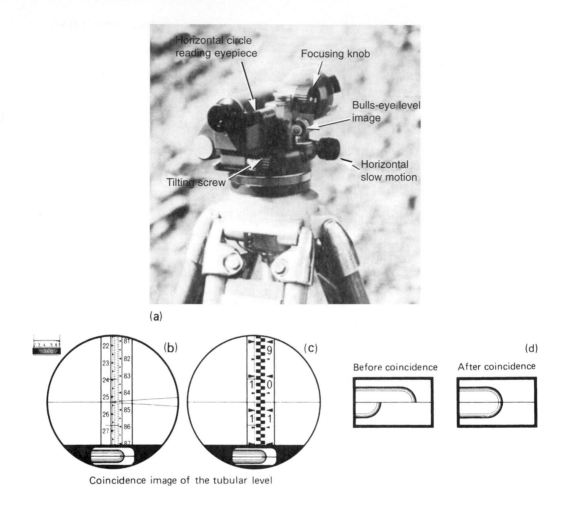

(a)

(b)   (c)   (d)

Before coincidence   After coincidence

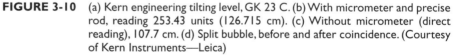

Coincidence image of the tubular level

FIGURE 3-10 (a) Kern engineering tilting level, GK 23 C. (b) With micrometer and precise rod, reading 253.43 units (126.715 cm). (c) Without micrometer (direct reading), 107.7 cm. (d) Split bubble, before and after coincidence. (Courtesy of Kern Instruments—Leica)

by fine wires. If a wire or fulcrum breaks, the compensator will become inoperative, and all subsequent rod readings will be incorrect.

The operation of the compensator can be verified by tapping the end of the telescope or by slightly turning one of the leveling screws (one manufacturer provides a push button), causing the telescopic line of sight to veer from horizontal. If the compensator is operative, the crosshair will appear to deflect momentarily before returning to its original rod reading. The constant checking of the compensator will avoid costly mistakes.

Levels used to establish or densify vertical control are manufactured so as to give precise results. These levels can be tilting levels or automatic levels. The magnifying power, setting accuracy of the tubular level or compensator, quality of optics, and so on are

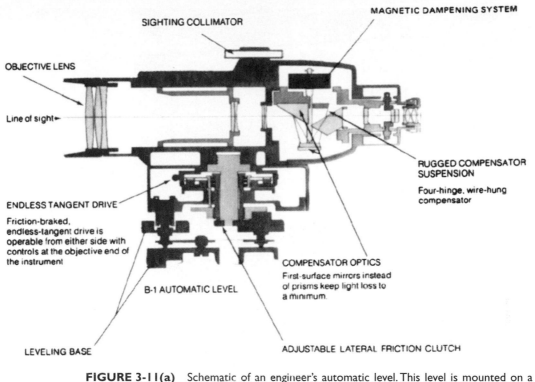

FIGURE 3-11(a)   Schematic of an engineer's automatic level. This level is mounted on a domed-head tripod, which permits rapid setup. (Courtesy Sokkia Co. Ltd.)

all improved to provide for precise rod readings. The least count on leveling rods is 0.01 ft or 0.001 m. Usually, precise levels are equipped with optical micrometers so that readings can be determined one or two places beyond the least count.

Many automatic levels utilize a concave base, which, when attached to its domed-head tripod top, can be roughly leveled by sliding the instrument on the tripod top. This rough leveling can be accomplished in a few seconds. If the bull's-eye bubble is nearly centered by this maneuver and the compensator activated, the leveling screws may not be needed at all to level the instrument.

3-4-4   Digital Level

Figure 3-11(b) shows a digital level and bar code rod. This level features digital, electronic image-processing for determining heights and distances with the automatic recording of data—for later transfer to the computer.

The digital level is an automatic level (pendulum compensator), capable of normal optical leveling with a rod graduated in feet or meters. However, this level, when used in electronic mode with the rod face graduated in bar code, will, with the press of a button, capture and process the image of the bar code rod. This processed image of the rod reading is then compared with the image of the whole rod, which is permanently stored in the level,

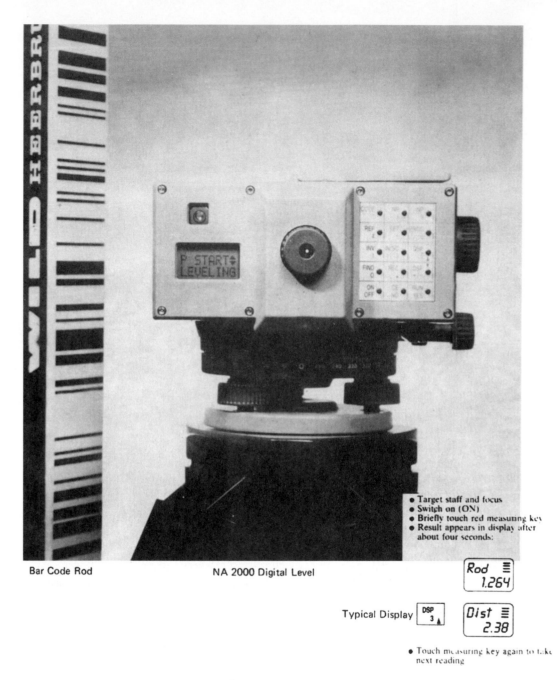

Bar Code Rod   NA 2000 Digital Level

- Target staff and focus
- Switch on (ON)
- Briefly touch red measuring key
- Result appears in display after about four seconds:

Typical Display

- Touch measuring key again to take next reading

FIGURE 3-11(b)   Wild NA 2000 Digital level and bar code rod. (Courtesy of Leica Co., Toronto)

in order to determine height and distance values. The rod shown in Figure 3-11(b) is 4.05 m long; it is graduated in bar code on one side and in either feet or meters on the other side.

After the instrument has been leveled, the image of the bar code must be properly focused by the operator; next, the operator presses the "measure" button to begin the image processing—which takes about 4 seconds [see Figure 3-11(b) for typical displays]. Although the heights and distances are automatically determined and recorded (if desired), the horizontal angles, in this case, must be read and recorded manually.

Preprogrammed functions include level loop survey, two-peg test, self-test, set time, and set units. Coding can be the same as used with Total Stations (see Chapter 5— which means that the processed leveling data can be transferred directly to the computer data base. The bar code can be read in the range of 1.8 to 100 m away from the instrument; optically the rod can be read as close as 0.5 cm. If the rod is not plumb or is being held upside down, an error message will flash on the screen. Other error messages include "instrument not level," "low battery," and "memory almost full." Rechargeable batteries are said to last for 2000 measurements. Distance accuracy is in the range of 1/2500 to 1/3000, whereas leveling accuracy is stated as having a standard deviation for a 1-km double run of 1.5 mm for electronic measurement and 2.0 mm for optical measurement.

3-5 Leveling Rods

Leveling rods are manufactured from wood, metal, or fiberglass and are graduated in feet or meters. The foot rod can be read directly to 0.01 ft, whereas the metric rod can usually be read only to 0.01 m, with millimeters being estimated. Metric rod readings are normally booked to the closest 1/3 cm (i.e., 0.000, 0.003, 0.005, 0.007, and 0.010); more precise values can be obtained by using an optical micrometer.

One-piece rods are used for more precise work. The most precise work requires the face of the rod to be an invar strip held in place under temperature-compensating spring tension.

Normal leveling utilizes two- or three-piece rods graduated in either feet or meters. The sole of the rod is a metal plate that will withstand the constant wear and tear of leveling. The zero mark is at the bottom of the metal plate. The rods are graduated in a wide variety of patterns, all of which readily respond to logical analysis; the surveyor is well advised to study an unfamiliar rod at close quarters prior to leveling to ensure that the graduations are thoroughly understood (see Figure 3-12 for a variety of graduation markings).

The rectangular sectioned rods are of either the folding (hinged) or the sliding variety. Newer fiberglass rods have oval or circular cross sections and fit telescopically together for heights of 3, 5, and 7 m, from a stored height of 1.5 m (equivalent foot rods are also available).

Benchmark leveling utilizes foldings rods or invar rods, both of which have built-in handles and rod levels. When the bubble is centered, the rod is plumb. All other rods can be plumbed by using a rod level (Figure 3-13).

Level Rod Faces

Rod faces pictured are approximately one-half actual size.

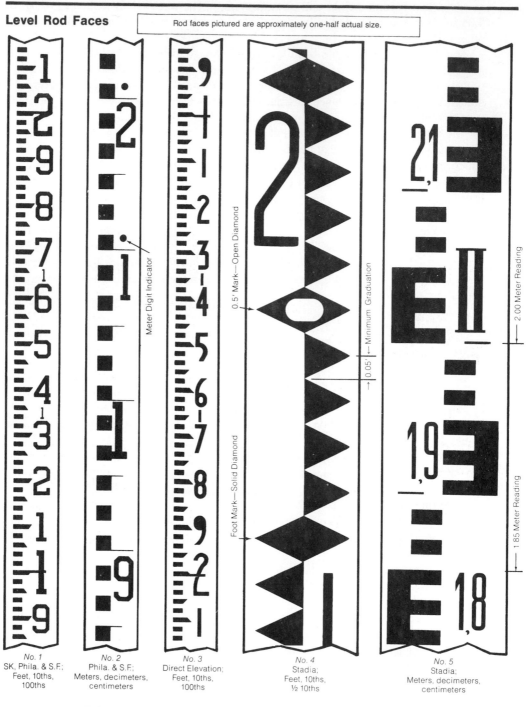

No. 1	No. 2	No. 3	No. 4	No. 5
SK, Phila. & S.F.; Feet, 10ths, 100ths	Phila. & S.F.; Meters, decimeters, centimeters	Direct Elevation; Feet, 10ths, 100ths	Stadia; Feet, 10ths, ½ 10ths	Stadia; Meters, decimeters, centimeters

FIGURE 3-12 Traditional rectangular cross-section leveling rods showing a variety of graduation markings. (Courtesy of Sokkia Co. Ltd.)

FIGURE 3-13 Circular rod level.
(Courtesy of Keuffel & Esser Co.)

3-6 Definitions for Leveling

A **benchmark (BM)** is a permanent point of known elevation. Benchmarks are established by using precise leveling techniques and instrumentation. Benchmarks are bronze disks or plugs usually set into vertical wall faces. It is important that the benchmark be placed in a structure that has substantial footings (at least below minimum frost depth penetration). Benchmark elevations and locations are published by federal, state or provincial, and municipal agencies and are available to surveyors for a nominal fee.

A **temporary benchmark (TBM)** is a semipermanent point of known elevation. TBMs can be flange bolts on fire hydrants, nails in the roots of trees, top corners of concrete culvert headwalls, and so on. The elevations of TBMs are not normally published, but are available in the field notes of various surveying agencies.

A **turning point (TP)** is a point temporarily used to transfer an elevation (see Figure 3-16).

A **backsight (BS)** is a rod reading taken on a point of known elevation in order to establish the elevation of the instrument line of sight.

The **height of instrument (HI)** is the elevation of the line of sight through the level (i.e., elevation of BM + BS = HI).

A **foresight (FS)** is a rod reading taken on a turning point, benchmark, or temporary benchmark in order to determine its elevation (i.e., HI − FS = elevation of TP (or BM or TBM).

An **intermediate foresight (IS)** is a rod reading taken at any other point where the elevation is required.

$$HI - IS = elevation$$

Most engineering leveling projects are initiated to determine the elevations of intermediate points (as in profiles, cross sections, etc.).

The addition of backsights to elevations to obtain heights of instrument and the subtraction of foresights from heights of instrument to obtain new elevations are known as note reductions.

3-7 Techniques of Leveling

In leveling, as opposed to transit work, the instrument can usually be set up in a relatively convenient location. If the level has to be set up on a hard surface, such as asphalt or concrete, the tripod legs will be spread out to provide a more stable setup. When the level is to be set up on a soft surface (e.g., turf), the tripod is first set up so that the tripod top is nearly horizontal, and then the tripod legs are firmly pushed into the earth. The tripod legs are snugly tightened to the tripod top so that a leg, when raised, will just fall back under the force of its own weight. Undertightening can cause an unsteady setup, just as overtightening can cause an unsteady setup due to torque strain. On hills, it is customary to place one leg uphill and two legs downhill; the instrument operator stands facing uphill while setting up the instrument.

The tripod legs can be adjustable or straight-leg; the straight-leg tripod is recommended for leveling, as it contributes to a more stable setup. After the tripod has been set roughly level, with the feet firmly pushed into the ground, the instrument can be leveled.

Four-screw instruments attach to the tripod via a threaded base and are leveled by rotating the telescope until it is directly over a pair of opposite leveling screws and then by proceeding as described in Section 3-4-1 and Figure 3-8.

Three-screw instruments are attached to the tripod via a threaded bolt that projects up from the tripod top into the leveling base of the instrument. The three-screw instrument, which usually has a circular bull's-eye bubble level, is leveled as described in Section 3-4-2 and Figure 3-9. Unlike the four-screw instrument, the three-screw instrument can be manipulated by moving the screws one at a time, although experienced surveyors will usually manipulate at least two at a time, and often all three are manipulated at the same time. After the bubble has been centered, the instrument can be revolved to check that the circular bubble remains centered.

Once the level has been set up, preparation for the rod readings can take place. The eyepiece lenses (see Figures 3-5 and 3-6, E) are focused by turning the eyepiece focusing ring (F) until the crosshairs are as black and as sharp as possible (it helps to have the telescope pointing to a light-colored background for this operation). Next, the rod is brought into focus by turning the telescope focusing screw (Figure 3-6, C) until the rod graduations are as clear as possible. If both of these focusing operations have been carried out correctly, it will appear that the crosshairs are superimposed on the leveling rod. If either focusing operation (eyepiece or rod focus) has not been properly carried out, it will appear that the crosshair is moving slightly up and down as the observer's head moves slightly up and down. The apparent movement of the crosshair can result in incorrect readings. The condition where one or both focus adjustments have been improperly made, and the resultant error, is known as *parallax*.

Figure 3-14 shows one complete leveling cycle; actual leveling operations are no more complicated than that shown. Leveling operations typically involve numerous repe-

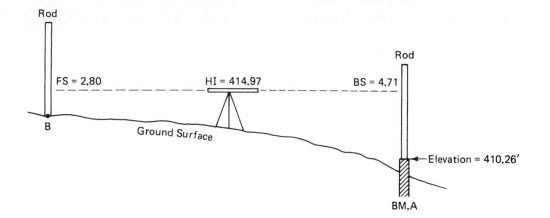

FIGURE 3-14 Leveling procedure: one setup.

titions of this leveling cycle, with some operations requiring that additional (intermediate) rod readings be taken at each instrument setup.

$$\text{Existing elevation} + \text{BS} = \text{HI} \tag{3-5}$$

$$\text{HI} - \text{FS} = \text{new elevation} \tag{3-6}$$

These two statements completely describe the differential leveling process.

When one is leveling between benchmarks or turning points, the level is set approximately midway between the BS and FS locations to eliminate (or minimize) errors due to curvature and refraction (Section 3-3) and errors due to a faulty line of sight (Section 3-11).

To ensure that the rod is plumb, either a rod level (Figure 3-13) is used, or the surveyor gently "waves the rod" toward and away from the instrument. The correct rod reading will be the lowest reading observed. The surveyor must ensure that the rod does not sit up on the back edge of the base and effectively raise the zero mark on the rod off the BM (or TP). The instrument operator is sure that the rod has been properly waved if the readings decrease to a minimum value and then increase in value (see Figure 3-15).

To determine elevation of B

Elevation pt. *A*   410.26

Backsight rod reading at *A*   +4.71 BS

Height (elevation) of instrument line of sight = 414.97 HI

Foresight rod reading at *B*   −2.80 FS

Elevation pt. *B* = 412.17

After the rod reading of 4.71 is taken at *A*, the elevation of the line of sight of the instrument is known to be 414.97 (410.26 + 4.71). The elevation of point *B* can be determined by holding the rod at *B*, sighting the rod with the instrument, and reading the rod

(a)

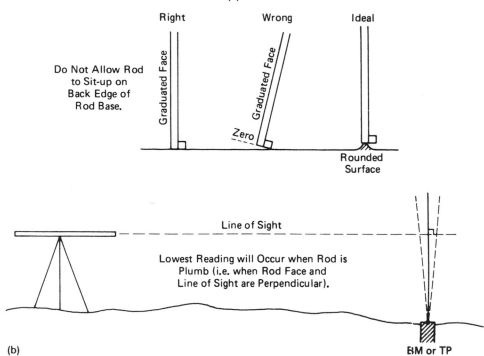

Right   Wrong   Ideal

Do Not Allow Rod
to Sit-up on
Back Edge of
Rod Base.

Graduated Face

Graduated Face

Zero

Rounded
Surface

Line of Sight

Lowest Reading will Occur when Rod is
Plumb (i.e. when Rod Face and
Line of Sight are Perpendicular).

BM or TP

(b)

FIGURE 3-15   (a) Waving the rod. (b) Waving the rod slightly to and from the instrument allows the instrument operator to take the most precise (lowest) reading.

(2.80 ft). The elevation of *B* is therefore $414.97 - 2.80 = 412.17$ ft. In addition to determining the elevation of point *B*, the elevations of any other points lower than the line of sight and visible from the level can be determined in a similar manner.

The situation depicted in Figure 3-16 shows the technique used when the point whose elevation is to be determined (BM 461) is too far from the point of known elevation (BM 460) for a one-setup solution. The elevation of an intermediate point (TP 1) is determined, allowing the surveyor to move the level to a location where BM 461 can be seen. Real-life situations may require numerous setups and the determination of the elevation of many intermediate points before getting close enough to determine the elevation of the desired point. When the elevation of the desired point has been determined, the surveyor must then either continue the survey to a point (BM) of known elevation or return (loop) the survey to the point of commencement. The survey must be closed onto a point of known elevation so that the accuracy and acceptability of the survey can be determined. If the closure is not within allowable limits, the survey must be repeated.

The arithmetic can be verified by performing the arithmetic check (page check). Since all BS are added and all FS are subtracted, when the sum of BS is added to the original elevation and then the sum of FS is subtracted from that total, the remainder should be the same as the final elevation calculated (see Figure 3-17). Arithmetic check:

$$\text{Original elevation} + \Sigma\, \text{BS} - \Sigma\, \text{FS} = \text{new elevation}$$

In the 1800s and early 1900s, leveling procedures like the one described here were used to survey locations for railroads that traversed North America between the Atlantic Ocean and the Pacific Ocean.

3-8 Benchmark Leveling (Vertical Control Surveys)

Benchmark leveling is the type of leveling employed when a system of benchmarks is to be established or when an existing system of benchmarks is to be extended or densified (e.g., perhaps a benchmark is required in a new location, or perhaps an existing benchmark has been destroyed and a suitable replacement is required). Benchmark leveling is typified by the relatively high level of precision specified, both for the instrumentation and for the technique itself.

The specifications shown in Tables 8-3 and 8-4 cover the techniques of precise leveling. Precise levels with coincidence tubular bubbles of a sensitivity of 10 seconds per 2-mm division (or equivalent for automatic levels) and with parallel-plate micrometers are used almost exclusively for this type of work. Invar rods, together with a base plate, rod level, and supports, are used in pairs to minimize the time required for successive readings. Tripods for this type of work are longer than usual, enabling the surveyor to keep the line of sight farther above the ground, thus minimizing interference and errors due to refraction. Ideally the work is performed on a cloudy, windless day, although work can proceed on a sunny day if the instrument is protected from the sun and its possible differential thermal effects on the instrument.

At the national level, benchmarks are established by federal agencies utilizing first-order methods and first-order instruments. The same high requirements are also specified for state and provincial grids; but as work proceeds from the whole to the part (i.e., down

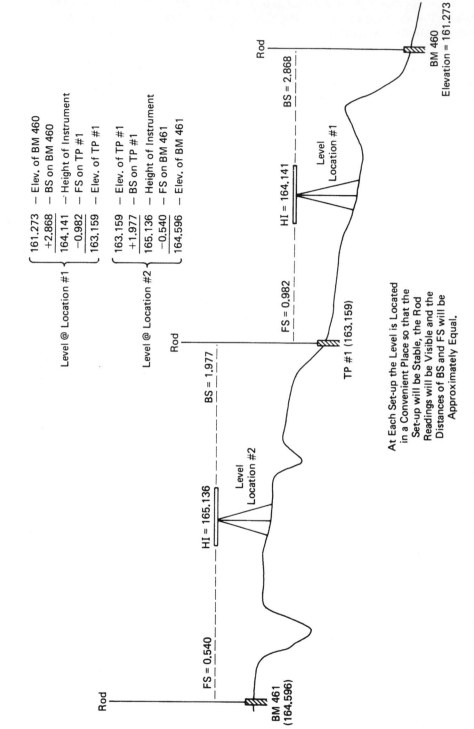

Level @ Location #1
$$\left\{\begin{array}{ll} 161.273 & -\text{ Elev. of BM 460} \\ +2.868 & -\text{ BS on BM 460} \\ \hline 164.141 & -\text{ Height of Instrument} \\ -0.982 & -\text{ FS on TP \#1} \\ \hline 163.159 & -\text{ Elev. of TP \#1} \end{array}\right.$$

Level @ Location #2
$$\left\{\begin{array}{ll} 163.159 & -\text{ Elev. of TP \#1} \\ +1.977 & -\text{ BS on TP \#1} \\ \hline 165.136 & -\text{ Height of Instrument} \\ -0.540 & -\text{ FS on BM 461} \\ \hline 164.596 & -\text{ Elev. of BM 461} \end{array}\right.$$

At Each Set-up the Level is Located in a Convenient Place so that the Set-up will be Stable, the Rod Readings will be Visible and the Distances of BS and FS will be Approximately Equal.

FIGURE 3-16 Leveling procedure: more than one setup.

BENCHMARK VERIFICATION
BM460 to BM461

KANEN – π
Job SOMERVILLE–ROD, LEVEL #09 19°C, CLOUDY
Date MAY 11, 2000 Page 62

STA	B.S. (+)	H.I.		F.S. (−)	ELEV.	DESCRIPTION
BM 460	2.868	164.141			161.273	BRONZE PLATE SET IN --- ETC.
T.P. #1	1.977	165.136		0.982	163.159	NAIL IN ROOT OF MAPLE --- ETC.
BM 461				0.540	164.596	BRONZE PLATE SET IN --- ETC.
Σ	4.845			1.522	✓	
ARITHMETIC CHECK:						
	161.273	+ 4.845	− 1.522	=	164.596	

FIGURE 3-17 Leveling field notes and arithmetic check (data from Figure 3-16).

to municipal or regional grids), the rigid specifications are relaxed somewhat. For most engineering works, benchmarks are established (from the municipal or regional grid) at third-order specifications. Benchmarks established to control isolated construction projects may be at an even lower order of accuracy.

It is customary in benchmark leveling at all orders of accuracy to first verify that the starting benchmark's elevation is correct. This can be done by two-way leveling to the closest adjacent benchmark.

This check is particularly important when the survey loops back to close on the starting benchmark and no other verification is planned.

3-9 Profile and Cross-Section Leveling

In engineering surveying, we often consider a route (road, sewer pipeline, channel, etc.) from three distinct perspectives. The *plan view* of route location is the same as if we were in an aircraft looking straight down. The *profile* of the route is a side view or elevation (see Figures 3-18 and 3-19) in which the longitudinal surfaces are highlighted (e.g., road, top and bottom of pipelines). The *cross section* shows the end view of a section at a point

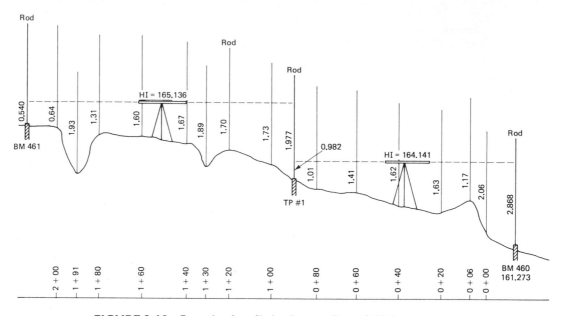

FIGURE 3-18 Example of profile leveling; see Figure 3-19 for survey notes.

(0 + 60 in Figure 3-20) and is at right angles to the centerline. These three views taken together completely define the route in *X, Y,* and *Z* coordinates.

Profile levels are taken along a path that holds interest for the designer. In road-work, preliminary surveys often profile the proposed location of the centerline (₵) (see Figure 3-18). The proposed ₵ is staked out at an even interval (50 to 100 ft or 20 to 30 m). The level is set up in a convenient location so that the benchmark and as many interme-diate points as possible can be sighted. Rod readings are taken at the even station loca-tions and at any other point where the ground surface has a significant change in slope. When the rod is moved to a new location and it cannot be seen from the instrument, a turning point is called for so that the instrument can be moved ahead and the remaining stations leveled.

The turning point can be taken on a wood stake, the corner of concrete step or con-crete headwall, a lug on the flange of a hydrant, and so on. The turning point should be a solid, well-defined point that can be precisely described and, it is hoped, found again at a future date. In the case of leveling across fields, it usually is not possible to find turning point features of any permanence; in that case, stakes are driven in and then abandoned when the survey is finished. In the example shown in Figure 3-19, the survey was closed acceptably to BM 461; had there been no benchmark at the end of the profile, the surveyor would have looped back and closed into the initial benchmark.

The field notes for the profile leveling shown in Figure 3-18 are shown in Fig-ure 3-19. The intermediate sights (IS) are shown in a separate column, and the elevations at the intermediate sights show the same number of decimals as shown in the rod readings. Rod readings on turf, ground, and the like are usually taken to the closest 0.1 ft or 0.01 m.

SMITH—NOTES
BROWN—π
JONES—ROD

Job 21 °C — SUNNY   LEVEL #L-14
Date .... AUG 3 1999 .... Page 72

STA.	B.S.	H.I.	I.S	F.S.	ELEV.	DESCRIPTION
BM 460	2.868	164.141			161.273	BRONZE PLATE SET IN --- ETC.
0 + 00			2.06		162.08	₵
0 + 06			1.17		162.97	₵ -TOP OF BERM
0 + 20			1.63		162.51	₵
0 + 40			1.62		162.52	₵
0 + 60			1.41		162.73	₵
0 + 80			1.01		163.13	₵
T.P. #1	1.977	165.136		0.982	163.159	NAIL IN ROOT OF MAPLE --- ETC.
1 + 00			1.73		163.41	₵
1 + 20			1.70		163.44	₵
1 + 30			1.89		163.25	₵ BOTTOM OF GULLY
1 + 40			1.67		163.47	₵
1 + 60			1.60		163.54	₵
1 + 80			1.31		163.83	₵
1 + 91			1.93		163.21	₵ BOTTOM OF GULLY
2 + 00			0.64		164.50	₵
BM 461				0.540	164.596	BRONZE PLATE SET IN --- ETC.

$\Sigma = 4.845$ $\Sigma = 1.522$

ARITHMETIC CHECK: $161.273 + 4.845 - 1.522 = 164.596$

164.591 — PUBLISHED ELEV.

$E = 164.596$

164.591

0.005

ALLOWABLE ERROR (3RD ORDER)

$= 12 \text{ mm } \sqrt{K}, = .012\sqrt{.2} = .0054 \text{ m}$

ABOVE ERROR (.005) SATISFIES 3RD ORDER.

FIGURE 3-19 Profile field notes.

Rod readings taken on concrete, steel, asphalt, and so on are usually taken to the closest 0.01 ft or 0.003 m.

It is a waste of time and money to read the rod more precisely than conditions warrant.

The reader is referred to Chapter 7 for details on plotting the profile.

When the final route of the facility has been agreed on, further surveying is required. Once again the ₵ is staked (if necessary), and cross sections are taken at all even stations. In roadwork, rod readings are taken along a line perpendicular to ₵ at each even station. The rod is held at each significant change in surface slope and at the limits (₤ of the job. In uniformly sloping land areas, it is often the case that the only rod readings required at each cross-sectioned station are at ₵ and the two ₤'s. Chapter 15 shows how the cross sections are plotted and then utilized to compute volumes of cut and fill (₤ denotes the streetline or property line and ₵ the centerline).

Figure 3-21 illustrates the rod positions required to suitably define the ground surface at 2 + 60, at right angles to ₵. Figure 3-22 shows typical *cross-section* note forms

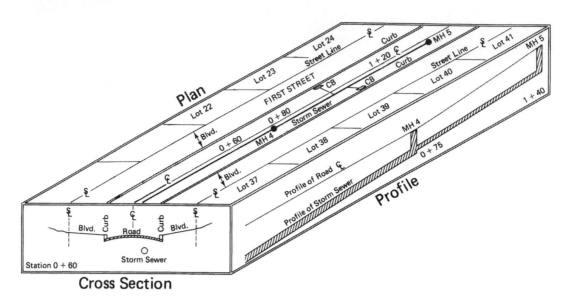

Cross Section

FIGURE 3-20 Relationship of plan, profile, and cross-section views.

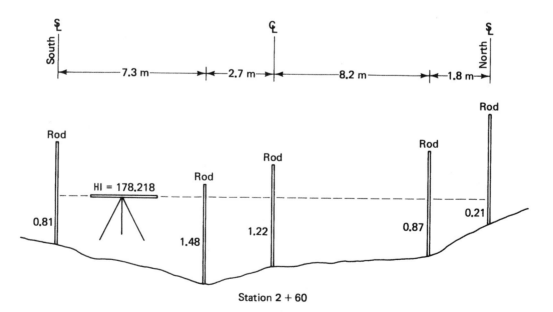

Station 2 + 60

FIGURE 3-21 Cross-section surveying.

Chap. 3   Leveling

SMITH−NOTES   JONES−ROD
BROWN−π   TYLER−TAPE
LEVEL #6

CROSS−SECTIONS FOR PROPOSED ....
LOCATION OF DUNCAN ROAD ....

Job .. 14 °C .. CLOUDY
Date .... NOV 24 2000 .... Page 23

STA.	B.S.	H.I.	I.S.	F.S.	ELEV.	DESCRIPTION
BM #28	2.011	178.218			176.207	BRONZE PLATE SET IN SOUTH WALL, 0.50m.
		(178.22)				ABOVE GROUND, CIVIC #2242, 23RD AVE.
2 + 60						
10 m LT			0.81		177.41	S . ₵
2.7 m LT			1.48		176.74	BOTTOM OF SWALE
₵			1.22		177.00	₵
8.2 m RT			0.87		177.35	CHANGE IN SLOPE
10 m RT			0.21		178.01	N . ₵
2 + 80						
10 m LT			1.02		177.20	S . ₵
3.8 m LT			1.64		176.58	BOTTOM OF SWALE
₵			1.51		176.71	₵
7.8 m RT			1.10		177.12	CHANGE IN SLOPE
10 m RT			0.43		177.79	N . ₵

FIGURE 3-22 Cross-section notes (municipal format).

employed in many municipalities. Figure 3-23 shows typical *cross-section* note forms favored by many highway agencies.

The student will note that the HI (178.218) has been rounded to two decimals (178.22) to facilitate reduction of the two-decimal rod readings. The rounded value is placed in brackets to distinguish it from the correct HI, from which the next FS will be subtracted.

Road and highway construction often requires the location of granular (sand, gravel) deposits for use in the highway road bed. These *borrow pits* (gravel pits) are surveyed to determine the volume of material "borrowed" and transported to the site. Before any excavation takes place, one or more reference baselines are established, and two benchmarks (at minimum) are located in convenient locations. The reference lines are located in secure locations where neither the stripping and stockpiling of topsoil nor the actual excavation of the granular material will endanger the stakes (Figure 3-24). Cross sections are taken over (and beyond) the area of proposed excavation. These original **cross sections** will be used as data against which interim and final excavations will be measured. The volumes calculated from the **cross sections** (see Chapter 15) are often converted to tons (tonnes) for payment purposes. In many locations, weigh scales are located at the pit to aid in converting the volumes and as a check on the calculated quantities.

CROSS-SECTIONS FOR PROPOSED

LOCATION OF DUNCAN HIGHWAY

SMITH—NOTES   JONES—ROD
BROWN—π   TYLER—TAPE
Job 14 °C   CLOUDY   LEVEL #6
Date NOV 24 2000   Page 23

STA.	B.S.	H.I.	I.S	F.S.	ELEV.	
	2.011	178.218			176.207	BRONZE PLATE SET IN SOUTH WALL
		(178.22)				0.50 ABOVE GROUND, CIVIC #2242, 23RD AVE.
						LEFT ℄ RIGHT
						10.0 2.7 8.2 10.0
2+60						0.81 1.48 1.22 0.87 0.21
						177.41 176.74 177.00 177.35 178.01
						10.0 3.8 7.8 10.0
2+80						1.02 1.64 1.51 1.10 0.43
						177.20 176.58 176.71 177.12 177.79

FIGURE 3-23 Cross-section notes (highway format).

The original **cross sections** are taken over a grid at 50-ft (20-m) intervals. As the excavation proceeds, additional rod readings (in addition to 50-ft grid readings) for top and bottom of excavation are required. Permanent targets can be established to assist in the alignment of the cross-section lines running perpendicular to the baseline at each 50-ft station. If permanent targets have not been erected, a surveyor on the baseline can keep the rod on line by using a prism or estimated right angles.

3-10   Reciprocal Leveling

Section 3-7 advises the surveyor to keep BS and FS distances roughly equal so that instrumental and natural errors will cancel out. In some situations, such as river or valley crossings, it is not always possible to balance BS and FS distances. The reciprocal leveling technique is illustrated in Figure 3-25. The level is set up and readings are taken on TP 23 and TP 24. (Precision can be improved by taking several readings on the far point, TP 24, and then averaging the results.) The level is then moved to the far side of the river, and the process is repeated. The differences in elevation thus obtained are averaged to obtain the

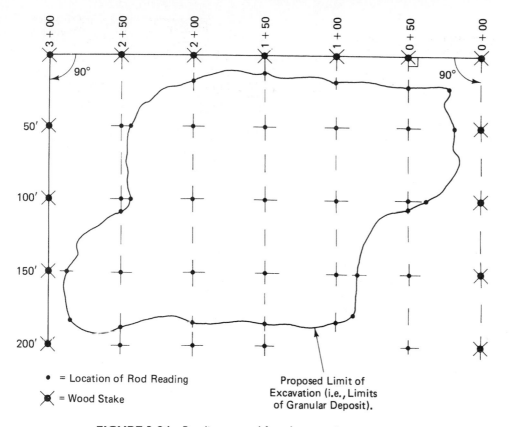

3 + 00   2 + 50   2 + 00   1 + 50   1 + 00   0 + 50   0 + 00

90°   90°

50'

100'

150'

200'

• = Location of Rod Reading

✖ = Wood Stake

Proposed Limit of
Excavation (i.e., Limits
of Granular Deposit).

FIGURE 3-24 Baseline control for a borrow pit survey.

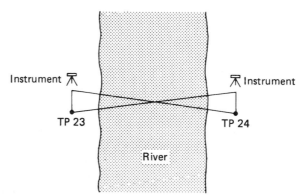

Instrument 📷   📷 Instrument

TP 23   TP 24

River

FIGURE 3-25 Reciprocal leveling.

Sec. 3-10   Reciprocal Leveling   77

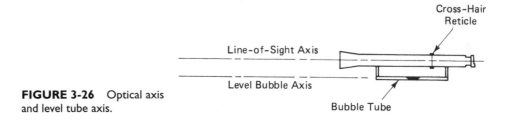

FIGURE 3-26 Optical axis and level tube axis.

Line-of-Sight Axis

Level Bubble Axis

Cross-Hair Reticle

Bubble Tube

final result. The averaging process will eliminate instrumental errors and natural errors, such as curvature. Errors due to refraction can be minimized by ensuring that the elapsed time for the process is kept to a minimum.

3-11   Peg Test

The purpose of the peg test is to check that the line of sight through the level is horizontal (i.e., parallel to the axis of the bubble tube). The line of sight axis is defined by the location of the horizontal crosshair (see Figure 3-26). The reader is referred to Chapter 4 for a description of the horizontal crosshair orientation adjustment.

To perform the peg test, the surveyor first places two stakes at a distance of 200 to 300 ft (60 to 90 m) apart. The level is set up midway (paced) between the two stakes, and rod readings are taken at both locations (see Figure 3-27, first setup).

If the line of sight through the level is not horizontal, the errors in rod readings (Δe_1) at both points A and B will be identical, as the level is halfway between the points. Since the errors are identical, the calculated difference in elevation between points A and B (difference in rod readings) will be the *true* difference in elevation.

The level is then moved to one of the points (A) and set up so that the eyepiece of the telescope just touches the rod as it is being held plumb at point A. The rod reading (a_2) can be determined by sighting backward through the objective lens at a pencil point that is being moved slowly up and down the rod. The pencil point can be precisely centered, even though the crosshairs are not visible, because the circular field of view is relatively small. Once that reverse rod reading has been determined and booked, the rod is held at B and a normal rod reading obtained. (The reverse rod reading at A will not contain any line-of-sight error because the crosshair was not used to obtain the rod reading.)

■ EXAMPLE 3-2

First setup: Rod reading at A, $a_1 = 1.075$

Rod reading at B, $b_1 = \underline{1.247}$

True difference in elevations $= 0.172$

Second setup: Rod reading at A, $a_2 = 1.783$

Rod reading at B, $b_2 = \underline{1.946*}$

Apparent difference in elevation $= 0.163$

Error (Δe_2) in 60 m $= 0.009$

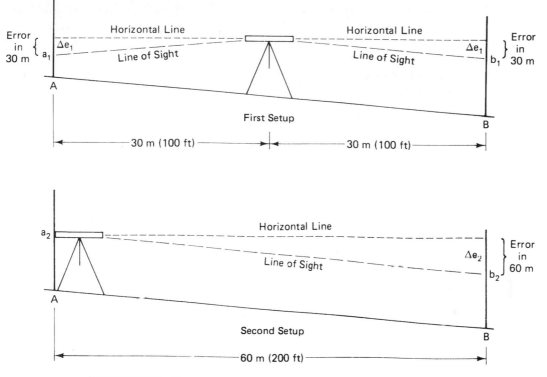

FIGURE 3-27 Peg test.

This is an error of -0.00015 m/m. Therefore, the **collimation correction** (C factor) $= +0.00015$ m/m. (*Had there been *no* error in the instrument line of sight, the rod reading at b_2 would have been 1.955, i.e., $1.783 + 0.172$.)

In Section 3-7, the reader was advised to try to keep the BS and FS distances equal; the peg test illustrates clearly the benefits to be gained by use of this technique. If the BS and FS distances are kept roughly equal, errors due to a faulty line of sight simply do not have the opportunity to develop.

■ EXAMPLE 3-3

If the level used in the peg test of Example 3-2 is used in the field with a BS distance of 80 m and an FS distance of 70 m, the net error in the rod readings will be $10 \times 0.00015 = 0.0015$ (0.002). That is, for a relatively large differential in distances and a large line-of-sight error (0.009 for 60 m), the effect on the survey is negligible for ordinary work.

The peg test can also be accomplished by using the techniques of reciprocal leveling (Section 3-10).

3-12 Three-Wire Leveling

Leveling can be performed by utilizing the stadia crosshairs found on most levels (all theodolites). See Figure 3-28. Each backsight (BS) and foresight (FS) is recorded by reading the stadia hairs in addition to the horizontal crosshair. The three readings thus obtained are averaged to obtain the desired value.

The stadia hairs (wires) are positioned an equal distance above and below the main crosshair and are spaced to give 1.00 ft (m) of interval for each 100 ft (m) of horizontal distance that the rod is away from the level.

The recording of three readings at each sighting enables the surveyor to perform a relatively precise survey while utilizing ordinary levels. Readings to the closest thousandth of a foot (mm) are estimated and recorded. The leveling rod used for this type of work should be calibrated to ensure its integrity. Use of an invar rod is recommended.

Figure 3-29 shows typical notes for benchmark leveling. A realistic survey would include a completed loop or a check into another BM of known elevation.

If the collimation correction as calculated in Section 3-11 (+0.00015 m/m) is applied to the survey shown in Figure 3-29, the correction to the elevation is as follows:

$$C = +0.00015 \times (62.9 - 61.5) = +0.0002$$

Sum of FS corrected to $5.7196 + 0.0002 = 5.7198$

Elevation of BM 201

$$
\begin{aligned}
\text{Elev. BM 17} &= 186.2830 \\
+ \, \Sigma \, \text{BS} &= \underline{+2.4143} \\
&\ 188.6973 \\
- \Sigma \, \text{FS (corrected)} &\ \underline{-5.7198} \\
\text{Elev. BM 201} &= 182.9775 \text{ (corrected for collimation)}
\end{aligned}
$$

When levels are being used for precise purposes, it is customary to determine the collimation correction at least once each day.

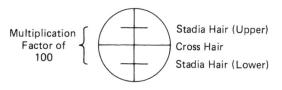

FIGURE 3-28 Reticle crosshairs. i.e. 100 × Stadia Hair Interval = Distance

B.M. LEVELING—3 WIRE
B.M. #17 to B.M. 201
(RETURN RUN ON P.48)
JONES—NOTES
SMITH—$\overline{\wedge}$
BROWN—ROD
GREEN—ROD
Job ROD #19;   INST. #L.33   8°C CLOUDY
Date MAR 3 2000   Page 47

STA.	B.S.	DIST.	F.S.	DIST.	ELEV.	DESCRIPTION
BM #17					186.2830	BRONZE PLATE SET IN WALL --- ETC.
	0.825		1.775			
	0.725	10.0	1.673	10.2	+0.7253	
	0.626	9.9	1.572	10.1	187.0083	
	2.176	19.9	5.020	20.3	−1.6733	
	+0.7253		−1.6733			
T.P. #1					185.3350	N.LUG TOP FLANGE FIRE HYD. N/S
	0.698		1.750			MAIN ST. OPP. CIVIC #181.
	0.571	12.7	1.620	13.0	+0.5710	
	0.444	12.7	1.490	13.0	185.9060	
	1.713	25.4	4.860	26.0	−1.6200	
	+0.5710		−1.6200			
T.P. #2					184.2860	N.LUG TOP FLANGE FIRE HYD. N/S
	1.199		2.509			MAIN ST. OPP. CIVIC #163.
	1.118	8.1	2.427	8.2	+1.1180	
	1.037	8.1	2.343	8.4	185.4040	
	3.354	16.2	7.279	16.6	−2.4263	
	+1.1180		−2.4263			
BM. 201					182.9777	BRONZE PLATE SET IN ESTLY FACE
						OF RETAINING WALL --- ETC.
Σ	+2.4143	61.5m	−5.7196	62.9m		

ARITHMETIC CHECK: 186.283 + 2.4143 − 5.7196 = √

182.9777

FIGURE 3-29 Survey notes for three-wire leveling.

3-13   Trigonometric Leveling

The difference in elevation between A and B (Figure 3-30) can be determined if the vertical angle (α) and the slope distance (S) are measured.

$$V = S \sin \alpha \tag{3-7}$$

$$\text{Elevation at } \overline{\wedge} + \text{hi} \pm V - \text{RR} = \text{elevation at rod} \tag{3-8}$$

Note: The hi in this case is not the elevation of the line of sight as it is in differential leveling, but instead hi here refers to the distance from point A up to the optical center of the theodolite, measured with a steel tape or rod. See also Chapter 7.

Trigonometric leveling can be used where it is not feasible to use a level. For example, a survey crew running ₵ profile for a route survey comes to a point where the ₵ runs off a cliff; in that case, a theodolite can be set up on ₵ with the angle and distance measured to a ₵ station at the lower elevation.

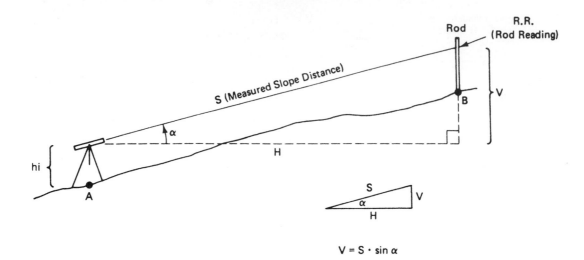

$$V = S \cdot \sin \alpha$$

FIGURE 3-30 Trigonometric leveling.

The slope distance can be determined by using a steel tape, stadia methods (Chapter 7), or EDM methods (Chapter 5). The angle is normally measured by use of a theodolite, but for lower-order surveys, a clinometer (Section 2-5-2) could be used.

For long distances (associated with EDM), curvature and refraction errors must be eliminated. These matters are discussed in Chapter 5.

■ **EXAMPLE 3-4**
See Figure 3-31.

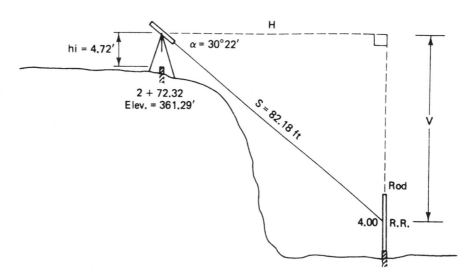

FIGURE 3-31 Example of trigonometric leveling (see Section 3-13).

$$V = S \sin \alpha \qquad (3\text{-}7)$$
$$= 82.18 \sin 30°22'$$
$$= 41.54 \text{ ft}$$

$$\text{Elev. at } \overline{\wedge} + hi \pm V - RR = \text{elevation at rod} \qquad (3\text{-}8)$$
$$361.29 + 4.72 - 41.54 - 4.00 =$$
$$320.47 =$$

Note: The RR *could* have been 4.72, the value of the hi. If that reading had been visible, the surveyor would have sighted on it in order to eliminate $+hi$ and $-RR$ from the calculation. That is,

$$\text{Elev. at } \overline{\wedge} \pm V = \text{elevation at rod} \qquad (3\text{-}8a)$$

In this example, the station (chainage) of the rod station could also be determined.

See Section 5-9 for a discussion of trigonometric leveling using Total Stations.

3-14 Suggestions for Rod Work

1. The rod should be properly extended and clamped; care should be taken to ensure that the bottom of the sole plate does not become encrusted with mud and the like, which could result in mistaken readings. If a rod target is being used, care must be exercised to ensure that it is properly positioned and that it cannot slip.

2. The rod should be held plumb for all rod readings. Either a rod level will be used, or the rod will be gently waved to and from the instrument so that the lowest (indicating a plumb rod) reading can be determined. This practice is particularly important for all backsights and foresights.

3. The surveyor should ensure that all points used as turning points are suitable (i.e., describable, identifiable, and capable of having the elevation determined to the closest 0.01 ft or 0.001 m). The TP should be nearly equidistant from the two proposed instrument locations.

4. Care should be taken to ensure that the rod is held in precisely the same position for the backsight as it was for the foresight for all turning points.

5. If the rod is temporarily being held near to, but not on, a required location, the face of the rod should be turned away from the instrument so that the instrument operator cannot take a mistaken reading. This type of mistaken reading usually occurs when the distance between the two surveyors is too far to allow for voice communication and sometimes even for good visual contact.

3-15 Suggestions for Instrument Work

1. Use a straight-leg (nonadjustable) tripod, if possible.

2. Tripod legs should be tightened so that when one leg is extended horizontally, it falls slowly back to the ground under its own weight.

3. The instrument can be comfortably carried resting on one shoulder; if tree branches or other obstructions (e.g., door frames) threaten the safety of the instrument, it should be carried cradled under one arm with the instrument forward, where it can be seen.

4. When setting up the instrument, gently force the legs into the ground by applying weight on the tripod shoe spurs. On rigid surfaces (e.g., concrete), the tripod legs should be spread farther apart to increase stability.

5. When the tripod is to be set up on a hillside, two legs should be placed downhill and the third leg placed uphill. The instrument can be set up roughly leveled by careful manipulation of the third, uphill leg.

6. The location of the level setup should be chosen wisely with respect to the ability to "see" the maximum number of rod locations, particularly BS and FS locations.

7. Prior to taking rod readings, the crosshair should be sharply focused; it helps to point the instrument toward a light-colored background.

8. When the surveyor observes apparent movement of the crosshairs on the rod (parallax), he or she should carefully check the crosshair focus adjustment and the objective focus adjustment for consistent results.

9. The surveyor should consistently read the rod at either the top or the bottom of the crosshair.

10. Never move the level before a foresight is taken; otherwise, all work done from that HI will have to be repeated.

11. Check to ensure that the level bubble remains centered or that the compensating device (in automatic levels) is operating.

12. Rod readings (and the line of sight) should be kept at least 18 in. (0.5 m) above the ground surface to help minimize refraction errors when one is performing a precise level survey.

3-16   Mistakes in Leveling

Mistakes in level loops can be detected by performing arithmetic checks and also by closing in on the starting BM or on any other BM whose elevation is known.

Mistakes in rod readings that do not form part of a level loop, such as intermediate sights taken in profiles, cross sections, or construction grades, are a much more irksome problem. It is bad enough to discover that a level loop contains mistakes and must be repeated, but it is a far more serious problem to have to redesign a highway profile because a key elevation contains a mistake or to have to break out a concrete bridge abutment (the day after the concrete was poured) because the grade stake elevation contained a mistake.

Since intermediate rod readings cannot be inherently checked, it is essential that the opportunities for mistakes be minimized.

Common mistakes in leveling include the following: misreading the foot (meter) value, transposing figures, not holding the rod in the correct location, resting the hands on the tripod while reading the rod and causing the instrument to go off level, entering the rod readings incorrectly (i.e., switching BS and FS), giving a correct rod reading the wrong station identification, and making mistakes in the note reduction arithmetic.

Mistakes in arithmetic can be largely eliminated by having the other crew members check the reductions and initial each page of notes checked. Mistakes in the leveling operation cannot be totally eliminated, but they can be minimized if the crew members are aware that mistakes can (and probably will) occur. All crew members should be constantly alert as to the possible occurrence of mistakes, and all crew members should try to develop rigid routines for doing their work so that mistakes, when they do eventually occur, will be all the more noticeable.

Problems

3-1. Compute the error due to curvature and refraction for the following distances:
    (a) 400 ft   **(b)** 1200 ft   **(c)** 300 m
    (d) 4 miles   **(e)** 2000 m   **(f)** 4 kilometers

3-2. Determine the rod readings indicated on the foot and metric rod illustrations shown. The foot readings are to the closest 0.01 ft, and the metric readings are to the closest half or third centimeter.

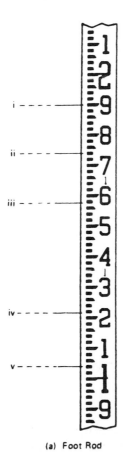

(a) Foot Rod

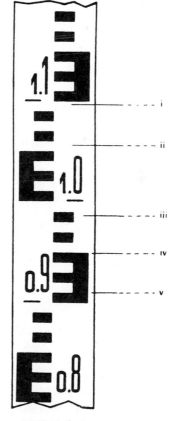

(b) Metric Rod

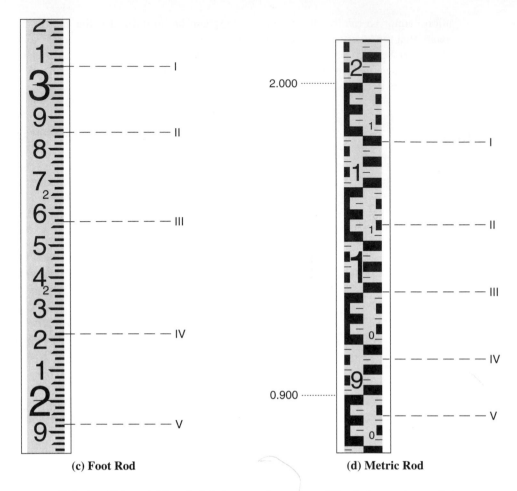

(c) Foot Rod **(d) Metric Rod**

3-3. An offshore drilling rig is being towed out to sea. What is the maximum distance away that the navigation lights can still be seen by an observer standing at the shoreline? The observer's eye height is 5′9″, and the uppermost navigation light is 225 ft above the water.

3-4. Prepare a set of level notes for the survey illustrated. Show the arithmetic check.

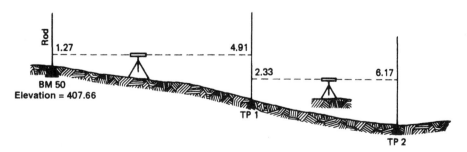

3-5. Prepare a set of profile leveling notes for the survey illustrated. In addition to computing all elevations, show the arithmetic check and the resulting error in closure.

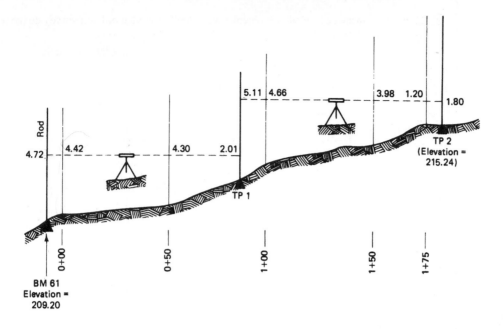

3-6. Complete the accompanying set of differential leveling notes, and perform the arithmetic check.

Station	BS	HI	FS	Elevation
BM 3	1.613			183.723
TP 1	1.425		1.927	
TP 2	1.307		1.710	
TP 3	1.340		1.273	
BM 3			0.780	

3-7. If the loop distance in Problem 3-6 is 700 m, for what order of survey do the results qualify? (Use Table 8-2 or Table 8-3.)

3-8. Reduce the accompanying set of differential leveling notes, and perform the arithmetic check.

Station	BS	HI	FS	Elevation
BM 100	2.71			611.68
TP 1	3.62		4.88	
TP 2	3.51		3.97	
TP 3	3.17		2.81	
TP 4	1.47		1.62	
BM 100			1.21	

3-9. If the distance leveled in Problem 3-8 is 1000 ft, for what order of survey do the results qualify? (See Tables 8-3 and 8-4.)

3-10. Reduce the accompanying set of profile notes, and perform the arithmetic check.

Station	BS	HI	IS	FS	Elevation
BM S. 101	0.475				212.815
0 + 000			0.02		
0 + 020			0.41		
0 + 040			0.73		
0 + 060			0.70		
0 + 066.28			0.726		
0 + 080			1.38		
0 + 100			1.75		
0 + 120			2.47		
TP 1	0.666			2.993	
0 + 140			0.57		
0 + 143.78			0.634		
0 + 147.02			0.681		
0 + 160			0.71		
0 + 180			0.69		
0 + 200			1.37		
TP 2	0.033			1.705	
BM S. 102				2.891	

3-11. Reduce the accompanying set of municipal cross-section notes.

Station	BS	HI	IS	FS	Elevation
BM 41	6.21				177.49
TP 13	4.10			0.89	
12 + 00					
50 ft left			3.9		
18.3 ft left			4.6		
℄			6.33		
20.1 ft right			7.9		
50 ft right			8.2		
13 + 00					
50 ft left			5.0		
19.6 ft left			5.7		
℄			7.54		
20.7 ft right			7.9		
50 ft right			8.4		
TP 14	7.39			1.12	
BM S. 22				2.41	

3-12. Complete the accompanying set of level notes, and perform the arithmetic check.

Station	BS	HI	IS	FS	Elevation
BM 102	10.62				236.63
TP 1	9.45			3.99	
TP 2	7.77			3.10	
0 + 00			2.7		
0 + 50			2.1		
1 + 00			0.2		
TP 3	5.78			2.75	
1 + 50			1.7		
1 + 71.20			1.38		
2 + 00			0.6		
BM 103				2.44	

3-13. Complete the accompanying set of profile level notes, and perform the arithmetic check.

Station	BS	HI	IS	FS	Elevation
BM 5	1.447				155.440
0 + 000			0.17		
0 + 020			0.37		
0 + 040			0.65		
0 + 060			0.69		
0 + 080			0.72		
0 + 090.30			0.733		
0 + 100			0.79		
TP 1	1.880			1.925	
0 + 120			0.98		
0 + 137.33			0.913		
0 + 140			0.88		
0 + 160			0.83		
0 + 180			0.80		
0 + 200			0.71		
TP 2	0.823			1.675	
BM 6				1.390	

3-14. Complete the accompanying set of municipal cross-section notes.

Station	BS	HI	IS	FS	Elevation
BM 21	4.26				672.18
TP 4	6.11			6.83	
6 + 00					
25 ft left			2.7		
15 ft left			3.8		
₵			3.1		
15 ft right			3.7		
25 ft right			2.6		
7 + 00					
25 ft left			4.1		
15 ft left			5.3		
₵			4.7		
15 ft right			5.3		
25 ft right			3.8		
TP 5	8.47			7.29	
BM 22				9.77	

3-15. Complete the accompanying set of highway cross-section notes.

Station	BS	HI	FS	Elevation	Left		℄	Right	
BM 107	7.71			522.68					
80 + 50					60' 9.7	28' 8.0	5.7	32' 4.3	60' 4.0
81 + 00					60' 10.1	25' 9.7	6.8	30' 6.0	60' 5.3
81 + 50					60' 11.7	27' 11.0	9.2	33' 8.3	60' 8.0
TP 1			10.17						

-- 3-16. A level is set up midway between two wood stakes that are about 300' apart. The rod reading on stake A is 8.72' and on stake B is 5.61'. The level is then moved to point B and set up so that the eyepiece end of the telescope is just touching the rod as it is held plumb on the stake. A reading of 5.42' is taken on the rod at B by sighting backwards through the telescope. The level is then sighted on the rod held on stake A, where a reading of 8.57' is noted.

(a) What is the correct difference in elevation between the tops of stakes A and B?

(b) If the level had been in perfect adjustment, what reading would have been observed at A from the second setup?

(c) What is the line-of-sight error in 300'?

(d) Describe how you would eliminate the line-of-sight error from the telescope.

— 3-17. A preengineering baseline was run down a very steep hill. Rather than measure horizontally downhill with the steel tape, the surveyor measured the vertical angle with a theodolite and the slope distance with a 200' steel tape. The vertical angle was $-21°26'$ turned to a point on a plumbed range pole 4.88' above the ground. The slope distance from the theodolite to the point on the range pole was 148.61'. The theodolite's optical center was 4.66' above the upper baseline station at 110 + 71.25.

(a) If the elevation of the upper station is 829.76, what is the elevation of the lower station?

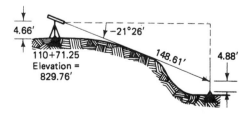

(b) What is the chainage of the lower station?

3-18. It is required to establish the elevation of point B from point A (elevation = 187.298 m); A and B are on opposite sides of a 12-lane highway.

Reciprocal leveling is used, with the following results:

Setup at A side of highway

   Rod reading on A = 0.673 m;

   Rod readings on B = 2.416 and 2.418 m

Setup at B side of highway

   Rod reading on B = 2.992 m;

   Rod readings on A = 1.254 and 1.250 m

(a) What is the elevation of point B?

(b) What is the leveling error?

Chapter 4

Transits and Theodolites

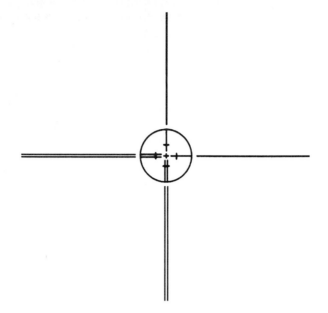

4-1 Introduction

As noted in Section 1.5, the term *transit* or *theodolite* (transiting theodolite) can be used to describe those survey instruments designed to precisely measure horizontal and vertical angles. In addition to measuring horizontal and vertical angles, transits/theodolites can be used to establish straight and curved alignments in the field.

Originally the instrument designed to measure angles was called a theodolite. As instrument design evolved, one of the notable modifications was the shortening of the long telescope, which permitted the telescope to be revolved 360° about its horizontal axis. This act of turning the telescope over, called *transiting* the telescope, sped up alignment work and permitted the averaging out of sighting and instrumental errors. The theodolite then became known as the *transiting theodolite,* but over time, it has come to be referred to simply as either transit or theodolite.

Transits/theodolites have, during the twentieth century, gone through three distinctive evolutionary stages:

1. The open face, vernier-equipped engineers' transit (American transit) with a four-screw leveling base (see Figure 4-1);
2. The enclosed, optical readout transit/theodolite with a direct digital readout or micrometer-equipped readout (for more precise readings), with a three-screw leveling base (see Figure 4-2); and
3. The enclosed electronic transit/theodolite with a direct readout, with a three-screw leveling base (see Figure 4-3).

Most recently manufactured transits are electronic, but many of the earlier optical instruments and even a few vernier instruments still survive in the field (and in the classroom)—no doubt a tribute to the excellent craftsmanship of the instrument makers. In past

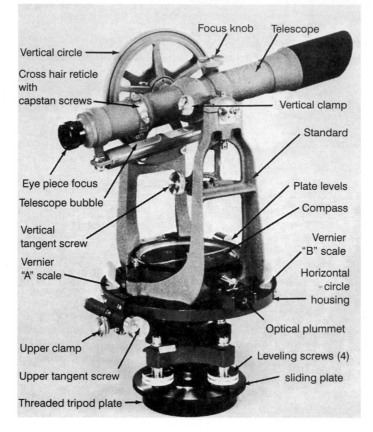

Focus knob   Telescope

Vertical circle

Cross hair reticle
with
capstan screws

Vertical clamp

Standard

Eye piece focus

Telescope bubble

Plate levels

Compass

Vertical
tangent screw

Vernier
"A" scale

Vernier
"B" scale

Horizontal
circle
housing

Optical plummet

Upper clamp

Leveling screws (4)

Upper tangent screw

sliding plate

Threaded tripod plate

FIGURE 4-1   Engineer's transit. (Courtesy of Keuffel & Esser Co.)

editions of this text, the instruments were introduced chronologically; however, in this edition, the vernier transits are discussed last—recognizing their fading importance.

The electronic transit will probably be the last in the line of transits/theodolites. Because of the versatility and lower cost of electronic equipment, future field instruments will be more along the line of the Total Station (see Chapter 5), which combines all the features of an electronic transit with the additional capabilities of electronically measuring horizontal and vertical distances and storing all measurements, along with relevant attribute data, for future transfer to the computer. Future "transits" may even include a Global Positioning System (GPS) receiver (see Chapter 9) to permit precise positioning—in both horizontal and vertical planes.

4-2   Vertical Angles

Figure 4-4 illustrates that vertical angles can be referenced to a horizontal line or to a vertical line. Vernier transits are designed to read plus or minus vertical angles from a

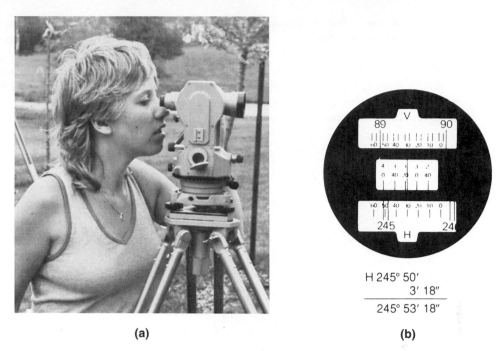

H 245° 50'
    3' 18"

245° 53' 18"

(a)   **(b)**

FIGURE 4-2   (a) Twenty-second micrometer theodolite, Sokkia TM 20. (b) Horizontal and vertical scales with micrometer scale.

FIGURE 4-3   Leica T-1600 digital electronic theodolite. This instrument has keyboards front and back, an angle accuracy of 1.5", automatic error monitoring, some surveying programs (e.g., "free stationing"), and interfaces that permit the addition of a data storage module and an electronic distance measurement device. (Courtesy of Leica Canada Co.)

horizontal line. Modern theodolites measure vertical angles from the zenith (a few theodolites measure from the nadir); a measurement of 90° or 270° indicates a horizontal line.

Zenith and *nadir* are terms describing points on a celestial sphere (i.e., a sphere of infinitely large radius with its center at the center of the earth). The zenith point is directly above the observer, and the nadir is directly below the observer; the zenith, nadir, and observer are all on the same vertical line.

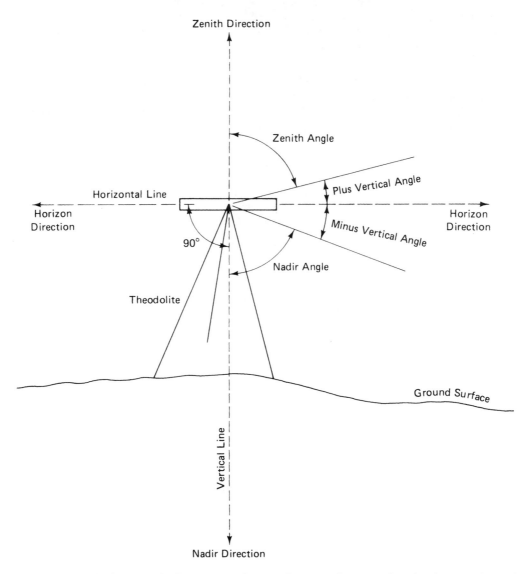

FIGURE 4-4 The three reference directions for vertical angles: horizontal, zenith, and nadir.

4-3   Horizontal Angles

4-3-1   Interior Angles

If the angles in a closed figure are to be measured, the interior angles are normally read. When all the interior angles have been recorded, the accuracy of the work can be determined by comparing the sum of the field angles with the theoretical value for a closed polygon.

For a closed polygon of n sides, the sum of the interior angles will be $(n - 2)180°$. In Figure 4-5, the interior angles in a five-sided polygon have been measured as shown. For a five-sided polygon, the sum of the interior angles must be $(5 - 2)180° = 540°$; the angles in Figure 4-5 do, in fact, total 540°. However, in field practice, the total is usually marginally more or less than $(n - 2)180°$, and it is then up to the surveyor to determine if the error of angular closure is within the tolerances specified for that survey. The balancing of acceptable errors is discussed later in this chapter.

In addition to interior angles, the surveyor can measure the exterior angles, as shown in Figure 4-5. Exterior angles are used to check interior angles or to define exterior tie-ins.

4-3-2   Deflection Angles

An open traverse is shown in Figure 4-6. The deflection angles shown are measured from the prolongation of the back line to the forward line. The angles are measured either to the left (L) or to the right (R); the direction (L or R) must be shown along with the numerical value.

It is possible to measure the same angle [see Figure 4-6(b)] by directly sighting the back line and then turning the angle left or right to the forward line. This technique is seldom used, as most surveying agencies prefer to use deflection angles; deflection angles

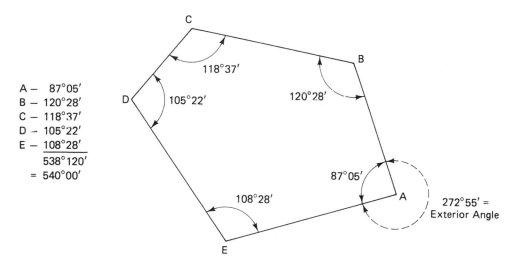

A — 87°05'
B — 120°28'
C — 118°37'
D — 105°22'
E — 108°28'
　　538°120'
　= 540°00'

FIGURE 4-5   Closed traverse showing the interior angles.

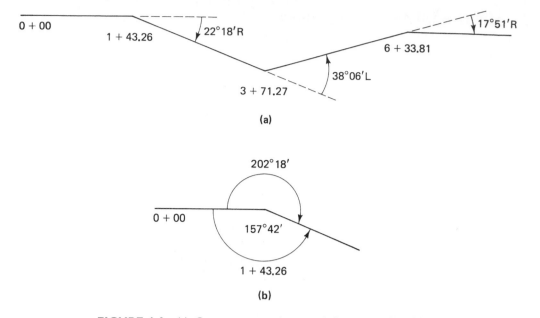

FIGURE 4-6   (a) Open traverse showing deflection angles. (b) Same traverse showing angle right (202° 18′) and angle left (157° 42′).

are normally small angles, which are easier to work with and are simpler to use when one is computing bearings and azimuths.

4-4   Electronic Theodolites

Electronic theodolites operate in a manner similar to that of optical theodolites; one major difference is that these instruments (most) have only one motion (upper) and accordingly have only one horizontal clamp and slow-motion screw. Angle readouts can be to 1″, with precisions from 0.5″ to 20″. The surveyor should check the specifications of new instruments to determine their precision rather than simply accepting the lowest readout as being relevant (some instruments with 1″ readouts may be capable only of 5″ precision). Digital readouts eliminate the uncertainty associated with the reading and interpolation of scale and micrometer settings. Electronic theodolites have zero-set buttons for quick instrument orientation *after* the backsight has been taken; horizontal angles can be turned left or right, and repeat-angle averaging is available on some models. Figures 4-3, 4-7, and 4-8 are typical of the more recently introduced theodolites. The display windows for horizontal, and vertical angles are located at both the front and the rear of the instruments for easy access.

The instruments shown in Figures 4-7 and 4-8 are basic electronic theodolites, whereas the instrument shown in Figure 4-3 has additional capabilities, including the ability to be expanded to Total Station capability with the inclusion of modular components such as EDM and data collection. Figure 4-7 also shows the operation keys and display area typical of many of these instruments. After turning on the instrument, the

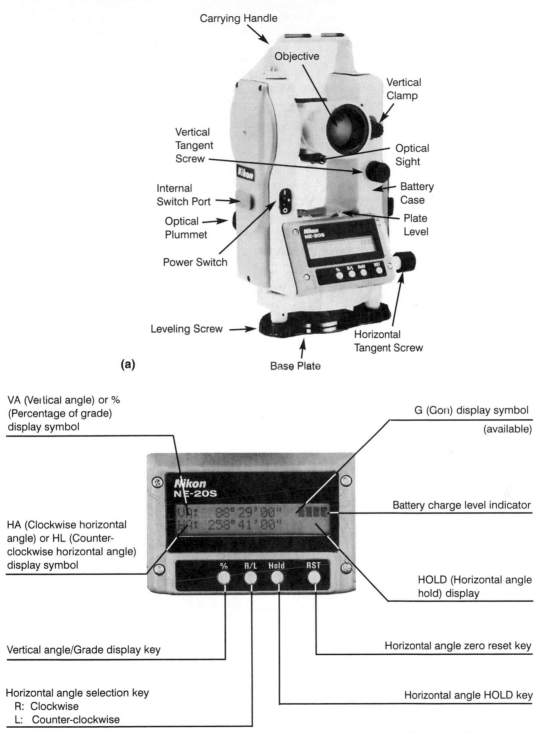

(a)

(b)

FIGURE 4-7 Nikon NE-20S electronic digital theodolite. (a) Theodolite. (b) Operation keys and display. (Courtesy of Nikon Inc., Melville, N.Y.)

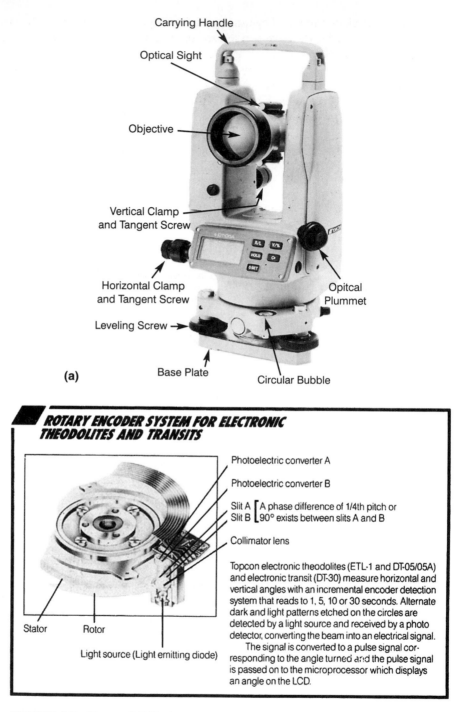

(a)

Carrying Handle

Optical Sight

Objective

Vertical Clamp
and Tangent Screw

Horizontal Clamp
and Tangent Screw

Leveling Screw

Base Plate

Opitcal
Plummet

Circular Bubble

ROTARY ENCODER SYSTEM FOR ELECTRONIC THEODOLITES AND TRANSITS

Photoelectric converter A

Photoelectric converter B

Slit A ⎡ A phase difference of 1/4th pitch or
Slit B ⎣ 90° exists between slits A and B

Collimator lens

Topcon electronic theodolites (ETL-1 and DT-05/05A) and electronic transit (DT-30) measure horizontal and vertical angles with an incremental encoder detection system that reads to 1, 5, 10 or 30 seconds. Alternate dark and light patterns etched on the circles are detected by a light source and received by a photo detector, converting the beam into an electrical signal.

The signal is converted to a pulse signal corresponding to the angle turned and the pulse signal is passed on to the microprocessor which displays an angle on the LCD.

Stator   Rotor

Light source (Light emitting diode)

(b)

FIGURE 4-8 Topcon DT-05 electronic digital theodolite. (a) Theodolite. (b) Encoder system for angle readouts. (Courtesy of Topcon Instrument Corp., Paramus, N.J.)

vertical circle is referenced by turning the telescope slowly through the horizon. The vertical circle can be set with zero at the zenith or at the horizon; the factory setting of zenith can be changed by setting the appropriate dip switch, as described in the instrument's manual. The status of the battery charge can be monitored on the display panel, giving the operator ample warning of the need to replace and/or recharge the battery.

A field angle can be turned and then "doubled" (see Section 4-8-6) by pressing the "hold" button after turning the first angle. When the clamp is then loosened (and the telescope transited), the original angle stays in the readout display until after the backsight has been resighted. To turn the "double" angle, simply release the "hold" button just prior to releasing the clamp.

Typical specifications include the following:

Magnification: 26× to 30×
Field of view: 1.5°
Shortest viewing distance: 1.0 m
Angle readout, direct: 10″ to 20″
Angle measurement: electronic and incremental [see Figure 4-8(b)]
Level sensitivity
    Plate: 40″/2 mm
    Circular: 10′/2 mm

These simple electronic theodolites are quickly replacing optical transits and theodolites (which themselves replaced the vernier transit). They are simpler to use and less expensive to purchase and repair. Their use of electronic components would seem to indicate a continuing lowering of both purchase costs and repair costs over the long term.

The theodolite shown in Figure 4-3 is typical of more complex and more capable instruments that can be converted into Total Stations with the addition of EDM instruments and data collectors. Additionally, some of these instruments have various built-in functions that can be independent of the data collector and that enable the operator to determine "remote object elevation" and "distance between remote points" (see Chapter 5). This instrumentation technology is evolving so rapidly that most new instruments on the market have been in production only for a year or two.

4-5   Repeating Optical Theodolites

Figures 4-2 and 4-9 show repeating *optical micrometer* theodolites. These instruments are characterized by three-screw leveling heads, optical plummets, light weight, and glass circles read with the aid of a microscope, which has its eyepiece adjacent to the telescope.

The theodolite in Figure 4-2 has the circles graduated in 10′ intervals; the location between the 10′ marks is determined by using the optical micrometer, which is read in the middle window. This instrument is set to zero *by first setting the micrometer scale to zero;* a knob on one of the standards controls the micrometer setting. Then, with both clamps loosened, the circle is revolved until the 0° mark (a double line) is close to the 0′ mark; with the upper clamp now tightened, the zeros are precisely matched by centering the 0′ mark in the middle of the double-line 0° mark. After an angle has been turned, clamped, and fine-adjusted, it will be noted that the micrometer scale is still set to zero and that the

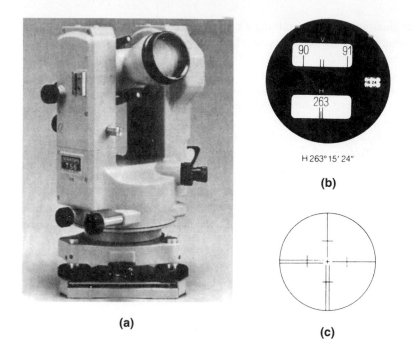

H 263° 15′ 24″

(b)

(a)

(c)

FIGURE 4-9 (a) Six-second repeating micrometer theodolite. (b) Horizontal circle and microm-eter reading. (c) Cross-hair reticle pattern. (Courtesy of Sokkia Co. Ltd.)

horizontal (or vertical) circle degree mark is between two of the 10′ marks. The degree mark (245° in Figure 4-2) is moved to precisely straddle the closest 10′ mark (50 in Figure 4-2) by turning the micrometer knob. The amount that the degree mark was moved can now be read in the middle micrometer window (3′18″ in Figure 4-2). This theodolite is usually read to the closest 20″, with estimates to the closest 10″. The vertical circle is read in the same way as is the horizontal circle—the same micrometer scale being used. If the vertical index is not automatically compensated (as it is for most repeating theodolites), the vertical circle index coincidence bubble must be centered by rotating the appropriate screw when vertical angles are being read.

The theodolite in Figure 4-9 is zeroed and set in a similar manner to that in Figure 4-2 and can be read directly to the closest 6″. The graduations of both circles are pro-jected—by prisms and mirrors—to a location where they can be viewed through the mi-croscope eyepiece. Light, which is necessary to view the graduations, is controlled by an adjustable mirror located on one of the standards. Light required for underground or night work (star observations) is directed through the mirror window, powered by at-tached battery packs.

Most of these theodolites come with a self-indexing feature that ensures that the vertical circle remains properly oriented with respect to the zenith, horizontal, and nadir directions.

The theodolite tripod, unlike the transit tripod with its threaded top, has a flat base through which a bolt is threaded up into the three-screw leveling base, thus securing the instrument to the tripod.

Most theodolites have a leveling head tribrach release feature, which permits the alidade and circle assemblies to be lifted from the leveling head and interchanged with a target or prism (see Figure 4-10). When the theodolite (minus its leveling head) is placed on another leveling head (which has been vacated by a target or prism), it will be instantly over the point and nearly level. This system, called *forced centering,* speeds up the work and reduces the centering errors that are associated with the multiple setups required by some traverse and general control surveys.

Similar to the engineers' transit, the optical theodolite—which is also a repeating instrument—has two independent motions (upper and lower), which necessitates upper and lower clamps with their attendant slow-motion screws. However, some theodolites come equipped with only one clamp and slow-motion screw; these instruments have a lever or switch device that transfers clamp operation from upper to lower motion and thus probably reduces the opportunity for mistakes due to wrong-screw manipulation.

Typical specifications for repeating optical theodolites include the following:

Magnification: $30\times$
Field of view: $1°30'$ (5.2 ft @ 100' or 5.2 m @ 100 m)
Shortest focusing distance: 5' or 1.5 m
Stadia multiplication constant: 100
Bubble sensitivity
   Circular bubble: 8' per 2 mm
   Plate vial: 30" or 40" per 2 mm (one plate vial only)
Direct scale reading: 1' (graduations both clockwise and counterclockwise)
Micrometer scale reading: direct reading to 20", 10", or 6"

FIGURE 4-10 A variety of tribrach-mounted traverse targets. Targets and theodolites can be easily interchanged to save setup time (forced centering system). (Courtesy of Sokkia Co. Ltd.)

4-6 Direction Optical Theodolites

The essential difference between a direction theodolite and a repeating theodolite is that the direction theodolite has only one motion (upper), whereas the repeating theodolite has two motions (upper and lower). Since it is difficult to precisely set angle values on direction theodolites, angles are usually determined by reading the initial direction and the final direction and then determining the difference between the two.

Direction theodolites are generally more precise; for example, the Wild T-2 shown in Figure 4-11 reads directly to 01″ and by estimation to 0.5″, whereas the Wild T-3 shown in Figure 4-12 reads directly to 0.2″ and by estimation to 0.1″.

In the case of the Wild T-2 (and the other 1″ theodolites), the micrometer is turned to force the index to read an even 10″ [the grid lines shown above (beside) the scale are brought to coincidence], and then the micrometer scale reading (02′44″) is added to the circle reading (94°10′) to give a result of 94°12′44″.

In the case of the T-3 (Figure 4-12), both sides of the circle are viewed simultaneously; one reading is shown erect, the other inverted. The micrometer knob is used to precisely align the erect and inverted circle markings. Each division on the circle is 04′; but if the lower scale is moved half a division, the upper also moves half a division, once again causing the markings to align—that is, *a movement of only 02′*. The circle index line is between the 73° and 74° marks indicating that the value being read is 73°. Minutes can be read on the circle by counting the number of divisions from the erect 73° to the inverted value that is 180° different than 73° (i.e., 253°). In this case, the number of divisions between these two numbers is 13, each having a value of 02′ (i.e., 26′).

On the micrometer, a value of 01′59.6″ can be read. The reading is therefore 73°27′59.6″.

Typical specifications for direction optical theodolites include the following:

Magnification: 30× to 32×
Field of view: 1°30′ (24 m to 29 m @ 1000 m)
Shortest focusing distance: 1.5 m to 2.2 m
Bubble sensitivity
   Circular bubble: 8′ per 2 mm
   Plate vial: 20″ per 2 mm
Micrometer scale reading directly to 1″

4-6-1 Angles Measured with a Direction Theodolite

As noted earlier, since it is not always possible to precisely set angles on a direction theodolite scale, directions are observed and then subtracted, one from the other, in order to determine angles. Furthermore, if several sightings are required for precision purposes, it is customary to distribute the initial settings around the circle to minimize the effect of possible circle graduation distortions. For example, if a direction theodolite is used where both sides of the circle are viewed simultaneously, the initial settings (positions) are distributed per 180/*n*, where *n* is the number of settings required by the precision specifications (specifications for precise surveys are published by the National Geodetic Survey in the United States and the Geodetic Surveys in Canada). To be consistent, not only should

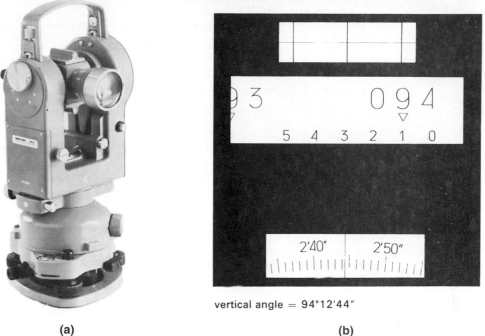

vertical angle = 94°12′44″

(a)   (b)

FIGURE 4-11 (a) Wild T-2, a 1-second optical direction theodolite. (b) Vertical circle reading. (Courtesy of Leica Canada Co.)

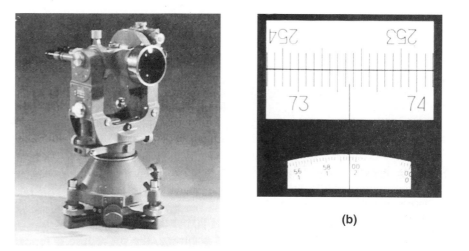

(b)

(a)

FIGURE 4-12 (a) Wild T-3 precise theodolite for first-order surveying. (b) Circle reading (least graduation is 0.2 seconds). (Courtesy of Leica Canada Co.) On the micrometer, a value of 01′59.6″ can be read. The reading is, therefore, 73°25′59.6″.

Table 4-1 APPROXIMATE INITIAL SCALE SETTINGS
FOR FOUR POSITIONS

10′ Micrometer, Wild T-2	2′ Micrometer, Wild T-3
0°00′00″	0°00′00″
45°02′30″	45°00′30″
90°05′00″	90°01′00″
135°07′30″	135°01′30″

the initial settings be uniformly distributed around the circle, but the range of micrometer scale should be noted as well and appropriately apportioned.

For example, if the scales shown in Figure 4-11 are used, the initial settings for four positions are near 0°, 45°, 90°, and 135° on the circle and near 00′00″, 02′30″, 05′00″, and 07′30″ on the micrometer.

For the instruments shown in Figures 4-11 and 4-12, the settings are as given in Table 4-1.

These initial settings are accomplished by setting the micrometer to zero (02′30″, 05′00″, 07′30″) and then setting the circle as closely to zero as is possible using the tangent screw. Precise coincidence of the zero (45, 90, 135) degree mark is achieved by using the micrometer knob, which moves the micrometer scale slightly off zero (2′30″, 5′00″, 7′30″, etc.).

The direct readings are taken first in a clockwise direction; the telescope is then transited (plunged), and the reverse readings are taken counterclockwise. In Figure 4-13, the last entry at position 1 is 180°00′12″ (R). If the angles (shown in the abstract) do not meet the required accuracy, the procedure is repeated while the instrument still occupies that station.

4-7 Theodolite Setup

The theodolite can be set up in much the same manner as described in Section 4-8-5 for the transit. The difference in setups is related to the use of *optical plummets* instead of plumb bobs to position the instrument over the point. Although the optical plummet results in a more precise positioning, it is, for the beginner, more difficult to use. Since the optical plummet can realistically give position only when the instrument is level (or nearly so), the beginning surveyor is often unaware of the relative location of the instrument until the setup procedure is almost complete, and if the instrument has not been properly positioned, the entire procedure must then be repeated. To reduce setup times, a systematic approach is recommended.

SETUP PROCEDURE

1. Place the instrument over the point with the tripod plate as level as possible and with two tripod legs on the downhill side, if applicable.
2. Stand back a pace or two, and see if the instrument appears to be over the station; if it does not, adjust the location, and check again from a pace or two away.

FOXLEA SUBDIVISION
DIRECTIONS FOR CONTROL EXTENSION

Job CLEAR 17 °C
Date MAR 13 2000

CRAWFORD – x̄
HABKIRK – NOTES
Page 28

WILD T-2 #4128-B

x̄@ STATION #481

STATION SIGHTED	D/R	READING	MEAN D/R	REDUCED DIRECTION
POSITION #1				
1001	D	0° 00' 08"		
	R	180° 00' 12"	10"	0° 00' 00"
778	D	40° 37' 44"		
	R	220° 37' 47"	46"	40° 37' 36"
779	D	78° 52' 19"		
	R	258° 52' 13"	16"	78° 52' 06"
POSITION #2				
1001	D	45° 02' 22"		
	R	225° 02' 26"	24"	0° 00' 00"
778	D	85° 40' 02"		
	R	265° 40' 05"	04"	40° 37' 40"
779	D	123° 54' 30"		
	R	303° 54' 36"	33"	78° 52' 09"
POSITION #3				
1001	D	90° 05' 03"		
	R	270° 05' 07"	05"	0° 00' 00"
778	D	130° 42' 44"		
	R	310° 42' 45"	44"	40° 37' 39"
779	D	168° 57' 10"		
	R	348° 57' 14"	12"	78° 52' 07"
POSITION #4				
	ETC.			

ABSTRACT OF ANGLES

POSITION	ANGLE 1001-778	ANGLE 778-779
1	40° 37' 36"	38° 14' 30"
2	40° 37' 40"	38° 14' 29"
3	40° 37' 39"	38° 14' 28"
4		

FIGURE 4-13 Field notes for directions.

3. Move to a position 90° opposed to the original inspection location and repeat step 2. *Note:* This simple act of "eyeing-in" the instrument from two directions, 90° opposed, takes only seconds, but could save a great deal of time in the long run.

4. Check to see that the station point can now be seen through the optical plumb and then firmly push in the tripod legs by pressing down on the tripod shoe spurs.

5. While looking through the optical plumb, manipulate the leveling screws (one, two, or all three at a time) until the crosshair (bull's-eye) of the optical plumb is directly on the station mark.

6. Now, level the theodolite circular bubble by adjusting the tripod legs up or down. This is accomplished by noting which leg, when slid up or down, will move the circular bubble into the bull's-eye. Upon adjusting the leg, the bubble will either move into the circle (the instrument is level) or slide around until it is exactly opposite another tripod leg. That leg is then adjusted up or down until the bubble moves into the circle. If the bubble does not move into the circle, adjust the leg until the bubble is directly opposite another leg, and repeat the process. If this manipulation has been done correctly, the bubble will be centered after the second leg has been adjusted; it is seldom necessary to adjust the legs more than three times.

Comfort can be taken from the fact that these manipulations take less time to perform than they do to read about.

7. A check through the optical plumb will now confirm that its crosshair (bull's-eye) is still quite close to being over the station mark.

8. The circular bubble is now exactly centered (if necessary) by turning one (or more) leveling screws.

9. The tripod clamp bolt is loosened a bit, and the instrument is slid on the flat tripod top until the optical plummet crosshair (bull's-eye) is exactly centered on the station mark. The tripod clamp bolt is retightened and the circular bubble reset, if necessary. When sliding the instrument on the tripod top, it is advised not to twist the instrument, but to move it in a rectangular fashion; this will ensure that the instrument will not go seriously off level if the tripod top itself is not close to being level.

10. The instrument can now be precisely leveled by centering the tubular bubble. The tubular bubble is set so that it is aligned in the same direction as two of the foot screws. These two screws can be turned (together or independently) until the bubble is centered. The instrument is then turned 90° and centered, at which point the tubular bubble will be aligned with the third leveling screw. After leveling in this position, the instrument now should be level, although it is always checked by turning the instrument through 180°.

4-8   Vernier Transits

Figure 4-1 shows a vernier transit. The lower clamp and lower tangent screw in this illustration are hidden behind the leveling head; the optical plummet shown is usually an optional accessory.

Figure 4-14 shows the three main assemblies of the transit. The upper assembly, called the *alidade,* comprises the standards, telescope, vertical circle and vernier, two opposite verniers for reading the horizontal circle, plate bubbles, compass, and upper tangent (slow-motion) screw.

The spindle of the alidade fits down into the hollow spindle of the circle assembly. The circle assembly consists of the horizontal circle (covered by the alidade plate except at the vernier windows), the upper clamp, and the hollow spindle previously mentioned.

The hollow spindle of the circle assembly fits down into the leveling head. The leveling head includes the four leveling screws, the half-ball joint about which opposing screws are manipulated to level the instrument, a threaded collar that permits attachment to the tripod, the lower clamp and lower tangent screw, and a chain, with attached hook, to accommodate the plumb bob string.

The upper clamp tightens the alidade to the circle, whereas the lower clamp tightens the circle to the leveling head. These two independent motions permit angles to be accumulated on the circle for repeated measurements. Transits having these two independent motions are called *repeating* transits.

All transits and most theodolites are repeating instruments. Precise theodolites (1″ readout or smaller) have only one motion; that is, each time the theodolite is turned, the angle value changes. These theodolites are called *direction instruments.* Electronic theodo-

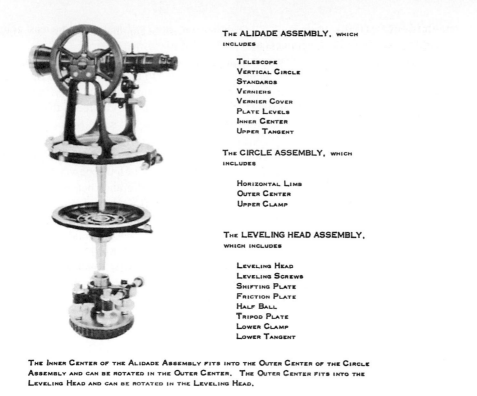

THE **ALIDADE ASSEMBLY**, WHICH INCLUDES

    TELESCOPE
    VERTICAL CIRCLE
    STANDARDS
    VERNIERS
    VERNIER COVER
    PLATE LEVELS
    INNER CENTER
    UPPER TANGENT

THE **CIRCLE ASSEMBLY**, WHICH INCLUDES

    HORIZONTAL LIMB
    OUTER CENTER
    UPPER CLAMP

THE **LEVELING HEAD ASSEMBLY**, WHICH INCLUDES

    LEVELING HEAD
    LEVELING SCREWS
    SHIFTING PLATE
    FRICTION PLATE
    HALF BALL
    TRIPOD PLATE
    LOWER CLAMP
    LOWER TANGENT

THE INNER CENTER OF THE ALIDADE ASSEMBLY FITS INTO THE OUTER CENTER OF THE CIRCLE ASSEMBLY AND CAN BE ROTATED IN THE OUTER CENTER. THE OUTER CENTER FITS INTO THE LEVELING HEAD AND CAN BE ROTATED IN THE LEVELING HEAD.

FIGURE 4-14 Three major-assemblies of the transit. (Courtesy of Sokkia Co. Ltd.)

lites are mostly direction instruments, although some manufacturers (e.g., Sokkia) market *repeating* electronic theodolites.

4-8-1 Circles and Verniers

The horizontal circle is usually graduated into degrees and half degrees (30′) (Figure 4-15), although it is not uncommon to find the horizontal circle graduated into degrees and

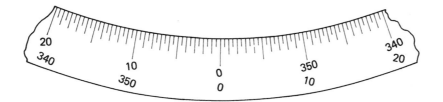

FIGURE 4-15 Part of a transit circle showing a least count of 30 minutes. The circle is graduated in both clockwise and counterclockwise directions, permitting the reading of angles turned to both the left and right.

one-third degrees (20′). To determine the angle value more precisely than the least count of the circle (i.e., 30′ or 20′), vernier scales are employed.

Figure 4-16 shows a double vernier scale alongside a transit circle. The left vernier scale is used for clockwise circle readings (angles turned to the right), and the right vernier scale is used for counterclockwise circle readings (angles turned to the left). To avoid confusion as to which vernier (left or right) scale is to be used, one can recall that the vernier to be used is the one whose graduations are increasing in the same direction as are the circle graduations.

The vernier scale is constructed so that 30 vernier divisions cover the same length of arc as do 29 divisions (half degrees) on the circle. The width of one vernier division is (29/30) × 30′ = 29′ on the circle. Therefore, the space difference between one division on the circle and one division on the vernier represents 01′; with reference to Figure 4-16, the first division on the vernier (left or right of the index mark) fails to exactly line up with the first division on the circle (left or right) by 01′. The second division on the vernier fails to line up with the corresponding circle division by 02′, and so on. If the vernier is moved so that its first division exactly lines up with the first circle division (30′ mark), the reading is 01′; if the vernier again is moved the same distance at arc (1′), the second vernier mark now lines up with the appropriate circle division line, indicating a vernier reading of 02′.

Generally the vernier is read by finding which vernier division line exactly coincides with any circle line and then adding the value of the vernier line to the value of the angle obtained from reading the circle to the closest 30′ (in this example).

In Figure 4-17, the circle is divided into degrees and half degrees (30′). Before even looking at the vernier, we know that its range will be 30′ (left or right) to cover the least count of the circle. Inspection of the vernier shows that 30 marks cover the range of 30′, indicating that the value of each mark is 01′. (Had each of the minute marks been further subdivided into two or three intervals, the angle could then have been read to the closest 30″ or 20″.)

If we consider the clockwise circle readings (field angle turned left to right), we see that the zero mark is between 184° and 184°30′; the circle reading is therefore 184°. Now, to find the value to the closest minute, we use the left side vernier, and, moving from the zero mark, we look for the vernier line that exactly lines up with a circle line. In this case, the 08′ mark lines up; this is confirmed by noting that both the 07′ and the 09′ marks do

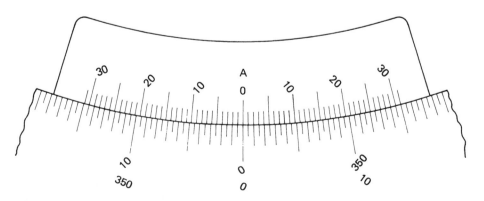

FIGURE 4-16 Double vernier scale set to zero on the horizontal circle.

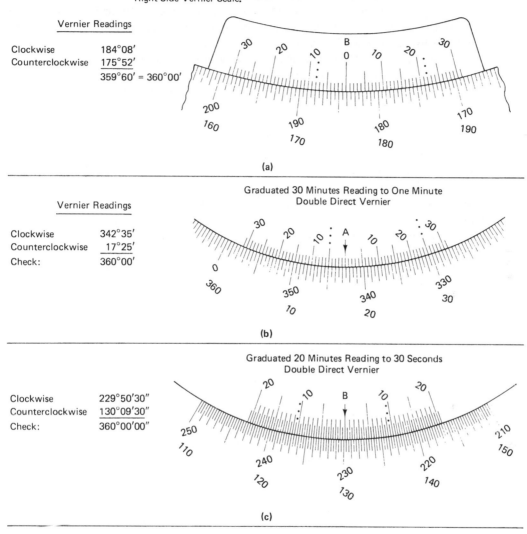

Note: Clockwise Angles (i.e. Angles Turned to the Right) Utilize Only the Left Side Vernier Scale. Counterclockwise Angles (i.e. Angles Turned to the Left) Utilize Only the Right Side Vernier Scale.

Vernier Readings

Clockwise	184°08'
Counterclockwise	175°52'
	359°60' = 360°00'

(a)

Graduated 30 Minutes Reading to One Minute
Double Direct Vernier

Vernier Readings

Clockwise	342°35'
Counterclockwise	17°25'
Check:	360°00'

(b)

Graduated 20 Minutes Reading to 30 Seconds
Double Direct Vernier

Clockwise	229°50'30"
Counterclockwise	130°09'30"
Check:	360°00'00"

(c)

FIGURE 4-17 Sample vernier readings. Triple dots identify aligned vernier graduations. Note: Appropriate vernier scale graduation numerals are angled in the same direction as the referenced circle graduation numerals.

not line up with their corresponding circle marks, both by the same amount. The angle for this illustration is 184° + 08' = 184°08'.

If we consider the counterclockwise circle reading in Figure 4-17, we see that the zero mark is between 175°30' and 176°; the circle reading is therefore 175°30', and to that value, we add the right side vernier reading of 22' to give an angle of 175°52'. As a check, the sum of the clockwise and counterclockwise readings should be 360°00'.

All transits are equipped with two double verniers (A and B) located 180° apart. Although increased precision theoretically can be obtained by reading both verniers for each angle, usually only one vernier is employed. Furthermore, to avoid costly mistakes, most surveying agencies favor use of the same vernier, the A vernier, at all times.

As noted earlier, the double vernier permits angles to be turned to the right (left vernier) or to the left (right vernier). However, by convention, field angles are normally turned only to the right. The exceptions to this occur when deflection angles are being employed, as in route surveys, or when construction layouts necessitate angles to the left, as in some curve deflections. There are a few more specialized cases (e.g., star observations) where it is advantageous to turn angles to the left, but as stated earlier, the bulk of surveying experience favors angles turned to the right. This type of consistency provides the routine required to foster a climate where fewer mistakes occur and where mistakes that do occur can be readily recognized and eliminated.

The graduations of the circles and verniers illustrated are in wide use in the survey field. However, there are several variations to both circle graduations and vernier graduations. Typically the circle is graduated to the closest 30' (as illustrated), 20', or 10' (rarely). The vernier has a range in minutes covering the smallest division on the circle (30', 20', or 10') and can be further graduated to half minute (30") or one-third minute (20") divisions. A few minutes spent observing the circle and vernier graduations of an unfamiliar transit will easily disclose the proper technique required for reading. See also Figure 4-17(b) and (c).

The use of a magnifying glass (5×) is recommended for reading the scales, particularly for the 30" and 20" verniers.

4-8-2   Telescope

The telescope (see Figures 4-18 and 4-19) in the transit is somewhat shorter than that in a level with a reduced magnifying power (26×). The telescope axis is supported by the standards, which are of sufficient height to permit the telescope to be revolved (transited) 360° about the axis. A level vial tube is attached to the telescope so that, if desired, it may be used as a level.

The telescope level has a sensitivity of 30" to 40" per 2-mm graduation, compared to a level sensitivity of about 20" for a dumpy level. When the telescope is positioned so that the level tube is under the telescope, it is said to be in the *direct* (normal) position; when

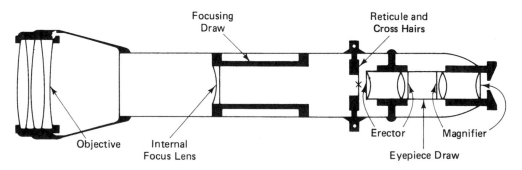

FIGURE 4-18   Transit telescope. (Courtesy of Sokkia Co. Ltd.)

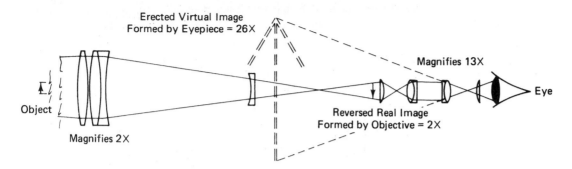

FIGURE 4-19 Diagram of optical system. (Courtesy of Sokkia Co. Ltd.)

the level tube is on top of the telescope, the telescope is said to be in a *reversed* (inverted) position. The eyepiece focus is always located at the eyepiece end of the telescope, whereas the object focus can be located on the telescope barrel just ahead of the eyepiece focus, midway along the telescope, or on the horizontal telescope axis at the standard.

4-8-3 Leveling Head

The leveling head supports the instrument; proper manipulation of the leveling screws (Section 3-4-1) allows the horizontal circle and telescope axis to be placed in a horizontal plane, which forces the alidade and circle assembly spindles to be placed in a vertical direction.

When the leveling screws are loosened, the pressure on the tripod plate is removed, permitting the instrument to be shifted laterally a short distance (3/8 in.). This shifting capability permits the surveyor to precisely position the transit center over the desired point.

4-8-4 Plate Levels

Transits come equipped with two plate levels set at 90° to each other. Plate levels have a sensitivity range of 60″ to 80″ per 2-mm division on the level tube, depending on the overall precision requirements of the instrument.

4-8-5 Transit Setup

The transit is removed from its case, held by the standards or leveling base (never by the telescope), and placed on a tripod by screwing the transit snugly to the threaded tripod top. When the transit is carried indoors or near obstructions (e.g., tree branches), it is carried cradled under the arm, with the instrument forward, where it can be seen. Otherwise, the transit and tripod can be carried on the shoulder. Total Stations (Chapter 5) should always be removed from the tripod and carried by the handle or in the instrument case.

The instrument is placed roughly over the desired point and the tripod legs adjusted so that (1) the instrument is at a convenient height and (2) the tripod plate is nearly level.

Usually two legs are first placed on the ground, and the instrument is roughly leveled by manipulation of the third leg. If the instrument is to be set up on a hill, the instrument operator faces uphill and places two of the legs in the lower position; the third leg is placed in the upper position and then manipulated to roughly level the instrument. The wing nuts on the tripod legs are tightened, and a plumb bob is attached to the plumb bob chain, which hangs down from the leveling head. The plumb bob is attached by means of a slip knot, which allows placement of the plumb bob point immediately over the mark. If it appears that the instrument placement is reasonably close to its final position, the tripod legs are pushed into the ground, taking care not to jar the instrument.

If necessary, the length of plumb bob string is adjusted as the setup procedure advances. If after pushing in the tripod legs the instrument is not centered, one leg is either pushed in farther or pulled out and repositioned until the plumb bob is very nearly over the point or until it becomes obvious that manipulation of another leg would be more productive. When the plumb bob is within 1/4 in. of the desired location, the instrument is then leveled.

Now, two adjacent leveling screws are loosened so that pressure is removed from the tripod plate and the transit can be shifted laterally until it is precisely over the point. If the same two adjacent leveling screws are now retightened, the instrument will return to its level (or nearly so) position. Final adjustments to the leveling screws at this stage will not be large enough to displace the plumb bob from its position directly over the desired point.

The actual leveling procedure for a transit is a faster operation than that for a level. The transit has two plate levels, which means that the transit can be leveled in two directions, 90° opposed, without rotating the instrument. When both bubbles have been carefully centered, it remains only for the instrument to be turned through 180° to check the adjustment of the plate bubbles. If one (or both) bubble(s) does not center after turning 180°, the discrepancy is noted, and the bubble is brought to half the discrepancy by means of the leveling screws. If this has been done correctly, the bubbles will remain in the same position as the instrument is revolved—indicating that the instrument is level.

4-8-6   Measuring Angles by Repetition (Vernier Transit)

With the assumption that the instrument is placed over the point and is level, the following procedure is used to turn and "double" an angle. *Turning the angle at least twice permits the elimination of mistakes and increases precision, owing to the elimination of most instrumental errors.*

It is recommended that only the A vernier scale be used.

1. *Set the scales to zero.* Loosen both the upper and the lower motion clamps. While holding the alidade stationary, revolve the circle by pushing on the circle underside with the fingertips. When the zero on the scale is close to the vernier zero, tighten (snug) the upper clamp. Then, with the aid of a magnifying glass, turn the upper tangent screw (slow-motion screw) until the zeros are precisely set. It is good practice to make the last turn of the tangent screw against the tangent screw spring so that spring tension is assured.

2. *Sight the initial point* (see Figure 4-20 and assume the instrument at station *A* and an angle from *B* to *E*). With the upper clamp tightened and the lower clamp loose, turn and point at station *B,* and then tighten the lower clamp. At this point, check the eye-

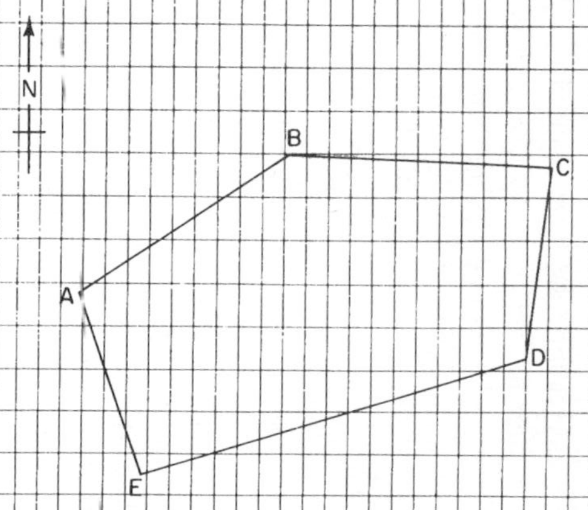

FIGURE 4-20 Field notes for repeated angles.

The following content is the field notes shown within the figure:

TRIDELL HOLDINGS LTD.
SITE "E" CONTROL TRAVERSE

Job CLEAR 26°C
Date JUNE 2 2000
ZEISS TH 43-007

DAWES-X
DAVIDOFF-NOTES
Page 12

STATION	DIRECT	DOUBLE	MEAN
A	101°24'00"	202°48'00"	101°24'00"
B	149°13'00"	298°26'00"	149°13'00"
C	80°58'00"	161°57'00"	80°58'30"
D	116°20'00"	232°38'00"	116°19'00"
E	92°04'00"	184°09'00"	92°04'30"
			538°119'00"
			= 539°59'00"

ANGULAR CLOSURE
(N-2)180
= 3 x 180 = 540° 00'
ERROR = 01'00"

115

piece focus and object focus to eliminate parallax (Section 3-6). If the sight is being given by a range pole, or even a pencil, always sight as close to the ground level as possible to eliminate plumbing errors. If the sight is being given with a plumb bob, sight high on the plumb bob string to minimize the effect of plumb bob oscillations. Using the lower tangent screw, position the vertical crosshair on the target, once again making the last adjustment motion against the tangent screw spring.

3. *Turn the angle.* Loosen the upper clamp, and turn clockwise to the final point (*E.*) When the sight is close to *E*, tighten the upper clamp. Using the upper tangent screw, set the vertical crosshair precisely on the target, using techniques already described. Read the angle by utilizing (in this case) the left side vernier, and book the value in the appropriate column in the field notes (see Figure 4-20).

4. *Repeat the angle.* After the initial angle has been booked, *transit (plunge) the telescope,* loosen the lower motion, and sight at the initial target, station *B.* The simple act of transiting the telescope removes nearly all the potential instrumental errors associated with the transit.

The procedure described in the first three steps is repeated in step 4, the only differences being that the telescope is now inverted and that the initial horizontal angle setting is 98°53′ instead of 0°00′. The angle that is read as a result of this repeating procedure should be approximately double the initial angle. This "double" angle is booked and then divided by 2 to find the mean value, which is also booked.

If the procedure has been executed properly, the mean value should be the same as the direct reading or half the least count (30″) different. In practice, a discrepancy equal to the least count (01′) is normally permitted. Although doubling the angle is sufficient for most engineering projects, precision can be increased by *repeating* the angle a number of times. Due to personal errors of sighting and scale reading, this procedure has practical constraints as to improvement in precision. It is generally agreed that **repetitions beyond six or perhaps eight times will not further improve the precision.**

When multiple repetitions are being used, only the first angle and the final value are recorded. The final value is divided by the number of repetitions to arrive at the mean value. It may be necessary to augment the final reading by 360° or multiples of 360° prior to determining the mean. The proper value can be roughly determined by multiplying the first angle recorded by the number of repetitions.

Figure 4-20 shows typical field notes for repeated angles. It can be seen that the angle at *A* and the other four angles were satisfactorily doubled. That is, the mean (half the double) was, in each case, within 30″ of the original angle.

These notes also illustrate that the interior angles of a closed figure are immediately summed to demonstrate geometric closure [$(n - 2)180$] and that acceptable errors are removed from the work by adjusting the field angles so that they do sum to $(n - 2)180$.

4-9   Laying Off Angles

Case 1.   The angle is to be laid out no more precisely than the least count of the transit or theodolite.

Assume a route survey where a deflection angle (31°12′R) has been determined photogrammetrically to position the ℄ clear of natural obstructions [see Figure 4-21(a)]. The

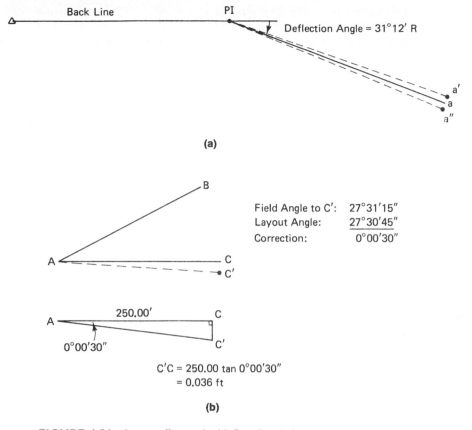

(a)

Field Angle to C':   27°31'15"
Layout Angle: 27°30'45"
Correction: 0°00'30"

C'C = 250.00 tan 0°00'30"
    = 0.036 ft

(b)

FIGURE 4-21   Laying off an angle. (a) Case I, angle laid out to the least count of instrument. (b) Case 2, angle to be laid out more precisely than the least count the instrument will permit.

surveyor sets the instrument at the PI (point of intersection of the tangents) and sights the back line with the telescope reversed and the horizontal circle set to zero. Next, the surveyor transits (plunges) the telescope, turns off the required deflection angle, and sets a point on line. The deflection angle is 31°12'R, and a point is set at a'. The surveyor then loosens the lower motion (repeating instruments), sights again at the back line, transits the telescope, and turns off the required value (31°12' × 2 = 62°24'). It is very likely that this line of sight will not precisely match the first sighting at a'; if the line does not cross a', a new mark, a'', is made and the instrumentation given a sighting on the correct point a, which is midway between a' and a''.

Case 2.   The angle is to laid out more precisely than the least count of the instrument will directly permit.

Assume that an angle of 27°30'45" is required in a heavy construction layout and that a 1' transit is being used. In Figure 4-21(b), the transit is set up at A zeroed on B with an angle of 27°31' turned to set point C'. The angle is then repeated to point C' a suitable number of times so that an accurate value of that angle can be determined. Let's assume that the scale reading after four repetitions is 110°05′, giving a mean angle value of 27°31′15″ for angle BAC'.

If the layout distance of AC is 250.00 ft, point C can be precisely located by measuring from C' a distance of $C'C$:

$$C'C = 250.00 \tan 0°00′30″$$
$$= 0.036 \text{ ft}$$

After point C has been located, its position can be verified by repeating angles to it from point B.

4-10 Prolonging a Straight Line (Double Centering)

Prolonging a straight line (also known as *double centering*) is a common survey procedure used every time a straight line must be prolonged. The best example of this requirement is in route surveying, where straight lines are routinely prolonged over long distances and often over very difficult terrain. The technique of reversion (the same technique as used in repeating angles) is used to ensure that the straight line is properly prolonged.

With reference to Figure 4-22, the straight line BA is to be prolonged to B' [see also Figure 4-28(a)]. With the instrument at A, a sight is carefully made on station B. The telescope is transited, and a temporary point is set at C. The transit is revolved back to station B, and a new sighting is made (the telescope is in a position reversed to the original sighting). The telescope is transited, and a temporary mark is made at D, adjacent to C.

Note: Over short distances, well-adjusted transits will show no appreciable displacement between points C and D however, over the longer distances normally encountered in this type of work, all transits will display a displacement between direct and reversed sightings; the longer the forward sighting, the greater the displacement.

The correct location of station B' is established midway between C and D by measuring with a steel tape.

4-11 Interlining (Balancing In)

It is sometimes necessary to establish a straight line between two points that themselves are not intervisible (i.e., a transit set up at one point cannot be sighted at the other required point because of an intervening hill). It is usually possible to find an intermediate position from which both points can be seen.

In Figure 4-23, points A and B are not intervisible, but point C is in an area from which both A and B can be seen. The interlining procedure is as follows: The transit is set up in the area of C (at C_1) and as close to line AB as is possible to estimate. The transit is roughly leveled, and a sight is taken on point A; then the telescope is transited and a sight taken toward B. The line of sight will, of course, be not on B, but on point B_1, some distance away. Noting roughly the distance B_1B and the position of the transit between A and

FIGURE 4-22 Double centering to prolong a straight line.

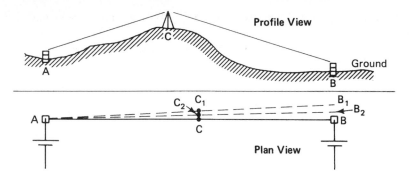

FIGURE 4-23   Interlining (balancing in).

B (e.g., one-half, one-third, or one-quarter of the distance AB), one makes an estimate as to proportionately how far the instrument is to be moved in order to be on the line AB. The transit is once again roughly leveled (position C_2), and the sighting procedure is repeated.

   This trial-and-error technique is repeated until, after sighting A, the transited line of sight falls on point B or close enough to point B that it can be precisely set by shifting the transit on the leveling head shifting plate. When the line has been established, a point is set at or near point C so that the position can be saved for future use.

   The entire procedure of interlining can be accomplished in a surprisingly short period of time. All but the final instrument setups are only roughly leveled, and at no time does the instrument have to be set up over a point.

4-12   Intersection of Two Straight Lines

The intersection of two straight lines is also a very common survey technique. In municipal surveying, street surveys usually begin (0 + 00) at the intersection of the ₵s of two streets, and the chainage and angle of the intersections of all subsequent street ₵s are routinely determined.

   Figure 4-24(a) illustrates the need for intersecting points on a municipal survey, and Figure 4-24(b) illustrates just how the intersection point is located. With reference to Figure 4-24(b), with the instrument set on a Main St. station and a sight taken also on Main St. ₵ (the longer the sight, the more precise the sighting), two points (2 to 4 ft apart) are established on Main St. ₵, one point on either side of where the surveyor estimates that 2nd Ave. ₵ will intersect. The instrument is then moved to a 2nd Ave. station, and a sight is taken some distance away, on the far side of Main St. ₵. The surveyor can stretch a plumb bob string over the two points (A and B) established on Main St. ₵, and the instrument operator can note where on the string 2nd Ave. ₵ intersects. If the two points (A and B) are reasonably close together (2 to 3 ft), the surveyor can use the plumb bob itself to take line from the instrument operator on the plumb bob string; otherwise, the instrument operator can take line with a pencil or any other suitable sighting target.

   The intersection point is then suitably marked (e.g., nail and flagging on asphalt, wood stake with tack on ground), and then the angle of intersection and the chainage of the point can be determined. After the intersection point is marked, temporary markers A and B are removed.

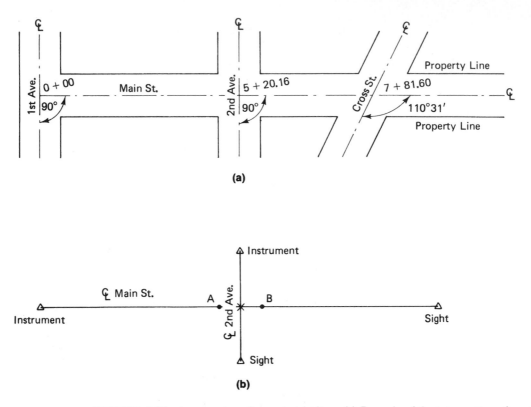

FIGURE 4-24 Intersection of two straight lines. (a) Example of the intersection of center lines of streets. (b) Intersecting technique.

4-13   Prolonging a Survey Line by Triangulation Techniques

In route surveying, obstacles, such as rivers or chasms, must be traversed. Whereas the alignment can be conveniently prolonged by double centering, the stationing may be deduced from the construction of a geometric figure. In Figure 4-25(a), the distance from 1 + 121.271 to the station established on the far side of the river can be determined by solving the constructed triangle (triangulation).

The ideal (strongest) triangle is one having angles close to 60° (equilateral), although angles as small as 20° may be acceptable. The presence of rugged terrain and heavy tree cover adjacent to the river often results in a less than optimal geometric figure.

The baseline and a minimum of two angles are measured so that the missing distance can be calculated. The third angle (on the far side of the river) should also be measured to check for mistakes and to reduce errors.

In Figure 4-25(b), the line must be prolonged past an obstacle, a large tree. In this case, a triangle is constructed with the three angles and two distances measured as shown. As noted earlier, the closer the constructed triangle is to equilateral, the stronger will be the calculated distance (*BD*).

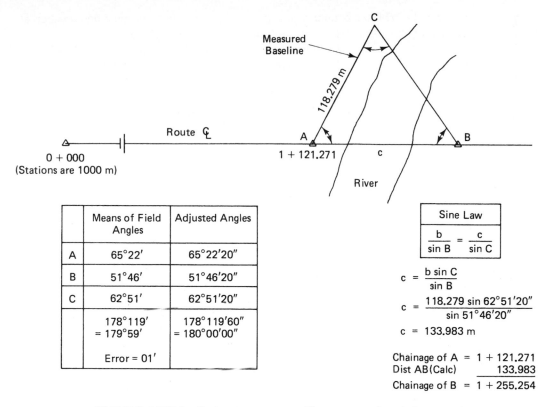

FIGURE 4-25(a) Prolonging a measured line over an obstacle by triangulation.

	Means of Field Angles	Adjusted Angles
A	65°22'	65°22'20"
B	51°46'	51°46'20"
C	62°51'	62°51'20"
	178°119' = 179°59'	178°119'60" = 180°00'00"
	Error = 01'	

$$\boxed{\begin{array}{c} \text{Sine Law} \\[4pt] \dfrac{b}{\sin B} = \dfrac{c}{\sin C} \end{array}}$$

$$c = \frac{b \sin C}{\sin B}$$

$$c = \frac{118.279 \sin 62°51'20"}{\sin 51°46'20"}$$

$$c = 133.983 \text{ m}$$

Chainage of A = 1 + 121.271
Dist AB(Calc)   133.983
Chainage of B = 1 + 255.254

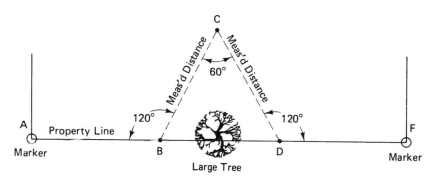

FIGURE 4-25(b) Prolonging a line past an obstacle by triangulation.

4-14 Prolonging a Survey Line Past an Obstacle

It often occurs in property surveying that obstacles, such as trees, block the path of the survey. Whereas in route surveying it is customary for the surveyor to cut down the offending trees (later construction will require them to be removed in any case), in property surveying the owner would be quite upset to find valuable trees destroyed just so the surveyor could establish a boundary line. Accordingly the surveyor must find an alternate method of providing distances and/or locations for blocked survey lines.

In Figure 4-26(a), the technique of right-angle offset is illustrated. Boundary line *AF* cannot be run because of the wooded area. The survey continues normally to point *B* just clear of the wooded area. At *B,* a right angle is turned (and doubled), and point *C* is located a sufficient distance away from *B* to provide a clear parallel line to the boundary line. The transit is set at *C* and sighted at *B* (great care must be exercised because of the short sighting distance); an angle of 90° is turned to locate point *D*. Point *E* is located on the boundary line by using a right angle and the offset distance used for *BC*. The survey can then continue to *F.* If distance *CD* is measured, then the required boundary distance (*AF*) is *AB* + *CD* + *EF.*

If intermediate points are required on the boundary line between *B* and *E* (e.g., fencing layout), a right angle can be turned from a convenient location on *CD,* and the offset distance (*BC*) is used to measure back to the boundary line. Use of a technique like this will minimize the destruction of trees and other obstructions.

In Figure 4-26(b), trees are scattered over the area, preventing the establishment of a right-angle offset line. In this case, a random line (open traverse) is run (by deflection angles) through the scattered trees. The distance *AF* is the sum of *AB, EF,* and the resultant of *BE* (see Chapter 6 for appropriate computation techniques for problems such as this).

It was noted that the technique of right-angle offsets has larger potential for error due to the weaknesses associated with several short sightings, but at the same time, this technique gives a simple and direct method for establishing intermediate points on the boundary line. In contrast, the random line and triangulation methods provide for stronger geo-

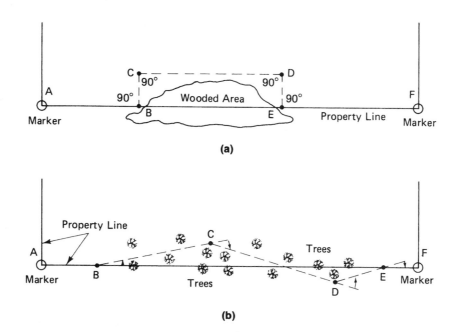

FIGURE 4-26 Prolonging a line past an obstacle. (a) Right-angle offset method. (b) Random-line method.

metric solutions to the missing property line distances, but they also require less direct and much more cumbersome calculations for the placement of intermediate on-line points (e.g., fence layouts).

4-15 Instrument Adjustments

4-15-1 Geometry of the Transit/Theodolite

The vertical axis of the transit goes up through the center of the spindles and is oriented over a specific point on the earth's surface. The circle assembly and alidade revolve about this axis. The horizontal axis of the telescope is perpendicular to the vertical axis, and the telescope and vertical circle revolve about it. The line of sight (line of collimation) is a line joining the intersection of the reticle crosshairs and the center of the objective lens. The line of sight is perpendicular to the horizontal axis and should be truly horizontal when the telescope level bubble is centered and when the vertical circle is set at zero.

4-15-2 Adjustment of the Transit/Theodolite—General

Figure 4-27 shows the geometric features of the transit. The most important relationships are as follows:

1. The vertical crosshair should be perpendicular to the horizontal axis (tilting axis).
2. The axis of the *plate bubble* should be in a plane perpendicular to the vertical axis.
3. The *line of sight* should be perpendicular to the horizontal axis.
4. The horizontal axis should be perpendicular to the vertical axis *(standards adjustment)*.

   In addition to the above, the following secondary features must be considered:

5. The axis of the telescope and the axis of the *telescope bubble* should be parallel.
6. The *vertical circle vernier* zero mark should be aligned with the vertical circle zero mark when the plate bubbles and the telescope bubble are centered (transits).

   These features are discussed in the following paragraphs.

4-15-3 Vertical Crosshair

If the vertical crosshair is perpendicular to the horizontal axis, all parts of the vertical crosshair can be used for line and angle sightings. This adjustment can be checked by sighting a well-defined distant point and then clamping the horizontal movements. The telescope is now moved up and down so that the point sighted appears to move on the vertical crosshair. If the point appears to move off the vertical crosshair, an error exists, and the crosshair reticle must be rotated slightly until the sighted point appears to stay on the vertical crosshair as it is being revolved. The reticle can be adjusted slightly by loosening two adjacent capstan screws, rotating the reticle, and then retightening the same two capstan screws.

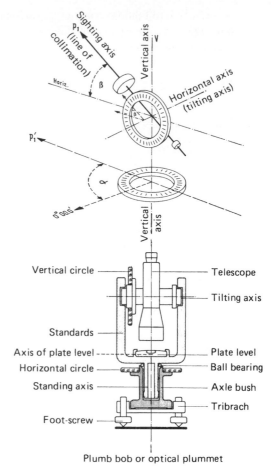

FIGURE 4-27 Geometry of the theodolite. (Courtesy of Leica Co. Ltd.)

This same crosshair orientation adjustment is performed on the *dumpy level*, but in the case of the level, the horizontal crosshair is of prime importance. The horizontal crosshair is checked by sighting a distant point on the horizontal crosshair with the vertical clamp set and then moving the telescope left and right, checking to see that the sighted point remains on the horizontal crosshair; the adjustment for any maladjustment of the reticle is performed as described previously.

4-15-4   Plate Bubbles

It has been previously noted (Section 4-8-5) that after a bubble has been centered, its position is checked by rotating the instrument through 180°; if the bubble does not remain centered, it can be properly set by bringing the bubble halfway back by using the foot screws. For example, if, when a bubble position is checked, it is out by four division marks, the bubble can now be properly set by turning the foot screws until the bubble is only two division marks off center.

The bubble should remain in this off-center position as the telescope is rotated, indicating that the instrument is, in fact, level. Although the instrument can now be safely used, it is customary to remove the error by adjusting the bubble tube.

The bubble tube can now be adjusted by turning the capstan screws at one end of the bubble tube until the bubble becomes precisely centered. The entire leveling and adjusting procedure is repeated until the bubble remains centered as the instrument is rotated and checked in all positions. All capstan-screw adjustments are best done in small increments. That is, if the end of the bubble tube is to be lowered, first loosen the lower capstan screw a slight turn (say, one-eighth), and then tighten (snug) the top capstan screw to close the gap. This incremental adjustment is continued until the bubble is precisely centered.

4-15-5 Line of Sight

Vertical Crosshair.   The vertical line of sight should be perpendicular to the horizontal axis so that a vertical plane is formed by the complete revolution of the telescope on its axis. The technique for testing for this adjustment is known as **double centering** (Section 4-10).

The transit is set over a point A [Figure 4-28(a)] and leveled. A backsight is taken on any distant well-defined point B (a well-defined point on the horizon is best); the telescope is transited (plunged), and a point C is set on the opposite side of the transit 300 to 400 ft away and at roughly the same elevation as the transit station. Now loosen either the upper or lower plate clamp, and revolve the transit back toward point B. With the telescope still inverted, sight B and then transit the telescope and sight toward point C previously set. It is highly probable that the new line of sight will not fall precisely on point C and that a new point, D, will be set adjacent to C. The correct location of line AB produced is at B′, which is located midway between points C and D. Since the distance CB′ or B′D is double the sighting error, the line-of-sight correction is accomplished by setting point E midway between B and D (or one-quarter of the way from D to C) and by moving the vertical crosshair onto point E.

The vertical crosshair is adjusted laterally by first loosening the left or right reticle capstan screw and then tightening the opposite screw. This procedure is repeated until the spread CD is eliminated or, as is more usually the case, CD is reduced to a manageable size—say, 0.5 ft at 1000 ft for normal engineering work. (Some surveyors, knowing that this error cannot be totally eliminated, prefer to have an error large enough to warrant continual correction.).

Horizontal Crosshair.   The horizontal crosshair must be adjusted so that it lies on the optical axis of the telescope. To test this relationship, set up the transit at point A [Figure 4-28(b)], and place two stakes, B and C, in a straight line, with B about 25 ft away and C about 300 ft away. With the vertical motion clamped, take a reading first on C(K) and then on B(J). Transit (plunge) the telescope, set the horizontal crosshair on the previous rod reading (J) at B, and then take a reading at point C. If the transit is in perfect adjustment, the two rod readings at C will be the same; if the crosshair is out of adjustment, the rod reading at C will be at some reading L instead of K. To adjust the crosshair, adjust the crosshair reticle up or down by first loosening and then tightening the appropriate opposing capstan screws until the crosshair lines up with the average of the two readings (M).

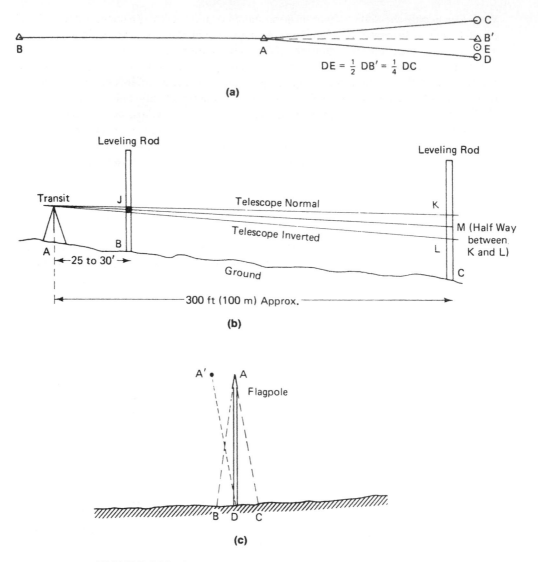

$$DE = \tfrac{1}{2} DB' = \tfrac{1}{4} DC$$

(a)

(b)

(c)

FIGURE 4-28   Instrument adjustments. (a) Line of sight perpendicular to horizontal axis (double centering). (b) Horizontal crosshair adjustment. (c) Standards adjustment.

4-15-6   Standards Adjustment

The horizontal axis should be perpendicular to the vertical axis. The standards are checked for proper adjustment by first setting up the transit and then sighting a high (at least 30° altitude) point [point *A* in Figure 4-28(c)]. After clamping the instrument in that position, the telescope is depressed, and point *B* is marked on the ground. The telescope is then transited (plunged), a lower clamp is loosened, and the transit is turned and once again set precisely on point *A*. The telescope is again depressed, and if the standards are properly adjusted, the vertical crosshair will fall on point *B;* if the standards are not in adjustment, a new point *C* is established. The discrepancy between *B* and *C* is double the error resulting from the standards maladjustment. Point *D,* which is now established midway between *B* and *C,* will be in the same vertical plane as point *A.* The error is removed by sighting point *D* and then elevating the telescope to *A',* adjacent to *A.* The adjustable end of the horizontal axis is then raised or lowered until the line of sight falls on point *A.* When the adjustment is complete, care is taken in retightening the upper friction screws so that the telescope revolves with proper tension.

4-15-7   Telescope Bubble

If the transit is to be used for leveling work, the axis of the telescope bubble and the axis of the telescope must be parallel. To check this relationship, the bubble is centered with the telescope clamped, and the peg test (Section 3-11) is performed. When the proper rod reading has been determined at the final setup, the horizontal crosshair is set on that rod reading by moving the telescope with the vertical tangent (slow motion) screw. The telescope bubble is then centered by means of the capstan screws located at one (or both) end(s) of the bubble tube.

4-15-8   Vertical Circle Vernier (Transits)

When the transit has been carefully leveled (plate bubbles) and the telescope bubble has been centered, the vertical circle should read zero. If a slight error (index error) exists, the screws holding the vernier are loosened, the vernier is tapped into its proper position, and then the screws are retightened so that the vernier is once again just touching, without binding, the vertical circle.

4-15-9   Circular Level (Theodolites)

Optical and electronic theodolites utilize a circular level for rough leveling as well as one or more plate levels for fine leveling. After the plate level has been set and adjusted, the circular bubble can be adjusted (centered) by turning one or more of the three adjusting screws around the bubble, as described in Section 4-15-4.

4-15-10   Optical Plummet

The optical axis of the plummet is aligned with the vertical axis of the theodolite if, when the instrument is revolved through 180°, the reticle of the optical plummet stays superimposed on the ground mark. If the reticle does not stay on the mark, the plummet can be adjusted in the following manner: The reticle is put over the ground mark by adjusting the leveling screws [see Figure 4-29(a)]. If the plummet is not in adjustment, the reticle will appear to be in a new location (*X*) after the theodolite is turned about 180°; point *P* is marked halfway between the two locations. The adjusting screws [Figure 4-29(b)] are turned until the reticle image is over *P,* indicating that the plummet is now in adjustment.

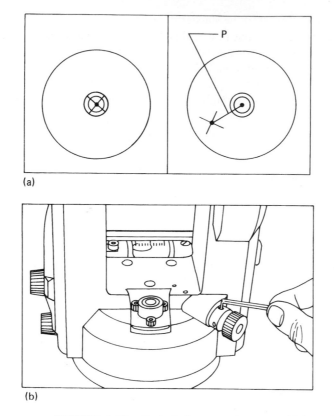

(a)

(b)

FIGURE 4-29 Optical plummet adjustment. (a) Point P is marked halfway between original position (·) and 180° position (X). (b) Plummet adjusting screws are
turned until X becomes superimposed on P. (Courtesy of Nikon Inc.,
Melville, N.Y.)

4-15-11   Vertical Index Error for Electronic Theodolites

CHECKING

1. Set up the instrument on the tripod, and level it.
2. With the telescope in its face-left position, sight an arbitrary target P, positioned within ±45° from the horizontal plane, and take a reading of the vertical angle: r.
3. Reverse the telescope's position, and once again sight target P, taking a reading of the vertical angle: l.
4. If $r + l$ equals 360° when the internal switch has been used to set the *zenith angle to 0°,* or if $r + l$ equals 180° (or 540°) when the internal switch has been used to set the horizontal angle to 0°, no adjustment will be required. Otherwise, refer to the following adjustment procedure.

ADJUSTMENT

1. Set the telescope in the face-left position, and sight target P, positioned within $\pm 45°$ from the horizontal plane.

$r = 76°15'20''$

```
VA:   76° 15' 20"   ████
HA:   30° 00' 00"
```

2. Set the telescope in the face-right position, and sight target P again.

$l = 283°45'20''$

```
VA: 283° 45' 20"   ████
HA:  30° 00' 00"
```

3. Calculate $\epsilon = \frac{1}{2}(r + l - 360°)$
   (Zenith 0°)
   assuming, in this case, $l = 283°45'20''$ and $\epsilon = 20''$.

4. Remove the internal switch cover. (Refer to Figure 4-7.)

5. Calculate l_0, the correct vertical angle at the face-right position:

$$l_0 = l - \epsilon = 283°45'00''$$

6. Turn the right-hand rotary switch (20″/div.*) until the display reads

$$l_0 = 283°45'00''$$

7. Check again.

   *If adjustment cannot be made using only the 20″/div. switch, turn the left-hand switch (320″/div.) one step in either direction, and try again.

The description here is for the Nikon theodolite. Other theodolites can be adjusted in a similar manner, as described in their manufacturers' manuals.

Chapter 5

Electronic Surveying Measurement

5-1 General

5-1-1 Electronic Distance Measurement

Electronic distance measurement (EDM), first introduced in the 1950s by the Geodimeter Inc. founders, has since those early days undergone continual refinement. The early instruments, which were capable of very precise measurements over long distances, were large, heavy, complicated, and expensive. Rapid advances in related technologies have provided lighter, simpler, and less expensive instruments—these EDM instruments (EDMIs) are manufactured for use with theodolites and as modular components of *Total Station* instruments. Technological advances in electronics continue at a rapid rate—as evidenced by recent market surveys that indicate that most new electronic instruments have been on the market for less than two years.

Current EDMIs use infrared light, laser light, or microwaves. The microwave systems use a receiver/transmitter at both ends of the measured line, whereas infrared and laser systems utilize a transmitter at one end of the measured line and a reflecting prism at the other end. Some laser EDMIs will measure short distances (100–350 m) without a reflecting prism—reflecting the light directly off the feature (e.g., building wall) being measured. Microwave instruments are often used in hydrographic surveys and have a usual upper measuring range of 50 km. Although microwave systems can be used in poorer weather conditions (fog, rain, etc.) than can infrared and laser systems, the uncertainties caused by varying humidity conditions over the length of the measured line may result in lower accuracy expectations. Hydrographic measuring and positioning techniques have, in a few short years, been largely supplanted by Global Positioning System (GPS) techniques (see Chapter 9).

Infrared and laser EDMIs come in long range (10–20 km), medium range (3–10 km) and short range (0.5 to 3 km).

EDMIs can be mounted on the standards or the telescope of most theodolites; additionally, they can be mounted directly in a tribrach. When used with an electronic theodolite, the combined instruments can provide both the horizontal and the vertical position of one point relative to another. The slope distance provided by an add-on EDMI can be reduced to its horizontal and vertical equivalents by utilizing the slope angle provided by the theodolite—in *Total Station* instruments, this reduction is accomplished automatically.

5-1-2 Electronic Angle Measurement

The electronic digital theodolite, first introduced in the late 1960s (Carl Zeiss Inc.), set the stage for modern field data collection and processing. See Figure 4.8, which shows electronic angle measurement using a rotary encoder and photoelectric converters.

When the electronic theodolite is used with a built-in EDMI, (e.g., Zeiss Elta, Figure 5-1) or an add-on and interfaced EDMI (e.g., Wild T-1000, Figure 5-2), the surveyor has a very powerful instrument. Add to that instrument an on-board microprocessor that automatically monitors the instrument's operating status and manages built-in surveying programs and a data collector (built-in or interfaced) that stores and processes measurements and attribute data, and you have what is known as a *Total Station*.

FIGURE 5-1 Zeiss Total Stations. The Elta 45 and 55 have on-board data storage (1,900 data lines), whereas the Elta 50 requires an interfaced data collector. On-board programs include coordinates, free stationing, polar points, heights of objects, connecting distances (between remote points), and setting out. Angle accuracy from 3 to 5 seconds and EDM distances to 1,500 m (single prism). (Courtesy of Carl Zeiss Inc., Thornwood, N.Y.)

FIGURE 5-2 Wild T-1000 electronic theodolite, shown with DI 1000 Distomat EDM and the GRE 3 data collector. (Courtesy of Leica Co. Inc., Toronto)

5-2 Principles of Electronic Distance Measurement (EDM)

Figure 5-3 shows a wave of wavelength λ. The wave is traveling along the *x* axis with a velocity of 299, 792.5 ± 0.4 km/s (in vacuum). The frequency of the wave is the time taken for one complete wavelength.

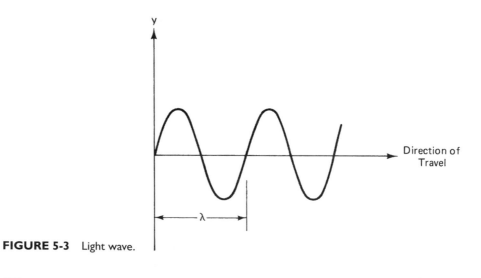

FIGURE 5-3 Light wave.

$$\lambda = \frac{c}{f} \qquad (5\text{-}1)$$

where
λ = wavelength in meters

c = velocity in km/s

f = frequency in hertz (one cycle per second)

Figure 5-4 shows the modulated electromagnetic wave leaving the EDMI and being reflected (lightwaves) or retransmitted (microwaves) back to the EDMI. It can be seen that the double distance ($2L$) is equal to a whole number of wavelengths ($n \lambda$), plus the partial wavelength (ϕ) occurring at the EDMI.

$$L = \frac{n\lambda + \phi}{2} \text{ meters} \qquad (5\text{-}2)$$

The partial wavelength (ϕ) is determined in the instrument by noting the phase delay required to precisely match up the transmitted and reflected or retransmitted waves. The instrument (e.g., Wild Distomat) can count the number of full wavelengths ($n\lambda$), or, instead, the instrument can send out a series (three or four) of modulated waves at different frequencies. (The frequency is typically reduced each time by a factor of 10, and, of course, the wavelength is increased each time also by a factor of 10.) By substituting the resulting values of λ and ϕ into Equation (5-2), the value of n can be found. The

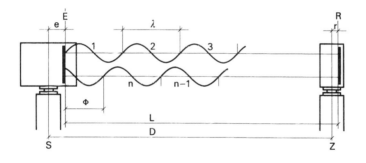

S   Station
Z   Target
E   Reference plane within the distance
    meter for phase comparison
    between transmitted and received
    wave
R   Reference plane for the reflection
    of the wave transmitted by the
    distance meter
a   Addition constant
e   Distance meter component of
    addition constant
r   Reflector component of addition
    constant
λ Modulation wave length
ϕ Fraction to be measured of a whole
    wave length of modulation ($\triangle \lambda$)

The addition constant a applies to a measuring equipment consisting of distance meter and reflector. The components e and r are only auxiliary quantities.

FIGURE 5-4 Principles of EDM measurement. (Courtesy of Kern Instruments—Leica)

instruments are designed to carry out this procedure in a matter of seconds and then to display the value of L in digital form.

The velocity of light (including infrared) through the atmosphere can be affected by (1) temperature, (2) atmospheric pressure, and (3) water vapor content. In practice, the corrections for temperature and pressure can be performed manually by consulting nomographs similar to that shown in Figure 5-5, or the corrections can be performed automatically on some EDMIs by the on-board processor/calculator after the values for temperature and pressure have been entered.

For short distances using lightwave EDMIs, atmospheric corrections have a relatively small significance. For long distances using lightwave instruments and especially microwave instruments, atmospheric corrections can become quite important. The following chart shows the comparative effects of the atmosphere on both lightwaves and microwaves.

| Parameter | Error | Error (parts per million) | |
		Light Wave	Microwave
t, temperature	$+1°C$	-1.0	-1.25
p, pressure	$+1$ mm Hg	$+0.4$	$+0.4$
e, partial water-vapor pressure	1 mm Hg	-0.05	$+7$ at $20°C$ $+17$ at $45°C$

At this point, it is also worth noting that several studies of general EDM use show that more than 90 percent of all distance determinations involve distances of 1000 m or less and that more than 95 percent of all layout measurements involve distances of 400 m or less. The values in the preceding chart would seem to indicate that, for the type of measurements normally encountered in the construction and civil field, instrumental errors and centering errors hold much more significance than do the atmosphere-related errors.

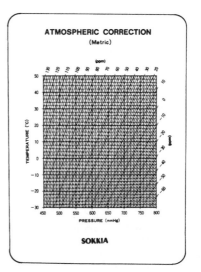

FIGURE 5-5 Atmospheric correction graph. (Courtesy of Sokkia Co. Ltd.)

5-3 EDMI Characteristics

Following are the characteristics of recent models of add-on *EDMI*s. Generally the more expensive instruments have longer distance ranges and higher precision.

Distance range: 800 m to 1 km (single prism with average atmospheric conditions)
        Short-range *EDMI*s can be extended to 1300 m using 3 prisms
        Long-range *EDMI*s can be extended to 15 km using 11 prisms
        (Leica Co.)
Accuracy range: ±(15 mm + 5ppm) for short-range *EDMI*s
        ±(3mm + 1ppm) for long-range *EDMI*s
Measuring time: 1.5 seconds for short-range *EDMI*s to 3.5 seconds for long-range
        *EDMI*s
        Both accuracy and time are considerably reduced for *tracking mode* measurements
Slope reduction: manual or automatic on some models
Average of repeated measurements: available on some models
Battery capability: 1400 to 4200 measurements, depending on the size of the battery
        and the temperature
Temperature range: −20°C to +50°C
Nonprism measurements: available on some models; distances from 100 to 350 m (3 to 5 km with prisms) (see Section 5-8)

5-4 Prisms

Prisms are used with electro-optical EDMIs (light, laser, and infrared) to reflect the transmitted signals (see Figure 5-6). A single reflector is a cube corner prism that has the characteristic of reflecting light rays back precisely in the same direction as they are received. This retro-direct capability means that the prism can be somewhat misaligned with respect

FIGURE 5-6 Various target and reflector systems in tribrach mounts. (Courtesy of Topcon Instrument Corp., Paramus, N.J.)

to the EDMI and still be effective. A cube corner prism is formed by cutting the corners off a solid glass cube; the quality of the prism is determined by the flatness of the surfaces and the perpendicularity of the 90° surfaces.

Prisms can be tribrach-mounted on a tripod, centered by optical plummet, or attached to a prism pole held vertical on a point with the aid of a bull's-eye level; however, prisms must be tribrach-mounted if a higher level of accuracy is required.

In control surveys, tribrach-mounted prisms can be detached from their tribrachs and then interchanged with a theodolite (and EDMI) similarly mounted at the other end of the line being measured. This interchangeability of prism and theodolite (also targets) speeds up the work, as the tribrach mounted on the tripod is centered and leveled only one time. Equipment that can be interchanged and mounted on tribrachs already set up is known as *forced-centering equipment.*

Prisms mounted on adjustable-length prism poles are very portable and, as such, are particularly suited for stakeout surveys. Figure 5-7 shows the prism pole being steadied with the aid of an additional target pole. The height of the prism is normally set to equal the height of the instrument. It is particularly important that prisms mounted on poles or tribrachs be permitted to tilt up/down so that they can be perpendicular to infrared signals that are being sent from much higher or lower positions.

FIGURE 5-7 Steadying the EDM reflector with the aid of a second target pole.

5-5 EDMI Accuracies

EDMI accuracies are stated in terms of a constant instrumental error and a measuring error proportional to the distance being measured.

Typically accuracy is claimed as $\pm$[5 mm + 5 parts per million (ppm)] or $\pm$(0.02 ft + 5 ppm). The $\pm$5 mm (0.02 ft) is the instrument error that is independent of the length of the measurement, whereas the 5 ppm (5 mm/km) denotes the distance-related error.

Most instruments now on the market have claimed accuracies in the range of $\pm$(3mm + 1 ppm) to $\pm$(10 mm + 10 ppm). The proportional part error (ppm) is insignificant for most work, and the constant part of the error assumes less significance as the distances being measured lengthen: At 100 m, an error of $\pm$5 mm represents 1/20,000 accuracy, whereas at 1,000 m, the same instrumental error represents 1/200,000 accuracy.

When one is dealing with accuracy, it should be noted that both the EDMI and the prism reflectors must be corrected for off-center characteristics. The measurement being recorded goes from the electrical center of the EDMI to the back of the prism (allowing for refraction through glass) and then back to the electrical center of the EDMI. The difference between the electrical center of the EDMI and the plumb line through the tribrach center is compensated for by the EDMI manufacturer at the factory. The prism constant (30 to 40 mm) is eliminated either by the EDMI manufacturer at the factory or in the field.

The EDMI/prism constant value can be field-checked in the following manner: A long line (> 1 km) is laid out with end stations and an intermediate station (see Figure 5-8). The overall distance AC is measured, along with partial lengths AB and BC. The constant value will be present in all measurements; therefore,

$$AC - AB - BC = \text{instrument/prism constant} \qquad (5\text{-}3)$$

Alternatively, the constant can be determined by measuring a known baseline if one can be conveniently accessed.

5-6 EDMI Operation

Figures 5-9 to 5-11 show a variety of first-generation short- to medium-range EDMIs. The operation of all EDMIs involves the following basic steps: (1) set up, (2) aim, (3) measure, (4) record.

5-6-1 Set Up

Tribrach-mounted EDMIs are simply inserted into the tribrach (forced centering) after the tribrach has been set over the point—by means of the optical plummet. Telescope or theodolite yoke-mounted EDMIs are simply attached to the theodolite either before or

FIGURE 5-8 Method of determining the instrument-reflector constant.

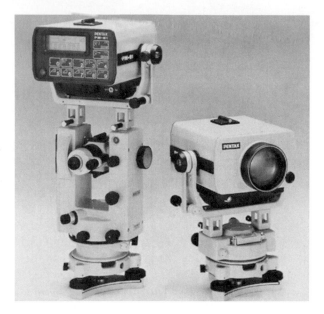

FIGURE 5-9 Pentax PM 81 EDM mounted on a 6-second Pentax theodolite and also shown as tribrach-mounted. EDM has a triple-prism range of 2 km (6,600 ft) with SE = +/-(5 mm + 5 ppm). (Courtesy of Pentax Corp., Colo.)

after the theodolite has been set over the point. Prisms are set over the remote station point either by inserting the prism into an already setup tribrach (forced centering) or by holding the prism vertically over the point on a prism pole. The EDMI is turned on, and a quick check is made to ensure that it is in good working order—for example, battery, display, and the like. The height of the instrument (telescope axis) and the height of the prism (center) are measured and recorded; the prism is usually set to the height of the theodolite when it is mounted on an adjustable prism pole.

5-6-2   Aim

The EDMI is aimed at the prism by using either the built-in sighting devices on the EDMI or the theodolite telescope. Telescope or yoke-mount EDMIs will have the optical line of sight a bit lower than the electronic signal. Some electronic tacheometer instruments (ETIs) have a sighting telescope mounted on top of the instrument; in those cases, the optical line of sight will be a bit higher than the electronic signal.

Most instrument manufacturers provide prism/target assemblies, which permit fast optical sightings for both optical and electronic alignment (see Figure 5-6). That is, when the crosshair is on target, the electronic signal will be maximized at the center of the prism.

The surveyor can (if necessary) set the electronic signal precisely on the prism center by adjusting the appropriate horizontal and vertical slow-motion screws until a maximum signal intensity is indicated on the display (this display is not available on all EDMIs). Some older EDMIs have an attenuator that must be adjusted for varying distances—the signal strength is reduced for short distances so that the receiving electronics are not over-loaded. Newer EDMIs have automatic signal attenuation.

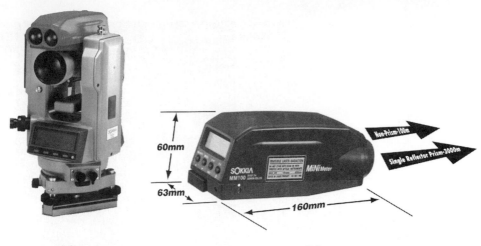

(a)   (b)

Mounting on the "DT4F" is by convenient hot-shoe

Connection via which power supply and data communication are provided.

(c)   (d)

FIGURE 5-10 Sokkia MiNi Meter MM100 laser add-on EDM. (a) EDM shown mounted on the telescope of Sokkia DT4F electronic 5″ theodolite. (b) MiNi Meter dimensions. (c) Display screen showing menu button, which provides access to programs permitting input for atmospheric corrections, height measurements, horizontal and vertical distances, self diagnostics, etc. (d) Illustration showing "hot shoe" electronics connection and counterweight. (e) MiNi Meter shown mounted directly into a tribrach-with attached sighting telescope, data output connector, and battery. (Courtesy of Sokkia Corporation, Overland Park, Kan.)

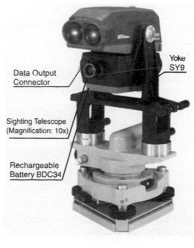

(e)

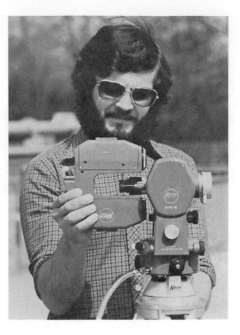

FIGURE 5-11 Kern DM 502 (infrared EDM) attaches readily to a theodolite, a DKM 2 1-second theodolite in this case. U-shaped design permits one sighting for both distance and angle measurement. Distance range is 2,000 m with the Kern single prism. See Figure 8.12 for the Kern prism. (Courtesy of Kern Instruments—Leica Co.)

5-6-3 Measure

The slope distance measurement is accomplished by simply pressing the "measure" button and waiting the few seconds for the result to appear in the display. The displays are either LCD (most) or LED. The measurement is shown to two decimals of a foot or three decimals of a meter; a foot/meter switch readily switches from one system to the other. If no measurement appears in the display, the surveyor should check on the switch position, battery status, attenuation, and crosshair location (sometimes the stadia hair is mistakenly centered).

EDMIs with built-in calculators or microprocessors can now be used to compute horizontal and vertical distances, coordinates, and atmospheric, curvature, and prism constant corrections. The required input data (vertical angle, ppm, prism constant, etc.) are entered via the keyboard.

Most EDMIs have a tracking mode (very useful in layout surveys), which permits continuous distance updates as the prism is moved ever closer to its final layout position.

Handheld radios are useful for all EDM work, as the long distances put a halt to normal voice communications. In layout work, clear communications are essential if the points are to be properly located. All microwave EDMIs permit voice communication—which is carried right on the measuring signal.

Figure 5-12 shows a remote device (Kern RD 10), which is attached to the prism. The display on the EDMI is transmitted to the RD 10 so that the surveyor holding the prism is immediately aware of the results. In tracking mode, the RD 10 display will show the remaining left/right and near/far (+/−) layout distances so that the surveyor holding the prism can quickly proceed to the desired layout point—even on high-noise construction sites.

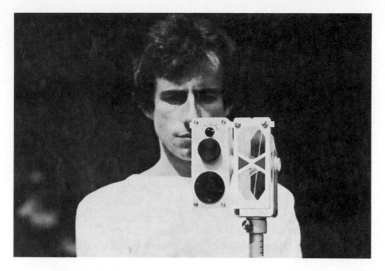

FIGURE 5-12 Kern RD 10 remote EDM display shown attached to EDM reflecting prism. Slope, horizontal, and vertical distances (from the EDM to the prism) are displayed on the RD 10. Maximum range is 1,300 feet (400 m).

5-6-4 Record

The measured data can be recorded conventionally in field note format, or they can be manually entered into an electronic data collector. The distance data must be accompanied by all relevant atmospheric and instrumental correction factors.

Total Station instruments, which have automatic data acquisition capabilities, are discussed in Section 5-9.

5-7 Geometry of Electronic Distance Measurements

Figure 5-13 illustrates the use of EDM when the optical target and the reflecting prism are at the same height (see Figure 5-6—single prism assembly). The slope distance (S) is mea-

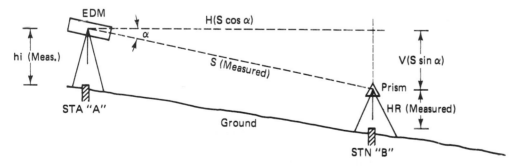

FIGURE 5-13 Geometry of an EDM calculation, general case.

sured by the EDMI, and the slope angle (α) is measured by the accompanying theodolite. The heights of the EDMI and theodolite (hi) are measured with a steel tape or by a graduated tripod centering rod; the height of the reflector/target is measured in a similar fashion. As noted earlier, adjustable-length prism poles permit the surveyor to set the height of the prism (HR) equal the height of the instrument (hi), thus simplifying the computations. From Figure 5-13, if the elevation of station A is known and the elevation of station B is required:

$$\text{Elev. STA. } B = \text{elev. STA. } A + \text{hi} \pm V - \text{HR} \qquad (5\text{-}4)$$

When the EDMI is mounted on the theodolite and the target is located beneath the prism the geometric relationship can be as shown in Figure 5-14.

The additional problem encountered in the situation depicted in Figure 5-14 is the computation of the correction to the vertical angle ($\Delta\alpha$) that occurs when Δhi and ΔHR are different. The precise size of the vertical angle is important, as it is used in conjunction with the measured slope distance to compute the horizontal and vertical distances.

In Figure 5-14, the difference between ΔHR and Δhi is X (i.e., ΔHR $-$ Δhi $= X$). The small triangle formed by extending S' [see Figure 5-14(b)] has the hypotenuse equal

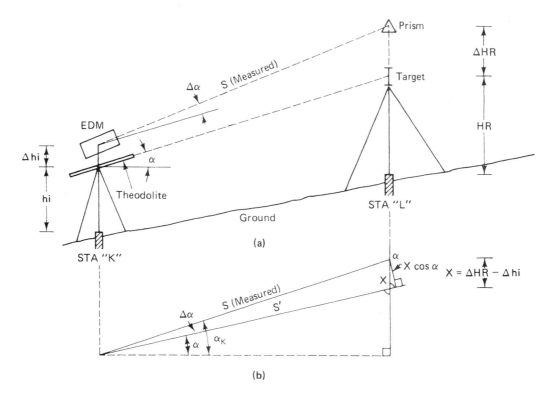

FIGURE 5-14 Geometry of an EDM calculation, usual case.

to X and an angle of α. This permits computation of the side $X \cos \alpha$, which can be used together with S to determine $\Delta \alpha$:

$$\frac{X \cos \alpha}{S} = \sin \Delta \alpha$$

■ **EXAMPLE 5-1**

An EDM slope distance AB is determined to be 561.276 m. The EDMI is 1.820 m above its station (A), and the prism is 1.986 m above its station (B). The EDMI is mounted on a theodolite whose optical center is 1.720 m above the station. The theodolite was used to measure the vertical angle ($+6°21'38''$) to a target on the prism pole; the target is 1.810 m above station B.

Compute both the horizontal distance AB and the elevation of station B, given that the elevation of station A = 186.275 m.

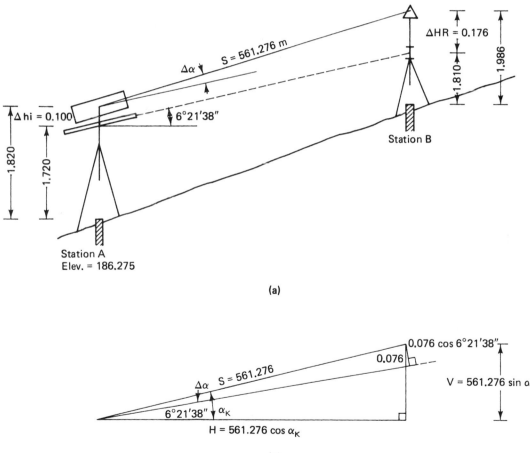

(a)

(b)

FIGURE 5-15   Illustration for Example 8.1

Solution

The given data are shown in Figure 5-15(a), and the resultant figure is shown in Figure 5-15(b). The X value introduced in Figure 5-14(b) is, in this case, determined as follows:

$$X = (1.986 - 1.810) - (1.820 - 1.720)$$
$$= 0.176 - 0.100$$
$$= 0.076 \text{ m}$$
$$\sin \Delta\alpha = \frac{0.076 \cos 6°21'38''}{561.276}$$
$$\Delta\alpha = 28''$$
$$\alpha_k = 6°22'06''$$
$$H = 561.276 \cos 6°22'06''$$
$$= 557.813 \text{ m}$$

If H had been computed by using the field vertical angle of $6°21'38''$, the result would have been 557.821 m, not a significant difference in this example.

$$\text{Elev. } B = \text{elev. } A + 1.820 + 561.276 \sin 6°22'06'' - 1.986$$
$$= 186.275 + 1.820 + 62.257 - 1.986$$
$$= 248.336 \text{ m}$$

If V had been computed by using $6°21'38''$, the result would have been 62.181 m instead of 62.257 m, a more significant discrepancy.

5-8 EDMI Without Reflecting Prisms

Some recently introduced EDMIs (see Figure 5-10 and 5-16) can measure distances without using reflecting prisms—the measuring surface itself is used as a reflector. Some manufacturers employ a timed-pulse infrared signal, transmitted by a laser diode. These instruments permit direct acquisition of distances from the target.

These instruments can be used conventionally with reflecting prisms for distances up to 4 km; when used without prisms, the range drops to 100 to 300 m, depending on the light conditions (cloudy days and night darkness provide the better measuring distances). With prisms, the available accuracy is about $\pm(3 \text{ mm} + 1 \text{ ppm})$; without prisms, the available accuracy drops to about ± 10 mm. Targets having light-colored and flat surfaces perpendicular to the measuring beam (e.g., building walls) provide the best ranges and accuracies.

These instruments provide quick results (0.8 s in rapid mode and 0.3 s in tracking mode), which means that applications for moving targets are possible; with increased acceptance into the surveying community, it is expected that applications will be developed in near-shore hydrographic surveying and in many areas of heavy construction. Already this technique is being used, with an interfaced data collector, to automatically measure cross sections in mining applications—with plotted cross sections and excavated volumes being automatically generated by digital plotter and computer.

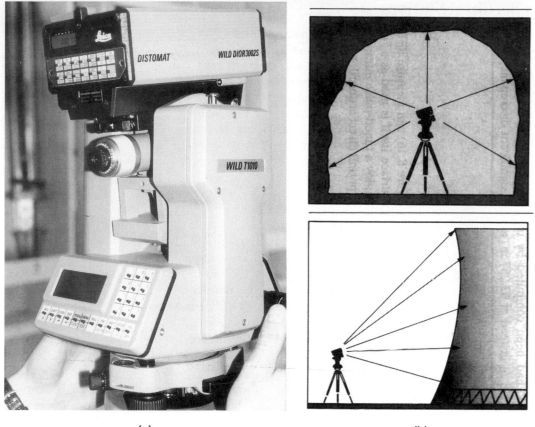

(a)   (b)

FIGURE 5-16   Distance measurement without reflectors. (a) Wild T1010 Electronic theodolite, together with an interfaced DIOR 3002S prismless EDM (angle accuracy is 3 seconds); (b) Illustrations of two possible uses for this technique. Upper: tunnel cross sections. Lower: profiling a difficult-access feature. (Courtesy of Leica Co., Toronto)

Other applications will include cross-sectioning above-ground excavated works and material stockpiles; measuring to dangerous or difficult access points—for example, bridge components, cooling towers, and dam faces; and automatically measuring liquid surfaces—for example, municipal water reservoirs and catchment ponds. It is conceivable that these new techniques may have some potential in industrial surveying, where production line rates require this type of monitoring.

These instruments are used with an attached laser, which helps to positively identify the feature being measured; that is, the visible laser beam is set on the desired feature so that the surveyor can be sure that the correct surface is being measured and not some feature just beside it or just behind it. Since the measurement is so fast, care must be taken not to mistakenly measure to some object that may temporarily intersect the measuring signal—for example, trucks or other traffic.

5-9 Total Stations

Electronic theodolites were introduced in Section 4-4. When these instruments are combined with interfaced EDMIs and electronic data collectors, they become electronic tacheometer instruments (ETIs)—also known as Total Stations. Figure 5-17 to 5-22 illustrate some additional Total Stations now in use.

These Total Stations can read and record horizontal and vertical angles together with slope distances. The microprocessors in the Total Stations can perform a variety of mathematical operations: for example, averaging multiple angle measurements; averaging multiple distance measurements; determining X, Y, Z coordinates, remote object elevations (i.e., heights of sighted features), and distances between remote points; and making atmospheric and instrumental corrections. The data collector can be a handheld device connected by cable to the tacheometer (see Figure 5-17 and 5-22), but many instruments come with the data collector built into the instrument. Figure 5-18 shows a Sokkia Powerset Total Station, a series of instruments that have angle accuracies from 0.5 to 5 seconds, distance ranges (one prism) from 1600 m to 2400 m, dual axis compensation, a wide variety of built-in programs, and a rapid battery charger, which can charge the battery in 70 minutes. Data are stored on-board in internal memory (about 1300 points) and/or on memory cards (about 2000 points per card). The data can be directly transferred to the computer from the Total Station via an RS-232 cable, or the data can be transferred from the data storage cards first to a card reader-writer and from there to the computer.

Figure 5-19 shows a Nikon DTM 750 Total Station having card readers for applications program cards (upper reader) and for data storage cards (lower reader). The data storage cards can be removed when full and read into a computer using standard PCMCIA

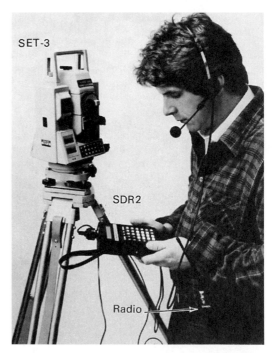

FIGURE 5-17 Sokkia Total Station Set 3 with cable-connected SDR2 electronic field book. Also shown is a two-way radio (2-mile range) with push-to-talk headset.

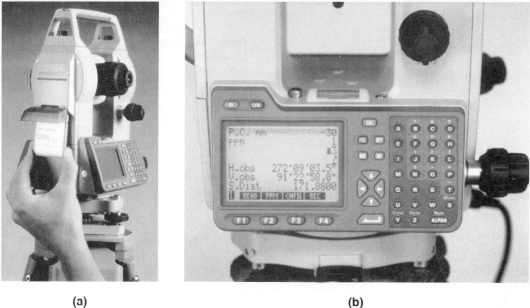

(a)

(b)

■ **Graphic "Bull's Eye" Level**

A graphically displayed "bull's-eye" lets you quickly and efficiently level the instrument.

(c)

FIGURE 5-18 (a) Sokkia SET 1000 Total Station having angle display of 0.5 seconds (1″ accuracy) and a distance range to 2,400 m using one prism. The instrument comes with a complete complement of surveying programs, dual-axis compensation, and the ability to measure (to 120 m) to reflective sheet targets—a feature suited to industrial surveying measurements. (b) Keyboard and LCD display. (c) Graphics bulls-eye level—allows you to level the instrument while observing the graphics display. (Courtesy of Sokkia Corp., Overland Park, Kan.)

(continued)

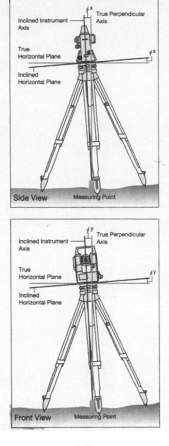

■ **Simultaneous Detection of Inclination in Two Directions And Automatic Compensation**

The built-in dual-axis tilt sensor constantly monitors the inclination of the vertical axis in two directions. It calculates the compensation value and automatically corrects the horizontal and vertical angles. (The compensation range is ±3'.)

FIGURE 5-18 *(continued)*
(d) Dual-axis compensation illustration. (Courtesy of Sokkia Corp., Overland Park, Kan.)

(d)

card readers—now standard on most "notebook" computers. Total Station operating software is MS-DOS compatible, permitting user-defined additions to applications software.

All the data collectors described here are capable of doing much more than just collecting data. The capabilities vary a great deal from one manufacturer to another. Similarly the computational characteristics of the electronic theodolites themselves also vary widely. Some EDM/electronic theodolites (without the data collector) simply show the horizontal and vertical angles together with the slope distance, whereas others also show the resultant

FIGURE 5-19 (a) Nikon DTM 750 Total Station featuring: on-board storage on PCMCIA computer cards; applications software on PCMCIA cards (upper drive); guidelight for layout work (to 100 m); dual-axis tilt sensor; EDM range of 2,700 m (8,900 ft) to one prism; angle precision of 1 second to 5 seconds; distance precision of +/−(2 mm + 2 ppm); operating system is MS-DOS compatible. (b) Menu schematic for the Nikon DTM 750. (Courtesy of Cansell Survey Equipment Co., Toronto)

(a)

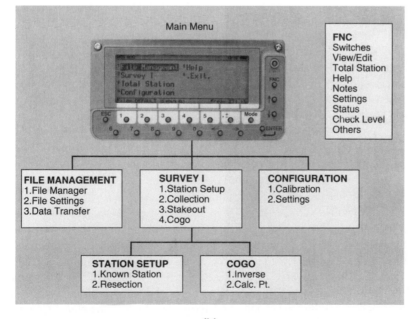

(b)

horizontal and vertical distances. Some electronic theodolites can compute remote elevations and distances between remote points, whereas others require the interfaced data collector to perform those functions.

Many data collectors are really handheld computers, very sophisticated and very expensive—in excess of $2500. If the Total Station is being used alone, the capability of performing all survey computations—including closures and adjustments—is highly desirable. However, if the Total Station is being used as a part of a system (field data collection/data processing/digital plotting), then the computational capacity of the data collectors becomes less important. If the Total Station is being used as part of a system, the data collector then can be designed to collect only the basic information—that is, slope distance, horizontal angle, vertical angle, or coordinates—and attribute data, such as point number, point type, and operation code (see Section 5-10). Computations and adjustments are then performed by one of the many coordinate geometry programs now available for surveyors and engineers.

Most early models and some current models use the absolute method for reading angles; these instruments are essentially optical coincidence instruments with photoelectronic sensors to scan and read the circles, which are divided into preassigned values—from 0 to 360 degrees (or 0 to 400 grad or gon).

Some later models employ an incremental method of angle measurement (see Figure 4-8). These instruments have a circle divided into many graduations, with both sides of the circle being scanned simultaneously; a portion of the circle is slightly magnified and superimposed on the opposite side of the circle. As a result, a moiré pattern is developed that can be analyzed (with the aid of photodiodes) to read the circles.

Both systems enable the surveyor to conveniently assign zero degrees (or any other value) to an instrument sighting **after** the instrument has been sighted in.

Most Total Stations have coaxial electronic and optical systems (see Figure 5-1 and 5-17 to 5-22), which permit one sighting for both electronic and optical orientation. Other Total Stations have the telescope mounted a bit below or above the EDMI (see Figure 5-2 and 5-16). These instruments employ a specific target/prism assembly similar to that shown in Figure 5.6 (left side)—the assembly is designed so that when the crosshairs are centered on the target, the EDMI measuring beam is exactly on the prism.

The Total Station has an on-board microprocessor that monitors the instrument status (e.g., level and plumb orientation, battery status, return signal strength) and makes corrections to measured data for the first of these conditions, when warranted. In addition, the microprocessor controls the acquisition of angles and distances and then computes horizontal distances, vertical distances, coordinates, and the like.

Many Total Stations are designed so that the data stored in the data collector can be automatically downloaded to a computer via an RS 232 interface. The download program is usually supplied by the manufacturer; a second program is required to translate the raw data into a format that is compatible with the surveyor's coordinate geometry (i.e., processing) programs. The system computer could be a mainframe, a mini, or a desktop, although lower costs and increased capabilities have recently made the desktop computer the choice of many surveyors and engineers.

Also, most Total Stations enable the surveyor to capture the slope distance and the horizontal and vertical angles to a point by simply pressing one button; the point number

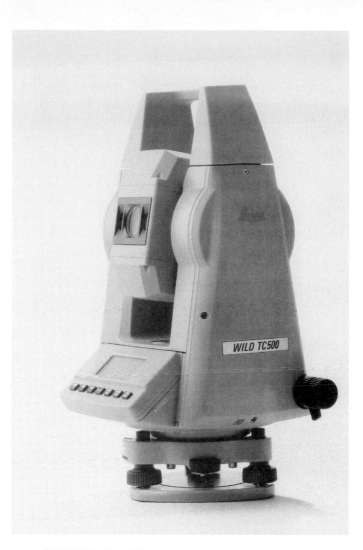

FIGURE 5-20 Wild TC500 Total Station featuring angles to 5 seconds and distances to one prism to 700 m (2,300 ft) at $+/-$(5 mm + 5 ppm) accuracy. Data are stored in attached data collector (Wild GPCI field computer). Used in construction and engineering surveys. (Courtesy of Leica, Switzerland)

and point description for that point can then be recorded. **In addition, the wise surveyor will prepare a sketch showing the overall detail and the individual point locations.** This sketch will help keep track of the completeness of the work and will be invaluable at a later date when the plot file is prepared.

Total Stations and/or their attached data collectors have been programmed to perform a wide variety of surveying functions. Some programs require that the proposed instrument station's coordinates and elevation—as well as the coordinates and elevations for proposed reference stations—be up-loaded into the Total Station prior to the field work.

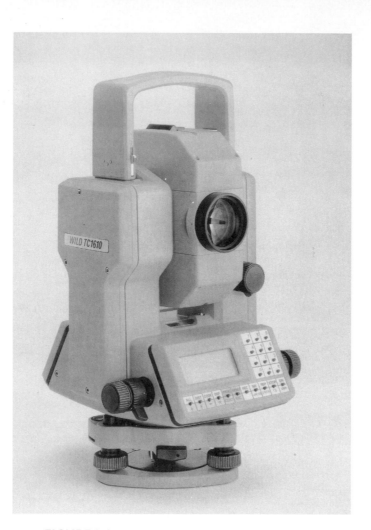

FIGURE 5-21   Wild TC1610 Total Station with on-board removable data storage modules (module reader required to effect transfer to computer).Angles are read to within 1.5 seconds and distances to one prism to 2.5 km (8,200 ft) at +/−(2 mm + 2 ppm) accuracy. (Courtesy of Leica Co. Inc.,Toronto)

After setup, the instrument station must be identified as such, and the hi and prism heights must be measured and entered. Typical Total Station programs include:

- *northing, easting, and elevation* determination.
- *missing line measurement*—this program enables the surveyor to determine the horizontal and slope distances between any two sighted points as well as the directions of the lines joining the sighted points.
- *resection*—this technique permits the surveyor to set up the Total Station at any convenient position and then determine the coordinates and elevation of that position by sighting previously coordinated reference stations. When sighting two points of

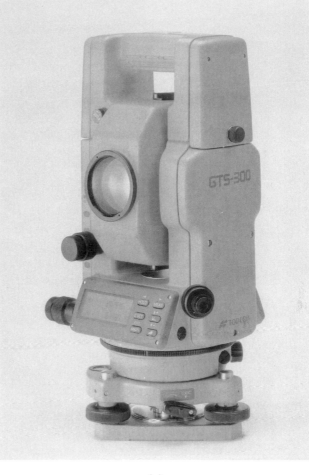

FIGURE 5-22 (a) Topcon GTS 300 Total Station. The 300 Series instruments have angle accuracies from I second to I0 seconds and single prism distances from 1,200 m (3,900 ft) to 2,400 m (7,900 ft) at +/−(2 mm + 2 ppm) accuracy.

(continued)

(a)

known position, it is necessary to measure both the distances and angle between the reference points; when sighting several points (three or more) of known position, it is only necessary to measure the angles between the points. It is important to stress that most surveyors take more readings than are minimally necessary to obtain a solution. These redundant measurements give the surveyor increased precision and a check on the accuracy of the results.

- *azimuth*—the azimuth of the line joining a sighted point from the instrument station is readily displayed.

- *remote object elevation*—the surveyor can determine the heights of inaccessible points (e.g., electricity conductors, bridge components, etc.) by simply sighting the pole-mounted prism as it is being held directly under the object. When the object itself is sighted, the object height can be promptly displayed (the prism height must first be entered into the Total Station; it is often set at the value of the instrument hi).

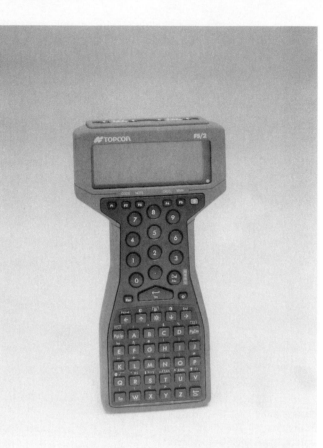

FIGURE 5-22 *(continued)*
(b) Topcon FS2 Data Collector for use with GTS 300 Series Total Stations. (Courtesy of Topcon Instrument Corp., Paramus, N.J.)

(b)

- *offset measurements* (a) *distance offsets*—when an object is hidden from the Total Station, a measurement can be taken to the prism held out in view of the Total Station and then the offset distance is measured. The angle (usually 90°) to the hidden object along with the measured distance are entered into the Total Station, enabling it to compute the position of the hidden object. (b) *angle offsets*—the prism is held to the left or right of the object being located (e.g., a concrete column). The prism is centered and then an angle is measured to the predetermined center of the object. The program will compute the coordinates of the center of the object (the concrete column, in this case).
- *layout or setting-out positions*—after the coordinates and elevations of the layout points have been up-loaded into the Total Station, the layout/setting-out software will enable the Total Station to display the left/right, forward/back, and up/down movements needed to place the prism in each of the desired positions. This capability is a great aid in property and construction layouts.

- *building face pickup*—this program permits the surveyor to define the vertical face of a building, including all cut-outs (doors and windows) by simply turning angles to each feature.

See Figure 5-23 for an illustration of these Total Station capabilities.

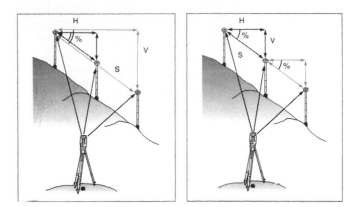

(a)

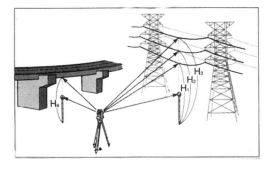

(b)

FIGURE 5-23   Typical programmed Total Station operations. Note that for most of these operations, the instrument station's coordinates and the reference azimuth to the backsight station (or its coordinates) must first be entered into the Total Station. (Sketches courtesy of Sokkia Corporation, Overland Park, Kan.) (a) *Missing line measurement* permits the surveyor to determine the length, slope, and direction of a line joining any two points sighted in from the instrument station. (b) *Remote object elevation measurement* permits the surveyor to determine the heights of inaccessible points (e.g., electricity conductors, bridge components, etc.). The surveyor first sights the prism (the height of the prism on the prism pole has already been entered into the Total Station) while it is held directly under (over) the feature being measured, and then the surveyor sights directly on the feature; the resultant height is then displayed on the screen.

(continued)

FIGURE 5-23 *(continued)*
(c) *Offset measurements.* (i) *Distance offset* is measured to a hidden (from the Total Station) measuring point by measuring the offset distance and angle (usually 90°) between the measuring point and the prism; after the offset distance and angle have been entered into the Total Station, the software calculates the angle and distance from the instrument to the desired point, or it can calculate the coordinates of the desired point. (ii) *Angle offset* uses a prism set on either the left or right side of the measuring point (the theoretical center of a concrete column in this example); first the prism is sighted, and then the angle is turned to the center of the column. Either the angle and distance to the theoretical center are calculated, or the center's coordinates are calculated. (d) The *azimuth* from the instrument station to a reference station can be quickly displayed if the coordinates of both the instrument station and the reference station have already been entered into the Total Station (inversing). (e) *Resection* is a technique that permits the surveyor to set up the Total Station in any convenient point *(free station)* and then determine its location coordinates by sighting in at least two points of known location—whose coordinates have first been entered into the Total Station. When sighting two points of known location, both distance and angle must be measured. When sighting several points of known location, the resection solution can be accomplished by measuring only the angles. When more points are sighted than are needed for the solution, these redundant measurements permit the software to compute and display the positional accuracy of the solution.

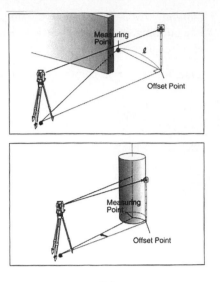

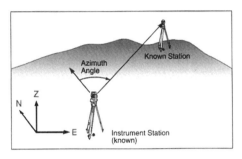

(c)

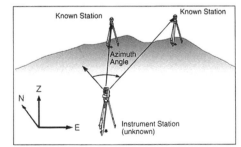

(d)

(e)

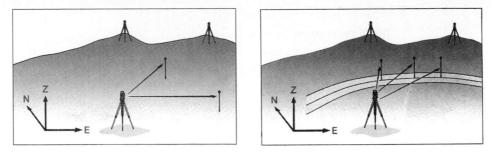

(f)   (g)

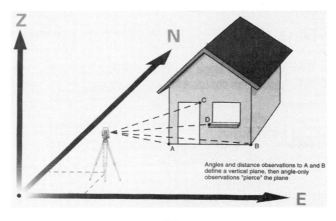

(h)

FIGURE 5-23 *(continued)* (f) *Northing, easting,* and *elevation* can be computed for any points sighted from the base station instrument. (g) *Setting out* in three dimensions (N, E, and Z) can be accomplished when the instrument has been properly oriented and the coordinates of the set-out points have been uploaded into the Total Station from the computer—or manually entered. The Total Station display tells the surveyor where the prism is located with respect to final set-out position with right/left, forward/backward, and up/down graphic displays—these directions can be communicated to the prism-holder via hand signals or radio. (h) *Building face pickup* allows for the coordination of points in a vertical plane using angle-only observations. The vertical plane must first be defined, as shown in the accompanying figure.

SUMMARY OF TYPICAL TOTAL STATION CHARACTERISTICS

  A. Parameter Input
    1. Angle units: degrees or gons
    2. Distance units: feet or meters

3. Pressure units: in HG or mm HG*

4. Temperature units: °F or °C*

5. Prism constant (usually −0.03 m)

6. Offset distance (used when the prism cannot be held at the center of the object)

7. Face 1 or Face 2 selection

8. Automatic point number incrementation

9. Height of instrument (hi)

10. Height of reflector (HR)

11. Point numbers and code numbers for occupied and sighted stations

12. Date and time settings—for Total Stations with on-board clocks

B. Capabilities (see Figure 5-23)

1. Monitor: battery status, signal attenuation, horizontal and vertical axes status, collimation factors

2. Compute coordinates—northing, easting, elevation

3. Traverse closure and adjustment, and areas

4. Topography reductions

5. Remote object elevation—that is, object heights

6. Distances between remote points (missing line measurement)

7. Inversing

8. Resection

9. Layout (setting out)

10. Horizontal and vertical collimation corrections

11. Vertical circle indexing

12. Records search and review

13. Programmable features—that is, load external programs

14. Transfer of data to the computer (downloading)

15. Transfer of computer files to the data collector (uploading) for layout purposes

*Newer instruments have built-in sensors that detect atmospheric effects and automatically correct readings for these natural errors.

5-10   Field Procedures for Total Stations in Topographic Surveys

Total Stations can be used in any type of preliminary survey, control survey, or layout survey. They are particularly well suited for topographic surveys, in which the surveyor can capture the *Y, X, Z* (northing, easting, elevation) positions of a large number of points—700 to 1000 points per day, which is two to three times the number that could be taken by using conventional techniques (theodolite and EDMI, or stadia). This significant increase in productivity means that in some medium-density areas ground surveys are once again competitive in cost to aerial surveys.

Although the increase in efficiency in the field survey is notable, an even more significant increase in efficiency can occur when the Total Station is part of a computerized surveying system—data collection, data processing (reductions and adjustments), and plotting. The concepts of a computerized surveying system are introduced in Section 5-12.

One of the notable advantages of using electronic surveying techniques is that data are recorded in the electronic field book; this cuts down considerably on the time required to record data and on the opportunity of making transcription mistakes. Does this mean that manual field notes are a thing of the past? The answer is no! Even in electronic surveys, there is a need for neat, comprehensive field notes. At the very least, such notes will contain the project title, field personnel, equipment description, date, weather, instrument setup station identification, and backsight station(s) identification. In addition, for topographic surveys, many surveyors include in the manual notes a sketch showing the area details—individual details, such as trees, catch basins, and poles, and stringed detail, such as water's edge, curbs, walks, and building outlines. As the survey proceeds, the surveyor will place all or selected point identification numbers directly on the sketch feature, thus clearly showing the type of detail being recorded. Later, after the data have been transferred to the computer, as the graphics features are being edited, the presence of manual field notes will be invaluable in clearing up problems associated with any incorrect, or ambiguous, labeling/numbering of survey points.

5-10-1   Initial Data Entry

Most data collectors are designed to prompt for, or accept, some or all of the following initial data:

- Project description
- Date and crew
- Temperature
- Pressure (some data collectors require a ppm correction input, which is read from a temperature/pressure graph—see Figure 5-5)
- Prism constant (-0.03 m is a typical value)
- Curvature and refraction settings (see Chapter 3)
- Sea level corrections (see Chapter 8)
- Number of measurement repetitions—angle or distance (the average value is computed)
- Choice of Face 1 and Face 2 positions
- Automatic point number incrementation
- Choice of foot units or SI units for all data

(Many of these prompts can be bypassed, causing the microprocessor to use "default" values, or settings, in its computations.) After the initial data have been entered, and the operation mode selected, most data collectors will prompt the operator for all station and measurement entries; see the following sections for typical procedures.

5-10-2 Survey Station Descriptors

Each survey station, or shot location (point), must be described with respect to surveying activity, station identification, and other attribute data.

Total Stations that come equipped with their own data collectors (e.g., Sokkia, Wild, Topcon) will, in many cases, prompt for the data entry (e.g., OCC, BS, FS) and then automatically assign appropriate labels, which will then show up on the survey printout. Point description data can be entered as alpha or numeric codes (see Table 5-1 and Figure 5-24). This descriptive data will also show up on the printout and can (if desired) be tagged to show up on the plotted drawing. Some data collectors are now equipped with bar code readers that, when used with prepared code sheets, permit instantaneous entry of descriptive data.

Some data collectors (see Figure 5-25) are designed to work with all (or most) Total Stations on the market. These data collectors have their own routines and coding requirements. As this technology continues to evolve and continues to take over many surveying functions, standardized procedures will hopefully develop.

A positive indication of the trend toward standardization surfaced with the 1990 Survey Data Management System (SDMS™) developed by the American Association of State Highway and Transportation Officials (AASHTO). The SDMS* identifies and defines all highway-related surveying tasks, activities, and data tags; SDMS can be used for manual, as well as computer-based, collection and processing. Since the tasks and activities in highway surveying are similar or identical to all surveying tasks and activities, this new system could have particular applications for general surveying situations in which third-party data collectors are being used or in which the nature of the data processing and plan preparation is such that coding standardization would provide demonstrable benefits.

Also, newer data collectors (and computer programs) permit the surveyor to enter not only the point code, but also various levels of attribute data for each coded point. For example, a tie-in to a utility pole could also tag the pole number, the use (e.g., electric, telephone), the material (e.g., wood, concrete, steel), connecting poles, year of installation,

*For more information on the SDMS Data Structure Guide, contact AASHTO Executive Office, 444 N. Capitol St., NW., Washington, D.C. 20001.

Table 5-1 TYPICAL ALPHA AND NUMERIC DESCRIPTORS*

Activity	Code (alpha)	Code (numeric)
Occupied station	OCC	10
Backsight	BS	20
Foresight	FS	30
Intermediate sight	IS	40

*Many newer data collectors automatically prompt the surveyor for these basic surveying activities, thus eliminating the need to identify them by code.

Operation Codes (typical)

10 occupied station (Occ)
20 backsight station (Bs)
30 foresight station (Fs)
40 intermediate sight (Is)
41 O/S right ⎫
42 O/S left ⎪ O/S (offset sightings) occur when
43 O/S in front of point ⎬ the prism cannot be held at the
44 O/S behind point ⎭ center of the object. The O/S value
                                 is manually entered into the data
                                 collector after the field data have been stored.

50 cross-section intermediate sights. This code is used when a computer program will be utilized for volume computations.

(a)

Point Identification Codes
(shown is part of Seneca dictionary)

Survey Points

01	BM	Bench Mark
02	CM	Concrete Monument
03	SIB	Standard Iron Bar
04	IB	Iron Bar
05	RIB	Round Iron Bar
06	IP	Iron Pipe
07	WS	Wooden Stake
08	MTR	Coordinate Monument
09	CC	Cut Cross
10	N&W	Nail and Washer
11	ROA	Roadway
12	SL	Street Line
13	EL	Easement Line
14	ROW	Right of Way
15	CL	Centerline

Topography

16	EW	Edge Walk
17	ESHLD	Edge Shoulder
18	C&G	Curb and Gutter
19	EWAT	Edge of Water
20	EP	Edge of Pavement
21	RD	CL Road
22	TS	Top of Slope
23	BS	Bottom of Slope
24	CSW	Concrete Sidewalk
25	ASW	Asphalt Sidewalk
26	RW	Retaining Wall
27	DECT	Deciduous Tree
28	CONT	Coniferous Tree
29	HDGE	Hedge
30	GDR	Guide Rail
31	DW	Driveway
32	CLF	Chain Link Fence
33	PWF	Post and Wire Fence
34	WDF	Wooden Fence

(b)

Code Sheet for Field Use

Topos Translator for Seneca. Dic.

1 BM	2 CM	3 SIB	4 IB	5 RIB
6 IP	7 WS	8 MTR	9 CC	10 N W
11 ROA	12 SL	13 EL	14 ROW	15 CL
16 EW	17 ESHL	18 C G	19 EWAT	20 EP
21 RD	22 TS	23 BS	24 CSW	25 ASW
26 RW	27 DECT	28 CONT	29 HDGE	30 GDR
31 DW	32 CLF	33 PWF	34 WDF	35 SIGN
36 MB	37 STM	38 HDW	39 CULV	40 SWLE
41 PSTA	42 SAN	43 BRTH	44 CB	45 DCB
46 HYD	47 V	48 V CH	49 M CH	50 ARV
51 WKEY	52 HP	53 UTV	54 LS	55 TP
56 PED	57 TMH	58 TB	59 BCM	60 GUY
61 TLG	62 BLDG	63 GAR	64 FDN	65 RWYX
66 RAIL	67 GASV	68 GSMH	69 G	70 GMRK
71 TL	72 PKMR	73 TSS	74 SCT	75 BR
76 ABUT	77 PIER	78 FTG	79 EDB	80 POR
81 SLS	82 WTT	83 STR	84 BUS	85 PLY
86 TEN	0	0	0	0
0	0	0	0	0
0	0	0	0	0

(c)

FIGURE 5-24 (a) Instrument operation codes. (b) Alphanumeric codes for sighted point descriptions. (c) Code sheet for field use.

FIGURE 5-25 CMT MC V Total Station data collector interfaced with a portable disk drive. The collector, used with Surveyor's Assistant software, permits data collection with most popular Total Stations and provides a variety of coordinate geometry operations and plotting routines. The portable disk drive (3 1/2" floppy disks) ensures unlimited memory storage for large, isolated projects. (Courtesy of Corvallis MicroTechnology Inc., Corvallis, Ore.)

and so on. This type of expanded attribute data is typical of the data collected for a Geographic Information System (GIS). See Section 5-13.

5-10-3   Occupied Point (Instrument Station) Entries

- Height of instrument (measured value is entered)
- Station number—for example, 111 (see example in Figure 5-26)
- Station identification code (see Code Sheet, Figure 5-24)
- Coordinates of occupied station—coordinates can be assumed, state plane, or Universal Transverse Merator (UTM)
- Coordinates of backsight (BS) station, **or** reference azimuth to BS station

Note: With some data collectors, the coordinates of the above stations may instead be entered in the system computer file just prior to the field data reductions and adjustments.

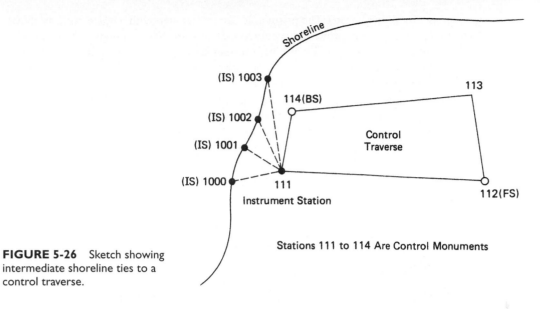

FIGURE 5-26 Sketch showing intermediate shoreline ties to a control traverse.

Stations 111 to 114 Are Control Monuments

5-10-4   Sighted Point Entries

- Operation code 20, 30, or 40—for BS, FS, or IS—for some Total Stations
- Height of prism/reflector (HR)—measured value is entered
- Station number—for example, 114 (BS) (see Figure 5-26)
- Station identification code (see Figure 5-24)

5-10-5   Procedures for the Example Shown in Figure 5-26

1. Enter the initial data and occupied station data, as shown in Sections 5-10-1 to 5-10-3.
2. Sight at station 114; zero the horizontal circle (any value can be set instead of zero). Most Total Stations have a zero-set button.
3. Enter code 20 (BS), or respond to the data collector prompt.
4. Measure and enter the height of prism/reflector (HR).
5. Press the appropriate **"measure"** buttons— for example, slope distance, horizontal angle, vertical angle (see step 6).
6. Press the **"record"** button after each measurement; most instruments measure and record these three measurements after the pressing of just one button (when they are in the **automatic** mode).
7. After the station measurements have been recorded, the data collector will prompt for the station point number (e.g., 114) and the station identification code (e.g., 02).
8. If appropriate, as in traverse surveys, the next sight is to the FS station (code 30); repeat steps 4, 5, 6, and 7, using correct data.
9. While at station 111, any number of IS (code 40) can be taken to define the topographic features being surveyed. The prism/reflector is usually mounted on an adjustable-length prism pole with the height of the prism (HR) being set to the height

of the Total Station (hi). The prism pole can be steadied with a brace pole, as shown in Figure 5-7, to improve the accuracy for more precise sightings. Some software permits the surveyor to identify, by a further code number, points that will be connected on the resultant plan (e.g., shoreline points in this example). This connect (on and off) feature permits the field surveyor to virtually prepare the plan (for graphics terminal or plotter) while performing the actual field survey. Alternately the surveyor can connect the points while in edit mode on the computer; **clear field notes** are essential for this activity.

10. When all the topographic detail in the area of the occupied station (111) has been collected, the Total Station can be moved* to the next traverse station (e.g., 112), and the data collection can proceed in the same manner as that already described. That is, BS @ STA.111, FS @ STA. 113, and take all relevant IS readings.

*When the Total Station is to be moved to another setup station, the instrument is always removed from the tripod and carried separately by its handle or in its case.

5-10-6   Data Transfer and Data Processing

In the example shown in Figure 5-26, the collected data now must be downloaded to a computer; the download computer program is normally supplied by the Total Station manufacturer, and the actual transfer is cabled through an RS 232 interface plug. Once the data are in the computer, the data must be sorted into a format that is compatible with the computer program that is to process the data; this *translation* program is usually written or purchased separately by the surveyor.

Modern Total Stations have data stored on-board, eliminating the costly data collectors. Some Wild instruments (e.g., Figure 5-21) store data on a module that can be transferred to a computer-connected reading device. Other instruments have the data stored on cards, which also require a reader. One manufacturer, Nikon, uses PCMCIA cards, which can be directly read into a computer through a PCMCIA reader (see Figure 5-19). Other Total Stations, including the geodimeter (see Figure 5-34), can be downloaded by connecting the instrument (or its keyboard) to the computer.

If the topographic data have been tied to a closed traverse, the traverse closure is calculated, and then all adjusted values for northings, eastings, and elevations (*Y, X, Z*) are computed. Some Total Stations have sophisticated data collectors (which are actually small computers) that can perform preliminary analysis, adjustments, and coordinate computations, whereas others require the computer program to perform these functions.

Once the field data have been stored in coordinate files, the data required for plotting by digital plotters can be assembled, and the survey can be quickly plotted at any desired scale. Additionally, the survey can be plotted at an interactive graphics terminal for graphics editing, using one of the many available computer-aided design (CAD) programs.

5-10-7   Field-Generated Graphics

Many surveying software programs permit the field surveyor to identify field data shots so that subsequent processing will produce appropriate computer graphics. For example, MicroSurvey International, Inc., software has a typical "description to graphics" feature, which enables the surveyor to join field shots, such as curbline shots [see Figure 5-27(a)]

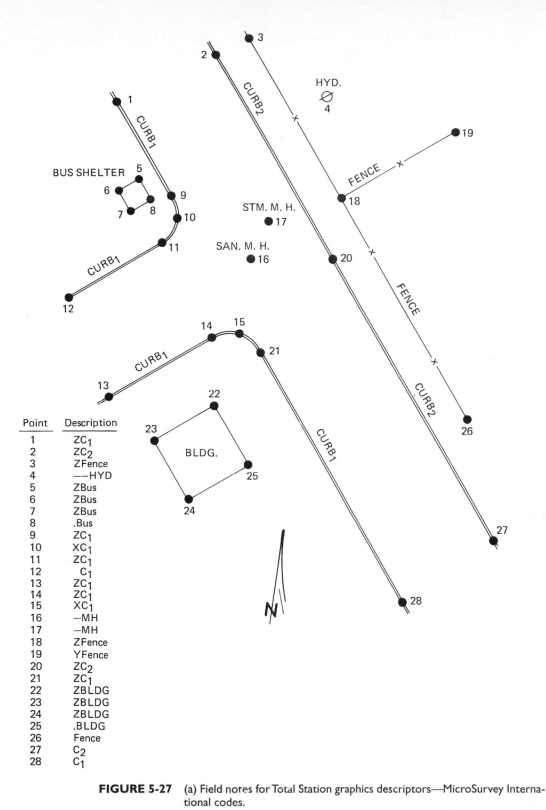

Point	Description
1	ZC_1
2	ZC_2
3	ZFence
4	——HYD
5	ZBus
6	ZBus
7	ZBus
8	.Bus
9	ZC_1
10	XC_1
11	ZC_1
12	C_1
13	ZC_1
14	ZC_1
15	XC_1
16	—MH
17	—MH
18	ZFence
19	YFence
20	ZC_2
21	ZC_1
22	ZBLDG
23	ZBLDG
24	ZBLDG
25	.BLDG
26	Fence
27	C_2
28	C_1

FIGURE 5-27 (a) Field notes for Total Station graphics descriptors—MicroSurvey International codes.

(continued)

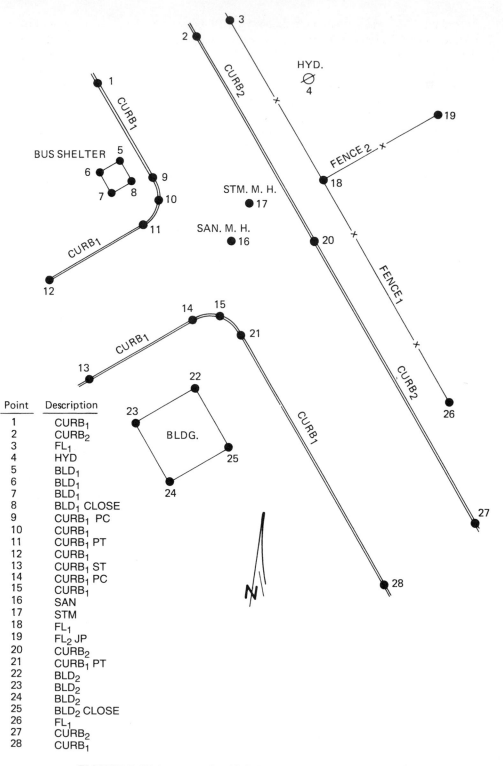

Point	Description
1	$CURB_1$
2	$CURB_2$
3	FL_1
4	HYD
5	BLD_1
6	BLD_1
7	BLD_1
8	BLD_1 CLOSE
9	$CURB_1$ PC
10	$CURB_1$
11	$CURB_1$ PT
12	$CURB_1$
13	$CURB_1$ ST
14	$CURB_1$ PC
15	$CURB_1$
16	SAN
17	STM
18	FL_1
19	FL_2 JP
20	$CURB_2$
21	$CURB_1$ PT
22	BLD_2
23	BLD_2
24	BLD_2
25	BLD_2 CLOSE
26	FL_1
27	$CURB_2$
28	$CURB_1$

FIGURE 5-27 (continued) (b) Field notes for Total Station graphics descriptors—Sokkia codes.

by adding a "Z" prefix to all but the last "CURB" descriptor. When the program first en-counters the "Z" prefix, it begins joining points with the same descriptors and then when the program encounters the first curb descriptor without the "Z" prefix, the joining of points is terminated; rounding (e.g., curved curbs) can be introduced by substituting an "X" prefix for the "Z" prefix [see Figure 5-27(a)].

Other typical graphics prefixes include the following:

"Y" joins the last identical descriptor by drawing a line at a right angle to the estab-lished line [see the fence line in Figure 5-27(a)].

"–" causes a dot to be created in the drawing file, which is later transferred to the plan. The dot on the plan can itself be replaced by inserting a previously created sym-bol block—for example, a tree, a manhole, a hydrant [see MH in Figure 5-27(a)]. If a second dash follows the first prefix dash, the ground elevation will **not** be trans-ferred to the graphics file [see HYD in Figure 5-27(a)], as some feature elevations may not be required.

"." instructs the system to close back on the first point of the string of descriptors with the same characters [see BLDG and BUS shelter in Figure 5-27(a) and POND in Figure 5-28].

Other software programs create graphic stringing by similar techniques. For example, Sokkia software gives the code itself a stringing capability (e.g., fence1, curb1, curb2, ₵), which the surveyor can easily turn on and off [see Figure 5-27(b)].

In some cases, it may be more efficient to assign the point descriptors from the com-puter keyboard *after* the survey has been completed. For example, the entry of descriptors is time consuming on some electronic field books (EFB), particularly in automatic mode. In addition, some topographic features (e.g., edge of water in a pond or lake) can be cap-tured in sequence, thus permitting the surveyor to edit in these descriptors efficiently from the computer in the processing stage. If the point descriptors are to be added at the com-puter, clear field notes are indispensable.

See Figure 5-28 for an illustration of this **stringing** technique. The pond edge has been picked up (defined) by 10 shots, beginning with #58 and ending with #67. Using the

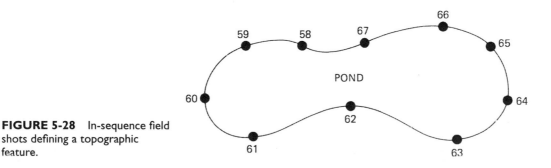

FIGURE 5-28 In-sequence field shots defining a topographic feature.

program introduced earlier, the point description edit feature is selected from the pull-down menu, and the following steps occur:

1. "Points to be described?" **58..66 enter**
2. "Description?" **ZPOND enter**
3. "Points to be described?" **67 enter**
4. "Description?" **.POND enter**

After the point descriptions have been suitably prefixed (either by direct field coding or by the editing technique shown here), a second command is accessed from another pull-down menu that simply (in one operation) converts the prefixed point description file so that the shape of the pond is produced in graphics. The four descriptor operations described here are less work than would be required to describe each point using field entries for the 10 points shown in this example. Larger features requiring many more field shots would be even more conducive to this type of postsurvey editing of descriptors.

It is safe to say that most projects requiring that graphics be developed from Total Station surveys will utilize a combination of point description field coding and postsurvey point description editing. It should be noted that the success of some of these modern surveys still depends to a significant degree on old-fashioned, reliable survey field notes.

It is becoming clear that the "drafting" of the plan of survey is increasingly becoming the responsibility of the surveyor, either through direct field coding techniques or through postsurvey data processing. All recently introduced surveying software programs enable the surveyor to produce a complete plan of survey.

5-11   Construction Layout Using Total Stations

We saw in the previous section that Total Stations are particularly well suited for collecting data in topographic surveys; we also noted that the collected data could be readily downloaded to a computer and processed into point coordinates—northing, easting, elevation (Y, X, Z)—along with point attribute data.

The significant increases in efficiency made possible with Total Station topographic surveys can be transferred to layout surveys when the original point coordinates exist in computer memory or floppy disk—together with the coordinates of all the key design points. To illustrate, consider the example of a road construction project.

First, the topographic detail is collected using Total Stations set up at various control points. The detail is then transferred to the computer; adjusted, if necessary; and converted into $Y, X,$ and Z coordinates. Various coordinate geometry and road design programs can then be used to design the proposed road. When the proposed horizontal, cross-section, and profile alignments have been established, the proposed coordinates ($Y, X,$ and Z) for all key horizontal and vertical (elevation) features can be computed and stored in computer files. The points coordinated will include top-of-curb and centerline positions at regular stations as well as all changes in direction or slope. Catch basins, traffic islands, and the like will also be included, as will all curved or irregular road components.

The computer files will now include coordinates of all control stations, all topographic detail, and, finally, all design component points. The layout will be accomplished by setting up at a control point, sighting another control point—with the correct azimuth on the horizontal circle—and then follow the display instructions (backward/forward, left/right, up/down) to locate the desired layout point. When the Total Station is set to tracking mode, the surveyor will set the prism on target by rapid trial-and-error measurements.

Figure 5-29 illustrates a computer printout for a road construction project. The Total Station is set at control monument CX-80 with a reference backsight on RAP (reference azimuth point) 2—point 957 on the printout. The surveyor has a choice of (1) setting the actual azimuth (213°57′01″, line 957) on the backsight and then turning the horizontal circle to the printed azimuths of the desired layout points or (2) setting zero degrees for the backsight and then turning the clockwise angle listed for each desired layout point. As a safeguard, after sighting the reference backsight, the surveyor usually sights a second or third control monument (see the top 12 points on the printout) to check the azimuth or angle setting. The computer printout also lists the point coordinates and baseline offsets for each layout point.

Figure 5-30 shows a portion of the construction drawing that accompanies the computer printout shown in Figure 5-29. The drawing (usually drawn by digital plotter from computer files) is an aid to the surveyor in the field in correctly laying out the works. All the layout points listed on the printout are also shown on the drawing, together with curve data and other explanatory notes.

Modern Total Stations offer an **even more efficient technique.** Instead of having the layout data only on a printout similar to that shown in Figure 5-29, the coordinates for all layout points can be uploaded into the Total Station microprocessor. The surveyor can then, in the field, identify the occupied control point and the reference backsight point(s), thus orienting the Total Station. The desired layout point number is then entered, with the required layout angle and distance being inversed from the stored coordinates and displayed. The layout can proceed by setting the correct azimuth, and then, by trial and error, the prism is moved to the layout distance (the Total Station is set to tracking mode for all but the final measurements); with some Total Stations, the prism is simply tracked with the remaining left/right ($\pm$) distance being displayed alongside the remaining near/far ($\pm$) distance. When the correct location has been reached, both displays show 0.000 m (0.00 ft).

If the instrument is set up at an unknown position *(free station),* its coordinates can be determined by sighting control stations whose coordinates have been previously uploaded into the Total Station microprocessor. This technique, known as *resection,* is available on all modern Total Stations. Sightings on two control points can locate the instrument station, although additional sightings (up to a total of four) are recommended to provide a stronger solution and an indication of the accuracy level achieved.

Some theodolites and Total Stations come equipped with a guide light, which can help move the prism holder on line very quickly. See Figures 5-31 and 5-32. The TC 800 is a Total Station that can be turned on and immediately used (no initialization procedure) and comes equipped with internal storage for 2000 points and a EGL1® guide light, which is very useful in layout surveys, as prism holders can quickly place themselves on-line by noting the colored lights sent from the Total Station. The flashing lights (yellow on the left and red on the right—as viewed by the prism holder), which are 12 m wide at a distance of 100 m, enable the prism holder to place the prism on-line with final adjustments as given by the instrument operator. With automatic target recognition (ATR—see Section 5-12-1), the sighting-in process is completed automatically.

THE MUNICIPALITY OF METROPOLITAN TORONTO - DEPARTMENT OF ROADS AND TRAFFIC

W.R. ALLEN ROAD FROM SHEPPARD AVENUE TO STANSTEAD DRIVE

ENGINEERING STAKEOUT

```
FROM STATION   269+80.00    TO STATION   271+30.00

BASE LINE

         INSTRUMENT ON  CONST CONTROL MON CX-80   AZIMUTH  213-57- 1

         SIGHTING       RAP #2 - ANTENNA C.F.B.
```

POINT NO.	STATION	DESCRIPTION	OFFSET FROM BASELINE	AZIMUTH DEG-MIN-SEC	DISTANCE	CLOCKWISE TURN ANGLE	ELEVATION	COORDINATES NORTH	EAST
876	269+89.355	CONST CONTROL MON CX-76	22.862 LEFT	170-49-16	80.430	316-52-15	0.0	4845374.460	307710.370
885	271+29.785	CONST CONTROL MON CX-85	22.857 LEFT	350-49- 8	60.000	136-52- 7	0.0	4845513.091	307687.967
877	269+95.164	CONST CONTROL MON CX-77	22.861 RIGHT	139-59-24	87.513	285-22-24	0.0	4845387.490	307754.580
878	269+97.098	CONST CONTROL MON CX-78	38.095 RIGHT	130-50-11	94.861	276-53-11	0.0	4845391.830	307769.310
879	270+27.530	CONST CONTROL MON CX-79	38.081 RIGHT	115-33-22	74.155	261-36-21	0.0	4845421.870	307764.440
881	270+69.932	CONST CONTROL MON CX-81	22.862 RIGHT	80-38- 4	45.719	226-41- 3	0.0	4845461.300	307742.650
958	290+51.899	RAP #3 - RADIO TOWER	294.749 LEFT	344-19-40	1990.850	130-22-40	0.0	4847370.697	307159.747
884	271+29.932	CONST CONTROL MON CX-84	22.862 RIGHT	28- 3-30	75.551	174- 6-29	0.0	4845520.531	307733.077
959	0+00.000	RAP #4 - CN TOWER	0.0	152-46-14	*********	298-49-14	0.0	4833410.793	313894.638
933	270+16.535	CONST CONTROL MON CX-133	61.272 RIGHT	113- 9- 1	99.566	259-12- 0	0.0	4845414.717	307789.088
956	271+72.134	RAP #1 - BILLBOARD FRAME	471.682 RIGHT	69- 7-32	505.019	215-10-31	0.0	4845633.810	308169.411
960	269+67.759	CONTROL MON MTR77-6119	9.329 RIGHT	153-18-33	106.983	299-21-32	196.768	4845358.277	307745.594
957	268+98.575	RAP #2 - ANTENNA C.F.B.	183.253 RIGHT	213-57- 1	234.606	0- 0- 0	0.0	4845259.249	307566.519
483	269+83.555	BC CORNER ROUND	25.637 LEFT	172-39-51	86.275	318-42-51	0.0	4845368.291	307708.556
753	269+83.622	CATCH BASIN GUTTER	25.142 LEFT	172-20- 0	86.193	318-23-11	0.0	4845368.437	307709.034
485	269+84.988	PI CORNER ROUND	13.500 LEFT	164-31-15	85.312	310-34-15	0.0	4845371.643	307720.309
486	269+88.075	MP CORNER ROUND	16.973 LEFT	166-41-56	81.922	312-44-55	0.0	4845374.136	307716.388
446	269+88.654	PI CORNER ROUND	13.500 RIGHT	146-40-47	88.906	292-43-46	0.0	4845379.569	307746.378
2103	269+90.000	C/L OF CONSTRUCTION	0.0	154-49-55	82.995	300-52-54	196.352	4845378.744	307731.744
444	269+90.625	BC CORNER ROUND	28.986 RIGHT	137-35-48	94.626	283-38-47	0.0	4845383.986	307761.351
754	269+91.351	CATCH BASIN GUTTER	34.690 RIGHT	134-33- 3	97.281	280-36- 2	0.0	4845385.613	307766.866
461	269+91.604	BC CORNER ROUND	36.674 RIGHT	133-35-51	98.267	279-34-50	0.0	4845386.179	307768.784
434	269+92.355	BULLNOSE TOP OF CURB	1.500 RIGHT	153-21-22	81.172	299-24-21	196.425	4845381.308	307733.941
437	269+93.105	BC BULLNOSE TOP OF CURB	2.250 RIGHT	152-41-18	80.687	298-44-17	196.395	4845382.168	307734.562
435	269+93.105	CP BULLNOSE TOP ISLAND	1.500 RIGHT	153-11-45	80.456	299-14-44	196.410	4845382.048	307733.821
436	269+93.105	EC BULLNOSE TOP OF CURB	0.750 RIGHT	153-42-23	80.233	299-45-22	196.425	4845381.929	307733.081
447	269+93.947	MP CORNER ROUND	18.162 RIGHT	142-24-37	86.221	288-27-36	0.0	4845385.538	307750.135
482	269+97.210	CENTER PT CORNER ROUND	27.250 LEFT	174-16-54	72.708	320-19-53	0.0	4845381.513	307704.785
484	269+97.210	EC CORNER ROUND-TOP CURB	13.500 LEFT	163-28-17	73.176	309-31-16	196.290	4845383.707	307718.358
755	269+98.000	CATCH BASIN TOP OF CURB	13.500 LEFT	163-23-29	72.392	309-26-28	196.270	4845384.488	307718.232
2107	270+00.000	TOP OF CURB	13.500 LEFT	163-10-51	70.410	309-13-51	196.036	4845386.462	307717.913
2106	270+00.000	C/L OF CONSTRUCTION	0.0	152-40-57	73.433	298-43-56	196.156	4845388.616	307731.240
443	270+04.265	CENTER PT CORNER ROUND	27.250 RIGHT	133-24-39	82.485	279-27-38	0.0	4845397.175	307757.460
445	270+04.265	EC CORNER ROUND-TOP CURB	13.500 RIGHT	141-47-32	74.932	287-50-31	196.050	4845394.981	307743.887
756	270+05.265	CATCH BASIN TOP OF CURB	13.500 RIGHT	141-25- 0	74.059	287-28- 0	196.110	4845395.968	307743.727
2111	270+10.000	TOP OF CURB	13.500 LEFT	139-30-47	69.973	285-33-46	195.854	4845400.642	307742.971
2110	270+10.000	TOP OF CURB	13.500 LEFT	161-55-21	60.513	307-58-20	195.974	4845396.334	307716.317
2109	270+10.000	C/L OF CONSTRUCTION	0.0	149-53-42	64.006	295-56-41	195.686	4845398.488	307729.644
2113	270+20.000	TOP OF CURB	13.500 LEFT	160-10-24	50.657	306-13-23		4845406.206	307714.722

FIGURE 5-29 Computer print-out of layout data for a road construction project. (Courtesy of Department of Roads and Traffic, City of Toronto)

CITY OF TORONTO
MANAGEMENT SERVICES DEPARMENT DATA PROCESSING CENTRE

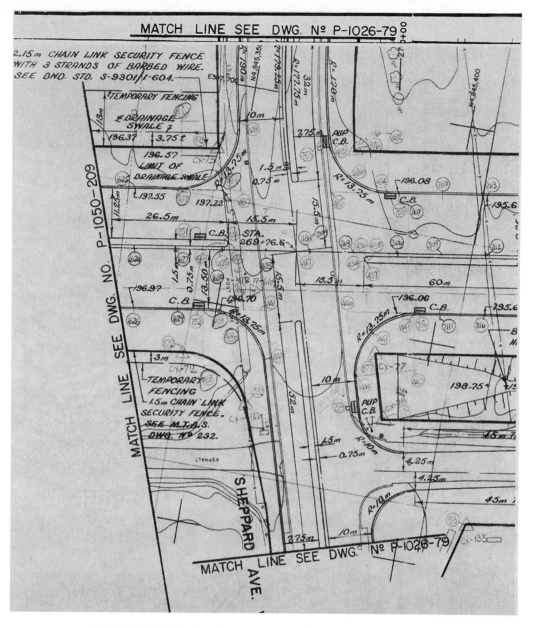

FIGURE 5-30 Portion of a construction plan showing layout points. (Courtesy of Department of Roads and Traffic, City of Toronto)

FIGURE 5-31   Leica TC 800 Total Station with EGLI guide light. (Courtesy of Leica Geosystems, Norcross, Ga.)

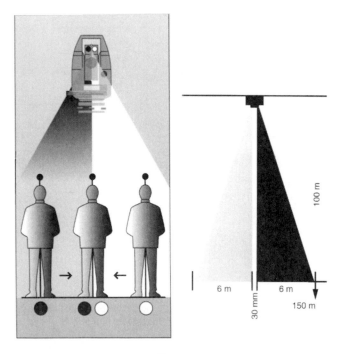

FIGURE 5-32   EGLI® guide light. (Courtesy of Leica Geosystems, Norcross, Ga.)

5-12   Motorized Total Stations

A recent (late 1980s) adaption of the Total Station is the addition of servomotors to drive both the horizontal and the vertical motions of these instruments. Motorized instruments have been designed to automatically search for prism targets and then precisely lock onto them, to automatically turn angles to designated points using the uploaded coordinates of those points along with the computational ability of the instrument, and to repeat angles by automatically double centering. These instruments, when combined with a remote controller held by the prism surveyor, enable the survey to proceed with a reduced need for field personnel.

5-12-1   Automatic Target Recognition (ATR)

Leica Geosystems Incorporated (among others) has designed an instrument with automatic target recognition, which utilizes an infrared light bundle that is sent coaxially through the telescope. First, the telescope must be roughly pointed at the target prism—either manually or under software control—and then the instrument does the rest. The ATR module is a digital camera that notes the offset of the reflected laser beam, permitting the instrument to then move automatically until the crosshairs have been electronically set precisely on the point. After the point has been precisely "sighted," the instrument can then read and record the angle and distance. Reports indicate that the time required for this process is only a third to a half of the time required to obtain the same results using conventional Total Station techniques. ATR comes with a lock-on mode, where the instrument, once sighted at the prism, will continue to follow the prism as it is moved from station to station. To ensure that the prism is always pointed to the instrument, Leica designed a 360° prism (see Figure 5-33), which greatly assists the surveyor in keeping the lock-on over a period of time. If lock-on is lost due to intervening obstacles, it is reestablished after manually roughly pointing at the prism. ATR recognizes targets up to 1000 m or 3300 ft away, will function in darkness, requires no focusing or fine pointing, works with all types of prisms, and maintains a lock on prisms moving up to speeds of 11 mph or 5 mps (at a distance of 100 m).

5-12-2   Remote Controlled Surveying

Geodimeter, the company that first introduced EDM equipment in the early 1950s, introduced in the late 1980s a survey system in which the Total Station (Geodimeter 4000, see Figure 5-34) has been equipped with motors to control both the horizontal and the vertical movements. This Total Station can be used as a conventional instrument, but when interfaced to a controller located with the prism, the station instrument can be remotely controlled by the surveyor at the prism station by means of radio telemetry. When the remote control feature button on the Total Station is activated, control of the station instrument is transferred to the remote controller, called the remote positioning unit (RPU) (see Figure 5-35). The RPU consists of the pole (with circular bubble), the prism, a data collector (up to 10,000 points), telemetry equipment for communicating with the station instrument, and a sighting telescope that, when aimed back at the station instrument, permits a sensing of the angle of inclination, which is then transmitted to the station instrument via radio

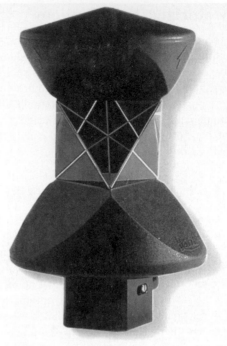

FIGURE 5-33 Leica 360° prism—used with remote-controlled Total Stations and with automatic target recognition (ATR) Total Stations. ATR eliminates fine pointing and focusing. The 360° feature means that the prism is always facing the instrument. (Courtesy of Leica Geosystems Inc., Norcross, Ga.)

communication. As a result, the instrument can automatically move its telescope to the proper angle of inclination, thus enabling the instrument to commence an automatic horizontal sweeping that results in the station instrument being locked precisely onto the prism.

A typical operation requires that the station unit be placed over a control station or over a free station whose coordinates can be determined using resection techniques (see Figure 5-23) and that a backsight be taken to another control point, thus fixing the location and orientation of the Total Station. The operation then begins with both units being activated at the RPU. The RPU sighting telescope is aimed at the station unit, and the sensed vertical angle is sent via telemetry to the station unit. The station unit then automatically sets its telescope at the correct angle in the vertical plane and begins a horizontal search for the RPU; the search area can be limited to a specific sector (e.g., 70°), thus reducing search time. The limiting range of this instrument is about 700 m. When the measurements (angle and distance) have been completed, the point number and attribute data codes can be entered into the data collector attached to the prism pole.

When used for setting out, the desired point number is entered at the RPU. The Total Station instrument then automatically turns the required angle, which it computes from previously uploaded coordinates held in storage (both the Total Station and the RPU have the points in storage). The RPU operator can position the prism roughly on line by noting the Track-Light®, which shows as red or green, depending on whether the operator is left or right of the line, and as white when the operator is on the line (see also the EGL1® guide light shown in Figure 5-32). Distance and angle readouts are then observed by the operator to position the prism pole precisely at the layout point location. Since the unit can fast-track (0.4 s) precise measurements and since it is also capable of averaging multiple

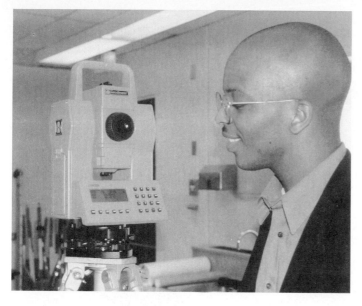

(a)

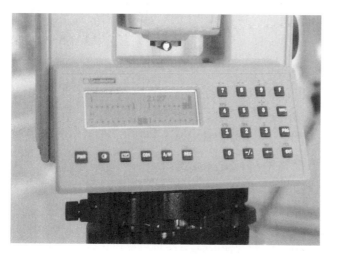

(b)

FIGURE 5-34 (a) Geodimeter 4400 Base Station. A Total Station equipped with servo motors controlling both the horizontal and vertical circle movements. Can be used alone as a conventional Total Station or as a robotic base station controlled by the RPU operator. (b) Geodimeter keyboard showing in-process electronic leveling. Upper cursor can also be centered by finally adjusting the third leveling screw.

FIGURE 5-35 Remote Positioning Unit (RPU)—a combination of prism, data collector, and radio communicator (with the base station) that permits the operator to engage in one-person surveys. (Courtesy of Geodimeter of Canada)

measurement readings, very precise results can be obtained when using the prism pole by slightly "waving" the pole left/right and back/forward in a deliberate pattern. Since all but the backsight reference are obtained using infrared and telemetry, the system can be effectively used after dark, permitting nighttime layouts for next-day construction and for surveys in high-volume traffic areas that can be accomplished efficiently only in low-volume periods.

Figure 5-36(a) shows a remotely controlled Total Station manufactured by Leica Geosystems Incorporated. This system utilizes ATR and the EGL1® to search for and then position the prism on the correct layout line—where the operator then notes the angle/distance readouts to determine the precise layout location.

Figure 5-36(b) shows a motorized Total Station manufactured by Carl Zeiss, Inc., which has many features—including remote control through RecLink-S radio control, FineLock (a coaxial prism sensor that quickly locks precisely on the target prism), PositionLight (a multicolored beam that provides a fast technique of positioning the prism holder in setting-out jobs), a full complement of computational and setting-out software in the DOS-based system, and a large display screen, together with a QWERTY keyboard. These instruments come with a 1-second accuracy (ELTA S 10) or a 3-second accuracy (ELTA S 20).

(a)

FIGURE 5-36 (a) Leica TPS System 1000, used for roadway stakeout. Surveyor is controlling the remote-controlled Total Station (TCA 1100) at the prism pole using the RCS 1000 controller together with a radio modem. Assistant is placing steel bar marker at previous set-out point. (Courtesy of Leica Geosystems Inc., Norcross, Ga.) (b) Zeiss ELTA S 10 motorized Total Station. (Courtesy of Carl Zeiss Inc., Thornwood, N.Y.)

(b)

5-13   Overview of Computerized Surveying Data Systems

Advances in computer science have had a tremendous impact on all aspects of modern technology. The effects on construction and engineering surveying have been significant. We have seen, in the previous section, how this new technology has changed the way field data can be collected and processed. To appreciate the full impact of this new technology, one has to view the overall operation—that is, from field to computer, computer processing, and data portrayal in the form of maps and plans. Figure 5-37 gives a schematic overview of an integrated survey data system.

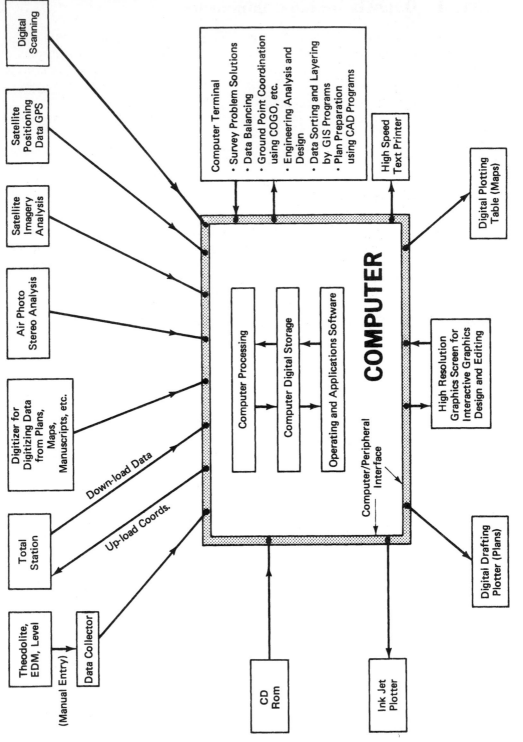

FIGURE 5-37 Computerized surveying data system.

5-13-1 Data-Gathering Components

The upper portion of the schematic shows the various ways that data can be collected and transferred to the computer. In addition to the Total Station techniques already described, field surveys can be performed using conventional surveying instruments (theodolites, EDMIs, and levels), with the field data entered into a data collector instead of conventional field books. This manual entry of field data lacks the speed associated with interfaced equipment, but after the data have been entered, all the advantages of electronic techniques are available to the surveyor. The raw field data, collected and stored by the Total Station, are transferred to the computer through a standard RS 232 interface connection; the raw data download program is supplied by the manufacturer, but the program required to translate the raw data into properly formated field data is the responsibility of the surveyor.

At this stage, coordinate geometry programs can be used to calculate traverse closures and adjust all acceptable data into Y, X, and Z values. If only topography was taken, there may be no need for adjustments, and the program can directly compute the required coordinates. Also at this stage, additional data points (e.g., inaccessible ground points) can be computed and added to the data file.

Figure 5-38 shows the translated field data [5-38(a)] and the computed point coordinates [5-38(b)]. The instrument location (OCC) coordinates and the backsight (BS) orientation can be entered into the data collector at the commencement of the survey, or they can be entered in a computer file, where they can be directly accessed for data processing. The data in Figure 5-38 are based on the survey shown in Figure 5-26.

Existing maps and plans have a wealth of data that may be relevant for an area survey. If such maps and plans are available, the data can be digitized on a digitizing table (see Figure 5-39) or by digital scanners and added to the Y, X, and Z coordinates files. In addition to distances and elevations, the digitizer can provide codes, identifications, and other attribute data for each digitized point. One of the more important features of the digitizer is its ability to digitize maps and plans at various scales and store the distances and elevations in the computer at their ground (or grid) values.

The stereo analysis of aerial photos is a very effective method of collecting topographic ground data, particularly in high-density areas, where the costs for conventional surveys would be high. Many municipalities routinely fly all major roads and develop plans and profiles that can be used for design and construction. With the advent of computerized surveying systems, the stereo analyzers can coordinate all horizontal and vertical features and transfer these Y, X, and Z coordinates to computer storage.

Satellite imagery is received from the U.S. Land Sat satellites and the French SPOT satellites and can be processed by a digital image analysis system that classifies terrain into categories of soil and rock types and vegetative cover; these and other data can be digitized and added to the computer storage.

Finally, precise position location can be determined by satellite observations. The United States has established a system of positioning satellites called NAVSTAR, which was developed for military navigational purposes. The NAVSTAR system of positioning will revolutionize the way control surveys (see Chapter 9) are performed.

In this section, several different ways of collecting topographic (and control) ground data have been outlined. The one element that they all have in common is that they are all

(a)

CODE	NUM	hi/HT	HCR	VCR	SDIST	OFFSET	LABEL
OCC	111	1.528					
BS	114	1.222	0.0000	90.2025	211.723	0.000	*CM
FS	112	1.365	91.5532	88.1458	261.271	0.000	*CM
IS	1000	1.528	262.4514	92.1323	41.247	0.000	*CM
IS	1001	1.528	277.1412	91.3404	58.478	0.550	*EDGE WATER
IS	1002	1.528	284.5856	90.2455	220.767	0.000	*EDGE WATER
IS	1003	1.528	341.5254	90.2225	245.444	0.000	*EDGE WATER
IS	1004	1.528	5.4526	90.1816	301.247	0.000	*EDGE WATER

(b)

PTNUM	NORTHING	EASTING	ELEVATION	LABEL
111	1000.000N	1000.000E	100.000	
112	991.225N	1261.001E	108.149	CM
114	1211.723N	1000.000E	98.743	CM
1000	994.801N	959.113E	98.400	CM
1001	1007.433N	941.464E	98.400	EDGE WATER
1002	1057.071N	786.743E	98.403	EDGE WATER
1003	1233.269N	923.673E	98.404	EDGE WATER
1004	1299.723N	1030.219E	98.406	EDGE WATER

FIGURE 5-38 Translated field data with computed coordinates. (a) Translated field data. (b) Northings, eastings, and elevations as computed by the coordinate geometry programs.

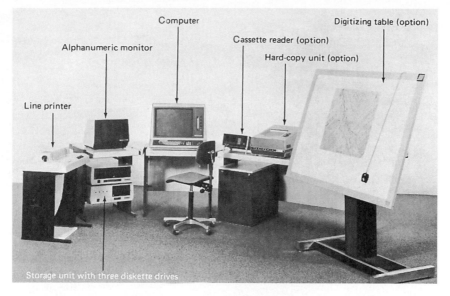

Computer

Alphanumeric monitor

Cassette reader (option)

Digitizing table (option)

Hard-copy unit (option)

Line printer

Storage unit with three diskette drives

FIGURE 5-39 Wild Geomap workstation. (Courtesy of Leica, Switzerland)

computer-based. This means that all the ground data for a specific area can be collected and stored in one computer. The collected data for an area are known as the **data base** for that area.

5-13-2 Data-Processing Components of the System

The central portion of the schematic (Figure 5-37) depicts the data-processing components of the system. Initially, as already described, the Total Station data can be closed and adjusted by means of various coordinate geometry programs. Additionally, missing data positions can be computed by using various intersection, resection, and interpolation techniques, with the resultant coordinates being added to the data base.

If the data are to be plotted, a *plot file* may be created that contains point plot commands (including symbols) and join commands for straight and curved lines; labels and other attribute data are also included.

Design programs are available for most construction endeavors. These programs can work with the stored coordinates to provide a variety of possible designs—which can then be quickly analyzed with respect to costs and other factors. Some design programs incorporate interactive graphics, which permit a plot of the survey to be shown to scale on a high-resolution graphics screen. Points and lines can be moved, created, edited, and so forth, with the final positions coordinated right on the screen and the new coordinates added to the coordinates files (see Figure 5-40).

5-13-3 Digital Plotting

Once the plotting files have been established, data can be plotted in a variety of ways. Data can be plotted onto a high-resolution graphics screen. The plot can be checked for com-

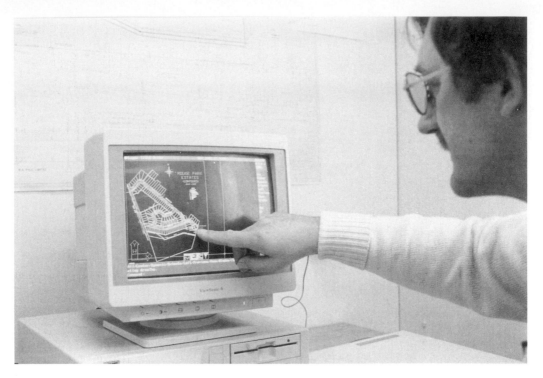

FIGURE 5-40 Land division design and editing on a desktop computer.

pleteness, accuracy, and so forth. If interactive graphics are available, the plotted features can be deleted, enhanced, corrected, crosshatched, labeled, dimensioned, and so on. At this stage, a hard copy of the screen display can be printed either on a simple printer or on an ink-jet color printer. Plot files can be plotted directly on a digital plotter similar to that shown in Figure 5-41. The resultant plan can be plotted to any desired scale, limited only by the paper size. Some plotters have only one or two pens, although plotters are available with four to eight pens; a variety of pens permits colored plotting or plotting using various line weights. Plans, and plan and profiles, drawn on digital plotters are becoming more common on construction sites.

Automatic plotting (with a digital plotter) can be used where the field data have been coordinated and stored in computer memory. Coordinated field data are a by-product of data collection by Total Stations, air photo stereo analysis, satellite imagery, and digitized, or scanned, data from existing plans and maps; see Figure 5-37.

A plot file can be created that includes the following typical commands:

- Title
- Scale
- Limits (e.g., can be defined by the southwesterly coordinates, northerly range, and easterly range)
- Plot all points

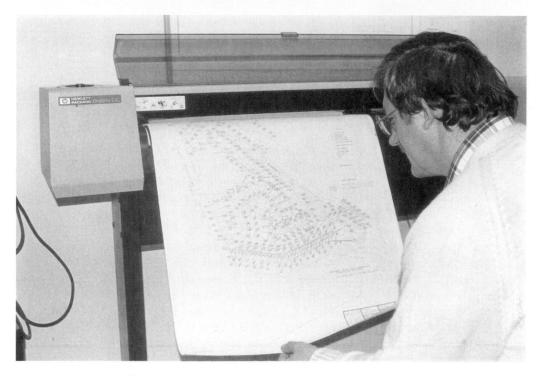

FIGURE 5-41   Land division plot on a Hewlett-Packard 8-pen digital plotter.

- Connect specific points (through feature coding or CAD commands)
- Pen number (various pens could have different line weights or colors—two to four pens are common)
- Symbol (symbols are predesigned and stored by identification number in a symbol "library")
- Height of characters (the heights of labels, text, coordinates, and symbols can be defined)

The actual plotting can be performed by simply keying in the plot command required by the specific computer and then by keying in the name of the plot file that is to be plotted. Figure 5-41 illustrates a typical digital plotter.

Alternatively, the coordinated field point files can be transferred to an interactive graphics terminal (see Figure 5-40), with the survey plot being created and edited graphically right on the high-resolution graphics screen. Some surveying software programs have this graphics capability, whereas others permit coordinate files to be transferred easily to an independent graphics program (e.g., "Autocad") for editing and plotting. Once the plot has been completed on the graphics screen (and all the point coordinates have been stored in the computer), the plot can be transferred to a digital plotter for final presentation.

This latter technique is now being successfully used in a wide variety of applications. In the not too distant future (as costs continue to decrease), most survey data processing will be handled in this or a similar manner. The savings in time and money are too great to be overlooked—especially when the actual engineering or construction design can be accomplished on the same graphics terminal, with all design elements also being stored in the computer files and all construction drawings being produced on the digital plotter.

5-14 Geographic Information Systems (GIS)

With the emergence of large data bases, which had been collected primarily for mapping, attention was given to new techniques for analyzing and querying the computer-stored data. The data in a data base were conventionally connected by spatial relationships (usually coordinates) and included attribute data (labels, etc.) unique to each point in the data base.

The introduction of topological techniques permitted the data to be connected in a relational sense, in addition to the spatial connection. It then became possible not only to determine where a point or a line (e.g., road) or an area was located, but also to analyze the features with respect to adjacency, connectivity (network analysis), and direction of vectors. **Adjacency, connectivity,** and **direction** opened the data base to a wider variety of analyzing and querying uses. For example, it is possible for a real estate promotion to display in map form all the industrially zoned parcels of land with rail-spur possibilities, within 3 miles of freeway access, in the range of 1.2 to 3.1 acres in size. Relational characteristics also permit the data base to be used for routing—emergency vehicles and vacationers.

Municipalities are putting Geographic Information Systems (GIS) to a wide variety of uses—including municipal street inventories where work orders are automatically generated for road, sewer, and waterworks maintenance.

GIS data can be assembled from existing data bases, digitized from existing maps and plans, or collected using conventional surveying techniques and/or Global Positioning System (GPS) surveying techniques. One GPS method that has recently become very popular for GIS data collection is that of Differential GPS—see Section 9-6. This technique utilizes a less expensive GPS receiver and radio signal corrections from a base station receiver to provide submeter accuracies that are acceptable for mapping and GIS data base inventories. See Figure 5-42 for Differential GPS equipment and Figure 5-43 for an illustration of handheld Total Stations that are useful in collecting additional data when GPS techniques cannot be used when the tree canopy or buildings obstruct satellite signals or when survey point locations cannot be conveniently accessed.

The ability to store data on feature-unique layers permits the simple production of special-feature maps. For example, maps can be produced that show only the property lines of an area; drainage and contour information, as well as other topographic information, can be added—in fact, any selected layer or combination of layers can be depicted on a map at any desired scale (see Figure 5-44).

5-15 The New Information Utility

Some of the by-products of the computer revolution were the simple procedures developed to compute and store the coordinates of any number of ground points. Surveyors, long accustomed to working with coordinates, quickly adapted their field and computation techniques for computer use. Computations for adjustments, areas, and others were made

FIGURE 5-42 Differential GPS, used here in data capture for a GIS data base. Note the collapsible tripod. (Courtesy of Trimble Navigation, Sunnyvale, Calif.)

quickly and with fewer mistakes. When Total Stations came into wide use in the early 1980s, the surveyor was able to locate field items with a single pointing and store the location data—coordinates, or slope distance, and horizontal and vertical angles—along with labels and other attribute data in the data collector. When the data collector was downloaded to the computer, all the field data were transferred, free of transcription errors. Once the data were in the computer, it was possible to process (coordinate) the data and plot them in the form of a plan. This information constituted the start of a data base for the area surveyed. Additional data could be retrieved from existing maps and plans (drawn to a wide variety of scales) covering the same area by using digitizing tables and scanners (see Section 5-13-1/Figure 5-39); the data base could be further augmented by the addition of digitized data from a wide variety of additional sources (see Figure 5-37) The total data in the data base (regardless of the capture technique) could be accessed for query and analysis using GIS programs or for plotting by digital plotters; in addition, the data could be manipulated, sorted, and delivered in a variety of report formats.

When municipalities first considered GIS purchases, the engineering or public works departments often provided the impetus for the acquisition of the technology. In a few years, it became obvious that the data in the data base could be used for many other purposes—that is, in addition to streets and street hardware inventories, municipalities could use coordinated data for land registration, street numbering, assessment data, and a wide variety of other municipal managerial and planning functions. For example, the unique

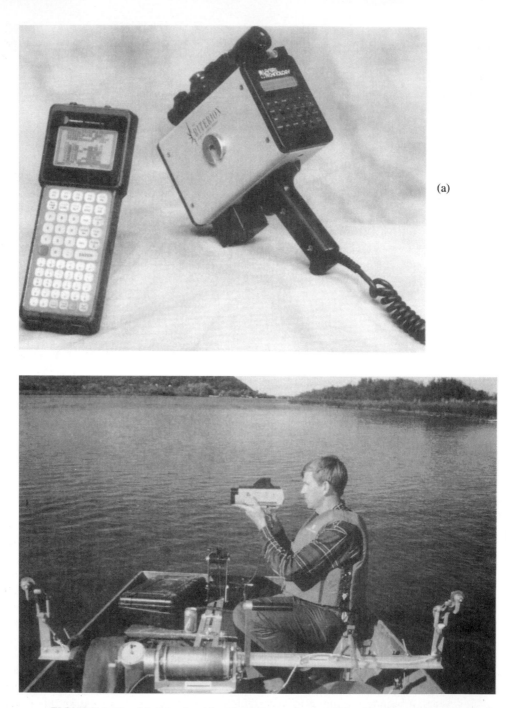

FIGURE 5-43 (a) Criterion Hand-held Survey Laser #300, with data collector; angles by flux-gate compass; distances without a prism to 1,500 ft (to 40,000 ft with a prism). This instrument is used to collect data with an accuracy of ±0.3° and ±0.3 ft for mapping and GIS data bases; it provides a good extension for canopy-obstructed GPS survey points. (Courtesy of Laser Technology Inc., Englewood, Colorado) (b) Prosurvey 1000 Hand-held Survey laser: used (without prisms) to record distances and angles to survey stations. Shown here determining river width in a hydrographic survey. (Courtesy of Laser Atlanta, Norcross, Georgia)

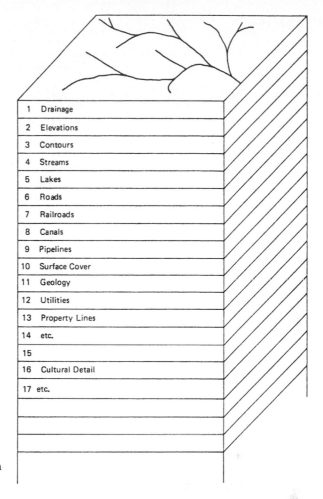

FIGURE 5-44 Schematic showing various data layers for a data base layer file.

The figure contains the following layers:

1 Drainage
2 Elevations
3 Contours
4 Streams
5 Lakes
6 Roads
7 Railroads
8 Canals
9 Pipelines
10 Surface Cover
11 Geology
12 Utilities
13 Property Lines
14 etc.
15
16 Cultural Detail
17 etc.

two-dimensional coordinates that identified a specific property could also include attribute data describing the type of dwelling, area of lot, floor area, number of occupants, taxes paid, zoning, and any other data relating to the property or to the owner. Three-dimensional coordinates could be used to precisely identify or register high-rise condominium commercial and residential ownership. When regional and federal census data (e.g., TIGER), which are now available from government agencies and private market-research companies (on CD ROM), are added to a local data base, the potential increases dramatically.

Add to all this static information the link to a dynamic positioning system, such as GPS (see Chapter 9), and you have what must be identified as a *new information utility*.

Just as the electric and the telephone utilities transformed society, so this new information utility will have a great impact on modern society. Land locations uniquely identified by their three-dimensional coordinates will in the future be thought of as addresses instead of targets. Moving vehicles—planes, trains, automobiles, and ships—will have their "addresses" updated as they move, with direction and time vectors to any other point in the data base being updated continuously. Applications are limited only by one's imagination.

Problems

5-1. In order to verify the constant of a particular prism, a straight line *EFG* is laid out. The EDMI is first set up at *E*, with the following measurements recorded:

$$EG = 586.645 \text{ m}, \qquad EF = 298.717 \text{ m}$$

The EDMI is then set up at *F*, where distance *FG* is recorded as 287.958 m. Determine the prism constant.

5-2. The EDM slope distance between two points is 5170.11 ft, and the vertical angle is +2°45′30″ (the vertical angles were read at both ends of the line and then averaged). If the elevation of the instrument station is 630.15 ft and the heights of the instrument, EDMI, target, and reflector are all equal to 5.26 ft, compute the elevation of the target station and the horizontal distance to that station.

5-3. A line *AB* is measured at both ends as follows:

⼏ @ *A*, slope distance = 1879.209 m;   vertical angle = +1°26′50″

⼏ @ *B*, slope distance = 1879.230 m;   vertical angle = −1°26′38″

The heights of the instrument, reflector, and target are equal for each observation.
(a) Compute the horizontal distance *AB*.
(b) If the elevation at *A* is 181.302 m, what is the elevation at *B?*

5-4. A coaxial EDMI at station *K* (elevation = 241.69 ft) is used to sight stations *L, M,* and *N,* with the heights of the instrument, target, and reflector equal for each sighting. The results are as follows:

@ STA. *L,* vertical angle = +3°30′,   EDM distance = 2000.00 ft

@ STA. *M,* vertical angle = −1°30′,   EDM distance = 2000.00 ft

@ STA. *N,* vertical angle = 0°00′,   EDM distance = 3000.00 ft

Compute the elevations of *L, M,* and *N* (correct for curvature and refraction).

5-5. With reference to Figure 5-15, a top-mounted EDMI is set up at STA. *A* (elevation = 110.222 m for this problem). Using the following values, compute the horizontal distance from *A* to *B* and the elevation of *B*.

The optical center of the theodolite is 1.601 m (hi) above station, and an angle of +4°18′30″ is measured to the target, which is 1.915 (HR) above station. The EDMI center is 0.100 m (Δhi) above the theodolite, and the reflecting prism is 0.150 m (ΔHR) above the target. The slope distance is measured to be 387.603 m.

5-6. With reference to Figure 5-15, a top-mounted EDMI is set up at STA. *A* (elevation = 531.49 ft for this problem). Using the following values, compute the horizontal distance from *A* to *B* and the elevation of *B*.

The optical center of the theodolite is 5.21 ft (hi) above station, and an angle of +3°14′30″ is measured to the target, which is 5.78 ft (HR) above station. The EDMI center is 0.31 ft (Δhi) above the theodolite, and the reflecting prism is 0.39 ft (ΔHR) above the target. The slope distance is recorded as 536.88 ft.

Chapter 6

Traverse Surveys

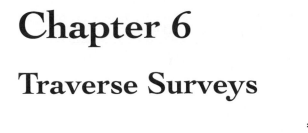

6-1   General

A traverse is a form of control survey that is used in a wide variety of engineering and property surveys. Essentially traverses are a series of established stations tied together by angle and distance. The angles are measured by transits or theodolites; the distances can be measured by steel tape, electronic distance measurement instrument (EDMI), or even stadia (see Chapter 7). Traverses can be *open,* as in route surveys, or *closed,* as in closed geometric figures (see Figures 6-1 and 6-2).

In engineering work, traverses are used as control surveys to (1) locate topographic detail for the preparation of plans, (2) lay out (locate) construction works, and (3) collect measurements needed for the determination of earthwork and other construction quantities.

6-1-1   Open Traverse

An open traverse (see Figure 6-1) is particularly useful as control for preliminary and construction surveys for roads, pipelines, electricity transmission lines, and the like. These surveys may be from a few hundred feet (meters) to many miles (kilometers) in length. The distances are normally measured by using steel tapes or EDMI. Each time the survey line changes direction, a deflection angle is measured with a transit (theodolite). Deflection angles are measured from the prolongation of the back line to the forward line (see Figure 6-1); the angles are measured either to the right or to the left, and the direction (L or R) is shown in the field notes along with the numerical values. Angles are measured at least twice (see Sections 4-4 and 4-8-6 for measuring angles by repetition) to eliminate mistakes and to improve accuracy.

The distances are shown in the form of stations (chainages), which are cumulative measurements referenced to the initial point of the survey, 0 + 00. See Figure 6-3 for typical field notes for a route survey.

Open traverses may extend for long distances without the opportunity for checking the accuracy of the ongoing work. Accordingly, all survey measurements are carefully

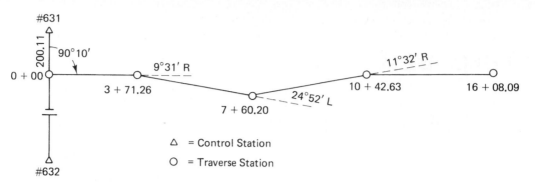

FIGURE 6-1 Open traverse.

repeated at the time of the work, and every opportunity for checking for position and direction is utilized (adjacent property surveys and intersecting road and railroad rights-of-way are checked when practicable). Global Positioning System (GPS) surveying techniques are now also being used to determine and verify traverse station positioning.

Many states and provinces are now providing densely placed control monuments as an extension to their coordinate grid systems. It is now possible to tie in the initial and terminal survey stations of a route survey to coordinate control monuments. Since the *Y* and *X* (and *Z*) coordinates of these monuments have been precisely determined, the route survey changes from an open traverse to a closed traverse and is then subject to geometric verification and analysis (see Sections 6-6 through 6-12).

6-1-2 Closed Traverse

A closed traverse is one that either begins and ends at the same point or begins and ends at points whose positions have been previously determined (as described above); in both

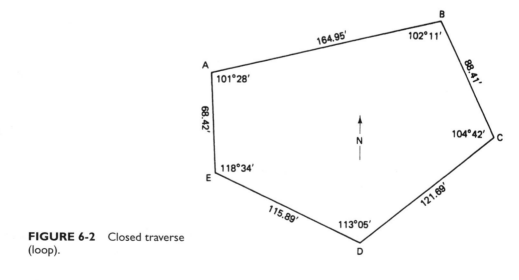

FIGURE 6-2 Closed traverse (loop).

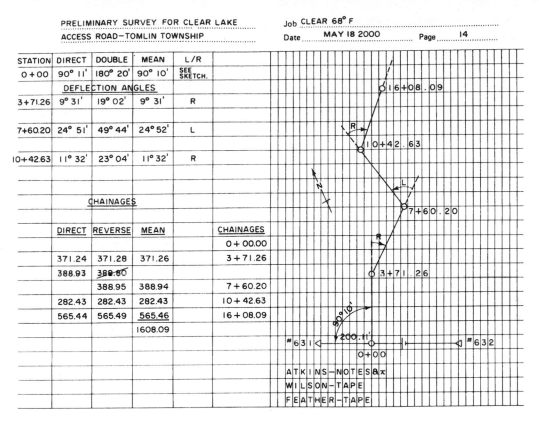

FIGURE 6-3 Field notes for an open traverse.

cases, the angles can be closed geometrically, and the position closure can be determined mathematically.

A closed traverse that begins and ends at the same point is called a loop traverse (see Figure 6-2). In this case, the distances are measured from one station to the next and verified, a steel tape or EDMI being used; the interior angle is measured at each station—each angle is measured at least twice. Figure 6-4 illustrates typical field notes for a loop traverse survey. In this type of survey, distances are booked simply as dimensions, not as stations or chainages.

6-2 Balancing Field Angles

For a closed polygon of n sides, the sum of the interior angles will be $(n - 2)180°$. In Figure 6-2, the interior angles of a five-sided polygon have been measured as shown in the field notes in Figure 6-4. For a five-sided closed figure, the sum of the interior angles must be $(5 - 2)180° = 540°$; in Figure 6-4, it is seen that the interior angles add to $540°01'$—an excess of one minute.

Before mathematical analysis can begin—that is, before the bearings or azimuths can be computed—the field angles must be adjusted so that their sum exactly equals the

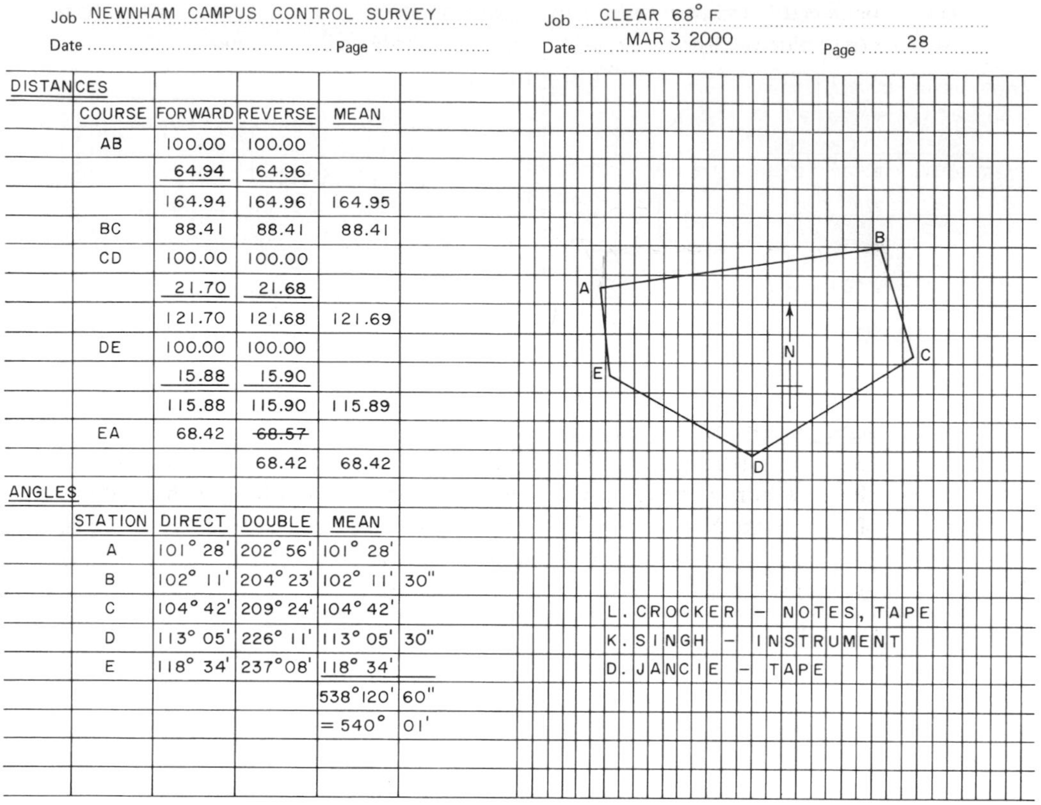

Job ....NEWNHAM CAMPUS CONTROL SURVEY..........   Job ....CLEAR 68° F..........

Date .... Page ....   Date .... MAR 3 2000 .... Page ....28........

DISTANCES				
	COURSE	FORWARD	REVERSE	MEAN
	AB	100.00	100.00	
		64.94	64.96	
		164.94	164.96	164.95
	BC	88.41	88.41	88.41
	CD	100.00	100.00	
		21.70	21.68	
		121.70	121.68	121.69
	DE	100.00	100.00	
		15.88	15.90	
		115.88	115.90	115.89
	EA	68.42	~~68.57~~	
		68.42	68.42	68.42

ANGLES				
	STATION	DIRECT	DOUBLE	MEAN
	A	101° 28'	202° 56'	101° 28'
	B	102° 11'	204° 23'	102° 11' 30"
	C	104° 42'	209° 24'	104° 42'
	D	113° 05'	226° 11'	113° 05' 30"
	E	118° 34'	237°08'	118° 34'
				538°120' 60"
				= 540° 01'

L. CROCKER — NOTES, TAPE

K. SINGH — INSTRUMENT

D. JANCIE — TAPE

FIGURE 6-4 Field notes for a closed traverse.

correct geometric total. The angles can be balanced by distributing the error evenly to each angle, or one or more angles can be arbitrarily adjusted to force the closure.

The total allowable error of angular closure is quite small (see Chapter 8); if the field results exceed the allowable error, the survey must be repeated.

The angles for the traverse in Figure 6-4 are shown in Table 6-1. Also shown are the results of equally balanced angles and arbitrarily balanced angles. The angles can be arbi-

Table 6-1 TWO METHODS OF ADJUSTING FIELD ANGLES

Station	Field Angle	Arbitrarily Balanced	Equally Balanced
A	101°28'	101°28'	101°27'48"
B	102°11'30"	102°11'	102°11'18"
C	104°42'	104°42'	104°41'48"
D	113°05'30"	113°05'	113°05'18"
E	118°34'	118°34'	118°33'48"
	= 538°120'60"	= 538°120'	= 538°117'180"
	= 540°01'00"	= 540°00'	= 540°00'00"

trarily balanced if the required precision will not be affected or if one or two setups are suspect (e.g., due to unstable ground, very short sighting).

6-3 Meridians

A line on the surface of the earth joining the north and south poles is called a *geographic,* astronomic, or "true" *meridian.* Figure 6-5 illustrates that geographic meridian is another term for a line of longitude. It is also illustrated that geographic meridians all converge at the poles.

Grid meridians are lines that are parallel to a grid reference meridian (central meridian—see Figure 6-5). Rectangular coordinate grids are discussed further in Chapter 8.

Magnetic meridians are lines parallel to the directions taken by freely moving magnetized needles, as in a compass. Whereas geographic and grid meridians are fixed, magnetic meridians may vary with time and location.

Geographic meridians can be established by tying into an existing survey line whose geographic direction is known or whose direction can be established by observations of the sun or of Polaris (the North Star). Grid meridians can be established by tying into an existing survey line whose grid direction is known or whose direction can be established by tying into coordinate grid monuments whose rectangular coordinates are known.

On small or isolated surveys of only limited importance, meridians are sometimes *assumed* (e.g., one of the survey lines is simply designated as being "due north"), and the whole survey is referenced to that assumed direction.

Meridians are important to the surveyor because they are used as reference directions for surveys. All survey lines can be related to each other and to the real world by angles related to meridians. These angles are called *bearings* and *azimuths.*

6-4 Bearings

A **bearing** is the direction of a line given by the **acute** angle between the line and a meridian. The bearing angle, which can be measured clockwise or counterclockwise from the north or south end of a meridian, is always accompanied by the letters that describe the quadrant in which the line is located (NE, SE, SW, and NW).

Figure 6-6 illustrates the concepts of bearings. The given angles for lines K-1 and K-4 are acute angles measured from the meridian and, as such, are bearing angles. The given angles for lines K-2 and K-3 are both measured from the E/W axis and therefore are not bearing angles; here, the given angles must be subtracted from 90° to determine the bearing angle.

All lines have two directions—forward and reverse. Figure 6-7 shows that to reverse a bearing, the letters are simply switched—that is, N/S and E/W. To illustrate, consider walking with a compass along a line in a northeasterly direction; if you were to stop and return along the same line, the compass would indicate that you would then be walking in a southwesterly direction. In Figure 6-7, when the meridian is drawn through point K, the line K-1 is being considered, and the bearing is NE; however, if the meridian is drawn through point 1, the line 1-K is being considered, and the bearing is SW. In computations, the direction of a line therefore depends on which end of the line the meridian is placed. When computing the bearings of adjacent sides—as in a closed

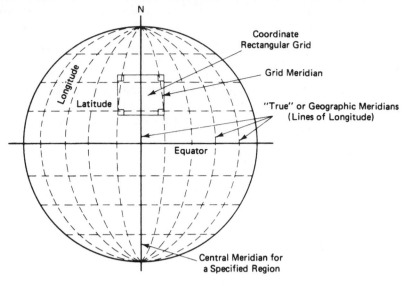

(a)

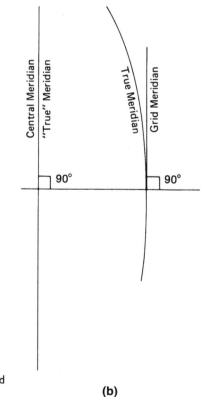

FIGURE 6-5 Relationship between "true" meridians and grid meridians.
(a) Illustration of geographic ("true") meridians and grid meridians.
(b) Illustration of geographic north and grid north.

(b)

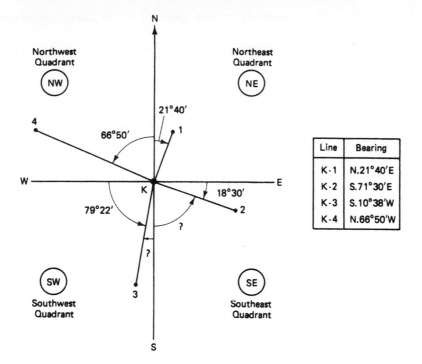

Line	Bearing
K-1	N.21°40'E
K-2	S.71°30'E
K-3	S.10°38'W
K-4	N.66°50'W

FIGURE 6-6 Bearings calculated from given data (answers in box).

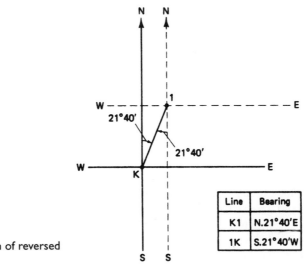

Line	Bearing
K1	N.21°40'E
1K	S.21°40'W

FIGURE 6-7 Illustration of reversed bearings.

traverse—the surveyor must routinely reverse bearings as the computations proceed around the traverse.

Figure 6-8 shows a five-sided traverse with geometrically closed angles and a given bearing for side *AE* of S 7°21′ E; the problem here is to compute the bearings of the remaining sides. To begin, the surveyor must decide whether to solve the problem going clockwise or counterclockwise; in this example, it was decided to work clockwise, and the bearing of side *AB* is first computed using the angle at *A*. Had the surveyor decided to work the computations counterclockwise, the first computation would be the bearing of side *ED*, using the angle at *E*.

To compute the bearing of side *AB*, the two sides *AB* and *AE* are drawn, together with a meridian through point *A*. The known data are then placed on the sketch, and a question mark is placed in the location of the required bearing angle. Step 1 on Figure 6-8 shows the bearing angle of 7°21′ and the interior angle at *A* of 101°28′. A question mark is placed in the position of the required bearing angle for side *AB*. If the sketch has been properly drawn and labeled, the procedure for the solution will become apparent. In step 1, it is apparent that the required bearing angle (*AB*) + the interior angle (*A*) + the bearing angle (*AE*) = 180°; that is, the bearing of *AB* = N 71°11′ E.

To compute the bearing of the next side, *BC*, the lines *BA* and *BC* are drawn, together with a meridian through point *B*. Once again, the known data are placed on the sketch, and a question mark is placed in the position of the required bearing angle for side *BC*. In step 1, the bearing of *AB* was computed as N 71°11′ E; when this information is to be shown on the sketch for step 2, it is obvious that something must be done to make these data comply with the new location of the meridian—that is, the bearing must be reversed. With the meridian through point *B,* the line being considered is *BA*—not *AB*—and the bearing becomes S 71°11′ W. It is apparent from the sketch and data shown in step 2 that the required bearing angle (*BC*) = the interior angle (*B*) − the bearing angle (*AB*), a value of S 31°00′ E.

The remaining bearings are computed in steps 3, 4, and 5. Step 5 involves the computation of the bearing for side *EA*. This last step provides the surveyor with a check on all the computations; that is, if the computed bearing turns out to be the same as the starting bearing (7°21′), the work is correct. If the computed bearing does not agree with the starting value, the work must be checked and the mistake found and corrected. If the work has been done with neat, well-labeled sketches similar to that shown in Figure 6-8, any mistake(s) will be quickly found and corrected.

6-5 Azimuths

An **azimuth** *is the direction of a line given by an angle measured clockwise from the north end of a meridian.* In some circumstances (some astronomic, geodetic, and state plane grid projects), azimuths are measured clockwise from the south end of the meridian. In this text, azimuths are referenced from north only. Azimuths can range in magnitude from 0° to 360°. Values in excess of 360°, which are sometimes encountered in computations, are valid, but are usually reduced by 360° before final listing.

Figure 6-9 illustrates the concepts of azimuths. The given angle for *K*-1 is a clockwise angle measured from the north end of the meridian and, as such, is the azimuth of *K*-1. The given angle for *K*-2 is measured clockwise from the easterly axis, which itself is

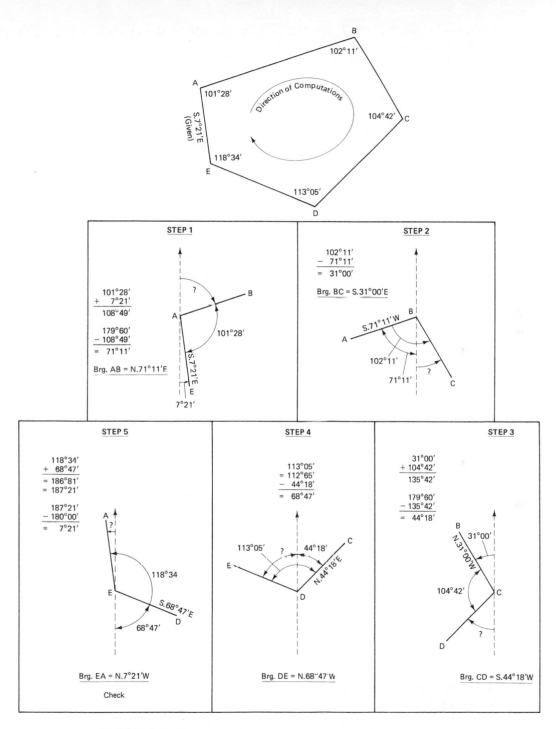

FIGURE 6-8 Bearing computations.

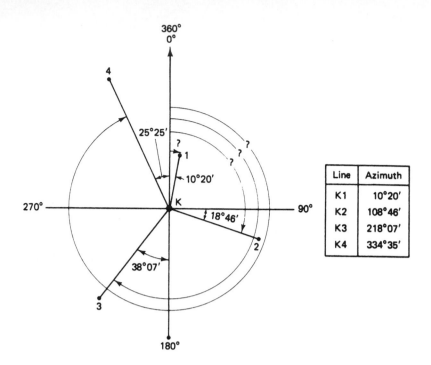

FIGURE 6-9 Azimuths calculated from given data (answers in box).

Line	Azimuth
K1	10°20′
K2	108°46′
K3	218°07′
K4	334°35′

already measured 90° from the north end of the meridian. The azimuth of *K*-2 is therefore 90° + 18°46′ = 108°46′.

The given angle for *K*-3 is measured clockwise from the south end of the meridian, which itself is 180° from the north end; the required azimuth of *K*-3 is therefore 180° + 38°07′ = 218°07′. The given angle for *K*-4 is measured counterclockwise from the north end of the meridian; the required azimuth is therefore 360° (359°60′) − 25°25′ = 334°35′.

It was noted in the previous section that each line has two directions—forward and reverse. In Figure 6-10, when the reference meridian is at point *K,* the line *K*-1 is being considered, and its azimuth is 10°20′. However, when the reference meridian is at point 1, the line 1-*K* is being considered, and the original azimuth must be reversed by 180°; its azimuth is now 190°20′.

To summarize, bearings are reversed by simply switching the direction letters, that is, N/S and E/W; azimuths are reversed by numerically changing the value by 180°.

Figure 6-11 shows a five-sided traverse with geometrically closed angles and a given azimuth for side *AE* of 172°39′. It should be noted that this azimuth of 172°39′ for *AE* is identical in direction to the bearing of S 7°21′ E for *AE* in Figure 6-8. In fact, the problems illustrated in Figures 6-8 and 6-11 are identical, except that the directions are given in bearings in Figure 6-8 and in azimuths in Figure 6-11.

If we wish to compute the azimuths also proceeding in a clockwise manner, we must first compute the azimuth of side *AB*. To compute the azimuth of *AB*, the two sides *AB* and

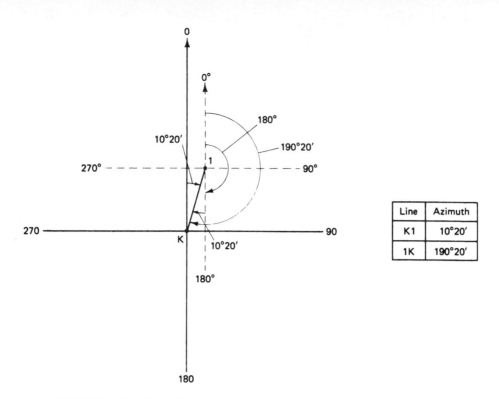

Line	Azimuth
K1	10°20'
1K	190°20'

FIGURE 6-10 Illustration of reversed azimuths.

AE are drawn, together with a meridian drawn through point *A*. The known data are then placed on the sketch along with a question mark in the position of the required azimuth. In step 1, it is apparent that the required azimuth (*AB*) = the given azimuth (*AE*) − the interior angle (*A*), a value of 71°11′.

To compute the azimuth of the next side, *BC,* the lines *BC* and *BA* are drawn, together with a meridian through point *B*. Once again, the known data are placed on the sketch, and a question mark is placed in the position of the required azimuth angle for side *BC*.

In step 1, the azimuth of *AB* was computed to be 71°11′; when this result is transferred to the sketch for step 2, it is obvious that it must be altered to comply with the new location of the meridian at point *B*. That is, with the meridian at *B*, the line *BA* is being considered, and the azimuth of line *AB* must be changed by 180°, resulting in a value of 251°11′; this "back azimuth" computation is shown in the boxes in the sketches for steps 2, 3, 4, and 5 (Figure 6-11).

The remaining azimuths are computed in steps 3, 4, and 5. Step 5 provides the azimuth for side *EA*. This last step gives the surveyor a check on all the computations, as the final azimuth (when reversed by 180°) should agree with the azimuth originally given for that line (*AE*). If the check does not work, all the computations must be reworked to find the mistake(s).

Sec. 6-5   Azimuths

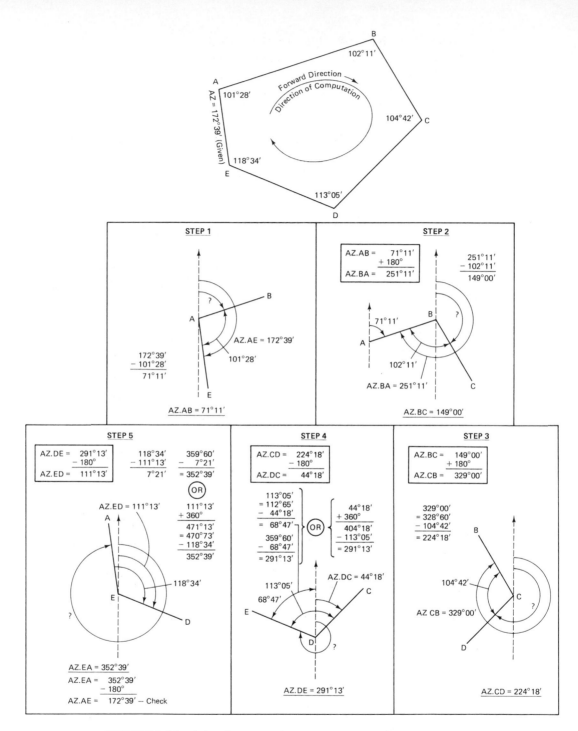

FIGURE 6-11 Azimuth computations.

Scrutiny of the five steps in Figure 6-11 reveals that the same procedure is involved in all the steps. That is, in each case, the desired azimuth is determined by *subtracting* the interior angle from the back azimuth of the previous course. This relationship is true every time the computations proceed in a *clockwise* direction.

If this problem had been solved by proceeding in a *counterclockwise* direction—that is, the azimuth of *ED* being computed first—it would have been noted that, in each case, the desired azimuth was computed by *adding* the interior angle to the back azimuth of the previous course.

The counterclockwise solution for azimuth computation is shown in Figure 6-12. It can be noted in Figure 6-12 that the computation follows a very systematic routine; it is so systematic that sketches are not required for each stage of the computation. A sketch is required at the beginning of the computation to give the overall sense of the problem and to ensure that the given azimuth is properly recognized as a forward or a back azimuth.

The terms *back azimuth* and *forward azimuth* are usually found only in computations; their directions depend entirely on the choice of clockwise or counterclockwise for the direction of the computation stages.

Normally surveying problems are worked out by using either bearings or azimuths for the directions of survey lines. The surveyor must be prepared to readily convert from one system to the other. Figure 6-13 illustrates and defines the relationships of bearings and azimuths in all four quadrants.

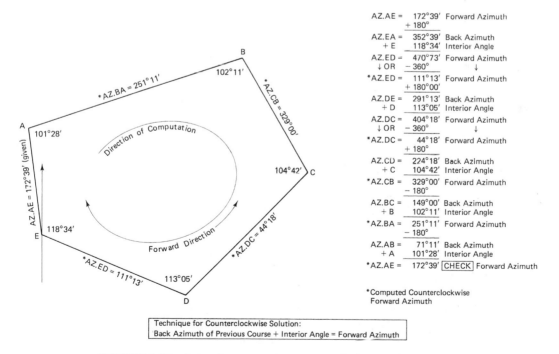

FIGURE 6-12 Azimuth computations, counterclockwise solution.

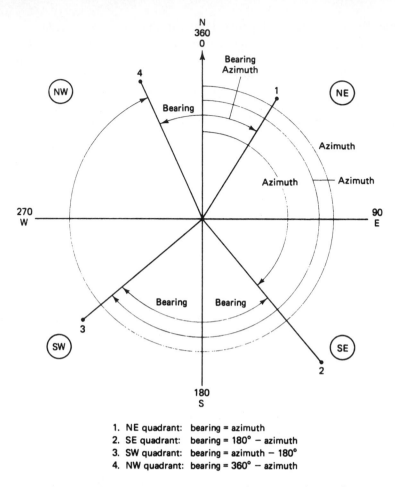

1. NE quadrant: bearing = azimuth
2. SE quadrant: bearing = 180° − azimuth
3. SW quadrant: bearing = azimuth − 180°
4. NW quadrant: bearing = 360° − azimuth

FIGURE 6-13   Relationships between bearings and azimuths.

6-6   Latitudes and Departures

In Chapter 1, we spoke of the need for the surveyor to check the survey measurements to ensure that the required accuracies were achieved and to ensure that mistakes were eliminated. Checking could consist of repeating the measurements in the field, and/or checking could be accomplished using mathematical techniques. One such mathematical technique involves the computation and analysis of latitudes and departures.

In Section 1-4, it was noted that a point could be located by polar ties (direction and distance) or by rectangular ties (two distances at 90°). In Figure 6-14(a), point B is located by polar ties from point A by direction (N 71°11′ E) and distance (164.95′). In Figure 6-14(b), point B is located by rectangular ties from point A by distance north ($\Delta N = 53.20′$) and distance east ($\Delta E = 156.13′$).

By definition, *latitude* is the north/south rectangular component of a line (ΔN). To differentiate direction, north is considered positive (+), and south is considered negative (−).

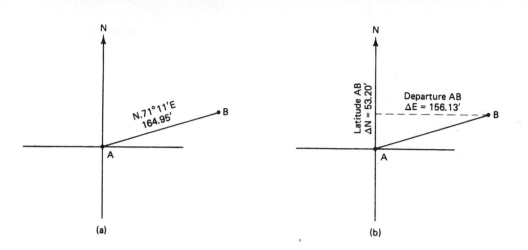

FIGURE 6-14 Location of a point. (a) Polar tie. (b) Rectangular tie.

Similarly, *departure* is the east/west rectangular component of a line (ΔE). To differentiate direction, east is considered positive ($+$), and west is considered negative ($-$).

When one is working with azimuths, the plus/minus designation is directly given by the appropriate trigonometric function.

$$\text{Latitude } (\Delta N) = \text{distance } (S) \cos \text{ bearing} \tag{6-1}$$

or

$$\text{Latitude } (\Delta N) = \text{distance } (S) \cos \text{ azimuth} \tag{6-2}$$

$$\text{Departure } (\Delta E) = \text{distance } (S) \sin \text{ bearing} \tag{6-3}$$

or

$$\text{Departure } (\Delta E) = \text{distance } (S) \sin \text{ azimuth} \tag{6-4}$$

Latitudes (lats) and departures (deps) can be used to compute the precision of a traverse survey by noting the plus/minus closure of both latitudes and departures. If the survey has been perfectly measured (angles and distances), the plus latitudes will equal the minus latitudes, and the plus departures will equal the minus departures.

In Figure 6-15, the survey has been analyzed in a clockwise manner (all algebraic signs and letter pairs would simply be reversed for a counterclockwise approach). Latitudes *DE, EA,* and *AB* are all positive and should precisely equal (if the survey measurements were perfect) the latitudes of *BC* and *CD,* which are negative. Departures *AB* and *BC* are positive and ideally should equal the departures *CD, DE,* and *EA,* which are negative.

The following sections in this chapter involve traverse computations that use trigonometric functions of direction angles—either bearings or azimuths—to compute latitudes and departures. When bearings are used, the algebraic signs of the lats and deps are assigned according to the N/S and E/W directions of the bearings. When azimuths are used, the algebraic signs of the lats and deps are given directly by the calculator, according to the trigonometric conventions illustrated in Figure 6-16.

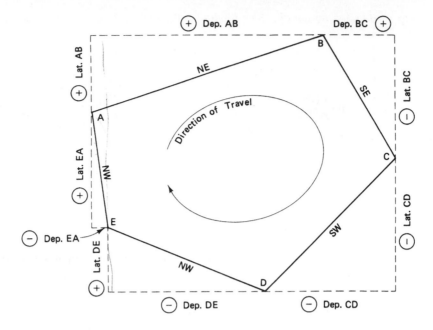

FIGURE 6-15 Closure of latitudes and departures (clockwise solution).

■ **EXAMPLE 6-1** *Computation of Latitudes and Departures to Determine the Error of Closure and the Precision Ratio of a Traverse Survey*

The survey data shown in Figure 6-2 will be used for this illustrative example. Following are all the steps required to adjust the field data and perform the necessary computations.

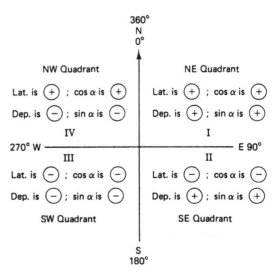

FIGURE 6-16 Algebraic signs of latitudes and departures by trigonometric functions where α is the azimuth.

Step 1. *Balance the angles.* See Table 6-1; the arbitrarily balanced angles will be used here.

Step 2. *Compute the bearings or azimuths.* See Figure 6-8 for bearings and Figure 6-11 or 6-12 for azimuths.

Step 3. *Compute the latitudes and departures.* Table 6-2 shows a typical format for a closed traverse computation. Columns are included for both bearings and azimuths, although only one of those direction angles is needed for computations. Table 6-2 shows that the latitudes fail to close by $+0.13'$ and that the departures fail to close by $-0.11'$.

Step 4. *Compute the linear error of closure.* See Figure 6-17 and Table 6-2. The linear error of closure is the net accumulation of the random errors associated with the traverse measurements. In Figure 6-17, the total error is showing up at A simply because the computation started at A. If the computation had started at any other station, the identical error of closure would have shown up at that station.

Line $A'A$ in Figure 6-17 is a graphical representation of the linear error of closure. The length of $A'A$ is the square root of the sums of the squares of the C lat and the C dep:

$$A'A = \sqrt{C\ \text{lat}^2 + C\ \text{dep}^2} = \sqrt{0.13^2 + 0.11^2} = 0.17'$$

C lat and C dep are equal to and opposite in sign to Σ lat and Σ dep and reflect the consistent direction (in this example) with the clockwise approach to this problem. It is sometimes advantageous to know the bearing of the linear error of closure. Reference to Figure 6-17 will show that C dep$/C$ lat $=$ tan bearing angle:

$$\text{Brg.}A'A = \text{S } 40°14'11'' \text{ E}$$

Table 6-2 CLOSED TRAVERSE COMPUTATIONS

Course	Distance	Bearing	Azimuth	Latitude	Departure
AB	164.95'	N 71°11' E	71°11'	+53.20	+156.13
BC	88.41'	S 31°00' E	149°00'	−75.78	+ 45.53
CD	121.69'	S 44°18' W	224°18'	−87.09	− 84.99
DE	115.89'	N 68°47' W	291°13'	+41.94	−108.03
EA	68.42'	N 7°21' W	352°39'	+67.86	− 8.75
	P = 559.36'			Σ lat = +0.13	Σ dep = −0.11

$$E = \sqrt{\Sigma\ \text{lat}^2 + \Sigma\ \text{dep}^2}, \quad E = \sqrt{0.13^2 + 0.11^2}, \quad E = 0.17'$$

where E is the linear error of closure

Precision ratio $= \dfrac{E}{P}$ (where P = the perimeter of the traverse)

Precision ratio $= \dfrac{0.17}{559.36} = \dfrac{1}{3290} \approx \dfrac{1}{3300}$

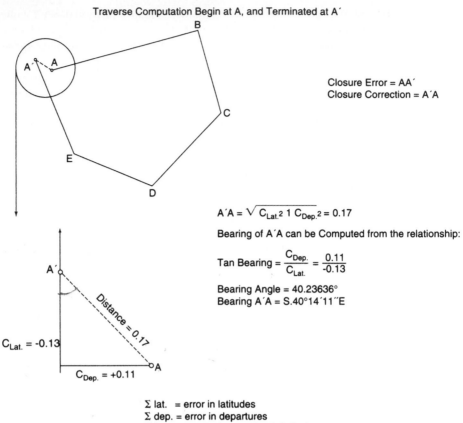

Traverse Computation Begin at A, and Terminated at A′

Closure Error = AA′
Closure Correction = A′A

$A'A = \sqrt{C_{Lat.}2\ 1\ C_{Dep.}2} = 0.17$

Bearing of A′A can be Computed from the relationship:

$Tan\ Bearing = \dfrac{C_{Dep.}}{C_{Lat.}} = \dfrac{0.11}{-0.13}$

Bearing Angle = 40.23636°
Bearing A′A = S.40°14′11″E

Σ lat. = error in latitudes
Σ dep. = error in departures
C lat. = required correction in latitudes
C dep. = required correction in departures

FIGURE 6-17 Closure error and closure correction.

Step 5. *Compute the precision ratio of the survey.* Table 6-2 shows that the precision ratio is the linear error of closure *(E)* divided by traverse perimeter *(P)*. The resultant fraction *(E/P)* is always expressed with a numerator of 1 and with the denominator rounded to the closest 100 units.

Precision ratio *(E/P)* = 0.17/559.36 = 1/3290 = 1/3300

The concept of an accuracy ratio was introduced in Section 1-12. Most states and provinces have these ratios legislated for minimally acceptable surveys for property boundaries. These values vary from one area to another, but are usually in the range of 1/5000 to 1/7500. In some cases, higher ratios (e.g., 1/10,000) are stipulated for high-cost downtown urban areas.

Engineering and construction surveys are performed at levels of 1/3000 to 1/10,000, depending on the importance of the work and the materials being used. For example, a ditched highway could well be surveyed at 1/3000, whereas overhead rails for a monorail transit system may require accuracies in the range of 1/7500 to

1/10,000. As noted in an earlier section, control surveys for both engineering and legal projects must be executed at higher levels of accuracy than are necessary for the actual location of the engineering or legal markers that are to be surveyed from those control surveys.

SUMMARY OF INITIAL TRAVERSE COMPUTATIONS
1. Balance the angles.
2. Compute the bearings and/or the azimuths.
3. Compute the latitudes and the departures
4. Compute the linear error of closure.
5. Compute the precision ratio of the survey.

If the precision ratio is satisfactory, further treatment of the data is possible—for example, coordinate and area computations. If the precision ratio is unsatisfactory (e.g., a precision ratio of only 1/2500 where 1/3000 was specified), complete the following steps:

1. Double-check all computations.
2. Double-check all field book entries.
3. Compute the bearing of the linear error of closure, and check to see if it is similar to one of the course bearings ($\pm$ 5°).*
4. Remeasure the sides of the traverse, beginning with a course having a bearing similar to the bearing of the linear error of closure (if there is one).
5. When a mistake (or error) is found, try the corrected value in the traverse computation to determine the new precision ratio.

*If a large error (or mistake) has been made on the measurement of one course, it will significantly affect the bearing of the linear error of closure. Accordingly, if a check on the field work is necessary, the surveyor first computes the bearing of the linear error of closure and checks that bearing against the course bearings. If a similarity exists ($\pm$ 5°), that course is the first course remeasured in the field.

The search for mistakes and errors is normally confined to only the distance measurements. The angle measurements are initially checked by doubling the angles (Section 4-4-6), and the angular geometric closure is checked at the conclusion of the survey for compliance to the survey specifications—that is, within a given tolerance of $(n - 2)180°$ (see Section 6-2).

6-7 Traverse Precision and Accuracy

The actual accuracy of a survey, as given by the precision ratio, can be misleading. The opportunity exists for significant errors to cancel out; this results in "high precision" closures from relatively imprecise field techniques. Many new surveying students are introduced to traverses by being asked to survey a traverse at the 1/3000 level of precision. Whereas most new student crews will struggle to achieve 1/3000, there always seems to be one crew (using the same equipment and techniques) that reports back with a substantially higher precision ratio—say 1/8000. In this case, it is safe to assume that the higher precision ratio obtained by the one crew is probably due to compensating errors rather than to superior skill.

For example, in a square-shaped traverse, systematic taping errors (e.g., long or short tape—Section 2-8-2) will be completely balanced and beyond mathematical detection. In fact, if a traverse has any two courses that are close to being parallel, identical systematic or random errors made on those courses will largely cancel out (the bearings will be reversed, and the nearly parallel latitudes and departures will have opposite algebraic signs).

In order to be sure that the resulting precision ratio truly reflects the field work, the traverse survey must be performed to specifications that will produce the desired results. For example, if a survey is to result in an accuracy of 1/5000, then the field distance-measuring techniques should resemble those specified in Table 2-2.

Further, the angle-measuring techniques should be consistent with the distance-measuring techniques. Figure 6-18 illustrates the relationship between angular and linear measurements; the survey specifications should be designed so that the maximum allowable error in angle (E_a). should be roughly equivalent to the maximum allowable error in distance (E_d).

If the linear accuracy is restricted to 1/5000, the angular error (θ) should be consistent;

$$1/5000 = \tan \theta$$
$$\theta = 0°00'41''$$

See Table 6-3 for additional linear and angular error relationships.

Point Y is to Be Set Out from Fixed Points X and Z

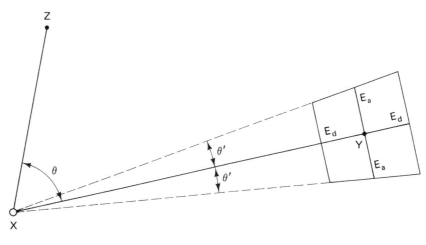

For the Line XY

E_d is the Possible Error in Distance Measurement and E_a is the Position Error Resulting from a Possible Angle Error of θ' in an Angle of θ.

FIGURE 6-18 Relationship between errors in linear and angular measurements.

Table 6-3 LINEAR AND ANGULAR ERROR RELATIONSHIPS

Linear Accuracy Ratio	Maximum Angular Error (E)	Least Count of Transit or Theodolite Scale
1/1000	0°03'26"	01'
1/3000	0°01'09"	01'
1/5000	0°00'41"	30"
1/7500	0°00'28"	20"
1/10,000	0°00'21"	20"
1/20,000	0°00'10"	10"

The overall allowable angular error in an n-angled closed traverse would be $E_a \sqrt{n}$. (Random errors accumulate as the square root of the number of observations.)

Thus, for a five-sided closed traverse with a specification for precision of 1/3000, the maximum angular error of closure would be $01' \sqrt{5} = 02'$ (to the closest minute), and for a specified precision of 1/5000, the maximum error of closure of the field angles would be $30'' \sqrt{5} = 01'$ (to the closest 30 seconds).

6-8   Compass Rule Adjustment

The compass rule is used in many survey computations. The compass rule distributes the errors in latitude and departure for each traverse course in the same proportion as the course distance is to the traverse perimeter. That is, generally,

$$\frac{C \text{ lat } AB}{\Sigma \text{ lat}} = \frac{AB}{P} \qquad \text{or} \qquad C \text{ lat } AB = \Sigma \text{ lat} \times \frac{AB}{P} \qquad (6\text{-}5)$$

where C lat AB = correction in latitude AB

Σ lat = error of closure in latitude

AB = distance AB

P = perimeter of traverse

and

$$\frac{C \text{ dep } AB}{\Sigma \text{ dep}} = \frac{AB}{P} \qquad \text{or} \qquad C \text{ dep } AB = \Sigma \text{ dep} \times \frac{AB}{P} \qquad (6\text{-}6)$$

where C dep AB = correction in departure AB

Σ dep = error of closure in departure

AB = distance AB

P = perimeter of traverse

With reference to Example 6-1, Table 6-2 has been expanded in Table 6-4 to provide space for traverse adjustments. The magnitudes of the individual corrections are shown next:

$$C \text{ lat } AB = \frac{0.13 \times 164.95}{559.36} = 0.04 \qquad C \text{ dep } AB = \frac{0.11 \times 164.95}{559.36} = 0.03$$

$$C \text{ lat } BC = \frac{0.13 \times 88.41}{559.36} = 0.02 \qquad C \text{ dep } BC = \frac{0.11 \times 88.41}{559.36} = 0.02$$

$$C \text{ lat } CD = \frac{0.13 \times 121.69}{559.36} = 0.03 \qquad C \text{ dep } CD = \frac{0.11 \times 121.69}{559.36} = 0.03$$

$$C \text{ lat } DE = \frac{0.13 \times 115.89}{559.36} = 0.03 \qquad C \text{ dep } DE = \frac{0.11 \times 115.89}{559.36} = 0.02$$

$$C \text{ lat } EA = \frac{0.13 \times 68.42}{559.36} = \underline{0.01} \qquad C \text{ dep } EA = \frac{0.11 \times 68.42}{559.36} = \underline{0.01}$$

$$\text{Check: } C \text{ lat} = 0.13 \qquad\qquad \text{Check: } C \text{ dep} = 0.11$$

These computations are normally performed on a handheld calculator with the constants 0.13/559.36 and 0.11/559.36 entered into storage for easy retrieval and thus quick computations.

It now only remains for the algebraic sign to be determined. Quite simply, **the corrections are opposite in sign to the errors.** Therefore, for this example, the latitude corrections are negative, and the departure corrections are positive. The corrections are now added algebraically to arrive at the balanced values. For example, in Table 6-4, the correction for latitude BC is -0.02, which is to be "added" to latitude BC_1, -75.78. Since the correction is the same sign as the latitude, the two values are added to get the answer. In the case of course AB, the latitude correction (-0.04) and the latitude ($+53.20$) have opposite signs, indicating that the difference between the two values is the desired value (i.e., subtract to get the answer).

To check the work, the balanced latitudes and balanced departures are totalled to see if their respective sums are zero. It sometimes happens that the balanced latitude or balanced departure totals fail to equal zero by one last-place unit (0.01 in this example). This discrepancy is probably caused by rounding off and is normally of no consequence; the discrepancy is removed by arbitrarily changing one of the values to force the total to zero.

Table 6-4 EXAMPLE 6-1, COMPASS RULE ADJUSTMENTS

Course	Distance	Bearing	Latitude	Departure	C lat.	C dep.	Balanced Latitudes	Balanced Departures
AB	164.95'	N 71°11' E	+53.20	+156.13	−0.04	+0.03	+53.16	+156.16
BC	88.41'	S 31°00' E	−75.78	+ 45.53	−0.02	+0.02	−75.80	+ 45.55
CD	121.69'	S 44°18' W	−87.09	− 84.99	−0.03	+0.03	−87.12	− 84.96
DE	115.89'	N 68°47' W	+41.94	−108.03	−0.03	+0.02	+41.91	−108.01
EA	68.42'	N 7°21' W	+67.86	− 8.75	−0.01	+0.01	+67.85	− 8.74
	P = 559.36'		Σ lat = +0.13	Σ dep = −0.11	C lat = −0.13	C dep = +0.11	0.00	0.00

Chap. 6   Traverse Surveys

It should be noted that when the error (in latitude or departure) to be distributed is quite small, the corrections can be arbitrarily assigned to appropriate courses. For example, if the error in latitude (or departure) is only 0.03 ft in a five-sided traverse, it is appropriate to apply corrections of 0.01 ft to the latitude of each of the three longest courses. Similarly, where the error in latitude for a five-sided traverse is +0.06, it is appropriate to apply a correction of −0.02 to the longest course latitude and a correction of −0.01 to each of the remaining four latitudes, the same solution provided by the compass rule.

Although the computations shown here are not tedious, the student will be pleased to know that the computation of latitudes and departures and all the adjustments to those computations are routinely performed on computers using a variety of computer programs based on coordinate geometry (COGO); some Total Station instruments also have these computational capabilities on board.

6-9 Effects of Traverse Adjustments on Measured Angles and Distances

Once the latitudes and departures have been adjusted, the original polar coordinates (distance and direction) will no longer be valid. In most cases, the adjustment required for polar coordinates is too small to warrant consideration. However, if the data are to be used for construction layout purposes, the corrected distances and directions should be used.

By way of example, consider the traverse data summarized in Table 6-4. We can use the corrected lats and deps to compute distances and bearings (azimuths) consistent with those corrected lats and deps. Figures 6-14 and 6-17 illustrate the trigonometric relationships among bearings, course distances, lats, and deps.

It is clear that a distance $= \sqrt{\text{lat}^2 + \text{dep}^2}$ and that the tangent of the course bearing (azimuth) = dep/lat.

In Example 6-1,

$$\text{Adjusted distance } AB = \sqrt{53.16^2 + 156.16^2} = 164.96'$$

$$\text{Tan of adjusted bearing } AB = 156.16/53.16$$

$$\text{Adjusted bearing } AB = \text{N } 71°12'01'' \text{ E}$$

The remaining corrected distances and bearings can be found in Table 6-5.

Table 6-5 ADJUSTMENT OF ORIGINAL DISTANCES AND BEARINGS

Course	Balanced Latitude	Balanced Departure	Adjusted Distance	Adjusted Bearing	Original Distance	Original Bearing
AB	+53.16	+156.16	164.96'	N 71°12'01'' E	164.95'	N 71°11' E
BC	−75.80	+ 45.55	88.43'	S 31°00'10'' E	88.41'	S 31°00' E
CD	−87.12	− 84.96	121.69'	S 44°16'51'' W	121.69'	S 44°18' W
DE	+41.91	−108.01	115.86'	N 68°47'34'' W	115.89'	N 68°47' W
EA	+67.85	− 8.74	68.41'	N 7°20'24'' W	68.42'	N 7°21' W
	0.00	0.00	P = 559.35'		P = 559.36'	

6-10   Omitted Measurement Computations

The techniques developed in the computation of latitudes and departures can be used to solve for missing course information on a closed traverse; these techniques also can be utilized to solve any surveying problem that can be arranged in the form of a closed traverse. The case of one missing course is illustrated in the following example and in Section 14-7, Dimension Verification. The case of one missing course requires the solution of a problem in which the bearing (azimuth) and distance for one course in a closed traverse are missing. Other variations of this problem include the case where the distance of one course and the bearing of another course are unknown; these cases can be solved by using missing course techniques (as outlined below), together with the sine law and/or cosine law (see Appendix A), which may be required for intermediate steps or cutoff lines.

■ **EXAMPLE 6-2**

In Figure 6-19, data for three of the four sides of the closed traverse are shown. In the field, the distances for *AB, BC,* and *CD* were measured; also, the interior angles at *B* and *C* were measured, and the bearing (azimuth) of *AB* was available from a previous survey. The bearings of *BC* and *CD* were computed from the given bearing and the measured angles at *B* and *C*.

Required are the distance *DA* and the bearing (azimuth) of *DA*. The problem is set up in the same manner as a closed traverse; see Table 6-6. When the latitudes and departures of *AB, BC,* and *CD* are computed and summed, the results indicate that the traverse failed to close by a line having a latitude of −202.82 and a departure of +276.13—line *AD* in Figure 6-19. To be consistent with direction (clockwise in this example), we can say that the missing course is line *DA* with a latitude of +202.82 and a departure of −276.13 (i.e., *C* lat and *C* dep, Figure 6-19).

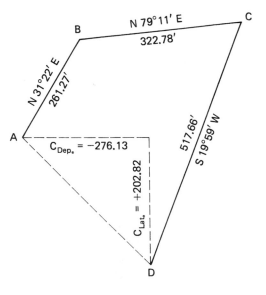

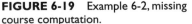

FIGURE 6-19   Example 6-2, missing course computation.

Table 6-6 EXAMPLE 6-2, MISSING COURSE

Course	Distance	Bearing	Latitude	Departure
AB	261.27	N 31°22' E	+223.09	+135.99
BC	322.78	N 79°11' E	+60.58	+317.05
CD	517.66	S 19°59' W	−486.49	−176.91
			Σ lat = −202.82	Σ dep = +276.13
DA			C lat = +202.82	C dep = −276.13

$$\text{Distance } DA = \sqrt{\text{lat } DA^2 + \text{dep } DA^2}$$
$$= \sqrt{202.82^2 + 276.13^2}$$
$$= 342.61'$$

$$\text{Tan brg. } DA = \frac{\text{dep } AD}{\text{lat } AD}$$
$$= \frac{-276.13}{+202.82}$$
$$= -1.3614535$$

Brg. DA = N 53°42' W (to the closest minute)

It should be noted that this technique does not permit a check on the accuracy ratio of the field work. Since DA is the closure course, its computed value will also contain all the accumulated errors in the field work—see Example 6-1, step 4).

6-11 Rectangular Coordinates of Traverse Stations

6-11-1 Coordinates Computed from Balanced Latitudes and Departures

Rectangular coordinates define the position of a point with respect to two perpendicular axes. Analytic geometry uses the concepts of a y axis (north-south) and an x axis (east-west), concepts that are obviously quite useful in surveying applications.

In Universal Transverse Mercator (UTM) grid systems, the x axis is often the equator, and the y axis is a central meridian through the middle of the zone in which the grid is located (see Chapter 8). For surveys of a limited nature, where a coordinate grid has not been established, the coordinate axes can be assumed.

If the axes are to be assumed, values are chosen such that the coordinates of all stations will be positive (i.e., stations will often be in the northeast quadrant).

The traverse tabulated in Table 6-4 will be used for illustrative purposes. Values for the coordinates of station A are assumed to be 1000.00 north and 1000.00 east.

To calculate the coordinates of the other traverse stations, it is simply a matter of applying the balanced latitudes and departures to the previously calculated coordinates. In Figure 6-20, the balanced latitude and departure of course AB are applied to the assumed

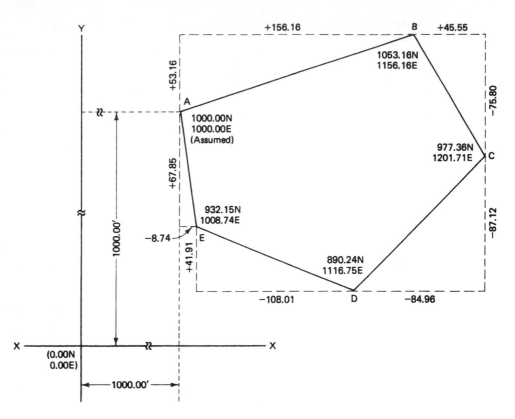

FIGURE 6-20   Station coordinates using balanced latitudes and departures.

coordinates of station *A* to determine the coordinates of station *B,* and so on. These simple computations are shown in Table 6-7.

A check on the computation is possible by using the last latitude and departure *(EA)* to recalculate the coordinates of station *A*.

If a scale drawing of the traverse is required, it can be accomplished by methods of rectangular coordinates, where each station is located independently of the other stations by scaling the appropriate north and east distances from the axes; or the traverse can be drawn by the direction and distance method of polar coordinates (i.e., by scaling the interior angle between courses and by scaling the course distances, the stations are located in counterclockwise or clockwise sequence).

Whereas in the rectangular coordinate system, plotting errors are isolated at each station, in the polar coordinate layout method, all angle and distance scale errors are accumulated and show up only when the last distance and angle are scaled to theoretically relocate the starting point. The resultant plotting error is similar in type to the linear error of traverse closure *(A'A')* illustrated in Figure 6-17.

The use of coordinates to define the positions of boundary markers has been steadily increasing over the years. The storage of property-corner coordinates in large-memory

Table 6-7 COMPUTATION OF COORDINATES USING BALANCED LATITUDES AND DEPARTURES

Course	Balanced Latitude	Balanced Departure	Station	Northing	Easting
			A	1000.00	1000.00
AB	+53.16	+156.16		+53.16	+156.16
			B	1053.16	1156.16
BC	−75.80	+ 45.55		−75.80	+45.55
			C	977.36	1201.71
CD	−87.12	− 84.96		−87.12	−84.96
			D	890.24	1116.75
DE	+41.91	−108.01		+41.91	−108.01
			E	932.15	1008.74
EA	+67.85	− 8.74		+67.85	−8.74
			A	1000.00	1000.00
				check	check

civic computers will, in the not so distant future, permit lawyers, municipal authorities, and others to have instant retrieval of current land registration assessment, and other municipal information, such as that concerning census and the level of municipal services. Although such use is important, the truly impressive impact of coordinate use results from the coordination of topographic detail (digitization), so that plans can be prepared by computer-assisted plotters (see Chapter 5), and the coordination of all legal and engineering details, so that not only will the plans be produced by computer-assisted plotters, but also the survey **layout** will be accomplished by sets of computer-generated coordinates (rectangular and polar) fed either manually or automatically through Total Stations (see Chapter 5). Complex layouts can then be accomplished quickly by a few surveyors from one or two centrally located control points, with a higher level of precision and a lower incidence of mistakes.

6-11-2 Adjusted Coordinates Computed from Raw-Data Coordinates

Section 6-8 demonstrated the adjustment of traverse errors by the adjustment of the individual ΔY's (northings) and ΔX's (eastings) for each traverse course using the compass rule. Although this traditional technique has been favored for many years, lately, because of the wide use of the computer in surveying solutions, coordinates are now often first computed from raw (unadjusted) bearing/distance data and then adjusted using the compass rule. Since we are now working with coordinates and not individual ΔY's and ΔX's, the distance factor to be used in the compass rule must be cumulative. This technique will be illustrated using the same field data from Section 6-6 (Example 6-1).

Corrections (C) to raw-data coordinates are shown in Tables 6-8 and 6-9.

Table 6-8 COMPUTATION OF RAW-DATA COORDINATES

Station/Course	Bearing	Distance	ΔY	ΔX	Coordinates (Raw-Data)	
					Northing	Easting
A					1000.00	1000.00
AB	N 71°11′ E	164.95	+53.20	+156.13		
B					1053.20	1156.13
BC	S 31°00′ E	88.41	−75.78	+ 45.53		
C					977.42	1201.66
CD	S 44°18′ W	121.69	−87.09	− 84.99		
D					890.33	1116.67
DE	N 68°47′ W	115.89	+41.94	−108.03		
E					932.27	1008.64
EA	N 7°21′ W	68.42	+67.86	− 8.75		
A					1000.13	999.89
			$\Sigma\Delta Y = +0.13$	$\Sigma\Delta X = -0.11$		

$C\Delta Y$ = correction in northing (latitude), and $C\Delta X$ = correction in easting (departure). Correction C is opposite in sign to errors ΣY and ΣX.

Station B

$C\Delta Y$ is $[AB/P]\ \Sigma\Delta Y = [164.95/559.36]\ 0.13 = -0.04$

$C\Delta X$ is $[AB/P]\ \Sigma\Delta X = [164.95/559.36]\ 0.11 = +0.03$

Table 6-9 COMPUTATION OF ADJUSTED COORDINATES

Station	Coordinates (Raw-Data)		$C\Delta Y$	$C\Delta X$	Coordinates (Adjusted)	
	Northing	Easting			Northing	Easting
A	1000.00	1000.00			1000.00	1000.00
B	1053.20	1156.13	−0.04	+0.03	1053.16	1156.16
C	977.42	1201.66	−0.06	+0.05	977.36	1201.71
D	890.33	1116.67	−0.09	+0.07	890.24	1116.74
E	932.27	1008.64	−0.11	+0.10	932.16	1008.74
A	1000.13	999.89	−0.13	+0.11	1000.00	1000.00

Station C

CΔY is $[(AB + BC)/P]\ \Sigma\Delta Y = [253.36/559.36]\ 0.13 = -0.06$
CΔX is $[(AB + BC)/P]\ \Sigma\Delta X = [253.36/559.36]\ 0.11 = +0.05$

Station D

CΔY is $[(AB + BC + CD)/P]\ \Sigma\Delta Y = [375.05/559.36]\ 0.13 = -0.09$
CΔX is $[(AB + BC + CD)/P]\ \Sigma\Delta Y = [375.05/559.36]\ 0.11 = +0.07$

Station E

CΔY is $[(AB + BC + CD + DE)/P]\ \Sigma\Delta Y = [490.94/559.36]\ 0.13 = -0.11$
CΔX is $[(AB + BC + CD + DE)/P]\ \Sigma\Delta X = [490.94/559.36]\ 0.11 = +0.10$

Station A

CΔY is $[(AB + BC + CD + DE + EA)/P]\ \Sigma\Delta Y = [559.36/559.36]\ 0.13 = -0.13$
CΔX is $[(AB + BC + CD + DE + EA)/P]\ \Sigma\Delta X = [559.36/559.36]\ 0.11 = +0.11$

6-12 Area of a Closed Traverse by the Coordinate Method

When the coordinates of the stations of a closed traverse are known, it is a simple matter to then compute the area within the traverse, either by computer or by handheld calculator. Figure 6-21(a) shows a closed traverse 1, 2, 3, 4 with the appropriate X and Y coordinate distances. Figure 6-21(b) illustrates the technique used to compute the traverse area.

With reference to Figure 6-21(b), it can be seen that the desired *area of the traverse is, in effect, area 2 minus area 1*. Area 2 is the sum of the areas of trapezoids 4'433' and 3'322'. Area 1 is the sum of trapezoids 4'411' and 1'122'.

$$\text{Area } 2 = \tfrac{1}{2}\ (X_4 + X_3)(Y_4 - Y_3) + \tfrac{1}{2}\ (X_3 + X_2)(Y_3 - Y_2)$$
$$\text{Area } 1 = \tfrac{1}{2}\ (X_4 + X_1)(Y_4 - Y_1) + \tfrac{1}{2}\ (X_1 + X_2)(Y_1 - Y_2)$$
$$2A = [(X_4 + X_3)(Y_4 - Y_3) + (X_3 + X_2)(Y_3 - Y_2)]$$
$$-[(X_4 + X_1)(Y_4 - Y_1) + (X_1 + X_2)(Y_1 - Y_2)]$$

Expand this expression, and collect the remaining terms:

$$2A = X_1(Y_2 - Y_4) + X_2(Y_3 - Y_1) + X_3(Y_4 - Y_2) + X_4(Y_1 - Y_3) \qquad (6\text{-}7)$$

Stated simply, the double area of a closed traverse is the algebraic sum of each X coordinate multiplied by the difference between the Y values of the adjacent stations.

The double area is divided by 2 to determine the final area. The final area can be positive or negative, reflecting only the direction of computation approach (clockwise or counterclockwise). The area is, of course, positive.

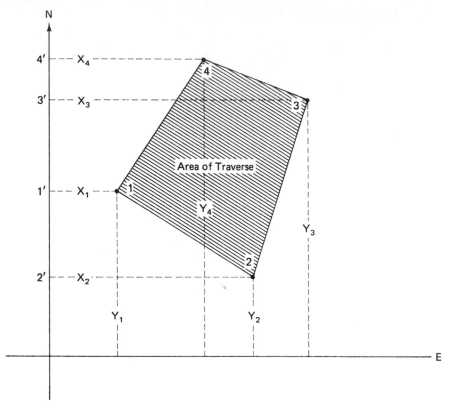

(a)

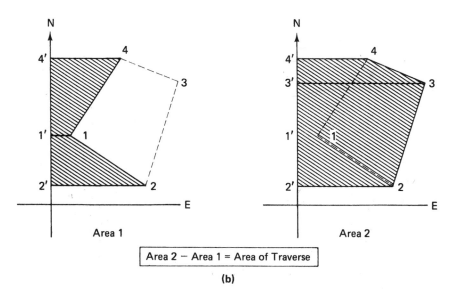

Area 2 − Area 1 = Area of Traverse

(b)

FIGURE 6-21 Area by rectangular coordinates.

Chap. 6   Traverse Surveys

■ **EXAMPLE 6-3** *Area Computation by Coordinates*

With reference to the traverse example (Example 6-1) in Section 6-6, as illustrated in Figure 6-20, the station coordinates are summarized below:

Station	Northing	Easting
A	1000.00	1000.00
B	1053.16	1156.16
C	977.36	1201.71
D	890.24	1116.75
E	932.15	1008.74

The double area computation uses the relationships developed earlier in this section. Equation (6-7) must be expanded from the four-sided traverse shown in the illustrative example to the five-sided traverse of Example 6-1:

$$2A = X_1(Y_5 - Y_2) + X_2(Y_1 - Y_3) + X_3(Y_2 - Y_4) + X_4(Y_3 - Y_5) + X_5(Y_4 - Y_1)$$

that is, for the double area, each X coordinate is multiplied by the difference between the Y coordinates of the adjacent stations.

Using the station letters instead of the general case numbers shown above, we find the solution:

$$XA(YE - YB) = 1000.00(932.15 - 1053.16) = -121,010$$
$$XB(YA - YC) = 1156.16(1000.00 - 977.36) = +26,175$$
$$XC(YB - YD) = 1201.71(1053.16 - 890.24) = +195,783$$
$$XD(YC - YE) = 1116.75(977.36 - 932.15) = +50,488$$
$$XE(YD - YA) = 1008.74(890.24 - 1000.00) = \underline{-110,719}$$

$$2A = +40,717 \text{ ft}^2$$
$$A = 20,358 \text{ ft}^2$$
$$A = \frac{20,358}{43,560} = 0.47 \text{ acre}$$

$$(1 \text{ acre} = 43,560 \text{ ft}^2)$$

Problems

6-1. A closed five-sided traverse has the following interior angles:
$A = 123°57'; B = 88°06'; C = 89°44'; D = 113°33'; E = ?$
Find the angle at E.

6-2. A five-sided closed traverse has the following interior angles:

$A = 79°46'30''$
$B = 132°41'30''$
$C = 91°22'00''$
$D = 111°21'30''$
$E = 124°46'00''$

Determine the angular error, and balance the angles by applying equal corrections to each angle.

6-3. Convert the following azimuths to bearings:
    (a) 215°33′   **(b)** 168°28′   **(c)** 339°15′50″   **(d)** 41°27′
    (e) 271°53′   **(f)** 166°59′

6-4. Convert the following bearings to azimuths:
    (a) N 15°18′ W   **(b)** N 66°51′ E   **(c)** S 39°41′ E   **(d)** S 8°19′ W
    (e) N 56°13′ W   **(f)** S 0°02′ E

6-5. Convert each of the azimuths given in Problem 6-3 to reverse (back) azimuths.

6-6. Convert each of the bearings given in Problem 6-4 to reverse (back) bearings.

6-7. An open traverse that runs from *A* to *H* has the following deflection angles:
    B = 1°11′R; *C* = 3°03′ R; *D* = 7°56′ L; *E* = 6°10′ L; *F* = 1°41′ R; *G* = 9°15′ L
    If the bearing of *AB* is N 25°10′ E, compute the bearings of the remaining sides.

6-8. Closed traverse *ABCD* has the following bearings:
    AB = N 71°31′ E; *BC* = S 69°18′ E; *CD* = S 2°19′ W; *DA* = N 60°16′ W
    Compute the interior angles, and show a geometric check for your work.

Use the following sketch and interior angles for Problems 6-9 through 6-11.

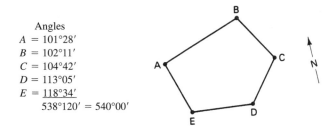

Angles
A = 101°28′
B = 102°11′
C = 104°42′
D = 113°05′
E = 118°34′
  538°120′ = 540°00′

6-9. If bearing *AB* is N 63°42′ E, compute the bearings of the remaining sides. Provide two solutions, one working clockwise and one working counterclockwise.

6-10. If the azimuth of *AB* is 59°28′, compute the azimuths of the remaining sides. Provide two solutions, one working clockwise and one working counterclockwise.

6-11. If the azimuth of *AB* is 70°09′, compute the azimuths of the remaining sides. Provide two solutions, one working clockwise and one working counterclockwise.

6-12. A four-sided closed traverse has the following angles and distances:

A = 51°23′   *AB* = 713.93 ft
B = 105°39′   *BC* = 606.06 ft
C = 78°11′   *CD* = 391.27 ft
D = 124°47′   *DA* = 781.18 ft

The bearing of *AB* is N 71°49′ E.
(a) Perform a check for angular closure.
(b) Compute both bearings and azimuths for all sides.
(c) Compute the latitudes and departures.
(d) Compute the linear error of closure and the precision ratio.

6-13. Using the data from Problem 6-12, balance the latitudes and departures using the compass rule. Compute corrected distances and directions.

6-14. Using the data from Problem 6-13, compute the coordinates of stations B, C, and D, assuming that the coordinates of station A are 1000.00 ft N and 1000.00 ft E.

6-15. Using the data from Problem 6-14, compute the area (in acres) enclosed by the traverse.

6-16. A five-sided closed traverse has the following angles and distances:

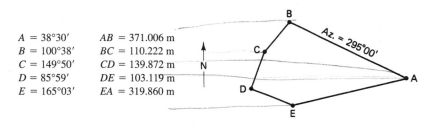

A = 38°30′	AB = 371.006 m
B = 100°38′	BC = 110.222 m
C = 149°50′	CD = 139.872 m
D = 85°59′	DE = 103.119 m
E = 165°03′	EA = 319.860 m

Side AB has an azimuth of 295°00′.
(a) Perform a check for angular closure.
(b) Compute both bearings and azimuths for all sides.
(c) Compute the latitudes and departures.
(d) Compute the linear error of closure and the precision ratio.

6-17. Using the data from Problem 6-16, balance the latitudes and departures using the compass rule.

6-18. Using the data from Problem 6-17, compute the coordinates of stations C, D, E, and A, assuming that the coordinates of station B are 1000.000 m N and 1000.000 m E.

6-19. Using the data from Problem 6-18, compute the area (in hectares) enclosed by the traverse.   5.27 ha

6-20. The two frontage corners (A and D) of a large tract of land are joined by the following open traverse:

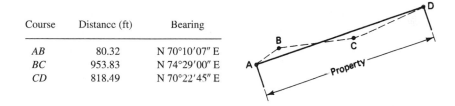

Course	Distance (ft)	Bearing
AB	80.32	N 70°10′07″ E
BC	953.83	N 74°29′00″ E
CD	818.49	N 70°22′45″ E

Compute the distance and bearing of the property frontage AD.

6-21. Given the following data for a closed property traverse, compute the missing data (i.e., distance CD and bearing DE).

Course	Distance (m)	Bearing
AB	537.144	N 37°10′49″ E
BC	1109.301	N 79°29′49″ E
CD	?	S 18°56′31″ W
DE	953.829	?
EA	483.669	N 26°58′31″ W

6-22. A six-sided traverse has the following station coordinates:
 A: 559.319 N, 207.453 E; *B:* 738.562 N, 666.737 E; *C:* 541.742 N, 688.350 E;
 D: 379.861 N, 839.008 E; *E:* 296.099 N, 604.048 E; *F:* 218.330 N, 323.936 E
 Compute the distance and bearing of each side.

6-23. Using the data from Problem 6-22, compute the area (hectares) enclosed by the traverse.

6-24. A theodolite with EDMI was set up at control station *K,* which is within the limits of a five-sided property. The coordinates of station *K* are 1990.000 N, 2033.000 E. Azimuth angles and polar distances to the five property corners are as follows:

Direction	Azimuth	Horizontal Distance (m)
KA	286°51′30″	34.482
KB	37°35′28″	31.892
KC	90°27′56″	38.286
KD	166°26′49″	30.916
KE	247°28′43″	32.585

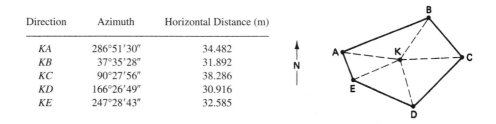

Compute the coordinates of the property corners *A, B, C, D,* and *E.*

6-25. Using the data from Problem 6-24, compute the area (hectares) of the property.

6-26. Using the data from Problem 6-24, compute the bearings (to the closest second) and distances (to three decimals) of the five sides of the property.

Chapter 7

Topographic Surveying and Drawing Using Traditional (Preelectronics) Techniques

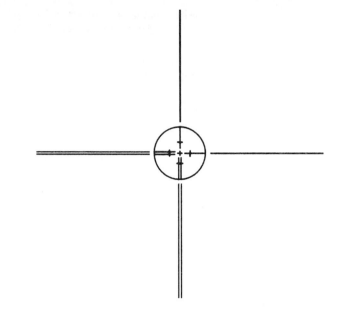

7-1 General

Topographic surveys are used to determine the positions of man-made and natural features (e.g., roads, buildings, trees, shorelines). These man-made and natural features can then be plotted to scale on a map or plan. In addition, topographic surveys include the determination of ground elevations, which can later be plotted in the form of contours, cross sections, profiles, or simply spot elevations. In engineering and construction work, topographic surveys are often called **preliminary** or **preengineering** surveys. Large-area topographic surveys are usually performed by aerial photography, with the resultant distances and elevations being derived from the photographs through the use of photogrammetric principles (see *Surveying: Principles and Applications,* Kavanagh and Bird). In this case, the survey plan is normally drawn on a digital plotter.

For smaller-area topographic surveys, various types of ground survey techniques can be employed. Ground surveys can be accomplished by using (1) transit and tape, (2) stadia, (3) Total Stations (see Sections 5-9 and 5-10), or (4) Global Positioning Systems (GPS) (see Chapter 9).

If the ground survey has been performed with the transit and tape or the stadia method, the survey drawing will usually be accomplished by conventional scale and protractor plotting techniques. On the other hand, if the survey has used the Total Station or GPS technique, the survey drawing will be drawn on a digital plotter (see Section 5-13).

The vast majority of topographic surveys are now performed using aerial surveying techniques, with the plans and digital elevation models (DEM) being constructed using modern computerized *photogrammetric* techniques. Smaller-scale surveys are often performed using electronic equipment, such as *Total Stations.* The horizontal location (X and Y) and the vertical (elevation) location (Z) can be easily captured with one sighting, with point descriptions and other attribute data being entered into electronic storage for later transfer to the computer. Electronic surveying techniques are discussed in detail in Chapter 5.

The focus in this chapter will be on the rectangular and polar surveying techniques, first introduced in Section 1-4, employing preelectronic field techniques. The rectangular technique discussed here utilizes right-angle offsets for detail location and cross sections for elevations and profiles. The polar technique discussed here utilizes *stadia* techniques for both horizontal location and elevation capture and contours for elevation depiction. Although *stadia* has been largely replaced by polar electronic techniques (see Chapter 5), many colleges and universities still employ these techniques as an introduction to surveying and mapping and as an excellent way for students to acquire field skills with surveying equipment.

The ground survey is taken from survey lines or stations that are part of, or tied into, the survey control. Horizontal survey control could consist of boundary lines—or offsets to boundary lines, such as centerlines—in road surveys; coordinate grid monuments; route survey traverses; or arbitrarily placed baselines or control monuments. Vertical survey control is based on benchmarks that already exist in the survey area or benchmarks that are established through differential leveling from other areas.

Surveyors are conscious of the need for accurate and well-referenced survey control. If the control is inaccurate, the survey and any resultant design will also be inaccurate. If the control is not well referenced, it will be costly (perhaps impossible) to precisely relocate the control points in the field once they are lost. In addition to providing control for the original survey, the survey control must be used if additional survey work is required to complete the preengineering project; and, of course, the original survey control must be used for subsequent construction layout surveys that may result from designs based on the original surveys. It is not unusual to have one or more years elapse between the preliminary survey and the related construction layout.

7-2 Precision Required for Topographic Surveys

If we consider plotting requirements only, the survey detail need only be located at a precision level consistent with standard plotting precision. Many municipal plans (including plan and profile) are drawn at 1 in. = 50 ft or 1 in. = 40 ft (1 : 500 metric). If we assume that points can be plotted to the closest 1/50 in. (0.5 mm), then location ties need only be to the closest 1 ft or 0.8 ft (0.25 m). For smaller-scale plans, the location precision can be relaxed even further.

In addition to providing plotting data, topographic surveys provide the designer with field dimensions that must be considered for related construction design. For example, when one is designing an extension to an existing storm sewer, the topographic survey must include the location and elevations of all connecting pipe inverts (see Chapter 13). These values are more precisely determined (0.01 ft or 0.005 m) because of design requirements.

In this regard, the following points should be considered with respect to levels of precision:

1. Some detail can be precisely defined and located—for example, building corners, railway tracks, bridge beam seats, and sewer and culvert inverts.
2. Some detail cannot be precisely defined or located—for example, stream banks, edges of gravel roads, limits of wooded areas, rock outcrops, and tops/bottoms of slopes.
3. Some detail can be located with only moderate precision, with normal techniques— for example, large single trees, manhole covers, and walkways.

When a topographic survey requires all three of the above levels of precision, the items in level 1 are located at a precision dictated by the design requirements; the items in levels 2 and 3 are usually located at the precision of level 3 (e.g., 0.1 ft or 0.01 m).

Since most natural features are themselves not precisely defined, topographic surveys in areas having only natural features—for example, stream or watercourse surveys, site development surveys, or large-scale mapping surveys—can be accomplished by using relatively imprecise survey methods (see stadia surveying Sections 7-5 to 7-10 and aerial Surveying Sections 11-1 and 12-1).

A topographic survey performed using a combination of preelectronics methods and electronic methods (such as Total Stations) routinely provides far more precision in measurements than is called for in typical topographic project specifications—and at no additional cost.

7-3   Tie-Ins at Right Angles to Baselines

Many ground-based topographic surveys, excluding mapping surveys, but including most preengineering surveys, utilize the right-angle offset technique to locate detail. This technique not only provides the location of plan detail, but also provides location for area elevations taken by cross sections (see Section 7-4).

Plan detail is located by measuring the distance perpendicularly from the baseline to the object and, in addition, measuring along the baseline to the point of perpendicularity. The baseline is laid out in the field with stakes (nails in pavement) placed at appropriate intervals, usually 100 ft or 20 to 30 m. A sketch is entered in the field book before the measuring commences. If the terrain is smooth, a tape can be laid on the ground between the station marks. This will permit the surveyor to move along the tape (toward the forward station), noting and booking the stations of the sketched detail on both sides of the baseline. The right angle for each location tie can be established by using a pentaprism (Figure 7-1), or a right angle can be approximately established in the following manner: The surveyor stands on the baseline facing the detail to be tied in and then points one arm down the baseline in one direction and the other arm down the baseline in the opposite direction; after checking both arms (pointed index fingers) for proper alignment, the surveyor closes his eyes while he swings his arms together in front of him, pointing (presumably) at the detail. If he is not pointing at the detail, the surveyor moves slightly along the baseline and repeats the procedure until the detail has been correctly sighted in. The station is then read off the tape and booked in the field notes. This approximate method is used a great deal in

FIGURE 7-1 Double right-angle prism. (Courtesy of Keuffel & Esser Co.)

route surveys and municipal surveys. This technique (swung-arm technique) provides good results over short offset distances (50 ft or 15 m). For longer offset distances or for very important detail, a pentaprism or even a transit can be used to determine the station.

Once all the stations have been booked for the interval (100 ft or 20 to 30 m), it remains only to measure the offsets left and right of the baseline. If the steel tape has been left lying on the ground during the determination of the stations, it is usually left in place to mark the baseline while the offsets are measured from it with another tape (e.g., a cloth tape).

Figure 7-2(a) illustrates topographic field notes that have been booked when a single baseline was used, and Figure 7-2(b) illustrates such notes when a split baseline was used. In Figure 7-2(a), the offsets are shown on the dimension lines, and the stations are shown opposite the dimension line or as close as possible to the actual tie point on the baseline.

In Figure 7-2(b), the baseline has been "split"; that is, two lines are drawn representing the baseline, leaving a space of zero dimension between them for the inclusion of stations. The split baseline technique is particularly valuable in densely detailed areas where single baseline notes would tend to become crowded and difficult to decipher. The earliest topographic surveyors in North America used the split-baseline method of note keeping (see Figure 7-3).

The most efficient ground-based surveying techniques for locating details are those using Total Stations or GPS equipment; see Chapters 5 and 9.

7-4 Cross Sections and Profiles

Cross sections are a series of elevations taken at *right angles to a baseline* at specific stations, whereas profiles are a series of elevations taken *along a baseline* at some specified repetitive station interval. The elevations thus determined can be plotted on maps and plans either as spot elevations or as contours, or they can be plotted as end areas for construction quantity estimating.

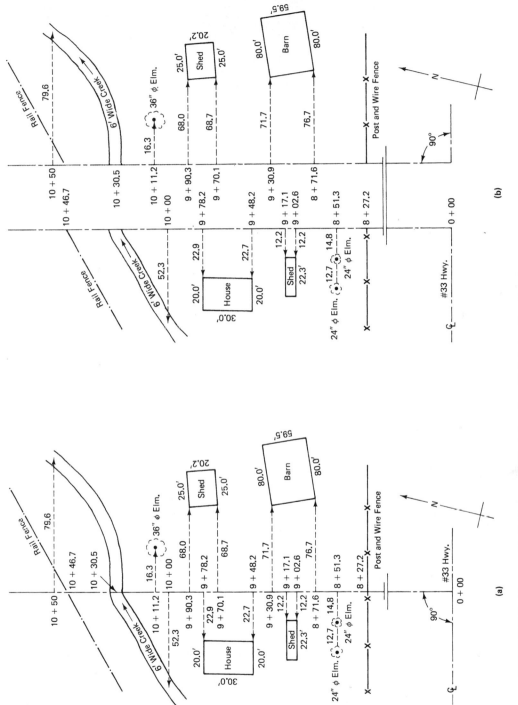

FIGURE 7-2 Topographic field notes. (a) Single baseline. (b) Split baseline.

227

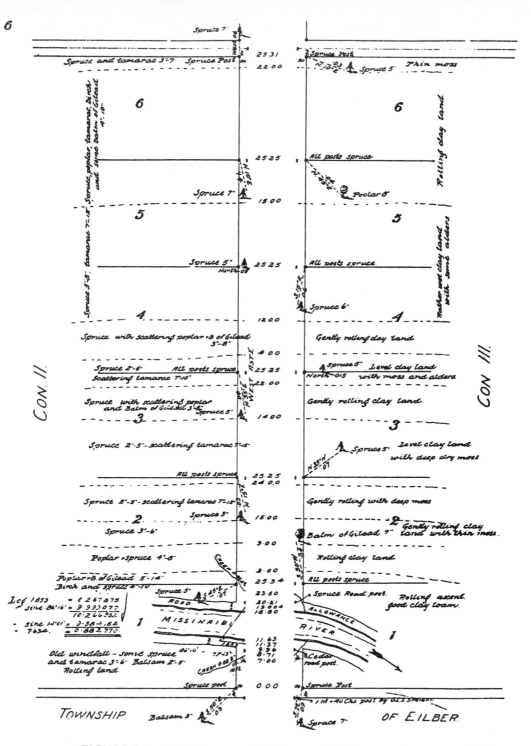

FIGURE 7-3 Original topographic field notes, 1907 (distances shown are in chains).

As in offset ties, the baseline interval is usually 100 ft (20 to 30 m), although in rapidly changing terrain the interval is usually smaller (e.g., 50 ft or 10 to 15 m). In addition to the regular intervals, cross sections are taken at each abrupt change in the terrain (top, bottom of slopes, etc.).

Figure 7-4 illustrates how the rod readings are used to define the ground surface. In Figure 7-4(a), the uniform slope permits a minimum (₵ and both limits of the survey) number of rod readings. In Figure 7-4(b), the varied slope requires several more (than the minimum) rod readings to adequately define the ground surface.

Figure 7-4(c) illustrates how cross sections are taken before and after construction. Chapter 16 covers how to calculate the end area (lined section) at each station and then the volumes of cut and fill.

The profile consists of a series of elevations along the baseline. If cross sections have been taken, the necessary data for plotting a profile will also have been taken. If cross sections are not planned for an area for which a profile is required, the profile elevations can be determined by simply taking rod readings along the line at regular intervals and at all points where the ground slope changes (see Figure 3-18).

Typical field notes for profile leveling are shown in Figure 3-19. Cross sections are booked in two different formats. Figure 3-22 shows cross sections booked in standard level note format. All the rod readings for one station (that can be "seen" from the HI) are booked together. In Figure 3-23, the same data are entered in a format popular with highway agencies. The latter format is more compact and thus takes less space in the field book; the former format takes more space in the field book, but allows for a description for each rod reading, an important consideration for municipal surveyors.

The assumption in this and the previous section is that the data are being collected by conventional offset ties and cross-section methods (i.e., steel and cloth tapes for the tie-ins and a level and rod for the cross sections). In municipal work, a crew of four surveyors can be efficiently utilized. While the party chief is making sketches for the detail tie-ins, the instrument operator (rod readings and bookings) and two rod holders (one on the tape, the other on the rod) can perform the cross sections.

In cases where the terrain is very rugged, making the level and rod work very time consuming (many instrument setups), the survey can be performed by stadia (see Section 7-5), all the elevation rod shots being kept on cross-section station lines. If stadia precision is sufficient, the plan detail location can also be accomplished by using stadia.

Chapter 5 describes Total Station instruments. These instruments, which use polar techniques similar to stadia, but much more effectively, can measure distances and differences in elevation very quickly; the surveyor holds a reflecting prism mounted on a range pole instead of holding a rod. Many of these instruments have the distance and elevation data recorded automatically for future computer processing, while others require that the data be manually entered into the data recorder. Either method could be used to advantage on a multitude of other surveying projects, including right-angle offset tie-ins and cross sections.

7-5 Stadia Principles

Stadia is a tacheometric form of distance measurement that relies on a fixed-angle intercept. Stadia is used on topographic surveys where a limiting accuracy of 1/400 will be

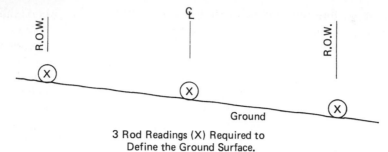

3 Rod Readings (X) Required to
Define the Ground Surface.

(a)

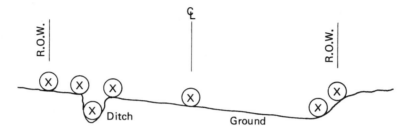

7 Rod Readings (X) Required to
Define this Ground Surface.

(b)

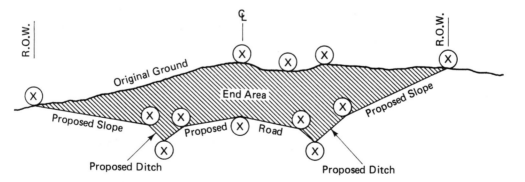

5 Rod Readings (X) Required to Define Original Ground Surface.
9 Rod Readings (X) Required to Define the Constructed Ground Surface.

(c)

FIGURE 7-4 Cross sections used to define ground surface. (a) Uniform slope. (b) Varied slope. (c) Ground surface before and after construction.

acceptable. As noted earlier, stadia is ideally suited for the location of natural features that themselves cannot be precisely defined or located.

The transit (some levels) crosshair reticle has, in addition to the normal crosshairs, two additional horizontal hairs [see Figure 7-5(a)], one above and the other below the main horizontal hair. The stadia hairs are positioned in the reticle so that, if a rod is held 100 ft (m) away from the transit (telescope level), the difference between the upper and lower stadia hair readings (rod interval) is exactly 1.00 ft (m). It can be seen [Figure 7-5(b)] that distances can be determined simply by sighting a rod with the telescope level and determining the rod interval; the rod interval is then multiplied by 100 to get the horizontal distance:

$$D = 100S \qquad (7\text{-}1)$$

Elevations can be determined by stadia in the manner illustrated in Figure 7-5(c). The elevation of the instrument station A is usually determined by using a level and rod. When the transit is set up on the station in preparation for a stadia survey, the height of the optical center of the instrument above the top of stake (hi) is measured with a tape and noted in the field book. A rod reading can then be taken on the rod with the telescope level. The elevation of the point B where the rod is being held is

$$\text{Elevation of station } A(\overline{\wedge}) + \text{hi} - \text{RR} = \text{elevation of point } B \text{ (rod)} \qquad (7\text{-}2)$$

Note: In stadia work, hi is the vertical distance from the station to the optical center of the transit, whereas in leveling work HI is the elevation of the line of sight through the level.

The optical center of the transit is at the center of the telescope at the horizontal axis. The exact point is marked with a cross, colored dot, or screw. Measuring the hi (height of instrument) with a tape is not exact because the tape must be bent over the circle assembly when one is measuring; however, the error encountered when this method is used will not significantly affect the stadia results. The hi can also be measured with the rod.

Figure 7-5(d) illustrates that the location of point B (rod) can be tied in by angle to a reference baseline X-A-Y. The plan location of point B can now be plotted using the angle from the reference line and the distance as determined by Equation (7-1). The elevation of point B can also be plotted, either as a spot elevation or as a component of a series of contours. It can be seen that the stadia method permits the surveyor to determine the three-dimensional location of any point with just one set of observations.

7-6 Inclined Stadia Measurements

The discussion so far has assumed that the stadia observations were taken with the telescope level; however, the stadia method is particularly well suited for the inclined measurements required by rolling topography.

When the telescope is inclined up or down, the computations must be modified to account for the effects of the sloped sighting. Inclined sights require consideration in two areas: (1) The distance from the instrument to the rod must be reduced from slope to horizontal, and (2) the rod interval of a sloped sighting must be reduced to what the interval would have been if the line of sight had been perpendicular to the rod.

Figure 7-6 illustrates these two considerations. The value of hi and the rod reading (RR) have been made equal to clarify the sketch. The geometric relationships are as

Cross Hair Reticle

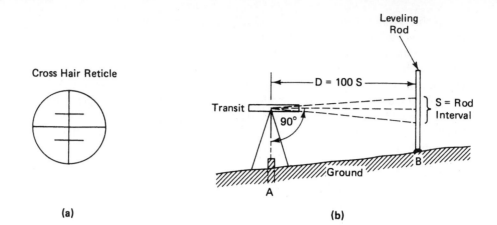

(a)

(b)

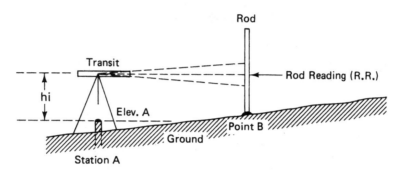

Elevation A. + hi − R.R. = Elevation B.

(c)

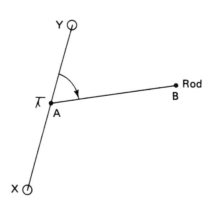

(d)

FIGURE 7-5 Stadia principles. (a) Stadia hairs. (b) Distance determination. (c) Elevation determination. (d) Angle determination.

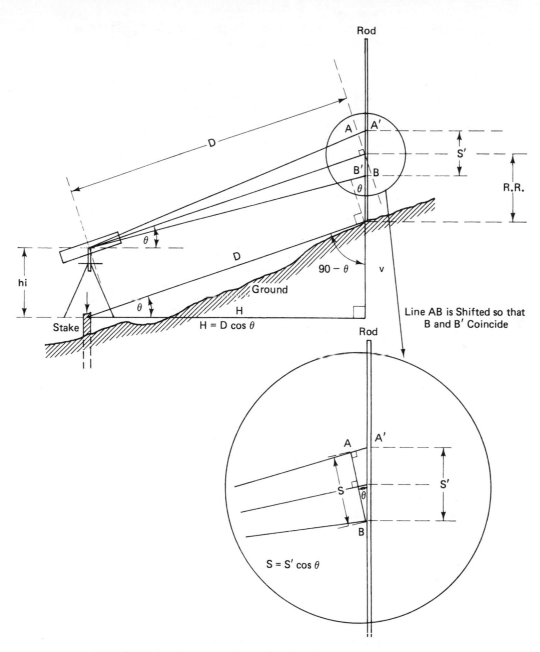

FIGURE 7-6 Geometry of an inclined stadia measurement.

follows: (1) S is the rod interval when the line of sight is horizontal, and (2) S' is the rod interval when the line of sight is inclined by angle θ.

$$D = 100S \qquad\qquad \text{Figure 7-5(b)} \qquad\qquad (7\text{-}1)$$

$$S = S' \cos \theta \qquad\qquad \text{Figure 7-6} \qquad\qquad (7\text{-}3)$$

$$D = 100S' \cos \theta \qquad\qquad \text{From Equations (7-3) and (7-1)} \qquad\qquad (7\text{-}4)$$

$$H = D \cos \theta \qquad\qquad \text{Figure 7-6} \qquad\qquad (7\text{-}5)$$

$$\boldsymbol{H = 100S' \cos^2\theta} \qquad\qquad \text{From Equations (7-4) and (7-5)} \qquad\qquad (7\text{-}6)$$

$$V = D \sin \theta \qquad\qquad \text{Figure 7-6} \qquad\qquad (7\text{-}7)$$

$$D = 100S' \cos \theta \qquad\qquad\qquad\qquad (7\text{-}4)$$

$$\boldsymbol{V = 100S' \cos \theta \sin \theta} \qquad \text{From Equations (7-7) and (7-4)} \qquad\qquad (7\text{-}8)$$

Since most modern theodolites will read only zenith angles $(90 - \theta)$, it is necessary to modify Equations (7-6) and (7-8).

$$\boldsymbol{H = 100 \; s' \sin^2 (90 - \theta)} \qquad\qquad (7\text{-}6a)$$

$$\boldsymbol{V = 100 \; s' \sin (90 - \theta) \cos (90 - \theta)} \qquad\qquad (7\text{-}8a)$$

Equations (7-6) and (7-8) can be used in computing the horizontal distance and difference in elevation for any inclined stadia measurement.

In the past, special slide rules and/or tables were used to compute H and V. However, with the universal use of handheld calculators, slide rules and stadia tables have become less popular. The computations can be accomplished just as quickly by working with Equations (7-6) and (7-8). Stadia reduction tables are given in Table 7-1. The table is entered at the value of the VCR (vertical circle reading), with the horizontal distance factor and the difference in elevation factor both being multiplied by the rod interval to give H and V. See Examples 7-1 and 7-2.

Figure 7-7 shows the general case of an inclined stadia measurement, which can be stated as follows:

$$\textbf{Elevation } (\overline{\wedge}) \textbf{ station } K + \textbf{hi} \pm V - \textbf{RR} = \textbf{elevation (rod) point } M \qquad (7\text{-}9)$$

The relationship is valid for every stadia measurement. If the hi and RR are equal, Equation (7-9) becomes

$$\textbf{Elevation } (\overline{\wedge}) \textbf{ station } K \pm V = \textbf{elevation (rod) point } M \qquad (7\text{-}10)$$

as the hi and RR cancel out each other. In practice, the surveyor will read the rod at the value of the hi unless that value is obscured (e.g., by a tree branch, vehicle, rise of land). If the hi value cannot be sighted, usually a value an even foot (decimeter) above or below is sighted, allowing for a mental correction to the calculation. Of course, if an even foot (decimeter) above or below the desired value cannot be read, *any value* can be read and Equation (7-9) is used.

Table 7-1 STADIA TABLES

Example: VCR = −3°21′
Rod interval = 0.123 m
From tables: $V = 5.83 \times 0.123 = 0.72$ m
$H = 99.66 \times 0.123 = 12.3$ m

Minutes	0°		1°		2°		3°	
	Hor. Dist.	Diff. Elev.	Hor. Dist.	Diff. Elev.	Hor. Dist.	Diff. Elev.	Hor. Dist.	Diff. Elev.
0	100.00	.00	99.97	1.74	99.88	3.49	99.73	5.23
2	100.00	.06	99.97	1.80	99.87	3.55	99.72	5.28
4	100.00	.12	99.97	1.86	99.87	3.60	99.71	5.34
6	100.00	.17	99.96	1.92	99.87	3.66	99.71	5.40
8	100.00	.23	99.96	1.98	99.86	3.72	99.70	5.46
10	100.00	.29	99.96	2.04	99.86	3.78	99.69	5.52
12	100.00	.35	99.96	2.09	99.85	3.84	99.69	5.57
14	100.00	.41	99.95	2.15	99.85	3.89	99.68	5.63
16	100.00	.47	99.95	2.21	99.84	3.95	99.68	5.69
18	100.00	.52	99.95	2.27	99.84	4.01	99.67	5.75
20	100.00	.58	99.95	2.33	99.83	4.07	99.66	5.80
22	100.00	.64	99.94	2.38	99.83	4.13	99.66	5.86
24	100.00	.70	99.94	2.44	99.82	4.18	99.65	5.92
26	99.99	.76	99.94	2.50	99.82	4.24	99.64	5.98
28	99.99	.81	99.93	2.56	99.81	4.30	99.63	6.04
30	99.99	.87	99.93	2.62	99.81	4.36	99.63	6.09
32	99.99	.93	99.93	2.67	99.80	4.42	99.62	6.15
34	99.99	.99	99.93	2.73	99.80	4.47	99.61	6.21
36	99.99	1.05	99.92	2.79	99.79	4.53	99.61	6.27
38	99.99	1.11	99.92	2.85	99.79	4.59	99.60	6.32
40	99.99	1.16	99.92	2.91	99.78	4.65	99.59	6.38
42	99.99	1.22	99.91	2.97	99.78	4.71	99.58	6.44
44	99.98	1.28	99.91	3.02	99.77	4.76	99.58	6.50
46	99.98	1.34	99.90	3.08	99.77	4.82	99.57	6.56
48	99.98	1.40	99.90	3.14	99.76	4.88	99.56	6.61
50	99.98	1.45	99.90	3.20	99.76	4.94	99.55	6.67
52	99.98	1.51	99.89	3.26	99.75	4.99	99.55	6.73
54	99.98	1.57	99.89	3.31	99.74	5.05	99.54	6.79
56	99.97	1.63	99.89	3.37	99.74	5.11	99.53	6.84
58	99.97	1.69	99.88	3.43	99.73	5.17	99.52	6.90
60	99.97	1.74	99.88	3.49	99.73	5.23	99.51	6.96

(continued)

Table 7-1 *(continued)*

Minutes	4° Hor. Dist.	4° Diff. Elev.	5° Hor. Dist.	5° Diff. Elev.	6° Hor. Dist.	6° Diff. Elev.	7° Hor. Dist.	7° Diff. Elev.
0	99.51	6.96	99.24	8.68	98.91	10.40	98.51	12.10
2	99.51	7.02	99.23	8.74	98.90	10.45	98.50	12.15
4	99.50	7.07	99.22	8.80	98.88	10.51	98.49	12.21
6	99.49	7.13	99.21	8.85	98.87	10.57	98.47	12.27
8	99.48	7.19	99.20	8.91	98.86	10.62	98.46	12.32
10	99.47	7.25	99.19	8.97	98.85	10.68	98.44	12.38
12	99.46	7.30	99.18	9.03	98.83	10.74	98.43	12.43
14	99.46	7.36	99.17	9.08	98.82	10.79	98.41	12.49
16	99.45	7.42	99.16	9.14	98.81	10.85	98.40	12.55
18	99.44	7.48	99.15	9.20	98.80	10.91	98.39	12.60
20	99.43	7.53	99.14	9.25	98.78	10.96	98.37	12.66
22	99.42	7.59	99.13	9.31	98.77	11.02	98.36	12.72
24	99.41	7.65	99.11	9.37	98.76	11.08	98.34	12.77
26	99.40	7.71	99.10	9.43	98.74	11.13	98.33	12.83
28	99.39	7.76	99.09	9.48	98.73	11.19	98.31	12.88
30	99.38	7.82	99.08	9.54	98.72	11.25	98.30	12.94
32	99.38	7.88	99.07	9.60	98.71	11.30	98.28	13.00
34	99.37	7.94	99.06	9.65	98.69	11.36	98.27	13.05
36	99.36	7.99	99.05	9.71	98.68	11.42	98.25	13.11
38	99.35	8.05	99.04	9.77	98.67	11.47	98.24	13.17
40	99.34	8.11	99.03	9.83	98.65	11.53	98.22	13.22
42	99.33	8.17	99.01	9.88	98.64	11.59	98.20	13.28
44	99.32	8.22	99.00	9.94	98.63	11.64	98.19	13.33
46	99.31	8.28	98.99	10.00	98.61	11.70	98.17	13.39
48	99.30	8.34	98.98	10.05	98.60	11.76	98.16	13.45
50	99.29	8.40	98.97	10.11	98.58	11.81	98.14	13.50
52	99.28	8.45	98.96	10.17	98.57	11.87	98.13	13.56
54	99.27	8.51	98.94	10.22	98.56	11.93	98.11	13.61
56	99.26	8.57	98.93	10.28	98.54	11.98	98.10	13.67
58	99.25	8.63	98.92	10.34	98.53	12.04	98.08	13.73
60	99.24	8.68	98.91	10.40	98.51	12.10	98.06	13.78

Table 7-1 *(continued)*

Minutes	8°		9°		10°		11°	
	Hor. Dist.	Diff. Elev.	Hor. Dist.	Diff. Elev.	Hor. Dist.	Diff. Elev.	Hor. Dist.	Diff. Elev.
0	98.06	13.78	97.55	15.45	96.98	17.10	96.36	18.73
2	98.05	13.84	97.53	15.51	96.96	17.16	96.34	18.78
4	98.03	13.89	97.52	15.56	96.94	17.21	96.32	18.84
6	98.01	13.95	97.50	15.62	96.92	17.26	56.29	18.89
8	98.00	14.01	97.48	15.67	96.90	17.32	96.27	18.95
10	97.98	14.06	97.46	15.73	96.88	17.37	96.25	19.00
12	97.97	14.12	97.44	15.78	96.86	17.43	96.23	19.05
14	97.95	14.17	97.43	15.84	96.84	17.48	96.21	19.11
16	97.93	14.23	97.41	15.89	96.82	17.54	96.18	19.10
18	97.92	14.28	97.39	15.95	96.80	17.59	96.16	19.21
20	97.90	14.34	97.37	16.00	96.78	17.65	96.14	19.27
22	97.88	14.40	97.35	16.06	96.76	17.70	96.12	19.32
24	97.87	14.45	97.33	16.11	96.74	17.76	96.09	19.38
26	97.85	14.51	97.31	16.17	96.72	17.81	96.07	19.43
28	97.83	14.56	97.29	16.22	96.70	17.86	96.05	19.48
30	97.82	14.62	97.28	16.28	96.68	17.92	96.03	19.54
32	97.80	14.67	97.26	16.33	96.66	17.97	96.00	19.59
34	97.78	14.73	97.24	16.39	96.64	18.03	95.98	19.64
36	97.76	14.79	97.22	16.44	96.62	18.08	95.96	19.70
38	97.75	14.84	97.20	16.50	96.60	18.14	95.93	19.75
40	97.73	14.90	97.18	16.55	96.57	18.19	95.91	19.80
42	97.71	14.95	97.16	16.61	96.55	18.24	95.89	19.86
44	97.69	15.01	97.14	16.66	96.53	18.30	95.86	19.91
46	97.68	15.06	97.12	16.72	96.51	18.35	95.84	19.96
48	97.66	15.12	97.10	16.77	96.49	18.41	95.82	20.02
50	97.64	15.17	97.08	16.83	96.47	18.46	95.79	20.07
52	97.62	15.23	97.06	16.88	96.45	18.51	95.77	20.12
54	97.61	15.28	97.04	16.94	96.42	18.57	95.75	20.18
56	97.59	15.34	97.02	16.99	96.40	18.62	95.72	20.23
58	97.57	15.40	97.00	17.05	96.38	18.68	95.70	20.28
60	97.55	15.45	96.98	17.10	96.36	18.73	95.68	20.34

(continued)

Table 7-1 (continued)

Minutes	12°		13°		14°		15°	
	Hor. Dist.	Diff. Elev.	Hor. Dist.	Diff. Elev.	Hor. Dist.	Diff. Elev.	Hor. Dist.	Diff. Elev.
0	95.68	20.34	94.94	21.92	94.15	23.47	93.30	25.00
2	95.65	20.39	94.91	21.97	94.12	23.52	93.27	25.05
4	95.63	20.44	94.89	22.02	94.09	23.58	93.24	25.10
6	95.61	20.50	94.86	22.08	94.07	23.63	93.21	25.15
8	95.58	20.55	94.84	22.13	94.04	23.68	93.18	25.20
10	95.56	20.60	94.81	22.18	94.01	23.73	93.16	25.25
12	95.53	20.66	94.79	22.23	93.98	23.78	93.13	25.30
14	95.51	20.71	94.76	22.28	93.95	23.83	93.10	25.35
16	95.49	20.76	94.73	22.34	93.93	23.88	93.07	25.40
18	95.46	20.81	94.71	22.39	93.90	23.93	93.04	25.45
20	95.44	20.87	94.68	22.44	93.87	23.99	93.01	25.50
22	95.41	20.92	94.66	22.49	93.84	24.04	92.98	25.55
24	95.39	20.97	94.63	22.54	93.82	24.09	92.95	25.60
26	95.36	21.03	94.60	22.60	93.79	24.14	92.92	25.65
28	95.34	21.08	94.58	22.65	93.76	24.19	92.89	25.70
30	95.32	21.13	94.55	22.70	93.73	24.24	92.86	25.75
32	95.29	21.18	94.52	22.75	93.70	24.29	92.83	25.80
34	95.27	21.24	94.50	22.80	93.67	24.34	92.80	25.85
36	95.24	21.29	94.47	22.85	93.65	24.39	92.77	25.90
38	95.22	21.34	94.44	22.91	93.62	24.44	92.74	25.95
40	95.19	21.39	94.42	22.96	93.59	24.49	92.71	26.00
42	95.17	21.45	94.39	23.01	93.56	24.55	92.68	26.05
44	95.14	21.50	94.36	23.06	93.53	24.60	92.65	26.10
46	95.12	21.55	94.34	23.11	93.50	24.65	92.62	26.15
48	95.09	21.60	94.31	23.16	93.47	24.70	92.59	26.20
50	95.07	21.66	94.28	23.22	93.45	24.75	92.56	26.25
52	95.04	21.71	94.26	23.27	93.42	24.80	92.53	26.30
54	95.02	21.76	94.23	23.32	93.39	24.85	92.49	26.35
56	94.99	21.81	94.20	23.37	93.36	24.90	92.46	26.40
58	94.97	21.87	94.17	23.42	93.33	24.95	92.43	26.45
60	94.94	21.92	94.15	23.47	93.30	25.00	92.40	26.50

7-7 Examples of Stadia Measurement Computations

There are three basic variations to a standard stadia measurement:

1. The rod reading is taken to be the same as the hi.
2. The rod reading is not the same as the hi.
3. The telescope is horizontal.

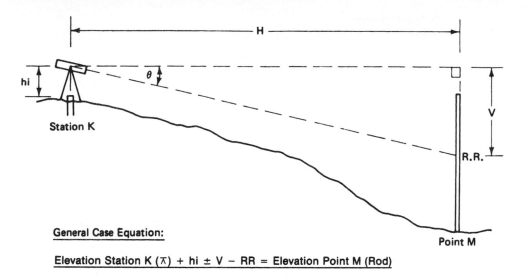

General Case Equation:

Elevation Station K ($\bar{\pi}$) + hi ± V − RR = Elevation Point M (Rod)

FIGURE 7-7 General case of an inclined stadia measurement.

■ **EXAMPLE 7-1**

This example, where the rod reading has been made to coincide with the value of the hi, is typical of 90 percent of all stadia measurements (see Figures 7-8 and 7-11). Here, the VCR is +1°36′, and the rod interval is 0.401. Both the hi and the rod reading are 1.72 m.

From Equation (7-6),

$$H = 100S'\cos^2\theta$$
$$= 100 \times 0.401 \times \cos^2 1°36'$$
$$= 40.1 \text{ m}$$

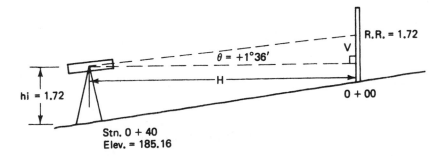

FIGURE 7-8 Example 7-1, RR = hi.

From Equation (7-8),

$$V = 100S' \cos \theta \sin \theta$$
$$= 100 \times 0.401 \times \cos 1°36' \times \sin 1°36'$$
$$= +1.12 \text{ m (algebraic sign is given by the VCR)}$$

From Equation (7-10),

$$\text{Elev. } (\overline{\wedge}) \pm V = \text{elev. (rod)}$$
$$185.16 + 1.12 = 186.28$$
$$\text{See STA. } 0 + 00 \text{ in Figure 7-11.}$$

From Table 7-1,

$$\text{VCR} = +1°36', \text{ rod interval} = 0.401$$
$$H = 99.92 \times 0.401 = 40.1 \text{ m}$$
$$V = 2.79 \times 0.401 = +1.12 \text{ m}$$

■ EXAMPLE 7-2

This example illustrates the case where the value of the hi cannot be seen on the rod due to some obstruction (see Figures 7-9 and 7-11). In this case, a rod reading of 2.72 with a vertical angle of −6°37′ was booked, along with the hi of 1.72 and a rod in-terval of 0.241.

From Equation (7-6),

$$H = 100S' \cos^2 \theta$$
$$= 100 \times 0.241 \times \cos^2 6°37'$$
$$= 23.8 \text{ m}$$

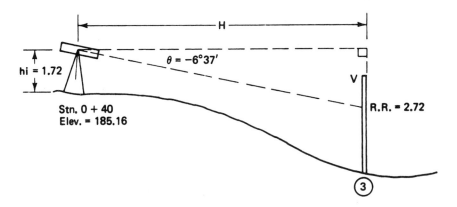

FIGURE 7-9   Example 7-2, RR ≠ hi.

From Equation (7-8),

$$V = 100S' \cos \theta \sin \theta$$
$$= 100 \times 0.241 \times \cos 6°37' \times \sin 6°37'$$
$$= -2.76 \text{ m (algebraic sign is given by the VCR)}$$

From Equation (7-9),

$$\text{Elev. } (\overline{\wedge}) + \text{hi} \pm V - \text{RR} = \text{elev. (rod)}$$
$$185.16 + 1.72 - 2.76 - 2.72 = 181.40$$

See STA. 3 in Figure 7-11.

From Table 7-1,

$$\text{VCR} = -6°37', \text{ rod interval} = 0.241$$
$$H = 98.675 \text{ (interpolated)} \times 0.241 = 23.8 \text{ m}$$
$$V = 11.445 \text{ (interpolated)} \times 0.241 = -2.76 \text{ m}$$

■ EXAMPLE 7-3

This example illustrates the situation where the ground is level enough to permit horizontal rod sightings (see Figures 7-10 and 7-11). The computations for this observation are quite simple; the horizontal distance is simply 100 times the rod interval [$D = 100S$, Equation (7-1)]. Since there is no vertical angle, there is no triangle to solve (i.e., $V = 0$). The difference in elevation is simply $+\text{hi} - \text{RR}$.

      If the survey is in a level area where many observations can be taken with the telescope level, this technique will speed up the survey computations and the field time. (Vertical angles are not read.) However, if the survey is in typical rolling topography, the surveyor normally will not spend the time necessary to see if a single horizontal observation can be made; the surveyor will instead continue sighting the rod at the hi value to maintain the momentum of the survey (a good instrument surveyor can keep two rod surveyors busy).

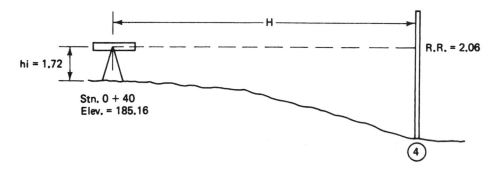

FIGURE 7-10 Example 7-3, telescope horizontal.

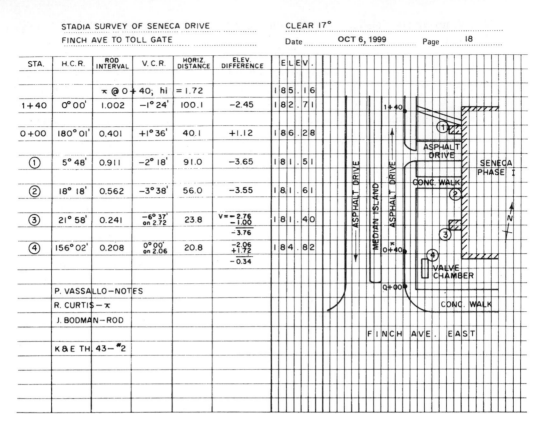

STADIA SURVEY OF SENECA DRIVE   CLEAR 17°

FINCH AVE TO TOLL GATE   Date   OCT 6, 1999   Page   18

STA.	H.C.R.	ROD INTERVAL	V.C.R.	HORIZ. DISTANCE	ELEV. DIFFERENCE	ELEV.
			⊼ @ 0 + 40; hi = 1.72			185.16
1+40	0° 00'	1.002	−1° 24'	100.1	−2.45	182.71
0 +00	180° 01'	0.401	+1° 36'	40.1	+1.12	186.28
①	5° 48'	0.911	−2° 18'	91.0	−3.65	181.51
②	18° 18'	0.562	−3° 38'	56.0	−3.55	181.61
③	21° 58'	0.241	−6° 37' on 2.72	23.8	V = −2.76 / −1.00 / −3.76	181.40
④	156° 02'	0.208	0° 00' on 2.06	20.8	−2.06 / +1.72 / −0.34	184.82
	P. VASSALLO−NOTES					
	R. CURTIS − ⊼					
	J. BODMAN−ROD					
	K & E TH. 43−#2					

FIGURE 7-11   Stadia field notes.

In this example, a rod interval of 0.208 was booked, together with the hi of 1.72 and a rod reading of 2.06. From Equation (7-1),

$$D = 100S$$
$$= 100 \times 0.208$$
$$= 20.8 \text{ m (horizontal distance)}$$

From Equation (7-9),

$$\text{Elev. } (\overline{\curvearrowleft}) + \text{hi} + V - RR = \text{elev. (rod)}$$
$$185.16 + 1.72 + 0 - 2.06 = 184.82$$
See STA. 4 on Figure 7-11.

7-8   Stadia Field Practice

In stadia work, the transit is set on a point for which the horizontal location and elevation have been determined. If necessary, the elevation of the transit station can be determined after setup by sighting on a point of known elevation and working backward through Equation (7-9).

The horizontal circle is zeroed, and a sight is taken on another control point (1 + 40 in Figure 7-11). All stadia pointings are accomplished by working on the circle utilizing the clamp and tangent screw. It is a good idea to periodically check the zero setting by sighting back on the original backsight; this will ensure that the setting has not been invalidated by inadvertent use of the clamp. At a bare minimum, a zero check is made just before the instrument is moved from the transit station; if the check proves that the setting has been inadvertently moved from zero, all the work must be repeated.

Before any observations are made, the hi is measured with a steel tape (sometimes with the leveling rod), and the value is booked, as shown in Figure 7-11.

The actual observation proceeds as follows: After the horizontal circle has been zeroed on the appropriate backsight station and with the circle clamp loosened, the rod is sighted; precise setting can be accomplished by the tangent screw after the clamp has been locked. The main crosshair is sighted approximately to the value of the hi, and then the telescope is revolved up or down until the lower stadia hair is on the closest even foot (decimeter) mark. The upper stadia hair is then read and the rod interval determined mentally by simply subtracting the lower hair reading from the upper hair reading. After the rod interval is booked (see Figure 7-11), the main crosshair is then moved to read the value of the hi on the rod. When this has been accomplished, the rod holder is waved off and begins walking to the next point, while the instrument operator reads and books the VCR and the HCR (horizontal circle reading) (see Figure 7-11). Usually the calculations for horizontal distance and elevation are performed after field hours.

The technique of temporarily moving the lower stadia hair to an even value to facilitate the determination of the rod interval introduces errors in the readings, but these errors are not large enough to significantly affect the results. The alternative to this technique would be to initially lock the main hair on the value of the hi and then read and book the upper and lower hair readings. When the lower hair is subtracted from the upper hair, the result can then be booked as the rod interval. This alternative technique is more precise, but it is far too cumbersome and time consuming for general use.

If the value of the hi cannot be seen on the rod, another value (e.g., even foot or decimeter above or below the hi) can be sighted, and that value is booked along with the vertical angle in the VCR column (see Figure 7-11, STA. 3).

If the telescope is level, the rod reading is booked in the VCR column alone or together with 0°00' (see Figure 7-11, STA. 4).

It sometimes happens that the entire rod interval cannot be seen on the rod (e.g., due to tree branches, intervening ground, extra-long shots); in this case, half the rod interval can be read and that value doubled and then entered in the rod interval column. Reading only half the rod interval reduces the precision considerably, so extra care should be taken when one is determining the half-interval.

Generally, if the relative accuracy ratio of 1/300 to 1/400 is to be maintained on long sights and on steeply inclined sights, extra care is required (particularly in reading the rod, plumbing the rod, etc.).

Stadia methods can be used to establish secondary control points or even to establish closed traverses that will be used for topographic stadia control. The technique essentially consists of taking stadia observations from both ends of each line and then averaging the results to obtain horizontal distances and differences in elevation. The double readings provide an increase in precision, which permits stations so established to be used as control for further stadia work.

7-9 Self-Reducing Stadia Theodolite

The self-reducing instrument (also known as a reduction tacheometer) is a theodolite designed specifically for stadia observations. Instead of the reticle with two stadia hairs and a main horizontal hair, the self-reducing stadia theodolite comes equipped with three curved lines of varying radii. As the telescope is moved up or down, the interval between the hairs changes. For example, the interval between the main (lower) hair and the upper hair moves in such a way that 100 times the rod interval automatically gives the horizontal distance, regardless of the vertical angle.

The middle hair is also moving, so that the interval between the middle hair (elevation curve) and the main hair, when multiplied by some factor, gives the difference in elevation. In some instruments, the elevation factor is 100. In other instruments, the elevation factor is shown in the telescopic field of view; in this case, the algebraic sign and magnitude of the elevation factor (as viewed in the telescope) change as the telescope is revolved (see Figure 7-12).

Some systems employ an extension to the stadia rod that permits the decimal portion of the hi value to be extended down from the zero mark of the rod. This facilitates the

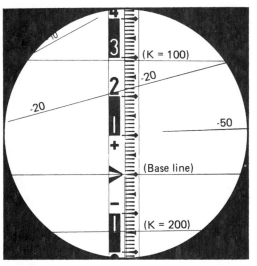

Reticule of the Dahlta 010A tacheometer.

FIGURE 7-12 Self-reducing stadia theodolite rod readings. (Courtesy of Zeiss JENA Instruments Ltd.)

Example:
1. Horizontal distance
   @ K = 100, interval = 0.292, distance = 29.2 m.
   @ K = 200, interval = 0.146, distance = 29.2 m.
2. Difference in elevation
   Elevation interval = 0.218
   Difference in elevation = 0.218 x (-20) = -4.36 m.

sighting of the hi value on the rod. For example, when this rod is used, if the hi is 1.201 m, the graduated extension to the rod is lowered 0.201 m, permitting the stadia surveyor to quickly sight 1.000 on the rod each time the hi value is to be sighted.

Essentially the advantage to the self-reducing technique is that the time-consuming, after-hours computations have been eliminated. The additional cost for a self-reducing stadia theodolite can be recouped quickly if many stadia surveys are required. When not being used for stadia work, the self-reducing stadia theodolite can be employed in the same manner as any 1″ theodolite.

7-10   Summary of Stadia Field Procedure

1. Set the theodolite over station.
2. Measure the hi with a steel tape.
3. Set the horizontal circle to zero.
4. Sight the reference station at 0°00′.
5. Sight the stadia point by loosening the clamp (clamp is tight).
6. Sight the main horizontal hair roughly on the value of the hi, then move the lower hair to the closest even foot (decimeter) mark.
7. Read the upper hair; determine the rod interval, and enter that value in the notes.
8. Sight the main horizontal hair precisely on the hi value.
9. Wave off the rod holder.
10. Read and book the horizontal (HCR) angle and the vertical (VCR) angle.
11. Check the zero setting for the horizontal angle before moving the instrument.
12. Reduce the notes (compute horizontal distances and elevations) after field hours; check the reductions.

NOTES

1. If the hi cannot be sighted, any point on the rod can be sighted, and that rod reading is then booked along with the vertical angle to that rod reading.
2. For modern theodolites, the zenith angle may be booked instead of the vertical angle, with the angle conversion taking place with the field notes reductions.
3. For self-reducing stadia theodolites, use of an extendable-foot rod permits all main-hair sightings to be at an even foot (decimeter) and greatly speeds up this method.

7-11   Survey Drafting

Survey drafting is a term that covers a wide range of scale graphics, including both manual and automatic plotting. *Maps,* which are usually drawn at a small scale, portray an inventory of all the topographic detail included in the survey specifications; on the other hand, *plans,* which are usually drawn at a much larger scale, not only show the existing terrain conditions, but also can contain proposed locations for newly designed construction works. Table 7-2 shows typical scales for maps and plans, and Table 7-3 shows standard drawing sizes for both the foot and the metric systems. See also Section 5-13-3.

Table 7-2 SUMMARY OF MAP SCALES AND CONTOUR INTERVALS

	Metric Scale	Foot/Inch Scale Equivalents	Contour Interval for Average Terrain*	Typical Uses
Large scale	1:10	1″ = 1′		Detail
	1:50	1/4″ = 1′, 1″ = 5′		Detail
	1:100	1/8″ = 1′, 1″ = 10′, 1″ = 8′		Detail, profiles
	1:200	1″ = 20′		Profiles
	1:500	1″ = 40′, 1″ = 50′	0.5 m, 1 ft	Municipal design plans
	1:1000	1″ = 80′, 1″ = 100′	1 m, 2 ft	Municipal services and site engineering
Intermediate scale	1:2000	1″ = 200′	2 m, 5 ft	Engineering studies and planning
	1:5000	1″ = 400′	5 m, 10 ft	(e.g., drainage areas, route planning)
	1:10 000	1″ = 800′	10 m, 20 ft	
Small scale	1:20 000	2 1/2″ = 1 mi		
	1:25 000			
	1:50 000	1″ = 1 mi		Topographic maps, Canada and United States
	1:100 000	1/2″ = 1 mi		Geological maps, Canada and United States
	1:200 000			
	1:250 000	1/4″ = 1 mi		Special purpose maps and atlases
	1:500 000	1/10″ = 1 mi		(e.g., climate, minerals)
	1:1 000 000	1/16″ = 1 mi		

*The contour interval chosen must reflect the scale of the plan or map, but, additionally, the terrain (flat or steeply inclined) and intended use of the plan are also factors in choosing the appropriate contour interval.

Table 7-3 STANDARD DRAWING SIZES

International Standards Organization (ISO)						ACSM* Recommendations	
Inch Drawing Sizes			Metric Drawing Sizes (millimeters)				
Drawing Size	Border Size	Overall Paper Size	Drawing Size	Border Size	Overall Paper Size		Paper Size
A	8.00 × 10.50	8.50 × 11.00	A4	195 × 282	210 × 297	—	150 × 200
B	10.50 × 16.50	11.00 × 17.00	A3	277 × 400	297 × 420	A4	200 × 300
C	16.00 × 21.00	17.00 × 22.00	A2	400 × 574	420 × 594	A3	300 × 400
D	21.00 × 33.00	22.00 × 34.00	A1	574 × 821	594 × 841	A2	400 × 600
E	33.00 × 43.00	34.00 × 44.00	A0	811 × 1159	841 × 1189	A1	600 × 800
						A0	800 × 1200

*American Congress on Surveying and Mapping Metric Workshop, March 14, 1975. Paper sizes rounded off for simplicity, still have cut-in-half characteristic.

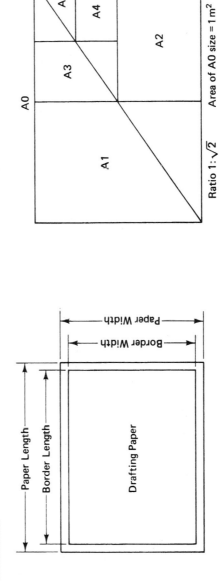

A0

A1

A3

A4

A4

A2

Ratio 1 : $\sqrt{2}$ Area of A0 size = 1 m²

Metric Drawing Paper

Paper Width

Border Width

Paper Length

Border Length

Drafting Paper

The size of drafting paper required can be determined by knowing the scale to be used and the area or length of the survey. Standard paper sizes are shown in Table 7-3. The title block is often a standard size and has a format similar to that shown in Figure 7-13. The title block is usually (depending on the filing system) placed in the lower right corner of the plan. Revisions to the plan are usually referenced immediately above the title block, showing the date and a brief description of the revision.

Many consulting firms and engineering departments attempt to limit the variety of their drawing sizes so that plan filing can be standardized. Some vertical-hold filing cabinets are designed so that title blocks in the upper right corner are more easily seen.

The actual plotting begins by first plotting the survey control (e.g., ℄ traverse line, coordinate grid) on the drawing. The control is plotted so that the data plot will be suitably centered on the available paper. Sometimes the data outline is roughly plotted first on tracing paper so that the plan's dimension requirements can be properly oriented on the available drafting paper. It is customary to orient the data plot so that north is toward the top of the plan; a north arrow is included on all property survey plans and many engineering drawings. The north direction on maps is clearly indicated by lines of longitude or by N-S, E-W grid lines. The plan portion of the plan and profile usually does not have a north indication; instead, local practice dictates the direction of increasing chainage (e.g., chainage increasing left to right for west to east and south to north directions).

Once the control has been plotted and checked, the features can be plotted by utilizing either rectangular (X, Y coordinates) or polar (r, θ coordinates) methods.

Rectangular plots (X, Y coordinates) can be laid out with a T-square and set square (right-angle triangle), although the parallel rule has now largely replaced the T-square. When either the parallel rule or the T-square is used, the paper is first set square and then taped with masking tape to the drawing board. Once the paper is square and secure, the parallel rule, together with a set square and scale, can be used to lay out and measure rec-

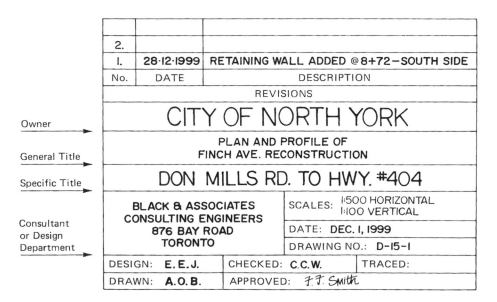

FIGURE 7-13 Typical title block.

tangular dimensions. Since rectangular plotting is more precise than polar plotting (plotting errors are not accumulated), this technique is used for precise work (e.g., control layout, important details) and for the plotting of details that have been tied into baselines with right-angle tie-ins (see Section 7-3).

Polar plots are accomplished by using a protractor and a scale. The protractor can be a plastic graduated circle or half circle having various size diameters (the larger, the more precise), a paper full-circle protractor for use under or on the drafting paper, or a flexible-arm drafting machine complete with right-angle-mounted graduated scales. Field data that have been collected by using polar techniques (stadia is a good example) can be efficiently plotted by utilizing polar techniques. See Figures 7-14 and 7-15 for standard map and plan symbols.

7-12   Contours

Contours are lines drawn on a plan that connect points having the same elevation. Contour lines represent an even value (see Table 7-2), with the contour interval being selected consistent with the terrain, scale, and intended use of the plan. It is commonly accepted that elevations can be determined to half the contour interval; this permits, for example, a 10-ft contour interval on a plan where it is required to know elevations to the closest 5 ft.

Contours are plotted by scaling between two adjacent points of known elevation. In Figure 7-16(a), the scaled distance (any scale can be used) between points 1 and 2 is 0.75 unit, and the difference in elevation is 5.4 ft. The difference in elevation between point 1 and contour line 565 is 2.7 ft; therefore, the distance from point 1 to contour line 565 is

$$\frac{2.7}{5.4} \times 0.75 = 0.38 \text{ unit}$$

To verify this computation, the distance from contour line 565 to point 2 is

$$\frac{2.7}{5.4} \times 0.75 = 0.38 \text{ unit} \qquad 0.38 + 0.38 \approx 0.75 \qquad \text{Check}$$

The scaled distance between points 3 and 4 is 0.86 unit, and their difference in elevation is 5.2 ft. The difference in elevation between point 3 and contour line 565 is 1.7 ft; therefore, the distance from point 3 to contour line 565 is

$$\frac{1.7}{5.2} \times 0.86 = 0.28 \text{ unit}$$

This can be verified by computing the distance from contour line 565 to point 4:

$$\frac{3.5}{5.2} \times 0.86 = 0.58 \text{ unit} \qquad 0.58 + 0.28 = 0.86 \qquad \text{Check}$$

The scaled distance between points 5 and 6 is 0.49 unit, and the difference in elevation is 5.6 ft. The difference in elevation between point 5 and contour line 565 is 0.9 ft; therefore, the distance from point 5 to contour line 565 is

$$\frac{0.9}{5.6} \times 0.49 = 0.08 \text{ unit}$$

Primary highway, hard surface	
Secondary highway, hard surface	
Light-duty road, hard or improved surface	
Unimproved road	
Road under construction, alignment known	
Proposed road	
Dual highway, dividing strip 25 feet or less	
Dual highway, dividing strip exceeding 25 feet	
Trail	

Railroad: single track and multiple track	
Railroads in juxtaposition	
Narrow gage: single track and multiple track	
Railroad in street and carline	
Bridge: road and railroad	
Drawbridge: road and railroad	
Footbridge	
Tunnel: road and railroad	
Overpass and underpass	
Small masonry or concrete dam	
Dam with lock	
Dam with road	
Canal with lock	

Buildings (dwelling, place of employment, etc.)	
School, church, and cemetery	Cem
Buildings (barn, warehouse, etc.)	
Power transmission line with located metal tower	
Telephone line, pipeline, etc. (labeled as to type)	
Wells other than water (labeled as to type)	o Oil . . . . . o Gas
Tanks: oil, water, etc. (labeled only if water)	o ● ● Water
Located or landmark object; windmill	o . . . . ⌶
Open pit, mine, or quarry; prospect	× x
Shaft and tunnel entrance	■ . . . . Y

Horizontal and vertical control station:

Tablet, spirit level elevation	BM △ 5653
Other recoverable mark, spirit level elevation	△ 5455
Horizontal control station: tablet, vertical angle elevation	VABM △ 95/9
Any recoverable mark, vertical angle or checked elevation	△ 3775
Vertical control station: tablet, spirit level elevation	BM × 957
Other recoverable mark, spirit level elevation	× 954
Spot elevation	× 7369 × 7369
Water elevation	670 670

Boundaries: National	
State	
County, parish, municipio	
Civil township, precinct, town, barrio	
Incorporated city, village, town, hamlet	
Reservation, National or State	
Small park, cemetery, airport, etc.	
Land grant	
Township or range line, United States land survey	
Township or range line, approximate location	
Section line, United States land survey	
Section line, approximate location	
Township line, not United States land survey	
Section line, not United States land survey	
Found corner: section and closing	
Boundary monument: land grant and other	
Fence or field line	

Index contour		Intermediate contour . . .	
Supplementary contour		Depression contours . . .	
Fill		Cut . . .	
Levee		Levee with road	
Mine dump		Wash . . .	
Tailings		Tailings pond	
Shifting sand or dunes		Intricate surface	
Sand area		Gravel beach	

Perennial streams		Intermittent streams . . .	
Elevated aqueduct		Aqueduct tunnel	
Water well and spring . o . . . . o~		Glacier . . .	
Small rapids		Small falls	
Large rapids		Large falls	
Intermittent lake		Dry lake bed	
Foreshore flat		Rock or coral reef . . .	
Sounding, depth curve . . . 10		Piling or dolphin	o
Exposed wreck		Sunken wreck	
Rock, bare or awash; dangerous to navigation			

Marsh (swamp)		Submerged marsh . . .	
Wooded marsh		Mangrove . . .	
Woods or brushwood . . .		Orchard . . .	
Vineyard		Scrub . . .	
Land subject to controlled inundation		Urban area	

FIGURE 7-14 Topographic map symbols. (Courtesy of U.S. Department of Interior, Geological Survey)

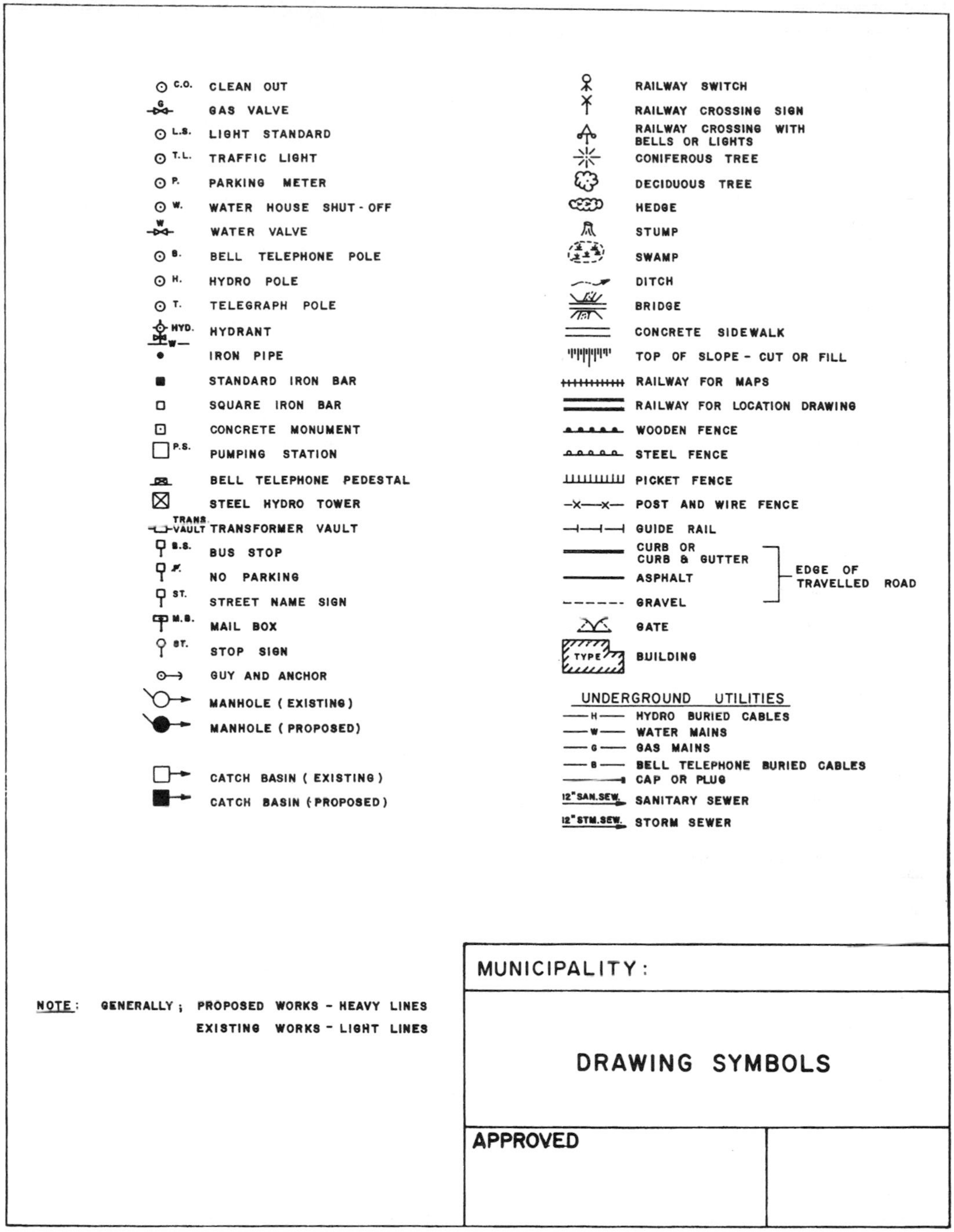

C.O.	CLEAN OUT			RAILWAY SWITCH
G	GAS VALVE			RAILWAY CROSSING SIGN
L.S.	LIGHT STANDARD			RAILWAY CROSSING WITH BELLS OR LIGHTS
T.L.	TRAFFIC LIGHT			CONIFEROUS TREE
P.	PARKING METER			DECIDUOUS TREE
W.	WATER HOUSE SHUT-OFF			HEDGE
W	WATER VALVE			STUMP
B.	BELL TELEPHONE POLE			SWAMP
H.	HYDRO POLE			DITCH
T.	TELEGRAPH POLE			BRIDGE
HYD.	HYDRANT			CONCRETE SIDEWALK
	IRON PIPE			TOP OF SLOPE - CUT OR FILL
	STANDARD IRON BAR			RAILWAY FOR MAPS
	SQUARE IRON BAR			RAILWAY FOR LOCATION DRAWING
	CONCRETE MONUMENT			WOODEN FENCE
P.S.	PUMPING STATION			STEEL FENCE
	BELL TELEPHONE PEDESTAL			PICKET FENCE
	STEEL HYDRO TOWER		—x—x—	POST AND WIRE FENCE
TRANS. VAULT	TRANSFORMER VAULT			GUIDE RAIL
B.S.	BUS STOP			CURB OR CURB & GUTTER
	NO PARKING			ASPHALT
ST.	STREET NAME SIGN			GRAVEL
M.B.	MAIL BOX			GATE
ST.	STOP SIGN		TYPE	BUILDING
	GUY AND ANCHOR			
	MANHOLE (EXISTING)		UNDERGROUND UTILITIES	
	MANHOLE (PROPOSED)		—H—	HYDRO BURIED CABLES
			—W—	WATER MAINS
	CATCH BASIN (EXISTING)		—G—	GAS MAINS
	CATCH BASIN (PROPOSED)		—B—	BELL TELEPHONE BURIED CABLES
				CAP OR PLUG
			12" SAN.SEW.	SANITARY SEWER
			12" STM.SEW.	STORM SEWER

EDGE OF TRAVELLED ROAD

NOTE: GENERALLY; PROPOSED WORKS - HEAVY LINES
EXISTING WORKS - LIGHT LINES

MUNICIPALITY:

DRAWING SYMBOLS

APPROVED

FIGURE 7-15 Municipal works plan symbols, including typical title block. (Courtesy of Municipal Engineers Association, Ontario)

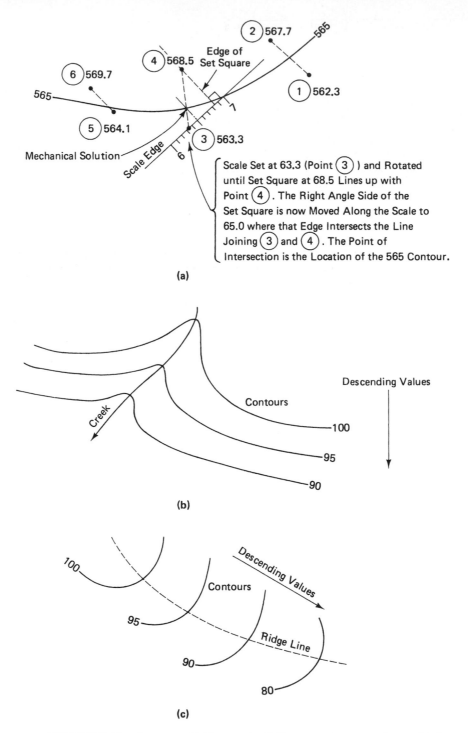

(a)

(b)

(c)

FIGURE 7-16 Contours. (a) Plotting the 565 contour by interpolation. (b) Contour deflections at a valley line. (c) Contour deflections at a ridge line.

and from line 565 to point 6 the distance is

$$\frac{4.7}{5.6} \times 0.49 = 0.41 \text{ unit}$$

In addition to the foregoing arithmetic solution, contours can be interpolated by using mechanical techniques. It is possible to scale off units on a barely taut elastic band and then stretch the elastic so that the marked-off units fit the interval being analyzed. Alternatively, the problem can be solved by rotating a scale, while a set square is used to line up the appropriate divisions with the field points. In Figure 7-16(a), a scale is set up at 63.3 on point 3 and then rotated until the 68.5 mark lines up with point 4, a set square being used on the scale. The set square is then slid along the scale until it lines up with 65.0; the intersection of the set square edge (90° to the scale) with the straight line joining points 3 and 4 yields the solution (i.e., the location of elevation at 565 ft). This latter technique is faster than the arithmetic technique.

Since contours are plotted by analyzing adjacent field points, it is essential that the ground slope be uniform between those points. An experienced survey crew will ensure that enough rod readings are taken to suitably define the ground surface. The survey crew can further define the terrain if care is taken in identifying and tying in valley lines and ridge lines. Figure 7-16(b) shows how contour lines bend uphill as they cross a valley; the steeper the valley is, the more the line diverges uphill. Figure 7-16(c) shows how contour lines bend downhill as they cross ridge lines. Figure 7-17 shows the plot of control, elevations, and valley and ridge lines. Figure 7-18 shows contours interpolated from the data in Figure 7-17.

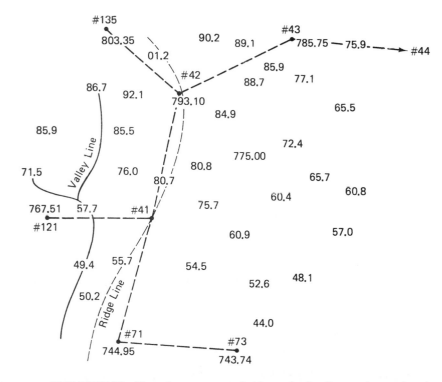

FIGURE 7-17   Plot of survey control, ridge and valley lines, and spot elevations.

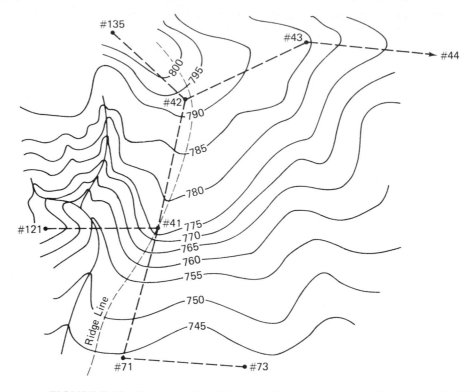

FIGURE 7-18 Contours plotted by interpolating between spot elevations, with additional plotting information given when the locations of ridge and valley lines are known.

Further, if the contours are to be plotted using computer software, additional information is required to permit the computer/plotter to produce contours that truly represent the surveyed ground surface. In addition to defining ridge and valley lines, as noted earlier, it is necessary for the surveyor to identify what are called **break lines**—they are lines that join points that define significant changes in slope, such as toe of slope, top/bottom of ditches and swales, ¢s, and the like. When the point numbers defining **break lines** are appropriately tagged—as required by the individual software—truly representative contours will be produced on the graphics screen and by the digital plotter.

SUMMARY OF CONTOUR CHARACTERISTICS

1. Closely spaced contours indicate steep slopes.
2. Widely spaced contours indicate moderate slopes (spacing here is a relative relationship).
3. Contours must be labeled to give the elevation value. Either each line is labeled, or every fifth line is drawn darker (wider) and labeled.
4. Contours are not shown going through buildings.

5. Contours crossing a man-made horizontal surface (roads, railroads) will be straight parallel lines as they cross the facility.

6. Since contours join points of equal elevation, contour lines cannot cross. (Caves present an exception.)

7. Contour lines cannot begin or end on the plan.

8. Depressions and hills look the same; one must note the contour value to distinguish the terrain (some agencies use hachures or shading to identify depressions).

9. Contours deflect uphill at valley lines and downhill at ridge lines; line crossings are perpendicular: U-shaped for ridge crossings, V-shaped for valley crossings.

10. Contour lines must close on themselves, either on the plan or in locations off the plan.

11. The ground slope between contour lines is uniform. Had the ground slope not been uniform between the points, additional readings (stadia or level) would have been taken at the time of the survey.

12. Important points can be further defined by including a "spot" elevation (height elevation).

13. Contour lines tend to parallel each other on uniform slopes.

Finally, the reader by now will have determined that the plotting of contours involves a great deal of time-consuming scaling operations. Fortunately, all the advantages of computer-based digital plotting are also available for the production of contour plans. In addition to contours, some software programs provide a three-dimensional perspective plot, which can portray the topography as viewed from any azimuth position and from various altitudes. See Figure 7-19 for a perspective view of a proposed road.

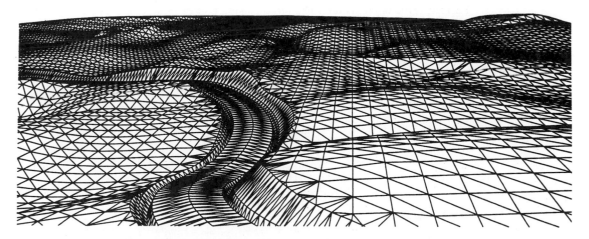

FIGURE 7-19   QuickSurf TGRID showing smoothed, rolling terrain coupled with road definition. (Courtesy of Schreiber U.S.A., Denver, CO)

Problems

7-1. Describe a technique to verify that the stadia multiplication constant for a particular instrument is, in fact, 100.

7-2. A transit (hi = 5.13 ft) at station 2 + 00 (elevation = 291.7 ft) is sighted at point 18 with the following results: bottom stadia hair = 4.43; top stadia hair = 5.83; crosshair rod reading = 5.13 with a vertical angle of +1°56′. Determine
(a) the horizontal distance from 2 + 00 to point 18 (1 decimal).
(b) the elevation of point 18 (1 decimal).

7-3. A transit (hi = 5.47 ft) at station K (elevation = 506.43 ft) is sighted at station M with the following results: stadia interval = 2.65 ft; crosshair rod reading = 9.33 ft with a vertical angle of −4°29′. Determine
(a) the horizontal distance of KM (1 decimal).
(b) the elevation of station M (1 decimal).

7-4. A transit (hi = 1.550 m) at station R (elevation = 160.605 m) is sighted at station T with the following results: stadia interval = 0.993 m; rod reading = 2.675 m with the telescope level. Determine
(a) the horizontal distance RT (1 decimal).
(b) the elevation of station T (2 decimals).

7-5. A transit (hi = 1.673 m) at control station A (elevation = 209.117 m) is sighted at control station B with the following results: stadia interval = 1.127 m; rod reading = 0.723 m with a vertical angle of +2°25′. The transit is then moved to station B (hi = 1.615 m) and sighted at station A with the following results: stadia interval = 1.127 m; rod reading = 2.555 with a vertical angle of −2°26′. Using average values, determine
(a) the horizontal distance AB (1 decimal).
(b) the elevation of station B (2 decimals).

7-6. The stadia data shown below were taken to profile a section of a gravel pit. Where the hi value could not be sighted on the rod, the sighted rod reading is booked along with the vertical angle. Where no rod reading is booked, the rod reading was made equal to the hi, which was 5.32 ft. The elevation of the transit station is 358.39 ft.

Point	Rod Interval	Vertical Angle
1	2.71	+1°58′
2	0.58	−3°;11′
3	0.91	0°00′ on 6.17
4	3.82	+3°38′ on 7.71
5	5.06	−2°19′ on 3.16
6	4.22	+12°32′
7	2.72	+16°30′

Compute the horizontal foot) and the elevations (1 decimal).

7-7. Reduce the following set of stadia notes, using either Equations (7-6) and (7-8) or Table 7-1.

Station	Horizontal Angle	Rod Interval	Vertical Angle	Horizontal Distance	Elevation Difference	Elevation
		⊼ @ STA. *J*, hi = 5.42′				583.83
K	0°00′	5.00	+1°30′			
1	14°28′	2.41	+2°10′			
2	18°01′	1.68	−1°51′			
3	54°46′	1.01	−4°22′			
4	87°10′	2.56	−4°10′ on 5.63			
5	82°31′	4.03	−3°21′			
6	65°08′	4.97	−2°51′			
7	51°10′	4.90	−2°27′			
8	42°30′	4.69	−2°;10′			
9	32°17′	4.10	0°00′ on 6.82			
10	18°20′	3.51	+0°40′ on 7.22			

7-8. Reduce the following cross-section notes.

Station	Horizontal Angle	Rod Interval	Vertical Angle	Horizontal Distance	Elevation Difference	Elevation
		⊼ @ CONTROL POINT *K*, hi = 1.82 m				211.19
L	0°00′					
0 + 00 ₵	34°15′	0.899	−18°10′			
S. ditch	33°31′	0.851	−21°08′			
N. ditch	37°08′	0.950	−19°52′			
0 + 50 ₵	68°17′	0.662	−15°07′			
S. ditch	64°10′	0.503	−19°32′			
N. ditch	70°48′	0.687	−18°44′			
1 + 00 ₵	113°07′	0.607	−12°51′			
S. ditch	109°52′	0.511	−15°58′			
N. ditch	116°14′	0.710	−13°47′			
1 + 50 ₵	139°55′	0.852	−9°00′			
S. ditch	135°11′	0.800	−10°15′			
N. ditch	144°16′	0.932	−9°20′			
2 + 00 ₵	152°18′	1.228	−5°49′			
S. ditch	155°43′	1.148	−7°05′			
N. ditch	147°00′	1.263	−6°32′			

7-9. A stadia traverse was used as control for a mapping survey. The elevation of station *A* is 206.08 m; all vertical angles were taken with the crosshair set to the hi value on the rod.

Transit Station	Rod Station	Rod Interval	Vertical Angle
A	B	0.682	+2°12′
	E	1.137	+1°58′
B	A	0.686	−2°11′
	C	0.826	+4°27′
C	B	0.827	−4°25′
	D	0.733	−2°33′
D	C	0.732	+2°33′
	E	0.606	−1°44′
E	D	0.606	+1°46′
	A	1.137	−1°57′

Using average values, determine
(a) the elevations of the traverse stations.
(b) the distances between the traverse stations.

7-10. A topographic survey was performed on a tract of land, leveling techniques were used to obtain elevations, and stadia techniques were used to locate the topographic detail. The accompanying sketch shows the traverse (*A* to *G*) used for stadia control and the grid baseline (0 + 00 @ *A*) used to control the leveling survey; offset distances are @ 90° to the baseline. All the necessary information is provided, including
(a) bearings and lengths of the traverse sides,
(b) grid elevations,
(c) angle and distance ties for the topographic detail, and
(d) northings and eastings of the stations.
Distances used can be in either foot units or metric units.

PART A

A-1. Establish the grid, plot the elevations (the decimal point is the plot point), and interpolate the data to establish contours at 1 m (ft) intervals. Scale @ 1:500 for metric units or 1 in. = 10 ft for foot units. Use pencil.

A-2. Compute the interior angles of the traverse and check for geometric closure [i.e., $(n - 2)180°$].

A-3. Plot the traverse using the interior angles and the given distances or using the coordinates (scale as in A-1).

A-4. Plot the stadia detail using the plotted traverse as control (scale as in A-1).

A-5. Determine the area enclosed by the traverse in m^2 (ft^2) by using *one* or more of the following methods.

(a) Use grid paper as an overlay or underlay; count the squares and partial squares enclosed by the traverse; determine the area represented by one square at the chosen scale, and from that relationship, determine the area enclosed by the traverse.

(b) Use a planimeter to determine the area.

(c) Divide the traverse into regular-shaped figures (squares, rectangles, trapezoids, triangles), using a scale to determine the figure dimensions. Calculate the areas of the individual figures, and sum them to produce the overall traverse area.

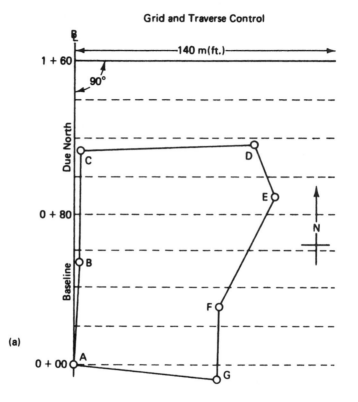

(d) Use the given balanced traverse data and the technique of coordinates to compute the traverse area.

Surveying Grid Elevations

STA.	℄	20 m (ft) E	40 m (ft)E	60 m (ft)E	80 m (ft)E	100 m (ft)E	120 m (ft)E	140 m (ft)E
1 + 60	68.97	69.51	70.05	70.53	70.32			
1 + 40	69.34	69.82	71.12	71.00	71.26	71.99		
1 + 20	69.29	70.75	69.98	71.24	72.07	72.53	72.61	
1 + 00	69.05	71.02	70.51	69.91	72.02	73.85	74.00	75.18
0 + 80	69.09	71.90	74.13	71.81	69.87	71.21	74.37	74.69
0 + 60	69.12	70.82	72.79	72.81	71.33	70.97	72.51	73.40
0 + 40	68.90	69.66	70.75	72.00	72.05	69.80	71.33	72.42
0 + 20	68.02	68.98	69.53	70.09	71.11	70.48	69.93	71.51
0 + 00 @ STA. A	67.15	68.11	68.55	69.55	69.92	71.02		

(b)

Balanced Traverse Data

Course	Bearing	Distance, m(ft)
AB	N 3°30′ E	56.05
BC	N 0°30′ W	61.92
CD	N 88°40′ E	100.02
DE	S 23°30′ E	31.78
EF	S 28°53′ W	69.11
FG	South	39.73
GA	N 83°37′ W	82.67

(c)

Station Coordinates

	Northing	Easting
A	1000.00	1000.00
B	1055.94	1003.42
C	1117.86	1002.88
D	1120.19	1102.87
E	1091.05	1115.54
F	1030.54	1082.16
G	990.81	1082.16

(d)

Stadia Notes (Problem 7-10, A-4)

STA.	Horizontal Angle	Distance, m(ft)	Description
	⊼ STA. *B* (sight *C*, 0°00′)		
1	8°15′	45.5	S. limit of treed area
2	17°00′	57.5	"
3	33°30′	66.0	"
4	37°20′	93.5	"
5	45°35′	93.0	"
6	49°30′	114.0	"
	⊼ @ STA. *A* (sight *B*, 0°00′)		
7	50°10′	73.5	℄ gravel road (8m ± width)
8	50°10′	86.0	"
9	51°30′	97.5	"
10	53°50′	94.5	N. limit of treed area
11	53°50′	109.0	"
12	55°00′	58.0	℄ gravel road
13	66°15′	32.0	N. limit of treed area
14	86°30′	19.0	"
	⊼ @ STA. *D* (sight *E*, 0°00′)		
15	0°00′	69.5	℄ gravel road
16	7°30′	90.0	N. limit of treed area
17	64°45′	38.8	N. E. corner of building
18	13°30′	75.0	N. limit of treed area
19	88°00′	39.4	N. W. corner of building
20	46°00′	85.0	N. limit of treed area

(e)

A highway is to be constructed to pass through points *A* and *E* of the traverse. The proposed highway ℄ grade is +2.30 percent rising from *A* to *E* (℄ elevation at *A* = 68.95). The proposed cut-and-fill sections are shown in Figures (a) and (b) below.

B-1. Draw profile *A-E*, showing both the existing ground and the proposed ℄ of the highway. Use the following scales: Metric: horizontal, 1:500; vertical, 1:100. Foot: horizontal, 1 in. = 10 ft or 15 ft; vertical, 1 in. = 2 ft or 3 ft.

B-2. Plot the highway ℄ and 16 m (ft) width on the plan (see Problems A-1, A-3, and A-4). Show the limits of cut and fill on the plan. Use the sections shown below.

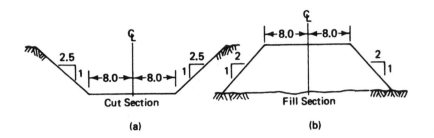

Cut Section   Fill Section

(a)   (b)

B-3. Combine Problems A-1, A-3, A-4, B-1, and B-2 on one sheet of drafting paper. Suitably arrange the plan and profile together with the balanced traverse data and a suitable title block. All line work is to be in ink. Use C or A2 size paper.

Chapter 8

Construction Control Surveys

8-1 General

We have seen in previous sections the need to tie our preliminary and construction surveys to some control fabric or network. The survey control stations must be permanent or readily replaceable and must be established at a relatively high level of accuracy.

The first major adjustment in control data was made in 1927, resulting in the North American datum (NAD). Since that time, a great deal more has been learned about the shape and mass of the earth; these new and expanded data come to us from releveling surveys, precise traverses, satellite positioning surveys, earth movement studies, and gravity surveys. The mass of data thus accumulated has been utilized to update and expand existing control data, and, as well, the new geodetic data have provided scientists with the means to more precisely define the actual geometric shape of the earth. The reference ellipsoid previously used for this purpose (the Clarke spheroid of 1866) has been modified to reflect our current knowledge of the earth. Accordingly, a World Geodetic System, first proposed in 1972 (WGS '72) and later endorsed in 1979 by the International Association of Geodesy (IAG), included proposals for an earth-mass-centered ellipsoid (GRS-80 ellipsoid), which would more closely represent the planet on which we live. Proposed parameters included a semimajor axis (equatorial radius) of 6,378,135 m (the Clarke spheroid has a semimajor axis of 6,378,206.4 m).

The new adjustment, NAD '83, covers the North American continent, including Greenland and parts of Central America. All individual control nets are included in a weighted simultaneous computation. A good tie to the global system is given by satellite positioning.

In most cases, the accuracies between NAD '83 first-order stations are better than 1:200,000, which would have been unquestioned in the pre–Global Positioning System (GPS) era. However, the increased use of very precise GPS surveys and the tremendous potential for new applications for this new technology have created a demand for high-precision upgrades of the control net, using GPS techniques.

The National Geodetic Survey (NGS) has software programs designed to assist the surveyor in several areas of geodetic inquiry. The reader is invited to look at the NGS Tool Kit, which is available at www.ngs.noaa.gov/TOOLS/. This site has online calculations capability for many of the geodetic activities listed below. To download PC software programs go to www.ngs.noaa.gov and click on the PC software icon.

- DEFLEC99   Computes deflections of the vertical at the surface of the earth for the conterminous United States, Alaska, Puerto Rico, Virgin Islands, and Hawaii
- G99SSS   Computes the gravimetric height values for the conterminous United States
- GEOID99   Computes geoid height values for the conterminous United States
- HTDP   Time-dependent horizontal positioning software that allows users to predict horizontal displacements and/or velocities at locations throughout the United States
- NADCON   Transforms geographic coordinates between the NAD 27, Old Hawaiian, Puerto Rico, or Alaska Island data and NAD 83 values
- State Plane Coordinate   GPPCGP: Converts NAD 27 state plane coordinates to NAD 27 geographic coordinates (latitudes and longitudes) and the converse
  SPCS83: Converts NAD 83 state plane coordinates to NAD 83 geographic positions and the converse
- Surface Gravity Prediction   Predicts surface gravity at specified geographic position and topographic height
- Tidal and Orthometric Elevations   The tidal information and orthometric elevations of a specific survey control mark can be viewed graphically—NAVD88, NGVD29, and Mean Lower Low Water (MLLW) data
- VERTCON   Computes the modeled difference in orthometric height between the North American Vertical Datum of 1988 (NAVD88) and the National Geodetic Vertical Datum of 1929 (NGVD29) for any given location specified by latitude and longitude

In Canada, software programs designed to assist the surveyor in a variety of geodetic applications are available on the Internet from the Canadian Geodetic Survey at www.geod.nrcan.gc.ca (in both English and French languages). Following is a selection of available services.

- Precise GPS Satellite Ephemerides
- GPS Satellite Clock Corrections
- GPS Constellation Information
- GPS Calendar
- National Gravity Program
- Universal Transverse Mercator (UTM) to/from geographic coordinate conversion (UTM is in 6° zones with a scale factor of 0.9996)*

*There is a charge for this program.

- Transverse Mercator (TM) to/from geographic coordinate conversion (TM is in 3° zones with a scale factor of 0.9999, similar to U.S. state plane grids)*
- GPS Height Transformation (based on GSD95; see Section 9-13)*

*There is a charge for this program.

A cooperative network upgrading program, including federal and state agencies, began in 1986, in Tennessee, and was completed, in Indiana, in 1997; about 16,000 survey stations were upgraded (horizontally) to either A-order or B-order status. Horizontal A-order stations have a relative accuracy of 5 mm +/− 1:10,000,000 relative to other A-order stations. Horizontal B-order stations have a relative accuracy of 8 mm +/− 1:1,000,000 relative to other A-order and B-order stations. Of the 16,000 survey stations, NGS has committed to maintaining about 1,400, named the Federal Base Network, and the various states will maintain the remainder. See Table 8-1 for accuracy standards for the new High Accuracy Reference Network (HARN).

With regard to traditional (pre-GPS) surveying instrumentation, in order to obtain high accuracy for conventional field control surveys, the surveyor must use high-precision equipment and high-precision techniques. High-precision equipment is illustrated in Figures 8-1, 8-2, and 8-3. Specifications for horizontal high-precision techniques stipulate the least angular count of the theodolite, the number of observations, the rejection of observations exceeding specified limits from the mean, the spacing of major stations, and the angular and positional closures. See Table 8-2 for traverse specifications.

Specifications for vertical high-precision techniques may stipulate the maximum length of a double run between closures, the sensitivity of the bubble vial or equivalent for

Table 8-1 POSITIONING ACCURACY STANDARDS

Survey Categories	Order	(95 percent confident level) Minimum Geometric Accuracy Standard		
		Base Error	Line-Length Dependent Error	
		e (cm)	p (ppm)	a (1:a)
Global-regional geodynamics	AA	0.3	0.01	1:100,000,000
National Geodetic Reference System, "primary" network	A	0.5	0.1	1: 10,000,000
National Geodetic Reference System, "secondary" networks	B	0.8	1	1: 1,000,000
National Geodetic Reference System (terrestrial based)	C			
	1	1.0	10	1: 100,000
	2-I	2.0	20	1: 50,000
	2-II	3.0	50	1: 20,000
	3	5.0	100	1: 10,000

From *Geometric Geodetic Accuracy Standards Using GPS Relative Positioning Techniques*. [Federal Geodetic Control Subcommittee (FGCS) 1988]. Publications available through the National Geodetic Survey (NGS), (301) 443-8631.

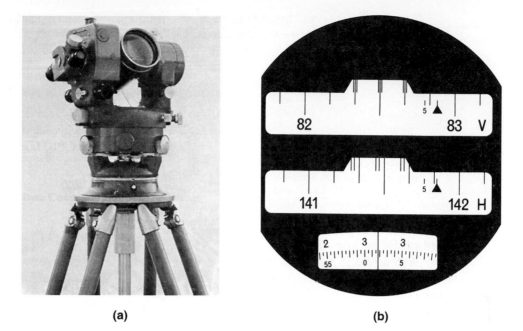

(a)   **(b)**

FIGURE 8-1   (a) Kern DKM 3 precise theodolite; angles directly read to 0.5 seconds, used in first-order surveys. (b) Kern DKM 3 scale reading (vertical angle- 82°53'01.8"). (Courtesy of Leica Co.)

FIGURE 8-2   Zeiss Ni I precise automatic level, featuring 40× magnification with a nominal accuracy of +0.2 mm √distance in kilometers. (Courtesy of Carl Zeiss—Oberkochen)

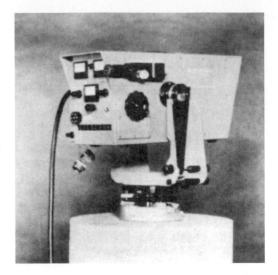

FIGURE 8-3 Kern Mekometer, ME 3000, a high-precision EDM [SE = ± (0.2 mm + 1 ppm)] with a triple-prism distance range of 2.5 km. Used wherever first-order results are required: for example, deformation studies, network surveys, plant engineering, and baseline calibration. (Courtesy of Kern Instruments)

automatic levels, the type of rod and rod markings, and the maximum closures. See Tables 8-3 and 8-4.

The American Congress on Surveying and Mapping (ACSM) and the American Land Title Association (ALTA) collaborated to produce new classifications for cadastral surveys based on present and proposed land use. These 1992 classifications (subject to state regulations) are shown in Table 8-5(a). Recognizing the impact of GPS techniques on all branches of surveying, in 1997 ACSM and ALTA published positional tolerances for different classes of surveys—see Table 8-5(b).

First-order specifications are seldom required for engineering or construction surveys—an extensive interstate highway control survey could be one example. Control for large-scale projects (e.g., interchanges, subdivisions) that are to be laid out using polar ties (angle/distance) by Total Stations may require accuracies in the range of

Table 8-2 TRAVERSE SPECIFICATIONS—UNITED STATES

| Classification | First Order | Second Order | | Third Order | |
		Class I	Class II	Class I	Class II
Recommended spacing of principal stations	Network stations 10–15 km; other surveys seldom less than 3 km	Principal stations seldom less than 4 km except in metropolitan area surveys, where the limitation is 0.3 km	Principal stations seldom less than 2 km except in metropolitan area surveys, where the limitation is 0.2 km	Seldom less than 0.1 km in tertiary surveys in metropolitan area surveys; as required for other surveys	
Position closure After azimuth adjustment	0.04 m $\sqrt{K}$ or 1:100,000	0.08 m $\sqrt{K}$ or 1:50,000	0.2 m $\sqrt{K}$ or 1:20,000	0.4 m $\sqrt{K}$ or 1:10,000	0.8 m $\sqrt{K}$ or 1:5000

Table 8-3 NATIONAL OCEAN SURVEY, U.S. COAST AND GEODETIC SURVEYS: CLASSIFICATION, STANDARDS OF ACCURACY, AND GENERAL SPECIFICATIONS FOR VERTICAL CONTROL

Classification	First Order Class I, Class II	Second Order		Third Order
		Class I	Class II	
Principal uses Minimum standards; higher accuracies may be used for special purposes	Basic framework of the National Network and of metropolitan area control	Secondary control of the National Network and of metropolitan area control	Control densification, usually adjusted to the National Network	Miscellaneous local control; may not be adjusted to the National Network
	Extensive engineering projects	Large engineering projects	Local engineering projects	Small engineering projects
	Regional crustal movement investigations	Local crustal movement and subsidence investigations	Topographic mapping	Small-scale topographic mapping
	Determining geopotential values	Support for lower-order control	Studies of rapid subsidence	Drainage studies and gradient establishment in mountainous areas
			Support for local surveys	
Maximum closures[a]				
Section: forward and backward	3 mm $\sqrt{K}$ *(Class I)* 4 mm $\sqrt{K}$ *(Class II)*	6 mm $\sqrt{K}$	8 mm $\sqrt{K}$	12 mm $\sqrt{K}$
Loop or line	4 mm $\sqrt{K}$ *(Class I)* 5 mm $\sqrt{K}$ *(Class II)*	6 mm $\sqrt{K}$	8 mm $\sqrt{K}$	12 mm $\sqrt{K}$

[a]Check between forward and backward runnings where K is the distance in kilometers.

Table 8-4 CLASSIFICATION, STANDARDS OF ACCURACY, AND GENERAL SPECIFICATIONS FOR VERTICAL CONTROL—CANADA

Classification	Special Order	First Order	Second Order (first-order procedures recommended)	Third Order	Fourth Order
Allowable discrepancy between forward and backward levelings	± 3 mm $\sqrt{K}$ ± 0.012 ft $\sqrt{m}$	± 4 mm $\sqrt{K}$ ± 0.017 ft $\sqrt{m}$	± 8 mm $\sqrt{K}$ ± 0.035 ft $\sqrt{m}$	± 24 mm $\sqrt{K}$ ± 0.10 ft $\sqrt{m}$	± 120 mm $\sqrt{K}$ ± 0.5 ft $\sqrt{m}$
Instruments:					
Self-leveling high-speed compensator	Equivalent to 10″/2mm level vial	Equivalent to 10″/2 mm level vial	Equivalent to 20″/2 mm level vial	Equivalent to sensitivity below	Equivalent to sensitivity below
Level vial	10″/2 mm	10″/2 mm	20″/2 mm	40″ to 50″/2 mm	40″ to 50″/2 mm
Telescopic magnification	40×	40×	40×		

Adapted from "Specifications and Recommendations for Control Surveys and Survey Markers" (Surveys and Mapping Branch, Department of Energy, Mines and Resources, Ottawa, Canada 1973).

Table 8-5(a) AMERICAN CONGRESS ON SURVEYING AND MAPPING MINIMUM ANGLE, DISTANCE, AND CLOSURE REQUIREMENTS FOR SURVEY MEASUREMENTS THAT CONTROL LAND BOUNDARIES FOR ALTA-ACSM LAND TITLE SURVEYS (1)

Dir. Reading of Instrument (2)	Instrument Reading Estimated (3)	Number of Observations per Station (4)	Spread from Mean of D&R Not to Exceed (5)	Angle Closure Where N = No. of Stations Not to Exceed	Linear Closure (6)	Distance Measurement (7)	Minimum Length of Measurements (8), (9), (10)
$20'' < 1'> \boxed{10''}$	$5'' < 0.1'> $N.A.	2 D&R	$5'' < 0.1'> \boxed{5''}$	$10'' \sqrt{N}$	1:15,000	EDM or doubletape with steel tape	(8) 81 m, (9) 153 m, (10) 20 m

Note (1) All requirements of each class must be satisfied in order to qualify for that particular class of survey. The use of a more precise instrument does not change the other requirements, such as number of angles turned, etc.

Note (2) Instrument must have a direct reading of at least the amount specified (not an estimated reading), i.e.: 20″ = Micrometer reading theodolite, <1′> = Scale reading theodolite, $\boxed{10''}$ = Electronic reading theodolite.

Note (3) Instrument must have the capability of allowing an estimated reading below the direct reading to the specified reading.

Note (4) D & R means the Direct and Reverse positions of the instrument telescope; i.e., Urban Surveys require that two angles in the direct and two angles in the reverse position be measured and meaned.

Note (5) Any angle measured that exceeds the specified amount from the mean must be rejected and the set of angles remeasured.

Note (6) Ratio of closure after angles are balanced and closure calculated.

Note (7) All distance measurements must be made with a properly calibrated EDM or steel tape, applying atmospheric, temperature, sag, tension, slope, scale factor, and sea level corrections as necessary.

Note (8) EDM having an error of 5 mm, independent of distance measured (manufacturer's specifications).

Note (9) EDM having an error of 10 mm, independent of distance measured (manufacturer's specifications).

Note (10) Calibrated steel tape.

Table 8-5(b) POSITIONAL TOLERANCES FOR LAND TITLE SURVEYS

Survey Class	
Urban	0.07 ft (or 20 mm) + 50 ppm
Suburban	0.13 ft (or 40 mm) + 100 ppm
Rural	0.26 ft (or 80 mm) + 200 ppm
Mountain/Marshl1and	0.66 ft (or 200 mm) + 200 ppm

From Classifications of ALTA–ACSM Land Title Surveys, as adopted by American Land Title Association and ACSM, 1997.

1/10,000 to 1/20,000, depending on the project, and would fall between second- and third-order accuracy specifications. The lowest requirements are reserved for small engineering projects that are limited in scope—for example, drainage studies and borrow pit volume surveys.

In Europe, positional accuracies are specified in ISO 4463 (International Organization for Standardization) and cover primary construction control stations, secondary construction control stations, and layout features.

Figure 8-4 shows a primary control net established to provide control for a construction site. The primary control stations are tied into a national, state, or provincial coordinate grid by a series of precise traverses or triangle networks. Points on baselines (secondary points) can be tied into the primary control net by polar ties, intersection, or resection. The actual layout points of the structure (columns, walls, footings, etc.) are established from these secondary points. ISO 4463 points out that the accuracy of key building or structural layout points should not be influenced by possible discrepancies in the state or provincial coordinate grid. For that reason, the primary project control net is analyzed and adjusted independently of the state or provincial coordinate grid. This "free net" is tied to the state or provincial coordinate grid without becoming an integrated adjusted component of that grid. The positional accuracy of project layout points relative to each other is more important than the positional accuracy of these layout points relative to a state or provincial coordinate grid.

8-2 Positional Accuracies (ISO 4463)

8-2-1 Primary System Control Stations

1. Permissible deviations of the distances and angles obtained when one is *measuring the positions of primary points, and those calculated from the adjusted coordinates of these points,* shall not exceed the following:

$$\text{Distance: } \pm\, 0.75\ \sqrt{L}\ \text{mm} \tag{8-1}$$

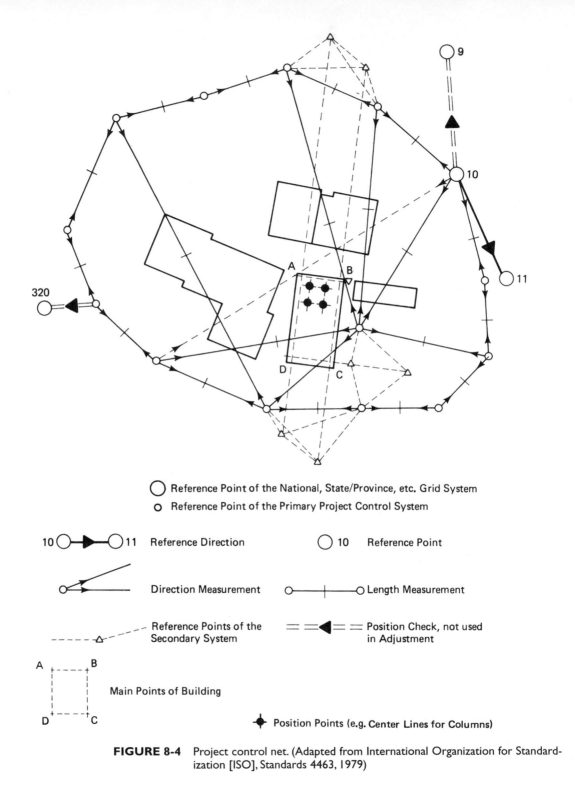

320

A B

D C

9

10

11

◯ Reference Point of the National, State/Province, etc. Grid System

o Reference Point of the Primary Project Control System

10 ◯━▶◯ 11   Reference Direction   ◯ 10   Reference Point

o╱━▶   Direction Measurement   o━━┼━━o Length Measurement

‒ ‒ ‒△‒ ‒   Reference Points of the   = =◀= = Position Check, not used
              Secondary System   in Adjustment

A┌ ‒ ‒ ‒┐B
 ¦   ¦   Main Points of Building
D└ ‒ ‒ ‒┘C

◆ Position Points (e.g. Center Lines for Columns)

FIGURE 8-4 Project control net. (Adapted from International Organization for Standardization [ISO], Standards 4463, 1979)

$$\text{Angles: } \pm \frac{0.045}{\sqrt{L}} \text{ degree or} \qquad (8\text{-}2)$$

$$\pm \frac{0.05}{\sqrt{L}} \text{ gon*}$$

where L is the distance in meters between primary stations; in the case of angles, L is the shorter side of the angle.

*1 revolution $= 360° = 400$ gon (also known as grad—a European angle unit). 1 gon $= 0.9$ degree (exactly).

2. Permissible deviations of the distances and angles obtained when one is *checking the positions of primary points* shall not exceed

$$\text{Distances: } \pm 2 \sqrt{L} \text{ mm} \qquad (8\text{-}3)$$

$$\text{Angles: } \pm \frac{0.135}{\sqrt{L}} \text{ degree or} \qquad (8\text{-}4)$$

$$\pm \frac{0.15}{\sqrt{L}} \text{ gon}$$

where L is the distance in meters between primary stations; in the case of angles, L is the length of the shorter side of the angle.

Angles are measured with a 1″ theodolite, with the measurements being made in two sets (each set is formed by two observations, one on each face of the instrument). See Figure 8-5.

Distances can be measured with steel tapes or electronic distance measurement instruments (EDMIs) and will be measured at least twice by either method. Steel tape measurements will be corrected for temperatures, sag, slope, and tension; a tension device will be used while taping is done. *EDMIs should be checked regularly against a range of known distances.*

8-2-2   Secondary System Control Stations

1. Secondary control stations and main layout points (e.g., *ABCD,* Figure 8-4) constitute the secondary system. The permissible deviations for a *checked distance from a given or calculated distance between a primary control station and a secondary point* shall not exceed

$$\text{Distances: } \pm 2 \sqrt{L} \text{ mm} \qquad (8\text{-}5)$$

2. Permissible deviations for *a checked distance from the given or calculated distance between two secondary points in the same system* shall not exceed

$$\text{Distances: } \pm 2 \sqrt{L} \text{ mm}$$

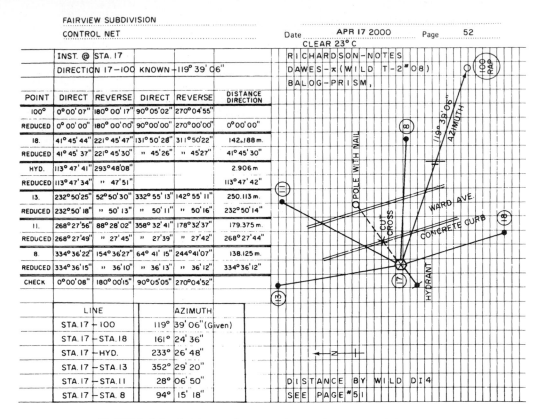

INST. @ STA.17
DIRECTION 17-100 KNOWN +119° 39' 06"

RICHARDSON-NOTES
DAWES-x(WILD T-2"08)
BALOG-PRISM,

POINT	DIRECT	REVERSE	DIRECT	REVERSE	DISTANCE DIRECTION
100°	0°00'07"	180°00'17"	90°05'02"	270°04'55"	
REDUCED	0°00'00"	180°00'00"	90°00'00"	270°00'00"	0°00'00"
18.	41°45'44"	221°45'47"	131°50'28"	311°50'22"	142.188m
REDUCED	41°45'37"	221°45'30"	" 45'26"	" 45'27"	41°45'30"
HYD.	113°47'41"	293°48'08"			2.906m
REDUCED	113°47'34"	" 47'51"			113°47'42"
13.	232°50'25"	52°50'30"	332°55'13"	142°55'11"	250.113m
REDUCED	232°50'18"	" 50'13"	" 50'11"	" 50'16"	232°50'14"
11.	268°27'56"	88°28'02"	358°32'41"	178°32'37"	179.375m
REDUCED	268°27'49"	" 27'45"	" 27'39"	" 27'42"	268°27'44"
8.	334°36'22"	154°36'27"	64°41'15"	244°41'07"	138.125m
REDUCED	334°36'15"	" 36'10"	" 36'13"	" 36'12"	334°36'12"
CHECK	0°00'08"	180°00'15"	90°05'05"	270°04'52"	

LINE	AZIMUTH
STA.17 - 100	119° 39' 06" (Given)
STA.17 - STA.18	161° 24' 36"
STA.17 - HYD.	233° 26' 48"
STA.17 - STA.13	352° 29' 20"
STA.17 - STA.11	28° 06' 50"
STA.17 - STA. 8	94° 15' 18"

DISTANCE BY WILD DI4
SEE PAGE #51

FIGURE 8-5 Field notes for control point directions and distances.

where L is the distance in meters. For L less than 10 m, permissible deviations are ±6 mm.

$$\text{Angles: } \pm \frac{0.135}{\sqrt{L}} \text{ degree or} \qquad (8\text{-}6)$$

$$\pm \frac{0.15}{\sqrt{L}} \text{ gon}$$

where L is the length in meters of the shorter side of the angle.

3. Permissible deviations for *a checked distance from the given or calculated distance between two points in different secondary systems for the same project* should not exceed

$$\pm K\sqrt{L} \text{ mm} \qquad (8\text{-}7)$$

where L is the distance in meters and K is a constant derived as shown in Table 8-6.

Table 8-6 ACCURACY REQUIREMENT CONSTANTS FOR LAYOUT SURVEYS

K	Application
10	Earthwork without any particular accuracy requirement (e.g., rough excavation, embankments)
5	Earthwork subject to accuracy requirements (e.g., roads, pipelines, structures)
2	Poured concrete structures (e.g., curbs, abutments)
1	Precast concrete structures, steel structures (e.g., bridges, buildings)

Adapted from Table 8-1, ISO 4463.

Angles are measured with a transit or theodolite reading to at least 1′. The measurement shall be made in at least one set (i.e., two observations, one on each face of the instrument).

Distances can be measured with steel tapes or EDMIs and will be measured at least twice by either method. Distances will be corrected for temperature, sag, slope, and tension: a tension device is to be used with the tape. EDMIs should be checked regularly against a range of known distances.

8-2-3 Layout Points

Permissible deviations for *a checked distance between a secondary point and a layout point, or between two layout points,* are

$$\pm\, K\, \sqrt{L} \text{ mm} \qquad (8\text{-}8)$$

where L is the specified distance in meters and K is a constant taken from Table 8-6. For L less than 5 m, permissible deviations are $\pm\, 2K$ mm.

Permissible deviations for *a checked angle between two lines, dependent on each other, through adjacent layout points* are

$$\pm\, \frac{0.0675}{\sqrt{L}}\, K \text{ degree or } \pm\, \frac{0.075}{\sqrt{L}}\, K \text{ gon} \qquad (8\text{-}9)$$

where L is the length in meters of the shorter side of the angle and K is a constant from Table 8-6.

Figure 8-6 illustrates the foregoing specifications for the case involving a stakeout for a curved concrete curb. The layout point on the curve has a permissible area of uncertainty generated by ± 0.015/m due to angle uncertainties and by ± 0.013/m due to distance uncertainties.

8-3 Specifications for Short Lines

A greater interest in urban control surveys and **engineering works control surveys** (in Canada) fostered a need for specifications that allowed for error propagation normally associated with short-line surveys. A control survey network that includes lines of less than

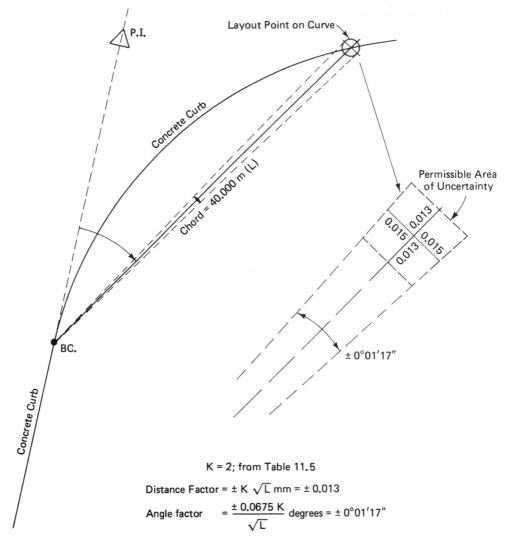

K = 2; from Table 11.5

Distance Factor = ± K $\sqrt{L}$ mm = ± 0.013

Angle factor $= \dfrac{\pm\,0.0675\,K}{\sqrt{L}}$ degrees = ± 0°01'17"

Angle Factor Converted to Distance =

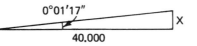

X = 40 tan 0°01'17" = 0.015 m

FIGURE 8-6 Accuracy analysis for a concrete curb layout point. (See ISO Standards 4463, 1979.)

3 km is classified according to whether the semimajor axis of the 95 percent confidence region for each station with respect to all other stations of the network is less than or equal to

$$r = c(d + 0.2) \qquad (8\text{-}10)$$

where r = radius in centimeters

d = distance in kilometers to any station

c = factor assigned according to the order of the survey

Table 8-7 shows values of r (cm) for various short distances. The table also shows comparative values for $d = 3.0$ km for the original specification $r = cd$ (1973) and the modified specification $r = c(d + 0.2)$ (1977). The modified specification reflects the fact that many errors (e.g., instrumental, centering, effects of network configuration) are simply not proportional to distance. The 1977 modification indicates that beyond a distance of 3 km, the disproportionate characteristics (with respect to distance) have largely been dissipated.

In addition to the specifications issued by the Surveys and Mapping Branch of the Canadian Department of Energy, Mines and Resources, local and provincial agencies have published suggested specifications. In many jurisdictions, the maximum allowable error for legal (property) surveys is set by law to be 1/5000. This could be stated as

$$r = 10(2d + 0.1) \text{ cm} \qquad (8\text{-}11)$$

Table 8-7 ACCURACY STANDARDS FOR HORIZONTAL CONTROL SURVEYS WITH SHORT LINES

		Semimajor Axis of 95% Confidence Region, $r = c(d + 0.2)$ (d is the distance between points)								
		$d = 0.1$ km			$d = 0.3$ km			$d = 1.0$ km		
Order	C	cm	ppm	Ratio	cm	ppm	Ratio	cm	ppm	Ratio
1	2	0.6	60	1/16,700	1.0	33	1/30,000	2.4	24	1/41,700
2	5	1.5	150	1/6700	2.5	83	1/12,000	6.0	60	1/16,700
3	12	3.6	360	1/2800	6.0	200	1/5000	14.4	144	1/6900
4	30	9.0	900	1/1100	15.0	500	1/2000	36.0	360	1/2800

		Semimajor Axis of 95% Confidence Region, $r = c(d + 0.2)$ (d is the distance between points)						$r = cd$ (1973 specs)		
		$d = 2.0$ km			$d = 3.0$ km			$d = 3.0$ km		
Order	C	cm	ppm	Ratio	cm	ppm	Ratio	cm	ppm	Ratio
1	2	4.4	22	1/45,500	6.4	21	1/46,900	6.0	20	1/50,000
2	5	11.0	55	1/18,200	16.0	53	1/18,800	15.0	50	1/20,000
3	12	26.4	132	1/7600	38.4	128	1/7800	36.0	120	1/8300
4	30	6.0	330	1/3000	96.0	320	1/3100	90.0	300	1/3300

Source: Surveys and Mapping Branch, Department of Energy, Mines and Resources, Ottawa, Canada, 1977.

where r (cm) is the maximum allowable error (MAE) and d is the distance in kilometers. For example, for 3 km,

$$r = 10(6.1) = 61 \text{ cm}$$
$$= 1/4900$$

For urban development, it has been suggested that the following formula apply:

$$r = 12(d^{2/3} + 0.1) \text{ cm} \tag{8-12}$$

Thus, for 3 km,

$$r = 12(3^{2/3} + 0.1) = 26 \text{ cm}$$
$$= 1/11500 \qquad \text{Class 3}$$

For intensely developed urban areas, it has been suggested that the following formula apply:

$$r = 5(d^{2/3} + 0.1)\text{cm} \tag{8-13}$$

For 3 km,

$$r = 5(3^{2/3} + 0.1) = 10.9 \text{ cm}$$
$$= 1/27500 \qquad \text{Class 2}$$

Formulas (8-11), (8-12), and (8-13) are included for illustrative purposes only—they have no official standing.

8-4 Coordinate Grid Systems

When the relative positions of control stations have been determined, it must be decided how best to tie in all these widely spaced points to a reference fabric. One basic reference fabric for the earth is the geodetic coordinate system employing latitude and longitude (ϕ, λ). Although this system is widely used for other purposes (e.g., navigation), it has been found too cumbersome for use in surveying; for example, the latitude and longitude angles must be expressed to four decimals of a second (01.0000″) to give position to the closest 0.01 ft. (At latitude 44°, 1″ latitude = 101 ft and 1″ longitude = 73 ft.)

To allow the surveyor to perform reasonably precise surveys and still use plane geometry and trigonometry for problem solutions, several forms of plane coordinate grids have been utilized.

8-5 Universal Transverse Mercator Grid System

The universal transverse Mercator (UTM) projection is developed by placing a cylinder around the earth with its circumference tangent to the earth along a meridian (central meridian). See Figure 8-7. When the cylinder is developed, a plane is established that can be used for grid purposes. It can be noted [Figures 8-7 and 8-9(a)] that at the central merid-

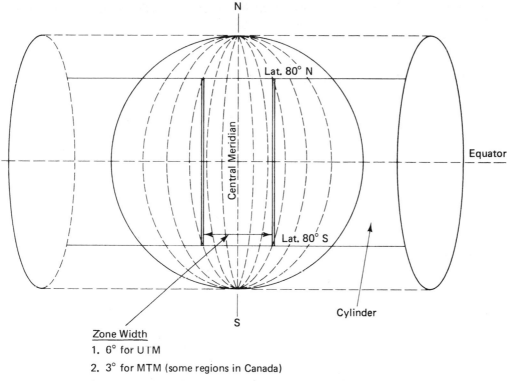

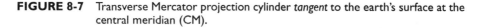

N

Lat. 80° N

Central Meridian

Equator

Lat. 80° S

Cylinder

S

<u>Zone Width</u>

1. 6° for UTM

2. 3° for MTM (some regions in Canada)

3. About 158 Miles for State Plane Coordinate Grid (U.S.A.)

FIGURE 8-7   Transverse Mercator projection cylinder *tangent* to the earth's surface at the central meridian (CM).

ian the scale is exact, and the scale becomes progressively more distorted as the distance from the central meridian increases. The distortion (which is always present when a spherical surface is projected onto a plane) can be minimized in two ways. First, the distortion can be minimized by keeping the zone width relatively narrow; second, the distortion can be lessened by reducing the radius of the projection cylinder so that, instead of being tangent to the earth's surface, the cylinder cuts through the earth's surface at an optimal distance on either side of the central meridian [see Figures 8-8 and 8-9(b)]. This means that the scale factor at the central meridian is less than unity; it is unity at the line of intersection and more than unity between the lines of intersection and the zone limit meridians. The plane surfaces developed from these tangent and secant cylinders are illustrated in Figure 8-9(a) and (b). Figure 8-10 shows a cross section of a UTM 6° zone. For full treatment of this topic, the reader is referred to texts on geodesy and cartography.

CHARACTERISTICS OF THE UNIVERSAL TRANSVERSE MERCATOR GRID SYSTEM

- Zone is 6° wide. Zone overlap is 0°30'.
- Latitude of the origin is the equator.
- Easting value of each central meridian = 500,000.000 m.

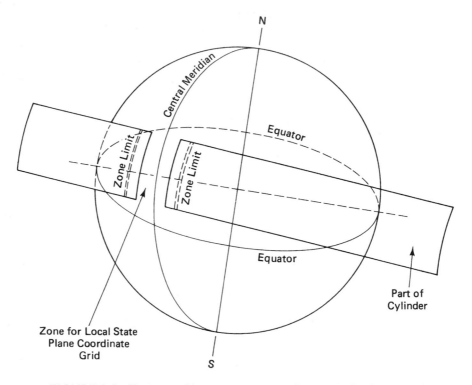

FIGURE 8-8 Transverse Mercator projection. *Secant* cylinder for state plane coordinate grids.

- Northing value of the equator = 0.000 m (10,000,000.000 m in the southern hemisphere).
- Scale factor at the central meridian is 0.9996 (i.e., 1/2500).
- Zone numbering commences with 1 in the zone 180° W to 174° W and increases eastward to zone 60 at the zone 174° E to 180° E.
- Projection limits of latitude are 80° S to 80° N.

8-6   State Plane Coordinate Grid Systems

Geodetic control surveys are based on the best estimates of the actual shape of the earth. For many years geodists used the Clarke 1866 spheroid as a base for their work, but as modernization occurred in both instrumentation and technology, it became clear that there was need for a more representative datum. Accordingly, a new spheroid, Geodetic Reference System 1980 (GRS80), was adopted.

To enable surveyors to avoid the more complicated three-dimensional computations required in geodesy, the National Geodetic Survey (NGS) devised state plane coordinate systems based on Lambert projections (conical) for states with a greater east/west dimension and on transverse Mercator projections (cylindrical) for states with a greater north/south dimension. To minimize distortion, the Lambert projection was limited to

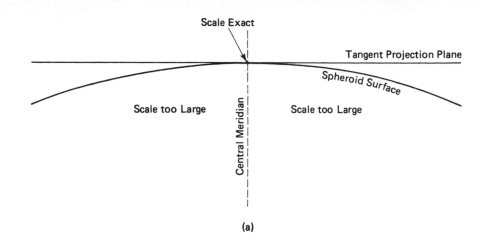

(a)

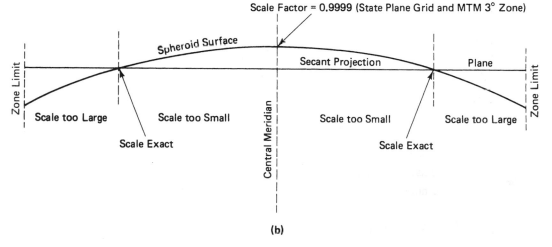

(b)

FIGURE 8-9 (a) Section view of the projection plane and the earth's surface (tangent projection). (b) Section view of the projection plane and the earth's surface (secant projection).

about 158 miles in a north/south direction, and the transverse Mercator projection was limited to about 158 miles in an east/west direction.

Initially, in 1933, NGS developed the State Plane Coordinate System (SPCS 27) using reference datum (NAD27) based on the Clarke 1866 ellipsoid. A new reference datum based on the GRS80 ellipsoid was created and called the North American Datum (NAD83); it was used as the basis for the new State Plane Coordinate System 1983 (SPCS 83). It seems likely that both systems will be used in the foreseeable future.

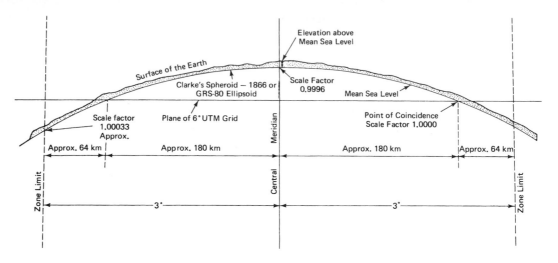

FIGURE 8-10 Cross section of a 6° zone (UTM).

Surveyors using both old and new SPCSs are able to compute position using tables published by the NGS. The SPCS 83, which enables the surveyor to work in a more precisely defined datum, uses similar mathematical approaches with some new nomenclature. For example, in the SPCS 27, the Lambert coordinates were expressed as *X* and *Y* with values given in feet (U.S. survey foot, see Table 1-1), and the convergence angle (between grid north and geodetic north) was displayed as θ; alternately, in the transverse Mercator grid, the convergence angle was designated by Δα. The SPCS 83, which has been adopted by most states, uses metric values for coordinates (designated as eastings and northings) as well as foot units (U.S. survey foot or international foot) in fewer states. The convergence angle is shown in both Lambert and transverse Mercator projections as γ.

The NGS, in addition to supplying tables for computations in SPCS 83, provides both interactive computations on the Internet (see the NGS Tool Kit, Section 8-1) and PC software available for downloading at www.ngs.noaa.gov. Many surveyors prefer computer-based computations to working with cumbersome tables. A manual that describes SPCS83 in detail, *NOAA Manual NOS NGS 5: State Plane Coordinate System of 1983,* is available from NGS.*

*To obtain NGS publications, contact: NOAA, National Geodetic Survey, N/NGS12, 1315 East-West Highway, Station 9202, Silver Springs, MD 20910-3282. Publications can also be ordered by phoning: (301) 713-3242.

8-6-1   Lambert Projection

The Lambert projection is a conical conformal projection. The apex of the cone is on the earth's axis of rotation above the north pole for northern hemisphere projections and below the south pole for southern hemisphere projections. The location of the apex (and the θ angle) depends on the area of the ellipsoid that is being projected. Reference to Figure 8-11 will confirm that although the east-west direction is relatively distortion-free, the

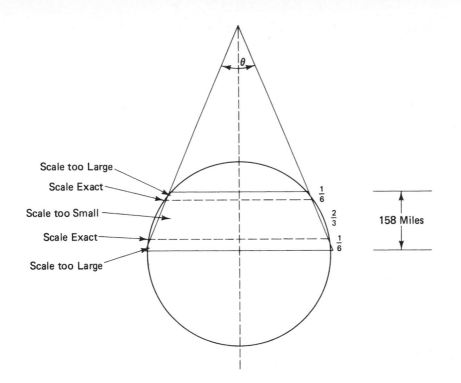

Scale too Large

Scale Exact

Scale too Small

Scale Exact

Scale too Large

$\frac{1}{6}$

$\frac{2}{3}$

$\frac{1}{6}$

158 Miles

FIGURE 8-11   Lambert secant projection.

north-south coverage must be restrained (e.g., to 158 miles) to maintain the integrity of the projection; therefore, the Lambert projection is used for states having a greater east-west dimension. Table 8-8 gives a list of all the states, indicating the type of projection being used; New York, Florida, and Alaska utilize both the transverse Mercator and the Lambert projections. The U.S. National Ocean Survey publishes tables for each state plane projection so that computations can be easily accomplished. These data have been revised to reflect the new reference spheroid (NAD '83) and new computer-based techniques for data manipulation. The National Ocean Survey publishes data (in meters) for both the state plane coordinate grid systems and the universal transverse Mercator grid system.

8-6-2   Computations for the Lambert Projection SPCS 27

Computations for the Lambert secant projection grid are illustrated in Figure 8-12. Most Lambert projection grids in the United States assign an X value at the central meridian (y axis) of 2,000,000 ft, and a Y value at the x axis of 0 ft.

The geographic coordinates (ϕ, latitude; λ, longitude) of point P are also shown. The distance R_b is the largest latitude radius of the zone and is obtained from the state plane tables. The angle θ is the angle between the meridian through point P and the central meridian. X_c is the X value assigned to the meridian (usually 2,000,000 ft) so that all the state X values will remain positive. The values of R are found in the state plane tables for the range of values for latitude, as are the values for θ for the range of values for longitude.

Table 8-8 STATE PLANE COORDINATE GRID SYSTEMS

Transverse Mercator System		Lambert System		Both Systems
Alabama	Mississippi	Arkansas	North Dakota	Alaska
Arizona	Missouri	California	Ohio	Florida
Delaware	Nevada	Colorado	Oklahoma	New York
Georgia	New Hampshire	Connecticut	Oregon	
Hawaii	New Jersey	Iowa	Pennsylvania	
Idaho	New Mexico	Kansas	South Carolina	
Illinois	Rhode Island	Kentucky	South Dakota	
Indiana	Vermont	Louisiana	Tennessee	
Maine	Wyoming	Maryland	Texas	
		Massachusetts	Utah	
		Michigan	Virginia	
		Minnesota	Washington	
		Montana	West Virginia	
		Nebraska	Wisconsin	
		North Carolina		

Using the relationships shown in Figure 8-12 and data from the appropriate state plane tables, we can compute the grid coordinates:

$$X_p = X_c + R \sin \theta \qquad (8\text{-}14)$$

$$Y_p = R_b - R \cos \theta \qquad (8\text{-}15)$$

The direction of a line can be analyzed by referring to Figure 8-13. It can be seen that the grid and geodetic meridians coincide at the central meridian and that the difference in azimuth between the grid meridian and the geodetic meridian is angle θ (convergence).

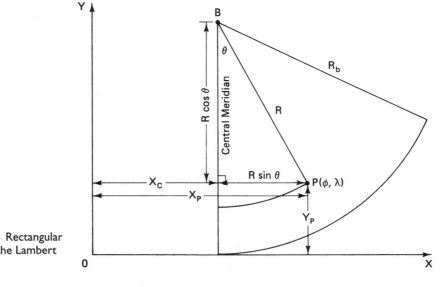

FIGURE 8-12 Rectangular coordinates on the Lambert projection.

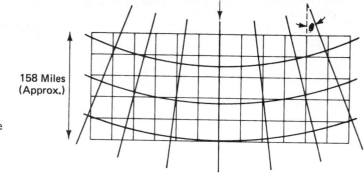

FIGURE 8-13 Lines of latitude (parallels) and lines of longitude (meridians) on the Lambert projection grid.

Angle θ becomes progressively larger as the distance from the central meridian increases (i.e., as the difference in longitude increases). See also Figure 6-5.

Angle θ is considered positive (+) if point P is east of the central meridian and negative if point P is west of the central meridian.

$$\text{Grid azimuth} = \text{geodetic azimuth} - \theta \qquad (8\text{-}16)$$

For distances of sights beyond 5 miles, a second term is added to θ to improve precision; the value of the second term is also available in the state plane tables.

If, in addition to limiting the north-south zone width to 158 miles, two-thirds of the zone width is between the secant lines (Figure 8-11), the distortion effect is kept to a level of 1/10,000 or better.

8-6-3   Computations for the Transverse Mercator Secant Projection SPCS 27

Most Mercator projection grids in the United States assign an X value to the central meridian (y axis) of 500,000 ft and a Y value to the x axis of 0 ft. The x axis is chosen so that all Y values for a specific state will be positive.

Using the relationships shown in Figure 8-14 and data from the appropriate state plane tables, we can compute the grid coordinates:

$$X'_p = H \cdot \Delta\lambda'' \pm ab \qquad (8\text{-}17)$$

$$X_p = X'_p + X_c \qquad (8\text{-}18)$$

(X_c is the X value assigned to the y axis for a specific state grid, usually 500,000 ft.)

$$YP = Y_0 + V\left(\frac{\Delta\lambda''}{100}\right)^2 \pm c \qquad (8\text{-}19)$$

Y_0, H, V, and a are based on the latitude and are found in the state zone tables. $\Delta\lambda''$ is the longitude of the central meridian minus the longitude of point P, given in seconds of arc; b and c are related to λ'' and are also found in the appropriate zone tables.

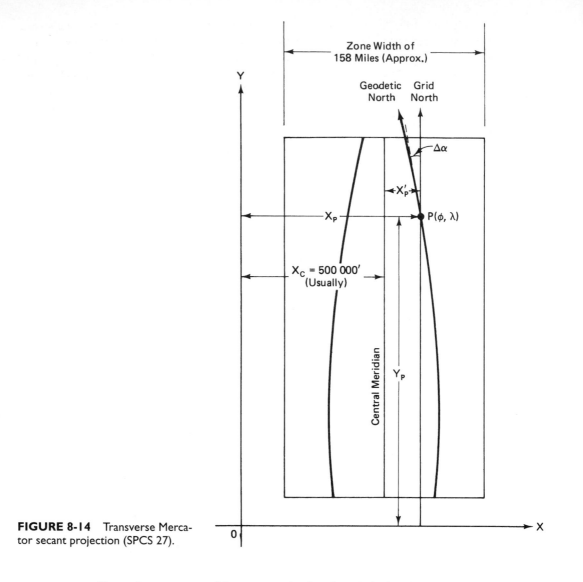

FIGURE 8-14 Transverse Mercator secant projection (SPCS 27).

Since the transverse Mercator projection is relatively distortion-free in the N-S direction, it is utilized for states having a predominantly N-S orientation (e.g., Indiana).

8-7 Utilization of Grid Coordinates

8-7-1 Elevation and Scale Factors

When local surveys (traverse or trilateration) are tied into coordinate grids, corrections must be provided so that (1) grid and ground distances can be reconciled and (2) grid and geodetic directions can be reconciled.

Figure 8-15 gives a section view of a state plane grid. It can be seen that a distance measured on the earth's surface must first be reduced for equivalency on the spheroid and then be further reduced (in this illustration) for equivalency on the projection plane. The first reduction involves multiplication by an elevation factor (sea level factor); the second reduction (adjustment) involves multiplication by the scale factor.

The elevation (sea level) factor can be determined by establishing a ratio, as is illustrated in Figure 8-16.

$$\text{Elevation factor} = \frac{\text{sea level distance}}{\text{ground distance}} = \frac{R}{R + H} \qquad (8\text{-}20)$$

where R is the average radius of the earth and H is the elevation above mean sea level.

For example, at 500 ft the elevation factor would be

$$\frac{20{,}906{,}000}{20{,}906{,}500} = 0.999976$$

and a ground distance of 800.00 ft at an average elevation of 500 ft would become $800 \times 0.999976 = 799.98$ at sea level.

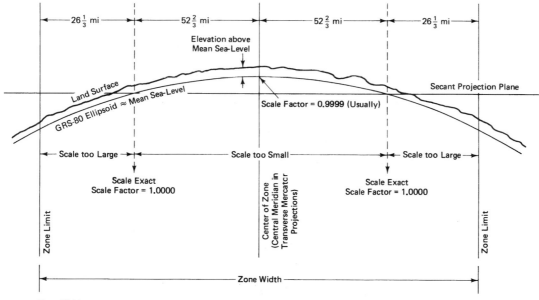

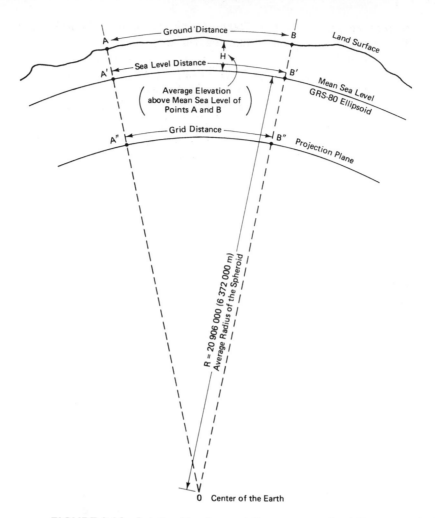

FIGURE 8-16 Relationship of ground distances to sea-level distances and grid distances.

For state plane projections, the published tables will give scale factors for positions of latitude difference (Lambert projection) or for distances east or west of the central meridian (transverse Mercator projections).

Scale factors for the transverse Mercator projections can also be computed by the formula

$$M_p = M_0 \left(1 + \frac{X^2}{2R^2} \right) \tag{8-21}$$

where M_p = scale factor at the survey station, M_0 = scale factor at the central meridian, X = east-west distance of the survey station from the central meridian, and R = average radius of the spheroid. ($X^2/2R^2$ can be expressed in feet, meters, miles, or kilometers.)

Chap. 8   Construction Control Surveys

For example, survey stations 12,000 ft from a central meridian having a scale factor of 0.9999 would have a scale factor determined as follows:

$$M_p = 0.9999 \left(1 + \frac{12,000^2}{2 \times 20,906,000^2}\right)$$

$$= 0.9999002$$

When the **elevation factor** is multiplied by the **scale factor,** the resultant is known as the **grid factor.** See Figure 8-17.

Ground distance $\times$ grid factor $=$ grid distance

Alternatively

$$\frac{\text{Grid distance}}{\text{Grid factor}} = \text{ground distance}$$

In practice, it is seldom necessary to use Formula (8-21), as tables are available for all state plane grids and the UTM grid (see Table 8-9). Grid factors can easily be interpolated (double interpolation) from these tables.

8-7-2 Convergence

Figures 6-5 and 8-14 illustrate the features of the transverse Mercator projection. The difference between grid north and geodetic north, also called convergence, is given by $\Delta\alpha$:

$$\Delta\alpha'' = \Delta\lambda'' \sin \phi p \qquad (8\text{-}22)$$

where $\Delta\lambda''$ is the difference in longitude in seconds between the central meridian and point P and ϕp is the latitude of point P. When long sights (> 5 miles) are taken, a second term (given in the state plane tables) is required to maintain directional accuracy. When the direction of a line from P_1 to P_2 is being considered, the expression becomes

$$\Delta\alpha'' = \Delta\lambda'' \sin \left(\frac{\phi P_1 + \phi P_2}{2}\right)$$

Alternatively, if the distance from the central meridian is known, the expression becomes

$$\theta'' = 52.13d \tan \phi \qquad (8\text{-}23)$$

or

$$\theta'' = 32.392\, dk \tan \phi$$

where θ = convergence angle in seconds

d = departure distance from the central meridian (CM) in miles (dk is the same distance in kilometers)

ϕ = average latitude of the line

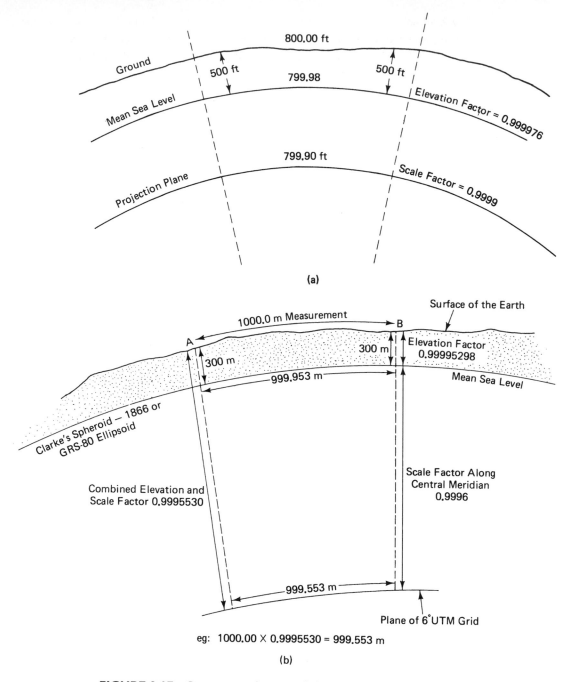

800.00 ft

Ground

500 ft

799.98

500 ft

Mean Sea Level

Elevation Factor = 0.999976

799.90 ft

Projection Plane

Scale Factor = 0.9999

(a)

Surface of the Earth

1000.0 m Measurement

B

A

300 m

Elevation Factor
0.99995298

300 m

999.953 m

Mean Sea Level

Clarke's Spheroid — 1866 or
GRS-80 Ellipsoid

Combined Elevation and
Scale Factor 0.9995530

Scale Factor Along
Central Meridian
0.9996

999.553 m

Plane of 6° UTM Grid

eg: 1000.00 × 0.9995530 = 999.553 m

(b)

FIGURE 8-17 Conversion of a ground distance to a grid distance using the elevation factor and the scale factor. (a) State plane grid. (b) Universal Transverse Mercator (UTM) grid, 6° zone.

■ EXAMPLE 8-1

Given the coordinates on the UTM coordinate grid of two horizontal control monuments (Mon. 113 and Mon. 115) and their elevations, compute the ground distance and geodetic direction between them (see Figure 8-18).

Station	Elevation	Northing	Easting
#113	181.926	4,849,872.066	632,885.760
#115	178.444	4,849,988.216	632,971.593

Zone 17 UTM; CM at 81° longitude West:

Scale factor at CM = 0.9996

ϕ (lat.) = 43°47′31″ ⎫ (scaled from topographic map for midpoint
λ (long.) = 79°20′35″ ⎭ of line joining Mon. 113 and Mon. 115)

By subtraction, coordinate distances are

$$\Delta N = 116.150 \text{ m}, \qquad \Delta E = 85.833 \text{ m}$$

1. Distance

$$\text{Mon. 113 to Mon. 115} = \sqrt{116.150^2 + 85.833^2} = 144.423 \text{ m}$$

2. Grid bearing

$$\text{Tan bearing} = \frac{\Delta E}{\Delta N} = \frac{85.833}{116.150}$$

$$\text{Bearing} = 36.463811°$$

$$\text{Grid bearing} = \text{N } 36°27′50″ \text{ E}$$

3. Convergence

$$\Delta\alpha'' = \Delta\lambda'' \sin \phi p \qquad\qquad (8\text{-}22)$$

$$= (81° - 79°20′35″) \sin 43°47′31″$$

$$= 4128″$$

$$= 1°08′48″$$

See Figure 8-18 for application of convergence.

4. Scale factor

$$\text{Scale factor at CM} = 0.9996$$

$$\text{Distance from CM} = \frac{132885.760 + 132971.593}{2}$$

$$= 132,928.677 \text{ m} = 132.929 \text{ km}$$

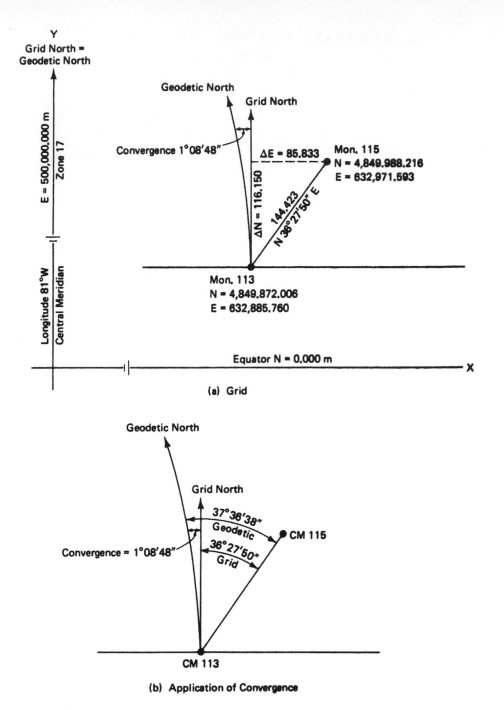

(a) Grid

(b) Application of Convergence

FIGURE 8-18 Illustration for Example 8-1. (a) Grid. (b) Application of convergence.

Scale factor at midpoint line Mon. 113–Mon. 115:

$$M_p = Mo \left(1 + \frac{X^2}{2R^2}\right) \tag{8-21}$$

$$= 0.9996 \left(1 + \frac{132.929^2}{2 \times 6372^{2*}}\right) = 0.999818$$

5. Elevation factor

$$\text{Elevation factor} = \frac{\text{sea level distance}}{\text{ground distance}} = \frac{R}{R + H^*} \tag{8-20}$$

$$= \frac{6372}{6372 + 0.180^\dagger} = 0.999972$$

6. Grid factor

$$\text{Grid factor} = \text{elevation factor} \times \text{scale factor}$$
$$= 0.999972 \times 0.999818 = 0.999790$$

or, using Table 8-9, Combined Scale and Elevation Factors (Grid Factors) —UTM,

	Distance from CM (km)		
Elev.	130	140	132.9 (Interpolated)
100	0.999792	0.999825	0.999802
200	0.999777	0.999810	0.999787

It now only remains to interpolate for the elevation value of 180 m; that is,

$$999,802 - \left(\frac{80}{100} \times 0.000015\right) = 0.999790$$

7. Ground distance

$$\text{Ground distance} = \frac{\text{grid distance}}{\text{grid factor}}$$

In this example,

$$\text{Ground distance Mon. 113–Mon. 115} = \frac{144.423}{0.999790} = 144.453 \text{ m}$$

*Average radius of sea level surface = 20,906,000 ft or 6,372,000 m.
†0.180 is the line midpoint elevation divided by 1000.

Table 8-9 COMBINED SCALE AND ELEVATION FACTORS (GRID FACTORS)—UTM

Distance from Central Meridian in Kilometers	Elevation above Mean Sea Level in Meters										
	0	100	200	300	400	500	600	700	800	900	1000
0	0.999600	0.999584	0.999569	0.999553	0.999537	0.999522	0.999506	0.999490	0.999475	0.999459	0.999443
10	0.999601	0.999586	0.999570	0.999554	0.999539	0.999523	0.999507	0.999492	0.999476	0.999460	0.999445
20	0.999605	0.999589	0.999574	0.999558	0.999542	0.999527	0.999511	0.999495	0.999480	0.999464	0.999448
30	0.999611	0.999595	0.999580	0.999564	0.999548	0.999533	0.999517	0.999501	0.999486	0.999470	0.999454
40	0.999620	0.999604	0.999588	0.999573	0.999557	0.999541	0.999526	0.999510	0.999494	0.999479	0.999463
50	0.999631	0.999615	0.999599	0.999584	0.999568	0.999552	0.999537	0.999521	0.999505	0.999490	0.999474
60	0.999644	0.999629	0.999613	0.999597	0.999582	0.999566	0.999550	0.999535	0.999519	0.999503	0.999488
70	0.999660	0.999645	0.999629	0.999613	0.999598	0.999582	0.999566	0.999551	0.999535	0.999519	0.999504
80	0.999679	0.999663	0.999647	0.999632	0.999616	0.999600	0.999585	0.999569	0.999553	0.999538	0.999522
90	0.999700	0.999684	0.999668	0.999653	0.999637	0.999621	0.999606	0.999590	0.999574	0.999559	0.999543
100	0.999723	0.999707	0.999692	0.999676	0.999660	0.999645	0.999629	0.999613	0.999598	0.999582	0.999566
110	0.999749	0.999733	0.999717	0.999702	0.999686	0.999670	0.999655	0.999639	0.999623	0.999608	0.999592
120	0.999777	0.999761	0.999746	0.999730	0.999714	0.999699	0.999683	0.999667	0.999652	0.999636	0.999620
130	0.999808	0.999792	0.999777	0.999761	0.999745	0.999730	0.999714	0.999698	0.999683	0.999667	0.999651
140	0.999841	0.999825	0.999810	0.999794	0.999778	0.999763	0.999747	0.999731	0.999716	0.999700	0.999684
150	0.999877	0.999861	0.999845	0.999830	0.999814	0.999798	0.999783	0.999767	0.999751	0.999736	0.999720
160	0.999915	0.999899	0.999884	0.999868	0.999852	0.999837	0.999821	0.999805	0.999790	0.999774	0.999758
170	0.999955	0.999940	0.999924	0.999908	0.999893	0.999877	0.999861	0.999846	0.999830	0.999814	0.999799
180	0.999999	0.999983	0.999967	0.999952	0.999936	0.999920	0.999905	0.999889	0.999873	0.999858	0.999842
190	1.000044	1.000028	1.000013	0.999997	0.999981	0.999966	0.999950	0.999934	0.999919	0.999903	0.999887
200	1.000092	1.000076	1.000061	1.000045	1.000029	1.000014	0.999998	0.999982	0.999967	0.999951	0.999935
210	1.000142	1.000127	1.000111	1.000095	1.000080	1.000064	1.000048	1.000033	1.000017	1.000001	0.999986
220	1.000195	1.000180	1.000164	1.000148	1.000133	1.000117	1.000101	1.000086	1.000070	1.000054	1.000039
230	1.000251	1.000235	1.000219	1.000204	1.000188	1.000172	1.000157	1.000141	1.000125	1.000110	1.000094
240	1.000309	1.000293	1.000277	1.000262	1.000246	1.000230	1.000215	1.000199	1.000183	1.000168	1.000152
250	1.000369	1.000353	1.000338	1.000322	1.000306	1.000290	1.000275	1.000259	1.000243	1.000228	1.000212

8-8 Project Control

Project control begins with either a boundary survey (e.g., residential developments) or an all-inclusive peripheral survey (e.g., construction sites). The boundary or site peripheral survey will, if possible, be tied into state or provincial grid control monuments so that reference can be made to the state or provincial coordinate grid systems. The peripheral survey is densified with judiciously placed control stations over the entire site. The survey data for all control points are entered into the computer for accuracy verification and error adjustment and, finally, for coordinate determination of all control points. All key layout points (e.g., lot corners, radius points, ₵ stations, curve points, construction points) are also coordinated with the computer by using coordinate geometry computer programs (e.g., COGO). Printout sheets, as shown in Figure 5-29, are used by the surveyor to lay out the proposed facility from coordinated control stations. The computer will give the surveyor the azimuth and distance from one, two, or perhaps three different control points to one layout point. Positioning a layout point from more than one control station provides an exceptional check on the accuracy of the work.

Generally a layout point can be positioned by simultaneous angle sightings from two control points, with the distance being established by EDM from one of those stations, or a layout point can be positioned by simultaneous angle sightings from three control points. Both techniques provide a redundancy in measurement that permits positional accuracy determination.

To ensure that the layout points have been accurately located (e.g., with an accuracy level of between 1/5000 and 1/10,000), the control points themselves must be located to an even higher level of accuracy. These accuracies can be achieved if EDMIs are used for distances and 1″ or 2″ theodolites are used for angle measurement.

As noted earlier, in addition to quality instrumentation, the surveyor must use "quality" geometrics in designing the shape of the control net; a series of interconnected equilateral triangles provides the strongest control net.

Control points are positioned keeping in mind the following:

1. Good visibility to other control points and an optimal number of layout points are required.
2. Not only is the visibility factor considered for existing ground conditions, but consideration is also given to all potential visibility lines during all stages of construction.
3. A minimum of two (three is preferred) reference ties is required for each control point so that it can be reestablished if destroyed. Consideration must be given to the availability of features suitable for referencing (i.e., features into which nails can be driven or cut-cross chiseled, etc.). Ideally the three ties would be each 120° apart. See Figure 11-4.
4. Control points should be placed in locations that will not be affected by primary or secondary construction activity. In addition to keeping clear of the actual construction site positions, the surveyor must anticipate temporary disruptions to the terrain resulting from access roads, materials stockpiling, and so on. If possible, control points are safely located adjacent to features that will *not* be moved (e.g., electrical towers, concrete walls, large valuable trees).

5. Control points must be established on solid ground (or rock). Swampy areas or loose fill areas must be avoided.

Once the control point locations have been tentatively chosen, they are plotted so that the quality of the control net geometrics can be considered. At this stage, it may be necessary to go back into the field and locate additional control points to strengthen weak geometric figures. When the locations have been finalized on paper, each station is given a unique identification code number, and then the control points are set in the field. Field notes, showing reference ties to each point, are carefully taken and then filed. Now the actual measurements of the distances and angles of the control net are taken. When all the field data have been collected, the closures and adjustments are computed. The coordinates of all layout points are then computed, with polar ties being generated for each layout point, from two or possibly three control stations.

Figure 8-19 shows a single layout point being positioned by angle only from three control sights. The three control sights could simply be referenced to the farthest away of the control points themselves (e.g., angles *A, B,* and *C*); or, if a reference azimuth point (RAP) has been identified and coordinated in the locality, it is preferred, as it no doubt would be farther away and thus capable of providing more precise sightings (e.g., angles

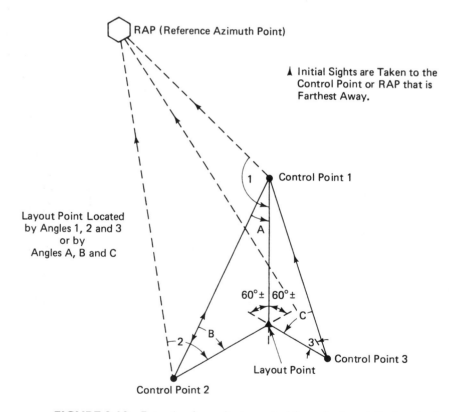

FIGURE 8-19 Example of coordinate control for polar layout. Single point layout, located by three angles. (Adapted from construction manual, Ministry of Transportation—Ontario)

1, 2, and 3). RAPs are typically communications towers, church spires, or other identifiable points that can be seen from widely scattered control stations. Coordinates of RAPs are computed by turning angles to the RAP from project control monuments or preferably from state or provincial control grid monuments (see Figure 5-29).

Figure 8-5 illustrates a method of recording angle directions and distances to control stations with a listing of derived azimuths. Station 17 can be quickly found by the surveyor from the distance and alignment ties to the hydrant, the cut cross on curb, and the nail in the pole. Had station 17 been destroyed, it could have been reestablished from these and other reference ties.

The bottom row, marked "check," indicates that the surveyor has "closed the horizon" by continuing to revolve the theodolite back to the initial target point (100, in this example) and then reading the horizontal circle. A difference of more than 5″ between the initial reading and the check reading usually means that the series of angles in that column must be repeated.

After the design of a facility has been coordinated, polar layout coordinates can be generated for layout points from selected stations. The surveyor can copy the computer data directly into the field book (see Figure 8-20) for later use in the field. On large projects

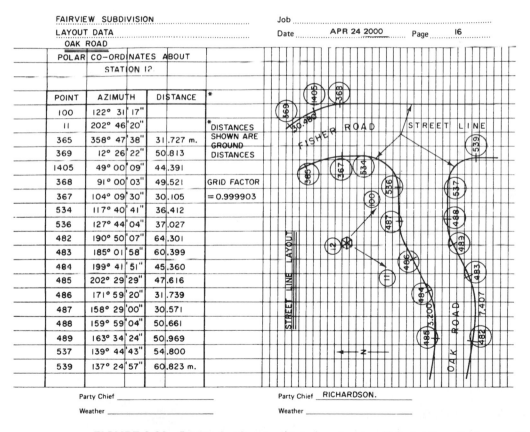

FAIRVIEW SUBDIVISION Job ....
LAYOUT DATA Date .... APR 24 2000 .... Page .... 16 ....
OAK ROAD

POLAR	CO-ORDINATES	ABOUT		
	STATION 12			
POINT	AZIMUTH	DISTANCE	*	
100	122° 31' 17"			
11	202° 46' 20"		*DISTANCES	
365	358° 47' 38"	31.727 m.	SHOWN ARE	
369	12° 26' 22"	50.813	GROUND DISTANCES	
1405	49° 00' 09"	44.391		
368	91° 00' 03"	49.521	GRID FACTOR	
367	104° 09' 30"	30.105	= 0.999903	
534	117° 40' 41"	36.412		
536	127° 44' 04"	37.027		
482	190° 50' 07"	64.301		
483	185° 01' 58"	60.399		
484	199° 41' 51"	45.360		
485	202° 29' 29"	47.616		
486	171° 59' 20"	31.739		
487	158° 29' 00"	30.571		
488	159° 59' 04"	50.661		
489	163° 34' 24"	50.969		
537	139° 44' 43"	54.800		
539	137° 24' 57"	60.823 m.		

Party Chief _____ Party Chief __RICHARDSON.__
Weather _____ Weather _____

FIGURE 8-20 Prepared polar coordinate layout notes. (Adapted from field notes, Marshall, Macklin, Monaghan, Surveyors and Engineers—Markham, Ontario)

(expressways, dams, etc.), it is common practice to have bound volumes printed that include polar coordinate data for all control stations and all layout points (see Figure 5-29). Most Total Stations, discussed in chapter 5, have automatic computer–to–Total Station layout data transfer capabilities. This means that the surveyor is able to store all the layout data for a project in the Total Station itself and is able to access specific data simply by entering the appropriate point identification code. The automatic transfer of polar layout data to the Total Station will eliminate transcription errors that can occur when the technique illustrated in Figure 8-20 is used.

In addition to providing rectangular coordinates (based on the coordinate grid) and polar coordinates (based on specific control stations), the computer program will generate direct distance and bearing data between layout points. These point-to-point data are valuable for checking the location of points already established by polar layout. These checks are usually accomplished by measuring the point-to-point distances, although angular checks are also possible.

8-9   Level Loop Adjustments

In Section 3-6, it was noted that level surveys had to be closed within acceptable tolerances or the survey would have to be repeated. The tolerances for various orders of surveys are shown in Tables 8-3 and 8-4.

If a level survey is performed in order to establish new benchmarks, it is desirable to suitably proportion any acceptable error throughout the length of the survey. Since the error tolerances shown in Tables 8-3 and 8-4 are based on the distances surveyed, adjustments to the level loop will be based on the relevant distances or on the number of instrument setups, which is a factor directly related to the distance surveyed.

■ EXAMPLE 8-2
A level circuit is shown in Figure 8-21. The survey, needed for local engineering projects, commenced at BM 20; the elevations of new benchmarks 201, 202, and 203 were determined; and then the level survey was looped back to BM 20, the point of commencement (the survey could have terminated at any established BM).

According to Table 8-3, the allowable error for a second-order, Class II (local engineering projects) survey is $0.008 \sqrt{K}$; thus, $0.008 \sqrt{4.7} = 0.017$ m is the permissible error.

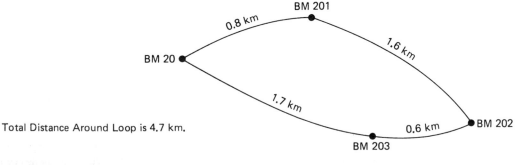

Total Distance Around Loop is 4.7 km.

FIGURE 8-21   Level loop.

The error in the survey was found to be -0.015 m over a total distance of 4.7 km—in this case, an acceptable error. It only remains for this acceptable error to be suitably distributed over the length of the survey. The error is proportioned according to the fraction of cumulative distance over total distance, as shown in the following table. More complex adjustments are normally performed by computer, utilizing the adjustment method of least squares.

BM	Loop Distance, Cumulative (km)	Elevation	Correction $\dfrac{\text{Cumulative Distance}}{\text{Total Distance}} \times C*$	Adjusted Elevation
20		186.273 (fixed)		186.273
201	0.8	184.242	$+0.8/4.7 \times 0.015 = +0.003 =$	184.245
202	2.4	182.297	$+2.4/4.7 \times 0.015 = +0.008 =$	182.305
203	3.0	184.227	$+3.0/4.7 \times 0.015 = +0.010 =$	184.237
20	4.7	186.258	$+4.7/4.7 \times 0.015 = +0.015 =$	186.273

$*C = 186.273 - 186.258 = +0.015$ m

Problems

Problems 8-1 to 8-5 utilize the following urban control monument data:

Monument	Elevation	Northing	Easting
A	179.832	4,850 296.103	317 104.062
B	181.356	4,850 218.330	316 823.936
C	188.976	4,850 182.348	316 600.889
D	187.452	4,850 184.986	316 806.910

Longitude @ monument $B = 79°21'00''$ West

Average latitude @ $43°47'30''$

Central meridian (CM) at longitude $79°30'$ West; scale factor = 0.9999, easting at CM = 304,800 m; northing at equator = 0.000 m.

8-1. Determine the grid distances and grid bearings of sides AB, BC, CD, and DA.

8-2. From the grid bearings computed in Problem 8-1, compute the interior angles (and their sum) of the traverse A, B, C, D, A, thus verifying the correctness of the grid bearing computations.

8-3. Determine the ground distances for the four traverse sides by applying the scale and elevation factors (i.e., grid factors).

8-4. Determine the convergence correction for each traverse side and the geodetic bearings for each traverse side.

8-5. From the geodetic bearings computed in Problem 8-4, compute the interior angles (and their sum) of the traverse A, B, C, D, A, thus verifying the correctness of the geodetic bearing computations.

8-6. Given the following level loop data:

BM	Cumulative Loop Distance	Elevation
102		171.277 (fixed)
	600 m	
1100		169.990
	1300 m	
1101		169.773
	2100 m	
1102		166.553
	2500 m	
1103		168.270
	2800 m	
1104		170.337
	3500 m	
102		171.215

(a) Compute the loop error.
(b) Determine the level of accuracy from Table 8-3 or Table 8-4.
(c) Adjust the elevations of the newly established benchmarks.

Chapter 9

Global Positioning
Systems (GPS)

9-1 Background

In the mid-1980s, the U.S. Department of Defense (DoD) began to implement a second-generation guidance system—*Navigation Satellite Timing and Ranging* (NAVSTAR) Global Positioning System *(GPS)*. In December 1993, the U.S. government officially declared that the system had reached its initial operational capability (IOC) with 26 satellites (23 Block II satellites) potentially then available for tracking. Additional Block II satellites continue to be launched (life span is thought to be about 7 years). Current *GPS* satellite status and the constellation configuration can be accessed via the Internet at http://www.ngs.noaa.gov/. Tables 9-1 and 9-2 are examples of satellite status reports.

Prior to NAVSTAR, precise positioning was usually determined by using low-altitude satellites or inertial guidance systems. The first-generation satellite positioning system, called TRANSIT, consisted of five satellites in polar orbit at an altitude of only 1000 km. Precise surveys, with positioning from 0.2 to 0.3 m, could be accomplished using **translocation** techniques —that is, one receiver occupied a position of known coordinates while another occupied an unknown position. Data received at the known position were used to model signal transmission and determine orbital errors, thus permitting more precise results. The positioning analysis techniques used in the TRANSIT system utilized a ground receiver capable of noting the change in satellite frequency transmission as the satellite first approached and then receded from the observer. The change in frequency was affected by the velocity of the satellite itself. The change in velocity of transmissions from the approaching and then receding satellite, known as the Doppler effect, is directly proportional to the shift in frequency of the transmitted signals and thus proportional to the change of distance between the satellite and the receiver over a given time interval. When the satellite's orbit was precisely known and the position of the satellite in that orbit was also precisely known through ephemeris data and universal time (UT), the position of the receiving station could be computed.

Table 9-1 GPS SATELLITE STATUS REPORT

SUBJ: GPS Status	17 Jan 2000

1. SATELLITES, PLANES, AND CLOCKS (CS=CESIUM RB=RUBIDIUM):
A. BLOCK I : NONE
B. BLOCK II: PRNS 1, 2, 3, 4, 5, 6, 7, 8, 9, 10, 11, 13, 14, 15,
    PLANE   : SLOT F4, B3, C2, D4, B4, C1, C4, A3, A1, E3, D2, F5, E1, D5,
    CLOCK   :   CS, CS, CS, RB, CS, CS, RB, CS, CS, CS, RB, RB, CS CS
    BLOCK II: PRNS 16, 17, 18, 19, 21, 22, 23, 24, 25, 26, 27, 29, 30, 31
    PLANE   : SLOT E5, D3, F3, A5, E2, B1, B4, D1, A2, F2, A4, F1, B2, C3
    CLOCK   :   CS, CS, CS, CS, CS, RB, CS, RB, CS, RB, CS, RB, CS, CS

Note: Daily status reports are available on the Internet at http://www.navcen.uscg.mol/gps/status/default.htm.

Table 9-2 GLONASS CONSTELLATION STATUS REPORT

GLONASS Constellation Status
(January 17, 2000)

GLONASS Number	Cosmos Number	Plane/ Slot	Frequ. Chann.	Launch Date	Intro Date	Status	Outage Date
758	2275	3/18	10	11.04.94	04.09.94	withdrawn	15.01.00
770	2288	2/14	9	11.08.94	04.09.94	withdrawn	15.01.00
775	2289	2/16	22	11.08.94	07.09.94	operating	
766	2308	3/22	10	07.03.95	05.04.95	operating	
781	2317	2/10	9	24.07.95	22.08.95	operating	
785	2318	2/11	4	24.07.95	22.08.95	operating	
776	2323	2/9	6	14.12.95	07.01.96	operating	
778	2324	2/15	11	14.12.95	26.04.99	operating	
782	2325	2/13	6	14.12.95	18.01.96	operating	
779	2364	1/1	2	30.12.98	18.02.99	operating	
784	2363	1/8	8	30.12.98	29.01.99	operating	
786	2362	1/7	7	30.12.98	29.01.99	operating	

Note: All the dates (DD.MM.YY) are given in Moscow Time [coordinated universal time (UTC) + 0300]. Daily updates are available on the GLONASS Internet site: http://mx.iki.rssi.ru/SFCSIC/english.html.

Another positioning system available is called the Inertial Surveying System (ISS). This system requires a vehicle (truck or helicopter) to occupy a point of known coordinates (northing, easting, and elevation) and remain stationary for a *zero velocity update.* As the vehicle moves, its location is constantly updated by the use of three computer-controlled accelerometers, each aligned to the north-south, east-west, or vertical axis. The accelerometer platform is oriented north-south, east-west, and plumb by means of three computer-controlled gyroscopes, each of which is aligned to one of three axes; see Figure 9-1. Analysis of acceleration data gives rectangular (latitude and longitude) displacement factors for horizontal movement, in addition to vertical displacement. The high cost of both the ISS equipment and its operation has resulted in its being largely replaced by **GPS** positioning techniques for all but very specialized applications.

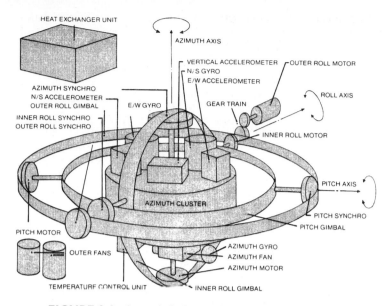

FIGURE 9-1 Inertial platform schematic. (Courtesy of Nortech, Canada)

9-2 Global Positioning

The current *GPS* is based on accurate ephemeris data on the real-time location of each satellite and on a very precisely kept time. It uses satellite signals, accurate time, and sophisticated algorithms to generate distances to ground receivers in order to provide "resectioned" positions anywhere on earth. GPS can also provide navigation data, such as the speed and direction of a mobile receiver, as well as estimated arrival times at specific locations.

The satellite orbits have been designed so that positioning can usually be determined at any location on earth at any time of the day or night. A minimum of four satellites must be tracked to solve the positioning intersection equations dealing with position (*X, Y,* and *Z* coordinates—which are later translated to easting, northing, and elevation) and with clock differences between the satellites and ground receivers. In reality, five or more satellites are tracked, if possible, to introduce additional redundancies and to strengthen the geometry of the satellite array. This not only provides more accurate positioning, but also, reduces the receiver occupation time at each survey station.

In addition to the satellites arrayed in space, the GPS includes tracking stations evenly spaced around the earth. Stations are located at Colorado Springs, Colorado (the master control station), and on the islands of Ascension, Diego Garcia, Kwajalein, and Hawaii. All satellites are observed at each station, with all the clock and ephemeris data being transmitted to the control station at Colorado Springs. The system is kept at peak efficiency, as corrective data are transmitted back to the satellites from Colorado Springs (and a few other ground stations) every few hours.

This system, originally designed for military guidance, has quickly attracted a wide variety of civilian users in the positioning and navigation applications fields. Already additional applications have been developed in commercial aviation navigation, boating and shipping navigation, trucking and railcar positioning, emergency routing, automobile dashboard electronic charts, and orienteering navigation. Also, there are plans to install GPS chips in cell phones to satisfy the 911 service requirement for precise caller locations.

9-3 Receivers

GPS receivers range in ability (and cost) from survey-level receivers capable of use in surveys requiring high accuracy and costing more than $20,000, to mapping and geographic information system (GIS) receivers (submeter accuracy) costing about $3,000 each, to marine navigation receivers (accuracy 100 to 200 m) costing about $1,000, and finally to orienteering (hiking) and low-precision mapping/GIS receivers costing only a few hundred dollars. See Figures 9-2 to 9-6 and Figures F-6 to F-8.

FIGURE 9-2 Ashtech Dimension GPS Receiver with Corvalis CMT-CV5 Data Collector. Featuring 12 channels. C/A code and carrier, 2 MB internal memory, two RS-232 I/O ports, and an internal microstrip antenna. (Courtesy of Ashtech, California)

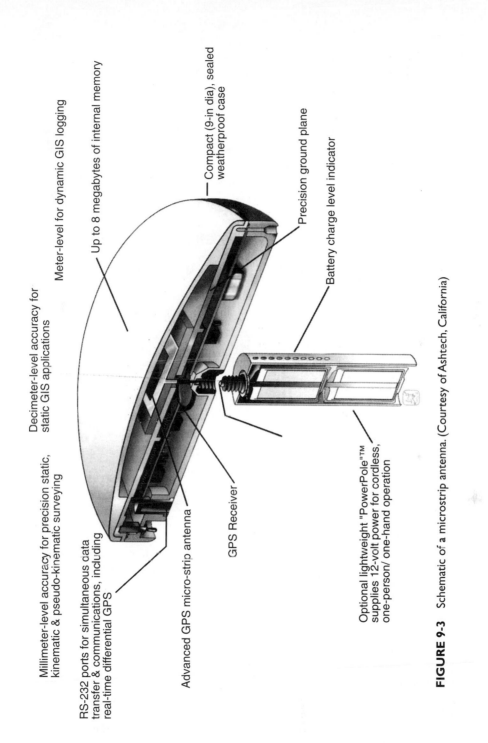

Millimeter-level accuracy for precision static, kinematic & pseudo-kinematic surveying

Decimeter-level accuracy for static GIS applications

Meter-level for dynamic GIS logging

Up to 8 megabytes of internal memory

Compact (9-in dia), sealed weatherproof case

Precision ground plane

Battery charge level indicator

RS-232 ports for simultaneous data transfer & communications, including real-time differential GPS

Advanced GPS micro-strip antenna

GPS Receiver

Optional lightweight "PowerPole"™ supplies 12-volt power for cordless, one-person/ one-hand operation

FIGURE 9-3 Schematic of a microstrip antenna. (Courtesy of Ashtech, California)

305

FIGURE 9-4 Leica SYS 300. System includes SR9400 GPS receiver (single frequency) with AT201 antenna, CR333 GPS controller (electronic field book) that collects data and provides software for real-time GPS surveying, and a radio modem. It can provide the following accuracies: 10 mm to 20 mm + 2 ppm using differential carrier techniques; and .30 m to .50 m using differential code measurements. (Courtesy of Leica Geosystems Inc., Norcross, Georgia)

The major differences in the receivers are the number of channels available (the number of satellites that can be tracked at one time) and whether or not the receiver can observe both L1 and L2 frequencies—code phase and carrier phase may also be measured. Generally speaking the higher-cost dual-frequency receivers require much shorter observation times for positioning measurements than do the less expensive single-frequency receivers. Low-end general-purpose GPS receivers track only one channel at a time (sequencing from satellite to satellite as tracking progresses); an improved low-end general-purpose receiver tracks on two channels, but still must sequence the tracking to other satellites to achieve positioning. Low-end surveying receivers can continuously observe on 5 channels (sequencing not required), whereas some high-end surveying receivers can observe on 12 channels. Some receivers can control photogrammetric camera operation, and some receivers can datalog every second, while others datalog every 15 seconds. The more expensive receivers can be used in all GPS survey modes with shorter observation times, whereas less expensive receivers can be restricted to a certain type of survey and will require longer observation times and perhaps longer processing times as well. As this is written, new software and hardware are being developed that will increase capabilities while reducing costs. GPS surveying has a very bright future.

The cost for three precise receivers, together with appropriate software, ranges up from $50,000—with expectations of lower costs as production increases and technology im-

Microstrip
Antenna

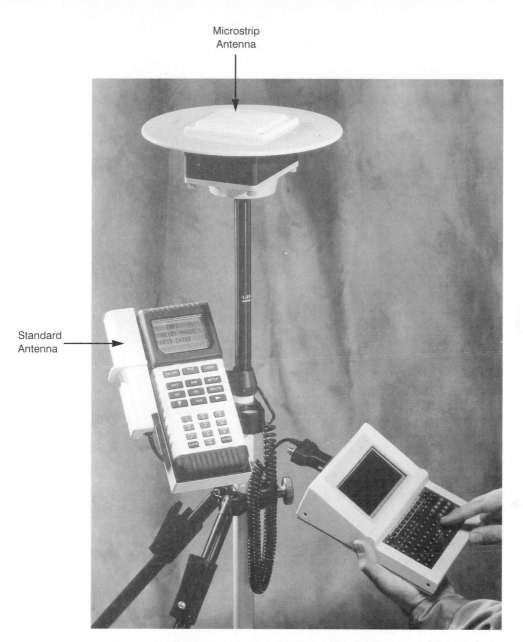

Standard
Antenna

FIGURE 9-5 Magellan 5-channel GPS NAVPRO 5000 receiver shown with multipath re-
sistant microstrip antenna and data collector (1 meg HP 95LXGPS). When
used with the large antenna in differential mode, sub-meter accuracy can be
achieved with 10 minutes of observations. (Courtesy of Magellan Systems
Corp., San Dimas, California)

FIGURE 9-6 Trimble navigation Total Station GPS. Real-time positioning for a wide variety of applications. Features include: GPS antenna and electronic field book at the adjustable pole; receiver, radio and radio antenna in the backpack. The receiver has been equipped with GPS processing software and the electronic field book has been equipped with the applications software (e.g., layout) thus permitting real time data capture or layout. (Courtesy of Trimble Navigation, Sunnyvale, California)

proves. In contrast, two lower-order receivers can be used in *relative positioning* mode to determine position to within a few meters—a precision that could be acceptable for selected mapping and GIS data bases. The total cost (including software) of this system can be as low as $7000. As noted in Section 9-6, surveys can be performed while using only one receiver if access is available to radio-transmitted corrections from a permanent receiver—as is the case with the U.S. Coast Guard's Differential Global Positioning System *(DGPS).*

One-receiver surveys, utilizing both code and carrier measurements, can also be performed utilizing the still developing national Global Positioning Systems in the United States and Canada—see Sections 9-8 and 9-9.

9-4   Satellites

GPS satellites (Figure 9-7) are manufactured by Rockwell International, weigh about 1900 pounds, span 17 feet (with solar panels deployed), and orbit the earth at 10,900 nautical

FIGURE 9-7 GPS satellite. (Courtesy of Leica Geosystems Inc., Norcross, Georgia)

miles (20,000 km) in a period of 12 hours (actually 11 hours, 58 minutes). The satellites' constellation (see Figure 9-8) consists of 24 satellites (including 3 spares) placed in six orbital planes. This configuration ensures that at least four satellites (the minimum number needed for precise measurements) are always potentially visible anywhere on earth.

Russia has also created a satellite constellation, called GLONASS, which consists of 24 satellites, placed in three orbital planes at 19,100 km with an orbit time of 11 hours, 15 minutes. As with GPS, GLONASS satellites continuously broadcast their own precise positions along with less precise positions for all other same-constellation satellites. Unlike

FIGURE 9-8 GPS satellites in orbit around the Earth.

GPS, GLONASS does not have selective availability (SA)—see Section 9-5—which permits more precise measurements under some conditions.

Tables 9-1 and 9-2 show the status for both GPS and GLONASS satellites. Daily updates of satellite status are available on the Internet at the addresses shown in the tables. (The reader will note that 10 satellites are listed as operational on the GLONASS Home Page, although all 12 satellites are listed as operational on the History Page.) Knowing the "health" of the satellites is critical to mission planning.

Many GPS receivers now are capable of tracking both GPS and GLONASS satellite signals. The advantages of using both constellations are these: (1) The increased number of visible satellites results in the potential for shorter observation times and increased accuracy, and (2) the increased number of satellites available to a receiver could mean that surveys interrupted by poor satellite geometry or by local obstructions caused by buildings, tree canopy, and the like while using only one constellation could continue uninterrupted by also tracking satellites from a second constellation.

9-5   Satellite Signals

GPS satellites transmit at two L-band frequencies with the following characteristics:

L1 FREQUENCY

L1 at 1575.42 MHz

$\lambda = c/f$ (5-1)

where λ is the wavelength, c is the speed of light, and f is the frequency.

$$\lambda = \frac{300,000,000 \text{ m/s}}{1,575,420,000 \text{ Hz}} = 0.190 \text{ m}$$

The wavelength is about 19 cm.

- C/A code

- P code

- Navigation message (clock corrections and orbital data)
- Y code (anti-spoofing code)

L2 FREQUENCY

L2 at 1227.60 MHz

$\lambda = c/f$ (5-1)

$$\lambda = \frac{300,000,000 \text{ m/s}}{1,227,600,000 \text{ Hz}} = 0.244 \text{ m}$$

The wavelength is about 24 cm.

- P code

- Navigation message (clock corrections and orbital data)
- Y code (anti-spoofing code)

The coarse acquisition (C/A) code is available to the public, whereas the P code is designed for military use. Only the P code is modulated on the L2 band. Although it was originally said that in times of national emergency the DoD could degrade the satellite signals, apparently this degradation (resulting in errors in the range of 100 m)—called selective availability (SA), which occurs on both L1 and L2, is now permanently activated. Another method of denying accuracy to the user is called anti-spoofing (A-S). Anti-spoofing occurs as the P code is encrypted to prevent tinkering by hostile forces. At present, both SA and A-S, along with most natural and other errors associated with the GPS measurements, can be eliminated by *relative positioning*. The more data collected, the faster and more accurate the solutions. For example, some GPS suppliers have computer programs designed to deal with some or all of the following: C/A code pseudorange on L1, both L1 and L2 P code pseudoranges, both carrier phases, both Doppler observations, and a measurement of the cross-correlation of the encrypted P code (Y code) on the L1 and L2 frequencies—to produce real-time or post processing solutions.

It was announced at the White House in early 1999 that provision was being made to add two additional civilian signals by 2005 on the next generation of satellites (Block IIF). Apparently one of the new signals will be located in the frequency of the current GPS L2 signal and one in some other location—perhaps L5. Additional civilian frequencies will make positioning faster and more accurate under many measuring conditions.

Finally, there are plans to establish another satellite constellation (called Galileo) in Europe. When this occurs, surveyors and other users will have a much expanded global positioning system. The combination of GPS, GLONASS, and Galileo is referred to as the Global Navigation Satellite System (GNSS).

One key dimension in positioning is the parameter of time. Time is kept on board the satellites by so-called atomic clocks—with a precision of 1 nanosecond (.0000000001 s). The ground receivers are equipped with less precise quartz clocks. Uncertainties caused by these less precise clocks are resolved when observing the signals from four satellites—instead of the basic three-satellite configuration required for *X/Y/Z* positioning.

9-6 Position Measurements

Position measurements generally fall into one of two categories: *code measurement* and *carrier phase measurement*. Civilian code measurement is restricted to the C/A code, which can only provide accuracies in the range of 100 m when used in *point positioning* and accuracies in the "submeter" to 10 m range, when used in various *relative positioning* techniques. P code measurements can apparently provide the military with much better accuracies.

Point positioning is the technique that employs one GPS receiver to track satellite code signals so that it can directly determine the coordinates of the receiver station. *Relative positioning* is a technique that employs at least two GPS receivers to track satellite code signals and/or satellite carrier phases to determine the baseline vector (ΔX, ΔY, and ΔZ) from one receiver to the other receiver. When one receiver is set up on a known base station and a roving receiver simultaneously measures signals from the same satellites, computed (post-processed) accuracies can be in the "submeter" to 10 m range, as previously noted for C/A code measurements, and in the millimeter range for carrier phase measurements. Some receivers, set up at base stations having known coordinates, are equipped with software capable of immediately determining range and/or carrier phase errors and with radios that can transmit the error correction data to the roving receiver(s). Roving receivers equipped with appropriate software can then determine the coordinates of their stations in *real time*.

The types of surveying where code pseudorange measurements or carrier measurements are made at a base station and then used to correct measurements made at another survey station are called *differential positioning*. Although the code measurement accuracies ("submeter" to 10 m) may not be sufficient for traditional control and layout surveys, they are ideal for most navigation needs and for many GIS and mapping surveys. The U.S. Coast Guard Maritime Differential GPS Service has created a code measurement differential system *(DGPS)*, consisting of 50 remote broadcast sites and 2 control centers, originally designed primarily to provide navigation data in coastal areas, the Great Lakes, and major river sites. The system includes continuously operating GPS receivers, at locations of known coordinates, that determine pseudorange values and then radio transmit the code error corrections to working navigators and surveyors at distances ranging from 100 to 400 km. The system uses international standards for its broadcasts—the Radio Technical Commission for Maritime (RTCM) services. Effectively the surveyor or navigator using the *DGPS* broadcasts along with his/her own receiver has the advantages normally found when using two receivers (relative positioning); and since the corrections for many of the errors (orbital and atmospheric) will be very similar for nearby receivers, the accuracies thus become much improved. Information on *DGPS* and on individual broadcast sites can be obtained on the Internet at the U.S. Coast Guard Navigation Center web site at www.navcen.uscg.mil/. Figure 9-9 shows typical data available—for Site #839, Youngstown, New York. See also Section 9-8 on the continuously operating reference station (CORS) network.

9-6-1 Code Measurements

As previously noted, military users can utilize both the P code and the C/A code. The C/A code is used by the military to quickly access the P code. The civilian user must be content with using only the C/A code.

Both codes are digital codes comprised of zeros and ones (see Figure 9-10), and each satellite transmits codes unique to that satellite. Although both codes are carefully structured, because the codes sound like random electronic "noise," they have been given the name *pseudo random noise (PRN)*. The PRN code number (see Table 9-1) indicates which of the 37 seven-day segments of the P code PRN signal is presently being used by each satellite (it takes the P code PRN signal 267 days to transmit). Each one-week segment of the P code is unique to each satellite and is reassigned each week (see Table 9-1). Receivers have replicas of all satellite codes in the on-board memory, which they use to identify the satellite and then to measure the time difference between the signals from the satellite to the receiver. Time is measured as the receiver moves the replica code (retrieved from memory) until a match between the transmitted code and the replica code is achieved. See Figure 9-10(b). Errors caused by the slowing effects of the atmosphere on the transmission of satellite radio waves can be corrected by simultaneously performing position measurements utilizing two different wavelengths—such as L1 and L2.

The distance, called *pseudorange,* is determined by multiplying the time factor by the speed of light.

$$\rho = t(300{,}000{,}000)$$

where ρ (lowercase Greek letter rho) = pseudorange

t = travel time of the satellite signal in seconds

$300{,}000{,}000$ = velocity of light in meters per second (actually 299,792,458 m/s)

When the *pseudorange* (ρ) is corrected for clock errors, atmospheric delay errors, multipath errors, and the like, it is then called the *range* and is abbreviated by the uppercase Greek letter rho, P; that is, P = (ρ + error corrections).

DGPS Status for Coverage Site 1/15/00 11:26 AM

The Latest Status for Site Number 839

DGPS BROADCAST SITE STATUS & OPERATING SPECIFICATIONS
STATUS AS OF 1/15/00

NOTE: Differential corrections are based on the NAD 83 position of the reference station (REFSTA) antenna. Positions obtained using DGPS should be referenced to NAD 83 coordinate system only. All sites are broadcasting RTCM Type 9-3 correction messages.

Back to the DGPS Coverage Page

YOUNGSTOWN, NY

Status:	Operational
RBn Antenna Location:	43,13.8N;78, 58.2W
REFSTA Ant Location (A):	43,13.8748N;78, 58.20992W
REFSTA Ant Location (B):	43, 13.87466N;78, 58.18778W
REFSTA RTCM SC-104 ID (B):	119
REFSTA FIRMWARE VERSION:	RD00-1C19
Broadcast Site ID:	839
Transmission Frequency:	322 KHZ
Transmission Rate:	100 BPS
Signal Strength:	75uV at 150 SM

Outages:
No current outages

http://www.navcen.uscg.mil/ado/DgpsCoverageStatus.asp?SiteID = 839

FIGURE 9-9 Status report for DGPS station. (Courtesy of the U.S. Coast Guard)

Figure 9-11 shows the geometry involved in point positioning. Computing three pseudoranges (ρ_{AR}, ρ_{BR}, ρ_{CR}) is enough to solve the intersection of three developed spheres—although this computation gives two points of intersection. One point (a superfluous point) will be obviously irrelevant; that is, it probably will not even fall on the surface of the earth. The fourth pseudorange (ρ_{DR}) is required to remove the fourth unknown—the receiver clock error.

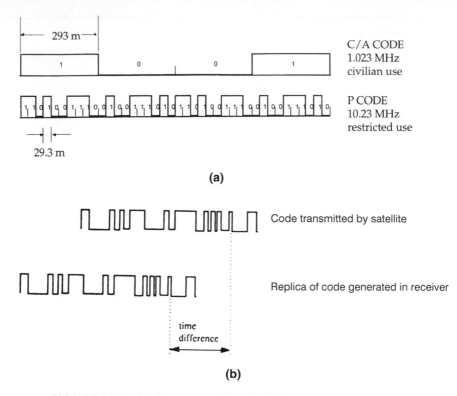

FIGURE 9-10 (a) C/A code and P code. (b) Time determination.

9-6-2 Carrier Phase Measurement

GPS codes, which are modulations of the carrier frequencies, are comparatively lengthy. Compare the C/A code at 293 m and the P code at 29.3 m (Figure 9-10) with the wavelengths of L1 and L2 at 0.19 m and 0.24 m, respectively. It follows that carrier phase measurements have the potential for much higher accuracies than do code measurements. Since carrier phase observations do not use codes in any way, SA (selective availability)—the intentional error that limits accuracy to about 100 m—is not a factor in this type of measurement.

We first encountered phase measurements in Chapter 5, when we observed how EDM equipment measured distances (see Figure 5-4). Essentially EDM distances are determined by measuring the phase delay required to match up the transmitted carrier wave signal with the return signal (two-way signaling).

$$L = \frac{n\lambda + \phi}{2} \tag{5-2}$$

where ϕ is the partial wavelength determined by measuring the phase delay (through comparison with an on-board reference), n is the number of complete wavelengths [from the electronic distance measurement instrument (EDMI) to the prism and back to the EDMI],

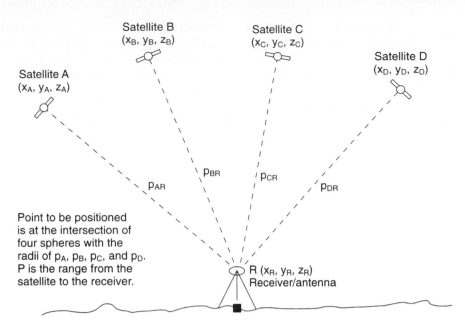

Satellite B
(x_B, y_B, z_B)

Satellite C
(x_C, y_C, z_C)

Satellite D
(x_D, y_D, z_D)

Satellite A
(x_A, y_A, z_A)

ρ_{BR}

ρ_{CR}

ρ_{AR}

ρ_{DR}

Point to be positioned
is at the intersection of
four spheres with the
radii of ρ_A, ρ_B, ρ_C, and ρ_D.
P is the range from the
satellite to the receiver.

R (x_R, y_R, z_R)
Receiver/antenna

FIGURE 9-11   Geometry of point positioning.

and λ is the wavelength. The integer number of wavelengths is determined as the EDMI successively sends out (and receives back) signals at different frequencies.

Since GPS ranging involves only one-way signaling, other techniques must be used to determine the number of full wavelengths. GPS receivers can measure the phase delay (through comparison with on-board carrier replicas) and count the full wavelengths after lock-on to the satellite has occurred, but more complex treatment is required to determine *N*—the *initial cycle ambiguity*. That is, *N* is the number of full wavelengths sent by the satellite prior to lock-on. Since a carrier signal is comprised of a continuous transmission of sine waves with no distinguishing features, the wave count cannot be accomplished directly.

$$P = \phi + N\lambda + errors$$

where P = satellite-receiver range

 ϕ = measured carrier phase

 λ = wavelength

 N = *initial ambiguity* (the number of full wavelengths at lock-on)

Once the cycle ambiguity between a receiver and a satellite has been resolved, it does not have to be addressed further unless a *loss of lock* occurs between the receiver and the satellite. When *loss of lock* occurs, the ambiguity must be resolved again. *Loss of lock* results in a loss of the integer number of cycles and is called a *cycle slip*. The surveyor is alerted to *loss of lock* when the receiver commences a beeping sequence. As an example, loss of lock can occur when a roving receiver passes under a bridge, a tree canopy, or any other obstruction that blocks all or some of the satellite signals.

Cycle ambiguity can be determined through the process of *differencing.* GPS measurements can be differenced between two satellites, between two receivers, and between two epochs. An epoch is an event in time—a short observation interval in a longer series of observations; after the initial epoch has been observed, later epochs will reflect the fact that the constellation has moved relative to the ground station and, as such, presents a new geometrical pattern and thus new intersection solutions. Generally, relative differencing among many satellites and among many epochs speeds up the positioning process and improves the accuracy of the position.

Differencing   *Relative positioning* occurs when two receivers are used to simultaneously observe satellite signals and to compute the vectors (known as a *baseline*) joining the two receivers. In *relative positioning,* the position of one point on earth is determined relative to the position of a known point, whereas in *point positioning,* the position of the occupied point is directly determined. *Relative positioning* can provide better accuracies because of the correlation possible between measurements simultaneously made over time by two or more different satellite receivers. Differencing is the technique of simultaneous baseline measurements and falls into the categories of *single difference, double difference* and *triple difference.*

- *Single difference:* When two receivers simultaneously observe the same satellite, it is possible to correct for most of the effects of satellite clock errors, orbit errors, and atmospheric delay. See Figure 9-12(a).
- *Double difference:* When one receiver observes two (or more) satellites, the measurements are free of receiver clock error, and atmospheric delay errors are also eliminated. Further, when using both differences (between the satellites and between the receivers), a double difference occurs. Clock errors, atmospheric delay errors, and orbit errors are all eliminated. See Figure 9-12(b).

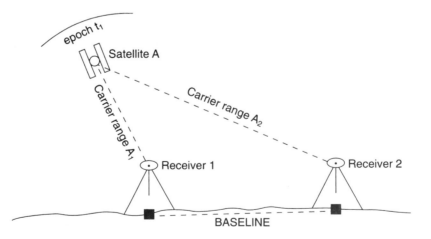

(a) Single difference. Two receivers simultaneously observing the same satellite (i.e., difference between receivers).

FIGURE 9-12   Differencing.

- *Triple difference:* The difference between two double differences is the triple difference. That is, the double differences are compared over two (or more) successive epochs. The triple difference (i.e., receiver differences, satellite differences, and epoch differences) permits the elimination of the cycle ambiguity. See Figure 9-12(c). This procedure is also effective in detecting and correcting *cycle slips.* Cycle ambiguities can also be resolved by utilizing both code and carrier phase measurements and the methods of kinematic surveying that utilize start-ups of *antenna swap, known*

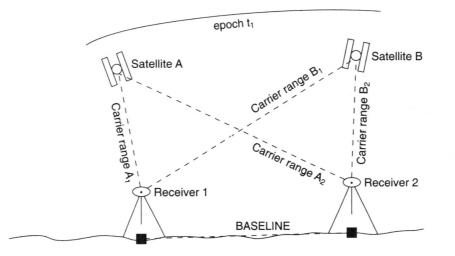

(b) Double difference. Two receivers simultaneously observing the same satellite(s) (i.e., difference between receivers and between satellites).

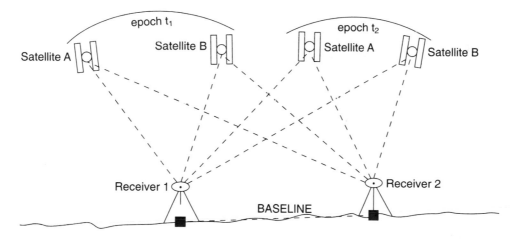

(c) Triple difference. The difference between two double differences (i.e., differences between receivers, satellites, and epochs).

FIGURE 9-12 (continued) Differencing.

location occupation, and on-the-fly (OTF) initialization—a technique that can be used while the roving receiver is in motion (see Section 9-11-3); see also the references at the end of this chapter for more on the theory of signal observations and ambiguity resolution.

9-7 Errors

The chief source of error in **GPS** are

1. Clock errors of the receivers.
2. Ionospheric (50 to 1000 km above earth) and tropospheric (earth's surface to 80 km above earth) refraction. Signals are slowed as they travel through these earth-centered layers. The errors worsen as satellite signals move from directly overhead to down near the horizon. These errors can be reduced by scheduling nighttime observations, by gathering sufficient redundant data and using reduced baseline lengths (1 to 5 km), or by collecting data on both frequencies over long (20 km or more) distances. Most surveying agencies do not record observations from satellites below 10° to 15° of elevation above the horizon.
3. Multipath interference—which is similar to the ghosting effect seen on TV, as some signals are received directly and others are received after they have been reflected from adjacent features. Recent improvements in antenna design have significantly reduced these errors.
4. A weak geometric figure that results from poorly located four-satellite signal intersections. This consideration is called the *dilution of precision (DOP)*. *DOP* can be optimized if many satellites (beyond the minimum of four) are tracked—with the additional data strengthening the position solution; most survey-level receivers are now capable of tracking 5 to 12 satellites simultaneously.

    GDOP refers to the general dilution of precision—the geometric effect of satellite vector measurement errors together with receiver clock errors. Elevation solutions require strong *GDOP*, and these solutions are strengthened when satellite elevations in excess of 70° are available for the observed satellite orbits. It used to be that observations were discontinued if the *GDOP* was above 7; now, some receiver manufacturers suggest that a *GDOP* of 8 can be acceptable.
5. Errors associated with the satellite orbital data.
6. Setup errors. Centering errors can be reduced if the equipment is checked to ensure that the optical plummet is true, and hi measuring errors can be reduced by utilizing equipment that provides a built-in (or accessory) measuring capability to directly or indirectly precisely measure the hi or by using fixed-length tripods and bipods.
7. Selected availability (SA)—denial of accuracy, as noted in Section 9-5.

Many of the effects of the above errors, including denial of accuracy by the DoD, can be surmounted by using *relative positioning* surveying techniques. Most of the discussion in this text is oriented to relatively short baselines; for long lines (> 150 km), more sophisticated processing is required to deal with natural and man-made errors.

9-8 Continuously Operating Reference Station (*CORS*)

The *DGPS* differential code measurement system developed by the U.S. Coast Guard (Section 9-6) has been adapted so it is now a nationwide differential positioning system— known as *CORS*. The continuously operating reference station (*CORS*) network includes stations set up by the National Geodetic Survey (NGS), the U.S. Coast Guard, the U.S. Army Corps of Engineers (USACE), and, more recently, stations set up by other federal and local agencies. The network, which in the late 1990s comprised more than 150 stations (expected to increase to 200 to 250 stations by 2005) is managed by the NGS, part of the National Oceanic and Atmospheric Administration. See Figure 9-13 for 1998 *CORS* coverage.

The coordinates at each site are computed from 24-hour data sets collected over a 10- to 15-day period. These highly accurate coordinates are then transformed into the NAD '83 horizontal datum for use by local surveyors. Each CORS continuously tracks GPS satellite signals and create files of both carrier measurements and code range measurements, which are available to the public via the Internet, to assist in positioning surveys. NGS converts all receiver data and individual site meteorological data to RINEX (Receiver Independent Exchange) format, version 2. The files can be accessed via the Internet at http://www.ngs.noaa.gov. Once in the web site, the new user should select "Products and Services" and then select "GPS Continuously Operating Reference Station (CORS)." The user is urged to download and read the "readme" files and the "frequently

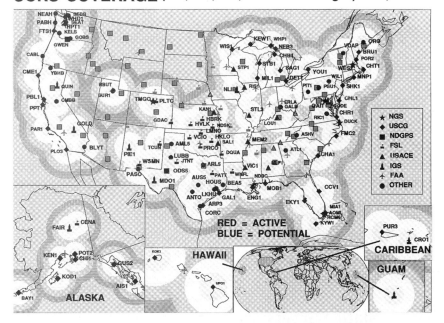

FIGURE 9-13 CORS coverage. Coverage maps are continually updated and are available on the Internet @ http://.ngs.noaa.gov/CORS/cors-data.html. (Courtesy of the National Geodetic Survey—NGS)

asked questions" file on the first visit. The NGS stores data from all sites for 31 days, and then the data are normally transferred to CD-ROMs, which are available for a fee. The data are usually collected at a 30-s epoch rate, although some sites collect data at 5-s and 15-s epoch rates. The local surveyor, armed with data sets in his or her locality at the time of an ongoing survey and having entered these data into his or her GPS program, has the equivalent of an additional dual-frequency GPS receiver. A surveyor with just one receiver can proceed as if two receivers were being used in the *relative positioning* mode.

9-9   Canadian Active Control System

The Geodetic Survey Division (GSD) of Geomatics Canada has combined with the Geological Survey of Canada to establish a network of *active control points* (ACP) in the Canadian Active Control System. The system includes 10 unattended dual-frequency tracking stations (ACPs) that continuously measure and record carrier phase and pseudorange measurements for all satellites in view at a 30-s sampling interval. A master ACP in Ottawa coordinates and controls the system. The data are archived in RINEX format and available on-line 4 hours after the end of the day. Precise ephemeris data, computed with input from 24 globally distributed core GPS tracking stations of the International GPS Service for Geodynamics (IGS), are available on-line within 2 to 5 days after the observations; precise clock corrections are also available in the 2- to 5-day time frame. The Canadian Active Control System is complemented by the Canadian Base Network, which provides 200-km coverage in Canada's southern latitudes for high accuracy control (centimeter accuracy). These control stations are used to evaluate and to complement a wide variety of control stations established by various government agencies over the years.

These products, which are available for a subscription fee, enable a surveyor to position any point in the country with a precision ranging from a centimeter to a few meters. Code observation positioning at the meter level, without the use of a base station, is possible using precise satellite corrections. Real time service at the meter level is also available. The data can be accessed on the web at http://www.geod.nrcan.gc.ca.

9-10   Survey Planning

Planning is important for GPS surveys so that almanac data can be analyzed to obtain optimal time sets when a geometrically strong array of satellites is available above 15° of elevation (above the horizon) and to identify topographic obstructions that may hinder signal reception. Planning software can graphically display GDOP (geometric dilution of precision) at each time of the day (GDOP of 7 or below is usually considered suitable for positioning—a value of 5 or lower is ideal). See Figures 9-14 to 9-18 for a variety of computer screen plots that the surveyor can use to help the mission-planning process—selecting not only the optimal days for the survey, but also the hours of the day that will result in the best data.

9-10-1   Static Surveys

For static surveys (see Section 9-11-2 for a definition), survey planning includes a visit to the field in order to inspect existing stations and to place monuments for new stations. A

FIGURE 9-14 GPS planning software. Graphical depiction of satellite availability, elevation, and GDOP almanac data, which are processed by SKI software for a specific day and location. (Courtesy of Leica, Canada)

compass and clinometer (Figure 2-7) are handy in sketching the location and elevation of potential obstructions at each station on a *visibility (obstruction) diagram* (see Figure 9-19) —these obstructions are entered into the software for later display. The coordinates (latitude and longitude) of stations should be scaled from a topographic map—scaled coordinates can help some receivers to more quickly lock onto the satellites.

Computer graphics displays include the number of satellites available (Figure 9-15); satellite orbits and obstructions—showing orbits of satellites as viewed at a specific station on a specific day (Figure 9-16); a visibility plot of all satellites over one day (Figure 9-17); and a polar plot of all visible satellites—at a moment in time (Figure 9-18). Figure 9-16 shows that for the location shown (latitude and longitude) most satellite orbits are in the southerly sky; accordingly survey stations at that location should be located south of high obstructions, where possible, to minimize topographic interference. Almanac data, used in survey planning, can be updated on a regular basis through satellite observations, and, as well, most software suppliers provide almanac updates via their computer bulletin boards.

Additionally, static surveys require decisions as to the type of receivers to be used— receivers should be of the same type; that is, they should have the same number of channels and signal processing techniques. Also, the sampling rate must be set; faster rates require more storage, but can be helpful in detecting cycle slips—particularly on longer

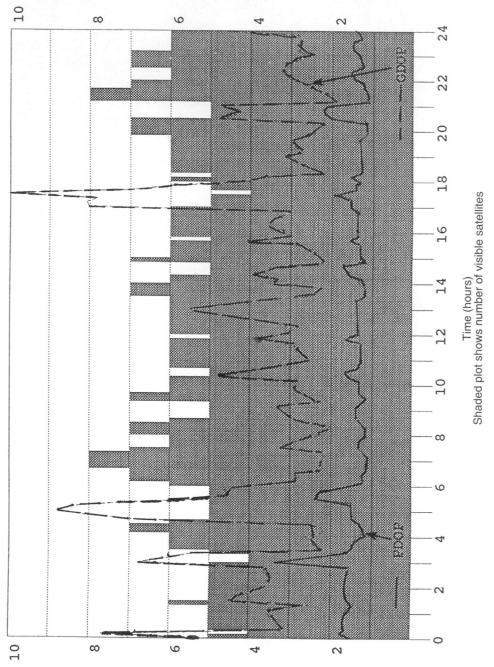

FIGURE 9-15 GPS planning software. GDOP and PDOP during a specific day. (Courtesy of Leica, Canada)

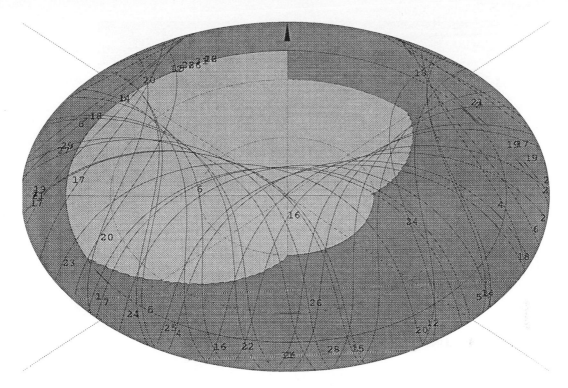

FIGURE 9-16 GPS planning software. Computer "sky plot" display showing satellite orbits and obstructions for a particular station (darker shading). (Courtesy of Leica, Canada)

lines (> 50 km). And the time (hours) of observation must be determined—given the available GDOP and the need for accuracy as well as the start/stop times for each session. All this information is entered into the software, with the results uploaded into the receivers.

9-10-2 Kinematic Surveys

Much of the discussion above, for planning static surveys, also applies to kinematic surveys (see Section 9-11-3 for definitions). For kinematic surveys, the route also must be planned for each roving receiver so that best use is made of control points, crews, and equipment. The type of receiver chosen will depend, to some degree, on the accuracy required. For topographic or GIS surveys, low-order (submeter) survey roving receivers (e.g., Figures 9-4 and 9-5) may be a good choice. For construction layout in real time, high-end roving receivers capable of centimeter or millimeter accuracy (e.g., Figure 9-6) may be selected. The base station receiver must be compatible with the survey mission and the roving receivers; one base station can support any number of roving receivers. The technique to be used for initial ambiguity resolution must be determined; that is, will it be *antenna swap,* or *known station occupation,* or *on-the-fly (OTF)?* And at which stations will this resolution take place?

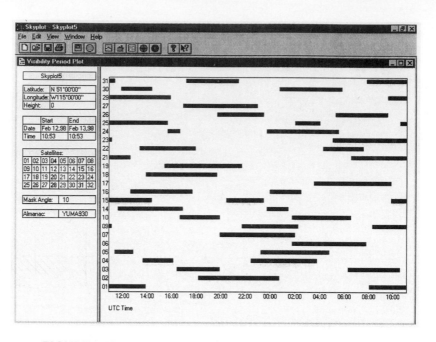

FIGURE 9-17 Visibility plot—from Skyplot series (color-coded in original format). (Courtesy of Position Inc., Calgary, Alberta)

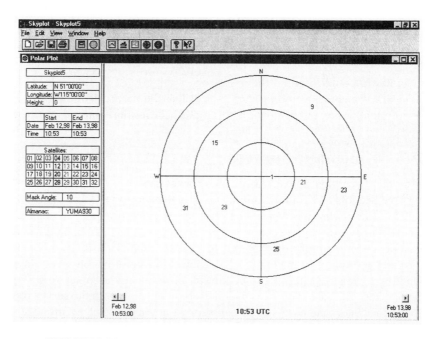

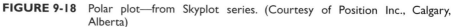

FIGURE 9-18 Polar plot—from Skyplot series. (Courtesy of Position Inc., Calgary, Alberta)

GPS STATION OBSTRUCTION DIAGRAM

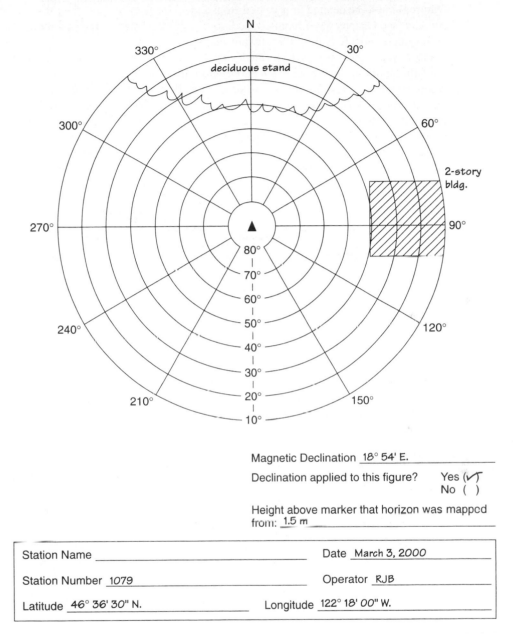

Magnetic Declination 18° 54' E.

Declination applied to this figure?   Yes (✓)
                                       No ( )

Height above marker that horizon was mapped
from: 1.5 m

Station Name _____	Date March 3, 2000
Station Number 1079	Operator RJB
Latitude 46° 36' 30" N.	Longitude 122° 18' 00" W.

FIGURE 9-19 Station visibility diagram.

If the survey is designed to locate topographic and built features, then the codes for the features should be defined or accessed from a symbols library—just the same as for EDM surveys (see Chapter 5). If required, additional asset data (attribute data) should be tied to each symbol; hopefully the GPS software will permit the entry of several layers of asset data. For example, if the feature to be located is a pole, the pole symbol can be backed up with pole use (illumination, electric wire, telephone, etc.); the type of pole can be booked (concrete, wood, metal, etc.); and the year of installation can be entered (municipal computers can automatically generate work orders for any facility's maintenance based on the original date of installation). Planning will ensure that when the roving surveyor is at the feature point, all possible prompts will be displayed to completely capture the data for each way point. The success of any kinematic survey depends a great deal on the thoroughness of the presurvey reconnoiter and on the preparation of the job file—using the GPS software.

9-11 GPS Field Procedures

9-11-1 Tripod-Mounted Antenna and Pole-Mounted Antenna Considerations

GPS antennas can be mounted directly to tripods via optical plummet–equipped tribrachs. All static survey occupations and base station occupations for all other types of GPS surveys require the use of a tripod. Care is taken to precisely center the antenna and to precisely measure the hi. All antennas have a direction mark (often an N or arrow, or a series of numbered notches along the outside perimeter of the antenna), which enables the surveyor to align the roving antenna in the same direction (usually north) as the base station antenna. This helps to eliminate any bias in the antennas. The measured hi (corrected or uncorrected) is entered into the receiver, and when a "lock" has been established to the satellites, a message is displayed on the receiver display, and observations begin. If the hi cannot be measured directly, then slant heights are measured. Some agencies measure in two or three locations and average the results. The vertical height can be computed using the Pythagorean theorem: $\text{hi} = \sqrt{\text{slant height}^2 - \text{antenna radius}^2}$ (see Figure 9-20).

GPS receiver antennas can also be mounted on adjustable-length poles (similar to prism poles) or bipods. These poles and fixed-length bipods may have built-in power supply conduits, a built-in circular bubble, and the ability to display the hi. When using poles, the GPS receiver program automatically prompts the surveyor to accept the last-used hi; if there has been no change in the antenna height, the surveyor simply accepts the prompted value. As with most surveys, field notes are important, both as backup and as confirmation of entered data. The hi at each station is booked along with equipment numbers, session times, crew, file (job) number, and any other pertinent data (see Figure 9-20).

9-11-2 Static Surveys

Traditional Static   This is the technique of relative GPS positioning where one base receiver antenna (single or dual frequency) is placed over a point of known coordinates (X, Y, Z) on a tripod, while others are placed, also on tripods, over permanent stations to be

GPS FIELD LOG

page 1 of __

GPS FIELD LOG

Project Name _____   Project Number _____

Receiver Model/No _____   Station Name _____
Receiver Software Version _____   Station Number _____
Data Logger Type/No _____   4-Char ID   _____
Antenna Model/No _____   Date   _____
Cable Length _____   Obs. Session   _____
Ground Plane Extensions Yes ( ) No ( )   Operator   _____

Data Collection

Collection Rate _____

Start Day/Time _____

End Day/Time _____

Receiver Position

Latitude _____

Longitude _____

Height _____

Obstruction or possible interference sources ___   _____

_____

General weather conditions _____

_____

Detailed meteorological observations recorded: Yes ( ) No ( )

Antenna Height Measurement

Show on sketch measurements taken to derive the antenna height. If slant measurements are taken, make measurement on two opposite sides of the antenna. Make measurements before and after observing session.

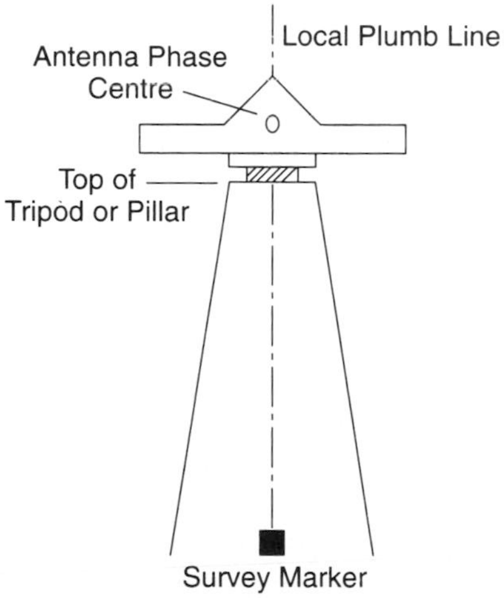

Local Plumb Line

Antenna Phase Centre

Top of Tripod or Pillar

Survey Marker

Vertical measurements ( )

Slant measurements ( ) : radius _____ m

BEFORE	AFTER
_____ m _____ in	_____ m _____ in
_____ m _____ in	_____ m _____ in

Mean   _____

Corrected to vertical
if slant measurement   _____

Vertical offset to
phase centre   _____

Other offset
(indicate on sketch)   _____

TOTAL HEIGHT   _____

Verified by: _____

FIGURE 9-20   GPS field log. (Courtesy of Geomatics, Canada)

positioned; observation times are 1 hour or more (perhaps days), depending on the receiver, the accuracy requirements, the satellites' geometric configuration, the length of line, and atmospheric conditions. This technique is used for long lines (> 20 km) in geodetic control, control densification, and photogrammetric control for aerial surveys and precise engineering surveys; it is also used as a fallback technique when the available geometric array of satellites is not compatible with other GPS techniques (see the sections describing GPS measurement methods). The preplanning of station locations takes into consideration potential obstructions presented by trees and buildings—which must be considered and minimized.

Rapid Static   This is a more recently developed technique (early 1990s) where dual-frequency receivers are used over short (up to 15 km) lines. As with static surveys, this technique requires one receiver antenna to be positioned (on a tripod) at a known base station while the roving surveyor moves from station to station with the antenna pole-mounted. With good geometry, initial phase ambiguities can be resolved within a minute (3 to 5 minutes for single-frequency receivers). With this technique, there is no need to maintain lock on the satellites while moving rover receivers—the roving receivers can even be turned off to preserve their batteries. Accuracies of a few millimeters are possible using this technique. Observation times of 5 to 10 minutes are typical.

Reoccupation (Also Called *Pseudo-Kinematic* and *Pseudo-Static*)   This technique can be used when fewer than four satellites are available or when *GDOP* is weak (above a value of 7 or 8). Survey stations are occupied on at least two different occasions at least 1 hour apart; the solution may be strengthened if the base station has been moved to another control station for the second set of observations. The processing software will combine the satellite observations to provide a solution; the data are processed as for a static survey. That is, if there are only three satellites available on the first occupation and another three available on the second occupation, the software will process the data as if six satellites are available at once. Observation times of 10 minutes are typical. Roving receivers have their antennas pole-mounted.

9-11-3   Kinematic Surveys

STOP and GO   This is an efficient way to survey detail points for engineering and topographic surveys.

This technique begins with both the base unit and the roving unit occupying a 10-km (or shorter) baseline (two *known positions*) until ambiguities are resolved—usually about 5 minutes. Alternatively, short baselines with one known position can be used where the distance between the stations is short enough to permit *antenna swapping*. Here, the base station and a nearby (within reach of the antenna cable) undefined station are occupied for a short period of time (say, 2 minutes) in the *static mode,* after which the antennas are swapped (while still receiving the satellite signals—but now in the *rove mode*) for a further few minutes of readings in the static mode (techniques may vary with different manufacturers).

After the antennas have been returned to their original tripods and after an additional short period of observations in the static mode, the roving receiver—in rove mode—then moves (on a pole, backpack, truck, boat, etc.) to position all required detail points—keeping a lock on the satellite signals. If the lock is lost, the receiver is held stationary until the ambiguities are once again resolved so that the survey can continue. Observation times of 2 or 3 seconds are all that is required to compute accurate positions. The base station stays in the static mode unless it is planned to "leapfrog" the base and rover stations.

Traditional Kinematic This technique computes a relative differential position at preset time intervals instead of at operator-selected points. Lock must be maintained to a minimum of four satellites, or it must be reestablished when lost. This technique is used for road profiling, ship positioning in sounding surveys, and aircraft positioning in aerial surveys. As an example of this technique, Leica (Canada) reported (1994) that a road profile survey was conducted using one of their antennas mounted on a 4-m adjustable arm attached to a highway truck capable of following the edge of the pavement to within 0.05 m. Measurements were taken every second with the truck traveling at 15 km/hr (4 m/s). The nearly 10,000 points collected were processed in about 8 hours. Control was provided by two master GPS stations, and, as well, the vehicle stopped over 22 control stations en route. The results showed, at the 95 percent confidence level, that there was a maximum spread of error ranging to 0.050 m in horizontal and to 0.070 m in vertical. Continuous surveying can be interrupted to take observations (a few epochs) at any required way points.

Real-Time Differential [Also Known as Real-Time Kinematic (RTK)]

The real-time combination of GPS receivers, mobile data communications, on-board data processing, and on-board applications software contributes to an exciting new era in surveying. As with the motorized Total Stations described in Section 5-12, real-time positioning offers the potential of a one-person capability in mapping and quantity surveys (the base station receiver can be unattended). Layout surveys need two surveyors—one to operate the receiver and one to mark the stations in the field. *RTK* requires a base station to measure the satellite signals, to process baseline corrections, and then to broadcast the corrections to any number the roving receivers via radio transmission. See Figure 9-21 for a typical radio and amplifier used in code and carrier differential surveys. This technique can commence without the rover first occupying a known baseline; the base station transmits code and carrier phase data to the roving receiver, which can use this data to help resolve ambiguities and to solve for change in coordinate differences between the reference and the roving receivers; the range of the radio transmission of the carrier phase data from the base to the rover can be extended by booster radios to a distance of about 10 km; longer ranges require commercially licensed radios—as do even shorter ranges in some countries. This technique can utilize either single-frequency or dual-frequency receivers; loss of signal lock can be regained by single-frequency receivers by reoccupying a point of known position, and by dual-frequency receivers either by remaining stationary for a few minutes or by using *OTF* resolution—while proceeding to the next survey position. With software being developed and upgraded constantly in this field, it seems that there is now a software solution to all surveying applications. When a second civilian frequency is provided, solutions will be much enhanced.

One example of extended applications comes from Trimble Navigation, with its GPS Total Station—see Figure 9-6. This system works generally as described above (base

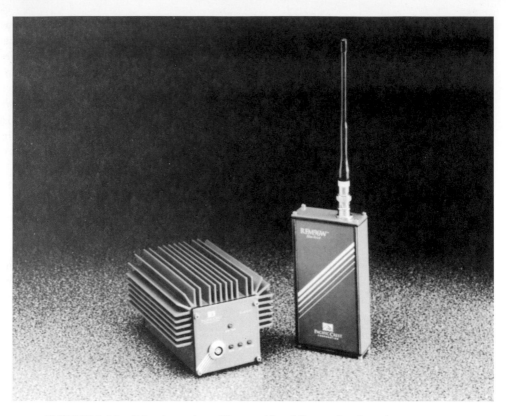

FIGURE 9-21　FM radio and amplifier used for differential code and carrier measurement surveys. (Courtesy of Pacific Crest Corporation, Santa Clara, California)

station and rovers) except that the field system has been expanded to include processing software and applications software for topographic and layout surveys. The *GPS Total Station* includes the antenna and data collector mounted on an adjustable-length pole, with the receiver, radio, and radio antenna mounted in the backpack—more recent models have all equipment mounted on the pole. This receiver (Model 4800) can track nine satellites and has storage for 50 hours of L1/L2 data while tracking six satellites continuously at 15-s epochs. The pole kit weighs only 8.5 pounds.

This system is available with both single-frequency and dual-frequency receivers— the more expensive dual-frequency receiver having the better potential for surveys in areas where satellite visibility may be reduced by topographic obstructions. The radio range on this system is 1 to 3 km, with a range of 10 km possible with booster radios (a range more than adequate for most engineering surveys).

9-12　GPS Applications

When in the field, the surveyor first sets the receiver over the point and then measures, records (in the field log), and enters the hi into the receiver. The session programming is verified, and the mode of operation is selected; satellite lock and position computation are then verified. As the observations proceed, the process is monitored, and, finally, when the session is complete, the receiver is turned off (base station) or moved to the next way point (roving receiver). The survey controller (data collector) has applications programs for topography, radial and linear stakeout, cut/fill, and intersections by bearing-bearing, bearing-distance, and distance-distance. In addition, the controller will perform inverse, sea level, curvature and refraction, datum transformations (Universal Transverse Mercator (UTM), state plane, Lambert, etc.), and geoid corrections. See Figure 9-22 for typical operations capability with data collectors that are used for both EDM Total Station surveys and GPS Total Station surveys.

Data Collection Software Functions

Job Creation & Review
Create/Open Job
Edit/View Coordinates
Create/Delete/View Raw Data
Delete Points/Job
Create Point List
Pop-up Descriptors
Pop-up Linework Commands
Edit/View Control

Direct Function Access Keys

Setup Functions
Total Stations
Rod-Height Prompt Option
Height of Instrument Prompt
Descriptor Prompt Option
Degrees/Grads Feet/Meters
Control File
Collimation Correction
Multiple Descriptor Files
Repetition: Angles & Distance
Radial Sideshots
Direct Record Mode
On-line Help

Printing
Coordinate
Raw Data
Cut Sheet
Spray Sheet

Coordinate Geometry
Area Computation
Intersections (all major types)
2- and 3-Point Resections
7-Point Least Squares Resection
Inverse by Points/Coords/Lines
Automatic PT#-PT# Inverse
Bench Mark (transfer elevation)
Compute Corner Angle
Triangle Solutions
Azimuth/Bearing Conversion
Zenith/Slope Dist. Conversion
Pre-Determined Area
Map Check

Curves
Horizontal Curves
Vertical Curves
Straight Grade
3-Point Curve Solution
2-Point & Radius Solution
Compute Radius by PC & PT
PC & Radius by PI & Tangent
Line Tangent to a Circle

Curves, cont.
Traverse on Curve
Layout by PC Deflections
   PI Deflections
   Tangent Offsets
   Chord Offsets
Spiral Curves

Data Collection
Traverse/Sideshot
Cross Section Topo
Backsight Check
Survey Notes
Point Protection
Automatic Next Point #
Course or Fine Distance Mode
Radial Sideshots
Reciprocal Zenith Traverse
Sun Shot Routines
Off-Center Shots
   Horiz/Vert-Angle/Dist
   Azimuth Distance
   D-D Intersection

Adjustments
Change Scale 2D or 3D
Translate/Rotate Coordinates
Vertical Closure
Scale Factor
Compass Rule
Angle Adjustment
Earth Curvature
Feet to Meters
Adjust to Latest Localization

Stakeout
Radial/Point Stakeout
Offset Stake Using Point List
Slope Staking Using Point List
DTM Stakeout
Stake to a Line
Stake a Line and Offset
Stake a Curve and Offset
Stake a Spiral and Offset
Cut/Fill to Design Grade
Stake/Store Reference Point
Turn Gun to 0
Store Cut Sheet
Locate Stake by Station
Where is Next Point
Graphical Staking Screens

Building Pad Stakeout
Auto-Compute X,Y,Z of Rod
Stakeout by X,Y,Z
Convert Decimal Feet to Ft/In

Leveling
Trigonometric
Differential
Bench
Leveling Stakeout

Earth Work
Average End Area
Borrow Pit

Road Layout
Horizontal Alignments
Vertical Alignments
Templates
Define Cross Section
Store/Recall Road
Grade Book
Point List to Road
Road to Point List

Screen Plot
Points, Lines, Pnt Number

File Transfer
Coordinates
Raw Data/Text
Point List
Road Alignment
Road Template
Transfer to/from PC
Transfer to/from other TDS DC
Transfer to/from Modem
DTM File

Robotic Total Station Support
Geodimeter 600 Series
Topcon APL1
Leica TPS Series

GPS Specific Functions
Base/Rover Setup
Local Horizontal and
Vertical Transformation
Real-Time Coordinate Generation
Satellite View
Residual Display
Data Collection
Automatic Accept
   w/User-Defined Tolerances
Do All Stakeout Functions
   w/GPS Receiver

FIGURE 9-22 Data collection and software functions of a typical data collector (controller). (Courtesy of Tripod Data Systems, Corvallis, Oregon)

When used for topographic surveys, detail is located by short occupation times and described with the input of appropriate coding; input may be by keying in, by using bar-code readers, or by utilizing prepared library codes. Line work may require no special coding (see Z codes, Section 5-10-7), as entities (curbs, fences, etc.) can be joined by their specific codes (curb2, fence3, etc.). Some software will display the precision of each observation for horizontal and vertical position, giving the surveyor the opportunity to take additional observations if the displayed accuracy does not meet job specifications. In addition to positioning random detail, this GPS technique permits the collection of data on specified profile, cross-section, and boundary locations—utilizing the navigation functions; contours may be readily plotted from the collected data. GPS is also useful when beginning the survey in locating boundary and control markers that may be covered by snow or other ground cover; if the marker's coordinates are in the receiver, the navigation mode will take the surveyor directly to its location. Data captured using these techniques can be added to a mapping or GIS data base or directly plotted to scale using a digital plotter (see Chapter 5).

For layout work, since the coordinates of all layout points have previously been entered from the computer, as each layout point number is keyed into the collector, the azimuth and distance to the required position are displayed on the screen. The surveyor, guided by these directions, eventually moves to the desired point—which is then staked. One base receiver will support any number of rover receivers, permitting the instantaneous layout of large-project boundaries, pipelines, roads, and building locations by several surveyors, each working only on a specific type of facility or by all roving surveyors working on all proposed facilities—but on selected sections of the project. As with topographic applications, the precision of the proposed location is displayed on the receiver as the antenna pole is held on the grade stake to confirm that layout specifications have been met; if the displayed accuracy is below specifications, the surveyor simply waits at the location until the processing of data from additional epochs provides the surveyor with the necessary accuracy. On road layouts, both line and grade can be given directly to the builder (by marking grade stakes), and progress in cut/fill can be monitored; slope stakes can be located without any need for intervisibility—the next logical stage, which is to mount antennas directly on various construction excavating equipment to directly provide line and grade control, has already been taken by some GPS receiver manufacturers.

When used for material inventory measurements, GPS techniques are particularly useful in open-pit mining, where original, in-progress, and final surveys can easily performed for quantity and payment purposes. As well, material stockpiles can be surveyed quickly and volumes computed using appropriate on-board software.

As with the accuracy/precision display previously mentioned, not only are cut/fill, grades, and the like displayed at each step along the way, but also a permanent record is kept on all of these data in case a review is required. Accuracy can also be confirmed by reoccupying selected layout stations and noting and recording the displayed measurements —an inexpensive, yet effective, method of quality control.

Unfortunately, for GPS topographic and layout work, there is no way to get around the fact that existing and proposed positions must be occupied by the antenna. If some of these specific locations are such that satellite visibility is impossible because obstructions are blocking the satellites' signals—even when using receivers capable of tracking both constellations—then ancillary surveying techniques (e.g., Total Stations, handheld "Total

Stations"—Section 5-14) must be used. We may soon see EDM Total Stations (with prism-less measuring ability) equipped with GPS chips and antennas so that all needed measurements can be performed by one instrument.

9-13 Vertical Positioning

Most surveyors have, until now, been able to ignore the implications of geodesy for normal engineering plane surveys. The distances encountered are so relatively short that global implications are negligible. However, the elevation coordinate *(h)* given by GPS solutions refers to the height from the surface of the reference ellipsoid (GRS80) (see Figure 9-23) to the ground station, whereas the surveyor needs the height *(H)* above *mean sea level (MSL)*. The ellipsoid is referenced to a spatial Cartesian coordinate system (Figure 9-24), called the International Terrestrial Reference Framework (ITRF94), in which the center (0, 0, 0) is the center of the mass of the earth, and the *x* axis is a line drawn from the origin through the equatorial plane to the Greenwich meridian. The *y* axis is in the equatorial plane perpendicular to the *x* axis, and the *z* axis is drawn from the origin perpendicular to the equatorial plane, as shown in Figure 9-24.

Essentially GPS observations permit the computation of *X, Y,* and *Z* Cartesian coordinates of a geocentric ellipsoid; these Cartesian coordinates can then be transformed to geodetic coordinates—latitude (φ), longitude (λ), and ellipsoidal height *(h)*. Finally, the geodetic coordinates can be transformed to UTM, state plane, Lambert, or other grids—together with geoid corrections (see Figure 9-25 and (Section 9-13-1)—to provide working coordinates (northing, easting, and elevation) for the field surveyor.

The ellipsoid presently used by many to portray the earth is the WGS84 (World Geodetic System), which is generally agreed to more accurately represent the earth than previous versions—ongoing satellite observations permitted scientists to improve their estimates as to the size and mass of the earth. An earlier reference ellipsoid (GRS80)—the Geodetic Reference System of the International Union of Geodesy and Geophysics (IUGG)—which was adopted in 1979 by that group as the model then best representing the earth, is the ellipsoid on which the horizontal datum NAD '83 (North American datum of 1983) is based (see Figure 9-23). In this system, the geographic coordinates are given by the ellipsoidal latitude (φ), longitude (λ), and height *(h)* above the ellipsoidal surface to the

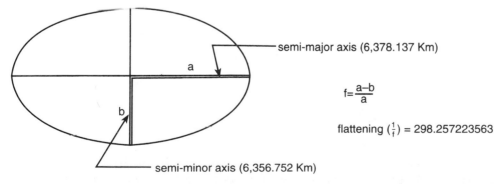

semi-major axis (6,378.137 Km)

$$f = \frac{a-b}{a}$$

flattening $(\frac{1}{f})$ = 298.257223563

semi-minor axis (6,356.752 Km)

FIGURE 9-23 Ellipse parameters of the GRS80 ellipsoid (flattening is exaggerated).

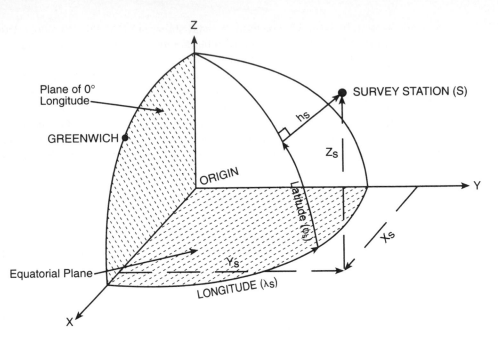

FIGURE 9-24   Cartesian (X,Y,Z) and geodetic (ϕ_s, λ_s, h_s) coordinates.

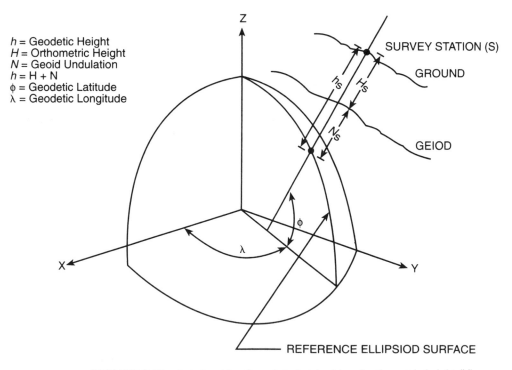

h = Geodetic Height
H = Orthometric Height
N = Geoid Undulation
$h = H + N$
ϕ = Geodetic Latitude
λ = Geodetic Longitude

FIGURE 9-25   Relationship of geodetic height *(h)* and orthometric height *(H)*.

ground station. The GEOID99 model (see Section 9-13-1) is based on known relationships between NAD '83 and the ITRF spatial reference frame, together with GPS height measurements on NAVD '88 (North American vertical datum of 1988) benchmarks.

Traditionally surveyors are used to working with spirit levels and reference orthometric heights *(H)* to the "average" surface of the earth—as depicted by MSL. The surface of mean sea level can be approximated by the equipotential surface of the earth's gravity field, called the *geoid*. The *geoid,* which has an irregular surface, is influenced by the density of adjacent land masses at any particular survey station, and, as such, its surface does not follow the surface of the ellipsoid; sometimes it is below the ellipsoid and other times above it—for most of the North American continent, the geoid is above the ellipsoid. Wherever the mass of the earth's crust changes, the *geoid's* gravitational potential also changes—resulting in a nonuniform and unpredictable *geoid* surface. Since the *geoid* does not lend itself to mathematical expression—as does the ellipsoid—*geoid undulation* (the difference between the *geoid* surface and the ellipsoid surface) must be measured at specific sites to determine the local *geoid undulation* value—see Figures 9-26 and 9-27.

9-13-1   Geoid Modeling

Geoid undulations can be determined both by gravimetric surveys and by the inclusion of points of known elevation in GPS surveys. When the average undulation of an area has been determined, it only remains to determine the residual undulations over the surveyed area. While residual undulations are usually less than 0.020 m over areas of 50 km^2, the undulation itself ranges from +75 m at New Guinea to −104 m at the south tip of India. In the United States, the undulation ranges from +53 m along the Atlantic Ocean to −5 m in the Rockies; in Canada, the undulation ranges from +40 m on the east coast to −20 m on the west coast.

After all the known *geoid* separations have been plotted, the *geoid undulations (N)* at any given survey station can be interpolated; the *orthometric height (H)* can be determined from the relationship $H = h - N$, where h is the ellipsoid height (N is positive when the geoid is above the ellipsoid and negative when below the ellipsoid)—see Figures 9-26 and 9-27. *Geoid* modeling data can be obtained from government agencies, and in many cases, GPS suppliers provide this data resident in their software.

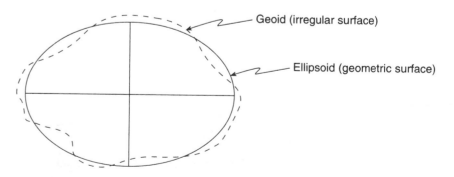

FIGURE 9-26   GRS80 ellipsoid and the geoid.

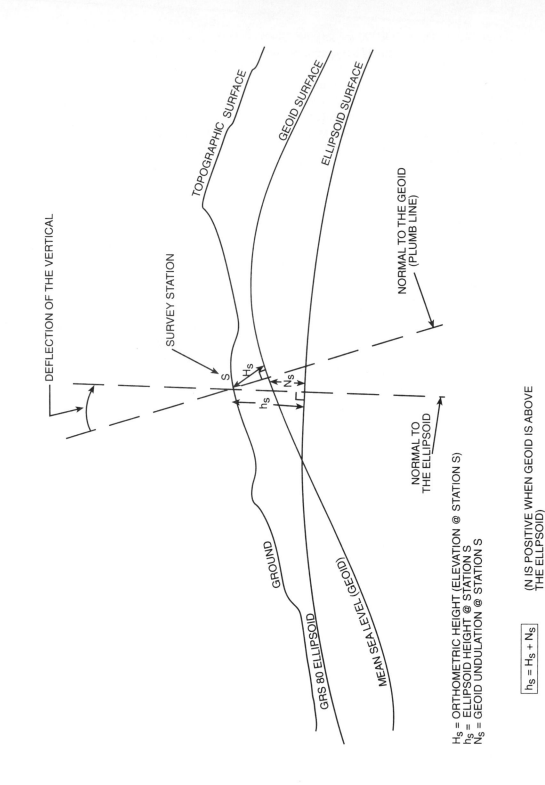

$$\boxed{h_S = H_S + N_S}$$

FIGURE 9-27 The three surfaces of geodesy (undulations are greatly exaggerated).

H_S = ORTHOMETRIC HEIGHT (ELEVATION @ STATION S)
h_S = ELLIPSOID HEIGHT @ STATION S
N_S = GEOID UNDULATION @ STATION S

(N IS POSITIVE WHEN GEOID IS ABOVE
THE ELLIPSOID)

Because of the uncertainties still inherent in geoid modeling, it is generally thought that accuracies in elevation are only about half the accuracies achievable in horizontal positioning. That is, if a horizontal accuracy is defined to be $\pm$(5 mm + 1 ppm), the vertical accuracy is probably close to $\pm$(10 mm + 2 ppm).

GSD95 Geoid (Canada)   The Ministry of Energy, Mines and Resources—Canada has developed a *geoid* model—GSD95 (a refinement of GSD91), which takes into account more than 700,000 surface gravity observations in Canada, with additional observations taken in the United States, Greenland, and Denmark. These data are available from the Ministry, located in Ottawa. The Canadian geoid separation program uses a quadratic interpolation algorithm to determine undulations within a relative accuracy of about 0.010 m over a 10-km separation. See also Section 8-1.

GEOID99 (United States)   GEOID99 (a refinement of GEOID96, GEOID93, and GEOID 90) is a geoid-elevation estimation model referenced to the GRS80 ellipsoid. It consists of computer software containing geoid undulation data, together with contour maps showing the undulations. These data, which have been developed by the National Geodetic Survey, cover the country in 2′ by 2′ grids (latitude and longitude); GEOID93 was in 3′ grids. GEOID99 has incorporated more than 2900 new GPS heights on known benchmarks; additionally, GEOID99 reflects the advances made in the new gravimetric geoid model (G99SSS), which incorporated almost two million gravity observations. Together, these advancements provide much better accuracies in converting directly from GPS heights to orthometric heights.

When values developed from GEOID99 are compared to values determined by spirit leveling, local orthometric datums can be established.

GEOID99 height grids are available in three overlapping files:

Eastern United States	24°–50° N,	66°–90° W
Central United States	24°–50° N,	83°–107° W
Western United States	24°–50° N,	101°–125° W

These files, together with the interpolation program (GEOID), are available from the National Geodetic Information Center, (301) 713-3242; further information is available from the NGS web site: http://www.ngs.noaa.gov/GEOID/GEOID99/geoid99.html. See also Section 8-1.

9-14   Conclusion

Table 9-3 provides a summary of the GPS positioning techniques described in this chapter. GPS techniques hold such promise that it is conceivable that all future horizontal and vertical control will be coordinated using these techniques. It is also likely that many engineering, mapping, and GIS surveying applications will be developed using emerging advances in real-time GPS data collection.

In the future, the collection of GPS data will be enhanced as more and more North American local and federal agencies install continuously operating receivers/transmitters,

Table 9-3 GPS MEASUREMENTS SUMMARY

Two basic modes

Code-based measurements: Satellite-to-receiver pseudorange is measured and then corrected to provide the range; four satellite ranges are required to determine position—by removing the uncertainties in *X, Y, Z,* and receiver clocks. Military can access both P code and C/A code; civilians can access only the C/A code—where the accuracy is degraded to the 100 m level.

Carrier-based measurements: The carrier waves themselves are used to compute the satellite(s)-to-receiver range; similar to EDM. Most carrier receivers utilize both code measurements and carrier measurements to compute positions.

Two basic techniques

Point positioning: Code measurements are used to directly compute the position of the receiver. Only one receiver required.

Relative positioning: Code and/or carrier measurements are used to compute the baseline vector ($\Delta X, \Delta Y, and \Delta Z$) from a point of known position to a point of unknown position, thus enabling the computation of the coordinates of the new position.

Relative positioning: Two receivers required—one occupying a point of known position.

Static: Accuracy—5 mm + 1 ppm. Observation times—1 hour to many hours. Use—control surveys; standard method when lines longer than 20 km. Uses dual- or single-frequency receivers.

Rapid static: Accuracy—5 to 10 mm + 1 ppm. Observation times—5 to 10 minutes. Initialization time of 1 minute for dual-frequency and about 3 to 5 minutes for single-frequency receivers. Receiver must have specialized rapid static observation capability. The roving receiver does not have to maintain lock on satellites (useful feature in areas with many obstructions). Used for control surveys, including photogrammetric control for lines 10 km or less. The receiver program determines the total length of the sessions, and the receiver screen displays "time remaining" at each station session.

Re-occupation (also known as pseudostatic and pseudo-kinematic): Accuracy—5 to 10 mm + 1 ppm. Observation times about 10 minutes, but each point must be re-occupied again after at least 1 hour, for another 10 minutes. No initialization time required. Useful when GDOP is poor. No need to maintain satellite lock. Same rover receivers must re-occupy the points they initially occupied. Moving the base station for the second occupation sessions may improve accuracy. Voice communications are needed to ensure simultaneous observations between base receiver and rover(s).

Kinematic: Accuracy—10 mm + 2 ppm. Observation times—1 to 4 epochs, (1 to 2 minutes on control points); the faster the rover speed, the quicker must be the observation (shorter epochs). Sampling rate is usually between 0.5 and 5 seconds. Initialization by occupying two known points—2 to 5 minutes, or by antenna swap—5 to 15 minutes. Lock must be maintained on 4 satellites (5 satellites are better in case one of them moves close to the horizon). Good technique for open areas (especially hydrographic surveys) and where large amounts of data are required quickly.

Stop and go: Accuracy—10 to 20 mm + 2 ppm. Observation times—a few seconds to a minute. Lock must be maintained to 4 satellites and if loss of lock occurs, it must be reinitialized [i.e., occupy known point, rapid static techniques, or on-the-fly (OTF) resolution—OTF requires dual-frequency receivers]. This technique is one of the more effective ways of locating topographic and built features, as for engineering surveys.

DGPS: The U.S. Coast Guard's system of providing differential code measurement surveys. Accuracy—sub-meter to 10 m. Roving receivers are equipped with radio receivers capable of receiving base station broadcasts of pseudorange corrections, using RTCM standards. For use by individual surveyors working within range of the transmitters (100 km to 400 km). Positions can be determined in real time. Surveyors using just one receiver have the equivalent of two receivers.

Real-time differential surveys: Also known as real-time kinematic, RTK. Accuracies—1 to 2 cm. Requires a base receiver occupying a known station, which then radio transmits error corrections to any number of roving receivers thus permitting them to perform data gathering and layout surveys in real time. All required software is onboard the roving receivers. Dual-frequency receivers permit OTF reinitialization after loss of lock. Baselines are restricted to about 10 km. Five satellites are required. This, or similar techniques, is without doubt the future for many engineering surveys.

CORS: Nationwide differential positioning system—using code and/or carrier observations. When fully implemented (by about the year 2005) this system of approximately 250 Continuously Operating Reference Stations will enable surveyors working with one GPS receiver to obtain the same results as if working with two. The CORS receiver is a highly accurate dual-frequency receiver. Surveyors can access station data for the appropriate location, date and time via the Internet—data is then input to the software to combine with the surveyor's own data to produce accurate (post-processed) positioning. Canada's nationwide system, Active Control System (ACS), provides base station data for a fee.

Notes: Observation times and accuracies are affected by the quality and capability of the GPS receivers, by signal errors, and by the geometric strength of the visible satellite array (GDOP). Vertical accuracies are about half the horizontal accuracies.

which provide positioning solutions for a wide variety of private and government agencies involved in surveying, mapping, planning, GIS-related surveying, and navigation.

Some refer to *GPS* positioning as a new utility. Whether *GPS* constitutes a new utility by itself or in combination with GIS and other spatially related data bases, there is no question that a new, dynamic, spatially related information utility is emerging. This utility will process information—both spatial data and relational data; it will also be capable of the real-time processing required for navigation and routing and thus significantly change the world as we know it.

Recommended Readings

Books and articles

Geomatics Canada. 1993. *GPS Positioning Guide.* Natural Resources Canada.

Leick, Alfred. 1995. *GPS Satellite Surveying,* 2nd ed. John Wiley & Sons.

Reilly, James P. "The GPS Observer" (ongoing columns), *Point of Beginning (POB).*

Spofford, Paul, and Neil Weston. 1998 "CORS—The National Geodetic Survey's Continuously Operating Reference Station Project." *ACSM Bulletin,* March/April 1998.

Trimble Navigation Co. 1989. *GPS, A Guide to the Next Utility.*

1992. *GPS, Surveyor's Field Guide.*

Jeff Hurn. 1993. *Differential GPS Explained.*

(Information on these and other Trimble publications is available at the Trimble web site shown on the following page.)

Van Sickle, Jan. 1996. *GPS for Land Surveyors.* Ann Arbor Press Inc.

Wells, David, et al. 1986. *Guide to GPS Positioning.* Canadian GPS Associates.

Magazines for general information (including archived articles)

ACSM Bulletin, American Congress on Surveying and Mapping
http://www.survmap.org/

GPS World http://www.gpsworld.com/

Point of Beginning (POB) http://www.pobonline.com/

Professional Surveyor http://www.profsurv.com

Web sites (general information, reference and web links, and GPS receiver manufacturers)

Ashtech http://www.ashtech.com/

Carl Zeiss http://www.zeiss.com/survey/

DGPS http://www.navcen.uscg.mil/ (U.S. Coast Guard Navigation Center)

GLONASS http://mx.iki.rssi.ru/SFCSIC/english.html

GPS Overview, Peter H. Dana, Department of Geography, University of Texas
http://www.utexas.edu/depts/grg/gcraft/notes/gps/gps.html

Land Surveying and Geomatics, Maynard H. Riley, PLS, Illinois
http://homepage.interaccess.com/~maynard/

Land Surveyors' Reference Page, Stan Thompson, PLS, Huntington Technology Group http://www.lsrp.com/

Leica   http://www.leica.com/
Natural Resources Canada   http://www.nrcan.gc.ca/
National Geodetic Survey (NGS)   http://www.ngs.noaa.gov/
Nikon   http://www.nikonusa.com/
Sokkia   http://www.sokkia.com/
Trimble   http://www.trimble.com/

Also see the list of Internet references in Appendix B.

PART II
Construction
Applications

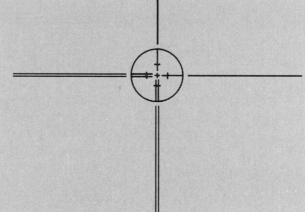

Construction surveys provide the horizontal and vertical layout for every key component of a construction project. This provision of **"line and grade"** can be accomplished only by experienced surveyors familiar with both the related project design and the appropriate construction techniques. A knowledge of related design is essential to effectively interpret the design drawings for layout purposes, and a knowledge of construction techniques is required to ensure that the layout is optimal for both **line and grade** transfer and construction scheduling.

We have seen that data can be gathered for engineering and other works in a variety of ways. Modern practice favors Total Station surveys for high density areas of limited size, and photogrammetric techniques for high density areas covering large tracts. Additionally, GPS techniques are now being successfully implemented in areas of moderate density. The technique chosen by a survey manager will usually be influenced by the costs (per point) and the reliability of the various techniques.

With regard to surveying applications, modern practice has become more dependent on the use of Total Stations, and recently, on the use of Global Positioning System (GPS) receivers working in "real" time (RTK techniques). In theory, GPS techniques seem to be ideal, as roving receiver-equipped surveyors quickly move to establish precise locations for layout points, in which both line and grade are promptly determined and marked.

Surveyors have found that to successfully utilize RTK surveying in construction surveying much care must be taken in establishing sufficient horizontal and vertical control monuments. In addition to the more stringent control requirements, surveyors must depend on an RTK system that has many components that can be cause for concern [e.g, short observation times, problems with radio transmissions, problems with satellite signal reception due to canopy obstructions (dual constellation receivers can help here), instrument calibration, multipath errors, and other errors (some of which will not be evident in error displays)].

For these reasons, points located through the use of GPS techniques must be verified, if possible, through independent surveys (e.g., check GPS surveys based on different control stations, take tape measurements from point to point where feasible, etc.). In the real world of construction works, the problems surrounding layout verification are compounded by the fact that the surveyor often doesn't have unlimited time to perform measurement checks—the contractor may actually be waiting on site to commence construction. All of this points to the need for a high level of planning and a rigid and systematic method (proven successful in past projects) of performing the GPS survey.

The elimination of mistakes and the achievement of required accuracy have been stressed in this text. In no area of surveying are these qualities more important than in construction surveying. All field measurements and calculations are suspect until they have been verified by independent means or by repeated checks. Mistakes have been known to escape detection in as many as three independent, conscientious checks by experienced personnel. These comments apply to all tape/EDM/GPS layouts.

Unlike other forms of surveying, construction surveying is often associated with speed of operation. Once contracts have been awarded, contractors may wish to commence construction immediately, as they will probably have definite commitments for their employees and equipment. They will not accept delay. A hurried surveyor is more likely to make mistakes in measurements and calculations, and thus even more vigilance than normal is required. Construction surveying is not an occupation for the faint of heart; the responsibilities are great and the working conditions often less than ideal. However, the sense of achievement when viewing the completed facility can be very rewarding.

Grade

Unfortunately the word *grade* has several different meanings. In construction work alone, it is often used in three distinctly different ways:

1. To refer to a proposed elevation.
2. To refer to the slope of profile line (i.e., gradient).
3. To refer to cuts and fills—vertical distances below or above grade stakes.

The surveyor should be aware of these different meanings and always note the context in which the word *grade* is being used.

Machine Guidance and Control

Regardless of the layout technique, layout activity often takes up much of surveyors' time and attention. Recent advances in machine guidance have resulted in techniques that significantly improve the efficiency of construction line and grade control. By reducing the need for as many layout surveyors and grade checkers near the working equipment, these techniques also provide an increased measure of safety.

Large tracts (e.g., airports, parking lots) can be brought to grade through the use of rotating lasers and machine-mounted laser detectors, which convey to the machine operator (bull dozer, grader, or scraper) the up/down operations required to bring the facility to the designed grade elevations. Rotating lasers can be set to define a horizontal plane or a sloped plane. The plane is usually referenced at some distance above the design grade.

Earth-work operations can now also be performed using backhoe excavators that are controlled by lasers. The signals received by the machine-mounted detectors are displayed in the machine cab where the operator can observe the location of the bucket's teeth with respect to the design grade in real time. In addition, audible tones permit the operator to keep focused on the work while guiding the excavation process up/down as needed. Accuracies are said to be as reliable as those used in most earth-work techniques. See Figure II-A.

Some manufacturers produce software that can integrate motorized theodolites and appropriately programmed PC computers to target machine-mounted reflecting prisms. These radio-controlled systems can monitor work progress and give real-time direction for line and grade operations of various construction equipment in a wide selection of engineering works (e.g., tunnels, road/railway construction, drilling). Manufacturers claim measurement standard deviations of 2 mm in height and 5 mm in position. See Figure II-B.

In addition to laser and computer-controlled Total Station techniques, machine guidance is also available, in real time, with the use of layout programs featuring GPS receivers. As with the Total Station techniques, receptors are mounted on the various construction equipment with the readings transmitted to the GPS controller or integrated PC

FIGURE II-A BucketPro Excavator cab display system used in machine-controlled excavation. (Courtesy of Spectra Precision, Dayton, Ohio)

FIGURE II-B   Paving machine operation controlled by a motorized Total Station/radio control modem/PC computer instrumentation package. (Courtesy of Leica Geosystems Inc., Norcross, Georgia)

computers. In-cab displays tell the operator how much up/down movement is needed on the cutting edge of the blade (grader or bull dozer) in order to maintain design alignment. This technique is used successfully in site preparation work, subbase placement, levelling, and even on superelevated curves.

The chapters in this section present the methods of construction line and grade determination. With machine guidance techniques, these line and grade determinations still have to be made, but instead of placing grade stakes, the surveyor may input the required data into guidance programs that operate directly from PC computers or from program design cards that are updated as the work progresses.

Chapter 10

Highway Curves

10-1 Route Surveys

Highway and railroad routes are chosen only after a complete and detailed study of all possible locations. Route selection usually involves the use of air photos, satellite imagery, and ground surveys and the analysis of existing plans and maps. The route is chosen because it satisfies all design requirements with minimal social, environmental, and financial impact.

The proposed centerline (₵) is laid out in a series of straight lines (tangents) beginning at 0 + 00 (0 + 000 metric) and continuing to the route terminal point. Each time the route changes direction, the deflection angle between the back tangent and forward tangent is measured and recorded. Existing detail that could have an effect on the highway design is tied in by conventional ground surveys, by aerial surveys, or by a combination of the two methods; typical detail would include lakes, streams, trees, structures, existing roads and railroads, and so on. In addition to the detail location, the surveyor will run levels along the proposed route, with elevations being taken across the route width at right angles to the ₵ at regular intervals (full stations, half stations, etc.) and at locations dictated by changes in the topography. These elevations will be used in the design of horizontal and vertical alignments; in addition, these elevations will form the basis for the calculation of construction cut-and-fill quantities (see Chapter 16).

The location of detail and the determination of elevations are normally confined to that relatively narrow strip of land representing the highway right-of-way (ROW). Exceptions would include potential river, highway, and railroad crossings, where approach profiles and sight lines (railroads) may be established.

10-2 Circular Curves: General

It was noted in the previous section that a highway route survey is initially laid out as a series of straight lines (tangents). Once the ₵ location alignment has been confirmed, the tangents are joined by circular curves that allow for smooth vehicle operation at the speeds for which the highway was designed. Figure 10-1 illustrates how two tangents are joined by a circular curve and shows some related circular curve terminology. The point at which the alignment changes from straight to circular is known as the BC (beginning of curve). The BC is located distance T (subtangent) from the PI (point of tangent intersection). The length of circular curve (L) is dependent on the central angle (Δ) and the value of R (radius). The tangent deflection angle (Δ) is equal to the curve's central angle (see Figure 10-2). The point at which the alignment changes from circular back to tangent is known as the EC (end of curve). Since the curve is symmetrical about the PI, the EC is also located distance T from the PI. From geometry, we recall that the radius of a circle is perpendicular to the tangent at the point of tangency. Therefore, the radius is perpendicular to the back tangent at the BC and to the forward tangent at the EC.

The terms BC and EC are also referred to by some agencies as PC (point of curve) and PT (point of tangency), and by others as TC (tangent to curve) and CT (curve to tangent).

10-3   Circular Curve Geometry

Most curve problems are calculated from field measurements (Δ and the chainage of PI) and from design parameters (R). Given R (which is dependent on the design speed) and Δ, all other curve components can be computed.

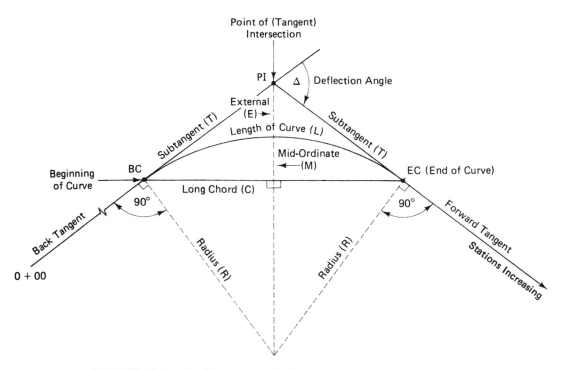

FIGURE 10-1   Circular curve terminology.

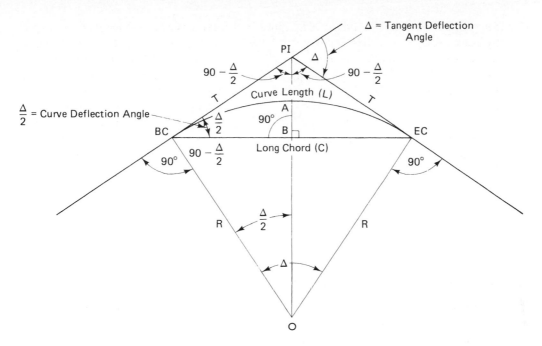

FIGURE 10-2 Geometry of the circle.

Analysis of Figure 10-2 will show that the curve deflection angle (PI, BC, EC) is $\Delta/2$ and that the central angle at O is equal to Δ, the tangent deflection.

The line (O − PI), joining the center of the curve to the PI, effectively bisects all related lines and angles.

Tangent: In triangle BC, O, PI,

$$\frac{T}{R} = \tan\frac{\Delta}{2}$$

$$\boldsymbol{T = R \tan\frac{\Delta}{2}} \tag{10-1}$$

Chord: In triangle BC, O, B,

$$\frac{1/2C}{R} = \sin\frac{\Delta}{2}$$

$$\boldsymbol{C = 2R \sin\frac{\Delta}{2}} \tag{10-2}$$

Mid-ordinate:

$$\frac{OB}{R} = \cos\frac{\Delta}{2}$$

$$OB = R \cos\frac{\Delta}{2}$$

But

$$OB = R - M$$

$$R - M = R \cos \frac{\Delta}{2}$$

$$M = R\left(1 - \cos \frac{\Delta}{2}\right) \tag{10-3}$$

External: In triangle BC, O, PI,

$$\text{O to PI} = R + E$$

$$\frac{R}{R + E} = \cos \frac{\Delta}{2}$$

$$E = R\left(\frac{1}{\cos (\Delta/2)} - 1\right) \tag{10-4}$$

$$= R\left(\sec \frac{\Delta}{2} - 1\right) \tag{alternate}$$

From Figure 10-3,

Arc: $\quad \dfrac{L}{2\pi R} = \dfrac{\Delta}{360},\qquad L = 2\pi R\,\dfrac{\Delta}{360}$ $\qquad\qquad$ (10-5)

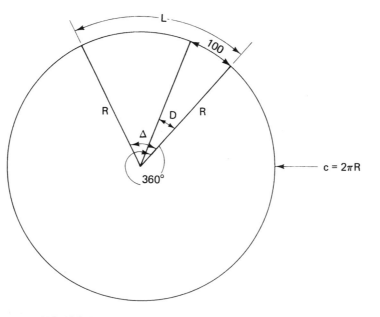

FIGURE 10-3 Relationship between the degree of curve (*D*) and the circle.

where Δ is expressed in degrees and decimals of a degree.

The sharpness of the curve is determined by the choice of the radius (R); large radius curves are relatively flat, whereas small radius curves are relatively sharp.

Many highway agencies use the concept of degree of curve (D) to define the sharpness of the curve. D is defined to be that central angle subtended by 100 ft of arc. (In railway design, D is defined to be the central angle subtended by 100 ft of chord.)

From Figure 10-3,

$$D \text{ and } R: \qquad \frac{D}{360} = \frac{100}{2\pi R}, \qquad D = \frac{5729.58}{R} \qquad\qquad (10\text{-}6)$$

$$\text{Arc:} \qquad \frac{L}{100} = \frac{\Delta}{D}, \qquad L = 100\,\frac{\Delta}{D} \qquad\qquad (10\text{-}7)$$

■ **EXAMPLE 10-1**

Refer to Figure 10-4. Given

$$\Delta = 16°38'$$
$$R = 1000 \text{ ft}$$
$$\text{PI at } 6 + 26.57$$

calculate the station of the BC and EC; also calculate lengths C, M, and E.

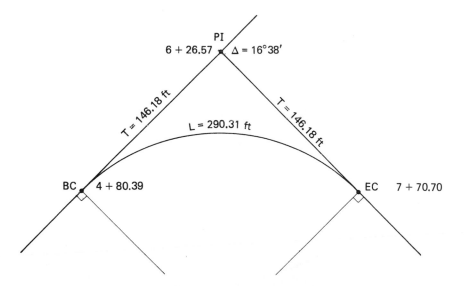

FIGURE 10-4 Sketch for Example 10-1. Note: To aid in comprehension, the magnitude of the Δ angle has been exaggerated in this section.

$$T = R \tan \frac{\Delta}{2} \qquad (10\text{-}1) \qquad\qquad L = 2\pi R \frac{\Delta}{360} \qquad\qquad (10\text{-}5)$$

$$= 1000 \tan 8°19' \qquad\qquad\qquad = 2\pi \times 1000 \times \frac{16.6333}{360}$$

$$= 146.18 \text{ ft} \qquad\qquad\qquad\qquad = 290.31 \text{ ft}$$

```
PI at    6 + 26.57
  −T     1    46.18
BC =  4 + 80.39
  +L     2 90.31
EC =  7 + 70.70
```

$$C = 2R \sin \frac{\Delta}{2} \qquad\qquad (10\text{-}2)$$

$$= 2 \times 1000 \times \sin 8°19'$$

$$= 289.29 \text{ ft}$$

$$M = R\left(1 - \cos \frac{\Delta}{2}\right) \qquad\qquad 10\text{-}3$$

$$= 1000(1 - \cos 8°19')$$

$$= 10.52 \text{ ft}$$

$$E = R(\sec \frac{\Delta}{2} - 1) \qquad\qquad 10\text{-}4$$

$$= 1000(\sec 8°19' - 1)$$

$$= 10.63 \text{ ft}$$

Note: A common mistake made by students first studying circular curves is to determine the station of the EC by adding the T distance to the PI. Although the EC is physically a distance of T from the PI, the stationing (chainage) must reflect the fact that the ₵ no longer goes through the PI. The ₵ now takes the shorter distance (L) from the BC to the EC.

■ EXAMPLE 10-2
Refer to Figure 10-5. Given

$$\Delta = 12°51'$$
$$R = 400 \text{ m}$$
$$\text{PI at } 0 + 241.782$$

calculate the station of the BC and EC.

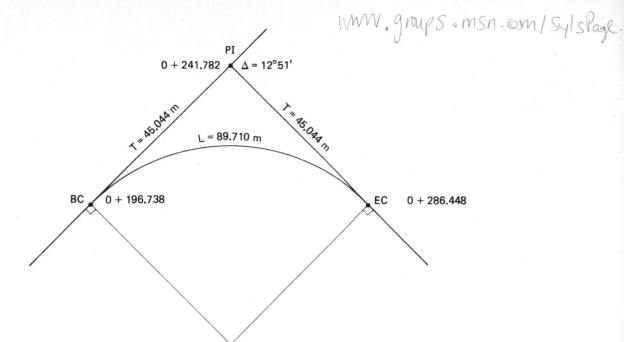

FIGURE 10-5 Sketch for Example 10-2.

$$T = R \tan \frac{\Delta}{2} \qquad (10\text{-}1) \qquad\qquad L = 2\pi R \frac{\Delta}{360} \qquad (10\text{-}5)$$

$$= 400 \tan 6°25'30'' \qquad 0.417 \quad 0.5 \qquad = 2\pi \times 400 \times \frac{12.850}{360}$$

$$= 45.044 \text{ m} \qquad\qquad\qquad = 89.710 \text{ m}$$

$$
\begin{array}{rl}
\text{PI at} & 0 + 241.782 \\
-T & \underline{\qquad 45.044} \\
\text{BC} = & 0 + 196.738 \\
+L & \underline{\qquad 89.710} \\
\text{EC} = & 0 + 286.448
\end{array}
$$

■ EXAMPLE 10-3

Refer to Figure 10-6. Given

$$\Delta = 11°21'35''$$
$$\text{PI at } 14 + 87.33$$
$$D = 6°$$

calculate the station of the BC and EC.

$$R = \frac{5729.58}{D} = 954.93 \text{ ft} \qquad (10\text{-}6)$$

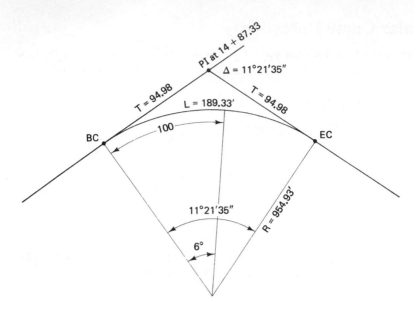

FIGURE 10-6 Sketch for Example 10-3.

$$T = R \tan \frac{\Delta}{2} \qquad (10\text{-}1)$$

$$= 954.93 \tan 5.679861°$$

$$= 94.98 \text{ ft}$$

$$L = 100 \frac{\Delta}{D} \qquad (10\text{-}7)$$

$$= \frac{100 \times 11.359722}{6}$$

$$= 189.33 \text{ ft}$$

or

$$L = \frac{2\pi R\Delta}{360} \qquad (10\text{-}5)$$

$$= 2\pi \times \frac{954.93 \times 11.359722}{360}$$

$$= 189.33 \text{ ft}$$

PI at	14 +	87.33
$-T$		94.98
BC =	13 +	92.35
$+L$	1	89.33
EC =	15 +	81.68

10-4 Circular Curve Deflections

A common method of locating a curve in the field is by deflection angles. Typically the theodolite is set up at the BC, and the deflection angles are turned from the tangent line (see Figure 10-7).

If we use the data from Example 10-2,

$$BC \text{ at } 0 + 196.738$$
$$EC \text{ at } 0 + 286.448$$
$$\frac{\Delta}{2} = 6°25'30'' = 6.4250°$$
$$L = 89.710$$
$$T = 45.044$$

And if the layout is to proceed at 20-m intervals, the procedure would be as follows. First, compute the deflection angles for the three required arc distances:

$$\text{Deflection angle} = \left(\frac{\text{arc}}{L}\right)\frac{\Delta}{2}$$

1. BC to first even station $(0 + 200)$: $([0 + 200] - [0 + 196.738] = 3.262)$:

$$\frac{6.4250}{89.710} \times 3.262 = 0.2336° = 0°14'01''$$

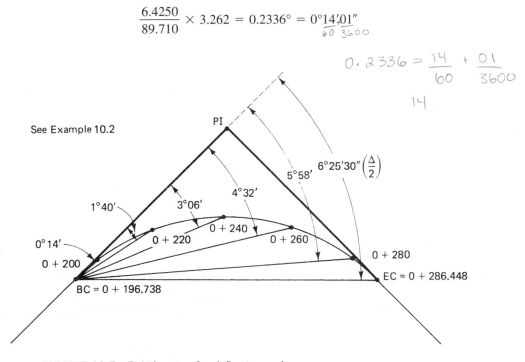

$$0.2336 = \frac{14}{60} + \frac{01}{3600}$$

$$14$$

See Example 10.2

FIGURE 10-7   Field location for deflection angles.

2. Even station interval:

$$\frac{6.4250}{89.710} \times 20 = 1.4324° = 1°25'57''$$

3. Last even station (0 + 280) to EC:

$$\frac{6.4250}{89.710} \times 6.448 = 0.4618° = 0°27'42''$$

Second, prepare a list of appropriate stations together with *cumulative* deflection angles.

Stations	Deflection Angles
BC 0 + 196.738	0°00'00''
0 + 200	0°14'01'' + 1°25'57''
0 + 220	1°39'58'' + 1°25'57''
0 + 240	3°05'55'' + 1°25'57''
0 + 260	4°31'52'' + 1°25'57''
0 + 280	5°57'49'' + 0°27'42''
EC 0 + 286.448	$6°25'31'' \approx 6°25'30'' = \frac{\Delta}{2}$

For most engineering layouts, the deflection angles are rounded to the closest minute or half-minute.

Another common method (see Chapter 5) of locating a curve in the field is by using the "setting out" feature of the Total Station. The coordinates of each station on the curve (or its offset) are first uploaded into the Total Station, permitting the processor to compute and display the angle and distance from the instrument station to each curve station—when prompted by the instrument operator.

10-5   Chord Calculations

In the previous example, it was determined that the deflection angle for station 0 + 200 was 0°14'01''; it follows that 0 + 200 could be located by placing a stake on the transit line at 0°14' and at a distance of 3.262 m (200 − 196.738) from the BC.

Furthermore, station 0 + 220 could be located by placing a stake on the transit line at 1°40' and at a distance of 20 m along the arc from the stake locating 0 + 200. The remaining stations could be located in a similar manner. However, it must be noted that the distances measured with a steel tape are not arc distances; they are straight lines known as *subchords*.

To calculate the subchord, Equation (10-2), $C = 2R \sin (\Delta/2)$, may be used. This equation, derived from Figure 10-2, is the special case of the long chord and the total deflection angle. The general case can be stated as follows:

$$C = 2R \sin \text{ deflection angle} \tag{10-8}$$

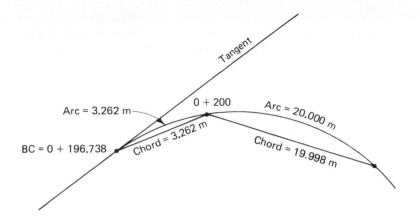

FIGURE 10-8 Curve arcs and chords.

and any subchord can be calculated if its deflection angle is known.

Relevant chords for the previous example can be calculated as follows (see Figure 10-8):

$$\text{First chord: } C = 2 \times 400 \times \sin 0°14'01'' = 3.2618 \text{ m}$$
$$= 3.262 \text{ m (at three decimals, chord} = \text{arc)}$$
$$\text{Even station chord: } C = 2 \times 400 \times \sin 1°25'57''$$
$$= 19.998 \text{ m}$$
$$\text{Last chord: } C = 2 \times 400 \times \sin 0°27'42''$$
$$= 6.448 \text{ m}$$

If these chord distances are used, the curve layout can proceed without error.

Note: Although the calculation of the first and last subchord shows the chord and arc to be equal (i.e., 3.262 m and 6.448 m), the chords are always marginally shorter than the arcs. In the case of short distances (above) and in the case of flat (large radius) curves, the arcs and chords can often appear to be equal. If more decimal places are introduced into the calculation, the marginal difference between arc and chord will become evident.

10-6 Metric Considerations

Countries that have switched from foot to metric (SI) units (e.g., Canada) have adopted for highway use a reference station of 1 km (e.g., 1 + 000); cross sections at 50-, 20-, and 10-m intervals; and a curvature design parameter based on a rational (even meter) value radius, as opposed to a rational value degree (even degree) of curve (*D*).

The degree of curve found favor with most highway agencies because of the somewhat simpler calculations associated with its use, a factor that was significant in the pre-electronics age, when most calculations were performed by using logarithms. A comparison of techniques involving both *D* and *R* (radius) shows that the only computation in which the rational aspect of *D* is carried through is that for the arc length—that is, $L = 100\Delta/D$, Equation (10-7)—and even in that one case, the ease of calculation depends on

Δ also being a rational number. In all other formulas, the inclusion of trigonometric functions or π ensures a more complex computation requiring the use of a calculator.

In field work, the use of D (as opposed to R) permits quick determination of the deflection angle for even stations. For example, in foot units, if the degree of curve is $2°$, the deflection angle for a full station (100 ft) is $D/2$ or $1°$; for 50 ft, the deflection is $0°30'$; and so on.

In metric units, the degree of curve is the central angle subtended by 100 m of arc, and the deflections are similarly computed. That is, for a metric D of $6°$, the deflections are as follows: for 100 m, $3°$; for 50 m, $1°30'$; for 20 m, $0°36'$; and for 10 m, $0°18'$. The metric curve deflections here are not quite as simple as in the foot system, but they are still uncomplicated and rational. However, curve stakeouts require more stations than just those on the even chainages. For example, the BC and EC, catch basins or culverts, vertical curve stations, and the like usually occur on odd chainages, and the deflection angles for those odd chainages involve irrational number calculations requiring the use of a calculator.

The widespread use of handheld calculators and office computers has greatly reduced the importance of techniques that permit only marginal reductions in computations. Surveyors are now routinely solving their problems with calculators and computers rather than using the seemingly endless array of tables that once characterized the back section of survey texts.

An additional reason for the lessening importance of D in computing deflection angles is that many curves (particularly at interchanges) are now being laid out by control-point-based polar or intersection techniques (i.e., angle/distance or angle/angle) instead of deflection angles (see Chapter 5).

Those countries using the metric system, almost without exception, use a rational value for the radius (R) as a design parameter.

10-7 Field Procedure

With the PI location and Δ angle measured in the field and with the radius or degree of curve (D) chosen consistent with the design speed, all curve computations can be completed. The surveyor then goes back out to the field and measures off the tangent (T) distance from the PI to locate the BC and EC on the appropriate tangent lines. The transit is then set up at the BC and zeroed and sighted in on the PI. The $\Delta/2$ angle ($6°25'30''$ in Example 10-2) is then turned off in the direction of the EC mark (wood stake, nail, etc.). If the computations for T and the field measurements of T have been performed correctly, the line of sight of the $\Delta/2$ angle will fall over the EC mark. If this does not occur, the T computations and then the field measurements are repeated.

Note: The $\Delta/2$ line of sight over the EC mark will, of necessity, contain some error. In each case, the surveyor will have to decide if the resultant alignment error is acceptable for the type of survey in question. For example, if the $\Delta/2$ line of sight misses the EC mark by 0.10 ft (30 mm) in a ditched highway ℄ survey, the surveyor will probably find the error acceptable and then proceed with the deflections. However, a similar error in the $\Delta/2$ line of sight in a survey to lay out an elevated portion of urban freeway will not be acceptable; in that case, an acceptable error will be roughly one-third of the preceding error (0.03 ft or 10 mm).

After the Δ/2 check has been satisfactorily completed, the curve stakes are set by turning off the deflection angle and measuring the chord distance for the appropriate stations. The theodolite is, if possible, left at the BC (see Section 10-8) for the entire curve stakeout, whereas the distance measuring moves continually forward from station to station. The rear surveyor keeps his or her body to the outside of the curve to avoid blocking the line of sight from the instrument.

A final verification of the work is available after the last even station has been set; the chord distance from the last even station to the EC stake is measured and compared to the theoretical value; if the check indicates an unacceptable discrepancy, the work is checked.

Finally, after the curve has been deflected in, the party chief usually walks the curve, looking for any abnormalities; if a mistake has been made (e.g., putting in two stations at the same deflection angle), it will probably be very evident. The circular curve's symmetry is such that even minor mistakes are obvious in a visual check.

It should be noted here that many highway agencies use polar layout for interchanges and other complex features. If the coordinates of centerline alignment stations are determined, they can be used to locate the facility. In this application, the Total Station is placed at a known (or resectioned) station and aligned with another known station so that the instrument's processor can compute and display the angle and distance needed for layout. See Chapter 5.

10-8 Moving Up on the Curve

The curve deflections shown in Section 10-4 are presented in a form suitable for deflecting in while set up at the BC, with a zero setting at the PI. However, it often occurs that the entire curve cannot be deflected in from the BC, and two or more instrument setups may be required before the entire curve has been located. The reasons for this include a loss of line of sight due to intervening obstacles (i.e., detail or elevation rises).

In Figure 10-9, the data of Example 10-2 are used to illustrate the geometric considerations in moving up on the curve. In this case, station 0 + 260 cannot be established with the theodolite at the BC (as were the previous stations). The line of sight from the BC to 0 + 260 is obscured by a large tree. To establish station 0 + 260, the instrument is moved forward to the last station (0 + 240) established from the BC. The horizontal circle is zeroed, and the BC is then sighted with the telescope in its inverted position. When the telescope is transited, the theodolite is once again oriented to the curve; that is, to set off the next (0 + 260) deflection, the surveyor refers to the previously prepared list of deflections and sets the appropriate deflection (4°32′) for the desired station location and then for all subsequent stations.

Figure 10-9 shows the geometry involved in this technique. A tangent to the curve is shown by a dashed line through station 0 + 240 (the proposed setup location). The angle from that tangent line to a line joining 0 + 240 to the BC is the deflection angle 3°06′. When the line from the BC is produced through station 0 + 240, the same angle (3°06′) occurs between that line and the tangent line through 0 + 240 (opposite angles). It was determined that the deflection angle for 20 m is 1°26′ (Section 10-4). When 1°26′ is added to 3°06′, the angle of 4°32′ for station 0 + 260 results, the same angle previously calculated for that station.

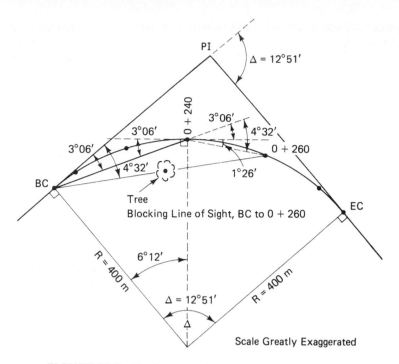

FIGURE 10-9 Moving up on the curve.

This discussion has limited the move up to one station; in fact, the move up can be repeated as often as is necessary to complete the curve layout. The technique can generally be stated as follows: *When the instrument is moved up on the curve and the instrument is backsighted, with the telescope inverted, at any other station, the theodolite will be "oriented to the curve" if the horizontal circle is first set to the value of the deflection angle for the sighted station;* that is, in the case of a BC sight, the deflection angle to be set is obviously zero; if the instrument is set on 0 + 260 and sighting 0 + 240, a deflection angle of 3°06′ is first set on the scale.

When the inverted telescope is transited to its normal position, all subsequent stations can then be sighted using the original list of deflections; this is the meaning of "theodolite oriented to the curve," and this is why the list of deflections can be made first, before the instrument setup stations have been determined and (as we shall see in Section 10-9) even before it has been decided whether to run in the curve centerline (₵) or whether it would be more appropriate to run in the curve on some offset line.

10-9 Offset Curves

Curves being laid out for construction purposes must be established on offsets so that the survey stakes are not disturbed by construction activities. Many highway agencies prefer to lay out the curve on ₵ (centerline) and then offset each ₵ stake a set distance left and right (left and right are oriented by facing to the forward station).

The stakes can be offset to one side by using the arm-swing technique described in Section 7.3, with the hand pointing to the two adjacent stations. If this is done with care, the offsets on that one side can be established on radial lines without too much error. After one side has been offset in this manner, the other side is then offset by lining up the established offset stake with the ₵ stake and measuring out the offset distance, ensuring that all three stakes are visually in a straight line. Keeping the three stakes in a straight line will ensure that any alignment error existing at the offset stakes will steadily diminish as one moves toward the ₵ and the construction works.

In the construction of most municipal roads, particularly curbed roads, the centerline may not be established; instead, the road alignment will be established directly on offset lines that are located a safe distance from the construction works. To illustrate, consider the curve in Example 10-2 used to construct a curbed road, as shown in Figure 10-10. The face of the curb is to be 4.00 m left and right of the centerline. Assume that the curb layout can be offset 2 m (each side) without interfering with construction (generally the less cut or fill required, the smaller the offset distance can be).

Figure 10-11 shows that if the layout is to be kept on radial lines through the ₵ stations, the station arc distances on the left-side (outside) curve will be longer than the corresponding ₵ arc distances, whereas the station arc distances on the right-side (inside) curve will be shorter than the corresponding ₵ arc distances. The figure also clearly shows that the ratio of the outside arc to the ₵ arc is identical to the ratio of the ₵ arc to the inside arc. (See arc computations in Section 10-10.) **By keeping the offset stations on radial lines, the surveyor is able to use the ₵ deflections previously computed.**

When using the "setting out" programs in Total Stations to locate offset curve stations in the field, the surveyor can simply identify the offset value (when prompted by the program) so that the processor can compute the coordinates and then inverse to determine and display the required angle and distance from the instrument station. Alternately

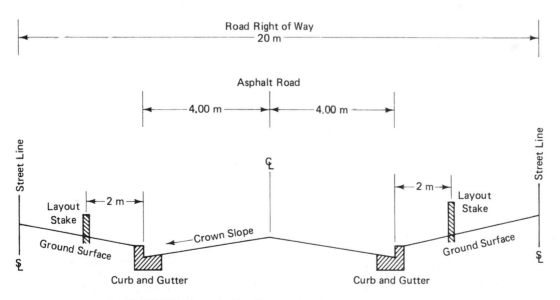

FIGURE 10-10 Municipal road cross section.

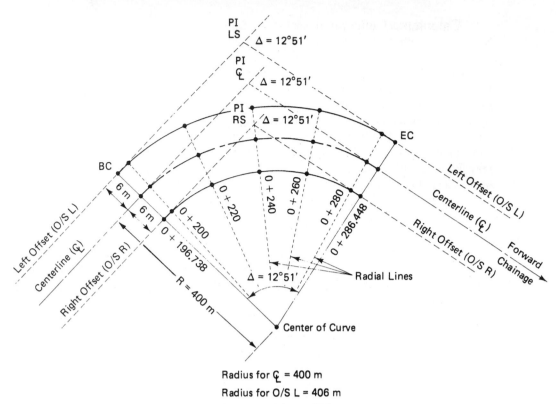

Radius for ℄ = 400 m
Radius for O/S L = 406 m
Radius for O/S R = 394 m

FIGURE 10-11 Offset curves.

civilian COGO-type software can be used to compute the coordinates of all offset stations and the layout angles and distances from selected proposed instrument stations before going out in the field.

■ **EXAMPLE 10-4** *Illustrative Problem for Offset Curves (Metric Units)*

Consider the problem of a construction offset layout using the data of Example 10-2, the deflections developed in Section 10-4, and the offset of 2 m introduced in Section 10-8.

$$\text{Given data: } \Delta = 12°51'$$
$$R = 400 \text{ m}$$
$$\text{PI at } 0 + 241.782$$

$$\text{Calculated data: } T = 45.044 \text{ m}$$
$$L = 89.710 \text{ m}$$
$$\text{BC at } 0 + 196.738$$
$$\text{EC at } 0 + 286.448$$

Required: Curbs to be laid out on 2-m offsets at 20-m stations.

Calculated Deflections

Station	Computed Deflection	Field Deflection
BC 0 + 196.738	0°00′00″	0°00′
0 + 200	0°14′01″	0°14′
0 + 220	1°39′58″	1°40′
0 + 240	3°05′55″	3°06′
0 + 260	4°31′52″	4°32′
0 + 280	5°57′49″	5°58′
EC 0 + 286.448	6°25′31″	6°25′30″ = $\frac{\Delta}{2}$; Check

Reference to Figures 10-10 and 10-11 will show that the left-side (outside) curb face will have a radius of 404 m. A 2-m offset for that curb will result in an offset radius of 406 m. Similarly the offset radius for the right-side (inside) curb will be $400 - 6 = 394$ m.

Since we are going to use the deflections already computed, it only remains to calculate the corresponding left-side arc or chord distances and the corresponding right-side arc or chord distances. Although layout procedure (angle and distance) indicates that chord distances will be required, for illustrative purposes we will compute both the arc and the chord distances on offset.

Arc Distance Computations. Reference to Figure 10-12 will show that the offset (o/s) arcs can be computed by direct ratio.

$$\frac{\text{o/s arc}}{\text{₵ arc}} = \frac{\text{o/s radius}}{\text{₵ radius}}$$

For the first arc (BC to 0 + 200),

$$\text{Left side: o/s arc} = 3.262 \times \frac{406}{400} = 3.311 \text{ m}$$

$$\text{Right side: o/s arc} = 3.262 \times \frac{394}{400} = 3.213 \text{ m}$$

For the even station arcs,

$$\text{Left side: o/s arc} = 20 \times \frac{406}{400} = 20.300 \text{ m}$$

$$\text{Right side: o/s arc} = 20 \times \frac{394}{400} = 19.700 \text{ m}$$

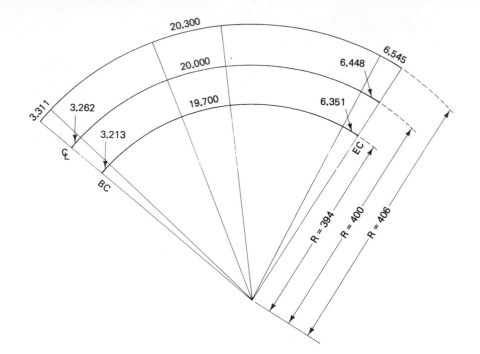

FIGURE 10-12 Offset arc lengths calculated by ratios.

For the last arc (0 + 280 to EC),

$$\text{Left side: o/s arc} = 6.448 \times \frac{406}{400} = 6.545 \text{ m}$$

$$\text{Right side: o/s arc} = 6.448 \times \frac{394}{400} = 6.351 \text{ m}$$

Arithmetic check: $LS - \math₡ = \math₡ - RS$.

Chord Distance Computations. Refer to Figure 10-13. For any deflection angle, the equation for chord length (see Section 10-5) is

$$C = 2R \sin \text{ deflection angle} \qquad (10\text{-}8)$$

In this problem, the deflection angles have been calculated previously, and it is the radius (R) that is the variable.

For the first chord (BC to 0 + 200),

$$\text{Left side: } C = 2 \times 406 \times \sin 0°14'01'' = 3.311 \text{ m}$$
$$\text{Right side: } C = 2 \times 394 \times \sin 0°14'01'' = 3.213 \text{ m}$$

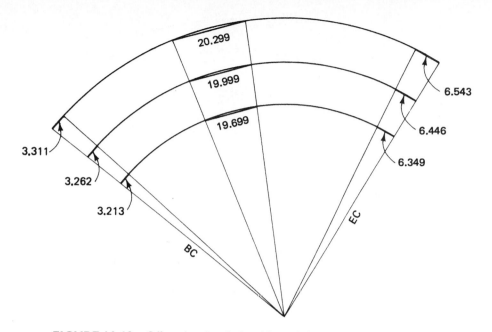

FIGURE 10-13 Offset chords calculated from deflection angles and offset radii.

For the even station chords,

$$\text{Left side: } C = 2 \times 406 \times \sin 1°25'57'' = 20.299 \text{ m}$$
$$\text{Right side: } C = 2 \times 394 \times \sin 1°25'57'' = 19.699 \text{ m}$$

See Section 10-4.

For the last chord,

$$\text{Left side: } C = 2 \times 406 \times \sin 0°27'42'' = 6.543 \text{ m}$$
$$\text{Right side: } C = 2 \times 394 \times \sin 0°27'42'' = 6.349 \text{ in}$$

Arithmetic check: *LS* chord − ℄ chord = ℄ chord − *RS* chord.

■ **EXAMPLE 10-5**   *Curve Problem (Foot Units)*

Given the following ℄ data,

$$D = 5°$$
$$\Delta = 16°28'30''$$
$$\text{PI at } 31 + 30.62$$

it is required to furnish stakeout information for the curve on 50-ft offsets left and right of ℄ at 50-ft stations.

$$R = \frac{5729.58}{D} \tag{10-6}$$

$$= 1145.92 \text{ ft}$$

$$T = R \tan \frac{\Delta}{2} \tag{10-1}$$

$$= 1145.92 \tan 8°14'15''$$

$$= 165.90 \text{ ft}$$

$$L = 100 \frac{\Delta}{D} \tag{10-7}$$

$$= \frac{100 \times 16.475}{5} = 329.50 \text{ ft}$$

Alternatively

$$L = 2\pi R \frac{\Delta}{360} = 329.50 \text{ ft} \tag{10-5}$$

$$
\begin{array}{rrr}
\text{PI at} & 31 & + 30.62 \\
-T & 1 & 65.90 \\
\hline
\text{BC} = & 29 & + 64.72 \\
+L & 3 & 29.50 \\
\hline
\text{EC} = & 32 & + 94.22 \\
\end{array}
$$

Computation of Deflections.

$$\text{Total deflection for curve} = \frac{\Delta}{2} = 8°14'15'' = 494.25'$$

$$\text{Deflection per foot} = \frac{494.25}{329.50} = 1.5'/\text{ft}$$

Alternatively, since $D = 5°$, the deflection for 100 ft is $D/2$ or $2°30' = 150'$. The deflection, therefore, for 1 ft is 150/100 or $1/5'/\text{ft}$.

Deflection for first station:

$$35.28 \times 1.5 = 52.92' = 0°52.9'$$

Deflection for even 50-ft stations:

$$50 \times 1.5 = 75' = 1°15'$$

Deflection for last station:

$$44.22 \times 1.5 = 66.33' = 1°06.3'$$

	Deflections (cumulative)	
Stations	Office	Field (closest minute)
BC 29 + 64.72	0°00.0′	0°00′
30 + 00	0°52.9′	0°53′
30 + 50	2°07.9′	2°08′
31 + 00	3°22.9′	3°23′
31 + 50	4°37.9′	4°38′
32 + 00	5°52.9′	5°53′
32 + 50	7°07.9′	7°08′
EC 32 + 94.22	8°14.2′	8°14′
	$\approx 8°14.25′$	
	$= \dfrac{\Delta}{2}$, Check	

Chord calculations for left- and right-side curves on 50-ft (from ℄) offsets (see the chord calculation table below and Figure 10-14):

$$\text{Radius for } ℄ = 1145.92 \text{ ft}$$
$$\text{Radius for LS} = 1195.92 \text{ ft}$$
$$\text{Radius for RS} = 1095.92 \text{ ft}$$

10-10 Compound Circular Curves

A compound curve consists of two (usually) or more circular arcs between two main tangents turning in the same direction and joining at common tangent points. Figure 10-15 shows a compound curve consisting of two circular arcs joined at a point of compound curve (PCC). The lower chainage curve is number 1, whereas the higher chainage curve is number 2.

CHORD CALCULATIONS FOR EXAMPLE 10-5

Interval	Left Side	℄	Right Side
BC to 30 + 00	$C = 2 \times 1195.92$ $\times \sin 0°52.9′$ $= 36.80$ ft	$C = 2 \times 1145.92$ $\times \sin 0°52.9′$ $= 35.27$ ft	$C = 2 \times 1095.92$ $\times \sin 0°52.9′$ $= 33.73$ ft
	Diff. = 1.53	Diff. = 1.54	
50-ft stations	$C = 2 \times 1195.92$ $\times \sin 1°15′$ $= 52.18$ ft	$C = 2 \times 1145.92$ $\times \sin 1°15′$ $= 50.00$ (to 2 decimals)	$C = 2 \times 1095.92$ $\times \sin 1°15′$ $= 47.81$ ft
	Diff. = 2.18	Diff. = 2.19	
32 + 50 EC	$C = 2 \times 1195.92$ $\times \sin 1°06.3′$ $= 46.13$ ft	$C = 2 \times 1145.92$ $\times \sin 1°06.3′$ $= 44.20$ ft	$C = 2 \times 1095.92$ $\times \sin 1°06.3′$ $= 42.27$ ft
	Diff. = 1.93	Diff. = 1.93	

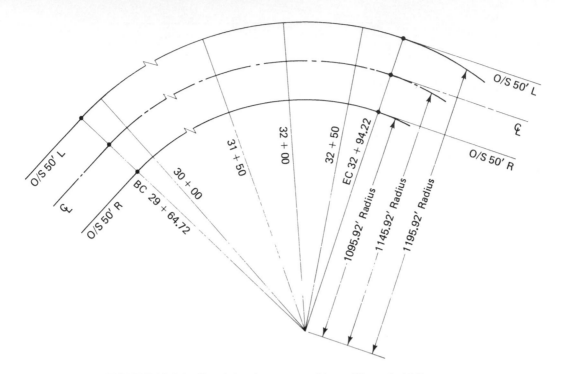

FIGURE 10-14 Sketch for the curve problem of Example 10-5.

The parameters are R_1, R_2, Δ_1, Δ_2 ($\Delta_1 + \Delta_2 = \Delta$), T_1, and T_2. If four of these six or seven parameters are known, the others can be solved. Under normal circumstances, Δ_1 and Δ_2, or Δ, are measured in the field, and R_1 and R_2 are given by design considerations, with minimum values governed by design speed.

Although compound curves can be manipulated to provide practically any vehicle path desired by the designer, they are not employed where simple curves or spiral curves can be used to achieve the same desired effect. Practically, compound curves are reserved for those applications where design constraints (topographic or cost of land) preclude the use of simple or spiral curves, and they are now usually found chiefly in the design of interchange loops and ramps. Smooth driving characteristics require that the larger radius be no more than 1-1/3 times larger than the smaller radius (this ratio increases to 1-1/2 when dealing with interchange curves).

Solutions to compound curve problems vary, as several possibilities exist as to which of the data are known in any one given problem. All problems can be solved by use of the sine law or cosine law or by the omitted measurement traverse technique illustrated in Example 6-10.

If the omitted measurement traverse technique is used, the problem becomes a five-sided traverse (see Figure 10-15) with sides R_1, T_1, T_2, R_2, and ($R_1 - R_2$) and with angles $90°$, $180 - \Delta°$, $90°$, $180 + \Delta°_2$, and $\Delta°_1$. An assumed azimuth can be chosen that will simplify the computations (i.e., set direction of R_1 to be $0°00'00''$).

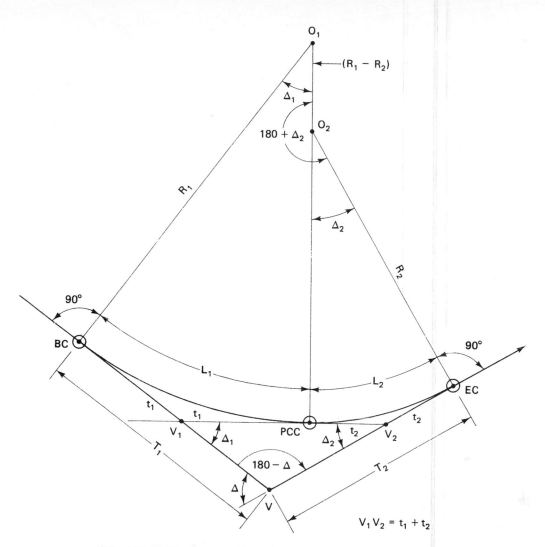

FIGURE 10-15 Compound circular curve.

10-11 Reverse Curves

Reverse curves [see Figure 10-16(a) and (b)] are seldom used in highway or railway alignment. The instantaneous change in direction occurring at the point of reverse curve (PRC) would cause discomfort and safety problems for all but the slowest of speeds. Additionally, since the change in curvature is instantaneous, there is no room to provide superelevation transition from cross-slope right to cross-slope left (see Sections 10-21 and 10-22). However, reverse curves can be used to advantage where the instantaneous change in direction poses no threat to safety or comfort.

The reverse curve is particularly pleasing to the eye and is used with great success on park roads, formal paths, waterway channels, and the like. This curve can be encountered

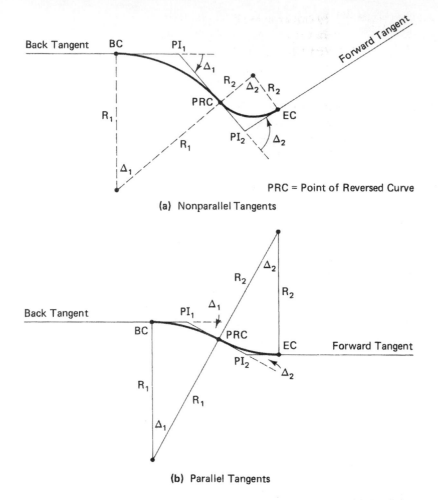

PRC = Point of Reversed Curve

(a) Nonparallel Tangents

(b) Parallel Tangents

FIGURE 10-16 Reverse curves. (a) Nonparallel tangents. (b) Parallel tangents.

in both situations illustrated in Figure 10-16(a) and (b); the parallel tangent application is particularly common (R_1 is often equal to R_2). As with compound curves, reverse curves have six independent parameters ($R_1, \Delta_1, T_1, R_2, \Delta_2, T_2$); the solution technique depends on which parameters are unknown, and the techniques noted for compound curves will also provide the solution to reverse curve problems.

10-12   Vertical Curves: General

Vertical curves are used in highway and street vertical alignment to provide a gradual change between two adjacent grade lines. Some highway and municipal agencies introduce vertical curves at every change in grade-line slope, whereas other agencies introduce vertical curves into the alignment only when the net change in slope direction exceeds a specific value (e.g., 1.5% or 2%).

In Figure 10-17, vertical curve terminology is introduced: g_1 is the slope (percentage) of the lower chainage grade line, g_2 is the slope of the higher chainage grade line, BVC is the beginning of the vertical curve, EVC is the end of the vertical curve, and PVI is the point of intersection of the two adjacent grade lines. The length of vertical curve (L) is the projection of the curve onto a horizontal surface and, as such, corresponds to plan distance.

The algebraic change in slope direction is A, where $A = g_2 - g_1$. For example, if $g_1 = +1.5$ percent and $g_2 = -3.2$ percent, A is equal to $(-3.2 - 1.5) = -4.7$.

The geometric curve used in vertical alignment design is the vertical axis parabola. The parabola has the desirable characteristics of (1) a constant rate of change of slope, which contributes to smooth alignment transition, and (2) ease of computation of vertical offsets, which permits easily computed curve elevations.

The general equation of the parabola is

$$y = ax^2 + bx + c \qquad (10\text{-}9)$$

The slope of this curve at any point is given by the first derivative,

$$\frac{dy}{dx} = 2ax + b \qquad (10\text{-}10)$$

and the rate of change of slope is given by the second derivative,

$$\frac{d^2y}{dx^2} = 2a \qquad (10\text{-}11)$$

which, as was previously noted, is a constant. The rate of change of slope ($2a$) can also be written as A/L.

If, for convenience, the origin of the axes is placed at the BVC (see Figure 10-18), the general equation becomes

$$y = ax^2 + bx$$

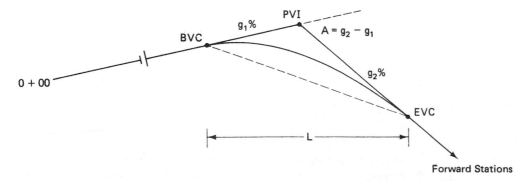

FIGURE 10-17   Vertical curve terminology (profile view shown).

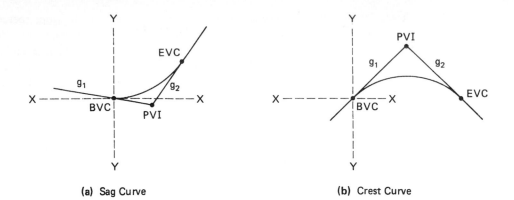

(a) Sag Curve   **(b) Crest Curve**

FIGURE 10-18 Types of vertical curves. (a) Sag curve. (b) Crest curve.

and because the slope at the origin is g_1, the expression for slope of the curve at any point becomes

$$\frac{dy}{dx} = \text{slope} = 2ax + g_1 \qquad\qquad (10\text{-}12)$$

The general equation can finally be written as

$$y = ax^2 + g_1x \qquad\qquad (10\text{-}13)$$

10-13   Geometric Properties of the Parabola

Figure 10-19 illustrates the following relationships:

1. The difference in elevation between the BVC and a point on the g_1 grade line at a distance of x units (feet or meters) is g_1x (g_1 is expressed as a decimal).
2. The tangent offset between the grade line and the curve is given by ax^2, where x is the horizontal distance from the BVC; that is, tangent offsets are proportional to the squares of the horizontal distances.
3. The elevation of the curve at distance X from the BVC is given by $\text{BVC} + g_1x - ax^2$ = curve elevation (the signs would be reversed in a sag curve).
4. The grade lines (g_1 and g_2) intersect midway between the BVC and the EVC; that is, BVC to $V = 1/2L = V$ to EVC.
5. Offsets from the two grade lines are symmetrical with respect to the PVI (V).
6. The curve lies midway between the PVI and the midpoint of the chord; that is, CM = MV.

10-14   Computation of the High or Low Point on a Vertical Curve

The locations of curve high and low points (if applicable) are important for drainage considerations; for example, on curbed streets, catch basins must be installed precisely at the drainage low points.

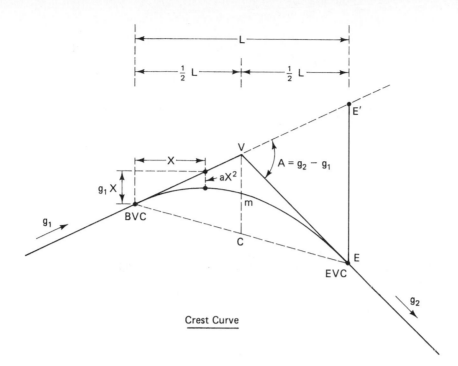

Crest Curve

FIGURE 10-19 Geometric properties of the parabola.

It was noted earlier that the slope was given by the equation

$$\text{Slope} = 2ax + g_1 \tag{10-12}$$

Figure 10-20 shows a sag vertical curve with a tangent drawn through the low point; it is obvious that the tangent line is horizontal with a slope of zero; that is,

$$2ax + g_1 = 0 \tag{10-14}$$

Had a crest curve been drawn, the tangent through the high point would have exhibited the same characteristics.

Since

$$2a = \frac{A}{L}$$

Equation (10-14) can be rewritten as

$$x = \frac{-g_1 L}{A} \tag{10-15}$$

where x is the distance from the BVC to the high or low point.

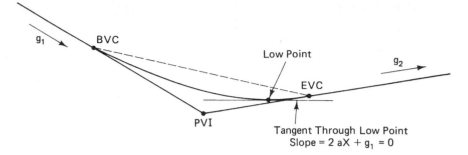

FIGURE 10-20 Tangent at curve low point.

10-15 Procedure for Computing a Vertical Curve

1. Compute the algebraic difference in grades: $A = g_2 - g_1$.
2. Compute the chainage of the BVC and EVC. If the chainage of the PVI is known, $\frac{1}{2}L$ is simply subtracted and added to the PVI chainage.
3. Compute the distance from the BVC to the high or low point (if applicable):

$$x = \frac{-g_1 L}{A} \tag{10-15}$$

and determine the station of the high/low point.
4. Compute the tangent grade-line elevation of the BVC and the EVC.
5. Compute the tangent grade-line elevation for each required station.
6. Compute the midpoint of chord elevation:

$$\frac{\text{Elevation of BVC} + \text{elevation of EVC}}{2}$$

7. Compute the tangent offset (d) at the PVI (i.e., distance VM in Figure 10-19):

$$d = \frac{\text{difference in elevation of PVI and midpoint of chord}}{2}$$

8. Compute the tangent offset for each individual station (see line ax^2 in Figure 10-19):

$$\text{Tangent offset} = d\left(\frac{x}{L/2}\right)^2 \quad \text{or} \quad \frac{4d}{L^2}(x^2) \tag{10-15}$$

where x is the distance from the BVC or EVC (whichever is closer) to the required station.
9. Compute the elevation on the curve at each required station by combining the tangent offsets with the appropriate tangent grade-line elevations—add for sag curves and subtract for crest curves.

Chap. 10   Highway Curves

■ **EXAMPLE 10-6**

The techniques used in vertical curve computations are illustrated in this example.

Given that $L = 300$ ft, $g_1 = -3.2\%$, $g_2 = +1.8\%$, PVI at $30 + 30$, and elevation $= 465.92$, determine the location of the low point and elevations on the curve at even stations as well as at the low point.

1. $A = 1.8 - (-3.2) = 5.0$
2. $PVI - \frac{1}{2}L = BVC$
   BVC at $(30 + 30) - 150 = 28 + 80.00$
   $PVI + \frac{1}{2}L = EVC$
   EVC $(30 + 30) + 150 = 31 + 80.00$
   $EVC - BVC = L$
   $(31 + 80) - (28 + 80) = 300$ Check
3. Elevation of PVI $= 465.92$
   150 ft at 3.2% $= 4.80$ (see Figure 10-21)
   Elevation BVC $= 470.72$
   Elevation PVI $= 465.92$
   150 ft at 1.8% $= 2.70$
   Elevation EVC $= 468.62$
4. Location of low point

$$x = \frac{-g_1 L}{A} \qquad (10\text{-}15)$$

$$= \frac{3.2 \times 300}{5} = 192.00 \text{ ft} \qquad \text{(from the BVC)}$$

5. Tangent grade-line computations are entered in Table 10-1(a). Example:

$$\text{Elevation at } 29 + 00 = 470.72 - (0.032 \times 20)$$
$$= 470.72 - 0.64$$
$$= 470.08$$

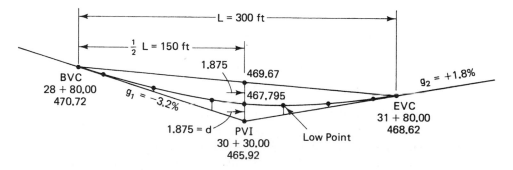

FIGURE 10-21 Sketch for Example 10-6.

Table 10-1(a) PARABOLIC CURVE ELEVATIONS BY TANGENT OFFSETS

Station	Tangent Elevation	+ Tangent Offset $\left(\frac{x}{\frac{1}{2}L}\right)^2 d*$	= Curve Elevation
BVC 28 + 80	470.72	$(0/150)^2 \times 1.875 = 0$	470.72
29 + 00	470.08	$(20/150)^2 \times 1.875 = .03$	470.11
30 + 00	466.88	$(120/150)^2 \times 1.875 = 1.20$	468.08
PVI 30 + 30	465.92	$(150/150)^2 \times 1.875 = 1.875$	467.80
Low 30 + 72	466.68	$(108/150)^2 \times 1.875 = .97$	467.65
31 + 00	467.18	$(80/150)^2 \times 1.875 = .53$	467.71
EVC 31 + 80	468.62	$(0/150)^2 \times 1.875 = 0$	468.62

See Section 10-16

⌈ 30 + 62	466.50	$(118/150)^2 \times 1.875 = 1.16$	467.66 ⌉
⟨ 30 + 72	466.68	$(108/150)^2 \times 1.875 = 0.97$	467.65 ⟩
⌊ 30 + 82	466.86	$(98/150)^2 \times 1.875 = 0.80$	467.66 ⌋

*Where x is distance from BVC or EVC, whichever is closer.

6. Mid-chord elevation:

$$\frac{470.72\ (\text{BVC}) + 468.62\ (\text{EVC})}{2} = 469.67$$

7. Tangent offset at PVI (d):

$$d = \frac{\text{difference in elevation of PVI and mid-chord}}{2}$$

$$= \frac{469.67 - 465.92}{2}$$

$$= \frac{3.75}{2}$$

$$= 1.875 \text{ ft}$$

8. Tangent offsets are computed by multiplying the distance ratio squared, $[x/(L/2)]^2$, by the maximum tangent offset (d). See Table 10-1(a).

9. The computed tangent offsets are added (in this example) to the tangent elevation in order to determine the curve elevation.

10-15-1 Parabolic Curve Elevations Computed Directly from the Equation

In addition to the tangent offset method shown earlier, vertical curve elevations can be computed directly from the general equation:

$$y = ax^2 + bx + c$$

Table 10-1(b) PARABOLIC CURVE ELEVATIONS COMPUTED FROM THE EQUATION
$y = ax^2 + bx + c$

Station	Distance from BVC	ax^2	bx	c	y (elevation on the curve)
BVC 28 + 80	0				470.72
29 + 00	20	0.03	−0.64	470.72	470.11
30 + 00	120	1.20	−3.84	470.72	468.08
PVI 30 + 30	150	1.88	−4.80	470.72	467.80
Low 30 + 72	192	3.07	−6.14	470.72	467.65
31 + 00	220	4.03	−7.04	470.72	467.71
EVC 31 + 80	300	7.50	−9.60	470.72	468.62

where $a = (g_2 - g_1)/2L$

L = horizontal length of vertical curve

$b = g_1$

c = elevation @ BVC

x = horizontal distance from BVC

y = elevation on the curve at distance x from the BVC

This technique is illustrated in Table 10-1(b), using the data from Example 10-6.

10-16   Design Considerations

From Section 10-14, $2a = A/L$ is an expression giving the constant rate of change of slope for the parabola. Another useful relationship is the inverse, or

$$K = \frac{L}{A} \tag{10-17}$$

where K is the horizontal distance required to effect a 1 percent change in slope on the vertical curve.

Substituting for L/A in Equation (10-15) yields

$$x = -g_1 K \tag{10-18}$$

(the result is always positive), where x is the distance to the low point from the BVC, or

$$x = +g_2 K \tag{10-19}$$

where x is the distance to the low point from the EVC.

In Figure 10-19, it is seen that EE' is the distance generated by the divergence of g_1 and g_2 over the distance $L/2$:

$$EE' = \frac{g_2 - g_1}{100} \times \frac{L}{2}$$

Also in Figure 10-19, it can be seen that $VC = 1/2\ EE'$ (similar triangles) and that $VM = d = 1/4\ EE'$; thus,

$$d = \frac{1}{4}\left(\frac{g_2 - g_1}{100}\right)\frac{L}{2}$$

$$= \frac{AL}{800} \qquad (10\text{-}20)$$

or, from Equation (10-17),

$$d = \frac{KA^2}{800} \qquad (10\text{-}21)$$

Equations (10-18), (10-19), and (10-21) are useful when design criteria are defined in terms of K.

Table 10-2 shows values of K for minimum stopping sight distances. On crest curves, it is assumed that the driver's eye height is at 1.05 m and the object that the driver must see is at least 0.38 m. The defining conditions for sag curves would be nighttime restrictions and relate to the field of view given by headlights with an angular beam divergence of 1°.

In practice, the length of vertical curve is rounded to the nearest even meter, and, if possible, the PVI is located at an even station so that the symmetrical characteristics of the curve can be fully used. To avoid the aesthetically unpleasing appearance of very short ver-

Table 10-2 TYPICAL DESIGN CONTROLS FOR CREST AND SAG VERTICAL CURVES BASED ON MINIMUM STOPPING SIGHT DISTANCES FOR VARIOUS DESIGN SPEEDS

Design Speed, V (km/h)	Min. Stopping Sight Distance, S (m)	K Factor	
		Crest (m)	Sag (m)
40	45	4	8
50	65	8	12
60	85	15	18
70	110	25	25
80	135	35	30
90	160	50	40
100	185	70	45
110	215	90	50
120	245	120	60
130	275	150	70
140	300	180	80

$$K_{crest} = \frac{S^2}{200\ h_1(1 + \sqrt{h_2/h_1})^2} \qquad\qquad K_{sag} = \frac{S^2}{200\ (h + S\ tan\alpha)}$$

$h_1 = 1.05$ m, height of driver's eye $\qquad\qquad h = 0.60$ m, height of headlights
$h_2 = 0.38$ m, height of object $\qquad\qquad\qquad \alpha = 1°$, angular spread of light beam
$L = KA$, from Equation (10-15), where L (m) cannot be less than V(km/h). When $KA < V$, use $L = V$.

Source: Vertical Curve Tables, Ministry of Transportation, Ontario.

tical curves, as a rule of thumb some agencies insist that the length of vertical curve (L) be at least as long in meters as the design velocity is in kilometers per hour.

Closer analysis of the data shown in Table 10-1 indicates a possible concern. Unfortunately the vertical curve at the low or high point has a relatively small change of slope. This is not a problem for crest curves or for sag curves for ditched roads and highways (ditches can have grade lines independent of the ¢ grade line). However, when sag curves are used for curbed municipal street design, a drainage problem is introduced. The curve elevations in brackets in Table 10-1(a) cover 10 ft either side of the low point. These data illustrate that for a distance of 20 ft there is virtually no change in elevation (i.e., only 0.01 ft). If the road were built according to the design, chances are that the low-point catch basin would not completely drain the extended low-point area. The solution to this problem is for the surveyor to arbitrarily lower the catch-basin grate (1 in. is often used) to ensure proper drainage or to install two catch basins, located in a manner that ensures adequate drainage of the entire low area.

10-17   Spiral Curves: General

A spiral is a curve with a uniformly changing radius. Spirals are used in highway and railroad alignment to overcome the abrupt change in direction that occurs when the alignment changes from tangent to circular curve, and vice versa. The length of the spiral curve is also used for the transition from normally crowned pavement to fully superelevated (banked) pavement.

Figure 10-22 illustrates how the spiral curve is inserted between tangent and circular curve alignment. It can be seen that at the beginning of the spiral (T.S. = tangent to spiral) the radius of the spiral is the radius of the tangent line (infinitely large) and that the radius of the spiral curve decreases at a uniform rate until, at the point where the circular curve

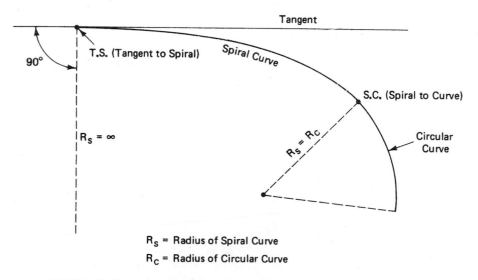

R_S = Radius of Spiral Curve
R_C = Radius of Circular Curve

FIGURE 10-22   Spiral curves.

begins (S.C. = spiral to curve), the radius of the spiral equals the radius of the circular curve. In the previous section, we noted that the parabola, which is used in vertical alignment, had the important property of having a uniform rate of change of slope. Here, we find that the spiral, used in horizontal alignment, has a uniform rate of change of radius (curvature). This property permits the driver to leave a tangent section of highway at a relatively high rate of speed without experiencing problems with safety or comfort.

Figure 10-23 illustrates how the circular curve is moved inward (toward the center of the curve), leaving room for the insertion of a spiral at either end of the shortened circular curve. The amount that the circular curve is shifted in from the main tangent line is known as P. This shift results in the curve center (O) being at the distance $(R + P)$ from the main tangent lines.

The spirals illustrated in this text reflect the common practice of using equal spirals to join the ends of a circular or compound curve to the main tangents. For more complex spiral applications, such as unequal spirals and spirals joining circular arcs, the reader is referred to a text on route surveying.

This text shows excerpts from spiral tables (see Tables 10-3, 10-4, and 10-5). Each state and province prepares and publishes similar tables for use by their personnel. A wide variety of spirals, both geometric and empirical, have been used to develop spiral tables. Geometric spirals include the cubic parabola and the clothoid curve, and empirical spirals include the A.R.E.A. 10-chord spiral, used by many railroads. Generally the use of tables is giving way to computer programs for spiral solutions. All spirals give essentially the same appearance when staked out in the field.

10-18   Spiral Curve Computations

Usually data for a spiral computation are obtained as follows:

1. Δ is determined in the field.
2. R or D (degree of curve) is given by design considerations (limited by design speed).
3. Chainage of PI is determined in the field.
4. L_s is chosen with respect to design speed and the number of traffic lanes.

All other spiral parameters can be determined by computation and/or by use of spiral tables.

Tangent to spiral:

$$T_s = (R + P) \tan \frac{\Delta}{2} + q \tag{10-22}$$

(See Figure 10-24.)

Spiral tangent deflection:

$$\Delta_s = \frac{L_s D}{200} \tag{10-23}$$

In circular curves, $\Delta = LD/100$ [see Equation (10-7)].

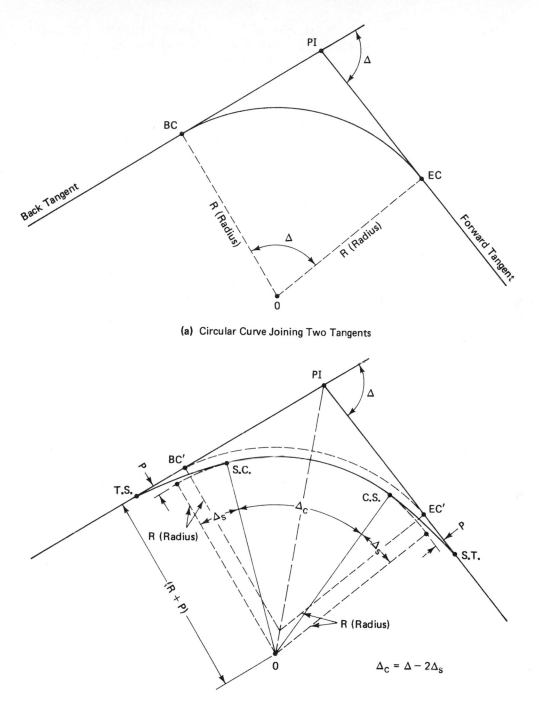

(a) Circular Curve Joining Two Tangents

$$\Delta_c = \Delta - 2\Delta_s$$

(b) Circular Curve Shown Shifted Inward to Permit Insertion
of Spiral Curves Within the Original Tangents

FIGURE 10-23 Shifting the circular curve to make room for the insertion of spirals.
(a) Circular curve joining two tangents. (b) Circular curve shifted inward
(toward curve center) to make room for the insertion of spiral curves at
either end of the circular curve.

Table 10-3 SPIRAL TABLES FOR L_s = 150 feet

D	Δ_s	R	p	R + p	q	LT	ST	Δ_s	X_c	Y_c	$\frac{D}{10\,L_s}$
7°30'	5°37'30"	763.9437	1.2268	765.1705	74.9759	100.0305	50.0459	5.62500°	149.86	4.91	0.00500
8°00'	6°00'00"	716.1972	1.3085	717.5057	74.9726	100.0575	50.0523	6.00000°	149.84	5.23	0.00533
30'	6°22'30"	674.0680	1.3902	675.4582	74.9691	100.0649	50.0590	6.37500°	149.81	5.56	0.00567
9°00'	6°45'00"	636.6198	1.4719	638.0917	74.9653	100.0728	50.0662	6.75000°	149.79	5.88	0.00600
30'	7°07'30"	603.1135	1.5536	604.6671	74.9614	100.0811	50.0738	7.12500°	149.77	6.21	0.00633
10°00'	7°30'00"	572.9578	1.6352	574.5930	74.9572	100.0899	50.0817	7.50000°	149.74	6.54	0.00667
30'	7°52'30"	545.6741	1.7169	547.3910	74.9528	100.0991	50.0901	7.87500°	149.72	6.86	0.00700
11°00'	8°15'00"	520.8707	1.7985	522.6692	74.9482	100.1088	50.0989	8.25000°	149.69	7.19	0.00733
30'	8°37'30"	498.2242	1.8802	500.1044	74.9434	100.1190	50.1082	8.62500°	149.66	7.51	0.00767
12°00'	9°00'00"	477.4648	1.9618	479.4266	74.9384	100.1295	50.1178	9.00000°	149.63	7.84	0.00800
13°00'	9°45'00"	440.7368	2.1249	442.8617	74.9277	100.1521	50.1383	9.75000°	149.57	8.49	0.00867
14°00'	10°30'00"	409.2556	2.2880	411.5436	74.9161	100.1765	50.1605	10.50000°	149.50	9.14	0.00933
15°00'	11°15'00"	381.9719	2.4510	384.4229	74.9037	100.2027	50.1843	11.25000°	149.42	9.79	0.01000
16°00'	12°00'00"	358.0986	2.6139	360.7125	74.8905	100.2307	50.2098	12.00000°	149.34	10.44	0.01067
17°00'	12°45'00"	337.0340	2.7767	339.8107	74.8764	100.2606	50.2370	12.75000°	149.26	11.09	0.01133
18°00'	13°30'00"	318.3099	2.9394	321.2493	74.8614	100.2924	50.2659	13.50000°	149.17	11.73	0.01200
19°00'	14°15'00"	301.5567	3.1020	304.6587	74.8456	100.3259	50.2964	14.25000°	149.07	12.38	0.01267
20°00'	15°00'00"	286.4789	3.2645	289.7434	74.8290	100.3614	50.3287	15.00000°	148.98	13.03	0.01333
21°00'	15°45'00"	272.8370	3.4269	276.2639	74.8115	100.3987	50.3627	15.75000°	148.87	13.67	0.01400
22°00'	16°30'00"	260.4354	3.5891	264.0245	74.7932	100.4379	50.3983	16.50000°	148.76	14.31	0.01467
23°00'	17°15'00"	249.1121	3.7512	252.8633	74.7740	100.4790	50.4357	17.25000°	148.65	14.96	0.01533
24°00'	18°00'00"	238.7324	3.9132	242.6456	74.7539	100.5219	50.4748	18.00000°	148.53	15.60	0.01600
25°00'	18°45'00"	229.1831	4.0750	233.2581	74.7331	100.5668	50.5157	18.75000°	148.40	16.26	0.01667
26°00'	19°30'00"	220.3684	4.2367	224.6051	74.7114	100.6135	50.5582	19.50000°	148.27	16.88	0.01733

Source: Spiral Tables (foot units), courtesy Ministry of Transportation, Ontario. L_s = 150.

Table 10-4(a) SPIRAL CURVE LENGTHS AND SUPERELEVATION RATES: SUPERELEVATION (e) MAXIMUM OF 0.06, TYPICAL FOR NORTHERN CLIMATES

| | V = 30 | | | | V = 40 | | | | V = 50 | | | | V = 60 | | | | V = 70 | | | | V = 80 | | |
| | | L, ft | | | | L, ft | | | | L, ft | | | | L, ft | | | | L, ft | | | | L, ft | |
D	e	2 Lane	4 Lane	e	2 Lane	4 Lane	e	2 Lane	4 Lane	e	2 Lane	4 Lane	e	2 Lane	4 Lane	e	2 Lane	4 Lane
0°15′	NC	0	0	NC	0	0	NC	0	0	NC	0	0	NC	0	0	RC	250	250
0°30′	NC	0	0	NC	0	0	NC	0	0	RC	200	200	RC	200	200	.023	250	250
0°45′	NC	0	0	NC	0	0	RC	150	150	.021	200	200	.026	200	200	.033	250	250
1°00′	NC	0	0	RC	150	150	.020	150	150	.027	200	200	.033	200	200	.041	250	250
1°30′	RC	100	100	.020	150	150	.028	150	150	.036	200	200	.044	200	200	.053	250	300
2°00′	RC	100	100	.026	150	150	.035	150	150	.044	200	200	.052	200	250	.059	250	300
2°30′	.020	100	100	.031	150	150	.040	150	150	.050	200	200	.057	200	300	.060	250	300
3°00′	.023	100	100	.035	150	150	.044	150	200	.054	200	250	.060	200	300	D_max = 2°30′		
3°30′	.026	100	100	.038	150	150	.048	150	200	.057	200	250	D_max = 3°00′					
4°00′	.029	100	100	.041	150	150	.051	150	200	.059	200	250						
5°00′	.034	100	100	.046	150	150	.056	150	200	.060	200	250						
6°00′	.038	100	100	.050	150	200	.059	150	250	D_max = 4°30′								
7°00′	.041	100	150	.054	150	200	.060	150	250									
8°00′	.043	100	150	.056	150	200	D_max = 7°00′											
9°00′	.046	100	150	.058	150	200												
10°00′	.048	100	150	.059	150	200												
11°00′	.050	100	150	.060	150	200												
12°00′	.052	100	150	D_max = 11°00′														
13°00′	.053	100	150															
14°00′	.055	100	150															
16°00′	.058	100	200															
18°00′	.059	150	200															
20°00′	.060	150	200															
21°00′	.060	150	200															
D_max = 21°00′																		

Source: Ministry of Transportation and Communications, Ontario.

Legend:

V, design speed, mph

e, rate of superelevation, feet per foot of pavement width

L, length of superelevation runoff or spiral curve

NC, normal crown section

RC, remove adverse crown, superelevate at normal crown slope

D, degree of circular curve

Above the heavy line spirals are not required but superelevation is to be run off in distances shown.

Table 10-4(b) SPIRAL CURVE LENGTHS (FEET) AND SUPERELEVATION RATES: SUPERELEVATION
(*e*) MAXIMUM OF 0.100, TYPICAL FOR SOUTHERN CLIMATES

| | | $V = 30$ | | | $V = 40$ | | | $V = 50$ | | | $V = 60$ | | | $V = 70$ | | |
| | | | L | | | L | | | L | | | L | | | L | |
D	R	e	2 Lane	4 Lane	e	2 Lane	4 Lane	e	2 Lane	4 Lane	e	2 Lane	4 Lane	e	2 Lane	4 Lane
0°15′	22918′	NC	0	0	NC	0	0	NC	0	0	NC	0	0	RC	200	200
0°30′	11459′	NC	0	0	NC	0	0	RC	150	150	RC	175	175	RC	200	200
0°45′	7639′	NC	0	0	RC	125	125	RC	150	150	0.018	175	175	0.020	200	200
1°00′	5730′	NC	0	0	RC	125	125	0.018	150	150	0.022	175	175	0.028	200	200
1°30′	3820′	RC	100	100	0.020	125	125	0.027	150	150	0.034	175	175	0.042	200	200
2°00′	2865′	RC	100	100	0.027	125	125	0.036	150	150	0.046	175	190	0.055	200	250
2°30′	2292′	0.020	100	100	0.033	125	125	0.045	150	160	0.059	175	240	0.069	210	310
3°00′	1910′	0.024	100	100	0.038	125	125	0.054	150	190	0.070	190	280	0.083	250	370
3°30′	1637′	0.027	100	100	0.045	125	140	0.063	150	230	0.081	220	330	0.096	290	430
4°00′	1432′	0.030	100	100	0.050	125	160	0.070	170	250	0.090	240	360	0.100	300	450
5°00′	1146′	0.038	100	100	0.060	130	190	0.083	200	300	0.099	270	400	$D_{max} = 3°9′$		
6°00′	955′	0.044	100	120	0.068	140	210	0.093	220	330	0.100	270	400			
7°00′	819′	0.050	100	140	0.076	160	240	0.097	230	350	$D_{max} = 5°5′$					
8°00′	716′	0.055	100	150	0.084	180	260	0.100	240	360						
9°00′	637′	0.061	110	160	0.089	190	280	0.100	240	360						
10°00′	573′	0.065	120	180	0.093	200	290	$D_{max} = 8.3°$								
11°00′	521′	0.070	130	190	0.096	200	300									
12°00′	477′	0.074	130	200	0.098	210	310									
13°00′	441′	0.078	140	210	0.099	210	310									
14°00′	409′	0.082	150	220	0.100	210	320									
16°00′	358′	0.087	160	240	$D_{max} = 13.4°$											
18°00′	318′	0.093	170	250												
20°00′	286′	0.096	170	260												
22°00′	260′	0.099	180	270												
24.8°	231′	0.100	180	270												
		$D_{max} = 24.8°$														

Source: American Association of State Highway and Transportation Officials (AASHTO).

Notes: NC = normal crown section. RC = remove adverse crown, superelevate at normal crown slope. Spirals desirable but not as essential above heavy line. Lengths rounded in multiples of 25 or 50 ft permit simpler calculations.
The higher *e* value (0.100) in Table 10-4(b) permits a sharper maximum curvature.

Since the spiral has a uniformly changing D, the spiral angle (Δ_s) = length of spiral (L_s) in stations times the average degree of curve (D/2).

Total length:

$$L = L_c + 2L_s \qquad (10\text{-}24)$$

See Figure 10-24, where L is the *total length of the curve system.*

Table 10-5 SPIRAL CURVE LENGTHS AND SUPERELEVATION RATES (METRIC)

Radius, m	40 e	40 A 2 lane	40 A 3 & 4 lane	50 e	50 A 2 lane	50 A 3 & 4 lane	60 e	60 A 2 lane	60 A 3 & 4 lane	70 e	70 A 2 lane	70 A 3 & 4 lane	80 e	80 A 2 lane	80 A 3 & 4 lane	90 e	90 A 2 lane	90 A 3 & 4 lane	100 e	100 A 2 lane	100 A 3 & 4 lane	110 e	110 A 2 lane	110 A 3 & 4 lane	120 e	120 A 2 lane	120 A 3 & 4 lane	130 e	130 A 2 lane	130 A 3 & 4 lane	140 e	140 A 2 lane	140 A 3 & 4 lane
7000	NC			NC			NC			NC			NC			NC			NC			NC			NC			NC			RC	700	700
5000	NC			NC			NC			NC			NC			NC			NC			NC			NC			RC	700	700	0.024	625	625
4000	NC			NC			NC			NC			NC			NC			RC	480	480	RC	500	500	RC	600	600	RC	600	600	0.028	560	560
3000	NC			NC			NC			NC			RC	300	300	RC	390	400	0.025	400	400	0.023	500	500	0.022	450	450	0.021	500	500	0.034	495	495
2000	NC			NC			NC			RC	275	275	RC	250	250	0.023	300	350	0.027	340	340	0.031	450	450	0.027	350	350	0.025	450	450	0.043	400	400
1500	NC			NC			RC	225	225	RC	250	250	0.024	225	225	0.029	270	275	0.033	300	300	0.037	350	350	0.035	300	300	0.030	400	400	0.050	345	340
1200	NC			NC			RC	200	200	0.023	225	225	0.028	200	200	0.033	240	240	0.038	250	250	0.042	300	300	0.041	285	285	0.039	330	330	0.056	330	330
1000	NC			RC	170	170	0.021	175	175	0.027	200	200	0.032	175	200	0.037	225	225	0.042	240	240	0.046	275	275	0.047	250	275	0.046	300	300	0.060	325	325
900	NC			RC	150	150	0.023	175	175	0.029	180	180	0.034	175	175	0.039	200	200	0.044	225	225	0.049	250	260	0.051	250	270	0.051	300	300	0.060	325	325
800	NC			RC	150	150	0.025	160	175	0.031	175	175	0.036	175	175	0.042	200	200	0.047	200	225	0.051	230	250	0.053	250	260	0.055	300	300			
700	NC			0.021	140	140	0.027	150	150	0.034	175	175	0.039	175	175	0.045	185	195	0.049	200	220	0.054	225	235	0.056	250	250	0.057	275	300			
600	NC	120	120	0.024	125	125	0.030	140	140	0.037	150	175	0.042	150	175	0.048	175	185	0.053	200	200	0.057	220	220	0.059	250	250	0.060	275	275			
500	RC	100	100	0.027	120	120	0.034	125	125	0.041	140	150	0.046	150	160	0.052	160	175	0.057	200	200	0.060	220	220	0.060	250	250						
400	0.023	90	90	0.031	100	100	0.038	115	120	0.045	125	150	0.051	135	150	0.057	160	165	0.060	200	200												
350	0.025	90	90	0.034	100	100	0.041	110	115	0.048	120	135	0.054	125	140	0.059	160	160															
300	0.028	80	80	0.037	90	100	0.044	100	110	0.051	120	125	0.057	125	135	0.060	160	160															
250	0.031	75	80	0.040	85	90	0.048	90	100	0.055	110	125	0.060	125	125																		
220	0.034	70	75	0.043	80	90	0.050	90	100	0.057	110	120	0.060	125	125																		
200	0.036	70	75	0.045	75	90	0.052	85	100	0.059	110	110																					
180	0.038	60	75	0.047	70	90	0.054	85	95	0.060	110	110																					
160	0.040	60	75	0.049	70	85	0.056	85	90																								
140	0.043	60	70	0.052	65	80	0.059	85	90																								
120	0.046	60	65	0.055	65	75	0.060	85	90																								
100	0.049	50	65	0.058	65	70																											
90	0.051	50	60	0.060	65	70																											
80	0.054	50	60																														
70	0.058	50	60																														
60	0.059	50	60																														

Minimum R: 40 → R = 55; 50 → R = 90; 60 → R = 130; 70 → R = 190; 80 → R = 250; 90 → R = 340; 100 → R = 420; 110 → R = 525; 120 → R = 650; 130 → R = 800; 140 → Minimum R = 1000.

Source: Roads and Transportation Association of Canada (RTAC).

Notes: $D_{max} = 0.06$
e is super elevation.
A is spiral parameter in meters.
NC is normal cross section.
RC is remove adverse crown and superelevate at normal rate.
Spiral length, $L = A^2 \div$ radius.
Spiral parameters are minimum and higher values should be used where possible.
Spirals are desirable but not essential above the heavy line.
For 6-lane pavement: above the dashed line use 4-lane values; below the dashed line use 4-lane values × 1.15.
A divided road having a median less than 7 m may be treated as a single pavement.

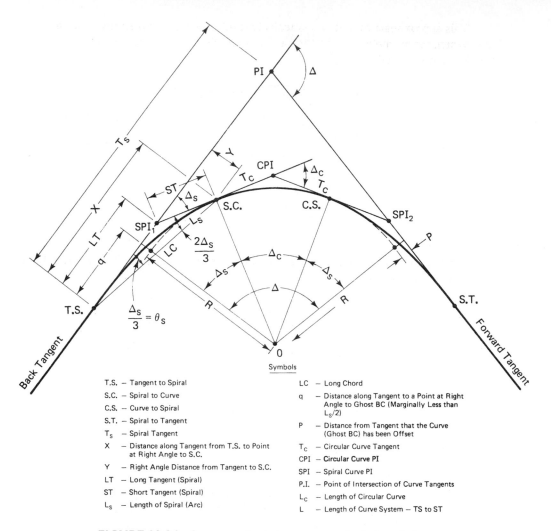

FIGURE 10-24 Summary of spiral geometry and spiral symbols.

Total deflection:

$$\Delta = \Delta_c + 2\Delta_s \qquad (10\text{-}25)$$

(See Figure 10-24.)

Spiral deflection:

$$\theta_s = \frac{\Delta_s}{3} \textbf{ (approx)} \qquad (10\text{-}26)$$

θ_s is the total spiral deflection angle; compare to circular curves where the deflection angle is $\Delta/2$.

This approximate formula gives realistic results for the vast majority of spiral problems. When, for example, Δ_s is as large as 21°—which is seldom the case—the correction to $\Delta_s/3$ is approximately $+30''$.

$$L_c = \frac{2\pi R \Delta_c}{360} \qquad \text{foot or meter units} \qquad (10\text{-}27)$$

$$L_c = \frac{100\Delta_c}{D} \qquad \text{foot units} \qquad (10\text{-}28)$$

$$\Delta_s = \frac{90}{\pi} \times \frac{L_s}{R} \qquad (10\text{-}29)$$

$$\phi = \left(\frac{l}{L_s}\right)^2 \theta_s \qquad (10\text{-}30)$$

from spiral definition, where ϕ is the deflection angle for any distance l, and ϕ and θ_s are in the same units. Practically

$$\phi' = l^2 \frac{\theta_s \times 60}{L_s^2}$$

where ϕ' is the deflection angle in minutes for any distance l measured from the T.S. or the S.T.

Other values, such as x, y, P, q, ST, and LT (see Figure 10-24), are routinely found in spiral tables issued by state and provincial highway agencies and can also be found in route surveying texts. For the past few years, solutions to these problems have almost exclusively been achieved by the use of computers and appropriate coordinate geometry computer software.

With the switchover to metric that took place in the 1970s in Canada, a decision was reached to work exclusively with the radius in defining horizontal curves. It was decided that new spiral tables, based solely on R definition, would be appropriate. The Roads and Transportation Association of Canada (RTAC) prepared spiral tables based on the spiral property defined as follows:

The product of any instantaneous radius r and the corresponding spiral length λ (i.e., l) from the beginning of the spiral to that point is equal to the product of the spiral end radius R and the entire length (L_s) of that spiral, which means it is a constant.

Thus,

$$r\lambda = RL_s = A^2 \qquad (10\text{-}31)$$

The constant is denoted as A^2 to retain dimensional consistency, since it represents a product of two lengths. It follows that

$$\frac{A}{R} = \frac{L_s}{A} \qquad (10\text{-}32)$$

The RTAC tables (see Table 10-5) are based on design speed and the number of traffic lanes, together with a design radius. The constant value A is taken from the table and used in conjunction with R to find all the spiral table curve parameters noted earlier (see Table 10-7).

It should be noted that, concurrent with the changeover to metric units, a major study in Ontario of highway geometrics resulted in spiral curve lengths that reflect design speed, attainment of superelevation, driver comfort, and aesthetics. Accordingly, the spiral lengths vary somewhat from the foot unit system to the metric system.

10-19 Spiral Layout Procedure Summary

Refer to Figure 10-24.

1. Select L_s (foot units) or A (metric units) in conjunction with the design speed, number of traffic lanes, and sharpness of the circular curve (radius or D).
2. From the spiral tables, determine P, q, x, y, and so on.
3. Compute the spiral tangent (T_s) [Equation (10-22)] and the circular tangent (T_c) [Equation (10-1)].
4. Compute the spiral angle Δ_s. Use Equation (10-23) for foot units or Equation (10-29) for metric units (or use tables).
5. Prepare a list of relevant layout stations. This list will include all horizontal alignment key points (e.g., T.S., S.C., C.S., and S.T.) as well as all vertical alignment key points, such as grade points, BVC, low point, and EVC.
6. Calculate the deflection angles. See Equation (10-30).
7. From the established PI, measure out the T_s distance to locate the T.S. and S.T.
8a. From the T.S., turn off the spiral deflection ($\theta_s = 1/3\ \Delta_s$ approximately), measure out the long chord (LC), and thus locate the S.C.
8b. Or, from the T.S., measure out the LT distance along the main tangent, and locate the spiral PI (SPI); the spiral angle (Δ_s) can now be turned and the ST distance measured out to locate the S.C.
9. From the S.C., measure out the circular tangent (T_c) along the line SPI_1–SC to establish the CPI.
10. The procedure to this point is repeated, starting at the S.T.
11. The key points are verified by checking all angles and redundant distances. Some surveyors prefer to locate the CPI by intersecting the two tangent lines (i.e., lines through SPI_1 and S.C. and through SPI_2 and C.S.). The locations can be verified by checking the angle Δ_c and by checking the two tangents (T_c).
12. Only after all key control points have been verified can the deflection angle stakeout commence. The lower chainage spiral is run in from the T.S., whereas the higher chainage spiral is run in from the S.T. The circular curve can be run in from the S.C., although it is common practice to run half the curve from the S.C. and the other half from the C.S. so that any acceptable errors that accumulate can be isolated in the middle of the circular arc, where, relatively speaking, they will be less troublesome.

■ **EXAMPLE 10-7** *Illustrative Spiral Problem: Foot Units*
Given the following data:

$$\Delta = 25°45' \ RT$$
$$V = 40 \text{ mph}$$
$$D = 9°$$
$$\text{PI at } 36 + 17.42$$
$$\text{Two-lane highway, 24 ft wide}$$

compute the key curve stations and deflections.

1. From Table 10-4(a),

$$L_s = 150 \text{ ft}$$
$$e = 0.058$$

See Section 10-21 for superelevation.
2. From Table 10-3,

$$\Delta_s = 6.75000°*$$
$$R = 636.6198 \text{ ft}$$
$$P = 1.4719 \text{ ft}$$
$$R + P = 638.0917 \text{ ft}$$
$$q = 74.9653 \text{ ft}$$
$$LT = 100.0728 \text{ ft}$$
$$ST = 50.0662 \text{ ft}$$
$$X = 149.79 \text{ ft}$$
$$Y = 5.88 \text{ ft}$$

*Alternatively

$$\Delta_s = \frac{L_sD}{200} \tag{10-23}$$
$$= \frac{150}{200} \times 9 = 6.75000°$$

3. Tangent to spiral:

$$T_s = (R + P) \tan \frac{\Delta}{2} + q \tag{10-22}$$
$$= 638.0917 \tan 12°52.5' + 74.9653$$
$$= 220.82 \text{ ft}$$

4.

$$\Delta_c = \Delta - 2\,\Delta_s$$
$$= 25°45' - 2(6°45')$$
$$= 12°15'$$

5.

$$L_c = \frac{100\Delta_c}{D} \qquad (10\text{-}7)$$
$$= \frac{100 \times 12.25}{9}$$
$$= 136.11 \text{ ft}$$

6. Key station computation:

PI at	36 +	17.42
$-T_s$	2	20.82
T.S. =	33 +	96.60
$+L_s$	1	50.00
S.C. =	35 +	46.60
$+L_c$	1	36.11
C.S. =	36 +	82.71
$+L_s$	1	50.00
S.T.	38 +	32.71

7. Spiral deflection:

$$\theta_s = \frac{\Delta_s}{3}$$
$$= \frac{6.75000°}{3}$$
$$= 2.25°$$
$$= 2°15'00''$$

Circular Curve Deflections. See Table 10-6.

$$\Delta_c = 12°15'$$
$$\frac{\Delta_c}{2} = 6°07.5'$$
$$= 367.5'$$

From Section 10-4, the deflection angle for one unit of distance is $(\Delta/2)/L$. Here, the deflection angle for 1 foot of arc (minutes) is

$$\frac{(\Delta_c/2)}{L_c} = \frac{367.5}{136.11} = 2.700'$$

Table 10-6 CURVE SYSTEM DEFLECTION ANGLES

Station	Distance from T.S. (or S.T.) I (ft)	I²	$\dfrac{\theta°_s \times 60}{L_s^2}$	$\dfrac{I^2\,(\theta_s \times 60)}{L_s^2}$ Deflection Angle (minutes)	Deflection
T.S. 33 + 96.60	0	0	0.006	0	0°00′00″
34 + 00	3.4	11.6	0.006	0.070	0°00′04″
34 + 50	53.4	2851.4	0.006	17.108	0°17′06″
35 + 00	103.4	10,691.6	0.006	64.149	1°04′09″
S.C. 35 + 45.60	150	22,500	0.006	135	$\theta_s = 2°15′00″$

	Circular Curve Data	Deflection Angle (cumulative)	Deflection
S.C. 35 + 46.60	$\Delta_c = 12°15′,\ \dfrac{\Delta_c}{2} = 6°07′30″$	0°00.00′	0°00′00″
35 + 50	Deflection for 3.40′ = 9.18′	0°09.18′	0°09′11″
36 + 00	Deflection for 50′ = 135′	2°24.18′	2°24′11″
36 + 50	Deflection for 32.71′ = 88.32′	4°39.18′	4°39′11″
C.S. 36 + 82.71		6°07.50′	6°07′30″

Station	I (ft)	I²	$\dfrac{\theta°_s \times 60}{L_s^2}$	Deflection Angle (minutes)	Deflection
C.S. 36 + 82.71	150*	22,500	0.006	135	$\theta_s = 2°15′00″$
37 + 00	132.71	17,611.9	0.006	105.672	1°45′40″
37 + 50	82.71	6840.9	0.006	41.046	0°41′03″
38 + 00	32.71	1069.9	0.006	6.420	0°06′25″
S.T. 38 + 32.71	0	0	0.006	0	0°00′00″

*Note that I is measured from the S.T.

Alternatively, since $D = 9°$, then the deflection for 100 ft is $D/2$ or $4°30′$, which is 270′. The deflection angle for 1 ft = 270/100 = 2.700′ (as previously). The required distances (from Table 10-6) are

$$(35 + 50) - (35 + 46.60) = 3.4′; \text{ deflection angle} = 3.4 \times 2.7 = 9.18′$$
$$\text{Even interval} = 50′; \text{ deflection angle} = 50 \times 2.7 = 135′$$
$$(36 + 82.71) - (36 + 50) = 32.71^1; \text{ deflection angle} = 32.71 \times 2.7 = 88.32′$$

These values are now entered cumulatively in Table 10-6.

■ **EXAMPLE 10-8** *Illustrative Spiral Problem: Metric Units*
Given the following data:

$$PI \text{ at } 1 + 086.271$$
$$V = 80 \text{ kmh}$$
$$R = 300 \text{ m}$$
$$\Delta = 16°00′ \ RT$$
$$\text{Two-lane road (7.5 m wide)}$$

compute the key stations and deflections.

From Table 10-5, $A = 125$ and $e = 0.057$. See Section 10-21 for a discussion of superelevation. From Table 10-7, we obtain the following:

Steps	For $A = 125$	and $R = 300$
1 and 2	$L_s = 52.083$ m	$LT = 34.736$ m
	$P = 0.377$ m	$ST = 17.374$ m
	$X = 52.044$ m	$\Delta_s = 4°58'24.9''$
	$Y = 1.506$ m	$\theta_s = 1/3\ \Delta_s = 1°39'27.9''$
	$q = 26.035$ m	$LC = 52.066$ m long chord

Also,

$$\Delta_s = \frac{90}{\pi} \times \frac{L_s}{R} \tag{10-29}$$

$$= \frac{90}{\pi} \times \frac{52.083}{300} = 4.9735601° = 4°58'24.8''$$

Step 3

$$T_s = (R + P) \tan \frac{\Delta}{2} + q \tag{10.22}$$

$$= 300.377 \tan 8° + 26.035$$

$$= 68.250 \text{ m}$$

Step 4

$$\Delta_c = \Delta - 2\Delta_s$$

$$= 16° - 2(4°58'24.8'')$$

$$= 6°03'10.2''$$

$$\frac{\Delta_c}{2} = 3°01'35.1''$$

Step 5

$$L_c = \frac{2\pi R \Delta_c}{360} \tag{10-5}$$

$$= \frac{2\pi \times 300 \times 6.052833}{360}$$

$$= 31.693 \text{ m}$$

Table 10-7 FUNCTIONS OF THE STANDARD SPIRAL* FOR A = 125 m

R (m)	A/R	L_s	X	Y	q Meters	P	LT	ST	L_c	Δ_s Deg.	Min.	Sec.	θ_s Deg.	Min.	Sec.
115	1.0870	135.870	131.204	26.095	67.152	6.606	92.293	46.851	133.774	33	50	48.3	11	14	55.1
120	1.0417	130.208	126.428	23.057	64.471	5.825	88.183	44.658	128.513	31	05	05.8	10	20	08.3
125	1.0000	125.000	121.911	20.464	61.983	5.162	84.451	42.685	123.617	28	38	52.4	9	31	44.3
130	0.9615	120.192	117.649	18.240	59.671	4.595	81.044	40.898	119.055	26	29	11.7	8	48	46.1
140	0.8929	111.607	109.847	14.661	55.509	3.686	75.034	37.755	110.821	22	50	16.5	7	36	08.5
150	0.8333	104.167	102.918	11.953	51.875	3.001	69.888	35.126	103.610	19	53	39.7	6	37	28.8
160	0.7813	97.656	96.751	9.868	48.677	2.475	65.425	32.844	97.253	17	29	07.0	5	49	25.8
170	0.7353	91.912	91.242	8.239	45.844	2.065	61.511	30.852	91.614	15	29	19.3	5	09	34.9
180	0.6944	86.086	86.302	6.948	43.319	1.741	58.048	29.096	86.581	13	48	55.9	4	36	10.5
190	0.6579	82.237	81.853	5.913	41.054	1.481	54.960	27.535	82.066	12	23	58.3	4	07	53.5
200	0.6250	78.125	77.828	5.072	39.013	1.270	52.188	26.137	77.993	11	11	26.1	3	43	44.4
210	0.5952	74.405	74.172	4.384	37.163	1.097	49.685	24.876	74.301	10	09	00.7	3	22	57.0
220	0.5682	71.023	70.838	3.814	35.481	0.954	47.413	23.733	70.941	9	14	54.3	3	04	55.6
230	0.5435	67.935	67.787	3.339	33.943	0.835	45.342	22.692	67.869	8	27	42.1	2	49	12.1
240	0.5208	65.104	64.984	2.940	32.532	0.735	43.455	21.739	65.051	7	46	16.5	2	35	24.0
250	0.5000	62.500	62.402	2.601	31.234	0.651	41.701	20.864	62.457	7	09	43.1	2	23	13.2
280	0.4464	55.804	55.748	1.852	27.983	0.463	37.222	18.619	55.779	5	24	34.1	1	54	10.8
300	0.4167	52.083	52.044	1.506	26.035	0.377	34.736	17.374	52.066	4	58	24.9	1	39	27.9
320	0.3906	48.828	48.800	1.241	24.409	0.310	32.562	16.285	48.815	4	22	16.8	1	27	25.3
340	0.3676	45.956	45.935	1.035	22.974	0.259	30.645	15.325	45.947	3	52	19.8	1	17	26.4
350	0.3571	44.643	44.625	0.949	22.318	0.237	29.768	14.887	44.635	3	39	14.6	1	13	04.7
380	0.3289	41.118	41.106	0.741	20.557	0.185	27.416	13.710	41.113	3	05	59.6	1	01	59.8
400	0.3125	39.063	39.063	0.636	19.530	0.159	26.045	13.024	39.058	2	47	51.5	0	55	57.1
420	0.2976	37.202	37.195	0.549	18.600	0.137	24.804	12.403	37.195	2	32	15.2	0	50	45.0
450	0.2778	34.722	34.717	0.446	17.360	0.112	23.150	11.576	34.720	2	12	37.7	0	44	12.5
475	0.2632	32.895	32.891	0.380	16.447	0.095	21.931	10.966	32.893	1	59	02.1	0	39	40.7
500	0.2500	31.250	31.247	0.325	15.624	0.081	20.834	10.418	31.249	1	47	25.8	0	35	48.6
525	0.2381	29.762	29.760	0.281	14.881	0.070	19.842	9.921	29.761	1	37	26.5	0	32	20.8
550	0.2273	28.409	28.407	0.245	14.204	0.061	18.940	9.470	28.408	1	28	47.1	0	29	35.7
575	0.2174	27.174	27.172	0.214	13.587	0.054	18.116	9.058	27.173	1	21	13.9	0	27	04.6

Source: Metric Curve Tables, Table IV, Roads and Transportation Association of Canada (RTAC).

*Short radius (i.e., < 150 m) may require a correction to $\Delta_s/3$ in order to determine precise value of θ_s.

Step 6 Key station computation:

$$
\begin{aligned}
\text{PI at} \quad & 1 + 086.271 \\
-T_s \quad & \underline{\quad\quad 68.250} \\
\text{T.S.} = \ & 1 + 018.021 \\
+L_s \quad & \underline{\quad\quad 52.083} \\
\text{S.C.} = \ & 1 + 070.104 \\
+L_c \quad & \underline{\quad\quad 31.693} \\
\text{C.S.} \quad & 1 + 101.797 \\
+L_s \quad & \underline{\quad\quad 52.083} \\
\text{S.T.} \quad & 1 + 153.880
\end{aligned}
$$

Circular Curve Deflections. See Table 10-8.

$$\Delta_c = 6°03'10''$$

$$\frac{\Delta_c}{2} = 3°01'35''$$

$$= 181.58'$$

Table 10-8 CURVE SYSTEM DEFLECTION ANGLES

Station	Distance from T.S. (or S.T.) I (m)	I^2	$\dfrac{\theta_s \times 60}{L_s^2}$	$\dfrac{I^2\,(\theta_s \times 60)}{L_s^2}$ Deflection Angle (minutes)	Deflection
T.S. 1 + 018.021	0	0			0°00'00''
1 + 020	1.979	3.9	0.036667	0.1436	0°00'09''
1 + 040	21.979	483.1	0.036667	17.71	0°17'43''
1 + 060	41.979	1762.2	0.036667	64.62	1°04'37''
S.C. 1 + 070.104	52.083	2712.6	0.036667	99.464	1°39'28''

Station	Circular Curve Data		Deflection Angle (cumulative)	Deflection
S.C. 1 + 070.104	$\Delta_c = 6°03'10'', \dfrac{\Delta_c}{2} = 3°01'35''$		0°00.00'	0°00'00''
1 + 080	Deflection for 9.896 m = 56.70'		0°56.70'	0°56'42''
1 + 100	Deflection for 20 m = 114.59'		2°51.29'	2°51'17''
C.S. 1 + 101.797	Deflection for 1.797 m = 10.30'		3°01.59'	3°01'35''

Station	I (m)	I^2	$\dfrac{\theta_s \times 60}{L_s^2}$	Deflection Angle (minutes)	Deflection
C.S. 1 + 101.797	52.083*	2712.6	0.036667	99.464	1°39'28''
1 + 120	33.880	1147.9	0.036667	42.09	0°42'05''
1 + 140	13.880	192.7	0.036667	7.06	0°07'04''
S.T. 1 + 153.880	0	0	0.036667	0	0°00'00''

*Note that I is measured from the S.T.

From Section 10-4, the deflection angle for one unit of distance is $(\Delta/2)/L$. Here, the deflection angle for 1 m or arc is

$$\frac{\Delta_c/2}{L_c} = \frac{181.58}{31.693} = 5.7293'$$

The required distances (deduced from Table 10-8) are

$(1 + 080) - (1 + 070.104) = 9.896$ m; deflection angle $= 5.7293 \times 9.896 = 56.70'$

Even interval $= 20.000$ m; deflection angle $= 5.7293 \times 20 = 114.59'$

$(1 + 101.797) - (1 + 100) = 1.797$ m; deflection angle $= 5.7293 \times 1.787 = 10.30'$

These values are now entered cumulatively in Table 10-8.

10-20 Approximate Solution for Spiral Problems

It is possible to lay out spirals by using the approximate relationships illustrated in Figure 10-25. Since $L_s \approx LC$ (long chord), the following can be assumed:

$$\frac{Y}{L_s} = \sin \theta_s, \qquad Y = L_s \sin \theta_s \tag{10-33}$$

$$X^2 = L_s^2 - Y^2$$

$$X = \sqrt{L_s^2 - Y^2} \tag{10-34}$$

$$q = \frac{1}{2}X \tag{10-35}$$

$$P = \frac{1}{4}Y \tag{10-36}$$

Using the sine law, we obtain

$$LT = \sin 2/3\ \Delta_s \times \frac{L_s}{\sin \Delta_s} \tag{10-37}$$

Using the sine law yields

$$ST = \sin 1/3\ \Delta_s \times \frac{L_s}{\sin \Delta_s} \tag{10-38}$$

For comparison, the values in Examples 10-7 and 10-8 are compared to the values obtained by the approximate methods.

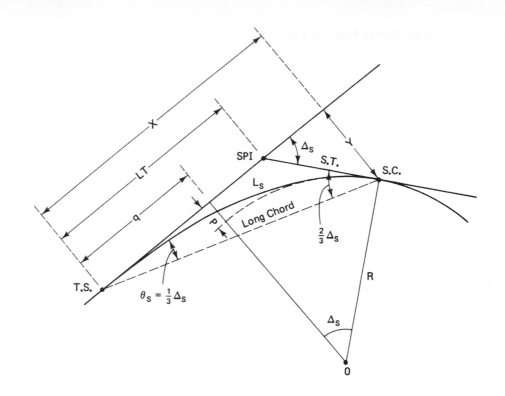

Basic Assumption: $L_s \approx$ Long Chord

FIGURE 10-25   Sketch for approximate formulas.

	Precise Methods		Approximate Methods	
Parameter	Example 10-23 (ft)	Example 10-24 (m)	Example 10-23 (ft)	Example 10-24 (m)
Y	5.88	1.506	5.89	1.507
X	149.79	52.044	149.88	52.061
q	74.97	26.035	74.94	26.031
P	1.47	0.377	1.47	0.377
LT	100.07	34.736	100.13	34.744
ST	50.07	17.374	50.10	17.379

It can be seen from the data summary that the precise and approximate values for Y, X, q, P, LT, and ST are quite similar. The largest discrepancy shows up in the X value, which is not required for spiral layout. The larger the Δ_s values are, the larger will be the discrepancy between the precise and approximate values. For the normal range of spirals in use, the approximate method could be adequate for the layout of an asphalt-surfaced ditched highway. For curbed highways or elevated highways, precise methods should be employed.

10-21 Superelevation: General

If a vehicle travels too fast on a horizontal curve, the vehicle may either skid off the road or overturn. The factors that cause this phenomenon are based on the radius of curvature and the velocity of the vehicle: the sharper the curve and the faster the velocity, the larger the centrifugal force requirement.

Two factors can be called on to help stabilize the radius and velocity factors: (1) side friction, which is always present to some degree between the vehicle tires and the pavement, and (2) superelevation, which is a banking of the pavement toward the center of the curve.

The side friction factor (f) has been found to vary linearly with velocity. Design values for f range from 0.16 at 30 mph (50 km/h) to 0.11 at 80 mph (130 km/h).

Superelevation must satisfy normal driving practices and climatic conditions. In practice, values for superelevation range from 0.125 (i.e., 0.125 ft/ft or 12.5% cross slope) in ice-free southern states to 0.06 in the northern states and Canadian provinces. Typical values for superelevation can be found in Table 10-4.

10-22 Superelevation Design

Figure 10-26 illustrates how the length of spiral (L_s) is used to change the pavement cross slope from normal crown to full superelevation. Figure 10-26(b) illustrates that the pavement can be revolved about the centerline, the usual case, or that the pavement can be revolved about the inside or outside edges, a technique that is often encountered on divided four-lane highways where a narrow median restricts drainage profile manipulation.

Figures 10-28(b) and 10-29 clearly show the technique used to achieve pavement superelevation when revolving the pavement edges about the centerline (℄) profile. At points A and A', the pavement is at normal crown cross section—with both edges (inside and outside) of pavement a set distance below the ℄ elevation. At points S.C. (D) and C.S. (D') the pavement is at full superelevation—with the outside edge a set distance above the ℄ elevation and the inside edge the same set distance below the ℄ elevation. The transition from normal crown cross section to full superelevation cross section proceeds as follows.

OUTSIDE EDGE

- From A to the T.S. (B), the outside edge rises at a ratio of 400:1—relative to the ℄ profile—and becomes equal in elevation to the ℄.
- From the T.S. (B), the outside edge rises (relative to the ℄ profile) at a uniform rate from being equal to the ℄ elevation at the T.S. (B) until it is at full superelevation above the ℄ elevation at the S.C. (D).

INSIDE EDGE

- From A, through the T.S. (B), to point C, the inside edge remains below the ℄ profile at normal crown depth.
- From C to the S.C. (D), the inside edge drops at a uniform rate from being at normal crown depth below the ℄ profile to being at full superelevation depth below the ℄ profile.

The transition from full superelevation at the C.S. (D') to normal cross section at A' proceeds in a manner reverse to that just described.

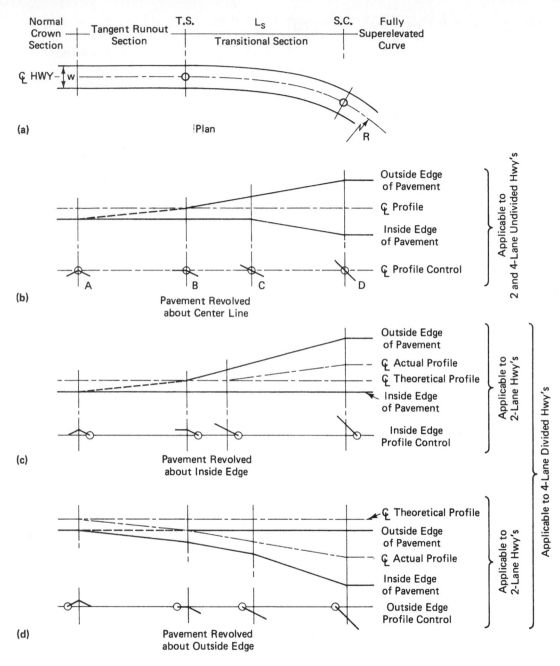

FIGURE 10-26 Methods of attaining superelevation for spiraled curves. (From *Geometric Design Standards for Ontario Highways,* Ministry of Transportation, Ontario)

See Figure 10-27 for vertical curve computations and Figures 10-28 and 10-29 for pavement superelevation computations. This problem uses the horizontal curve data of Example 10-7. Given data are as follows:

$$V = 40 \text{ mph}$$
$$\Delta = 25°45' \; RT$$
$$D = 9°$$
$$\text{PI at } 36 + 17.42$$

Two-lane highway, 24 ft wide, each lane 12 ft wide

Additional data are as follows:

PVI at 36 + 00

Elevation PVI = 450.00

$g_1 = -1.5\%$

$g_2 = +2\%$

$L = 300$ ft

Tangent runout at 400 : 1

Normal crown at 2%

Pavement revolved about the ₵

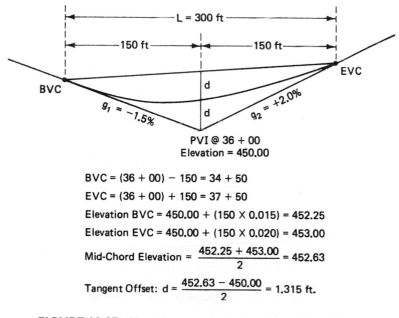

BVC = (36 + 00) − 150 = 34 + 50

EVC = (36 + 00) + 150 = 37 + 50

Elevation BVC = 450.00 + (150 X 0.015) = 452.25

Elevation EVC = 450.00 + (150 X 0.020) = 453.00

Mid-Chord Elevation = $\dfrac{452.25 + 453.00}{2}$ = 452.63

Tangent Offset: d = $\dfrac{452.63 - 450.00}{2}$ = 1.315 ft.

FIGURE 10-27   Vertical curve solution for the problem of Example 10-9.

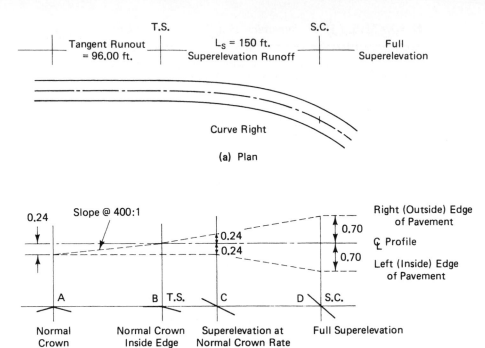

T.S.   S.C.

Tangent Runout L_S = 150 ft.   Full
= 96.00 ft.   Superelevation Runoff   Superelevation

Curve Right

(a) Plan

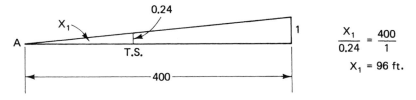

0.24   Slope @ 400:1   Right (Outside) Edge
of Pavement

0.70

0.24
                ₵ Profile
0.24

0.70

Left (Inside) Edge
of Pavement

A   B | T.S.   C   D | S.C.

Normal   Normal Crown   Superelevation at   Full Superelevation
Crown   Inside Edge   Normal Crown Rate

(b) Profile and Cross Sections

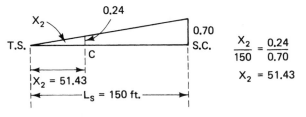

0.24

X_1

A

T.S.

1

400

$$\frac{X_1}{0.24} = \frac{400}{1}$$

$$X_1 = 96 \text{ ft.}$$

(c) Computation of Tangent Runout

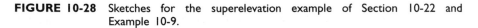

0.24

X_2

0.70

T.S.   S.C.

C

$$\frac{X_2}{150} = \frac{0.24}{0.70}$$

X_2 = 51.43

$$X_2 = 51.43$$

L_S = 150 ft.

(d) Location of Point C

FIGURE 10-28 Sketches for the superelevation example of Section 10-22 and
Example 10-9.

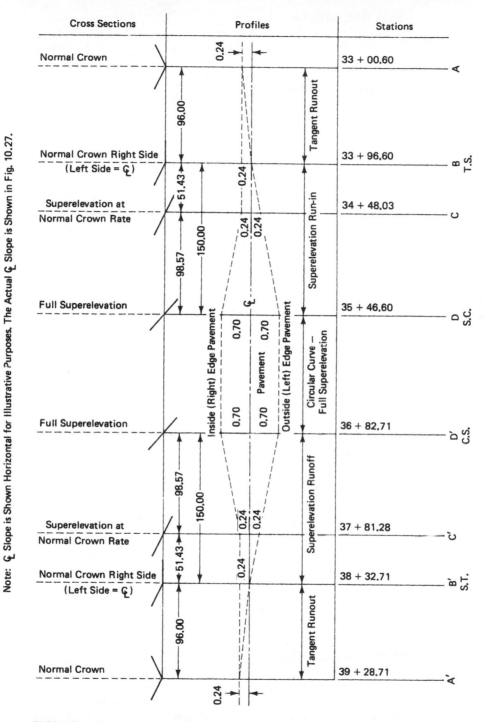

FIGURE 10-29 Superelevated pavement profiles and cross sections for the problem of Example 10-9.

From Table 10-4,

$$L_s = 150 \text{ ft}, \quad e = 0.058$$

Chainage of low point:

$$X = \frac{-g_1 L}{A}$$
$$= \frac{1.5 \times 300}{2 - (-1.5)}$$
$$= 128.57$$

$$
\begin{array}{rl}
\text{BVC at} & 34 + 50 \\
X = & 1 \quad 28.57 \\
\hline
\text{Low point} = & 35 + 78.57
\end{array}
$$

It is required to determine the ℂ and edge of pavement elevations for even 50-ft stations and all other key stations.

1. Compute the key horizontal alignment stations. (These stations have already been computed in Example 10-7.)
2. Solve the vertical curve for ℂ elevations at 50-ft stations and the low point, **plus any horizontal alignment key stations that may fall between the BVC and EVC.**
3. Begin preparation of Table 10-9, showing all key stations for both horizontal and vertical alignment. List the ℂ grade elevation for each station.
4. Compute station A; see Figure 10-28(c).

$$
\begin{array}{rl}
\text{Cross fall at 2\% for } 12' = 0.02 \times 12 &= 0.24 \text{ ft} \\
\text{Tangent runout} = \frac{400}{1} \times 0.24 &= 96 \text{ ft} \\
\text{Tangent runout} = & 96.00 \text{ ft} \\
\text{T.S.} = & 33 + 96.60 \\
X_1 \text{ (Tangent runout)} & \underline{\quad -96.00} \\
A = & 33 + 00.60
\end{array}
$$

Compute station A' (i.e., tangent runout at higher chainage spiral).

$$
\begin{array}{rl}
\text{S.T.} = & 38 + 32.71 \\
\text{Tangent runout} & \underline{\quad + 96.00} \\
A' = & 39 + 28.71
\end{array}
$$

Table 10-9 ¢ PAVEMENT ELEVATIONS

Station		Tangent Elevation	Tangent Offset $\left(\dfrac{X}{L/2}\right)^2 d$		¢ Elevation
A	33 + 00.60	454.49			454.49
	33 + 50	453.75			453.75
T.S.(B)	33 + 96.60	453.05			453.05
	34 + 00	453.00			453.00
C	34 + 48.03	452.28			452.28
BVC	34 + 50	452.25	$(0/150)^2 \times 1.32 =$	0	452.25
	35 + 00	451.50	$(50/150)^2 \times 1.32 =$	0.15	451.65
S.C.(D)	35 + 46.60	450.79	$(96.6/150)^2 \times 1.32 =$	0.55	451.35
	35 + 50	450.75	$(100/150)^2 \times 1.32 =$	0.58	451.33
Low point	35 + 78.57	450.32	$(128.6/150)^2 \times 1.32 =$	0.97	451.29
PVI	36 + 00	450.00	$(150/150)^2 \times 1.32 =$	1.32	451.32
	36 + 50	451.00	$(100/150)^2 \times 1.32 =$	0.58	451.58
C.S.(D')	36 + 82.71	451.65	$(67.3/150)^2 \times 1.32 =$	0.27	451.92
	37 + 00	452.00	$(50/150)^2 \times 1.32 =$	0.15	452.15
EVC	37 + 50	453.00	$(0/150)^2 \times 1.32 =$	0	453.00
C'	37 + 81.28	453.63			453.63
	38 + 00	454.00			454.00
S.T.(B')	38 + 32.71	454.65			454.65
	39 + 00	456.00			456.00
A'	39 + 28.71	456.57			456.57

5. Compute station C; see Figure 10-28(d).

$$\text{Cross fall at 5.8\% for 12-ft lane} = 0.058 \times 12 = 0.70 \text{ ft}$$

$$\text{Distance from T.S. to } C = 150 \times \frac{0.24}{0.70} = 51.43 \text{ ft}$$

$$\text{T.S.} = 33 + 96.60$$
$$X \text{ distance} = 51.43$$
$$C = 34 + 48.03$$

Compute station C' (i.c., at higher chainage spiral).

$$\text{S.T.} = 38 + 32.71$$
$$X_2 \text{ distance} = -51.43$$
$$C' = 37 + 81.28$$

6. Reference to Figure 10-29 will show that right-side pavement elevations are 0.24 ft below ¢ elevation from A to C and from C' to A' and 0.70 ft below ¢ from S.C. to C.S. Right-side pavement elevations between C and S.C. and C.S. and C' must be interpolated. Reference to Figure 10-29 will also show that left-side pavement elevations must be interpolated between A and T.S.,

between T.S. and S.C., between C.S. and S.T., and between S.T. and A'. Between S.C. and C.S., the left-side pavement elevation is 0.70 higher than the corresponding ℄ elevations.

7. Fill in the left- and right-edge pavement elevations (Table 10-10), where the computation simply involves adding or subtracting normal crown (0.24) or full superelevation (0.70).

8. Perform the computations necessary to interpolate for the missing pavement-edge elevations in Table 10-10 (values are underlined). See Figures 10-30 and 10-31.

Table 10-10 PAVEMENT ELEVATIONS FOR EXAMPLE 10-9

	Station	℄ Grade	Left-Edge Pavement Above/Below ℄	Left-Edge Pavement Elevation	Right-Edge Pavement Below ℄	Right-Edge Pavement Elevation
A	33 + 00.60	454.49	−0.24	454.25	−0.24	454.25
	33 + 50	453.75	−0.12	453.63	−0.24	453.51
T.S.(B)	33 + 96.60	453.05	0.00	453.05	−0.24	452.81
	34 + 00	453.00	+0.02	453.02	−0.24	452.76
C	34 + 48.03	452.28	+0.24	452.52	−0.24	452.04
BVC	34 + 50	452.25	+0.25	452.50	−0.25	452.00
	35 + 00	451.65	+0.48	452.13	−0.48	451.17
S.C.(D)	35 + 46.60	451.35	+0.70	452.05	−0.70	450.65
	35 + 50	451.33	+0.70	452.02	−0.70	450.62
Low pt.	35 + 78.57	451.29	+0.70	451.99	−0.70	450.59
PVI	36 + 00	451.32	+0.70	452.02	−0.70	450.62
	36 + 50	451.58	+0.70	452.28	−0.70	450.88
C.S.(D')	36 + 82.71	451.92	+0.70	452.62	−0.70	451.22
	37 + 00	452.15	+0.62	452.77	−0.62	451.53
EVC	37 + 50	453.00	+0.39	453.39	−0.39	452.61
C'	37 + 81.28	453.63	+0.24	453.87	−0.24	453.39
	38 + 00	454.00	+0.15	454.15	−0.24	453.76
S.T.(B')	38 + 32.71	454.65	0.00	454.65	−0.24	454.41
	38 + 50	455.00	−0.04	454.96	−0.24	454.76
	39 + 00	456.00	−0.17	455.83	−0.24	455.76
A'	39 + 28.71	456.57	−0.24	456.33	−0.24	456.33

Interpolated values are shown underlined.

Pavement revolved about the centerline (℄)

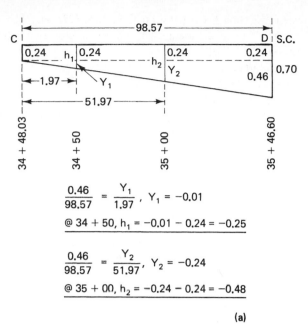

$$\frac{0.46}{98.57} = \frac{Y_1}{1.97} \ , \ Y_1 = -0.01$$

@ 34 + 50, $h_1 = -0.01 - 0.24 = -0.25$

$$\frac{0.46}{98.57} = \frac{Y_2}{51.97} \ , \ Y_2 = -0.24$$

@ 35 + 00, $h_2 = -0.24 - 0.24 = -0.48$

(a)

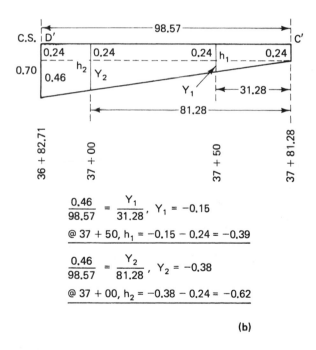

$$\frac{0.46}{98.57} = \frac{Y_1}{31.28} \ , \ Y_1 = -0.15$$

@ 37 + 50, $h_1 = -0.15 - 0.24 = -0.39$

$$\frac{0.46}{98.57} = \frac{Y_2}{81.28} \ , \ Y_2 = -0.38$$

@ 37 + 00, $h_2 = -0.38 - 0.24 = -0.62$

(b)

Note: Pavement Edge Differentials (with ₵) Between C and D or D′ and C′ are Identical at Each Station.

FIGURE 10-30 Right-edge pavement elevation interpolation for the problem of Example 10-9.

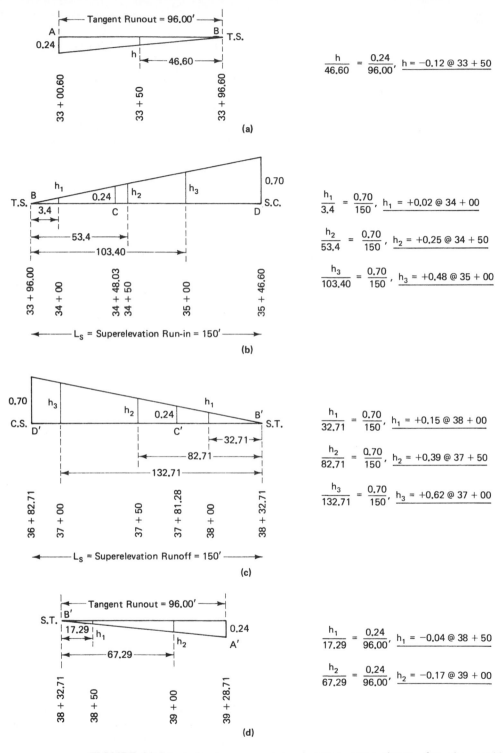

FIGURE 10-31 Left-edge pavement elevation interpolation for the problem of Example 10-9.

Problems

10-1. Given PI @ 9 + 27.26, $\Delta = 29°42'$, and $R = 700$ ft, compute tangent (T) and length of arc (L).

10-2. Given PI @ 15 + 88.10, $\Delta = 7°10'$, and $D = 8°$, compute tangent (T) and length of arc (L).

10-3. From the data in Problem 10-1, compute the stationing of the BC and EC.

10-4. From the data in Problem 10-2, compute the stationing of the BC and EC.

10-5. A straight-line route survey, which had PIs at 3 + 81.27 ($\Delta = 12°30'$) and 5 + 42.30 ($\Delta = 10°56'$), later had 600-ft-radius circular curves inserted at each PI. Compute the BC and EC chainage for each curve.

10-6. Given PI @ 5 + 862.789, $\Delta = 12°47'$, and $R = 300$ m, compute the deflections for even 20-m stations.

10-7. Given PI @ 8 + 272.311, $\Delta = 24°24'20''$, and $R = 500$ m, compute E (external), M (mid-ordinate) and the stations of the BC and EC.

10-8. Given PI @ 10 + 71.78, $\Delta = 36°10'30''$ RT, and $R = 1,150$ ft, compute the deflections for even 100-ft stations.

10-9. From the distances and deflections computed in Problem 10-6, compute the three key ₵ chord layout lengths: that is, (1) BC to first 20-m station, (2) chord distance for 20-m (arc) stations, and (3) from the last even 20-m station to the EC.

10-10. From the distances and deflections computed in Problem 10-8, compute the three key ₵ chord layout lengths: that is, (1) BC to first 100-ft station, (2) chord distance for 100-ft (arc) stations, and (3) from the last even 100-ft station to the EC.

10-11. From the distances and deflections computed in Problem 10-8, compute the six chords required for layout directly on offsets 50 ft right and 50 ft left of ₵.

10-12. It is required to join two highway ₵ tangents with a circular curve of radius 1000 ft. The PI is inaccessible, as its location falls in a river. Point A is established near the river on the back tangent, and point B is established near the river on the forward tangent. Distance AB is measured to be 615.27 ft. Angle $\alpha = 51°31'20''$, and angle $\beta = 32°02'45''$. Perform the calculations required to locate the BC and EC in the field.

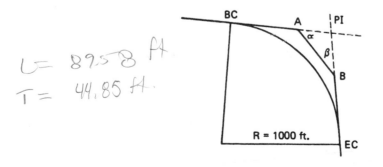

10-13. Two street curb lines intersect, with $\Delta = 71°36'$. A curb radius must be selected so that an existing catch basin (CB) will abut the future curb. The curb side of the catch basin ₵ is located from point V: V to CB = 8.713 m and angle E, V, CB = 21°41'. Compute the radius that will permit the curb to abut the existing catch basin.

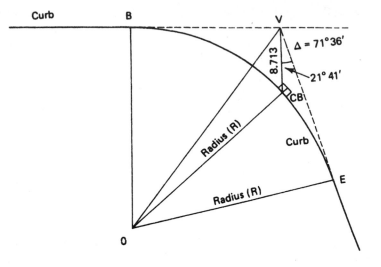

10-14. Given the following compound curve data: $R_1 = 200$ ft, $R_2 = 300$ ft, $\Delta_1 = 44''26'$, and $\Delta_2 = 45°18'$, compute T_1 and T_2 (see Figure 10-15).

10-15. Given the following vertical curve data: PVI @ 7 + 25.712, $L = 100$ m, $g_1 = -3.2\%$, $g_2 = +1.8\%$, and elevation of PVI = 210.440, compute the elevations of the curve low point and even 20-m stations.

10-16. Given the following vertical curve data: PVI; ca 19 + 00, $L = 500$ ft, $g_1 = +2.5\%$, $g_2 = -1\%$, and elevation @ PVI = 723.86 ft, compute the elevations of the curve summit and even full stations (i.e., 100-ft even stations).

10-17. Given the following vertical curve data: $g_1 = +3\%$, $g_2 = -1\%$, design speed = 110 km/h (from Table 10-2, $K = 90$ m), and PVI @ 0 + 360.100, with an elevation of 156.663, compute the elevations of the high point and even 50-m stations.

10-18. Given the following spiral curve data: $D = 8°$, $V = 40$ mph, $\Delta = 16°44'$, and PI @ 11 + 66.18, determine the value of each key spiral and circular curve component (L_s, R, P, q, LT, ST, X, Y, Δ_s, Δ_c, T_c, and L_c), and determine the stationing (chainage) of the T.S., S.C., C.S., and S.T.

10-19. Given the same data as in Problem 10-18, use the approximate equations [Equation (10-33) to Equation (10-38)] to compute X, Y, q, P, LT, and ST. Enter these values in a table together with equivalent values as determined in Problem 10-18 in order to compare the results.

10-20. Use the data from Problem 10-18 to compute the deflections for the curve system (spirals and circular curves) at even 50-ft stations.

10-21. Given the following spiral curve data: $R = 220$ m, $V = 80$ km/hr, $\Delta = 28°08'$ *RT*, two-lane road, and PI @ 1 + 286.441, determine the value of each key spiral and horizontal curve component (L_s, X, Y, q, P, LT, ST, LC, Δ_s, θ_s, Δ_c, T_c and L_c), and determine the chainage of the T.S., S.C., C.S., and S.T.

10-22. Given the same data as in Problem 10-21, use the approximate equations [Equation (10.33) to Equation (10.38)] to compute X, Y, q, P, LT, and ST. Enter these values in a table together with equivalent values as determined in Problem 10-21 in order to compare the results.

10-23. Use the data from Problem 10-21 to compute the deflections for the curve system (spirals and circular curve) at even 20-m stations.

10-24. Given the following vertical curve data: $g_1 = -1\%$, $g_2 = +3\%$, design speed $(V) =$ 80 km/h, PVI @ 1 + 300, and elevation = 210.400, compute the elevations of the low point and the even 20-m stations (use K minimum).

10-25. Combine the data from Problems 10-21 and 10-24, and add data for crown slope, tangent runout, and lane width:

$V = 80$ km/h	Lane width = 4 m
$R = 220$ m	Normal crown @ 2%
$\Delta = 28°08'$ RT	Tangent runout @ 400:1
PI @ 1 + 286.441	PVI @ 1 + 300
Two-lane road	$g_1 = -1\%$, $g_2 = +3\%$

Compute the elevations of the ₵ and edges of pavement at 20-m stations and at all key stations between 1 + 160 and 1 + 420. From Problem 10-21, the superelevation rate $(e) = 0.060$ (Table 10-5).

Chapter 11

Highway Construction Surveys

11-1 Preliminary (Preengineering) Surveys

Before the actual construction of a highway can begin, a great deal of investigative work has to be carried out. The final route chosen for the highway will reflect costs due to topography (cuts and fills); costs of relocating services; costs of rail, highway, and watercrossing bridges; environmental repair; and a host of other considerations.

Area information is first assembled from topographic maps, county maps, available aerial photography, and satellite imagery. More likely routes may be flown, with the resultant photogrammetric maps also being used to aid in the functional planning process. Figure 11-1 shows a simple stereo photo-analysis system, which corrects distortions in the photos (rectifies) and permits the operator to digitize the horizontal and vertical (elevations) positions of all required points.

When the route has been selected, lower level aerial photography will probably form the basis for the preliminary or preengineering survey. Figure 11-2 shows part of a general plan prepared for a new highway location; the actual design drawings—which will show much more detail—are often drawn at 1 in. = 50 ft (1:500 metric).

The proposed centerline is established in the field with the stationing carried through from the initial point to the terminal point. Each time the tangent centerline changes direction, the PI is referenced, and the deflection angle is measured and recorded. Figure 11-3 shows a split-angle tie to a PI. The highway designer will now be able to insert horizontal curves at each PI, with the radius or degree of curve being largely controlled by the design speed. At this point, the centerline stations are adjusted to account for the curve alignment—which, of course, is shorter than the tangent-only alignment.

Horizontal control monuments, and both permanent and temporary benchmarks, are established along the route; their placement intervals are usually less than 1000 ft (300 m). Control for proposed aerial photography may require even smaller intervals. These control monuments are targeted so that their locations will show up on the aerial photographs.

FIGURE 11-1 Zeiss G-2 Stereocord. Stereo-paired aerial photos are analyzed with horizontal and vertical data digitized for later plotting and analysis.

In addition to referencing the PIs, the centerline on tangent is referenced at regular intervals (500 to 1000 ft) to aid the surveyor in reestablishing the centerline alignment for further preliminary surveys, numerous layout surveys, interim payment surveys, and finally the as-built survey. See Figure 11-4 for typical tie-in techniques. Swing ties are referenced to spikes driven into trees or nails and washers driven into the roots of a tree. Strong swing ties intersect at angles near 120°; three ties are used so that if one is lost, the point can still be reestablished from the remaining two. In areas of sparse tree cover, centerline ties are usually taken at right angles to the centerline station and can be made to cut crosses in rock outcrops; iron bars driven into the ground (1″ reinforcing bars with brass caps), aluminum monuments, and even concrete monuments can be used for this purpose.

The plan, prepared from aerial photography, is upgraded in the field by the surveyor so that ambiguous or unknown features on the plan are properly identified—that is, types of fences, dimensions of structures, types of manholes (storm or sanitary), road and drive surfaces, and the like. Soundings are taken at all water crossings, and soil tests are taken at bridge sites and areas suspected of instability. All drainage crossings, watercourses, ditches, and so on are identified and tied in. Tree locations are fixed so that clearing and grubbing estimates can be prepared. Utility crossings (pipelines, conduits, and overhead cables) are located with respect to horizontal and vertical location (Total Station instruments are programmed to directly compute overhead clearances by *remote object elevation*).

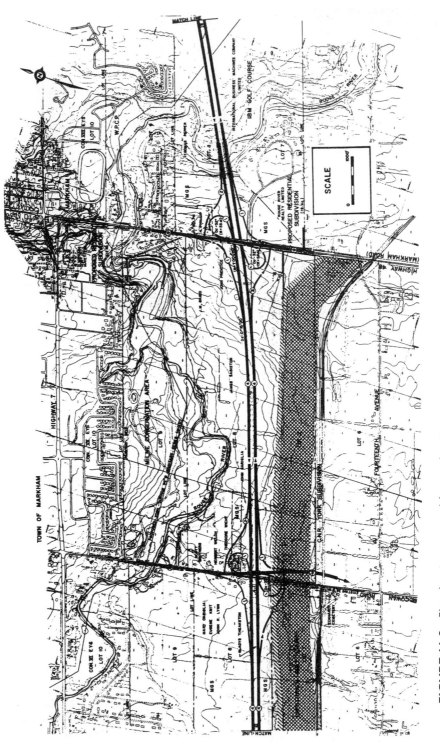

FIGURE 11-2 Plan showing proposed freeway location.

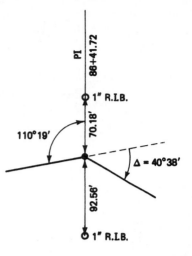

FIGURE 11-3 PI tie-in by split angle. Split angle in this example is $(180° + 40°38')/2 = 110°19'$.

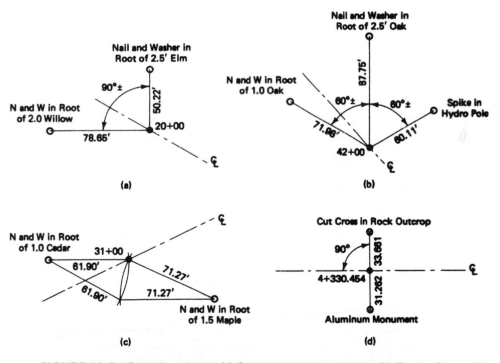

FIGURE 11-4 Centerline tie-ins. (a) Strong two-point swing tie. (b) Strong three-point swing tie. (c) Weak two-point swing tie, resulting in an ambiguous or poorly defined intersection. (d) 90° centerline tie-in (metric).

Railroad crossings require intersection angle and chainage, and track profiles a set distance right and left of the highway centerline. At-grade crossings require sight-line surveys for visibility patterns for set distances up the track ($\frac{1}{4}$ mile each way is not uncommon).

Road and other highway crossings require intersection angles and chainages, together with their centerline profiles left and right of the main centerline.

Cross sections are taken full-width at regular stations, typically 25 ft (10 m) in rock, 50 ft (20 m) in cut, and 100 ft (30 m) in fill. In addition, extra cross sections are taken at any significant changes in slope that occur between regular stations. Rod readings are usually taken to the closest 0.1 ft (0.01 m), and rod location is tied in to the closest foot (0.1 m) for both chainage and offset distances. Stations are at 100-ft intervals (e.g., 0 + 00, 1 + 00) in foot units and are at 1000-m intervals (e.g., 0 + 000, 1 + 000) in metric units.

11-2 Highway Design

The design of a highway depends on the type of service planned for the highway. Highways (and municipal streets) are classified as being *locals, collectors, arterials,* or *freeways*. The bulk of the highways, in mileage, are arterials that join towns and cities together in state or provincial networks.

Design parameters, such as number of lanes, actual lane width, thickness and type of granular material, thickness and type of surface (asphalt or concrete), maximum climbing grades, minimum radius of curvature (related to design speed), and other items, including driver comfort and roadside aesthetics, vary from the highest consideration, given for freeways, to the lowest consideration, reserved for locals.

Local highways have lower design speeds, narrower lanes, and sharper curves, reflecting the fact that locals' primary service function is that of property access. Freeways, on the other hand, have mobility as their primary service function, with vehicle access restricted to interchanges, which are often many miles apart. Freeways have relatively high design speeds, which require flatter curves and wider (and perhaps more) traffic lanes. Flatter climbing grades (5 percent maximum is often used) enable trucks to maintain their operating speeds, which helps in keeping the overall operating speed for all traffic close to the speed for which the facility was designed.

The highway designer will keep these service-related parameters in mind as the highway's profiles, cross sections, and horizontal geometrics are incorporated. Figure 11-5 shows a typical design cross section for a two-lane arterial highway.

Figure 11-6 is a plan and profile of an arterial two-lane highway, which shows the surveyor the horizontal and vertical geometrics, toe of slope location, and cut-and-fill quantities. This plan and profile and the appropriate cross section (e.g., Figure 11-5) are all the surveyor normally needs to provide line and grade to the contractor. Figure 11-7 is a plan showing interchange ramps with full-width pavement elevations at 25-ft stations; this level of detail is commonly provided for all superelevated sections of pavement.

Complex interchanges require special attention from the surveyor. Figure 11-8 shows some of the curve data and chainage coordinates for an interchange. All key curve stations (PI, BC, EC, CPI, T.S., S.T., SPI, etc.) are established and referenced as shown in Figures 11-3 and 11-4. The curves can be laid out by deflection angles (Chapter 10) or by polar layout (Sections 5-11 and 8-8). If the interchange is to be laid out by using polar ties,

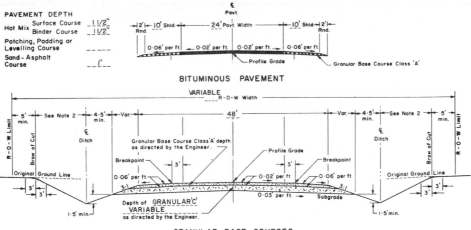

2 LANE HIGHWAYS
EARTH CUT SECTION

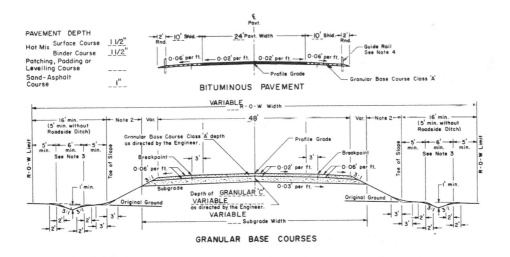

2 LANE HIGHWAYS
EARTH FILL SECTION

FIGURE 11-5 Typical cut and fill design cross sections for a two-lane arterial highway.

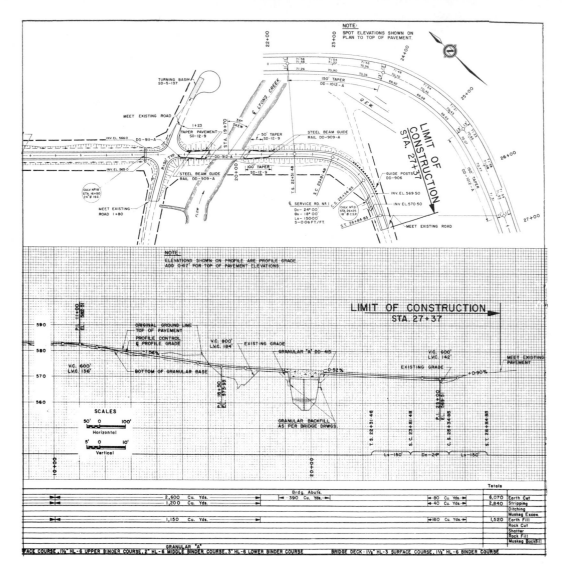

FIGURE 11-6 Plan and profile showing horizontal and vertical alignment, including pavement elevations through the superelevated section, cumulative quantities, and toe of slope locations.

then the surveyor will have to establish control monuments in protected areas, as discussed in Chapter 8.

Figure 11-8 also shows a creek diversion (Green Creek) necessitated by the interchange construction. Figure 11-8 gives the creek centerline alignment chainages and coordinates. Figure 11-9 shows some additional details for the creek diversion channel, including the centerline profile and cross sections, which can be used by the surveyor to provide line and grade for the channel.

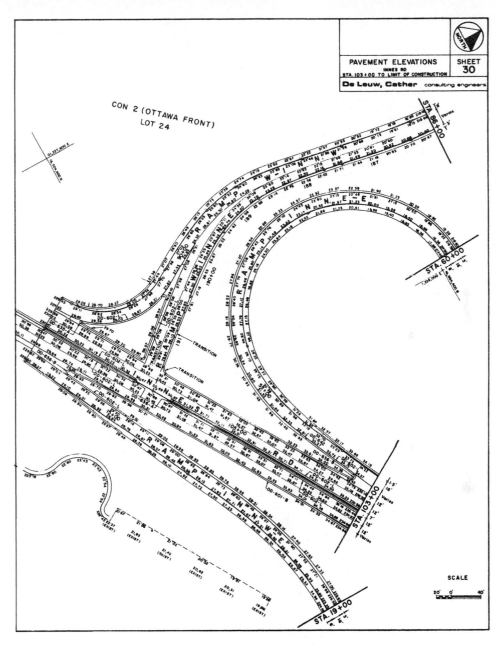

FIGURE 11-7 Interchange plan showing full-width pavement elevations at 25-ft station intervals.

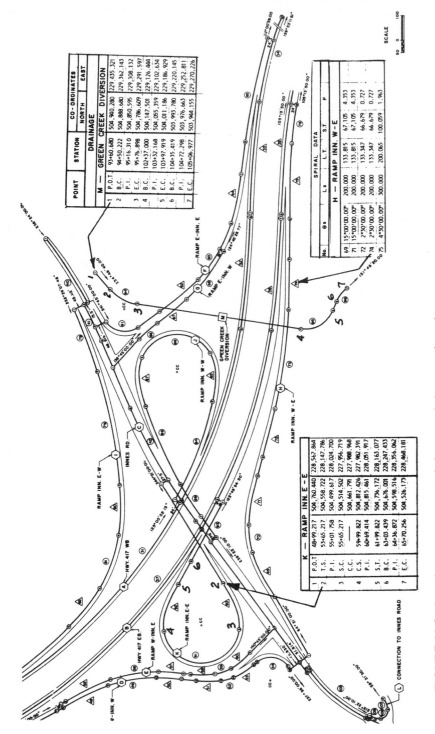

FIGURE 11-8 Interchange geometrics, including a creek diversion channel.

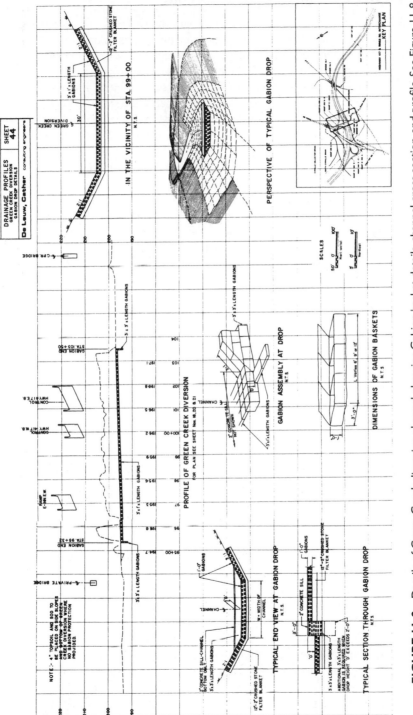

FIGURE 11-9 Details of Green Creek diversion channel, showing Gabion basket details, channel cross section, and profile. See Figure 11-8 for horizontal alignment.

11-3 Highway Construction Layout

When the decision is made to proceed with the highway construction, the surveyor goes back to the field to begin the stakeout. In some cases, months and even years may have passed since the preliminary survey was completed, and some of the control monuments (as well as their reference points) may have been destroyed.

However, if the preliminary survey has been properly referenced, sufficient horizontal and vertical control will be found to commence the stakeout. The centerline chainage is verified by measuring from referenced stations, by checking cross-road intersections, and by checking into any cross-road ties that were noted in the original survey.

Highways are laid out at 100-ft (30- or 40-m) stations, with additional stations being established at all changes in horizontal direction (e.g., BC, EC, T.S., S.T.) and all changes in vertical direction (e.g., BVC, ECV, low points, tangent runouts). The horizontal and vertical curve sections are often staked out at 50-ft (15- to 20-m) intervals to ensure that the finished product closely conforms to the design (25-ft intervals are often used on sharp-radius interchange ramps).

When foot units are used, the full stations are at 100-ft intervals (e.g., 0 + 00, 1 + 00). In metric units, municipalities use 100-m full-station intervals (0 + 00, 1 + 00), whereas most highway agencies use 1000-m (km) intervals for full "stations" (e.g., 0 + 000, 0 + 100, . . . , 1 + 000).

The $\mathcal{C}$ of construction is staked out by using a steel tape, GPS, or EDMI, with specifications designed for 1/3000 accuracy (minimum). The accuracy of $\mathcal{C}$ layout can be verified at reference monuments, road intersections, and the like.

Alternatively highways can be laid out from random coordinated stations using EDM instruments or Total Stations with polar layouts rather than rectangular layouts. Most interchanges are now laid out by polar methods, whereas most of the highways between interchanges are laid out with rectangular layout offsets. The methods of polar layout are covered in Chapters 5 and 8. GPS positioning techniques are now being used in many layout surveys, including highways.

The profile grade, shown on the contract drawing, can refer to the top of granular elevation, or it can refer to the top of asphalt elevation; the surveyor must ensure that he or she is using the proper reference before calculating subgrade elevations for the required cuts and fills.

11-4 Clearing, Grubbing, and Stripping Topsoil

Clearing and grubbing are the terms used to describe the cutting down of trees and the removal of all stumps. The full highway width is staked out, approximating the limits of cut and fill, so that the clearing and grubbing can be accomplished.

The first construction operation after clearing and grubbing is the stripping of topsoil. The topsoil is usually stockpiled for later use. In cut sections, the topsoil is stripped for full width, which extends to the points at which the far-side ditch slopes intersect the original ground surface (OG). See Figure 11-10. In fill sections, the topsoil is usually stripped for the width of the highway embankment (see Figure 11-11). Some highway agencies do not strip the topsoil where heights of fill exceed 4 ft (1.2 m), believing that this water-bearing material cannot damage the road base below that depth.

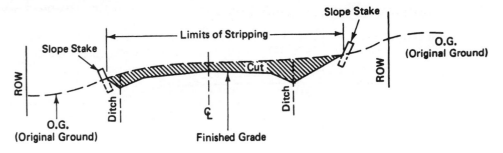

FIGURE11-10 Highway cut section.

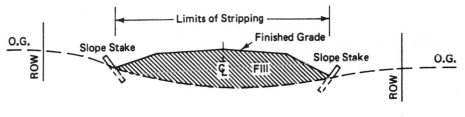

FIGURE 11-11 Highway fill section

The bottom of fills (toe of slope) and the top of cuts (top of slope) are marked by slope stakes. These stakes, which are angled away from ℄, not only delineate the limits of stripping, but also indicate the limits for cut and fill, such operations taking place immediately after the stripping operation. Lumber crayon (keel) or felt markers are used to show station and "s/s" (slope stake).

11-5 Placement of Slope Stakes

Figure 11-12 shows typical cut-and-fill sections in both foot and metric dimensions. The side slopes shown are 3:1, although most agencies use a steeper slope (2:1) for cuts and fills over 4 ft (1.2 m). To locate slope stakes, the difference in elevation between the profile grade at ℄ and the invert of ditch (cut section) or the toe of embankment (fill section) must first be determined. In Figure 11-12(a), the difference in elevation consists of

$$\text{Depth of granular} = 1.50 \text{ ft}$$
$$\text{Subgrade cross fall at 3\% over 24.5 ft} = 0.74 \text{ ft}$$
$$\underline{\text{Minimum depth of ditch} = 1.50 \text{ ft}}$$
$$\text{Total difference in elevation} = 3.74 \text{ ft}$$

The ℄ of this minimum-depth ditch would be 29.0 ft from the ℄ of construction.

In cases where the ditch is deeper than minimum values, the additional difference in elevation and the additional distance from ℄ of construction can be easily calculated by using the same slope values.

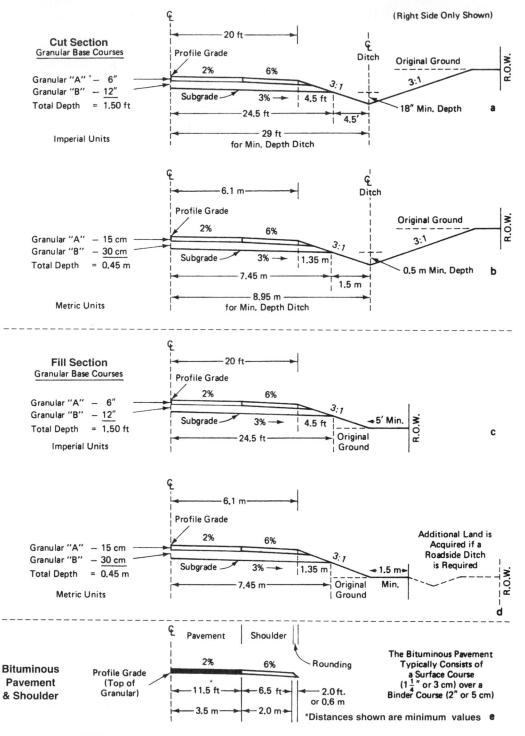

FIGURE 11-12 Typical two-lane highway cross section.

In Figure 11-12(b), the difference in elevation consists of

$$\begin{aligned}
\text{Depth of granular} &= 0.45 \text{ m} \\
\text{Fall at 3\% over 7.45 m} &= 0.22 \text{ m} \\
\text{Minimum depth of ditch} &= \underline{0.50 \text{ m}} \\
\text{Total difference in elevation} &= 1.17 \text{ m}
\end{aligned}$$

The ℄ of this minimum-depth ditch would be 8.95 m from the ℄ of construction.

In these two examples, only the distance from highway ℄ to ditch ℄ has been determined. See Example 11-1 for further treatment.

In Figure 11-12(c), the difference in elevation consists of

$$\begin{aligned}
\text{Depth of granular} &= 1.50 \text{ ft} \\
\text{Fall at 3\% over 24.5 ft} &= \underline{0.74 \text{ ft}} \\
\text{Total difference in elevation} &= 2.24 \text{ ft}
\end{aligned}$$

The difference from ℄ of construction to this point where the subgrade intersects the side slope is 24.5 ft.

In Figure 11-12(d), the difference in elevation consists of

$$\begin{aligned}
\text{Depth of granular} &= 0.45 \text{ m} \\
\text{Fall at 3\% over 7.45 m} &= \underline{0.22 \text{ m}} \\
\text{Total difference in elevation} &= 0.67 \text{ m}
\end{aligned}$$

The distance from ℄ of construction to this point where the subgrade intersects the side slope is 7.45 m.

In the last two examples, the computed distance locates the slope stake.

Figure 11-12(e) shows the pavement and shoulder cross section, which is built on top of the granular cross sections shown in Figure 11-12(a), (b), (c), and (d) in the final stages of construction.

■ **EXAMPLE 11-1** *Location of a Slope Stake in a Cut Section*

Refer to Figure 11-13. Given that the profile grade (top of granular) is 480.00 and the HI = 486.28,

$$\begin{aligned}
\text{Ditch invert} &= 480.00 - 3.74 = 476.26 \\
\text{Grade rod} &= 486.28 - 476.26 = 10.02 \\
\text{Depth of cut} &= \text{grade rod} - \text{ground rod}
\end{aligned}$$

The following equation must be satisfied by trial-and-error ground rod readings:

$$x = (\text{depth of cut} \times 3) + 29.0$$

The rod holder, holding a cloth tape as well as the rod, estimates the desired location and gives a rod reading. For this example, assume that the rod reading is 6.0 ft at a distance of 35 ft from ℄

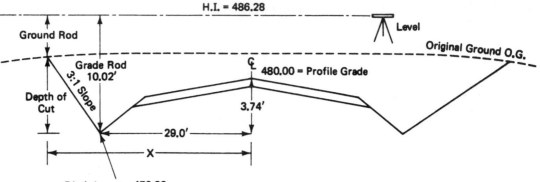

FIGURE 11-13 Location of a slope stake in cut section.

$$\text{Depth of cut} = 10.02 - 6.0 = 4.02$$
$$x = (4.02 \times 3) + 29.0 = 41.06 \text{ ft}$$

Since the rod holder is only 35 ft from the $\mathbb{C}$, he/she must move farther out. At the next point, 43 ft from $\mathbb{C}$, a reading of 6.26 is obtained.

$$\text{Depth of cut} = 10.02 - 6.26 = 3.76$$
$$x = (3.76 \times 3) + 29.0 = 40.3$$

Since the rod holder is at 43 ft, he/she is too far out.

The rod holder moves closer in and gives a rod reading of 6.10 at 41 ft from $\mathbb{C}$. Now

$$\text{Depth of cut} = 10.02 - 6.10 = 3.92$$
$$x = (3.92 \times 3) + 29 = 40.8$$

This location is close enough for placing the slope stake; the error of 0.2 ft is not significant in this type of work. Usually two or three trials are required to locate the slope stake properly.

Figures 11-14 and 11-15 illustrate the techniques used when one is establishing slope stakes in fill sections. Alternatively the slope stake distance from centerline can be scaled from cross sections or topographic plans. In most cases, cross sections (see Chapter 16) are drawn at even stations (100 ft or 30 to 40 m). The cross sections are necessary to calculate the volume estimates used in contract tendering. The location of the slope stakes can be scaled from the cross-section plan. In addition, highway contract plans are now usually developed photogrammetrically from aerial photos; these plans show contours that are precise enough for most slope-stake purposes. One can usually scale off the required distances from $\mathbb{C}$ by using either the cross-section plan or the contour plan to the closest 1.0 ft or 0.3 m. The cost savings effected by having this information determined in the office should usually outweigh any resultant loss of accuracy. It is now possible to increase the

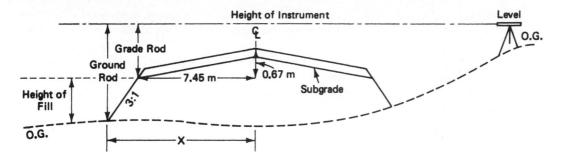

FIGURE 11-14 Location of slope stakes in a fill section. Case 1: instrument HI above subgrade.

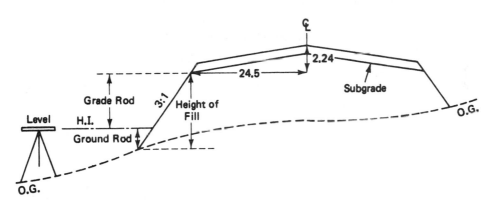

FIGURE 11-15 Location of slope stakes in a fill section. Case 2: instrument HI below subgrade.

precision through advances in computers and photogrammetric equipment. Occasional field checks can be used to check on these "scale" methods.

If scale methods are employed, trigonometric leveling or EDM instruments and vertical angles can be used to establish the horizontal distance from ℄ to the slope stake. These methods will be more accurate than using a cloth tape on deep cuts or high fills when "breaking tape" may be required several times.

11-6 Layout for Line and Grade

In municipal work, it is often possible to put the grade stakes on offset, issue a grade sheet, and then go on to other work. The surveyor may be called back to replace the odd stake knocked over by construction equipment, but usually the layout is thought to be a one-time occurrence.

In highway work, the surveyor must accept the fact that the grade stakes will be laid out several times. The chief difference between the two types of work is the large values for cut and fill. For the grade stakes to be in a "safe" location, they must be located beyond the slope stakes. Although this location is used for the initial layout, as the work progresses this distance back to ₵ becomes too cumbersome to allow for accurate transfer of alignment and grade.

As a result, as the work progresses, the offset lines are moved ever closer to the ₵ of construction, until the final location for the offsets is 2 to 3 ft (1 m) from each edge of the proposed pavement. The number of times that the layout must be repeated is a direct function of the height of fill or depth of cut involved.

In highway work, the centerline is laid out at the appropriate stations. The centerline points are then individually offset at convenient distances on both sides of ₵. For the initial layout, the ₵ stakes, offset stakes, and slope stakes are all put in at the same time. The cuts and fills are written on the grade stakes, referenced either to the top of the stake or to a mark on the side of the stake that will give even foot (even decimeter) values. The cuts and fills are written on that side of the stake facing ₵, whereas, as previously noted, the stations are written on that side of the stake facing back to the 0 + 00 location.

The highway designer attempts to balance cuts and fills so that the overall costs are kept lower. Most highway projects employ scrapers (see Figure 11-16) to first cut the material that must be removed and then transport the material to the fill area, where it is discharged. The grade supervisor keeps checking the scraper cutting-and-filling operations by checking back to the grade stakes. See Section 11-7 for grade-transfer techniques.

In rocky areas, blasting is required to loosen the rock fragments, which can then be loaded into haulers for disposal—either in fill areas or in shoulder or off-site areas.

FIGURE 11-16 Scraper (shown being assisted by a bulldozer) used for efficient transfer of cut material to fill areas. (Courtesy of Caterpillar, Inc., Peoria, Illinois)

Figure 11-17 shows a typical dump hauler, larger versions of which can accommodate up to 140 yd³ of material.

As the work progresses and the cuts and fills become more pronounced, care should be taken in breaking tape when laying out grade stakes so that the horizontal distance is maintained. The centerline stakes are offset by turning 90°, either with a right-angle prism or, more usually, by the swung-arm method. Cloth tapes are used to lay out the slope stakes and offset stakes. Once a ℄ station has been offset on one side, care is taken when offsetting to the other side to ensure that the two offsets and the ℄ stake are all in a straight line.

As in cross sectioning for preliminary surveys, the optimal size of the survey crew is four: the party chief to take notes, the instrument operator to run the instrument, one surveyor to hold one end (zero) of the tape on ℄, and the other surveyor to establish the stakes, using the other end of the tape to tie in rod readings for slope and grade stakes.

When the cut and/or fill operations have brought the work to the proposed subgrade (bottom of granular elevations), the subgrade must be verified by cross sections before the contractor is permitted to place the granular material. Usually a tolerance of 0.10 ft (30 mm) is allowed. Once the top of granular profile has been reached, layout for pavement (sometimes a separate contract) can commence. Figure 11-18 shows a road grader shaping the crushed stone with the guidance of a rotating laser.

The final layout for pavement is usually on a very close offset (3 ft or 1 m). If the pavement is to be concrete, more precise alignment is provided by nails driven into the tops of the stakes.

When the highway construction has been completed, a final survey is performed. The final survey includes cross sections and locations that are used for final payments to

FIGURE 11-17 Euclid R35 hauler, capacity of 30.5 cubic yards. (Courtesy of VME Americas Inc., Cleveland, Ohio)

FIGURE 11-18 Rotating laser shown controlling fine grading operations by a road grader. (Courtesy of Laser Alignment, Inc., Grand Rapids, Michigan)

the contractor and for a completion of the as-built drawings. The final cross sections are taken at the same stations used in the preliminary survey.

The description here has referred to two-lane highways. The procedure for layout of a four-lane divided highway is very similar. The same control is used for both sections; grade stakes can be offset to the center of the median and used for both sections. When the lane separation becomes large and the vertical alignment is different for each direction, the project can be approached as being two independent highways.

The layout for elevated highways, often found in downtown urban areas, follows the procedures used for structures layout.

11-7   Grade Transfer

The grade stakes can be set so that the tops of the stakes are at "grade." Stakes set to grade are colored red or blue on the top to differentiate them from all other stakes. This procedure is time consuming and often impractical except for final pavement layout. Generally the larger the offset distance is, the more difficult it is to drive the tops of the stakes to grade.

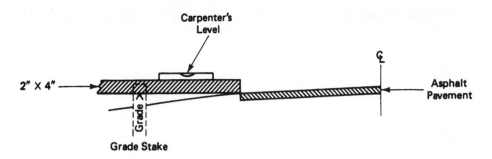

FIGURE 11-19 Grade transfer using a carpenter's level.

As noted earlier, the cut and fill can refer to the top of the grade stake or to a mark on the side of the grade stake referring to an even number of feet (decimeters) of cut or fill. The mark on the side of the stake is located by sliding the rod up and down the side of the stake until a value is read on the rod that will give the cut or fill to an even foot (decimeter). This procedure of marking the side of the stake is best performed by two workers, one to hold the rod and the other to steady the bottom of the rod and then to make the mark on the stake. The cut or fill can be written on the stake or entered on a grade sheet, one copy of which is given to the contractor.

To transfer the grade (cut or fill) from the grade stake to the area of construction, a means of transferring the stake elevation in a horizontal manner is required. When the grade stake is close (within 6 ft or 2 m), the grade transfer can be accomplished using a carpenter's level set on a piece of sturdy lumber (see Figure 11-19). When the grade stake is far from the area of construction, a string line level can be used to transfer the grade (cut or fill) (see Figure 11-20). In this case, a fill of 1 ft 0 in. is marked on the grade stake (in addition to the offset distance). A guard stake has been placed adjacent to the grade stake, and the grade mark is transferred to the guard stake. A 1-ft distance is measured up the guard stake, and the grade elevation is marked.

A string line is attached to the guard stake at the grade elevation mark; then a line level is hung from the string (near the halfway mark), and the string is pulled taut so as to eliminate most of the sag (it is not possible to eliminate all the sag). The string line is adjusted up and down until the bubble in the line level is centered; with the bubble centered,

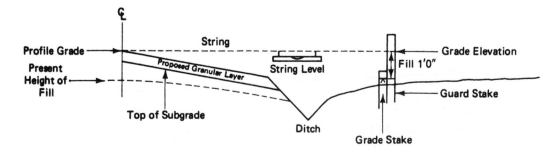

FIGURE 11-20 Grade transfer using a string level.

it can be quickly seen at ℄ how much more fill may be required to bring the highway, at that point, to grade.

It can be seen in Figure 11-20 that more fill is required to bring the total fill to the top of subgrade elevation. The surveyor can convey this information to the grade inspector so that the fill can be properly increased. As the height of fill approaches the proper elevation (top of subgrade), the grade checks become more frequent.

In the preceding example, the grade fill was 1 ft 0 in.; had the grade been cut 1 ft, the procedure with respect to the guard stake would have been the same: that is, measure up the guard stake 1 ft so that the mark now on the guard stake is 2 ft *above* the ℄ grade. The surveyor or inspector simply measures, at centerline, down 2 ft using a tape measure from the level string at ℄. If the measurement down to the "present" height of fill exceeds 2 ft, it indicates that more fill is required; if the measurement down to the "present" height of fill is less than 2 ft, it indicates that too much fill had been placed and that an appropriate depth of fill must be removed.

Another method of grade transfer used when the offset is large and the cuts or fills significant is the use of boning rods (batter boards). See Figure 11-21. In the preceding example, a fill grade is transferred from the grade stake to the guard stake; the fill grade is measured up the guard stake, and the grade elevation is marked (any even foot/decimeter cut or fill mark can be used, so long as the relationship to profile grade is clearly marked).

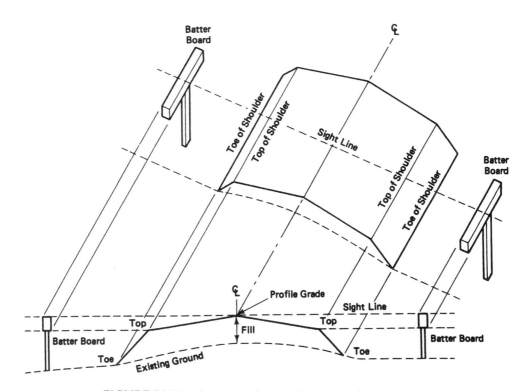

FIGURE 11-21   Grade transfer using batter boards.

FIGURE 11-22 A multilane divided highway, showing center drainage with grade stakes.

A crosspiece is nailed on the guard stake at the grade mark and parallel to ℄. A similar guard stake and crosspiece are established on the opposite side of ℄. The surveyor or grade inspector can then sight over the two crosspieces to establish profile grade datum at that point. Another worker can move across the section with a rod, and the progress of the fill (cut) operation can be visually checked. Figure 11-22 shows a divided highway with grade stakes on either side of the ℄ swale, controlling grades on both sections of highway.

In some cases, two crosspieces are used on each guard stake, the upper one indicating ℄ profile grade and the lower one indicating the shoulder elevation.

11-8   Ditch Construction

The ditch profile often parallels the ℄ profile, especially in cut sections. When the ditch profile does parallel the ℄ profile, no additional grades are required to assist the contractor in construction. However, it is quite possible to have the ℄ profile at one slope (even 0 percent) and the ditch profile at another slope (0.3 percent is often taken as a minimum slope to give adequate drainage). If the ditch grades are independent of ℄ profile, the contractor must be given these cut or fill grades, either from the existing grade stakes or from grade stakes specifically referencing the ditch line.

In the extreme case (e.g., a spiralled and superelevated highway going over the brow of the hill), the contractor may require five separate grades at one station (i.e., ℄, two edges of pavement, and two different ditch grades); it is even possible in this extreme case to have the two ditches flowing in opposite directions for a short distance.

Chapter 12

Municipal Street Construction Surveys

12-1 General

Preengineering surveys for a street or an area are requested when there is a strong likelihood that planned construction will be approved for the following year's budgeted works. The surveys manager must choose between aerial surveys and ground surveys for the preparation of the engineering drawings. On the basis of past experience, the surveys manager will know the cost per mile or kilometer for both ground and aerial surveys for various levels of urban density; the more densely packed topographic and man-made detail can usually be more efficiently picked up using aerial methods. However, the introduction of Total Stations, described in Chapter 5, and Global Positioning System (GPS) techniques, described in Chapter 9, has made ground surveys competitive with aerial surveys for certain levels of detail density. A survey crew, using a Total Station and two prism poles, can capture as many as 1000 points (X, Y, and Z coordinates) a day. Add to this tremendous increase in data acquisition the automatic transfer of data to the computer and the field note plot, which requires little additional work, and you have a highly efficient survey operation.

See Tables 7-2 and 7-3 for typical scales for maps, and plans, used in municipal and highways projects.

As with highways, preliminary surveys for municipal streets include all topographic detail within the road allowance. Buried electric power lines, gas lines, telephone lines, and water services are usually staked out by the respective utility. Failure to request a stakeout can result in a broken utility and an expensive repair—not counting delays in the construction process.

Railroad crossings are profiled left and right of the street right of way (ROW), with additional sight-line data being acquired as required by the railroad or municipality. Water crossings and other road crossings are intersected, tied in, and profiled left and right of the street ROW as described for highways. Proposed connections to existing works (bridges, sewers, pipelines, streets, etc.) are carefully and precisely surveyed to ensure that an accurate connection is made by the contractor.

In short, all topographic and works data that may have an effect on the cost estimates, the works design, or the construction of the proposed facility are tied in. Cross sections are taken full-width at all regular stations and at any change in grade that may occur
between them. Elevations are carefully determined for any connecting points (sewers,
curbs, street centerlines, etc.).

Reconstruction of existing roads may require drilling to determine the extent of any
granular material that could be recycled. Road drilling is usually scheduled during the off-
season.

Municipal benchmarks are utilized; care must be taken to always check into adjacent
or subsequent benchmarks. As the preliminary survey proceeds, temporary benchmarks
(TBMs) are established—and carefully referenced—to aid in subsequent preliminary and
construction surveys.

12-2   Classification of Roads and Streets

The plan shown in Figure 12-1 depicts a typical municipal road pattern. The **local** roads
shown have the primary purpose of providing access to individual residential lots. The **collector** roads (both major and minor) provide the dual service of lot access and traffic
movement. The collector roads connect the local roads to **arterial** roads; the main purpose
of the arterial roads is to provide a relatively high level of traffic movement service.

Municipal works engineers base their road design on the level of service to be provided. The proposed cross sections and geometric alignments vary in complexity and cost
from the fundamental local roads to the more complex arterials. The highest level of
service is given by the **freeways,** which provide high-velocity, high-volume routes with
limited access (interchanges only), ensuring continuous traffic flow when design conditions prevail.

12-3   Road Allowances

The road allowance varies in width from 40 ft (12 m) for small locals to 120 ft (35 m) for
major arterials. In parts of North America, including most of Canada, the local road
allowances originally were 66 ft wide (one Gunter's chain), and when widening was
required due to increased traffic volumes, it was common to take 10-ft widenings on each
side, initially resulting in an 86-ft road allowance for major collectors and minor arterials.
Further widenings left major arterials at 100- and 120-ft widths.

12-4   Road Cross Sections

A full-service municipal road allowance will usually have asphalt pavement, curbs, storm
and sanitary sewers, water distribution pipes, hydrants, catch basins, and sidewalks. Additional utilities, such as natural gas pipelines, electrical supply cables, and cable TV, are
also often located on the road allowance. The essential differences between local cross sections and arterial cross sections are the widths of pavement and the quality and depths of
pavement materials. The construction layout of sewers and pipelines is covered in Chapter
13. See Figure 12-2 for a typical municipal road cross section.

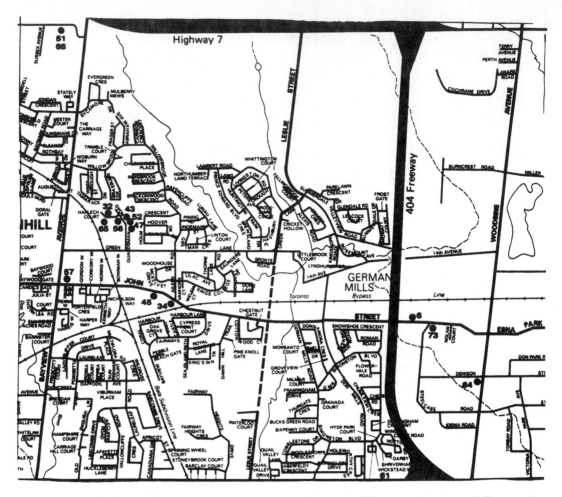

FIGURE 12-1 Municipal road pattern. (Courtesy of Fine Line Graphic and Cartographic Services, Markham, Ontario)

The cross fall (height of crown) used on the pavement varies from one municipality to another, but is usually close to a 2 percent slope. The curb face is often 6 in. (150 mm) high except at driveways and crosswalks, where the height is restricted to about 2 in. (50 mm) for vehicle and pedestrian access. The slope on the boulevard from the curb to the street line usually rises at a 2 percent minimum slope, thus ensuring that roadway storm drainage does not run onto private property.

12-5 Plan and Profile

A typical plan and profile are shown in Figure 12-3. The plan and profile, which usually also show the cross-section details and construction notes, are the "blueprint" from which the construction is accomplished. The plan and profile, together with the contract specifications, spell out in detail precisely where and how the road (in this example) is to be built.

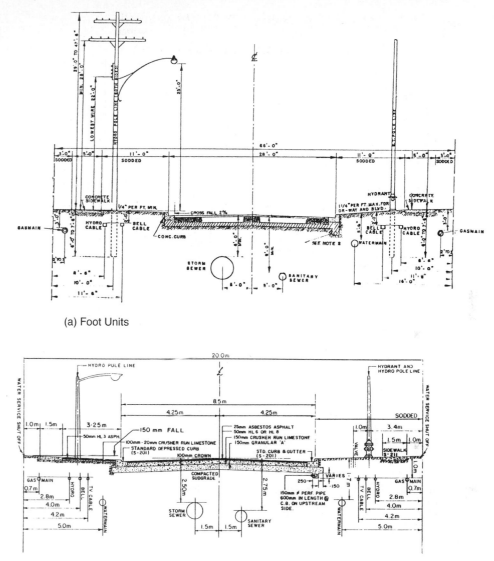

(a) Foot Units

(b) Metric Units

FIGURE 12-2 Typical cross section of a local residential road. Gas and water services shown under boulevards are normally installed on only one side of the roadway; far-side house connections are located under the road and boulevard but above the sewer pipes. (a) Foot units. (b) Metric units.

The plan portion of the plan and profile gives the horizontal location of the facility, including curve radii, whereas the profile portion shows the key elevations and slopes along the road centerline, including vertical curve information. Both the plan and the profile relate all data to the project stationing established as horizontal control.

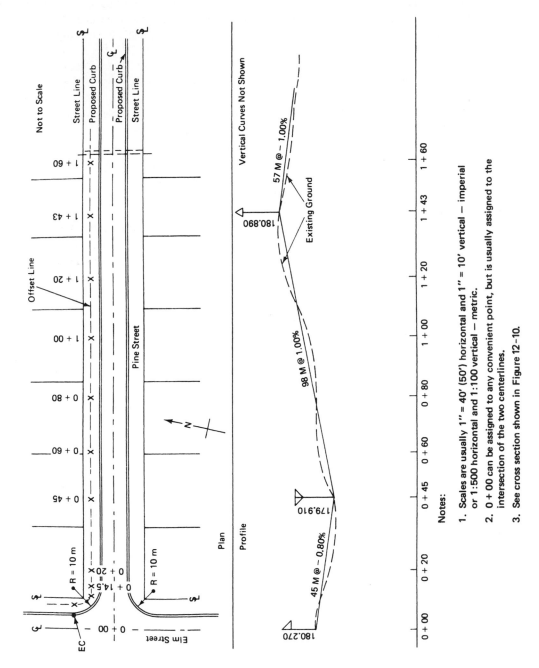

Notes:

1. Scales are usually 1″ = 40′ (50′) horizontal and 1″ = 10′ vertical – imperial or 1:500 horizontal and 1:100 vertical – metric.

2. 0 + 00 can be assigned to any convenient point, but is usually assigned to the intersection of the two centerlines.

3. See cross section shown in Figure 12–10.

FIGURE 12-3 Plan and profile.

434

12-6 Establishing Centerline (¢)

Let us use the example of a ditched residential road being upgraded to a paved and curbed road. The first job for the construction surveyor is to reestablish the centerline (¢) of the roadway. Usually this entails finding several property markers delineating street line (♯). Fence and hedge lines can be used initially to guide the surveyor to the approximate locations of the property markers. When the surveyor finds one property marker, he or she can measure out the frontage distances shown on the property plan (plat) to locate a sufficient number of additional markers. Usually the construction surveyor has the notes from the preliminary survey showing the location of property markers used in the original survey. If possible, the construction surveyor will utilize the same evidence used in the preliminary survey, taking the time, of course, to verify the resultant alignment. If the evidence used in the preliminary survey has been destroyed, as is often the case when a year or more elapse between the two surveys, the construction surveyor will take great care to see to it that the new results are not appreciably different from those of the original survey unless, of course, a blunder occurred on the original survey.

The property markers can be square or round iron bars (including rebars) or round iron or aluminum pipes, magnetically capped. The markers can vary from 1 1/2 to 4 ft in length. It is not unusual for the surveyor to have to use a shovel, as the tops of the markers are often buried. The surveyor can use a magneticmetal detector to aid in locating buried markers.

Sometimes even an exhaustive search of an area will not turn up a sufficient number of markers to establish ¢. The surveyor must then extend the search to adjacent blocks or backyards in order to reestablish the missing markers. Alternatively the surveyor can approach the home owners in the affected area and inquire as to the existence of a "mortgage survey plan" (see Figure 12-4) for the specific property. Such a plan is required in most areas before a financial institution will provide mortgage financing. The mortgage survey plan shows dimensions from the building foundation to the street line and to both sidelines. Information thus gained can be used to narrow the search for a missing marker or can be used directly to establish points on the street line.

Once a number of points have been established on both sides of the roadway, the ¢ can be marked from each of these points by measuring (at right angles) half the width of the road allowance. The surveyor then sets up the transit on a ¢ mark near one of the project extremities and sights in on the ¢ marker nearest the other project extremity. It can then be seen if all the markers line up in a straight line (assuming tangent alignment) (see Figure 12-5). If the markers do not all line up, the surveyor will check the affected measurements; if discrepancies still occur (as often is the case), the surveyor will make the "best fit" of the available evidence. Depending on the length of roadway involved and the quantity of ¢ markers established, the number of markers lining up perfectly will vary. Three well-spaced, perfectly aligned markers is the absolute minimum number required for the establishment of ¢. The reason that all markers do not line up is that over the years most lots are resurveyed; some lots may be resurveyed a number of times. Land surveyors' prime area of concern is that area of the plan immediately adjacent to their client's property, and they must ensure that the property stakeout is consistent for both evidence and plan intentions. Over a number of years, cumulative errors and mistakes can significantly affect the overall alignment of the ¢ markers.

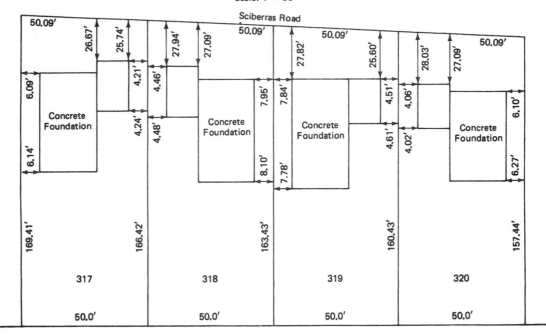

FIGURE 12-4 House survey (plat).

If, as in this example, the ℄ is being marked on an existing road, the surveyor will use nails with washers and red plastic flagging to establish the marks. The nails can be driven into gravel, asphalt, and, in some cases, concrete surfaces. The washers will keep the nails from sinking below the road surface, and the red flagging will help in relocation.

If the project had involved a new curbed road in a new subdivision, the establishment of the ℄ would have been much simplified. The recently set property markers would be intact for the most part, and discrepancies between markers would be minimal (as all markers would have been set in the same comprehensive survey operation). The ℄ in this case would be marked by wood stakes 2″ × 2″ or 2″ × 1″ and 18 in. long.

12-7 Establishing Offset Lines and Construction Control

In this present example, the legal fabric of the road allowance as given by the property markers constitutes the horizontal control. Construction control would consist of offset lines referenced to the *proposed curbs* with respect to line and grade. In the case of ditched roads and most highways, the offset lines are referenced to the *proposed centerline* with respect to line and grade.

The offset lines are placed as close to the proposed location of the curbs as possible. It is essential that the offset stakes not interfere with equipment and form work; it is also

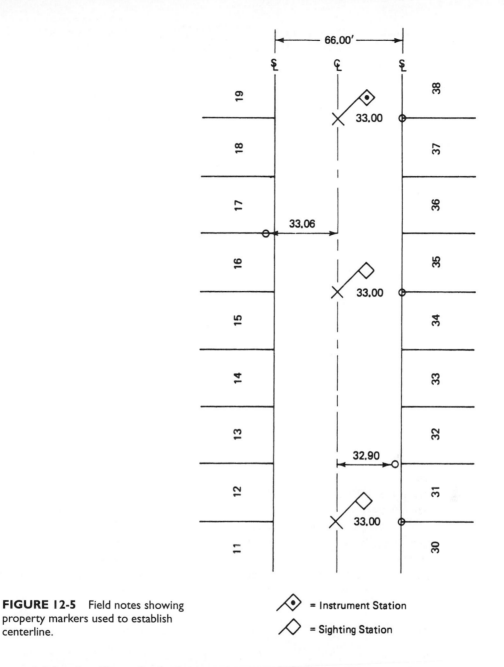

FIGURE 12-5 Field notes showing property markers used to establish centerline.

◇ = Instrument Station

◇ = Sighting Station

essential that the offset stakes be far enough removed that they are not destroyed during cut or fill operations. Ideally the offset stakes, once established, will remain in place for the duration of construction. This ideal can often be realized in municipal road construction, but it is seldom realized in highway construction, due to the significant size of cuts and fills. If cuts and fills are not too large, offset lines for curbs can be 3 to 5 ft (1 to 2 m) from the proposed face of curb. An offset line this close allows for very efficient transfer of line and grade (see Section 11-7). Figure 12-6 shows concrete curb and gutter being installed by a slip-form concrete curber. The curber is kept on line and grade by keeping in contact with a guide string or wire, which is established by measurements from the grade stakes.

In the case of a ditched gravel road being upgraded to a curbed paved road, the offset line will have to be placed far enough away on the boulevard to avoid the ditch filling operation and any additional cut and fill that may be required. In the worst case, it may be necessary to place the offset line on the street line, an 18- to 25-ft (6- to 7-m) offset. Figure 12-7 shows a grade supervisor checking the status of excavation by sighting over crossrails referenced to the finished grade and set at right angles to the street. These sight rails (also called batter boards) are erected by measuring from the grade stakes placed by the surveyor.

When the street pavement is to be concrete, the pavement can be placed first, before the curbs are installed. Figure 12-8 shows a concrete-paving operation being controlled by a guide wire precisely positioned in line and grade by the surveyor, working from previously placed grade stakes. After the pavement is in place, the curb—or curb and gutter—can be placed adjacent to the new concrete pavement.

When the street pavement is to be asphalt, the curbs—or curb and gutter—are always constructed first by measurements from the grade stakes. If curb and gutter have been

Guide String Set
From Grade Stakes

FIGURE 12-6 Slip-form concrete curber; line and grade are provided by the guide string (can also be guided by laser). Precision of 1/8 in. or .01 ft. (Courtesy of Puckett Bros. Mfg. Co. Inc., Georgia)

FIGURE 12-7 Progress of street construction being monitored by the use of sight rails (batter boards).

placed, the subsequent asphalt pavement is simply placed adjacent to the edge of the concrete gutter. If curb alone has been installed, the subsequent paving operation is guided by keel marks on the curb face a set distance below the top of the new curb (a 6-in. curb face is common). Figure 12-9 shows an asphalt-paving operation at an interchange; the asphalt is being placed adjacent to a barrier curb to the design profile marked on the curb face.

12-8 Construction Grades for a Curbed Street

The offset stakes (with nails or tacks for precise alignment) are usually placed at 50-ft (20-m) stations and at any critical alignment change points. The elevations of the tops of the stakes are determined by rod and level, based on the vertical control established for the project. It is then necessary to determine the proposed elevation for the top of curb at each offset station.

Referring to Figure 12-3, the reader can see that elevations and slopes have been designed for a portion of the project; the plan and profile have been simplified for illustrative purposes, and offsets are shown for one curb line only.

Given the ℄ elevation data, the construction surveyor must calculate the proposed curb elevations. He or she can proceed by calculating the relevant elevations on ℄ and then

FIGURE 12-8 Concrete paver controlled for line and grade by guide wire established from grade stakes. (Courtesy of Caterpillar Inc., Peoria, Illinois)

FIGURE 12-9 Asphalt spreader laying asphalt to finished grade as marked on the curb face. (Courtesy of Barber-Greene Co., Aurora, Illinois)

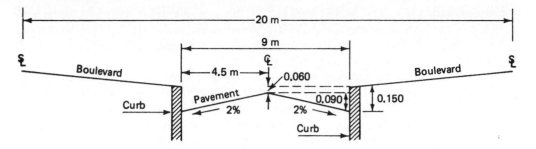

FIGURE 12-10 Cross section showing the relationship between centerline and the top of curb elevations.

adjusting for crown and curb height differential, or by applying the differential first and working out the curb elevations directly.

To determine the difference in elevation between ℄ and top of curb, the surveyor must analyze the appropriate cross section. In Figure 12-10, it can be seen that the cross fall is $4.5 \times 0.02 = 0.090$ m (90 mm). The face on the curb is 150 mm; therefore, the top of curb is 60 mm above the ℄ elevation.

A list of key stations (see Table 12-1) is prepared, and the ℄ elevation at each station is calculated. The ℄ elevations are then adjusted to produce curb elevations. Since

Table 12-1 GRADE SHEET COMPUTATIONS

Station	℄ Elevation		Curb Elevation
0 + 00	180.270		
	−0.116		
BC 0 + 14.5	180.154	+0.060	180.214
	−0.044		
0 + 20	180.110	+0.060	180.170
	−0.160		
0 + 40	179.950	+0.060	180.010
	−0.040		
0 + 45	179.910	+0.060	179.970
	+0.150		
0 + 60	180.060	+0.060	180.120
	+0.200		
0 + 80	180.260	+0.060	180.320
	+0.200		
1 + 00	180.460	+0.060	180.520
	+0.200		
1 + 20	180.660	+0.060	180.720
	+0.200		
1 + 40	180.860	+0.060	180.920
	+0.030		
1 + 43	180.890	+0.060	180.950
etc.			

superelevation is seldom used in municipal design, it is safe to say that the curbs on both sides of the road are normally parallel in line and grade. A notable exception to this can occur when intersections of collectors and arterials are widened to allow for turn lanes and both line and grade are affected.

The construction surveyor can then prepare a grade sheet (see Table 12-2), copies of which are given to the contractor and the project inspector. The tops of stake elevations, determined by level and rod, are assumed in this example.

The grade sheet, signed by the construction surveyor, also includes the street name, date, limits of the contract, and, most important, the offset distance to the face of the curb.

It should be noted that the construction grades (cut and fill) refer only to the vertical distance to be measured down or up from the grade stake to locate the proposed elevation. Construction grades do not define with certainty whether the contractor is in a cut or fill situation at any given point. For example (see Figure 12-11), at 0 + 20, a construction grade of cut 0.145 is given, whereas the contractor is actually in a fill situation (i.e., the proposed top of curb is *above* the existing ground at that station). This lack of correlation between construction grades and the construction process can become more pronounced as the offset distance lengthens. For example, if the grade stake at station 1 + 40 had been located at the street line, the construction grade would have been cut, whereas the construction process is almost entirely in a fill operation.

When the layout is performed using foot units, the basic station interval is 50 ft. The dimensions are recorded and calculated to the closest one-hundredth (0.01) of a foot. Although all survey measurements are in feet and decimals of a foot, for the contractor's purposes the final cuts and fills are often expressed in feet and inches. The decimal-inch relationships are soon committed to memory by surveyors working in the construction field (see Table 12-3). Cuts and fills are usually expressed to the closest 1/8 in. for concrete, steel, and pipelines and to the closest 1/4 in. for highways, granular surfaces, and ditch lines.

The grade sheet in Table 12-4 illustrates the foot-inch relationships. The first column and the last two columns are all that are required by the contractor, in addition to the offset distance, to construct the facility properly.

Table 12-2 GRADE SHEET

Station	Curb Elevation	Stake Elevation	Cut	Fill
0 + 14.5	180.214	180.325	0.111	
0 + 20	180.170	180.315	0.145	
0 + 40	180.010	180.225	0.215	
0 + 45	179.970	180.110	0.140	
0 + 60	180.120	180.185	0.065	
0 + 80	180.320	180.320	On grade	
1 + 00	180.520	180.475		0.045
1 + 20	180.720	180.710		0.010
1 + 40	180.920	180.865		0.055
1 + 43	180.950	180.900		0.050
etc.				

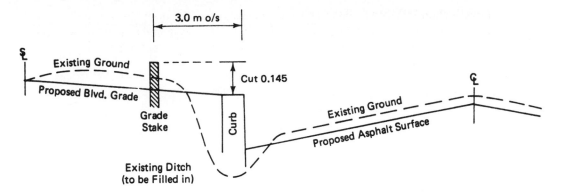

Station 0 + 20 Cut Grade

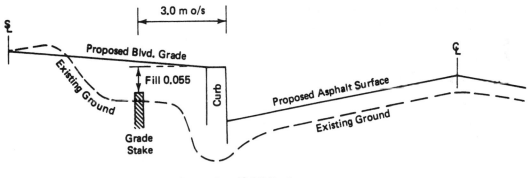

Station 1 + 40 Fill Grade

FIGURE 12-11 Cross sections showing cut and fill grades.

Table 12-3 DECIMAL FOOT-INCH CONVERSION

$1' = 12''$	$1'' = 1/12' = 0.083'$	
$1'' = 0.08(3)'$	$7'' = 0.58'$	$1/8'' = 0.01'$
$2'' = 0.17'$	$8'' = 0.67'$	$1/4'' = 0.02'$
$3'' = 0.25'$	$9'' = 0.75'$	$1/2'' = 0.04'$
$4'' = 0.33'$	$10'' = 0.83'$	$3/4'' = 0.06'$
$5'' = 0.42'$	$11'' = 0.92'$	
$6'' = 0.50'$	$12'' = 1.00'$	

In some cases, the cuts and fills (grades) are written directly on the appropriate grade stakes. This information, written with lumber crayon (keel) or felt marker, is always written on the side of the stake facing the construction. The station is also written on each stake and is placed on that side of each stake *facing the lower chainage* (station).

Table 12-4 GRADE SHEET (FOOT UNITS)

Station	Curb Elev.	Stake Elev.	Cut	Fill	Cut	Fill
0 + 30	470.20	471.30	1.10		1'1¼"	
0 + 50	470.40	470.95	0.55		0'6⅝"	
1 + 00	470.90	470.90	On grade		On grade	
1 + 50	471.40	471.23		0.17		0'2"
2 + 00	471.90	471.46		0.44		0'5¼"
2 + 50	472.40	472.06		0.34		0'4⅛"

12-9 Street Intersections

An intersection curb radius can range from 30 ft (10 m), for two local streets intersecting, to 60 ft (18 m), for two arterial streets intersecting. The angle of intersection is ideally 90° (for good sight lines); however, the range from 70° to 110° is often permitted for practical purposes. See Figure 12-12.

Street intersections require special attention from the surveyor for both line and grade. The curved curb lines (shown at the intersection of Pine Street and Elm Street in Figure 12-3) are often established in the field, not by the deflection angle technique of Chapter 10, but instead by first establishing the curve center and then establishing the arc by swinging off the curve radius. More on this later.

Additionally, the profile of this curved section of proposed curb requires analysis because this section of curb does not fit the profile of Pine Street or of Elm Street. We can determine the curb elevation at the BC on Pine Street; it is 180.214 @ 0 + 14.5 (Table 12-1).

At this point, the surveyor must obtain the plan and profile of Elm Street and determine the chainage at the EC (see Figure 12-3) of the curb coming from the BC at 0 + 14.5, on the north side of Pine Street. Once this station has been determined, the proposed curb elevation at the EC on Elm Street can be computed. Let's assume this value to be 180.100 m. This procedure has to be repeated to determine the curb elevation on Elm Street at the EC of the curve coming from the BC on the south side of Pine Street—if that curb is also being constructed.

The surveyor, knowing the elevation of both the BC on Pine Street and the EC on Elm Street, can compute the length of arc between the BC and the EC and then compute the profile grade for that particular section of curved curb. The procedure is as follows.

The curb elevation at the BC (180.214) is determined from the plan and profile of Pine Street (see Figure 12-3 and Table 12-1). The curb elevation at the EC is determined from the plan and profile of Elm Street (assume EC elevation = 180.100). The length of curb can be calculated:

$$L = \frac{\pi R \Delta}{180} \tag{10-5}$$

$$= 15.708 \text{ m}$$

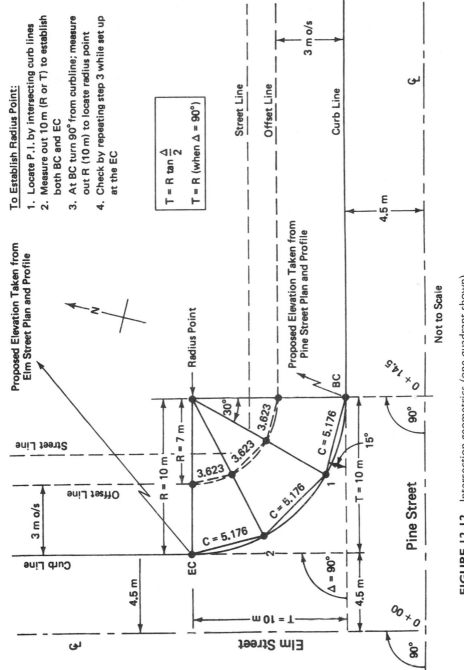

FIGURE 12-12 Intersection geometrics (one quadrant shown).

445

The slope from BC to EC can be determined:

$$180.214 - 180.100 = 0.114 \text{ m}$$

The fall is 0.114 over an arc distance of 15.708 m, which is −0.73 percent.

These calculations indicate that a satisfactory slope (0.5 percent is the usual minimum) joins the two points. The intersection curve is located by four offset stakes, BC, EC, and two intermediate points. In this case, 15.708 ÷ 3 = 5.236 m, the distance measured from the BC to locate the first intermediate point, the distance measured from the first intermediate point to the second intermediate point, and the distance used as a check from the second intermediate point to the EC.

In actual practice, the chord distance is used rather than the arc distance. Since $\Delta/2 = 45°$ and we are using a factor of 1/3, the corresponding deflection angle for one-third of the arc would be 15°.

$$C = 2R \sin (\text{deflection angle})$$
$$= 2 \times 10 \times \sin 15° = 5.176 \text{ m}$$

These intermediate points can be deflected in from the BC or EC, or they can be located by the use of two tapes, with one surveyor at the radius point (holding 10 m, in this case) and another surveyor at the BC or intermediate point (holding 5.176), while the stake surveyor holds the zero point of both tapes. The latter technique is the most often used on these small-radius problems. The only occasions when these curves are deflected in by transit occur when the radius point (curve center) is inaccessible (due to fuel pump islands, front porches, etc.).

The proposed curb elevations on the arc are as follows:

$$
\begin{aligned}
\text{BC} \quad 0 + 14.5 &= 180.214 \\
& -0.038 \\
\text{No. 1} &= 180.176 \\
& -0.038 \\
\text{No. 2} &= 180.138 \\
& -0.038 \\
\text{EC} &= 180.100 \\
\text{Arc interval} &= 5.236 \text{ m} \\
\text{Difference in elevation} &= 5.236 \times 0.0073 = 0.038
\end{aligned}
$$

Grade information for the curve can be included on the grade sheet.

The offset curve can be established in the same manner after making allowances for the shortened radius (see Figure 12-12).

For an offset (o/s) of 3 m, the radius becomes 7 m. The chords required can be calculated as follows:

$$C = 2R \sin (\text{deflection})$$
$$= 2 \times 7 \times \sin 15°$$
$$= 3.623 \text{ m}$$

12-10   Sidewalk Construction

The sidewalk is constructed adjacent to the curb or at some set distance from the street line. If the sidewalk is adjacent to the curb, no additional layout is required, as the curb itself gives line and grade for construction. In some cases, the concrete for this curb and sidewalk is placed in one operation.

When the sidewalk is to be located at some set distance from street line (℄), a separate layout is required. Sidewalks located near the ℄ give the advantages of increased pedestrian safety and boulevard space for the stockpiling of a winter's accumulation of plowed snow in northern regions. See Figure 12-13, which shows the typical location of sidewalk on road allowance.

Sidewalk construction usually takes place after the curbs have been built and the boulevard has been brought to sod grade. The offset distance for the grade stakes can be quite short (1 to 3 ft). If the sidewalk is located within 1 to 3 ft of the ℄, the ℄ is an ideal location for the offset line. In many cases, only line is required for construction, as the grade is already established by boulevard grading and the permanent elevations at ℄ (existing elevations on private property are seldom adjusted in municipal work). The cross slope (toward the curb) is usually given as being 1/4 in./ft (2 percent).

12-11   Site Grading

Every construction site, whether it be small, as in a residential house construction, or large, as in an airport construction, requires a site grading plan showing proposed (and existing) ground elevations. These ground elevations have been designed to (1) ensure proper drainage for storm-water runoff, (2) provide convenient pedestrian and vehicular access, and (3) optimally balance cut and fill.

Figure 12-14 shows part of a site grading plan for a residential development. The existing ground elevations are shown in brackets below each proposed elevation at all lot corners. With this plan, the surveyor can determine the runoff flow direction for each lot and set grade stakes at the lot corners to define finished ground grade. Figure 12-15 shows

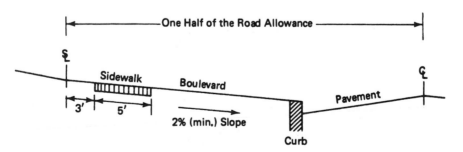

Note: The Sidewalk is Always Constructed so that it Slopes Toward the Road — Usually @ 1/4" per foot (2%)

FIGURE 12-13   Typical location of sidewalk on the road allowance.

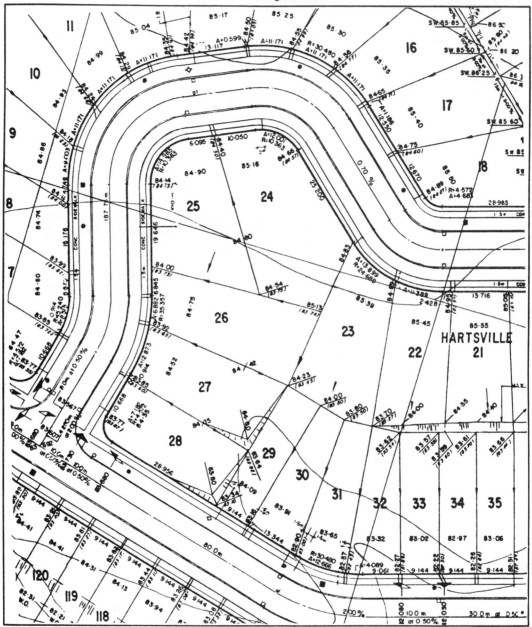

FIGURE 12-14 Site grading plan. Proposed elevation: 84.23. Existing elevation: 83.45.

FIGURE 12-15 Rough grading by backhoe-loader. (Courtesy of MF Industrial Ltd., Manchester, England)

a backhoe/loader roughly shaping up the ground behind a housing development, and Figure 12-16 shows another loader with a landscaping/pulverizing attachment bringing the ground to its final elevation just prior to sodding or seeding.

Grade control can be provided by rotating lasers or electronic levels, as described in Chapter 15; also see Figure 11-18. Grade can also be given by grade stakes or grade stakes with batter boards. Large-scale projects, with deep cuts or fills, may require several layouts before finally being brought to grade.

Typical municipal projects that require grading surveys include residential, commercial, or industrial developments; sanitary landfill sites; parks or greenbelts; and boulevards and the like, as with street construction.

FIGURE 12-16 Fine grading by landscaping attachment on loader. (Courtesy of John Deere Ltd., Grimsby, Ontario)

Problems

12-1. A new road is to be constructed beginning at an existing road (℄ elevation = 472.70 ft) for a distance of 600 ft. The ℄ gradient is to rise at 1.18 percent. The elevations of the offset grade stakes are as follows: 0 + 00 = 472.60; 1 + 00 = 472.36; 2 + 00 = 473.92; 3 + 00 = 475.58; 4 + 00 = 478.33; 5 + 00 = 479.77; 6 + 00 = 480.82. Prepare a grade sheet (see Table 12-4) showing the cuts and fills in feet and inches.

12-2. A new road is to be constructed to connect two existing roads. The ℄ intersection with the east road (0 + 00) is at an elevation of 210.666 m, and the ℄ intersection at the west road (1 + 32.562) is at an elevation of 209.446 m. The elevations of the offset grade stakes are as follows: 0 + 00 = 210.831; 0 + 20 = 210.600; 0 + 40 = 211.307; 0 + 60 = 210.114; 0 + 80 = 209.772; 1 + 00 = 209.621; 1 + 20 = 209.308; 1 + 32.562 = 209.400. Prepare a grade sheet (see Table 12-2) showing cuts and fills in meters.

Use Figure 12-17 for Problems 12-3 to 12-8.

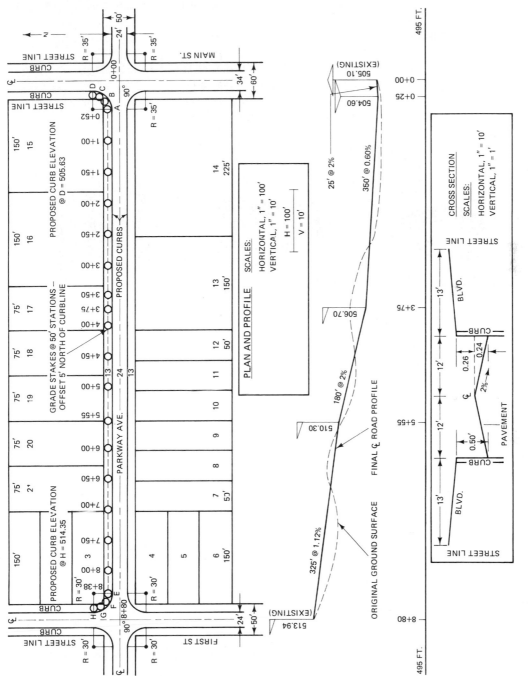

FIGURE 12-17 Plan, profile, and cross section for pavement and curbs, Parkway Avenue (foot units). Also see Figure 13-24.

451

12-3. Figure 12-17 shows proposed curb locations, together with grade stakes offset from the north-side curb. The straight section of curb begins at 0 + 52 and ends at 8 + 38 (centerline stations). Show, with the aid of a sketch, how these two chainages were determined.

12-4. Compute the final centerline road elevations at the points of curve (PC)—that is, 0 + 52 and 8 + 38—and at all even 50-ft stations.

12-5. Compute the top-of-curb elevations from 0 + 52 to 8 + 38; see Figure 12-17 (cross section) for the centerline/top-of-curb relationship.

12-6. Using the grade stake elevations shown here, prepare a grade sheet showing cuts/fills (ft and in.) for the proposed curb from 0 + 52 to 8 + 38.

Grade Stake Elevations

PC	0 + 52	504.71		4 + 50	508.46
	1 + 00	504.78		5 + 00	508.77
	1 + 50	504.93		5 + 55	510.61
	2 + 00	504.98		6 + 00	511.73
	2 + 50	505.82		6 + 50	512.00
	3 + 00	506.99		7 + 00	512.02
	3 + 50	507.61		7 + 50	512.11
	3 + 75	507.87		8 + 00	512.24
	4 + 00	508.26	PC	8 + 38	512.73

12-7. For the intersection curve ($R = 35$ ft) at Main Street, station A (0 + 52) to station D:
(a) Compute the length of arc.
(b) Determine the curb-line gradient (percentage) from A to D.
(c) Determine the proposed curb elevations at stations B and C; B and C divide the arc into three equal sections: $AB = BC = CD$.
(d) Using the grade stake elevations shown here, determine the cuts/fills (ft and in.) for stations B, C, and D.

Grade Stake Elevations

A	504.71	C	506.37
B	506.22	D	506.71

12-8. For the intersection curve ($R = 30$ ft) at First Street, station E (8 + 38) to station H:
(a) Compute the length of arc.
(b) Determine the curb-line gradient (percentage) from E to H.
(c) Determine the proposed curb elevations at stations F and G; F and G divide the arc into three equal sections: $EF = FG = GH$.
(d) Using the grade stake elevations shown here, determine the cuts/fills (ft and in.) for stations F, G, and H.

Grade Stake Elevations

E	512.73	G	512.88
F	512.62	H	513.27

Use Figure 12-18 for Problems 12-9 to 12-14.

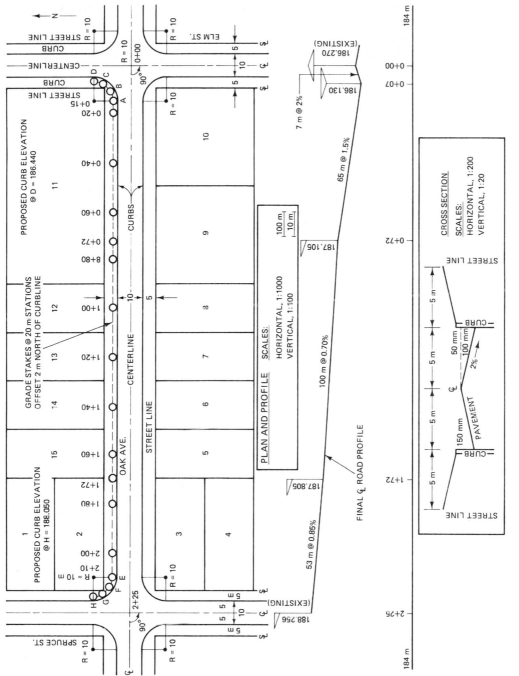

FIGURE 12-18 Plan, profile, and cross section for pavement and curbs, Oak Avenue (metric units). Also see Figure 13-25.

12-9. Figure 12-18 shows proposed curb locations, together with offset stakes for the north-side curb. The straight section of curb begins at station $0 + 15$ and ends at station $2 + 10$. Show, with the aid of a sketch, how these two chainages were determined.

12-10. Compute the final centerline road elevations at the points of curve (PC)—that is, $0 + 15$ and $2 + 10$—and at all even 20-m stations.

12-11. Compute the top-of-curb elevations from $0 + 15$ to $2 + 10$; see Figure 12-18 (cross section) for the centerline/top-of-curb relationship.

12-12. Using the grade stake elevations shown here, calculate the cuts/fills for the proposed curb from $0 + 15$ to $2 + 10$.

Grade Stake Elevations

PC	0 + 15	186.720		1 + 20	188.025
	0 + 20	186.387		1 + 40	188.003
	0 + 40	185.923		1 + 60	187.627
	0 + 60	186.425		1 + 72	187.455
	0 + 72	186.707		1 + 80	187.907
	0 + 80	187.200		2 + 00	187.993
	1 + 00	187.527	PC	2 + 10	188.125

12-13. For the intersection curve ($R = 10$ m) at Elm Street, station A ($0 + 15$) to station D:
(a) Compute the length of arc.
(b) Determine the curb-line gradient (percentage) from A to D.
(c) Determine the proposed curb elevations at stations B, C, and D; B and C divide the arc into three equal sections; that is, $AB = BC = CD$.
(d) Using the grade stake elevations shown here, determine the cuts/fills for stations B, C, and D.

Grade Stake Elevations

A	186.720	C	186.575
B	186.447	D	186.567

12-14. For the intersection curve ($R = 10$ m) at Spruce Street, station E ($2 + 10$) to station H:
(a) Determine the curb-line gradient (percentage) from E to H.
(b) Determine the proposed curb elevations at stations F, G, and H; F and G divide the arc into three equal sections: $EF = FG = GH$.
(c) Using the grade stake elevations shown here, determine the cuts/fills for stations F, G, and H.

Grade Stake Elevations

E	188.125	G	188.015
F	188.007	H	188.010

12-15. With reference to Figure 12-14 (site grading plan), a grade stake was set near the middle of Lot #26, and the stake-top elevation was determined to be 84.15 m. Compute the cut/fill at each lot corner.

Chapter 13

Pipeline and Tunnel Construction Surveys

13-1 Pipeline Construction

Pipelines are designed to carry water, oil, and natural gas while under pressure. Because pressure systems do not require close attention to grade lines, the layout for pipelines can proceed at a much lower order of precision than is required for gravity pipes. Pipelines are usually designed so that the cover over the crown is adequate for the loading conditions expected and also adequate to prevent damage due to frost penetration, erosion, and the like.

The pipeline location can be determined from the contract drawings; the line and grade stakes are offset an optimal distance from the pipe ¢ and are placed at 50- to 100-ft (15- to 30-m) intervals. When existing ground elevations are not being altered, the standard cuts required can be simply measured down from the ground surface (required cuts in this case would equal the specified cover over the crown plus the pipe diameter plus the bedding, if applicable). See Figure 13-1, Trench A.

In the case of proposed general cuts and fills, grades must be given to establish suitable crown elevation so that **final** cover is as specified. See Figure 13-1, Trench B. Additional considerations and higher precisions are required at major crossings (e.g., rivers, highways, utilities).

Figure 13-2(a) shows a pipeline being installed a set distance below existing ground (as in Trench A, Figure 13-1). Material cast from the trench is shown on the right side of the trench, and the installation equipment is shown on the left side of the trench. The surveyor, in consultation with the contractor, determines a location for the line and grade stakes that will not interfere with either the cast material or the installation equipment.

Figure 13-2(b) shows a pipe-jacking operation. The carrier pipe is installed at the same time that the tunnel is being excavated. Line and grade are provided by a construction laser that has been set to the design slope and horizontal alignment. This type

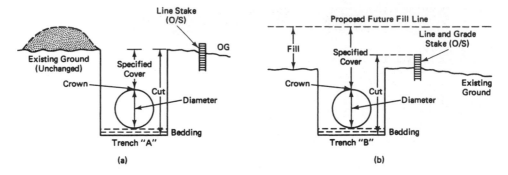

FIGURE 13-1 Pipeline construction. (a) Existing ground to be unchanged. (b) Existing ground to be altered.

(a)

FIGURE 13-2 (a) Pipeline installation. (Courtesy of Caterpillar, Inc., Peoria, Illinois)

(b)

FIGURE 13-2 (continued)   (b) Pipe-jacking operation. (Courtesy of American Augers, Inc., Ohio)

of operation is used where an open cut would be unacceptable—for example, across important roads or highways.

Final surveys show the actual location of the pipe and appurtenances (valves and the like). As-built drawings, produced from final surveys, are especially important in urban areas, where it seems there is no end to underground construction.

13-2   Sewer Construction

Sewers are usually described as being in one of two categories. Sanitary sewers collect domestic and industrial liquid waste and convey these wastes (sewage) to a treatment plant.

Storm sewers are designed to collect runoff from rainfall and to transport this water (sewage) to the nearest natural receiving body (e.g., creek, river, lake). The rainwater enters the storm-sewer system through ditch inlets or through catch basins located at the curb line on paved roads.

The design and construction of sanitary and storm sewers are similar in the respect that the flow of sewage is usually governed by gravity. Since the sewer grade lines (flow lines) depend on gravity, it is essential that construction grades be precisely given.

Figure 13-3(a) shows a typical cross section for a municipal roadway. The two sewers are typically located 5 ft (1.5 m) on either side of ₵. The sanitary sewer is usually deeper than the storm sewer, as it must be deep enough to allow for all house connections. The sanitary house connection is usually at a 2 percent (minimum) slope. If sanitary sewers are being added to an existing residential road, the preliminary survey must include the basement floor elevations. The floor elevations are determined by taking a rod reading on the window sill and then, after getting permission to enter the house, measuring from the window sill down to the basement floor. As a result of deep basements and long setbacks from ₵, sanitary sewers often have to be at least 9 ft (2.75 m) below ₵ grade.

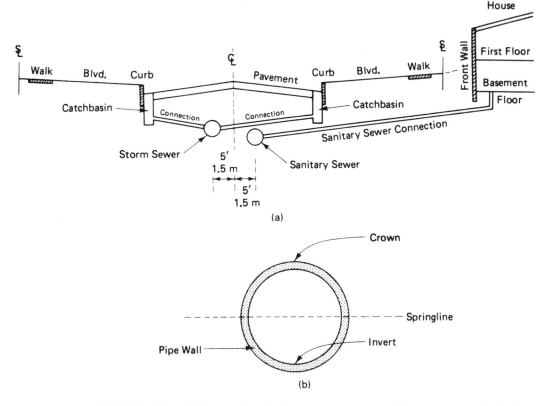

FIGURE 13-3 (a) Municipal road allowance showing typical service locations. (b) Sewer pipe section.

The minimum depth of storm sewers below ₵ grade depends, in the southern United States, on the traffic loading and, in the northern United States and most of Canada, on the depth of frost penetration. The minimum depth of storm sewers ranges from 3 ft (1 m) in some areas in the south to 8 ft (2.5 m) in the north. The design of the inlets and catch basins depends on the depth of sewer and the quality of the effluent.

The minimum slope for storm sewers is usually 0.50 percent, whereas the minimum slope for sanitary sewers is often set at 0.67 percent. In either case, the designers try to achieve self-cleaning velocity (i.e., a minimum of 2.5 to 3 ft/s or 0.8 to 0.9 m/s) to avoid excessive sewer maintenance costs.

Manholes are located at each change in direction, slope, or pipe size. In addition, manholes are located at 300- to 450-ft (100- to 140-m) maximum intervals.

Catch basins are located at 300-ft (100-m) maximum intervals; they are also located at the high side of intersections and at all low points. The 300-ft (100-m) maximum interval is reduced as the slope on the road increases.

For construction purposes, sewer layout is considered only from one manhole to the next. The stationing (0 + 00) commences at the first (existing) manhole (or outlet) and proceeds only to the next manhole. If a second leg is also to be constructed, station 0 + 00 is assigned to the downstream manhole and proceeds upstream only to the next manhole. Each manhole is described by a unique manhole number to avoid confusion with the stations for extensive sewer projects. Figure 13-3(b) shows a section of sewer pipe. The **invert** is the inside bottom of the pipe. The invert grade is the **controlling grade** for construction and design. The sewer pipes may consist of vitrified clay, steel, some of the newer "plastics," or, as usually is the case, concrete.

The pipe wall thickness depends on the diameter of the pipe. For storm sewers, 12 in. (300 mm) is usually taken as minimum diameter. The *spring line* of the pipe is at the halfway mark, and connections are made above this reference line. The **crown** is the outside top of the pipe. Although this term is relatively unimportant (sewer cover is measured to the crown) for sewer construction, it is important for pipeline (pressurized pipes) construction, as it gives the **controlling grade** for that type of construction.

13-3 Layout for Line and Grade

As in other construction work, offset stakes are used to provide line and grade for the construction of sewers; grade can also be defined by the use of in-trench lasers. Before deciding on the offset location, it is wise to discuss the matter with the contractor. The contractor will be excavating the trench and casting the material to one side or loading it into trucks for removal from the site. Additionally, the sewer pipe will be delivered to the site and positioned conveniently alongside its future location. The position of the offset stakes should not interfere with either of these operations.

The surveyor will position the offset line as close to the pipe centerline as possible, but seldom is it possible to locate the offset line closer than 15 ft (5 m) away. 0 + 00 is assigned to the downstream manhole or outlet, the chainage proceeding upstream to the next manhole. The centerline of construction is laid out with stakes marking the location of the two terminal points of the sewer leg. The surveyor will use survey techniques giving 1/3000 accuracy as a minimum for most sewer projects. Large-diameter (6-ft or 2-m) sewers require increased precision and accuracy.

The two terminal points on ₵ are occupied by transit or theodolite, and right angles are turned to precisely locate the terminal points at the assigned offset distance. 0 + 00 on offset is occupied by a transit or theodolite, and a sight is taken on the other terminal offset point. Stakes are then located at 50-ft (20-m) intervals; checking in at the terminal point verifies accuracy.

The tops of the offset stakes are surveyed and their elevations determined, the surveyor taking care to see that his or her leveling is accurate; the existing invert elevation of MH 3 (Figure 13-4), shown on the contract plan and profile, is verified at the same time. The surveyor next calculates the sewer invert elevations for the 50-ft (20-m) stations. He or she then prepares a grade sheet showing the stations, stake elevations, invert grades, and cuts. The following examples will illustrate the techniques used.

Assume that an existing sewer (Figure 13-4) is to be extended from existing MH 3 to proposed MH 4. The horizontal alignment will be a straight-line production of the sewer leg from MH 2 to MH 3. The vertical alignment is taken from the contract plan and profile (Figure 13-4).

The straight line is produced by setting up the transit or theodolite at MH 3, sighting MH 2, and double centering to the location of MH 4. The layout then proceeds as described previously.

The stake elevations, as determined by differential leveling, are shown in Table 13-1.

At station 1 + 50, the cut is 8 ft 3 7/8 in. (see Figure 13-5). To set a cross-trench batter board at the next even foot, measure up 0 ft 8 1/8 in. to the top of the batter board. The offset distance of 15 ft can be measured and marked at the top of the batter board over the pipe ₵ and a distance of 9 ft measured down to establish the invert elevation. This even foot measurement from the top of the batter board to the invert is known as the *grade rod distance*. A value can be picked for the grade rod so that it is the same value at each station. In this example, 9 ft appears to be suitable for each station, as it is larger than the largest

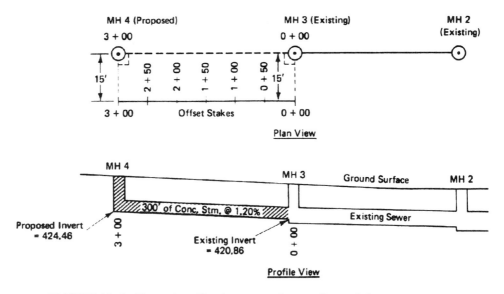

FIGURE 13-4 Plan and profile of a proposed sewer (foot units).

Table 13-1 SEWER GRADE SHEET: FOOT UNITS*

Station		Invert Elev.	Stake Elev.	Cut	Cut
MH 3	0 + 00	420.86	429.27	8.41	8'4 7/8"
	0 + 50	421.46	429.90	8.44	8'5 1/4"
	1 + 00	422.06	430.41	8.35	8'4 1/4"
	1 + 50	422.66	430.98	8.32	8'3 7/8"
	2 + 00	423.26	431.72	8.46	8'5 1/2"
	2 + 50	423.86	431.82	7.96	7'11 1/2"
MH 4	3 + 00	424.46	432.56	8.10	8'1 1/4"

*Refer to Table 12-3 for foot-inch conversion.

cut. The arithmetic shown for station 1 + 50 is performed at each station so that the batter boards can be set at 50-ft intervals. The grade rod (a 2 × 2 in. length of lumber held by a worker in the trench) has a foot piece attached to the bottom at a right angle to the rod so that the foot piece can be inserted into the pipe and allows measurement precisely from the invert.

This method of line and grade transfer has been shown first because of its simplicity; it has **not,** however, been widely used in the field in recent years. With the introduction of larger and faster trenching equipment, which can dig deeper and wider trenches, this method would only slow the work down, as it involves batter boards spanning the trench at 50-ft intervals. Many grade transfers are now accomplished by freestanding offset batter boards or laser alignment devices. Using the data from the previous example, we can illustrate how the technique of freestanding batter boards is utilized (see Figure 13-6).

These batter boards (3 ft or 1 m wide) are erected at each grade stake. As in the previous example, the batter boards are set at a height that will result in a grade rod that is an even number of feet (decimeters) long. However, with this technique, the grade rod distance will be longer, as the top of the batter board should be at a comfortable eye height for the inspector. The works inspector usually checks the work while standing at the lower

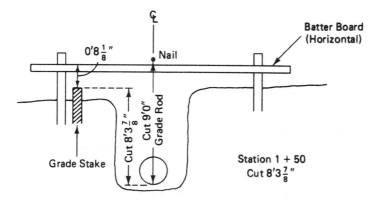

FIGURE 13-5 Use of cross-trench batter boards.

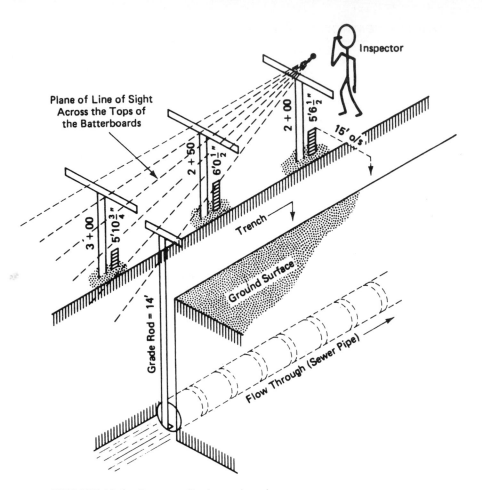

FIGURE 13-6 Free-standing batter boards.

chainage stakes and sighting forward to the higher chainage stakes. The line of sight over the batter boards is a straight line parallel to the invert profile, and in this example (see Figure 13-6), the line of sight over the batter boards is rising at 1.20 percent.

As the inspector sights over the batter boards, he or she can include in the field of view the top of the grade rod, which is being held on the most recently installed pipe length. The top of the grade rod has a horizontal board attached to it in a similar fashion to the batter boards. The inspector can visually determine whether the line over the batter boards and the line over the grade rod are in the same plane. If an adjustment up or down is required, the worker in the trench makes the necessary adjustment and has the work rechecked. Grades can be checked to the closest 1/4 in. (6 mm) in this manner. The preceding example is now worked out using a grade rod of 14 ft (see Table 13-2).

The grade rod of 14 ft requires an eye height of 5 ft 7 1/8 in. at 0 + 00; if this is considered too high, a grade rod of 13 ft can be used, which results in an eye height of

Table 13-2 SEWER GRADE SHEET—WITH BATTER BOARDS

Station		Invert Elev.	Stake Elev.	Cut	Stake to Batter Board	Stake to Batter Board
MH 3	0 + 00	420.86	429.27	8.41	5.59	5′7 1/8″
	0 + 50	421.46	429.90	8.44	5.56	5′7 3/4″
	1 + 00	422.06	430.41	8.35	5.65	5′7 3/4″
	1 + 50	422.66	430.98	8.32	5.68	5′8 1/8″
	2 + 00	423.26	431.72	8.46	5.54	5′6 1/2″
	2 + 50	423.86	431.82	7.96	6.04	6′ 0 1/2″
MH 4	3 + 00	424.46	432.56	8.10	5.90	5′10 3/4″

4 ft 7 1/8 in. at the first batter board. The grade rod height is chosen to suit the needs of the inspector.

In some cases, an additional station is put in before 0 + 00 (i.e., 0 − 50). The grade stake and batter board refer to the theoretical pipe ℄ and invert profile produced back through the first manhole. This batter board will, of course, line up with all the others and will be useful in checking the grade of the first few pipe lengths placed. Pipes are not installed unless a minimum of three batter boards (also known as sight rails) can be viewed simultaneously.

It should also be noted that many agencies use 25-ft (10-m) stations rather than the 50-ft (20-m) stations used in this example. The smaller intervals allow for much better grade control.

One distinct advantage to the use of batter boards in construction work is that an immediate check is available on all the survey work involved in the layout. The line of sight over the tops of the batter boards (which is actually a vertical offset line) must be a straight line. If, upon completion of the batter boards, all the boards do not line up precisely, it is obvious that a mistake has been made. The surveyor will check the work by first verifying all grade computations and by then releveling the tops of the grade stakes. Once the boards are in alignment, the surveyor can move on to other projects.

When the layout is performed in foot units, the basic station interval is 50 ft. The dimensions are recorded and calculated to the closest one-hundredth (0.01) of a foot. Although all survey measurements are in feet and decimals of a foot, for the contractor's purposes, the final cuts and fills are often expressed in feet and inches. The decimal-inch relationships are soon committed to memory by surveyors working in the construction field (see Table 12-3). Cuts and fills are usually expressed to the closest 1/8 in. for concrete, steel, and pipelines and to the closest 1/4 in. for highway granular surfaces and ditchlines.

Figure 13-7 includes a sketched plan and profile, design slope and inverts, and assumed elevations for the tops of the grade stakes. Also shown are the cuts and stake–to–batter board distances, based on a 5.0-m grade rod. All values are in metric (SI) units. Figures 13-8 and 13-9 show the installation of steel and concrete sewer pipes.

13-3-1 Laser Alignment

Laser devices are widely used in most forms of construction work. Lasers are normally used in a fixed direction and slope mode or in a revolving horizontal pattern. One such

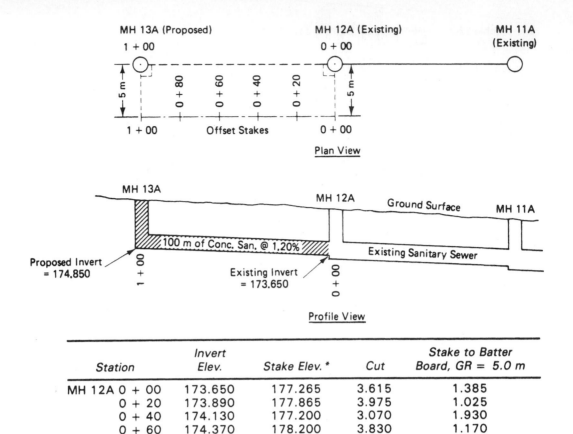

Station	Invert Elev.	Stake Elev.*	Cut	Stake to Batter Board, GR = 5.0 m
MH 12A 0 + 00	173.650	177.265	3.615	1.385
0 + 20	173.890	177.865	3.975	1.025
0 + 40	174.130	177.200	3.070	1.930
0 + 60	174.370	178.200	3.830	1.170
0 + 80	174.610	178.005	3.395	1.605
MH 13A 1 + 00	174.850	178.500	3.650	1.350

*Stake elevations and computations are normally carried out to the closest 5 mm.

FIGURE 13-7 Sewer construction example using metric units. An existing sanitary sewer is being extended from MH 12A to MH 13A. Five-meter offset (o/s) stakes were surveyed with the resultant stake elevations shown in the Stake Elev. Column.

device (Figure 13-10) can be mounted in a sewer manhole, aligned for direction and slope, and used with a target for the laying of sewer pipe. Since the laser beam can be deflected by dust or high humidity, care must be taken to overcome these factors.

Lasers used in sewer trenches can be accompanied by blowers that remove the dusty or humid air. Additionally the laser can be used above grade with a signal-sensing target rod. Working above ground not only eliminates the humidity factor, but also allows for more accurate and quicker horizontal alignment. These devices allow for setting slope within the limits of −10° to 30°. Some devices have automatic shutoff capabilities when the device is disturbed from its desired setting.

FIGURE 13-8   Corrugated steel sewer pipe, showing both tangent and curved sections. Only two batter boards are visible in this view, along with the grade rod leaning against the side of the trench. (Courtesy of the Corrugated Steel Pipe Institute)

■ **EXAMPLE 13-1**   *Sewer Grade Sheet*

Figure 13-11 is a reproduction of a plan and profile sheet from a book of contract documents, showing plan and profile data for a new storm sewer that terminates in a cross culvert at MH 44. The sewer runs up from the culvert @ 418 + 50 through MHs 42, 40, and 39.

As the sewer proceeds downstream toward the culvert outlet, the pipes must be of increasingly larger diameter to accommodate the cumulative flow being collected by each additional leg of the sewer.

Figures 13-11 and 13-12 show that the sewer flowline drops as it passes through each manhole; that is, the west invert in each case is at a higher elevation than is the east invert. This flowline drop at each manhole provides additional head, which is utilized to overcome flow losses caused by turbulence in manholes.

When the sewer pipes increase in diameter, as the sewer proceeds through a manhole, the required flowline drop is achieved by simply keeping the crowns of the incoming and outgoing pipes at the same elevation. That is, at MH (manhole) 40, the incoming pipe's diameter is 27 in., whereas the outgoing pipe's diameter is 30 in. If the crowns are kept at the same elevation, the flowline inverts drop 3 in., or 0.25 ft.

Location of Next
Upstream Manhole

FIGURE 13-9 John Deere 792 Excavator shown lowering a concrete sewer pipe into position on the prepoured concrete bedding, which was specified to alleviate unstable ground conditions. (Courtesy of John Deere Ltd., Grimsby, Ontario)

In order to compute the sewer grade sheets, the surveyor can summarize pertinent plan and profile data from the contract document, as in Figure 13-11, onto a layout sketch, as shown in Figure 13-12. In this example, it is assumed that three legs of the sewer are being constructed: MH 44 (culvert) to MH 42, MH 42 to MH 40, and MH 40 to MH 39.

The field surveyor first lays out the proposed sewer line manholes (42, 40, and 39). By setting up at each manhole stake and turning off 90° and then measuring out the appropriate offset distance, the manholes are located on offset. The offset sewer line can then be staked out at 50-ft stations, from one manhole to the next. The elevations of the tops of the offset stakes are then surveyed with a rod and level; the surveyor will, if possible, check into a second benchmark to ensure the accuracy of the work. In this example, the elevations of the tops of the stakes are assumed and are shown in Table 13-3.

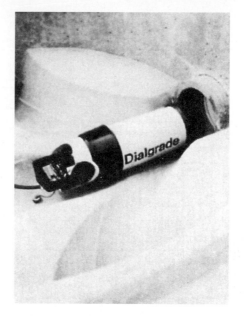

FIGURE 13-10 Pipeline laser, mounted in storm-pipe manhole. (Courtesy of Spectra Physics, Inc., Dayton, Ohio)

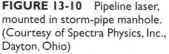

The surveyor next calculates the pipe invert elevation at each station that has been staked out. 0 + 00 is taken to be the lower manhole station, with the chainage proceeding to the upper manhole of that leg. For the second leg, 0 + 00 is taken to be the station of the lower manhole, and once again the chainage proceeds upstream to the next manhole. This procedure is repeated for the length of the sewer. Sewers are always constructed working upstream from the outlet (culvert, in this case) so that the trench can be drained during all phases of construction.

Table 13-3 shows the computed invert grades, the assumed stake elevations, and the resultant cut values. Using the techniques of freestanding batter boards as depicted in Figure 13-6, a grade rod is selected for each leg of the sewer that will give the works inspector a comfortable eye height—12 ft for the first two legs and 13 ft for the third leg. The stake–to–batter board dimension is computed for each station and then converted to feet and inches for use by the contractor.

13-4   Catch-Basin Construction Layout

Catch basins are constructed along with the storm sewer or at a later date, just prior to curb construction. Usually the catch basin (CB) is located by two grade stakes, one on each side of the CB. The two stakes are on curb line and are usually 5 ft (2 m) from the center of the catch basin. The cut or fill grade is referenced to the CB grate elevation at the curb face. The ℄ pavement elevation is calculated, and from it, the crown height is subtracted to arrive at the top of grate elevation (see Figures 13-13 and 13-14).

At low points, particularly at vertical curve low points, it is usual practice for the surveyor to arbitrarily lower the CB grate elevation to ensure that ponding does not occur on either side of the completed catch basin. It is noted in Chapter 10 that the longitudinal

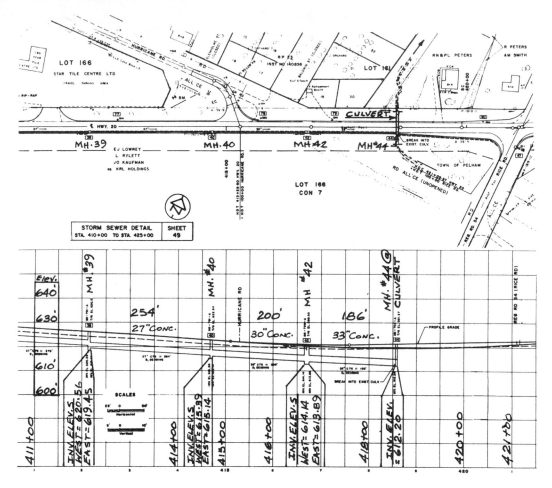

FIGURE 13-11   Plan and profile of Highway 20 (adapted).

slope at vertical curve low points is virtually flat for a significant distance. The CB grate elevation can be arbitrarily lowered as much as 1 in. (25 mm) to ensure that the gutter drainage goes directly into the catch basin without ponding. The catch basin, which can be of concrete poured in place, but is more often prefabricated and delivered to the job site, is set below finished grade until the curbs are constructed. At the time of curb construction, the finished grade for the grate is achieved by one or more courses of brick or concrete shim collars, laid on top of the concrete walls.

13-5   Tunnel Construction

Tunnels are used in road, sewer, and pipeline construction when the cost of working at or near the ground surface becomes prohibitive. For example, sewers are tunneled when they must be at a depth that would make open cut too expensive (or operationally unfeasible),

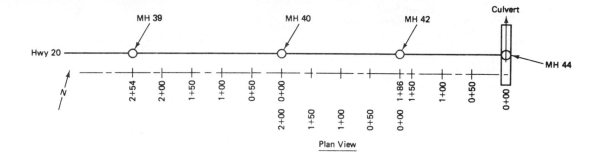

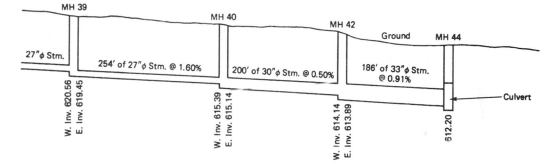

FIGURE 13-12 Layout sketch for sewer construction. Adapted from plan and profile of Highway 20 (slope percentages computed from given inverts and distances).

Table 13-3 GRADE SHEETS FOR SEWER CONSTRUCTION (SEE FIGURES 13-11 AND 13-12)

Station		Pipe Elev.	Stake Elev. (assumed)	Cut	Stake to BB (ft)	Stake to BB (ft and in.)	
MH 44	0 + 00	612.20	618.71	6.51	5.49	5'5 7/8"	
	0 + 50	612.65	618.98	6.33	5.67	5'8"	GRADE
	1 + 00	613.11	619.40	6.29	5.71	5'8 1/2"	ROD
	1 + 50	613.56	619.87	6.31	5.69	5'8 1/4"	= 12 ft
MH 42	1 + 86	613.89	620.33	6.44	5.55	5'6 5/8"	
MH 42	0 + 00	614.14	620.33	6.19	5.81	5'9 3/4"	
	0 + 50	614.39	620.60	6.21	5.79	5'9 1/2"	GRADE
	1 + 00	614.64	620.91	6.27	5.73	5'8 3/4"	ROD
	1 + 50	614.89	621.63	6.74	5.26	5'3 1/8"	= 12 ft
MH 40	2 + 00	615.14	622.60	7.46	4.54	4'6 1/2"	
MH 40	0 + 00	615.39	622.60	7.21	5.79	5'9 1/2"	
	0 + 50	616.19	623.81	7.62	5.38	5'4 5/8"	GRADE
	1 + 00	616.99	624.57	7.58	5.42	5'5"	ROD
	1 + 50	617.79	625.79	8.00	5.00	5'0"	= 13 ft
	2 + 00	618.59	626.93	8.34	4.66	4'7 7/8"	
MH 39	2 + 54	619.45	627.55	8.10	4.90	4'10 7/8"	

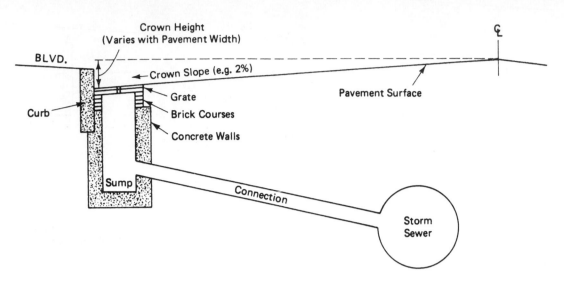

FIGURE 13-13 Typical catch basin (with sump), section view.

or sewers may be tunneled to avoid disruption of services on the surface such as would occur if an open cut were put through a busy expressway. Roads and railroads are tunneled through large hills and mountains in order to maintain optimal grade lines.

Control surveys for tunnel layouts are performed on the surface, joining the terminal points of the tunnel. These control surveys use triangulation, precise traverse survey methods, or Global Positioning System (GPS) techniques and allow for the computation of coordinates for all key points (see Figure 13-15).

In the case of highway (railway) tunnels, the ℄ can be run directly into the tunnel and is usually located on the roof either at ℄ or at a convenient offset (see Figure 13-16). If the tunnel is long, intermediate shafts could be sunk to provide access for materials, ventilation, and alignment verification. Conventional engineering theodolites are illustrated in Figure 13-16; for cramped quarters, a suspension theodolite (Figure 13-17) can be used. Levels can also be run directly into the tunnel, and temporary benchmarks are established in the floor or roof of the tunnel.

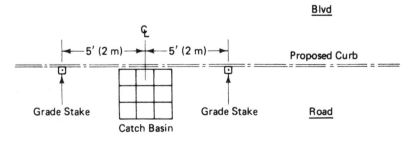

FIGURE 13-14 Catch basin layout, plan view.

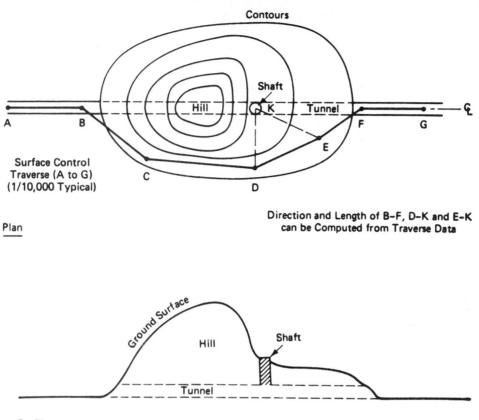

Contours

Shaft

Hill

Tunnel

A

B

Surface Control
Traverse (A to G)
(1/10,000 Typical)

C

D

E

F

G

Direction and Length of B-F, D-K and E-K
can be Computed from Traverse Data

Plan

Ground Surface

Hill

Shaft

Tunnel

Profile

FIGURE 13-15   Plan and profile of tunnel location.

In the case of long tunnels, work can proceed from both ends, meeting somewhere near the middle. Constant vigilance with respect to errors and mistakes is of prime importance.

In the case of a deep sewer tunnel, mining surveying techniques must be employed to establish line and grade (Figure 13-18). The surface ₵ projection *AB* is carefully established on beams overhanging the shaft opening. Plumb lines (piano wire) are hung down the shaft, and the tunnel ₵ is developed by overaligning the transit or theodolite in the tunnel. A great deal of care is required in overaligning, as this very short backsight will produce relatively long distances, thus magnifying any sighting errors.

The plumb lines usually employ heavy plumb bobs (capable of taking additional weights if required). Sometimes the plumb bobs are submerged in heavy oil in order to dampen the swing oscillations. If the plumb-line swing oscillations cannot be eliminated, the oscillations must be measured and then averaged.

Some tunnels are pressurized in order to control groundwater seepage; the air locks associated with pressure systems will cut down considerably on the clear dimensions in the shaft, making the plumbed-line transfer even more difficult.

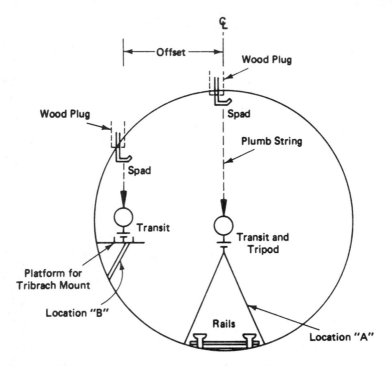

Tunnel ₵ is usually located in the roof (location "A") and then can be offset (location "B") to provide space for excavation and materials movement. Line and grade can be provided by a single laser beam which has been oriented for both alignment and slope.

FIGURE 13-16 Establishing "line" in a tunnel.

Transferring ₵ from surface to underground locations by use of plumb lines is an effective—although outdated—technique. Modern survey practice favors the use of precise optical plummets (see Figure 13-19) to accomplish the line transfer. These plummets are designed for use in zenith or nadir directions, or—as illustrated in Figure 13-19—in both zenith and nadir directions. The accuracy of this technique can be as high as 1 or 2 mm in 100 m.

Gyrotheodolites have also been used successfully for underground alignment control. Several surveying equipment manufacturers produce gyro attachments for use with repeating theodolites. Figure 13-20 shows a gyro attachment mounted on a 20″ theodolite.

The gyro attachment (also called a gyrocompass) consists of a wire-hung pendulum supporting a high-speed, perfectly balanced gyro motor capable of attaining the required speed of 12,000 rpm in 1 min. Basically the rotation of the earth affects the orientation of the spin axis of the gyroscope such that the gyroscope spin axis orients itself toward the pole in an oscillating motion that is observed and measured in a plane perpendicular to the pendulum. This north-seeking oscillation, which is known as *precession,* is measured on

FIGURE 13-17 Breithaupt mining suspension theodolite; can be used with a tripod or can be suspended from a steel punch in the ceilings of cramped galleries or drifts. (Courtesy of Keuffel & Esser Co.)

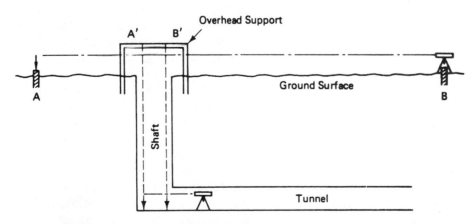

FIGURE 13-18 Transfer of surface alignment to the tunnel.

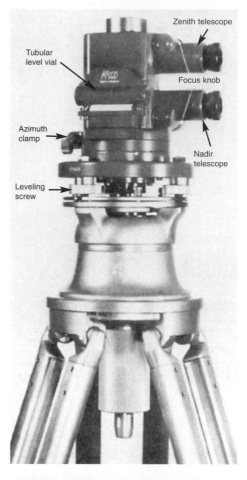

FIGURE 13-19 Kern OL precise optical plummet. SE in 100 m for a single measurement (zenith or nadir) = ±1 mm (using coincidence level). Used in highrise construction, towers, shafts, and the like. (Courtesy of Kern Instruments-Leica, Toronto, Ontario)

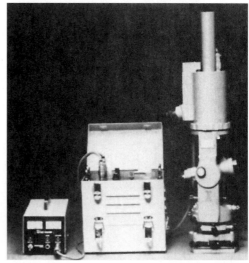

FIGURE 13-20 Gyro attachment, mounted on a 20-second theodolite. Shown with battery charger and control unit. (Courtesy of Sokkisha Canada, Markham, Ontario)

the horizontal circle of the theodolite; extreme left (west) and right (east) readings are averaged to arrive at the meridian direction.

The theodolite with gyro attachment is set up and oriented approximately to north, using a compass; the gyro motor is engaged until the proper angular velocity has been reached (about 12,000 rpm for the instrument shown in Figure 13-20), and then the gyroscope is released. The precession oscillations are observed through the gyro-attachment viewing eyepiece, and the theodolite is adjusted closer to the northerly direction if necessary. When the theodolite is pointed to within a few minutes of north, the extreme precession positions (west and east) are noted in the viewing eyepiece and then recorded on the horizontal circle; as noted earlier, the position of the meridian is the value of the averaged precession readings. This technique, which takes about a half hour to complete, is accurate to within 20″ of azimuth. These instruments can be used in most tunneling applications, where tolerances of 25 mm are common for both line and grade.

Lasers have been used for a wide variety of tunneling projects. Figure 13-21 shows a large-diameter boring machine, which is kept aligned (both line and grade) by keeping the

FIGURE 13-21 Laser-guided tunnel boring machine. (Courtesy of the Robbins Company, Kent, Washington)

laser beam centered in the two targets mounted near the front and rear of the tunnel boring machine.

A more recent addition to the high-technology scene is the automated profile scanner shown in Figure 13-22. This system uses a Wild DIOR 3001 EDM, which can measure distances from 0.3 m to 50 m (without using a reflecting prism) with an accuracy of 5 to 10 mm. An attached laser is used to physically mark the feature being measured so that the operator can verify the work.

The profiler is set up at key tunnel stations so that a 360° profile of the tunnel can be measured and recorded on a cassette. The number of measurements taken as the profiler revolves through 360° can be preset in the profiler, or it can be controlled manually by the remote controller.

The data on the cassette are then transferred to a microcomputer for processing. Figure 13-23 shows the station plot along with theoretical and excavated profiles. In addition to driving the digital plotter, the system software computes the area at each station and then computes the excavated volumes by averaging two adjacent areas and multiplying by the distance between them (see Chapter 16 for these computational techniques).

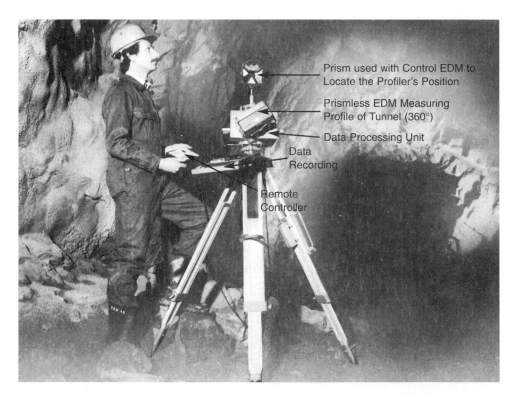

FIGURE 13-22 A.M.T. Profiler 2000 prismless EDM, used to measure tunnel profile at selected stations. (Courtesy of Amberg Measuring Technique Ltd. and Leica, Heerbrugg, Switzerland)

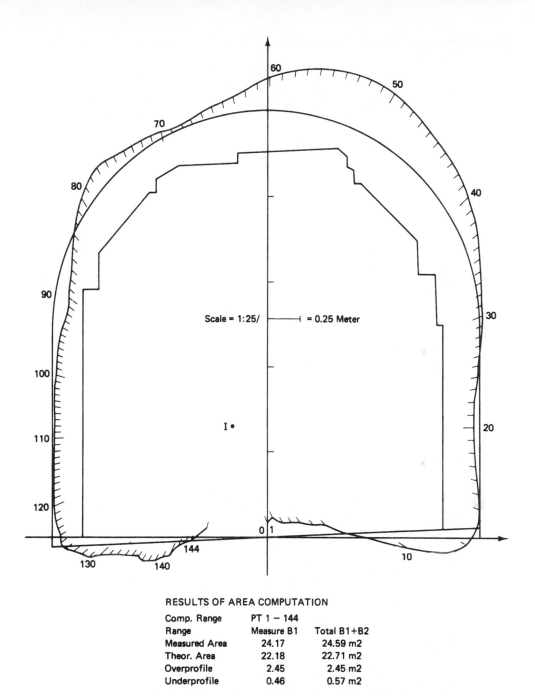

RESULTS OF AREA COMPUTATION		
Comp. Range	PT 1 – 144	
Range	Measure B1	Total B1+B2
Measured Area	24.17	24.59 m2
Theor. Area	22.18	22.71 m2
Overprofile	2.45	2.45 m2
Underprofile	0.46	0.57 m2

FIGURE 13-23 Computations and profile plot for profiler setup, where 144 prismless EDM readings were automatically taken and recorded. (Courtesy of Amberg Measuring Techniques)

Problems

13-1. A storm sewer is to be constructed from existing MH 8 (invert elevation = 360.21) @ +1.32 percent for a distance of 240 ft to proposed MH 9. The elevations of the offset grade stakes are as follows: 0 + 00 = 368.75; 0 + 50 = 368.81; 1 + 00 = 369.00; 1 + 50 = 369.77; 2 + 00 = 370.22; 2 + 40 = 371.91. Prepare a grade sheet (see Table 13.2) showing stake–to–batter board distances in ft and in.; use a 14-ft grade rod.

13-2. A sanitary sewer is to be constructed from existing manhole 4 (invert elevation = 150.810) @ +0.68 percent for a distance of 115 m to proposed MH 5. The elevations of the offset grade stakes are as follows: 0 + 00 = 152.933; 0 + 20 = 152.991; 0 + 40 = 153.626; 0 + 60 = 153.725; 0 + 80 = 153.888; 1 + 00 = 153.710; 1 + 15 = 153.600. Prepare a grade sheet (see Figure 13.7) showing stake–to–batter board distances in meters. Use a 4-m grade rod.

13-3. With reference to Figure 13.24 (plan and profile of Parkway Ave.), compute the sewer invert elevations, at 50-ft stations, from MH 9 (0 + 05, ₵) to MH 1 (3 + 05, ₵). Here, ₵ refers to roadway centerline stationing (not the sewer).

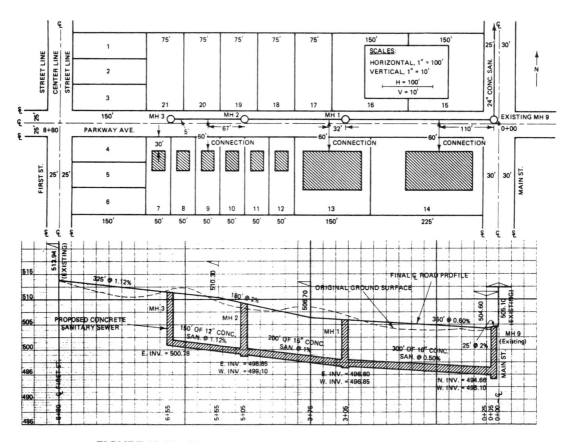

FIGURE 13-24 Plan and profile of Parkway Avenue (foot units). See also Figure 12-17.

13-4. Given the sewer grade stake elevations shown here, compute the "cut" distances at each 50-ft station for the section of sewer in Problem 13-3.

MH 9,	0 + 00	503.37		1 + 50	504.09
	0 + 50	503.32		2 + 00	504.10
	0 + 00	503.61		2 + 50	504.77
			MH 1,	3 + 00	504.83

13-5. Select a realistic grade rod, and prepare a grade sheet showing the stake–to–batter board dimensions both in feet and in feet and inches for the section of sewer in Problems 13-3 and 13-4.

13-6. With reference to Figure 13-24 (plan and profile of Parkway Ave.), for the sections of sewer from MH 1 (3 + 05, ₵) to MH 2 (5 + 05, ₵) and from MH 2 (5 + 05, ₵) to MH 3 (6 + 55, ₵), determine the following:
(a) The invert elevations of 50-ft stations.
(b) The cut distances from the top of the grade stake to invert at each 50-ft station.
(c) After selecting suitable grade rods, determine the stake–to–batter board distances at each stake.
Use the following grade stake elevations:

MH 1	0 + 00	504.83	MH 2	0 + 00	507.26
	0 + 50	505.21		0 + 50	507.43
	1 + 00	505.30		1 + 00	507.70
	1 + 50	506.17	MH 3	1 + 50	507.75
MH 2	2 + 00	507.26			

13-7. With reference to Figure 13-25 (plan and profile of Oak Ave.), compute the sewer invert elevations at 20-m stations from MH 13 (0 + 05, ₵) to MH 1 (1 + 05, ₵), and from MH 1 (1 + 05, ₵) to MH 2 (1 + 85, ₵).

13-8. Given the grade stake elevations shown below, compute the cut distances from stake to invert at each stake for both sections of sewer from Problem 13-7.

MH 13	0 + 00	186.713	MH 1	0 + 00	187.255
	0 + 20	186.720		0 + 20	187.310
	0 + 40	186.833		0 + 40	187.333
	0 + 60	186.877		0 + 60	187.340
	0 + 80	186.890	MH 2	0 + 80	187.625
MH 1	1 + 00	187.255			

13-9. Using the data in Problem 13-8, select suitable grade rods for both sewer legs, and compute the stake–to–batter board distance at each stake.

13-10. Referring to Section 13-2, Figure 13-3, and Figure 13-24, determine the minimum invert elevations for the sanitary-sewer building connections at the front-wall building lines for Lots 9, 13, and 14. (Use a minimum slope of 2 percent for sewer connection pipes.)

13-11. Referring to Section 13-2, Figure 13-3, and Figure 13-25, determine the minimum invert elevations for the sanitary-sewer building connections at the front-wall building lines for Lots 6 and 9. (Use a minimum slope of 2 percent for sewer connection pipes.)

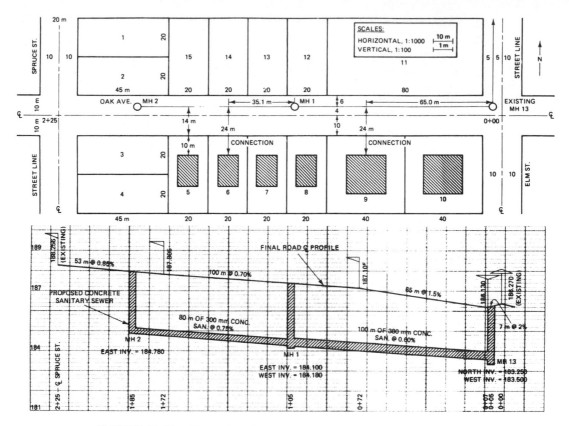

FIGURE 13-25 Plan and profile of Oak Avenue (metric units). See also Figure 12-18.

13-12. Figure 13-26 shows typical excavation equipment that can be used in pipeline and other construction projects. Write a report describing the types of construction projects in which each of the equipment can be effectively utilized. Describe why some excavation equipment is well suited for some specific roles and not at all well suited for others. Data can be obtained from the library, trade and professional journals, equipment dealers or manufacturers, and construction companies.

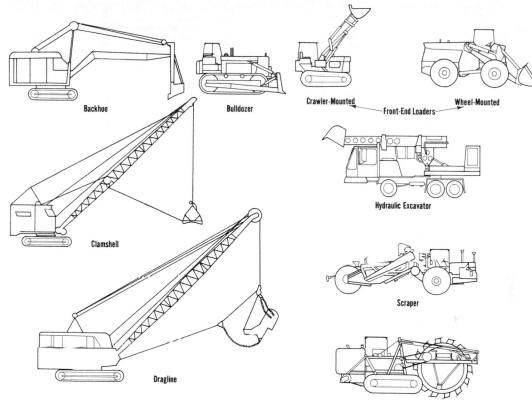

FIGURE 13-26 Typical excavation equipment. (Courtesy of the American Concrete Pipe Association)

Chapter 14

Culvert and Bridge Construction Surveys

14-1 Culvert Construction

The plan location and invert grade of culverts are shown on the construction plan and profile. The intersection of the culvert ₵ and the highway ₵ will be shown on the plan and will be identified by its highway stationing (chainage). In addition, when the proposed culvert is not perpendicular to the highway ₵, the skew number or skew angle will be shown (see Figure 14-1).

The construction plan will show the culvert location ₵ chainage, skew number, and length of culvert; the construction profile will show the inverts for each end of the culvert. One grade stake will be placed on the ₵ of the culvert, offset a safe distance from each end (see Figure 14-2).

The grade stake will reference the culvert ₵ and will give the cut or fill to the top of footing for open footing culverts, to the top of slab for concrete box culverts, or to the invert of pipe for pipe culverts. If the culvert is long, intermediate grade stakes may be required. The stakes may be offset 6 ft (2 m) or longer distances if site conditions warrant.

It is customary when concrete culverts are laid out to place two offset line stakes to define the end of the culvert, in addition to placing the grade stakes at either end of the culvert. These end lines are normally parallel to the ₵ of construction or perpendicular to the culvert ₵. See Figure 14-3 for types of culverts.

14-2 Culvert Reconstruction

Intensive urban development creates an increase in impervious surfaces—for example, roads, walks, drives, parking lots, and roofs. Prior to development, rainfall would have the opportunity to seep into the ground and eventually the water table, until the ground became saturated. After saturation, the rainfall would run off to the nearest watercourse, stream,

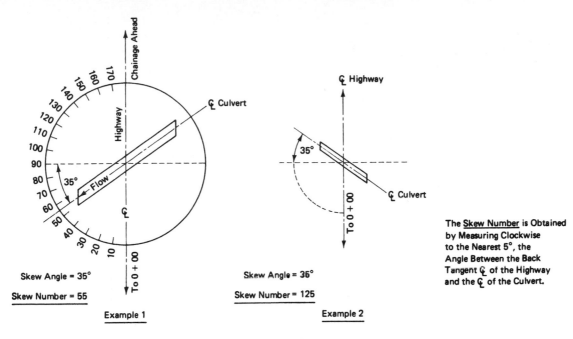

FIGURE 14-1 Culvert skew numbers, showing the relationship between the skew angle and the skew number.

river, or lake. The increase in impervious surfaces associated with urban development can result in a significant increase in surface runoff and thus cause flooding where the culverts, and sometimes bridges, are now no longer capable of handling the increased flow. Some municipalities demand that developers provide detention and storage facilities (e.g., ponds and oversized pipes) to keep increases in site runoff to a minimum.

Figure 14-4 shows a concrete box culvert being added to an existing box culvert, resulting in what is called a twin-cell culvert. The proposed centerline grade for the new culvert will be the same as for the existing culvert. The outside edge of the concrete slab was laid out on close offset (o/s), with the construction grade information (cuts to floor slab elevation) being referenced also from the o/s layout stakes. In addition, one edge (inside, in this case) of the wing wall footing is also laid out on close o/s, with the alignment and grade information referenced to the same o/s stakes. Wing walls are used to retain earth embankments adjacent to the ends of the culvert.

Figure 14-5 shows a situation where road improvements require the replacement of a cross culvert. The new culvert is skewed at #60 to better fit the natural stream orientation, the new culvert is longer (140 ft) to accommodate the new road width, and the new culvert is larger to provide increased capacity for present and future developments. Figure 14-5 shows plan and cross section of a detour that will permit the culvert to be constructed without closing the highway. The detour centerline curve data are described in detail in Chapter 10.

The suggested staging for the construction is shown in 18 steps. Essentially the traffic is kept to the east side of the highway while the west half of the old culvert is removed and the west half of the new culvert is constructed. Once the concrete in the west

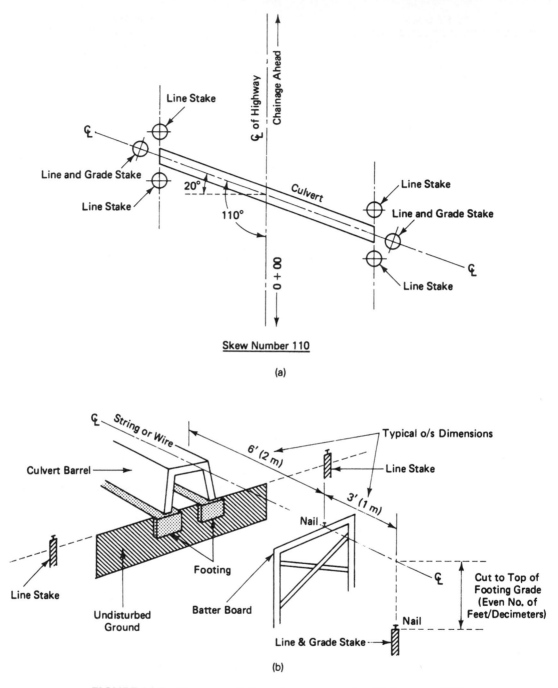

FIGURE 14-2 Line and grade for culvert construction. (a) Plan view. (b) Perspective view. (Courtesy of the Ministry of Transportation, Ontario)

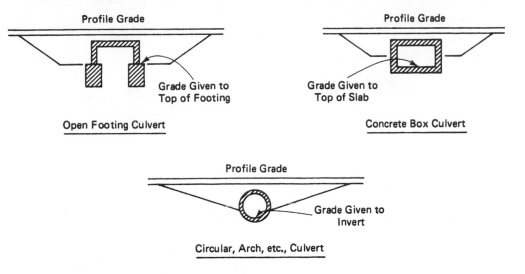

Profile Grade

Grade Given to
Top of Footing

Open Footing Culvert

Profile Grade

Grade Given to
Top of Slab

Concrete Box Culvert

Profile Grade

Grade Given to
Invert

Circular, Arch, etc., Culvert

FIGURE 14-3 Types of culverts.

half of the new culvert has gained sufficient strength (usually about 30 days), the detour can be constructed as shown in Figure 14-5. With the traffic now diverted to the detour, the east half of the old culvert is removed, and the east half of the new culvert is constructed. The improved road cross section can now be built over the completed culvert, and the detour and other temporary features can be removed.

14-3   Bridge Construction: General

Accuracy requirements for structure construction are generally of the highest order for survey layouts. Included in this topic are bridges, elevated expressways, and so on. Accuracy requirements for structure layouts range from 1/3000 for residential housing to 1/5000 for bridges and 1/10,000 for long-span bridges. The accuracy requirements depend on the complexity of the construction, the type of construction materials specified, and the ultimate design use of the facility. The accuracy required for any specific project could be specified in the contract documents, or it could be left to the common sense and experience of the surveyor.

Preliminary surveys for bridges include bore holes drilled for foundation investigation. The bridge designers will indicate on a highway design plan the location of a series of bore holes. The surveyor will locate the bore holes in the field by measuring centerline chainages, offsets, and ground elevations.

As the bridge design progresses, the surveyor may have to go back several times to the site to establish horizontal and vertical control for additional bore holes, which may be required for final footing design. Figure 14-6 shows the plan and profile location for a series of bore holes at abutment, pier, and intermediate locations. In addition, the coordinates of each bore hole location are shown, permitting the surveyor to establish the field points by *polar ties* from coordinated monuments; the surveyor may also establish the points by the more traditional *centerline chainage and offset measurements,* as previously noted, or by GPS techniques.

Existing Culvert

Telephone Cables
Temporarily Supported

Forms and Reinforcing Steel
for Outside Culvert Wall

Concrete Slab

Survey Layout Line
Outside of
Culvert Wall

Survey Layout Line
Inside Edge of
Retaining Wall Footing

FIGURE 14-4 Concrete culvert construction addition, showing floor slab, wing wall footing, and culvert walls—with reinforcing steel and forms.

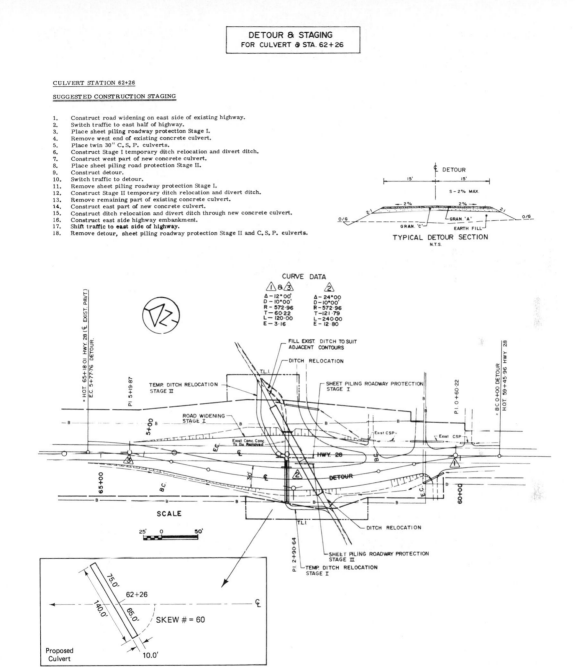

DETOUR & STAGING
FOR CULVERT @ STA. 62+26

CULVERT STATION 62+26

SUGGESTED CONSTRUCTION STAGING

1. Construct road widening on east side of existing highway.
2. Switch traffic to east half of highway.
3. Place sheet piling roadway protection Stage I.
4. Remove west end of existing concrete culvert.
5. Place twin 30" C. S. P. culverts.
6. Construct Stage I temporary ditch relocation and divert ditch.
7. Construct west part of new concrete culvert.
8. Place sheet piling road protection Stage II.
9. Construct detour.
10. Switch traffic to detour.
11. Remove sheet piling roadway protection Stage I.
12. Construct Stage II temporary ditch relocation and divert ditch.
13. Remove remaining part of existing concrete culvert.
14. Construct east part of new concrete culvert.
15. Construct ditch relocation and divert ditch through new concrete culvert.
16. Construct east side highway embankment.
17. Shift traffic to east side of highway.
18. Remove detour, sheet piling roadway protection Stage II and C. S. P. culverts.

TYPICAL DETOUR SECTION
N.T.S.

CURVE DATA

⚠ 1 & 3	⚠ 2
Δ – 12°00'	Δ – 24°00
D – 10°00'	D – 10°00'
R – 572·96	R – 572·96
T – 60·22	T – 121·79
L – 120·00	L – 240·00
E – 3·16	E – 12·80

SCALE

25'   0   50'

FIGURE 14-5 Detour and construction staging for culvert replacement and realignment.

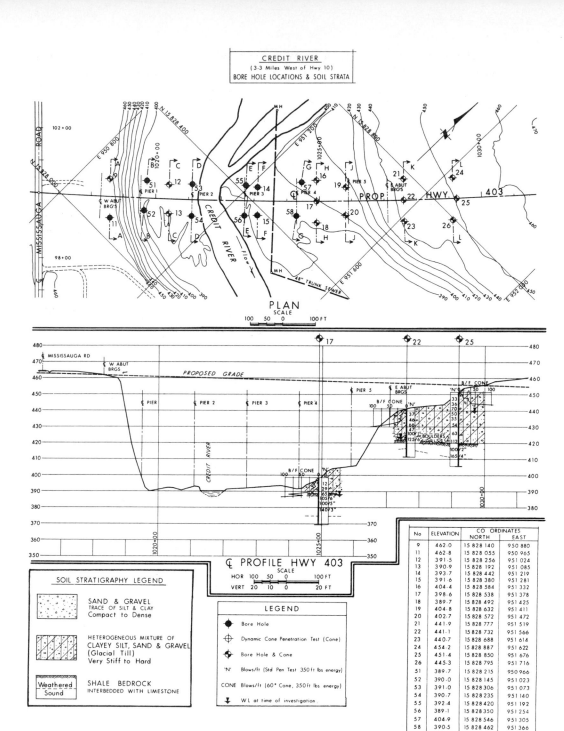

FIGURE 14-6 Bore hole locations.

The establishment of permanent, well-referenced construction control, as outlined in Chapters 8 and 9, will ensure that all aspects of the project—preliminary tie-ins and cross sections, bore holes, staged construction layouts, and final measurements—are all referenced to the same control net.

14-4 Contract Drawings

Contract drawings for bridge construction typically include general arrangement, foundation layout, abutment and pier details, beam details, deck details, and reinforcing steel schedules and could also include details on railings, wing walls, and the like. Whereas the contractor must utilize all drawings in the construction process, the construction surveyor is concerned only with those drawings that will facilitate the construction layout. Usually the entire layout can be accomplished by using only the general arrangement drawing (Figures 14-7 and 14-8) and the foundation layout drawing (Figure 14-9). These plans are

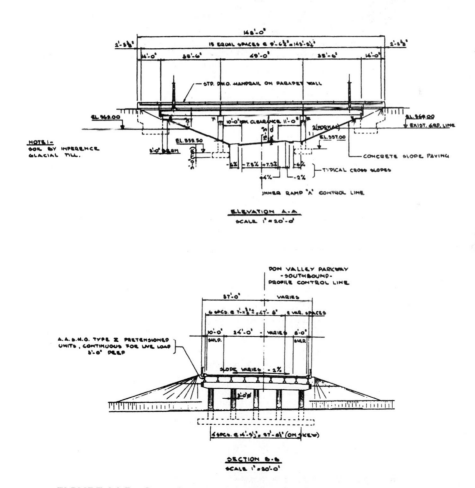

FIGURE 14-7 General arrangement plan for Bridge No. 5, Don Valley Parkway and Highway 401 East off ramp.

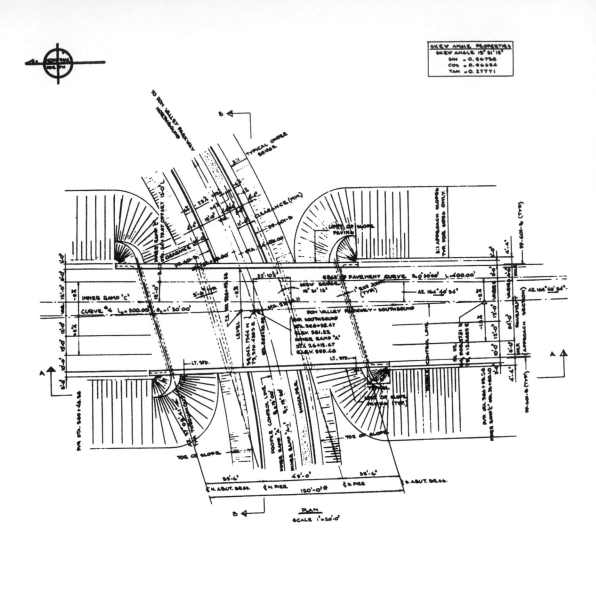

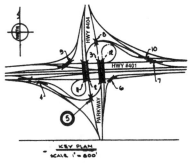

FIGURE 14-8 Key plan and general layout for Bridge No. 5, Don Valley Parkway and Highway 401 East off ramp. *See same dimension, Figure 14-9.

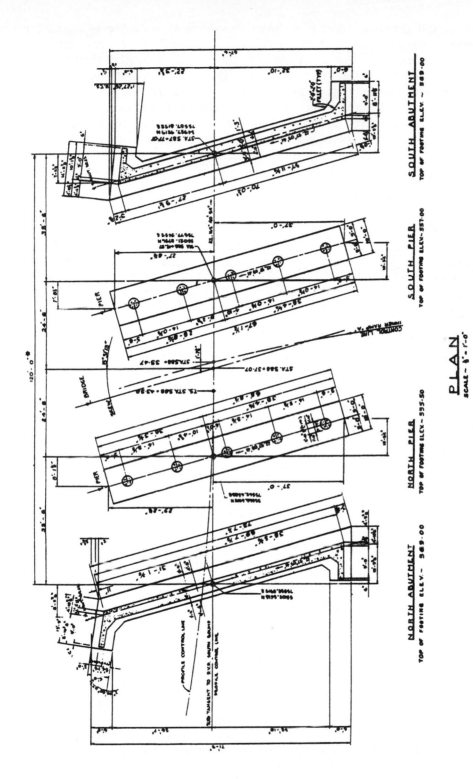

FIGURE 14-9 Foundation layout plan for bridge No. 5, Don Valley Parkway. *See same dimension, Figure 14-8.

491

analyzed to determine which of the many dimensions shown are to be utilized for construction layout.

The key dimensions are placed on foundation layout sketches (Figures 14-10 and 14-11), which will be the basis for the layout. The sketches show the location of the piers and the abutment bearing ₵, the location of each footing, and, in this case, the skew angle. Although most bridges have symmetrical foundation dimensions, the bridge in this example is asymmetrical due to the spiralled pavement requirements. This lack of symmetry does not pose any problems for the actual layout, but it does require additional work in establishing dimension check lines in the field.

14-5   Layout Computations

Chainage at ₵ of bridge	588s + 37.07	Chainage at ₵ of bridge	588 + 37.07
	+ 24.50		− 24.50
₵ north pier	588 + 61.57	₵ south pier	588 + 12.57
	+ 35.50		− 35.50
₵ north abut. brg.	588 + 97.07	₵ south abut. brg.	587 + 77.07

$$(588 + 97.07) - (587 + 77.07) = 120.00 \text{ ft Check}$$

Assume, for this example, that the offset lines are 5 ft south from the south footing faces of the north abutment and both piers, and 5 ft north from the north face of the south abutment. For this example, the offset stakes (1-in. reinforcing steel, 2 to 4 ft long) will be placed opposite the ends of the footings and a further 25 ft away on each offset line. The stakes can be placed by using right-angle ties from ₵ or by locating the offset line parallel to the footings.

In the latter case, it will be necessary to compute the ₵ stations for each offset line. With reference to Figure 14-10, it can be seen that the distance from abutment ₵ of bearings to face of footing is 4 ft 8 in. (4.67 ft). Along the N–S bridge ₵, this dimension becomes 4.84 ft (4.67 × secant 15°31′13″). Similarly the dimension from pier ₵ to face of pier footing is 5.00 ft; along the N–S bridge ₵, this dimension becomes 5.19 ft (5.00 × secant 15°31′13″). Along the N–S bridge ₵, the 5-ft offset distance also becomes 5.19 ft.

Accordingly, the stations for the offset lines at the N–S bridge ₵ become (refer to Figure 14-11)

$$\text{North abutment offset} = 588 + 97.07 - 10.03 = 588 + 87.04$$
$$\text{North pier offset} = 588 + 61.57 - 10.38 = 588 + 51.19$$
$$\text{South pier offset} = 588 + 12.57 - 10.38 = 588 + 02.19$$
$$\text{South abutment offset} = 587 + 77.07 + 10.03 = 587 + 87.10$$

14-6   Offset Distance Computations

The stations at which the offset lines intersect the bridge ₵ are each occupied with a transit (theodolite). The skew angle (15°31′13″) is turned and doubled (minimum), and the appropriate offset distances are measured out each side of the bridge ₵.

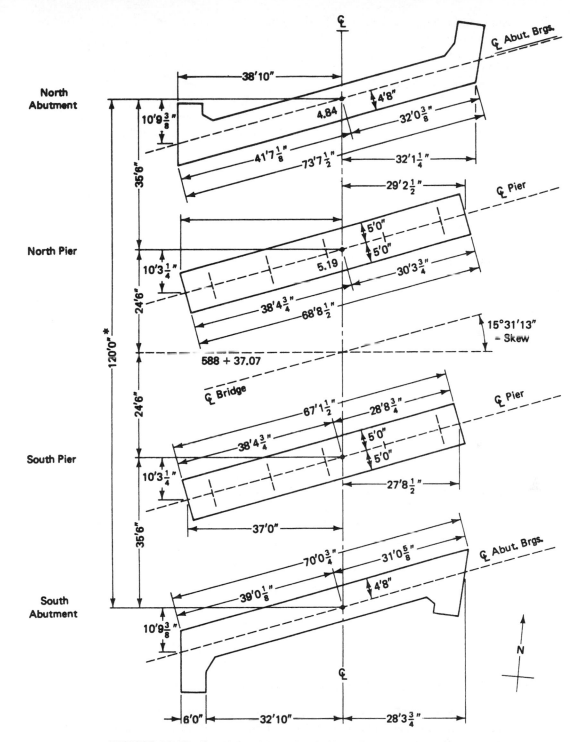

FIGURE 14-10 Foundation layout sketch. *See same dimension on Figures 14-8 and 14-9.

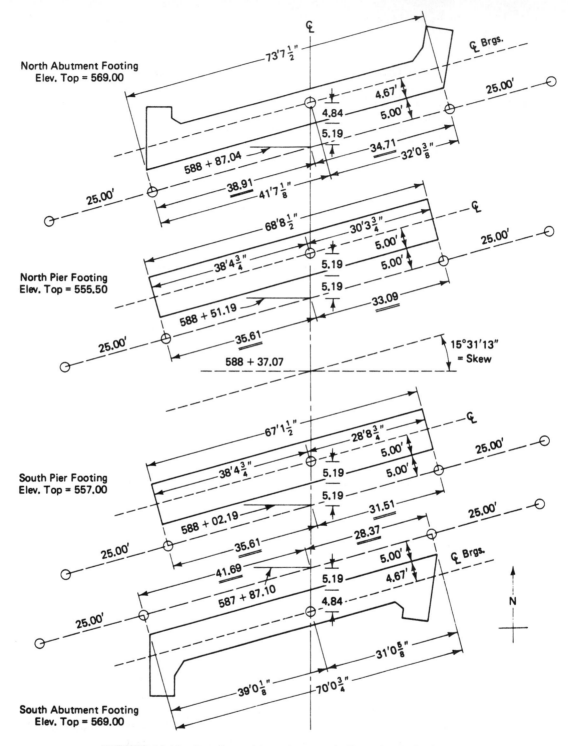

FIGURE 14-11 Foundation layout sketch and offsets sketch. Circles shown are ₵ and o/s layout bars.

For the north abutment offset line, the offset distance left is

$$41.59' \ (41'7 \ 1/8'') - (10.03 \times \sin 15°31'13'') = 38.91'$$

The offset distance right is 32.03 + 2.68 = 34.71 ft.

$$38.91 + 34.71 = 73.62' = 73'7 \ 1/2'' \quad \text{Check (see Figure 14-10)}$$

For the north pier offset line, the offset distance left is

$$38.39 \ (38'4 \ 3/4'') - (10.38 \sin 15°31'13'') = 35.61'$$

The offset distance right is 30.31 + 2.78 = 33.09 ft.

$$35.61 + 33.09 = 68.70 = 68'8 \ 1/2'' \quad \text{Check (see Figure 14-10)}$$

For the south pier offset line, the offset distance left is

$$38.39 - (10.38 \sin 15°31'13'') = 35.61'$$

The offset distance right is 28.73 (28'8 3/4'') + 2.78 = 31.51 ft.

$$35.61 + 31.51 = 67.12' = 67'1 \ 1/2'' \quad \text{Check (see Figure 14-10)}$$

For the south abutment offset line, the offset distance left is

$$39.01 \ (39'0 \ 1/8'') + (10.03 \times \sin 15°31'13'') = 41.69'$$

The offset distance right is 31.05 − 2.68 = 28.37 ft.

$$41.69 + 28.37 = 70.06' = 70'0 \ 3/4'' \quad \text{Check (see Figure 14-10)}$$

All these distances are shown on Figure 14-11 double underlined. Once these offsets and the stakes placed 25 ft farther on each offset line have been accurately located, the next step is to verify the offsets by some independent means.

As an alternative to the direct layout techniques described here, key layout points may be coordinated on the computer with all coordinates then uploaded into Total Stations and/or GPS receivers. The layout can then proceed using the polar layout and positioning techniques described in Chapters 5 and 9.

14-7 Dimension Verification

For this type of analysis, the technique described in Section 6-10 (omitted measurements) is especially useful. Bearings are **assumed** that will provide the simplest solution. See Figure 14-12.

These values are shown in Figure 14-12. The same techniques can be used to calculate any other series of diagonals if sight lines are not available for the diagonals shown.

In addition to diagonal check measurements, or even in place of them, check measurements can consist of right-angle ties from ₵, as shown in Figure 14-10. Additional calculations are required for the chainage and distance to the outside stakes.

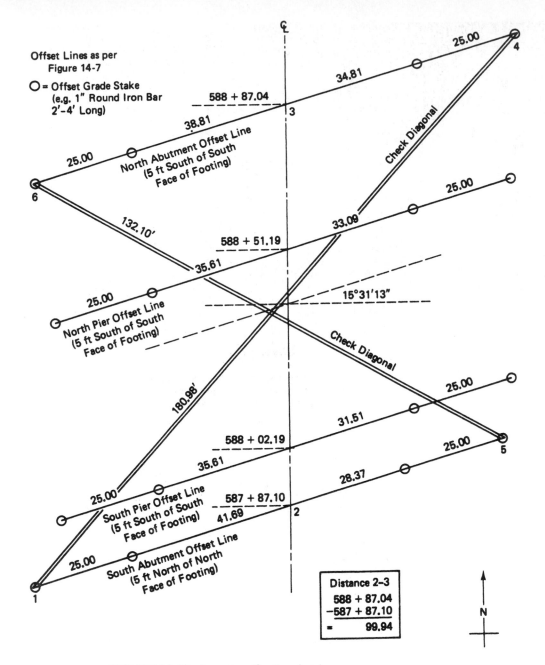

FIGURE 14-12 Layout verification sketch.

COMPUTATION FOR CHECK DIAGONAL 1–4

Line	Bearing	Distance	Lat.	Dep.
1–2	N 74°28′47″ E (90° skew angle chosen for convenience)	66.69	+17.84	+64.26
2–3	Due north	99.94	+99.94	+ 0.0
3–4	N 74°28′47″ E	59.81	+16.00	+57.63
1–4			+133.78	+121.89

Distance 1–4 = $\sqrt{133.78^2 + 121.89^2}$ = 180.98 ft

Allowable error = ±0.03 ft

COMPUTATION FOR CHECK DIAGONAL 5–6

Line	Bearing	Distance	Lat.	Dep.
5–2	S 74°28′47″ W	53.37	−14.28	−51.42
2–3	Due north	99.94	+99.94	− 0.0
3–6	S 74°28′47″ W	63.81	−17.07	−61.48
5–6			+68.59	−112.90

Distance 5–6 = $\sqrt{68.59^2 + 112.90^2}$ = 132.10 ft

Allowable error = ±0.02 ft

As in all construction layout work, great care must be exercised when the grade stakes are placed. The grade stakes (iron bars) should be driven flush with the surface (or deeper) to prevent deflection if heavy equipment were to cross over them. The grade stakes are protected by placing substantial guard stakes adjacent to them. The surveyor must bear in mind that, for many reasons, it is more difficult to place a marker in a specific location than it is to locate a set marker by field measurements. For example, it is difficult to drive a 3- or 4-ft steel bar into the ground while keeping it in its proper location with respect to line and distance. It is often the case that, as the top of the bar nears the ground surface, it becomes evident that the top is either off line or off distance. The solution to this problem is either to remove the bar and replace it or to wedge it into its proper location by driving a piece of rock into the ground adjacent to the bar. The latter solution will often prove unsuccessful, as the deflected bar can in time push the rock aside and return to near its original position. These problems can be avoided by taking great care during the original placement; continuous line and distance checks are advised.

In this example, an offset line was established 5 ft from the face of the footings. As foundation excavations are usually precisely excavated ("neat"), the value of 5 ft is quite realistic; however, the surveyor, in consultation with the contractor, must choose an offset that is optimal. As in all construction work, the shorter the offset distance is, the easier it is to accurately transfer line and grade to the structure.

14-8   Vertical Control

The 5-ft offset line in this example can be used not only to place the footings, but also to place the abutment walls and pier columns as the work proceeds above ground; the form work can be easily checked as the offset lines will be clear of all construction activity.

The proposed top-of-footing elevations are shown on the general arrangements plan (Figure 14-7) and in Figure 14-11. The elevations of the grade stakes opposite each end of the footings are determined by differential leveling, and the resultant "cuts" are given to the contractor in the form of either a grade sheet or batter boards.

A word of caution: It is often the case that a benchmark is located quite close to the work, and probably one instrument setup is sufficient to take the backsight, grade stake sights, and the foresight back to the benchmark. When this is the case, two potential problems should be considered. One problem is that after the grade stake sights have been determined, the foresight back to the benchmark will be taken—the surveyor, knowing the value of the backsight taken previously, will be influenced in reading the foresight, as he or she will expect to get the same value. In this case, the surveyor could well exercise less care in reading the foresight, using it only as a quick check reading; blunders have been known to occur in this situation. The second potential problem involves the use of automatic (self-leveling) levels, as sooner or later all automatic levels will become inoperative due to failure of the compensating device. This device is used to keep the line of sight horizontal and often relies on wires or bearings to achieve its purpose. If a wire breaks, the compensating device will produce a line of sight that is seriously in error. If the surveyor is unaware that the level is not functioning properly, the leveling work will be unacceptable, in spite of the fact that the final foresight will agree with the backsight.

The only safe way to deal with these potential problems is to always use two benchmarks when setting out grades. Start at one BM and check into the second BM. Even if additional instrument setups are required, the extra work is a small price to pay for this accuracy check. Each structure location should have three benchmarks established prior to construction so that, if one is destroyed, the minimum of two will remain for the completion of the project.

As the walls and piers are constructed above ground, the surveyor can check the forms (poured concrete bridges) for plumb by occupying one of the 25-ft offset stakes (Figures 14-11 and 15-8), sighting the other 25-ft offset stake, and then raising the telescope to sight-check measurements to the form work with the vertical crosshair. The 5-ft offset line should be far enough from the finished wall to allow for the line of sight to be clear of the concrete forms and other falsework supports. Realizing that steep vertical sightings can accentuate some instrumental errors, most surveyors will not take check sightings higher than 45° without double centering; see Sections 4-10 and 4-15.

For high bridges, instrument stations are moved farther away (farther than 25 ft, in this example) so that check sights with the theodolite are kept to relatively small vertical angles. In addition, offset stations are established, clear of the work, so that sights can be taken to the 90° (in this example) adjacent walls. See Figure 14-13 for typical locations for vertical control stations for the south pier of the bridge example.

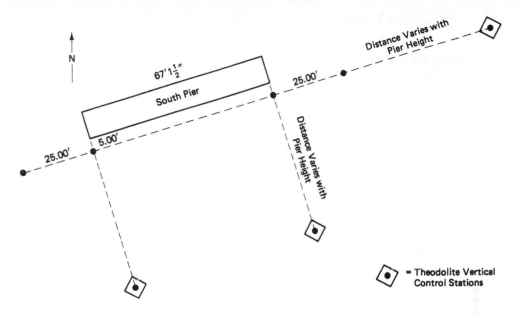

FIGURE 14-13 Showing theodolite stations that can be used for plumb checks as the construction rises above the ground. See also Figure 15-8.

14-9   Cross Sections for Footing Excavations

Original cross sections will have been taken prior to construction. As the excavation work proceeds, cross sections are taken, keeping the structural excavations (higher cost) separate from other cut-and-fill operations for the bridge site. When all work is completed, final cross sections are taken to be used for payments and final records.

The structural excavation quantities are determined by taking preliminary and final cross sections on each footing. The offset line for each footing is used as a baseline for individual footing cross sections.

Chapter 15

Building Construction Surveys

15-1 Building Construction: General

All buildings must be located with reference to the property limits. Accordingly, the initial stage of the building construction survey involves the careful retracing and verification of the property lines. Once the property lines are established, the building is located according to plan, with all corners marked in the field.

Large-scale building projects will have horizontal control points established, which are based on a state plane grid or a transverse Mercator grid. These horizontal control monuments will be tied into the project property lines as well as the state or provincial grid (see Section 8-2).

Temporary benchmarks will be surveyed onto all major sites from the closest benchmark, and then the work will be verified by closing the survey into another independent benchmark. The surveyor establishes a minimum of three temporary benchmarks at each site to ensure that, if one is destroyed, at least two will be available for all layout work (see Section 14-8).

15-2 Single-Story Construction

Construction surveys for single-story buildings may entail only survey layouts for the building footings—the contractor can often locate the rest of the building components to the footings for both line and grade; of course, site grading surveys will also be required in most circumstances.

Figure 15-1 includes (a) *Block Plan,* which shows the general area of the construction site; (b) *Site Plan,* which gives existing and proposed elevations, key building dimensions (16 m × 20 m), setbacks from front and side lines (5 m and 7.5 m, respectively), parking areas, walks, and so on: (c) *Ground Floor Plan,* which shows the basic dimensions

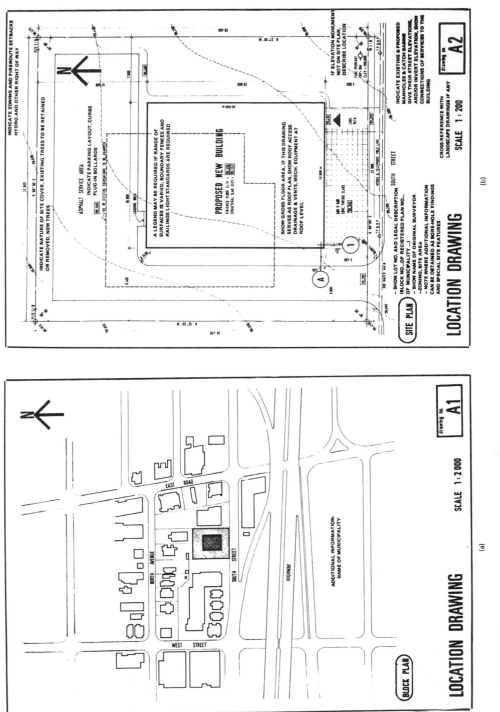

BLOCK PLAN

LOCATION DRAWING

SCALE 1:2000

(a)

ADDITIONAL INFORMATION:
NAME OF MUNICIPALITY

INDICATE ZONING AND FIREROUTE SETBACKS
HYDRO AND OTHER RIGHT OF WAY

INDICATE NATURE OF SITE COVER, EXISTING TREES TO BE RETAINED
OR REMOVED, NEW TREES

ASPHALT SERVICE AREA

INDICATE PARKING LAYOUT, CURBS
PLUG-IN BOLLARDS

A LEGEND MAY BE REQUIRED IF RANGE OF
SURFACES IS VARIED. BOUNDARY FENCES AND
RAILINGS LIGHT STANDARDS ARE REQUIRED

PROPOSED NEW BUILDING

SHOW GROSS FLOOR AREA, IF THIS DRAWING
SERVES AS ROOF PLAN, SHOW ROOF ACCESS
DRAINAGE & VENTS, MECH. EQUIPMENT AT
ROOF LEVEL

IF ELEVATION MONUMENT
NOT ON SITE PLAN,
DESCRIBE LOCATION

INDICATE EXISTING & PROPOSED
MANHOLES & CATCH BASINS
GIVE THEIR STREET ELEVATIONS,
AND/OR INVERT ELEVATION, SHOW
CONNECTIONS OF SERVICES TO THE
BUILDING

SITE PLAN

– SHOW LOT NO. AND LEGAL DESCRIPTION
(BLOCK NO...OF REGISTERED PLAN NO...)
– SHOW NAME OF MUNICIPALITY...
– SHOW NAME OF ORIGINAL SURVEYOR
– ZONING, SITE AREA
– NOTE WHERE ADDITIONAL INFORMATION
CAN BE OBTAINED AS BORE-HOLE FINDINGS
AND SPECIAL SITE FEATURES

LOCATION DRAWING

CROSS-REFERENCE WITH
LANDSCAPE DRAWINGS IF ANY

SCALE 1:200

(b)

(continued)

FIGURE 15-1 Location drawing for a single-story building. (a) Block plan. (b) Site plan.

501

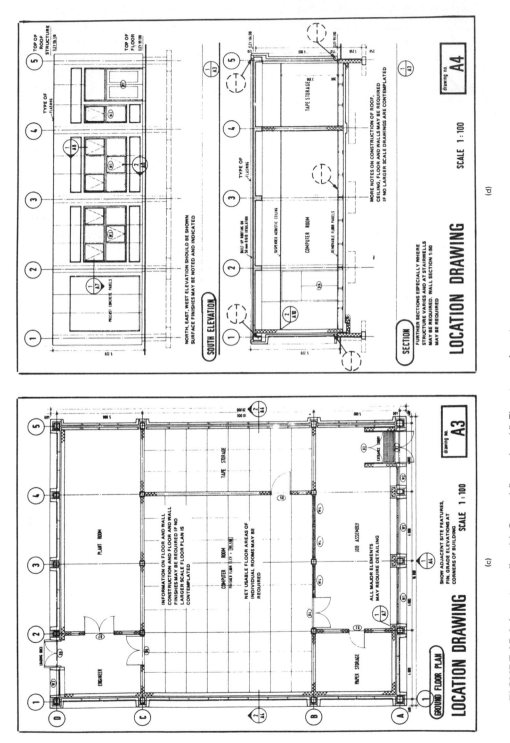

FIGURE 15-1 (continued). (c) Ground floor plan. (d) Elevation and section.

as well as first-floor elevations and column locations; and (d) *Elevation* (various) and *Section* (various), which show footing elevations, first-floor elevations, and roof elevations.

The surveyor sets up the property lines as shown on the site plan (a licensed surveyor may be required at this stage to establish the legal lines). The building corners are then set out by measuring the setbacks from the property lines. After the corners have been staked, diagonal distances (on line or offsets) can be measured to verify the layout—that is, for the building shown (16.000 m $\times$ 20.000 m), the diagonals should be $\sqrt{16.000^2 + 20.000^2} =$ 25.612 m. At an accuracy requirement of 1/5000, the diagonal tolerance would be $+0.005$ m (i.e., 0.005/25.612 = 1/5000). Once the corners have been laid out and verified, the offsets and batter boards can be laid out. Figure 15-2 shows the location of batter boards and string lines used for control of an L-shaped building; the batter boards and string lines are usually set at the first-floor elevation.

Figure 15-3 shows a combination transit and level that can be found on many small construction sites. Although this transit-level is not as precise as many of the instruments previously introduced in this text, its precision is well suited for small construction sites, where the instrument sights are relatively short—typically less than 150 ft or 50 m.

Figure 15-4 shows a backhoe beginning to excavate a basement and footings for a house; one set of corner batter boards can be seen in the photograph. Figure 15-5 shows a small bulldozer shaping up the site to conform to the site grading plan; this aspect of the

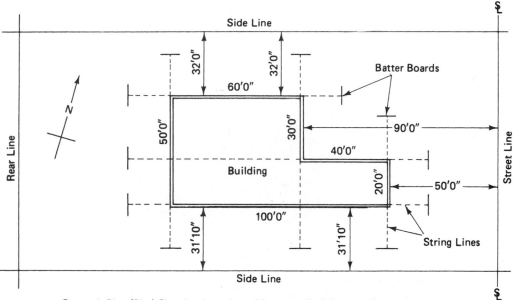

Property Plan (Plat) Showing Location of Proposed Building with Respect to the Property Lines.

This Plan also Shows the Location of the Batter Boards and the String Lines for Each Building Wall Footing.

FIGURE 15-2 Building layout.

FIGURE 15-3 David White LT8-300 level-transit. (Courtesy of David White Instruments, Germantown, Wisconsin)

Batter Boards

FIGURE 15-4   Excavation for house basement and footings. (Courtesy of John Deere Inc.)

building survey usually takes place only after the services have been trenched in from the street and the house has been erected. Figure 15-6 shows the steel work for a single-story commercial building. The columns shown have been bolted to the footing anchor bolts previously laid out by the surveyor. Figure 15-7 shows two different types of connections: Figure 15-7(a), the bolt connection, and Figure 15-7(b), the pocket connection. In both cases, a template can be utilized to properly align the bolt patterns to the column center-lines. The tolerance is usually set at 1/8 inch (3 or 4 mm) for each set of column bolts, with

Grade
Stakes

FIGURE 15-5   Site grading with a bulldozer. (Courtesy of John Deere Inc.)

FIGURE 15-6 Single-story building columns and column footings.

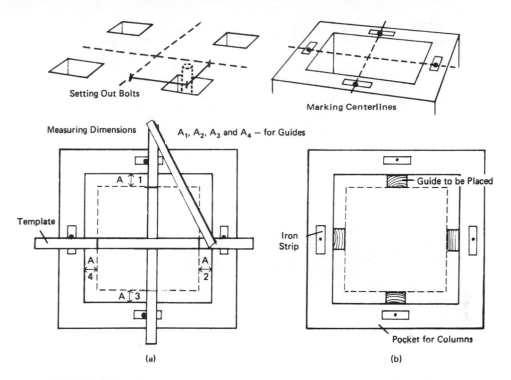

Setting Out Bolts

Marking Centerlines

Measuring Dimensions

A_1, A_2, A_3 and A_4 — for Guides

Template

A ↕ 1

A ↔ 4

A ↔ 2

A ↕ 3

Guide to be Placed

Iron Strip

Pocket for Columns

(a)   (b)

FIGURE 15-7 Connection of columns to footings. (a) Bolt connection. (b) Pocket connection. (Courtesy of National Swedish Institute for Building Research, FIG Report #69)

the overall tolerance for the length of the building set at 1/4 inch (6 mm). The columns can be plumbed with the aid of a transit, although for single-story construction, the columns can be satisfactorily plumbed with a spirit level (carpenters' level).

Once the steel is in place, the surveyor can mark the columns a set distance above the floor grade. In North America, the offset marks are set at 4 or 5 ft above the floor slab.

Masonry or concrete walls can be checked for plumb by setting the transit on an offset line, sighting a target set on the same offset line, and then checking all parts of the wall or concrete forms with the aid of precut offset boards, either held against the wall or nailed directly to the form. See Figure 15-8.

15-2-1 Construction Lasers and Electronic Levels

Lasers were introduced in Chapter 13 for control of line and grade in sewers [Figure 13-2(b) and 13-10] and for control of line and grade for a boring machine in tunnels (Figure 13-21). In both of these examples, a laser beam, fixed in slope and horizontal alignment, controlled the construction work. Figure 11.8 shows a rotating laser guiding grading operations.

In building construction, a rotating instrument, defining a horizontal or vertical plane, is used to control the construction. Figure 15-9(a) shows a surveyor marking the

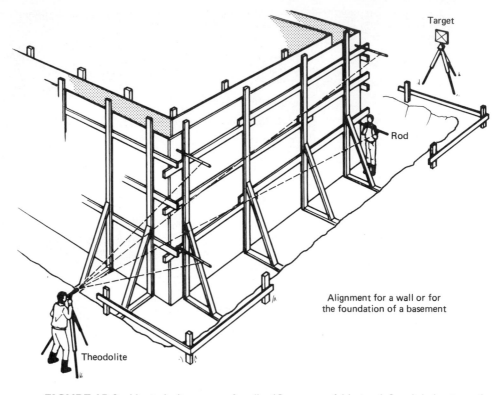

Target

Rod

Alignment for a wall or for
the foundation of a basement

Theodolite

FIGURE 15-8   Vertical alignment of walls. (Courtesy of National Swedish Institute for Building Research, FIG Report #69)

steel columns at the 4-ft mark with the aid of an electronic level; the rotating beam in this instrument is an *infrared beam* emitted by a laser diode. Figures 15-10 and 15-11 show rotating *lasers* controlling horizontal and vertical building components. A detection device, such as that shown in Figure 15-9(b), is used to capture the rotating beam. A detection device is required for the electronic level because the infrared beam is invisible, and it may be required for the rotating laser because the laser beam, when used in daylight, is not easily visible to the eye.

The word *laser* is an acronym for Light Amplification by Stimulated Emission of Radiation. Construction lasers, which have been used for the past generation, are of the helium-neon-gas type and are considered safe when in normal use.

The laser beam instrument can be used in darkened areas indoors without a beam detector, as the now-visible beam itself can be used as a reference line. For example, when false ceilings are installed, the column-mounted, rotating laser beam makes a laser mark on the ceiling hanger as it strikes its surface; the ceiling hanger is then marked or bent at the laser mark, ensuring a quick and horizontal installation for the ceiling channels.

Many rotating lasers and electronic levels can be battery-driven with a 10-hr operation, requiring overnight recharging. These instruments are also self-leveling when first set up to within 4° of level. These automatic instruments will stop rotating if knocked off

Anchor
Bolts

FIGURE 15-9 Electronic level. (a) Marking vertical control (4-foot marks on a steel column). (Courtesy of David White Instruments, Germantown, Wisconsin)

(continued)

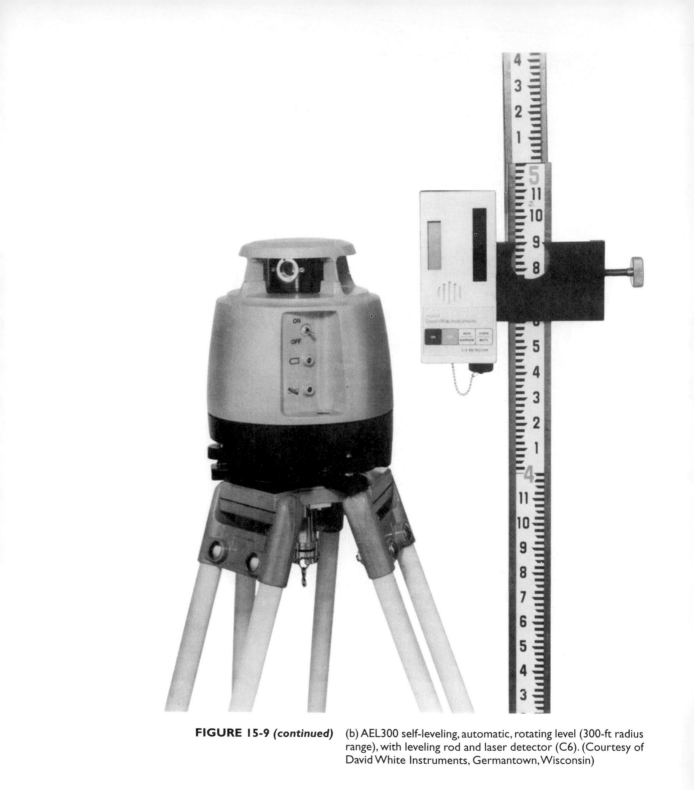

FIGURE 15-9 *(continued)*   (b) AEL300 self-leveling, automatic, rotating level (300-ft radius range), with leveling rod and laser detector (C6). (Courtesy of David White Instruments, Germantown, Wisconsin)

FIGURE 15-10 Rotating laser controlling the floor installation of a multistoried building complex. (Courtesy of Spectra Physics Inc., Dayton, Ohio)

level. The rotating speed can be varied from stop to 420 rpm. The instrument itself (Figure 15-9) can be set up on both threaded and bolt-type tripods and on any flat surface as well. The accuracy of the instrument shown in Figure 15-9 is 1/8 inch (0.01 ft) at 100 ft and 3/16 inch at 200 ft, with decreasing accuracy up to a limit of about 600 ft. The adjustment of the instrument can be checked by comparing results with a good-quality automatic or tilting level; if the electronic level is off by more than 1/8 inch in 100 ft, it is returned to the dealer for recalibration.

FIGURE 15-11 Rotating laser positioned to check plumb orientation of construction wall. (Courtesy of Laser Alignment Inc., Grand Rapids, Michigan)

When used for setting 4-ft marks, 1-m marks, or other floor reference marks, this technique is quite cost-effective. If a level and rod are used for this purpose, it will take two surveyors (instrument and rod) to do the job. When the electronic or laser level is used, the survey crew is reduced to just one surveyor; this eliminates communications and the chance for communication errors and, according to some reports, has resulted in a 50-percent increase in work accomplished along with the 50-percent decrease in work force. Figure 15-12 illustrates the ease with which one worker can check concrete footings prior to the concrete-block wall construction.

15-3   Multistory Construction

Multistory construction demands a high level of precision from the surveyor. As the building rises many stories, cumulative errors could cause serious delays and expense. Multistory columns are laid out by intersecting precisely established column lines, and the distances between columns are then checked in all directions. Templates are used to position anchor bolts or pockets, as shown in Figure 15-7.

Plumbness, or verticality, is checked by a theodolite sighted on premarked column centers or on the column edge. Column edges are sighted from stations set on offsets a distance of one-half the column width. Shim plates (up to 1/8 in.) are permitted in some specifications when one is plumbing columns that are mounted on anchor bolts. See

FIGURE 15-12 Autolaser 300, shown checking the footing elevations prior to construction of the concrete block walls. (Courtesy of David White Instruments, Germantown, Wisconsin)

Figures 15-7 and 15-13. Wedges are used to help plumb columns in pockets. Connecting beams will later hold the columns in their plumbed positions.

15-3-1 Vertical Control

Elevations are usually set two floors at a time. If the stairs are in place, the elevations can be carried up by differential leveling, as shown in Figure 15-14. Many building surveyors, however, prefer to transfer elevations upward by taking simultaneous readings from a properly tensioned, fully graduated steel tape, which can be hung down from the upper floor. The lower-floor surveyor, set up with a known height of instrument (HI), takes a reading on the suspended steel tape; at the same time (radios can be used for synchronization), the second surveyor, who has a level set up a floor or two higher, also takes a reading on the tape. The difference in readings is added to the lower HI to give the upper HI; temporary benchmarks are then set on the upper floor.

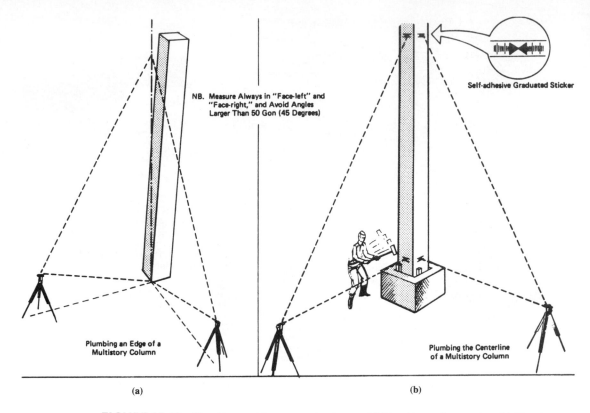

NB. Measure Always in "Face-left" and "Face-right," and Avoid Angles Larger Than 50 Gon (45 Degrees)

Self-adhesive Graduated Sticker

Plumbing an Edge of a Multistory Column

Plumbing the Centerline of a Multistory Column

(a)

(b)

FIGURE 15-13 Plumbing multistory steel columns. (a) Plumbing column edge. (b) Plumbing pretargeted column centerlines. (Courtesy of the National Swedish Institute for Building Research, FIG Report #69)

15-3-2 Horizontal Positioning

Horizontal control can be extended upward by downward plumbing through small (6-in.-square) through-floor ports onto the lower-floor control stations—or onto marks offset from control stations (see Figure 15-15). The plumbing operation is often accomplished by using optical plummets, as shown in Figure 13-19. Upward plumbing is dangerous, as material may be accidentally discharged through the floor port onto the surveyor below. In addition to using optical plummets, the surveyor can use heavy plumb bobs, with swing oscillations dampened in oil or water, as described in Section 13-5.

New layouts are constantly checked back to previously set layout points for both line and grade. All angles are doubled (face right and face left), and all distance tolerances are in the 5-mm (0.02-ft) range. As noted above, upper-floor control is checked back to control previously set on lower floors; when it becomes necessary to transfer control to higher floors from the ground, for steel structures, the survey work must be done early in the morning or on cloudy days so that the sun cannot heat and thus deform various parts of the structure, causing an erroneous layout.

Figure 15-16 illustrates the case where a theodolite is set up by interlining (wiggling in) between targets (see Section 4-11) set on adjacent structures. These permanent targets

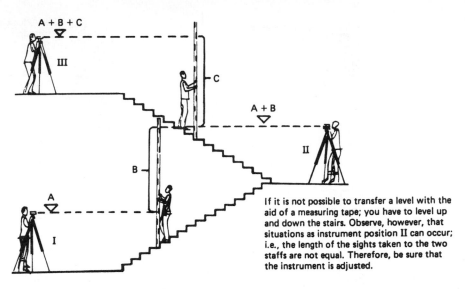

FIGURE 15-14 Transferring elevations in a multistory building. (Courtesy of the National Swedish Institute for Building Research, FIG Report #69)

were originally set from ground control before the project started. An alternative to this technique would be to set up on a control station located on a high building, sight a permanent target on another building, and then transfer this line down onto each new floor of the building as it is constructed.

15-3-3   Horizontal Alignment—Reference Azimuth Points (RAPs)

Figure 15-17 shows a survey station located on an upper floor by downward optical plumbing to a previously set control mark. Alignment is provided by sighting reference azimuth points (RAPs) where the coordinates have been determined (see Section 8-8). Knowing the coordinates of the instrument station and the coordinates of at least two RAPs, the surveyor can quickly determine the azimuth and distance to any of the coordinated building layout points (a third RAP is sighted to provide an accuracy check). If a programmed Total Station is being used, the coordinates of the layout points, the RAPs, and the instrument station can be loaded to the data collector, with the required layout distances and angles (polar ties) being calculated automatically.

15-3-4   Horizontal Alignment—Free Stations

Figure 15-18 illustrates *resection techniques* being used to provide the coordinates of the theodolite station. In this case, the theodolite or Total Station is set up at any convenient location (called a *free station*). Angles are then taken to a minimum of three coordinated control stations; a fourth control station could be taken to provide a second computation of the theodolite station as an accuracy check. If both angles and distances can be taken to the control stations, only two, or preferably three, stations are required. By using

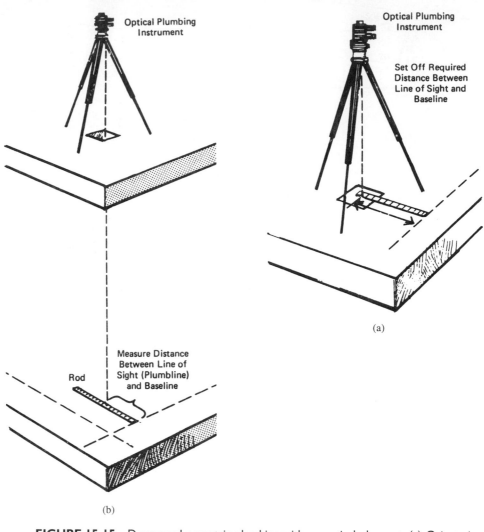

FIGURE 15-15 Downward eccentric plumbing with an optical plummet. (a) Orientation to lower floor. (b) Transfer lower floor position to instrument station floor. See Figure 13-19 for optical plummet. (Courtesy of the National Swedish Institute for Building Research, FIG Report #69)

trigonometric relationships (identities) to solve the resulting triangles, the coordinates of the theodolite station are computed—most Total Stations are now programmed to solve resection problems. Once the coordinates of the free station are solved, the Total Station programs can then compute the polar ties to any layout point, as described above.

Free stationing, which can be used for most layout surveys (not just building surveys) has several advantages: (1) The theodolite can be set up to avoid obstacles; (2) setup centering errors are eliminated; (3) fewer control stations are required; (4) the setup station can be located close to the current layout work; (5) if Total Stations are employed, the layout work is greatly accelerated.

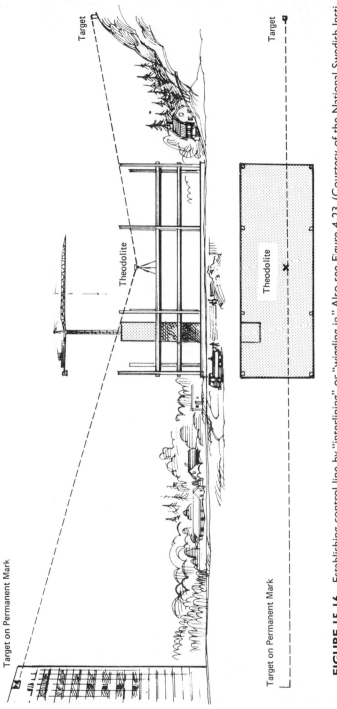

Target

Theodolite

Target on Permanent Mark

Target

Theodolite

Target on Permanent Mark

FIGURE 15-16 Establishing control line by "interlining" or "wiggling in." Also see Figure 4-23. (Courtesy of the National Swedish Institute for Building Research, FIG Report #69)

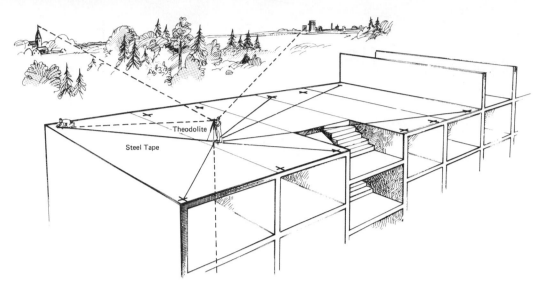

FIGURE 15-17 Optical plumbing combined with reference azimuth points for polar layouts. Also see Figure 13-19. (Courtesy of the National Swedish Institute for Building Research, FIG Report #69)

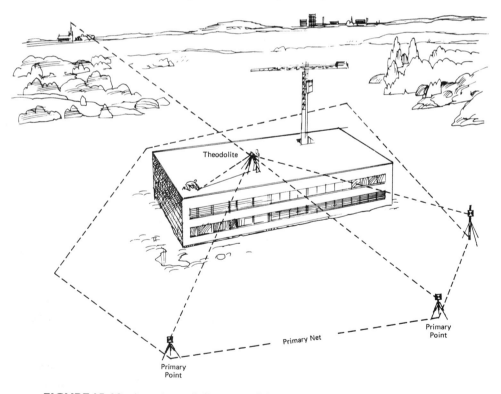

FIGURE 15-18 Location and alignment of theodolite by resection (free stationing). (Courtesy of the National Swedish Institute for Building Research, FIG Report #69)

Chapter 16

Quantity and Final Surveys

16-1 Construction Quantity Measurements: General

After the line and grade for a project have been established, the construction surveyor's next concern is to supply the project supervisor with survey measurements—and resultant quantities—that reflect the progress achieved by the contractor. Progress payments, which are based on quantities supplied by the surveyor and the construction inspector, are processed either at the end of a regular time period (e.g., monthly) or at the completion of previously agreed-upon project stages. The contractor usually also employs a surveyor to provide similar data; this ensures that questionable quantities are quickly discovered and remeasured.

Some construction projects are bid on a lump-sum basis; this is where the contractor's one-price bid covers all the work required to complete a project. The demolition of a structure is a good example of a situation where a lump-sum bid is appropriate. Here, the owner (e.g., municipality, state, or province) simply wants the structure removed; the demolition technique is of little importance to the owner (blasting would be an exception). The owner simply wants the job done as cheaply and expeditiously as possible.

However, most construction projects are bid on a unit-price basis, where all the facets of the job are defined in detail. The owner (e.g., municipality, highway department, developer, railroad) specifies the line and grade of the facility, the construction materials to be used, the qualities of the finished product (e.g., compressive strength of concrete), the compaction level of earth and granular fills, and the appearance of the finished product.

The owner will list all categories (units) of materials and operations and will prepare an estimate as to the total quantities for each item—that is, total cut and fill, total length of fence, total volume of concrete placed, total area of sod or seeding, and the like. See Table 16-1 for other typical construction categories, with tendering units. The contractor bids a price against each unit item; all items are then added to compute the total unit bid. Finally, these individual total bids are summed to produce the grand total for the contract bid.

Table 16-1 TYPICAL CONSTRUCTION CATEGORIES WITH TENDERING UNITS

Lineal (ft, m)	Area (ft², m², acres, ha)	Volume (ft³, m³)	Weight (tons, tonnes)*
Curb	Clearing	Concrete–in structures	Granular material
Curb and gutter	Grubbing	Cuts	Crushed stone
Sewer pipe	Sodding	Fills	Steel
Pipeline	Seeding	Borrow material	Asphalt
Pipe jacking	Mulching	Water	
Height of manhole	Road surfaces	Dust control chemicals	
Depth of pile		Various excavation operations	
Guide rail		Riprap	
Noise barrier		Gabions	
		Blasting (rock)	

*1 ton = 2000 lbs = 0.907 metric tons (tonnes)

The contractor is paid for the work as it is completed (progress payments) and when all the work is completed (final payments); usually the owner will hold back a certain percentage of the final payment until after the guarantee period (two years is typical) has elapsed.

Table 16-2 shows typical measuring precision, in both feet and meters, for layout and quantity surveys. Surveyors, working for both the owner and the contractor, record the progress payment measurements in their field notes; these notes must be accurate, complete, and unambiguous. Figures 16-1 to 16-4 illustrate typical survey notes for quantity surveys.

Table 16-2 TYPICAL MEASUREMENT PRECISION FOR VARIOUS CONSTRUCTION QUANTITIES (ADAPTED FROM *CONSTRUCTION MANUAL,* MINISTRY OF TRANSPORTATION AND COMMUNICATIONS, ONTARIO)

Measurement Precision Construction Survey		
Activity	Foot	Metric
CROSS SECTIONS		
Backsight and foresight readings to be taken to the nearest:	0.01 ft	1 mm
Maximum sight distance with level	300 ft.	90 m
Maximum allowable error between adjacent benchmarks	0.08 ft	20 mm
Intermediate rod readings to be taken to the nearest:	0.10 ft	10 mm
Intervals:		
earth cut	100 ft	25 m
rock cut	50 ft	10 m
rock cut with overburden	50 ft	10 m
muskeg excavation	100 ft	25 m
fills with stripping, subexcavation, or ditching	100 ft	25 m
transition from cut to fill	100 ft	25 m
fills	100 ft	25 m
earth or rock fills	100 ft	25 m
borrow pits	50 ft	25 m

Table 16-2 *(continued)*

Measurement Precision Construction Survey

Activity	Foot	Metric
Maximum transverse interval for cross-section elevations:		
earth	100 ft	25 m
rock	50 ft	10 m
borrow	50 ft	25 m
Offset distances to be measured to the closest:	1.0 ft	0.1 m
GRADE AND SUPERELEVATION CALCULATIONS		
Calculate grade percentage	to two decimal places	to three decimal places
Calculate grade elevation to the nearest:	0.01 ft	1 mm
Calculate lull superelevation cross fall to the nearest:	0.0001 ft	0.0001 m
Calculate the rate of rise or fall to the nearest:	0.00001 ft/ft	0.0001 m/m
Chainage of T.S., S.C., C.S., S.T. to be recorded to the nearest:	0.01 ft	1 mm
Layout/intervals:		
rock ⎰ With the exception of plus sections, layout is normally at the	50 ft	10 m
earth ⎱ same interval as the cross sections/grade calculations.	100 ft	25 m
Maximum interval for setting structure footing grades	25 ft	10 m
Structure grades to be set to an accuracy of:	0.01 ft	1 mm
Adjustment to slope stake distances to allow for grubbing losses	1 ft	300 mm
Set grades for earth grading to the nearest:	0.10 ft	10 mm
Set grades for granular to the nearest:	0.01 ft	5 mm
Layout stake offset for curb and gutter (ideal)	6 ft	2 m
Layout stake interval for curb and gutter	50/25 ft	20/10 m
Set curb and gutter grades to the nearest:	0.01 ft	1 mm
Maximum staking interval for layout of a radius (intersections)	10 ft	3 m
Layout stake offset for concrete pavement (ideal)	6 ft	2 m
Set grades for concrete pavement to an accuracy of:	0.01 ft	1 mm
Calculate individual cleaning and grubbing areas to the nearest:	ft^2	$0.10\ m^2$
Convert the total clearing area to the nearest:	0.01 acre	0.01 ha
Calculate earth, rock, or borrow end areas to the nearest:	ft^2	$0.10\ m^2$
Convert the total volume per cut to pit to the nearest:	yd^3	m^3
The quantity of blast cover, paid by box measurement, will not exceed:	$1500\ yd^3$	$1000\ m^3$
Truck box volumes shall be calculated to the nearest:	$0.10\ yd^3$	$0.10\ m^3$
The item total for "Water" shall be taken to the closest:	1000 gal	m^3
Water tank volumes shall be calculated to the closest:	gal	$0.01\ m^3$
Item totals for calcium chloride shall be taken to the closest:	0.01 ton	0.01 t
Culvert and structures excavation end areas shall be calculated to the nearest:	ft^2	$0.10\ m^2$
Volumes per culvert and structure site shall be calculated to the nearest:	yd^3	m^3
Linear dimensions for calculation of culvert and structure concrete volumes shall be to the closest:	0.01 ft	1 mm
Trigonometric functions shall be:	5-place tables	5-place tables
Volume calculations for concrete culverts and structures shall be to the closest:	$0.50\ ft^3$	$0.01\ m^3$
Concrete culvert and structure items totals shall be taken to the closest:	$0.10\ yd^3$	$0.10\ m^3$
Pipe culvert placement shall be measured to the closest:	ft	100 mm
Pipe removal shall be measured to the closest:	ft	100 mm
Sewer trench measurements shall be taken at maximum intervals of:	100 ft	30 m

(continued)

Table 16-2 *(continued)*

Measurement Precision Construction Survey

Activity	Foot	Metric
The height of manholes and catch basins shall be measured to:	0.10 ft	10 mm
Concrete in manholes and catch basins shall be calculated to the nearest:	0.01 yd^3	0.01 m^3
Excavation and backfill for sewer systems shall be calculated to the nearest:		
(a) end area	ft^2	0.10 m^2
(b) item total	yd^3	m^3
Sewer pipe and subdrains shall be measured to the closest:	ft	100 mm
Concrete pavement, sidewalk area (placing and removal) shall be calculated to the nearest:	ft^2	0.10 m^2
The item total for concrete pavements, sidewalk area (placing and removal) shall be rounded to the nearest:	yd^2	m^2
Curb and gutter, fence, guide rail (placing and removal) shall be measured to the closest:	ft	100 mm
and the item totaled to the closest:	ft	1.0 m
Seeding and mulching, and sodding shall be calculated to the closest:	ft^2	0.10 m^2
and the item totaled to the closest:	yd^2	1.0m^2
Topsoil stockpile and areas shall be calculated to the closest:	ft^2	0.10 m^2
and the stockpile volume calculated to the closest:	yd^3	1.0 m^3
RIPRAP		
Depth to be measured to the closest:	0.10 ft	10 mm
Length and width measured to the closest:	ft	100 mm
Volume calculated to the nearest:	ft^3	0.10 m^3
Item total to nearest:	yd^3	1.0 m^3
Reinforcing steel shall be totaled to the nearest:	0.01 ton	0.01 t
The length of each pile driven shall be measured to the nearest:	in.	10 mm
The pile driving item total shall be taken to the closest:	ft	0.10 m
The area of restored roadway surface shall be calculated to the nearest:	ft^2	0.10 m^2
and the item totaled to the nearest:	yd^2	1.0 m^2
Width measurements shall be taken to the closest:	pavement width plus	
	1 ft	300 mm
and length to the closest:	1 ft	300 mm
Field measurements of length and width for clearing and grubbing shall be taken to the closest:	ft.	100 mm
Measurements to establish truck box volume shall be taken to the closest:	0.10 ft	10 mm
Measurements to establish water truck tank volume shall be taken to the closest:	0.10 ft	10 mm
Measurements to establish boulder volume shall be taken to the closest:	0.10 ft	10 mm
Field measurements for concrete pavement and sidewalk shall be taken to the closest:	0.10 ft	10 mm
Field measurements for seeding and mulching and sodding shall be taken to the closest:	0.1 ft	100 mm
Field measurements for asphalt sidewalk and hot mix miscellaneous shall be taken to the closest:	foot-length	10 mm-length
	0.10 ft-width	10 mm-width

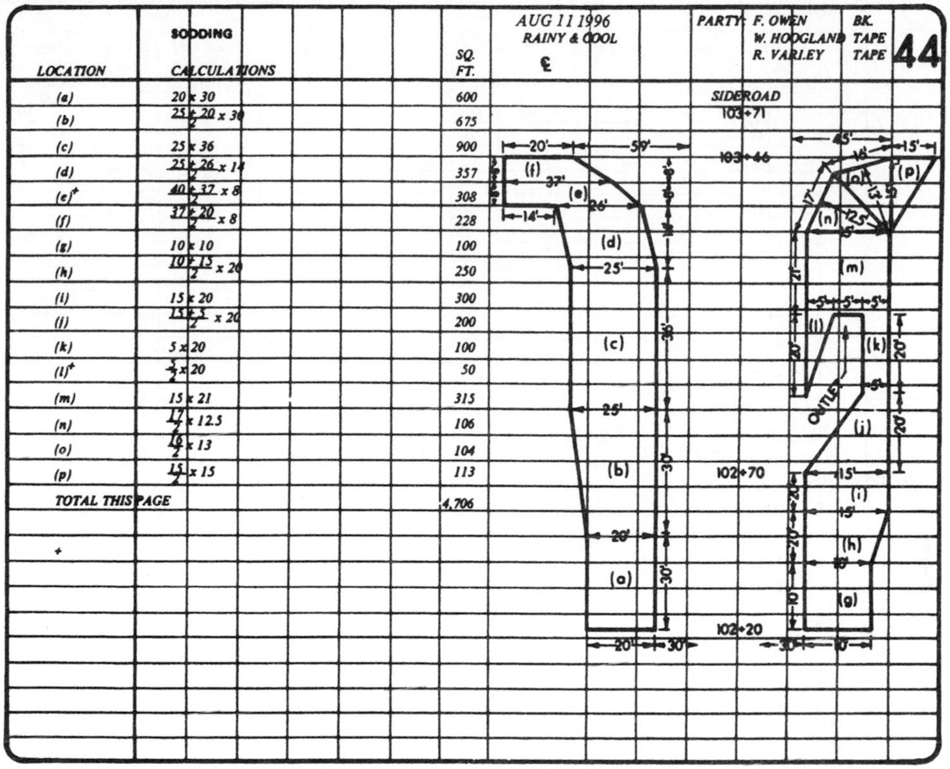

LOCATION	SODDING CALCULATIONS	SQ. FT.
(a)	20 x 30	600
(b)	$\frac{25+20}{2}$ x 30	675
(c)	25 x 36	900
(d)	$\frac{25+26}{2}$ x 14	357
(e)+	$\frac{40+37}{2}$ x 8	308
(f)	$\frac{37+20}{2}$ x 8	228
(g)	10 x 10	100
(h)	$\frac{10+15}{2}$ x 20	250
(i)	15 x 20	300
(j)	$\frac{15+5}{2}$ x 20	200
(k)	5 x 20	100
(l)+	$\frac{5}{2}$ x 20	50
(m)	15 x 21	315
(n)	$\frac{17}{2}$ x 12.5	106
(o)	$\frac{16}{2}$ x 13	104
(p)	$\frac{15}{2}$ x 15	113
TOTAL THIS PAGE		4,706
+		

AUG 11 1996
RAINY & COOL
PARTY: F. OWEN
W. HOOGLAND TAPE
R. VARLEY TAPE
BK.
44
SIDEROAD
103+71
103+46
102+70
102+20
OUTLET

FIGURE 16-1 Example of the method of recording sodding measurements. (From *Construction Manual,* Ministry of Transportation and Communications, Ontario)

Lineal units, as shown in Table 16-1, are added to obtain final quantities; similarly weight units are totaled by simply adding the scale tickets for the various items. However, both the area and the volume units require additional work from the surveyor before the unit totals can be determined. The following sections illustrate the more commonly used techniques for both area and volume computations.

16-2 Area Computations

Areas enclosed by closed traverses can be computed by using the coordinate method (Section 6-12). Reference to Figure 16-5 will illustrate two additional area computation techniques.

16-2-1 Trapezoidal Technique

The area in Figure 16-5 was measured using a cloth tape for the offset distances. A common interval of 15 ft was chosen to suitably delineate the riverbank. Had the riverbank been more uniform, a larger interval could have been used, and had the riverbank been

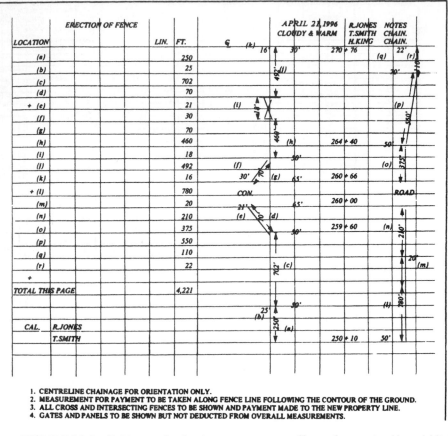

LOCATION	ERECTION OF FENCE			LIN.	FT.			APRIL 21, 1996 CLOUDY & WARM	R.JONES T.SMITH H.KING	NOTES CHAIN. CHAIN.
(a)					250		16'	30'	270 + 76	22'
(b)					25					
(c)					702					
(d)					70					
+ (e)					21					
(f)					30					
(g)					70					
(h)					460				264 + 40	50'
(i)					18					
(j)					492		30'		260 + 66	
(k)					16					
+ (l)					780		CON.		260 + 00	ROAD
(m)					20					
(n)					210				259 + 60	
(o)					375					
(p)					550					
(q)					110					
(r)					22					
+										
TOTAL THIS PAGE					4,221					
CAL.	R.JONES									
	T.SMITH								250 + 10	50'

1. CENTRELINE CHAINAGE FOR ORIENTATION ONLY.
2. MEASUREMENT FOR PAYMENT TO BE TAKEN ALONG FENCE LINE FOLLOWING THE CONTOUR OF THE GROUND.
3. ALL CROSS AND INTERSECTING FENCES TO BE SHOWN AND PAYMENT MADE TO THE NEW PROPERTY LINE.
4. GATES AND PANELS TO BE SHOWN BUT NOT DEDUCTED FROM OVERALL MEASUREMENTS.

FIGURE 16-2 Field notes for fencing measurements. (From *Construction Manual*, Ministry of Transportation and Communications, Ontario)

even more irregular, a smaller interval would have been appropriate. The trapezoidal technique assumes that the lines joining the ends of each offset line are straight lines (the smaller the common interval, the more valid this assumption).

The end sections can be treated as triangles:

$$A = (8.1 \times 26.1)/2 \; = 106 \text{ ft}^2$$

and
$$A = (11.1 \times 20.0)/2 = \underline{111 \text{ ft}^2}$$
$$217 \text{ ft}^2 = \text{subtotal}$$

The remaining areas can be treated as trapezoids. The trapezoidal rule is stated as follows:

$$\text{Area} = X \left(\frac{h_1 + h_n}{2} + h_2 + \cdots + h_{n-1} \right) \tag{16-1}$$

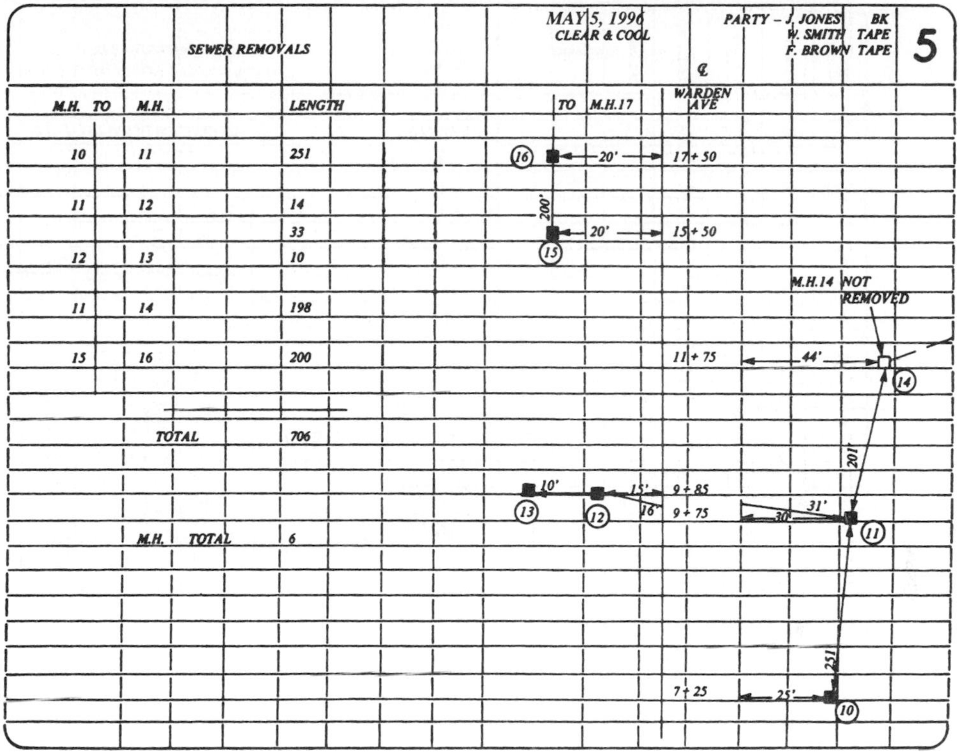

FIGURE 16-3 Example of field book entries regarding removal of sewer pipe, etc. (From *Construction Manual,* Ministry of Transportation and Communications, Ontario)

where X = common interval between the offset lines

h = offset measurement

n = number of offset measurements

$$A = 15\left(\frac{26.1 + 20.0}{2} + 35.2 + 34.8 + 41.8 + 45.1 + 40.5 + 30.3 + 25.0\right)$$

$$= 4136 \text{ ft}^2$$

Total area = 4136 + 217 = 4353 ft^2

16-2-2   Simpson's One-Third Rule

This technique gives more precise results than the trapezoidal technique and is used where one boundary is irregular in the manner shown in Figure 16-5. The rule assumes that an odd number of offsets are involved and that the lines joining the ends of three successive offset lines are parabolic in configuration.

PILE NUMBER	LENGTH	CUT OFF	IN PLACE	SPLICES	REMARKS	DATE DRIVEN	DRIVING TUBE PILES WEST ABUTMENT BRIDGE NO. 2
1	20'	5'	15'			03/14/96	CONTRACTOR USING DELMAG D-12
2	20'	5'-6"	14'-6"			"	
3	20'	4'	16'			"	
4	20'	3'	17'			"	
5	20'	5'	15'			"	
6	20'	5'-6"	14'-6"			"	
7	20'	4'	16'			"	
8	20'	2'	18'			03/18/96	
9	20'	1'	19'			"	
10	20+20=40	15'	25'	1		"	
11	20+20=40	12'	28'	1		"	
12	20+20=40	10'	30'	1		"	
13	20+20=40	15'	25'	1		"	
14	20+20=40	16'	24'	1		"	
15	20+20=40	16'	24'	1		"	
16	20'	-	20'		DRIVEN TO GRADE	03/22/96	
17	20'	-	20'	"	"	"	
18	20'	4'	16'			"	
19	20'	3'	17'			"	
20	20'	2'	18'			"	
	520'	128'	392'	6 TOTAL			

CONTINUED ON PAGE 6

WHEN SHEET PILES ARE DRIVEN – SHOW NUMBER AND TYPE ALONG
EACH SIDE – NUMBERED CONTINUOUSLY AROUND THE PERIMETER.

FIGURE 16-4 Example of field notes for pile driving. (From *Construction Manual,* Ministry of Transportation and Communications, Ontario)

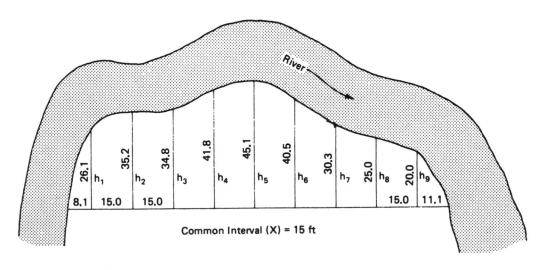

FIGURE 16-5 Irregular-area computation.

Simpson's one-third rule is stated as follows:

$$A = \frac{\text{interval}}{3} (h_1 + h_n + 2 \Sigma h \text{ odd} + 4 \Sigma h \text{ even}) \qquad (16\text{-}2)$$

that is, one-third of the common interval times the sum of the first and last offsets ($h_1 + h_n$) plus twice the sum of the other odd-numbered offsets (Σh odd) plus four times the sum of the even-numbered offsets (Σh even). From Figure 16-5,

$$A = \frac{15}{3} [26.1 + 20.0 + 2(34.8 + 45.1 + 30.3) \qquad (16\text{-}2)$$
$$+ 4(35.2 + 41.8 + 40.5 + 25.0)]$$
$$= 4183 \text{ ft}^2$$
$$\text{Total area} = 4183 + 217 \text{ (from preceding example)}$$
$$= 4400 \text{ ft}^2$$

If a problem is encountered with an even number of offsets, the area between the odd number of offsets is determined by Simpson's one-third rule, with the remaining area being determined by using the trapezoidal technique.

The discrepancy between the trapezoidal technique and Simpson's one-third rule is 30 ft^2 in a total of 4400 ft^2 (about 1 percent in this case).

16-2-3   Areas by Trigonometric and Geometric Formulas

Some construction quantities can be separated into geometric figures, which can then be analyzed by trigonometric and geometric formulas. These formulas are given in Figures 16-6 and 16-7 and are further illustrated by the worked-out examples in Figure 16-8.

16-3   Area by Graphical Analysis

We have seen that areas can be determined very precisely by using coordinates (Chapter 6), and less precisely by using the somewhat approximate methods illustrated by the trapezoidal rule and Simpson's one-third rule. Areas can also be determined by analyzing plotted data on plans and maps. For example, if a transparent sheet is marked off in grid squares to some known scale, an area outlined on a map can be determined by placing the squared paper over (sometimes under) the map and counting the number of squares and partial squares within the boundary limits shown on the map. The smaller the squares are, the more precise will be the result.

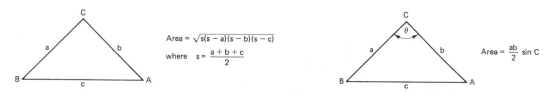

FIGURE 16-6   Areas by trigonometric formulas.

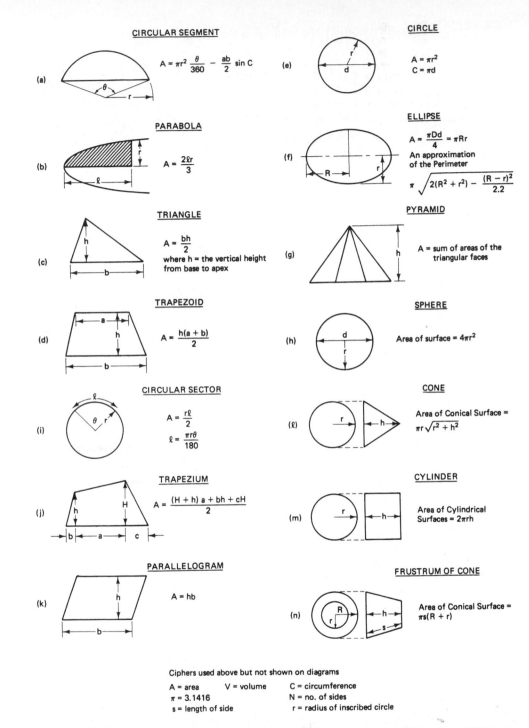

CIRCULAR SEGMENT

$$A = \pi r^2 \frac{\theta}{360} - \frac{ab}{2} \sin C$$

(a)

CIRCLE

$$A = \pi r^2$$
$$C = \pi d$$

(e)

PARABOLA

$$A = \frac{2\ell r}{3}$$

(b)

ELLIPSE

$$A = \frac{\pi D d}{4} = \pi R r$$

An approximation of the Perimeter

$$\pi \sqrt{2(R^2 + r^2) - \frac{(R - r)^2}{2.2}}$$

(f)

TRIANGLE

$$A = \frac{bh}{2}$$

where h = the vertical height from base to apex

(c)

PYRAMID

A = sum of areas of the triangular faces

(g)

TRAPEZOID

$$A = \frac{h(a + b)}{2}$$

(d)

SPHERE

Area of surface = $4\pi r^2$

(h)

CIRCULAR SECTOR

$$A = \frac{r\ell}{2}$$
$$\ell = \frac{\pi r \theta}{180}$$

(i)

CONE

Area of Conical Surface = $\pi r \sqrt{r^2 + h^2}$

(ℓ)

TRAPEZIUM

$$A = \frac{(H + h)\, a + bh + cH}{2}$$

(j)

CYLINDER

Area of Cylindrical Surfaces = $2\pi rh$

(m)

PARALLELOGRAM

$$A = hb$$

(k)

FRUSTRUM OF CONE

Area of Conical Surface = $\pi s(R + r)$

(n)

Ciphers used above but not shown on diagrams

A = area	V = volume	C = circumference
π = 3.1416		N = no. of sides
s = length of side		r = radius of inscribed circle

FIGURE 16-7 Areas by geometric formulas. (a) Circular segment. (b) Parabola. (c) Triangle. (d) Trapezoid. (e) Circle. (f) Ellipse. (g) Pyramid. (h) Sphere. (i) Circular sector. (j) Trapezium. (k) Parallelogram. (l) Cone. (m) Cylinder. (n) Frustum of cone. (From *Construction Manual,* Ministry of Transportation and Communications, Ontario)

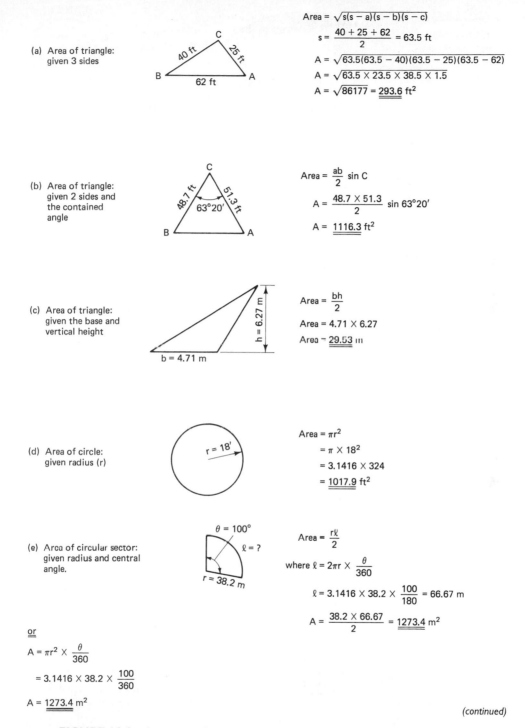

(a) Area of triangle: given 3 sides

$$\text{Area} = \sqrt{s(s-a)(s-b)(s-c)}$$

$$s = \frac{40 + 25 + 62}{2} = 63.5 \text{ ft}$$

$$A = \sqrt{63.5(63.5-40)(63.5-25)(63.5-62)}$$

$$A = \sqrt{63.5 \times 23.5 \times 38.5 \times 1.5}$$

$$A = \sqrt{86177} = \underline{293.6} \text{ ft}^2$$

(b) Area of triangle: given 2 sides and the contained angle

$$\text{Area} = \frac{ab}{2} \sin C$$

$$A = \frac{48.7 \times 51.3}{2} \sin 63°20'$$

$$A = \underline{1116.3} \text{ ft}^2$$

(c) Area of triangle: given the base and vertical height

$$\text{Area} = \frac{bh}{2}$$

$$\text{Area} = 4.71 \times 6.27$$

$$\text{Area} = \underline{29.53} \text{ m}$$

(d) Area of circle: given radius (r)

$$\text{Area} = \pi r^2$$

$$= \pi \times 18^2$$

$$= 3.1416 \times 324$$

$$= \underline{1017.9} \text{ ft}^2$$

(e) Area of circular sector: given radius and central angle.

$$\text{Area} = \frac{r\ell}{2}$$

$$\text{where } \ell = 2\pi r \times \frac{\theta}{360}$$

$$\ell = 3.1416 \times 38.2 \times \frac{100}{180} = 66.67 \text{ m}$$

$$A = \frac{38.2 \times 66.67}{2} = \underline{1273.4} \text{ m}^2$$

or

$$A = \pi r^2 \times \frac{\theta}{360}$$

$$= 3.1416 \times 38.2 \times \frac{100}{360}$$

$$A = \underline{\underline{1273.4}} \text{ m}^2$$

(continued)

FIGURE 16-8 Area examples.

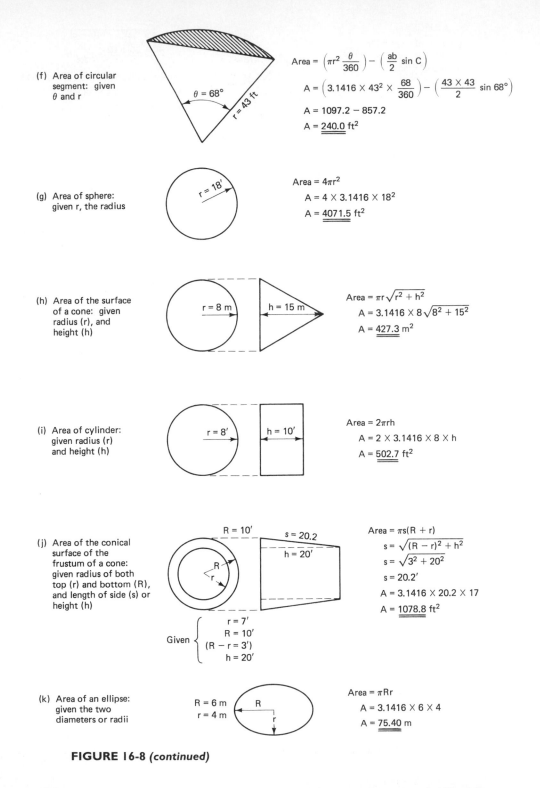

(f) Area of circular segment: given θ and r

$$\text{Area} = \left(\pi r^2 \frac{\theta}{360}\right) - \left(\frac{ab}{2} \sin C\right)$$

$$A = \left(3.1416 \times 43^2 \times \frac{68}{360}\right) - \left(\frac{43 \times 43}{2} \sin 68°\right)$$

$$A = 1097.2 - 857.2$$

$$A = \underline{\underline{240.0 \text{ ft}^2}}$$

$\theta = 68°$ $r = 43$ ft

(g) Area of sphere: given r, the radius

$r = 18'$

$$\text{Area} = 4\pi r^2$$

$$A = 4 \times 3.1416 \times 18^2$$

$$A = \underline{\underline{4071.5 \text{ ft}^2}}$$

(h) Area of the surface of a cone: given radius (r), and height (h)

$r = 8$ m $h = 15$ m

$$\text{Area} = \pi r \sqrt{r^2 + h^2}$$

$$A = 3.1416 \times 8 \sqrt{8^2 + 15^2}$$

$$A = \underline{\underline{427.3 \text{ m}^2}}$$

(i) Area of cylinder: given radius (r) and height (h)

$r = 8'$ $h = 10'$

$$\text{Area} = 2\pi r h$$

$$A = 2 \times 3.1416 \times 8 \times h$$

$$A = \underline{\underline{502.7 \text{ ft}^2}}$$

(j) Area of the conical surface of the frustum of a cone: given radius of both top (r) and bottom (R), and length of side (s) or height (h)

$R = 10'$ $s = 20.2$ $h = 20'$

$$\text{Area} = \pi s (R + r)$$

$$s = \sqrt{(R - r)^2 + h^2}$$

$$s = \sqrt{3^2 + 20^2}$$

$$s = 20.2'$$

$$A = 3.1416 \times 20.2 \times 17$$

$$A = \underline{\underline{1078.8 \text{ ft}^2}}$$

Given $\begin{cases} r = 7' \\ R = 10' \\ (R - r = 3') \\ h = 20' \end{cases}$

(k) Area of an ellipse: given the two diameters or radii

$R = 6$ m $r = 4$ m

$$\text{Area} = \pi R r$$

$$A = 3.1416 \times 6 \times 4$$

$$A = \underline{\underline{75.40 \text{ m}}}$$

FIGURE 16-8 *(continued)*

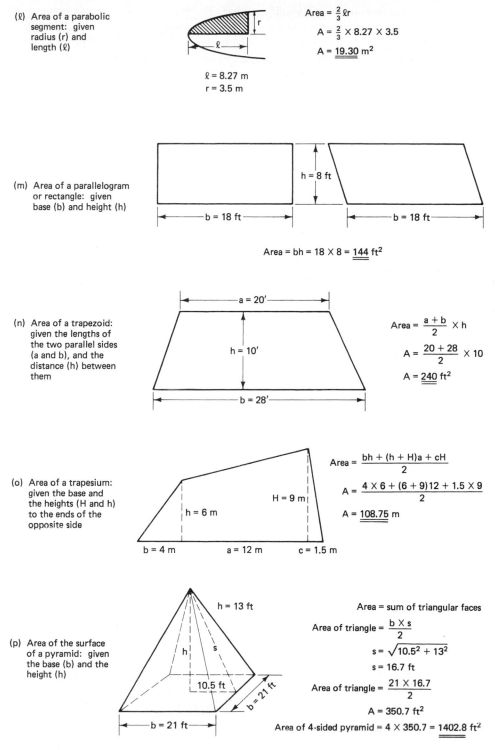

(ℓ) Area of a parabolic
segment: given
radius (r) and
length (ℓ)

$\ell = 8.27$ m
$r = 3.5$ m

Area $= \frac{2}{3}\ell r$

$A = \frac{2}{3} \times 8.27 \times 3.5$

$A = \underline{19.30}$ m²

(m) Area of a parallelogram
or rectangle: given
base (b) and height (h)

$h = 8$ ft

$b = 18$ ft

$b = 18$ ft

Area $= bh = 18 \times 8 = \underline{144}$ ft²

(n) Area of a trapezoid:
given the lengths of
the two parallel sides
(a and b), and the
distance (h) between
them

$a = 20'$

$h = 10'$

$b = 28'$

Area $= \dfrac{a+b}{2} \times h$

$A = \dfrac{20+28}{2} \times 10$

$A = \underline{240}$ ft²

(o) Area of a trapesium:
given the base and
the heights (H and h)
to the ends of the
opposite side

$H = 9$ m
$h = 6$ m

$b = 4$ m $a = 12$ m $c = 1.5$ m

Area $= \dfrac{bh + (h+H)a + cH}{2}$

$A = \dfrac{4 \times 6 + (6+9)12 + 1.5 \times 9}{2}$

$A = \underline{108.75}$ m

(p) Area of the surface
of a pyramid: given
the base (b) and the
height (h)

$h = 13$ ft

h s

10.5 ft

$b = 21$ ft

$b = 21$ ft

Area = sum of triangular faces

Area of triangle $= \dfrac{b \times s}{2}$

$s = \sqrt{10.5^2 + 13^2}$

$s = 16.7$ ft

Area of triangle $= \dfrac{21 \times 16.7}{2}$

$A = 350.7$ ft²

Area of 4-sided pyramid $= 4 \times 350.7 = \underline{1402.8}$ ft²

FIGURE 16-8 *(continued)*

Another method of graphic analysis involves the use of a planimeter (Figures 16-9 and 16-10). A planimeter consists of a graduated measuring drum attached to an adjustable or fixed tracing arm, which itself is attached to a pole arm, one end of which is anchored to the working surface by a needle. The graduated measuring drum gives partial revolution readings, while a disc keeps count of the number of full revolutions as the area outlined is traced.

Areas are determined by placing the pole-arm needle in a convenient location, setting the measuring drum and revolution counter to zero (some planimeters require recording an initial reading), and then tracing (using the tracing pin) the outline of the area being measured. As the tracing proceeds, the drum, which is also in contact with the working surface, revolves, measuring a value that is proportional to the area being measured. Some planimeters measure directly in square inches, while others can be set to map scales. When in doubt, or as a check on planimeter operation, the surveyor can measure out a scaled figure [e.g., 4-in. (100-mm) square] and then measure the area (16 in.^{2}) with a planimeter so that the planimeter area can be compared with the actual area laid off by scale. If the planimeter gives a result in square inches—say, 51.2 in.^{2}—and the map is at a scale of 1 in. = 100 ft, the actual ground area portrayed by 51.2 in.^{2} would be 51.2 × 100^2 = 512,000 ft^2 = 11.8 acres.

The planimeter is normally used with the pole-arm anchor point outside the area being traced. If it is necessary to locate the pole-arm anchor point inside the area being

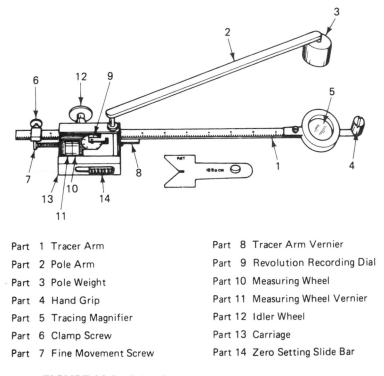

Part 1 Tracer Arm	Part 8 Tracer Arm Vernier
Part 2 Pole Arm	Part 9 Revolution Recording Dial
Part 3 Pole Weight	Part 10 Measuring Wheel
Part 4 Hand Grip	Part 11 Measuring Wheel Vernier
Part 5 Tracing Magnifier	Part 12 Idler Wheel
Part 6 Clamp Screw	Part 13 Carriage
Part 7 Fine Movement Screw	Part 14 Zero Setting Slide Bar

FIGURE 16-9 Polar planimeter.

FIGURE 16-10 Area takeoff by polar planimeter.

measured, as in the case of a relatively large area, the area of the zero circle of the planimeter must be added to the planimeter readings.

This constant is supplied by the manufacturer or can be deduced by simply measuring a large area twice, once with the anchor point outside the area and once with the anchor inside the area.

Planimeters are particularly useful in measuring end areas (Section 16-4) used in volume computations. Planimeters are also effectively used in measuring watershed areas, as a check on various construction quantities (e.g., areas of sod, asphalt), and as a check on areas determined by coordinates.

Electronic planimeters (Figure 16-11) measure larger areas in less time than traditional polar planimeters. Computer software is available for highways and other earthworks applications (e.g., cross sections) and for drainage basin areas. The planimeter shown in Figure 16-11 has a 36 × 30 in. working-area capability with a measuring resolution of 0.01 in.^{3} (0.02-in.^{2} accuracy).

16-4 Construction Volumes

In highway construction, for economic reasons, the designers try to optimally balance cut-and-fill volumes. Cut and fill cannot be precisely balanced because of geometric and aesthetic design considerations and because of the unpredictable effects of shrinkage and swell. *Shrinkage* occurs when a cubic yard (meter) is excavated and then placed while being compacted. The same material formerly occupying 1 yd^3 (m^3) volume now occupies a smaller volume. Shrinkage reflects an increase in density of the material and is obviously greater for silts, clays, and loams than it is for granular materials, such as sand and gravel.

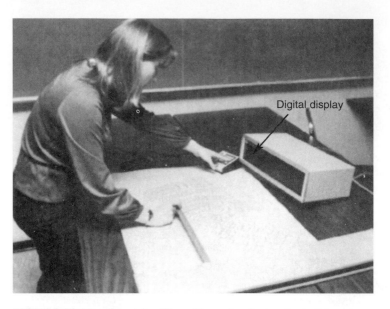

FIGURE 16-11 Area takeoff by a Numonics electronic planimeter.

Swell is a term used to describe the placing of shattered (blasted) rock. Obviously 1 yd^3 (m^3) of solid rock will expand significantly when shattered. Swell is usually in the 15 to 20 percent range, whereas shrinkage is in the 10 to 15 percent range, although values as high as 40 percent are possible with organic material in wet areas.

To keep track of cumulative cuts and fills as the profile design proceeds, the cumulative cuts (plus) and fills (minus) are shown graphically in a mass diagram. The total cut-minus-fill is plotted at each station directly below the profile plot. The mass diagram is an excellent method of determining *waste* or borrow volumes and can be adapted to show haul (transportation) considerations (Figure 16-12).

Large fills require *borrow* material, usually taken from a nearby *borrow pit*. Borrow-pit leveling procedures are described in Section 3-9 and Figure 3-24. The borrow pit in Figure 3-24 was laid out on a 50-ft grid. The volume of a grid square is the average height $(a + b + c + d)/4$ times the area of the base (50^2). The partial grid volumes (along the perimeter of the borrow pit) can be computed by forcing the perimeter volumes into regular geometric shapes (wedge shapes or quarter-cones).

When high precision is less important, volumes can be determined by analysis of contour plans; the smaller the contour interval, the more precise the result. The areas enclosed by a contour line can be taken off by planimeter; electronic planimeters are very useful for this purpose:

$$V = I \left(\frac{C_1 + C_2}{2} \right) \tag{16-3}$$

V is the volume (ft^3 or m^3) of earth or water, C_1 and C_2 are areas of adjacent contours, and I is the contour interval. The prismoidal formula (see Section 16-6) can be used if m is an

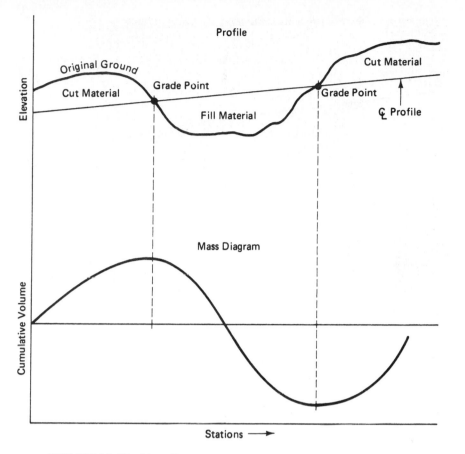

FIGURE 16-12 Mass diagram.

intervening contour (C_2) between C_1 and C_3. This method is well suited for many water-storage volume computations.

Finally, perhaps the most popular present-day volume computation technique involves the use of computers utilizing any one of a large number of available software programs. The computer programmer uses techniques similar to those described here, but the surveyor's duties may end with proper data entry to the computer (see Chapter 5).

16-5   Cross Sections, End Areas, and Volumes

Cross sections establish ground elevations at right angles to a proposed route. Cross sections can be developed from a contour plan as were profiles in the previous section, although it is common to have cross sections taken by field surveys. Chapter 5 introduced a computerized system that permits generation of profiles and cross sections from a general data base.

Cross sections are useful in determining quantities of cut and fill in construction design. If the original ground cross section is plotted and then the as-constructed cross

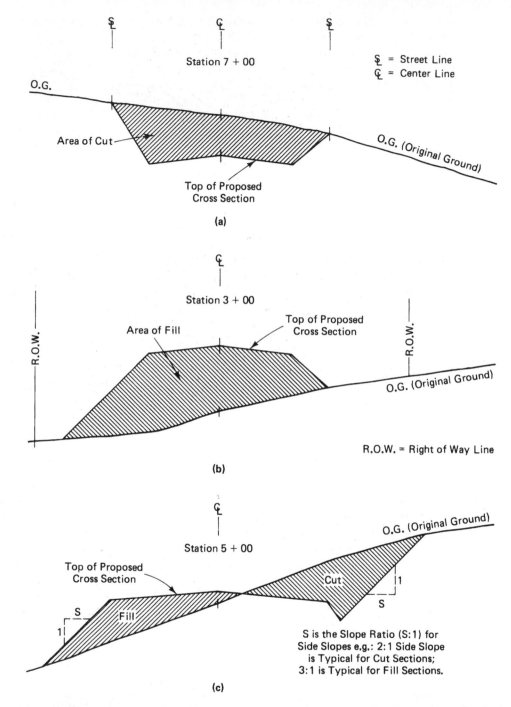

FIGURE 16-13 End areas. (a) Cut section. (b) Fill section. (c) Transition section (i.e., both cut and fill).

section is also plotted, the *end area* at that particular station can be computed. In Figure 16-13(a), the proposed road at STA 7 + 00 is at an elevation below existing ground. This indicates a *cut* situation (i.e., the contractor will cut out that amount of soil shown between the proposed section and the original section). In Figure 16-13(b), the proposed road elevation at STA 3 + 00 is above the existing ground, indicating a *fill* situation (i.e., the contractor will bring in or fill in that amount of soil shown). Figure 16-13(c) shows a transition section between cut-and-fill sections.

When the end areas of cut or fill have been computed for adjacent stations, the volume of cut or fill between those stations can be computed by simply averaging the end areas and multiplying the average end area by the distance between the end area stations; Figure 16-14 illustrates this concept.

$$V = \left(\frac{A_1 + A_2}{2}\right)L \qquad (16\text{-}4)$$

Formula (16-4) gives the general case for volume computation, where A_1 and A_2 are the end areas of two adjacent stations and L is the distance (feet or meters) between the stations. The answer in cubic feet is divided by 27 to give the answer in cubic yards; when metric units are used, the answer is left in cubic meters.

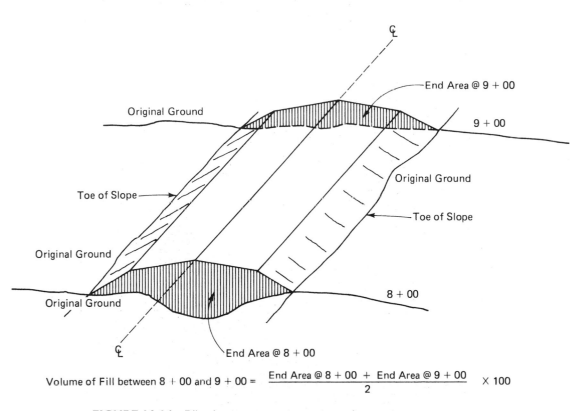

$$\text{Volume of Fill between 8 + 00 and 9 + 00} = \frac{\text{End Area @ 8 + 00 + End Area @ 9 + 00}}{2} \times 100$$

FIGURE 16-14 Fill volume computations using end areas.

The average end area method of computing volumes is entirely valid only when the area of the midsection is, in fact, the average of the two end areas. This is seldom the case in actual earthwork computations; however, the error in volume resulting from this assumption is insignificant for the usual earthwork quantities of cut and fill. For special earthwork quantities (e.g., expensive structures excavation) or for higher-priced materials (e.g., concrete in place), a more precise method of volume computation, the prismoidal formula, must be used.

■ **EXAMPLE 16-1** *Volume Computations by End Areas*

Figure 16-15(a) shows a pavement cross section for a proposed four-lane curbed road. As shown, the total pavement depth is 605 mm, the total width is 16.30 m, the subgrade is sloping to the side at 2 percent, and the top of the curb is 20 mm below the elevation of ℄. This proposed cross section is shown in Figure 16-15(b) along with the existing ground cross section at station 0 + 340. It can be seen that all subgrade elevations were derived from the proposed cross section, together with the ℄ design elevation of 221.43. The desired end area is the area shown below the original ground plot and above the subgrade plot.

At this point, an elevation datum line is arbitrarily chosen (220.00). The datum line chosen can be any elevation value rounded to the closest foot, meter, or 5-ft value that is lower than the lowest elevation in the plotted cross section.

Figure 16-16 illustrates that end area computations involve the computation of two areas:

1. Area between the ground cross section and the datum line.
2. Area between the subgrade cross section and the datum line.

The desired end area (cut) is area 1 minus area 2. For fill situations, the desired end area is area 2 minus area 1.

The end area computation can be determined as follows:

Station	Plus		Subarea	Minus		Subarea
0 + 340	$\frac{1.55 + 1.50}{2} \times 4.5$	=	6.86	$\frac{1.55 + 1.41}{2} \times 2.35$	=	3.48
	$\frac{1.50 + 2.00}{2} \times 6.0$	=	10.50	$\frac{0.66 + 0.82}{2} \times 8.15$	=	6.03
	$\frac{2.00 + 1.50}{2} \times 7.0$	=	12.25	$\frac{0.82 + 0.66}{2} \times 8.15$	=	6.03
	$\frac{1.50 + 1.59}{2} \times 3.5$	=	5.41	$\frac{1.41 + 1.59}{2} \times 2.35$	=	3.53
	Check: 21m		35.02 m²	Check: 21m		19.07 m²

End area = $35.02 - 19.07 = 15.95 \text{ m}^2$

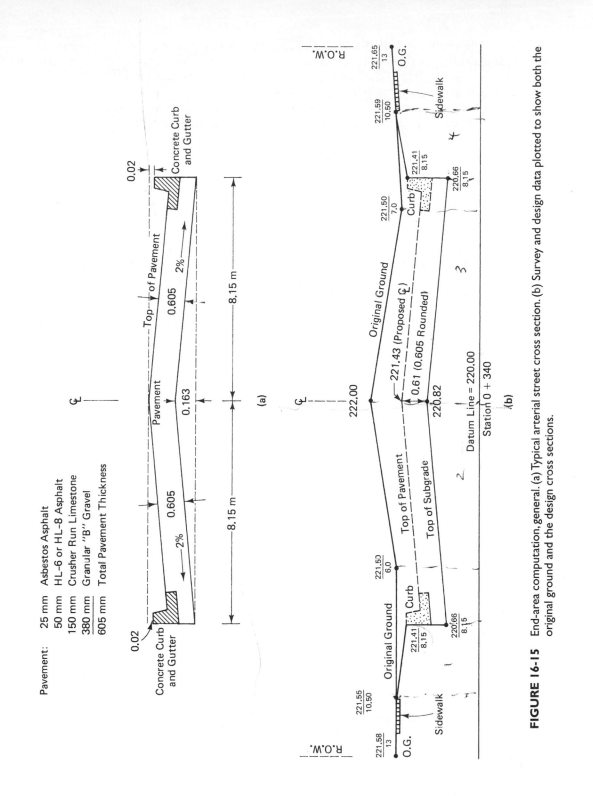

FIGURE 16-15 End-area computation, general. (a) Typical arterial street cross section. (b) Survey and design data plotted to show both the original ground and the design cross sections.

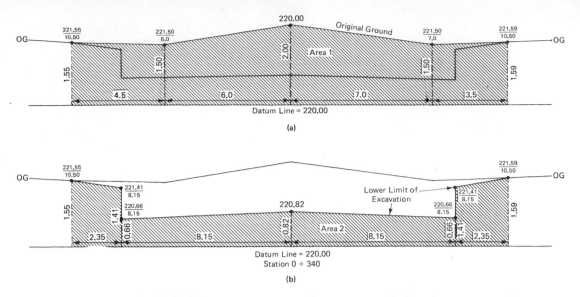

FIGURE 16-16 End-area computations for cut areas. (a) Area between ground cross section and datum line. (b) Area between subgrade cross section and datum line.

Assuming that the end area at 0 + 300 has been computed to be 18.05 m², we can now compute the volume of cut between 0 + 300 and 0 + 340:

$$V = \frac{18.05 + 15.95}{2} \times 40 = 680 \text{ m}^3 \qquad (16.4)$$

16-6 Prismoidal Formula

If values more precise than end area volumes are required, the prismoidal formula can be used. A prismoid is a solid with parallel ends joined by plane or continuously warped surfaces. The prismoidal formula is

$$V = L\frac{(A_1 + 4A_m + A_2)}{6} \text{ ft}^3 \text{ or m}^3 \qquad (16-5)$$

where A_1 and A_2 are the two end areas, A_m is the area of a section midway between A_1 and A_2, and L is the distance from A_1 to A_2. A_m is not the average of A_1 and A_2, but is derived from distances that are the average of corresponding distances required for A_1 and A_2 computations.

This formula is also used for other geometric solids (e.g., truncated prisms, cylinders, and cones). To justify its use, the surveyor must refine the field measurements to reflect the increase in precision being sought. A typical application of the prismoidal formula would be the computation of in-place volumes of concrete. The difference in cost between a cubic yard or meter of concrete and a cubic yard or meter of earth cut or fill is sufficient reason for the increased precision.

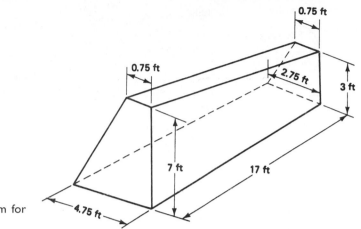

FIGURE 16-17 Sketch of prism for Example 16-2.

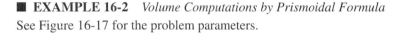

■ **EXAMPLE 16-2** *Volume Computations by Prismoidal Formula*
See Figure 16-17 for the problem parameters.

$$\text{Volume } (V) = \frac{L}{6}(A_1 + 4A_m + A_2) \quad (16\text{-}5)$$

$$= \frac{17}{6}(19.25 + 4 \times 11.25 + 5.25)$$

$$= \frac{17}{6}(19.25 + 45.00 + 5.25)$$

$$= \frac{17}{6} \times 69.50$$

$$= \frac{1181.50}{6}$$

$$= 196.92 \text{ ft}^3$$

$$= 7.29 \text{ yd}^3$$

$$\begin{bmatrix} A_1 = \dfrac{0.75 + 4.75}{2} \times 7 = 19.25 \text{ ft}^2 \\[2mm] A_m = \dfrac{0.75 + 3.75}{2} \times 5 = 11.25 \text{ ft}^2 \\[2mm] A_2 = \dfrac{0.75 + 2.75}{2} \times 3 = 5.25 \text{ ft}^2 \end{bmatrix}$$

16-7 Volume Computations by Geometric Formulas

Some construction items can be broken into solid geometric figures for analysis and quantity computations. Structural concrete quantities, material stockpiles, and construction liquids (e.g., dust control) are some quantities that lend themselves to this sort of analysis. Figures 16-18 and 16-19 illustrate some of these formulas and their use.

16-8 Final (As-Built) Surveys

Similar to preliminary surveys, final surveys tie in features—features that have just been built; these measurements provide a record of construction and a check that the construction has proceeded according to the design plan.

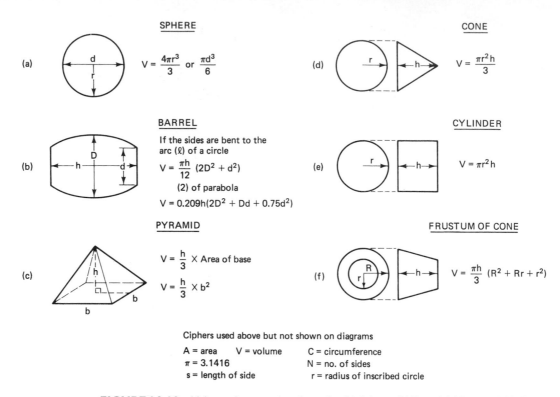

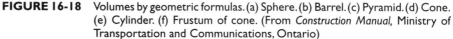

Ciphers used above but not shown on diagrams

A = area V = volume	C = circumference
π = 3.1416	N = no. of sides
s = length of side	r = radius of inscribed circle

FIGURE 16-18 Volumes by geometric formulas. (a) Sphere. (b) Barrel. (c) Pyramid. (d) Cone. (e) Cylinder. (f) Frustum of cone. (From *Construction Manual*, Ministry of Transportation and Communications, Ontario)

The **final plan,** drawn from the as-built survey, will be quite similar to the **design plan,** except for the revisions that are made to reflect the changes that are invariably required during the construction process. Design changes occur when problems are encountered that are apparent only after the construction has commenced—for example, unexpected underground pipes, conduits, or structures that interfere with the designed facility. It is difficult, especially in complex projects, to plan for every eventuality that may be encountered. However, if the preliminary surveyor, the construction surveyor, and the designer have all done their jobs well, the **design plan** and the **as-built drawing** will be quite similar with respect to the horizontal and vertical position of all detail.

The as-built survey is usually begun after all the construction work has been completed. The horizontal and vertical control points used in the preliminary and construction surveys are reestablished and rereferenced if necessary. The cross sections taken for the final payment survey are incorporated into the as-built survey. All detail is tied in, as in a preliminary survey.

Pipelines and sewers are surveyed before the trenches are backfilled. It is particularly important at this stage to tie in (horizontally and vertically) any unexpected pipes, conduits, or structures that are encountered in the trench. **As-built drawings,** produced from

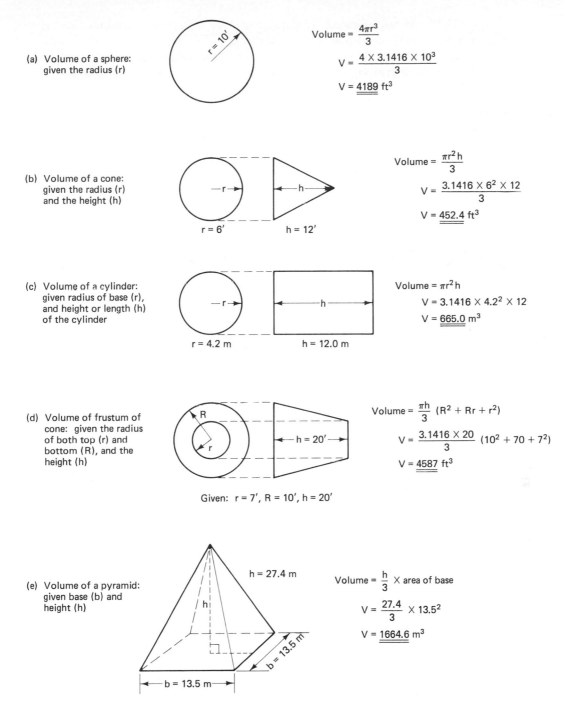

(a) Volume of a sphere: given the radius (r)

$$\text{Volume} = \frac{4\pi r^3}{3}$$

$$V = \frac{4 \times 3.1416 \times 10^3}{3}$$

$$V = \underline{4189} \text{ ft}^3$$

r = 10'

(b) Volume of a cone: given the radius (r) and the height (h)

$$\text{Volume} = \frac{\pi r^2 h}{3}$$

$$V = \frac{3.1416 \times 6^2 \times 12}{3}$$

$$V = \underline{452.4} \text{ ft}^3$$

r = 6'   h = 12'

(c) Volume of a cylinder: given radius of base (r), and height or length (h) of the cylinder

$$\text{Volume} = \pi r^2 h$$

$$V = 3.1416 \times 4.2^2 \times 12$$

$$V = \underline{665.0} \text{ m}^3$$

r = 4.2 m   h = 12.0 m

(d) Volume of frustum of cone: given the radius of both top (r) and bottom (R), and the height (h)

$$\text{Volume} = \frac{\pi h}{3}(R^2 + Rr + r^2)$$

$$V = \frac{3.1416 \times 20}{3}(10^2 + 70 + 7^2)$$

$$V = \underline{4587} \text{ ft}^3$$

Given: r = 7', R = 10', h = 20'

(e) Volume of a pyramid: given base (b) and height (h)

h = 27.4 m

$$\text{Volume} = \frac{h}{3} \times \text{area of base}$$

$$V = \frac{27.4}{3} \times 13.5^2$$

$$V = \underline{1664.6} \text{ m}^3$$

b = 13.5 m   b = 13.5 m

FIGURE 16-19 Examples of volume computations.

final (as-built) surveys, are especially valuable in urban areas, where, it seems, there is no end to underground construction and reconstruction.

After the completion of the contracted work and the expiration of the guarantee period, the **as-built drawing** is often transferred to microfilm for permanent storage.

Problems

16-1. The field measurements (in feet) for an irregularly shaped sodded area are shown below. Calculate the area of sod to the closest square yard, using (a) the trapezoidal technique; (b) Simpson's one-third rule.

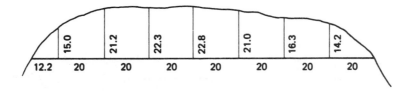

16-2. The field measurements (in feet) for an irregularly shaped paved area are shown below. Calculate the area of pavement to the closest square yard.

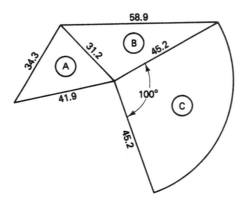

16-3. Calculate the end areas at stations 3 + 60 and 3 + 80, and then determine the volume (m³) of cut required in that section of road. For the end area at 3 + 60, use 180 m as the datum elevation, and for the end area at 3 + 80, use 181 m as the datum elevation.

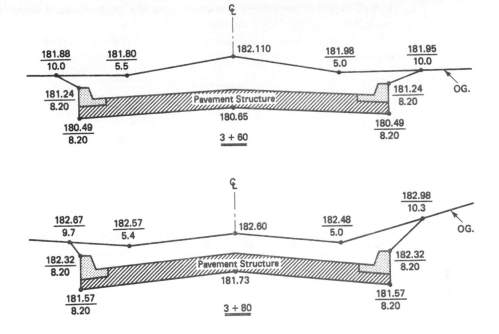

16-4. Use the prismoidal formula to compute the volume (yd^3) of concrete contained in the figure below.

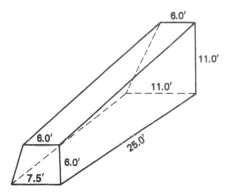

16-5. A stockpile of highway crushed stone is shaped into a conical figure; the base has a diameter of 72 ft, and the height of the stockpile is 52.5 ft. Compute the volume (yd^3) of stone in the stockpile.

16-6. Compute the volume (yd^3) contained in the footing and abutment shown in the figure below.

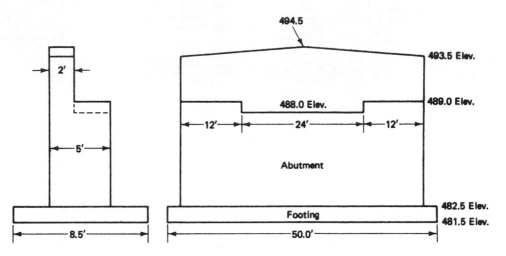

Appendix A

Trigonometry and Coordinate Geometry Review

A-1 Trigonometric Definitions and Identities

A-1-1 Right Triangles

BASIC FUNCTION DEFINITIONS (SEE FIGURE A-1)

$$\sin A = \frac{a}{c} = \cos B \qquad\qquad \text{(A-1)}$$

$$\cos A = \frac{b}{c} = \sin B \qquad\qquad \text{(A-2)}$$

$$\tan A = \frac{a}{b} = \cot B \qquad\qquad \text{(A-3)}$$

$$\sec A = \frac{c}{b} = \operatorname{cosec} B \qquad\qquad \text{(A-4)}$$

$$\operatorname{cosec} A = \frac{c}{a} = \sec B \qquad\qquad \text{(A-5)}$$

$$\cot A = \frac{b}{a} = \tan B \qquad\qquad \text{(A-6)}$$

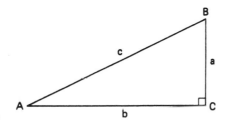

FIGURE A-1 Right triangle.

$$a = c \sin A = c \cos B = b \tan A = b \cot B = \sqrt{c^2 - b^2}$$

$$b = c \cos A = c \sin B = a \cot A = a \tan B = \sqrt{c^2 - a^2}$$

$$c = \frac{a}{\sin A} = \frac{a}{\cos B} = \frac{b}{\sin B} = \frac{b}{\cos A} = \sqrt{a^2 + b^2}$$

Note: The quadrant numbers in Figure A-2 reflect the traditional geometry approach (counterclockwise) to quadrant analysis. In surveying, the quadrants are numbered 1 (N.E.), 2 (S.E.), 3 (S.W.), and 4 (N.W.). The analysis of algebraic signs for the trigonometric functions (as shown) remains valid. Handheld calculators will automatically provide the correct algebraic sign if the angle direction is entered in the calculator in its azimuth form.

A-1-2   Oblique Triangles (See Figure A-3)

SINE LAW

$$\frac{a}{\sin A} = \frac{b}{\sin B} = \frac{c}{\sin C} \tag{A-7}$$

COSINE LAW

$$a^2 = b^2 + c^2 - 2bc \cos A \tag{A-8}$$

$$b^2 = a^2 + c^2 - 2ac \cos B \tag{A-9}$$

$$c^2 = a^2 + b^2 - 2ab \cos C \tag{A-10}$$

Given	Required	Formulas
A, B, a	C, b, c	$c = 180 - (A + B); b = \dfrac{a}{\sin A} \sin B; c = \dfrac{a}{\sin A} \sin C$
A, b, c	a	$a^2 = -b^2 + c^2 - 2bc \cos A$
a, b, c	A	$\cos A = \dfrac{b^2 + c^2 - a^2}{2\,bc}$
a, b, c	Area	Area $= \sqrt{s(s - a)(s - b)(s - c)}$ where $s = 1/2(a + b + c)$
C, a, b	Area	Area $= 1/2\,ab \sin C$

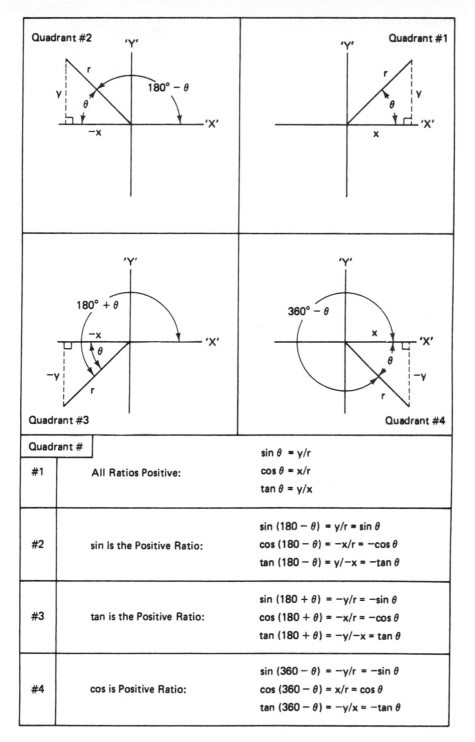

FIGURE A-2   Algebraic signs for primary trigonometric functions.

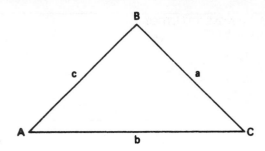

FIGURE A-3 Oblique triangle.

A-1-3 General Trigonometric Formulas

$$\sin A = 2 \sin \tfrac{1}{2}A \cos \tfrac{1}{2}A = \sqrt{1 - \cos^2 A} = \tan A \cos A \qquad \text{(A-11)}$$

$$\cos A = 2 \cos^2 \tfrac{1}{2}A - 1 = 1 - 2 \sin^2 \tfrac{1}{2}A$$
$$= \cos^2 \tfrac{1}{2}A - \sin^2 \tfrac{1}{2}A = \sqrt{1 - \sin^2 A} \qquad \text{(A-12)}$$

$$\tan A = \frac{\sin A}{\cos A} = \frac{\sin 2A}{1 + \cos 2A} = \sec^2 A - 1 \qquad \text{(A-13)}$$

ADDITION AND SUBTRACTION IDENTITIES

$$\sin (A \pm B) = \sin A \cos B \pm \sin B \cos A \qquad \text{(A-14)}$$

$$\cos (A \pm B) = \cos A \cos B \pm \sin A \sin B \qquad \text{(A-15)}$$

$$\tan (A \pm B) = \frac{\tan A \mp \tan B}{1 \mp \tan A \tan B} \qquad \text{(A-16)}$$

$$\sin A + \sin B = 2 \sin \tfrac{1}{2}(A + B) \sin \tfrac{1}{2}(A - B) \qquad \text{(A-17)}$$

$$\sin A - \sin B = 2 \cos \tfrac{1}{2}(A + B) \sin \tfrac{1}{2}(A - B) \qquad \text{(A-18)}$$

$$\cos A + \cos B = 2 \cos \tfrac{1}{2}(A + B) \cos \tfrac{1}{2}(A - B) \qquad \text{(A-19)}$$

$$\cos A - \cos B = 2 \sin \tfrac{1}{2}(A + B) \sin \tfrac{1}{2}(A - B) \qquad \text{(A-20)}$$

DOUBLE-ANGLE IDENTITIES

$$\sin 2A = 2 \sin A \cos A \qquad \text{(A-21)}$$

$$\cos 2A = \cos^2 A - \sin^2 A = 1 - 2 \sin^2 A = 2 \cos^2 A - 1 \qquad \text{(A-22)}$$

$$\tan 2A = \frac{2 \tan A}{1 - \tan^2 A} \qquad \text{(A-23)}$$

$$\sin \frac{A}{2} = \sqrt{\frac{1 - \cos A}{2}} \qquad \text{(A-24)}$$

$$\cos \frac{A}{2} = \sqrt{\frac{1 + \cos A}{2}} \qquad \text{(A-25)}$$

$$\tan \frac{A}{2} = \frac{\sin A}{1 + \cos A} \qquad \text{(A-26)}$$

A-2   Coordinate Geometry

Coordinate geometry was introduced in Section 6-11, where traverse station coordinates were computed along with the area enclosed by the traverse. This section describes the basics of coordinate geometry along with some applications. An understanding of these concepts will help the reader understand the fundamentals underlying coordinate geometry software programs that are now used to process most electronic surveying field data. See Chapter 5.

A-2-1   Geometry of Rectangular Coordinates

Figure A-4 shows two points $P_1(x_1, y_1)$ and $P_2(x_2, y_2)$ and their rectangular relationships to the x and y axes.

$$\text{Length } P_1P_2 = \sqrt{(x_2 - x_1)^2 + (y_2 - y_1)^2} \qquad \text{(A-27)}$$

$$\tan \alpha = \frac{x_2 - x_1}{y_2 - y_1} \qquad \text{(A-28)}$$

where α is the bearing or azimuth of P_1P_2.
    Also:

$$\text{Length } P_2P_2 = \frac{x_2 - x_1}{\sin \alpha} \qquad \text{(A-29)}$$

$$\text{Length } P_1P_2 = \frac{y_2 - y_1}{\cos \alpha} \qquad \text{(A-30)}$$

Use the equation having the larger numerical value of $(x_2 - x_1)$ or $(y_2 - y_1)$.
    It will be clear from Figure A-4 that $(x_2 - x_1)$ is the departure of P_1P_2 and that $(y_2 - y_1)$ is the latitude of P_1P_2. In survey work, the y value (latitude) is known as the northing, and the x value (departure) is known as the easting.
    From analytic geometry, the slope of a straight line is $m = \tan (90 - \alpha)$, where $(90 - \alpha)$ is the angle of the straight line with the x axis (Figure A-4); that is,

$$m = \cot \alpha$$

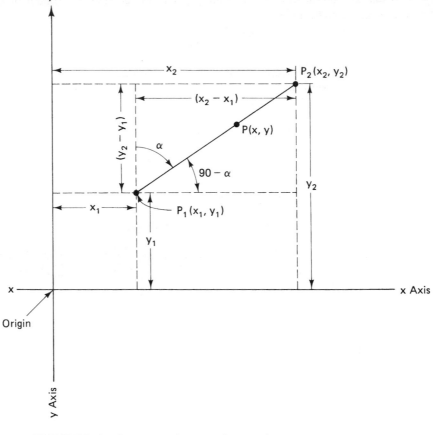

FIGURE A-4 Geometry of rectangular coordinates.

From coordinate geometry, the equation of straight line P_1P_2, where the coordinates of P_1 and P_2, are known, is

$$\frac{y - y_1}{y_2 - y_1} = \frac{x - x_1}{x_2 - x_1} \tag{A-31}$$

This can be written

$$y - y_1 = \frac{y_2 - y_1}{x_2 - x_1}(x - x_1)$$

where $(y_2 - y_1)/(x_2 - x_1) = \cot \alpha = m$ (from analytic geometry), the slope.

Analysis of Figure A-4 also shows that slope = rise/run = $(y_2 - y_1)/(x_2 - x_1) = \tan (90 - \alpha)$.

When the coordinates of one point (P_1) and the bearing or azimuth of a line are known, the equation becomes

$$y - y_1 = \cot \alpha \, (x - x_1) \qquad \text{(A-32)}$$

where α is the azimuth or bearing of the line through $P_1 \, (x_1, y_1)$

Also from analytical geometry,

$$y - y_1 = \frac{-1}{\cot \alpha} \, (x - x_1) \qquad \text{(A-33)}$$

which represents a line **perpendicular** to the line represented by Equation (A-32); that is, the slopes of perpendicular lines are negative reciprocals.

Equations for circular curves are quadratics in the form of

$$(x - H)^2 + (y - K)^2 = r^2 \qquad \text{(A-34)}$$

where r is the curve radius, (H, K) are the coordinates of the center, and (x, y) are the coordinates of point P, which locates the circle (see Figure A-5). When the circle center is at the origin, the equation becomes

$$x^2 + y^2 = r^2 \qquad \text{(A-35)}$$

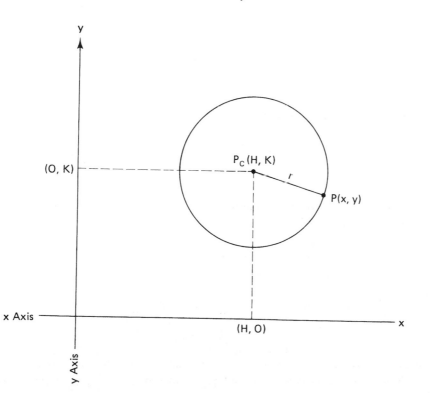

FIGURE A-5 Circular curve coordinates.

A-2-2 Illustrative Problems in Rectangular Coordinates

■ EXAMPLE A-1

From the information shown in Figure A-6, calculate the coordinates of the point of intersection (K_1) of lines EC and DB. From Equation (A-31), the equation of EC is

$$\frac{y - 688.89}{1302.96 - 688.69} = \frac{x - 1160.27}{1692.14 - 1160.27} \tag{1}$$

$$y - 688.69 = \frac{1302.96 - 688.69}{1692.14 - 1160.27}(x - 1160.27)$$

$$y - 688.69 = 1.15492508x - 1340.025$$

$$y = 1.15492508x - 651.335 \tag{1A}$$

The equation of DB is

$$\frac{y - 934.77}{1250.73 - 934.77} = \frac{x - 1684.54}{1313.61 - 1684.54} \tag{2}$$

$$y - 934.77 = \frac{1250.73 - 934.77}{1313.61 - 1684.54}(x - 1684.54)$$

$$y - 934.77 = -0.8518049x + 1434.899$$

$$y = -0.8518049x + 2369.669 \tag{2A}$$

Substitute for y:

$$1.15492508x - 651.335 = -0.08518049x + 2369.669$$

$$x = 1505.436$$

Substitute the value of x in either (1A) or (2A):

$$y = 1087.33$$

Therefore, the coordinates of point of intersection K_1 are (1087.33 N, 1505.44 E).

Note: Coordinates are shown as (N, E) or (E, N), depending on local practice.

■ EXAMPLE A-2

From the information shown in Figure A-6, calculate (a) the coordinates of K_2, the point of intersection of line ED and a line *perpendicular to ED* running through station B; and (b) distances K_2D and K_2E.

(a) From Equation (A-31), the equation of ED is

$$\frac{y - 688.69}{934.77 - 688.69} = \frac{x - 1160.27}{1684.54 - 1160.27} \tag{1}$$

$$y - 688.69 = \frac{246.08}{524.27}(x - 1160.27) \tag{1A}$$

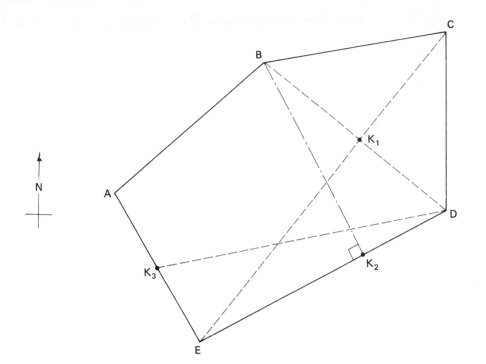

FIGURE A-6 Coordinates for traverse problem.

	Coordinates	
Station	North	East
A	1000.00	1000.00
B	1250.73	1313.61
C	1302.96	1692.14
D	934.77	1684.54
E	688.69	1160.27

From Equation (A-32), the equation of BK_2 is

$$y - 1250.73 - \frac{524.27}{246.08}(x - 1313.61) \qquad (2)$$

Simplifying, we find that these equations become (use five decimals to avoid rounding errors)

$$ED: \ 0.46938x - y = -144.09 \qquad (1B)$$

$$BK_2: \ 2.13049\,x + y = 4049.36 \qquad (2B)$$

$$2.59987x = 3905.27 \qquad\qquad (1B + 2B)$$
$$x = 1502.102$$

Substitute the value of x in Equation (1A), and check the results in Equation (2):

$$y = 849.15$$

Therefore, the coordinates of K_2 are (849.15 N, 1502.10 E).

(b) Figure A-7 shows the coordinates for stations E and D and intermediate point K_2 from Equation (A-27):

$$\text{Length } K_2D = \sqrt{85.62^2 + 182.44^2} = 201.53$$

and

$$\text{Length } K_2E = \sqrt{160.46^2 + 341.83^2} = 377.62$$
$$K_2D + K_2E = ED = 579.15$$

Check

$$\text{Length } ED = \sqrt{246.08^2 + 524.27^2} = 579.15$$

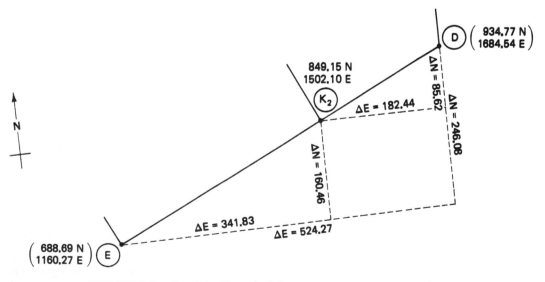

FIGURE A-7 Sketch for Example A-2.

■ EXAMPLE A-3

From the information shown in Figure A-6, calculate the coordinates of the point of intersection (K_3) on the line EA of a *line parallel to CB* running from station D to line EA. From Equation (A-31),

$$CB: \frac{y - 1302.96}{1250.73 - 1302.96} = \frac{x - 1692.14}{1313.16 - 1692.14}$$

$$y - 1302.96 = \frac{-52.23}{-378.53} (x - 1692.14)$$

$$\text{Slope (cot } \alpha) \text{ of } CB = \frac{-52.23}{-378.53}$$

Since DK_3 is parallel to BC,

$$\text{Slope (cot } \alpha) \text{ of } DK_3 = \frac{-52.23}{-378.53}$$

$$DK_3: y - 934.77 = \frac{52.23}{378.53} (x - 1684.54) \tag{1}$$

$$EA: \frac{y - 688.69}{1000.00 - 688.69} = \frac{x - 1160.27}{1000.00 - 1160.27} \tag{2}$$

$$DK_3: 0.13798x - y = -702.34 \tag{1A}$$

$$EA: 1.94241x + y = +2942.41 \tag{2A}$$

$$2.08039x = +2240.07 \tag{1A + 2A}$$

$$x = 1076.7547$$

Substitute the value of x in Equation (1A), and check the results in Equation (2A):

$$y = 850.91$$

Therefore, the coordinates of K_3 are (850.91 N, 1076.75 E).

■ EXAMPLE A-4

From the information shown in Figure A-8, calculate the coordinates of the point of intersection *(L)* of the ₡ of Fisher Road with the ₡ of Elm Parkway.

The coordinates of station M on Fisher Road are (4,850,277.101 N, 316,909.433 E), and the bearing of the Fisher Road ₡ *(ML)* is S 75°10′30″ E. The coordinates of the center of the 350 M radius highway curve are (4,850,317.313 N, 317,112.656 E).

The coordinates here are referred to a coordinate grid system having 0.000 m north at the equator and 304,800.000 m east at longitude 79°30′ W.

The coordinate values are, of necessity, very large and would cause significant rounding error if they were used in the computations. Accordingly, an auxiliary set of

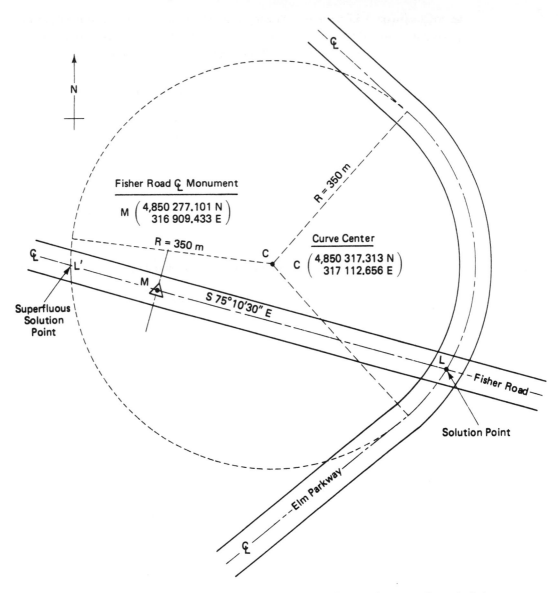

FIGURE A-8 Intersection of a straight line with a circular curve. Example A-4.

coordinate axes will be used, allowing the values of the given coordinates to be greatly reduced for the computations; the amount reduced will later be added to give the final coordinates. The summary of coordinates is shown next:

Station	Grid Coordinates		Reduced Coordinates	
	y	x	$y'(y - 4{,}850{,}000)$	$x'(x - 316{,}500)$
M	4,850,277.101	316,909.433	277.101	409.433
C	4,850,317.313	317,112.656	317.313	612.656

From Equation (A-32), the equation of the Fisher Road ₵ (*ML*) is

$$y' - 277.101 = \cot 75°10'30'' \, (x' - 409.433) \tag{1}$$

From Equation (A-34), the equation of the Elm Parkway ₵ is

$$(x' - 612.656)^2 + (y' - 317.313)^2 = 350.000^2 \tag{2}$$

Simplify Equation (1) to

$$y' - 277.101 = -0.2646782x' + 108.368$$
$$y' = -0.2646782x' + 385.469 \tag{1A}$$

Substitute the value of y' into Equation (2):

$$(x' - 612.656)^2 + (-0.2646782x' + 385.469 - 317.313)^2 - 350.000^2 = 0$$
$$(x' - 612.656)^2 + (-0.2646782x' + 68.156)^2 - 350.000^2 = 0$$
$$1.0700545x'^2 - 1261.391x' + 257492.61 = 0$$

This quadratic of the form $ax^2 + bx + c = 0$ has roots

$$x = \frac{-b \pm \sqrt{b^2 - 4ac}}{2a}$$

$$x' = \frac{1261.3908 \pm \sqrt{1{,}591{,}107.30 - 1{,}102{,}124.50}}{2.140109}$$

$$= \frac{1261.3908 \pm 699.27305}{2.140109}$$

$$= 916.1514 \text{ or } x' = 262.658$$

Solve for y' by substituting in Equation (1A):

$$y' = 142.984 \text{ or } y' = 315.949$$

When these coordinates are now enlarged by the amount of the original reduction, the following values are obtained:

Station	Reduced Coordinates		Grid Coordinates	
	y'	x'	$y(y' + 4,850,000)$	$x(x' + 316,500)$
L	142.984	916.151	4,850,142.984	317,416.151
L'	315.949	262.658	4,850,315.949	316,762.658

Analysis of Figure A-8 is required in order to determine which of the two solutions is the correct one. The sketch shows that the desired intersecton point L is south and east of station M. That is, L (4,850,142.984 N, 317 416.151 E) is the set of coordinates for the intersection of the ₵s of Elm Parkway and Fisher Road.

The other intersection point (L') solution is superfluous.

Appendix B

Surveying and Mapping Internet Web Sites

Allen Osborne Associates (GPS)   http://www.aoa-gps.com/
American Congress on Surveying and Mapping (ACSM)
   http://www.survmap.com
American Society for Photogrammetry and Remote Sensing
   http://www.asprs.org/asprs/
ARCINFO Tutorial   http://boris.qub.ac.uk/shane/arc/ARChome.html
Ashtech (Magellan)   http://www.ashtech.com
Beadle's (John) Introduction to GPS Applications
   http://ares.redsword.com/gps/apps
Bennett (Peter) NMEA-0183 and GPS Information
   http://vancouver-webpages.com/pub/peter/
Berntsen International, Inc. (surveying markers)   http://www.berntsen.com
Canadian Geodetic Survey   http://www.geod.nrcan.gc.ca
CORS Information   http://www.ngs.noaa.gov/CORS/cors-data.html
Corvallis Microtechnology   http://www.cmtinc.com
Dana (Peter H.) Global Positioning Overview
   http://www.utexas.edu/depts/grg/gcraft/notes/gps/gps.html
Differential GPS (DGPS)   http://www.navcen.uscg.mil/dgps/
Flatirons Surveying   http://www.flatsurv.com
Geotronics—Spectra Precision   http://www.geotronics.se/
GIS—Kingston University Center (U.K.)   http://www.kingston.ac.uk/geog/gis
Global Positioning System Resources (Sam Wormley)
   http://www.cnde.iastate.edu/gps.html
GLONASS (Russian Federation)   http://mx.iki.rssi.ru/SFCSIC/english.html
GPS World Magazine   http://www.gpsworld.com

Intergraph Corporation   http://www.intergraph.com/software/photogrammetry
Javad Positioning (GPS receivers)   http://www.javad.com
Land Surveying and Geomatics   http://homepage.interaccess.com/~maynard/
Land Surveyor Reference Page (Stan Thompson)   http://www.lsrp.com/index.html
Leica Geosystems Inc.   http://www.leica.com/
Leick GPS GLONASS GODESY
    http://www.spatial.maine.edu/~leick/gpshome.htm
LH Systems (digital photogrammetry)   http://www.lhsystemsgroup.com/
MAPINFO (mapping)   http:/www.mapinfo.com/
MicroSurvey Software   http://www.microsurvey.com/
NASA's GPS Applications Page   http://gpshome.scc.nasa.gov
NGS   http://www.ngs.noaa.gov/
Nikon   http://www.nikonusa.com
POB Point of Beginning Magazine   http://www.pobonline.com/
Professional Surveyor Magazine   http://www.profsurv.com
Sokkia   http://www.sokkia.com/
Spectra Precision (Geodimeter)   http://www.geodat.com
Spectra Precision (Terrasat—GPS/GIS)   http://www.terrasat.com
Surveyors Module International (SMI)   http://www.smi.com/
Tarr's (Paul) GPS WWW Resources List
    http://www.inmet.com/~pwt/gps_gen.html
Topcon Instrument Corporation   http:/www.topcon.com
Trimble   http://www.trimble.com
Tripod Data Systems (TDS)   http://www.tdsway.com
United States Coast Guard (USCG) Navigation Center
    http://www.navcen.uscg.mil
U.S. Geological Survey   http://usgs.gov/
University of Maine   http://www.spatial.maine.edu/
University NAVSTAR Consortium   www.unavco.ucar.edu/
Zeiss (Carl) Surveying   http://www.zeiss.com/survey/

Note: The web sites listed here cover surveying, GPS, photogrammetry, GIS, and mapping; some sites include web links to a variety of related sites. Although the web sites shown here were verified at the time of publication, some changes are inevitable; corrected site locations and new sites may be accessed by searching the web links shown at other sites listed here.

Appendix C

Glossary

Absolute Positioning (Point Positioning)   The direct determination of a station's coordinates by taking GPS observations on a minimum of four GPS satellites.

Abutment   That part of a bridge substructure that supports the end of the superstructure and retains the approach fill.

Accuracy   The conformity of a measurement to the "true" value.

Accuracy Ratio   The error in a measurement divided by the overall value of the measurement; that is, an error of 1 ft in 3000 ft would result in an accuracy ratio of 1/3000

Alignment   The location of the centerline of a survey or a facility.

Ambiguity   The integer number of carrier cycles between the GPS receiver and a satellite.

Arithmetic Check   A check on the reductions of differential leveling involving the sums of the backsights and the foresights.

Arterial Road (Highway)   A road mainly designed for traffic mobility—with some property access consideration.

As-Built (Final) Survey   A postconstruction survey that confirms design execution and records in-progress revisions

Automatic Level   A surveyors' level that has the line of sight automatically maintained in the horizontal plane once the instrument is roughly leveled.

Azimuth   The angle to a line of sight, measured clockwise from a north (usually meridian.

Backfill   Material used to fill an excavation.

Backsight   A sight taken with a level to a point of known elevation, thus permitting the surveyor to compute the elevation of the HI; in transit work, the backsight is a sighting taken to a point of known position to establish a reference direction.

Baseline   A line of reference for survey work; often the centerline, the street line, or the centerline of construction is used, although any line could be arbitrarily selected or established.

Batter Board   A horizontal cross piece on a grade stake or grade rod that refers to the proposed elevations.

Bearing   The direction of a line given by the acute angle from a meridian and accompanied by a cardinal compass direction.

Bearing Plate   A plate that is secured to the abutment seat or pier top on which the beams, girders, and the like rest.

Benchmark   A fixed solid reference point with a precisely determined published elevation.

Board Measure   A standard unit of timber measure; 1 board foot = 1 ft square by 1 in. thick.

Borrow Pit   A source of granular fill material that is located off the right of way.

Catch Basin   A structure designed to collect surface water and transfer it to a storm sewer.

Central Meridian   A reference meridian in the center of the zone covered by the plane coordinate grid—at every 6° of longitude in the UTM grid.

Circular Curve   A curve with a constant radius.

Clearing   The cutting and removal of trees from a construction site.

COGO (Coordinate Geometry)   Software programs that facilitate coordinate geometry computations used in surveying and civil engineering.

Collector Road (Highway)   A road designed to provide property access with some traffic mobility; it connects local roads to arterials.

Compass Rule   Used in traverse balancing, an adjustment that distributes the errors in latitude and departure for each traverse course in the same proportion as the course distance is to the traverse perimeter.

Compound Curve   Two or more circular arcs turning in the same direction and having common tangent points and different radii.

Construction Survey   A survey used to provide line and grade to a contractor for the construction of a facility.

Continuously Operating Reference Station   *See* CORS.

Contour   A line on a map joining points of similar elevation.

Control Survey   A survey used to establish reference points and lines for preliminary and construction surveys.

Coordinate Geometry   *See* COGO.

Coordinates   A set of numbers (*X, Y*) defining the two-dimensional position of a point given by the distances measured north and east of an origin reference point having coordinates of (0, 0).

CORS   [Continuously Operating Reference Station (GPS)] A station that transmits data that can be used by single-receiver surveyors and navigators to permit the higher-precision differential positioning normally only found in two-receiver (multi-receiver) surveys.

Cross Section   A profile of the ground or the like that is taken at right angles to a reference line.

Crown   The uppermost point on a road, or pipe, cross section—or the rate of cross fall on pavement.

Culvert   A structure designed to provide an opening under a road or the like, usually for the transportation of storm water.

Cut   In construction, the excavation of material; also the measurement down from a grade mark.

Cutoff Angle   *See* Mask Angle.

Data Collector   An electronic field book designed to accept field data—both measured and descriptive.

Datum   An assumed or a fixed reference plane.

Deck   The floor of a bridge.

Deflection Angle   The angle between the prolongation of the back line measured right (R) or left (L) to the forward line.

Departure   The change in easterly direction (ΔE) of a line.

Differential Leveling   A technique for determining the differences in elevation between points using a surveyors' level.

Differential Positioning   A technique using GPS measurements made at a known base station to correct measurements simultaneously taken at rover GPS receiving stations.

Digital Terrain Model   *See* DTM.

Double Centering   A technique of turning angles or producing straight lines involving a minimum of two sightings with a theodolite—once with the telescope direct and once with the telescope inverted.

Drainage   The collection and transportation of ground and storm water.

Drawing Exchange Format   *See* DXF.

DTM (Digital Terrain Model)   A three-dimensional depiction of a ground surface—usually produced by software programs (sometimes referred to as a DEM—digital elevation model).

DXF (Drawing Exchange Format)   An industry standard format that permits graphical data to be transferred among various data collector, CAD, GIS, and softcopy photogrammetry applications programs.

EDM (Electronic Distance Measurement A technique of determining distances that ultimately involves knowing the time taken for a light wave, sent from the EDM instrument (EDMI), to be reflected back from the other end of the line being measured; or, in the case of microwaves transmission, the time required for the signal to be received by a similar microwave instrument located at the other end of the line being measured.

EFB (Electronic Field Book) *See* Data Collector.

Electronic Distance Measurement *See* EDM.

Electronic Field Book *See* EFB.

Elevation The distance above, or below, a given datum.

Elevation Factor The factor used to convert ground distances to sea level distances.

Engineering Surveys Preliminary and layout surveys used for construction.

External Distance The distance from the mid-curve to the PI in a circular curve.

Fill Material used to raise the construction level, also the measurement up from a grade mark.

Final Survey *See* As-Built Survey.

Footing The part of the structure that is placed in, or on, the ground on which the main structure rests.

Foresight In leveling, a sight taken to a BM or TP to obtain a check on a leveling operation or to establish a transfer elevation.

Foundation The portion of the structure that rests on the footing.

4-Foot Mark A reference mark used in building construction that is 4 ft above the finished-floor elevation.

Free Station A conveniently located instrument station used for construction layout, the position of which is determined after occupation—through resection techniques.

Freeway A highway designed for traffic mobility with access restricted to interchanges with arterials and other freeways.

Gabion A wire basket filled with fragmented rocks or concrete, often used in erosion control.

GDOP (General Dilution of Precision) A measurement that indicates the relative uncertainty in position, using GPS measurements, caused by errors in time and satellite vector measurements. Widely spaced satellites at high elevations usually produce good results (i.e., a lower GDOP value).

General Dilution of Precision *See* GDOP.

Geodetic Datum A precisely established and maintained series of benchmarks referenced to mean sea level (MSL).

Geodetic Height (h) The distance from the ellipsoid surface to the ground surface.

Geographic Information System (GIS) A spatially and relationally referenced data base.

Geographic Meridian   A line on the surface of the earth joining the poles; that is, a line of longitude.

Geoid Height   *See* Geoid Undulation

Geoid Surface   A surface that is approximately represented by mean sea level (MSL) and is, in fact, the equipotential surface of the earth's gravity field.

Geoid Undulation (N)   The difference in elevation between the geoid surface and the ellipsoid surface; N is negative if the geoid surface is below the ellipsoid surface (also known as the geoid height).

GIS   *See* Geographic Information System.

Global Positioning System   *See* GPS.

GPS (Global Positioning System)   A ground positioning (Y, X, and Z) technique based on the reception and analysis of NAVSTAR satellite signals.

Grade Sheet   A construction report giving line and grade—that is, offsets—and cuts/fills at each station.

Grade Stake   A wood stake with a cut/fill reference mark to that portion of a proposed facility adjacent to the stake.

Grade Transfer   A technique of transferring cut/fill measurements to the facility; that is, carpenters' level, stringline level, laser, and batter boards.

Gradient   The slope of a gradeline.

Grid Distance   A distance on a coordinate grid.

Grid Factor   A factor used to convert ground distances to grid distances.

Grid Meridian   A meridian parallel to a central meridian on a coordinate grid.

Ground Distance   A distance as measured on the ground surface.

Grubbing   The removal of stumps, roots, and debris from a construction site.

Gunter's Chain   Early (1800s) steel measuring device consisting of 100 links, 66 ft long.

Haul   The distance that 1 cubic yard (meter) of cut material is transported to a fill location in highway construction.

Head Wall   A vertical wall at the end of a culvert that is used to keep fill material from falling into the creek or watercourse.

Hectare   10,000 square meters.

HI   The height of the line of sight of an instrument—above a datum (used in leveling).

hi   The height of an instrument (optical axis)—above the instrument station (used in stadia and Total Station work)

Interlining   A trial-and-error technique of establishing the theodolite on a line between two points that are not intervisible

Intermediate Sight   A sight taken by a level or transit to determine a feature elevation and/or location.

Invert   The inside bottom of a pipe or culvert.

Laser Alignment   The horizontal and/or vertical alignment given by a fixed or rotating laser.

Latitude (of a Course)   The change in northerly displacement (ΔN) of a line.

Latitude (Geographic)   An angular distance measured northerly or southerly at the earth's center from the equator.

Layout Survey   A construction survey.

Line and Grade   The horizontal and vertical position of a facility.

Linear Error of Closure   The line of traverse misclosure representing the resultant of the measuring errors.

Local Road (Highway)   A road designed for property access, connected to arterials by collectors.

Longitude   An angular distance measured in the plane of the equator from the reference meridian through Greenwich, England; lines of longitude show on globes as meridians.

Manhole   A structure that provides access to underground services.

Mask Angle   The vertical angle below which satellite signals are not recorded or not processed—often a value of 10° or 15° is used (also known as the cutoff angle).

Mass Diagram   A graphic representation of cumulative highway cuts and fills.

Mean sea level (MSL)   A reference datum for leveling.

Meridian   A north-south reference line.

Mid-ordinate Distance   The distance from the mid-chord to the mid-curve in a circular curve.

Mistake   A poor result due to carelessness or a misunderstanding.

Monument   A permanent reference point for horizontal and vertical positioning.

MSL   *See* Mean Sea Level.

Nadir   A vertical angle measured from the nadir direction (straight down) upward to a point.

NAVSTAR   A set of 24 orbiting satellites used in navigation and positioning.

Normal Tension   The amount of tension required in taping to offset the effects of sag.

Original Ground   The position of the ground surface prior to construction.

Page Check   An arithmetic check of leveling notes.

Parabolic Curve   A curve used in vertical alignment to join two adjacent gradelines.

Parallax   An error in sighting that occurs when the objective and/or the crosshairs are improperly focused.

Pier   A vertical column supporting beams, girders and the like between abutments.

Planimeter   A mechanical or electronic device used to measure area by tracing the outline of the area on the map or plan.

Polar Coordinates   The coordinates that locate a feature by angle and distance.

Precision   The degree of refinement with which a measurement is made.

Preengineering Survey   A preliminary survey that forms the basis for engineering design.

Property Survey   A survey to retrace or establish property lines or to establish the location of buildings with respect to property limits.

Pseudorange   The uncorrected distance from a GPS satellite to a ground receiver, determined by comparing the code transmitted from a satellite to the receiver's on-board replica code; in order to convert to the actual range (distance from satellite to receiver), corrections must be made for clock errors as well as natural and instrumental errors.

Rectangular Coordinates   Two distances, 90 degrees opposed, that locate a feature.

Relative Positioning   A technique used to determine the relative difference in position between two or more stations. This technique computes the baseline vector (x, y, and z) from the known-position base station to a rover station that is simultaneously receiving observations from the same satellites. This technique permits the cancellation of all errors that are common to both receivers.

Remote Object Elevation   The determination of the height of an object by a Total Station sighting, utilizing on-board applications software.

Resection   The solution of the coordinate determination of an occupied station by the angle sighting of three or more coordinated reference stations—two or more stations if both angles and distances are measured.

Retaining Wall   A wall built to hold back the embankment adjacent to the structure.

Right of Way (ROW)   The legal property limits of a utility or access route.

Route Surveys   Preliminary, control, and construction surveys that cover a long, but narrow area—as in highway and railroad construction.

ROW   *See* Right of Way.

Sag   The error caused when a measuring tape is supported only at the ends.

Scale Factor   The factor used to convert sea level distances to plane grid distances.

Sea Level Correction Factor   The factor used to convert ground distances to sea level equivalent distances.

Shaft   An opening of uniform cross section joining a tunnel to the surface—used for access and ventilation.

Skew Number   A clockwise angle (closest 5°) turned from the back tangent to the centerline of a culvert or bridge.

Slope Stake   A stake placed to identify the top or bottom of a slope.

Span   The unsupported length of a structure.

Spiral Curve   A transition curve of constantly changing radius placed between a high-speed tangent and a central curve—which permits a gradual speed adjustment.

Springline   The horizontal bisector of a sewer pipe—above which connections may be made.

Station   A point on a baseline that is a specified distance from the point of commencement; the point of commencement is identified as 0 + 00; 100 ft or 100 m are known as full stations (1000 m in some highway applications); 1 + 45.20 identifies a point 145.20 ft (m) distant from the point of commencement.

Stripping   The removal of topsoil from a construction site.

Superelevation   The banking of a curved section of road to help overcome the effects of centrifugal force.

Tangent   A straight line—often referred to with respect to a curve.

Three-Wire Leveling   A more precise technique of differential leveling in which rod readings are taken at the stadia hairs in addition to the main crosshair.

Toe of Slope   The bottom of a slope.

Total Station   An electronic theodolite combined with an EDM instrument and an electronic data collector.

Traverse   A continuous series of measured (angles and distances) lines.

Turning Point   A solid point used in leveling where an elevation is temporarily established so that the level may be relocated.

Universal Transverse Mercator System (UTM)   A worldwide grid system based on 60 zones, each 6° of longitude wide. The grid covers from 80° north latitude to 80° south latitude. Each central meridian, at the middle of the zone, has an x (easterly) value of 500,000.000 m, and the equator has a y (northerly) value of 0.000 m. The scale factor at the central meridian is 0.9996.

Vertical Angle   An angle in the vertical plane measured up (+) or down (−) from horizontal.

Vertical Curve   A parabolic curve joining two gradelines.

Waving the Rod   The slight waving of the leveling rod to and from the instrument, which permits the surveyor to take a more precise (lowest) rod reading.

Wing Wall   An abutment extension designed to retain the approach fill.

Zenith Angle   A vertical angle measured downward from the zenith (upward plumbline) direction; this is the vertical angle measured by most modern theodolites.

Appendix D
Typical Field Projects

The following projects can be performed in either foot units or metric units and can be adjusted in scope to fit the available time.

Survey field notes can be entered into a bound field book or on loose-leaf field note paper; if a bound field book is used, be sure to leave room for a Title, Index, and Diary at the front of the book—if they are required by your instructor.

SAMPLE FIELD BOOK INSTRUCTIONS AND LAYOUT

1. Write your name in ink on the outside cover.
2. Page numbers are to be on the right side only—for example 1 to 72.
3. All entries are to be in pencil, 2H or 3H.
4. Page 1:
5. Pages 2 and 3:
6. Pages 4, 5, 6 and 7:

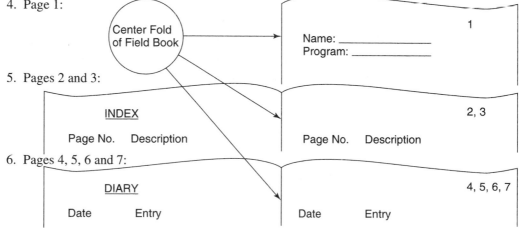

7. All entries are to be printed (uppercase, if permitted).

8. Calculations are to be checked and initialed.

9. Sketches are to be used to clarify field notes—orient the sketch so that the included north arrow is pointing toward the top of the page.

10. All field notes are to be brought up to date each day.

11. Show the word "copy" at the top of all copied pages.

12. Field notes are to be entered directly in the field book—not on scraps of paper to be copied later.

13. Mistakes in entered data are to lined out—not erased.

14. Spelling mistakes, calculation mistakes, and the like should be erased and reentered correctly.

15. Lettering is to be read from the bottom of the page or the right side.

16. The first page of each project will show the date, temperature, project title, crew duties, and so on.

17. The diary will show absentees, weather, description of work, and so on.

Project 1 Building Measurements

Description   The students will measure the selected walls of an indicated campus building with a cloth or fiberglass tape, and record the measurements on a sketch in the field book—as directed by the instructor (e.g., see Figure 2-15).

Equipment   Cloth or fiberglass tape (100 ft or 30 m).

Purpose   To introduce students to the fundamentals of note keeping and survey measurement.

Procedure   Use the measuring techniques described in class prior to going out.

One crew member will be appointed to take notes for this first project, and at the completion of the project (same day), the other crew members will copy the notes (ignoring erroneous data) into their field books—including diary and index data. Crew members will take equal turns acting as note keeper over the length of the program.

Draw (using a straightedge) a large sketch of the selected building walls on the right-hand (grid) side of your field book. Show the walls as they would appear in a plan view—for example, ignore overhangs, or show them as dashed lines. Keep the tape taut to remove sag, and try to keep the tape horizontal. If the building wall is longer than one tape length, make an intermediate mark (do not deface the building), and proceed from that point.

After completing all the measurements in one direction, start from the terminal point, and remeasure all the walls. If the second measurement agrees with the first measurement, put a check mark beside the entered data. If the second measurement agrees acceptably (e.g., within $+/- 0.10$ ft or 0.02 m), enter that measurement directly above or below the first entered measurement. If the second measurement disagrees with the first, (e.g., > 0.10 ft or 0.02 m), enter that value on the sketch, and measure that dimension a third time—discard the erroneous measurement by drawing a line (using a straightedge) through the erroneous value.

Discussion   If the class results are summarized on the chalkboard, it will be clear that all crews did not obtain the same results for specified building wall lengths; there will be much more agreement among crews on the lengths of the shorter building walls than on the lengths of the longer building walls (particularly the walls that were longer than one tape length).

Discuss and enumerate the types of mistakes and errors that could account for measurement discrepancies among survey crews working on this project.

Project 2   Experiment to Determine "Normal Tension"

Description   Project 2 is an experiment in which the students will determine the tension required to eliminate errors due to tension and sag for a 100-ft or 30-m steel tape—supported only at the ends. This tension is called *normal tension.*

Equipment   Steel tape (100.00 ft. or 30.000 m), two plumb bobs, and a tension handle.

Purpose   To introduce students to measurement techniques requiring the use of a steel tape and plumb bobs and to demonstrate the "feel" of the proper tension required when using a tape that is supported only at the ends (the usual case).

Procedure
- With a 100-ft or 30-m tape fully supported on the ground and under a tension of 10 lbs or 50 N *(standard tension),* as determined by use of a supplied tension handle, measure out from an initial mark and place a second mark at exactly100.00 ft or 30.000 m.
- Check this measurement by repeating the procedure (while switching personnel) and correcting if necessary. If this initial measurement is not performed correctly, much time will be wasted.
- Raise the tape off the ground and keep it parallel to the ground to eliminate slope errors.
- Using plumb bobs and the tension handle, determine how many pounds or Newtons of tension (see Table 2-1) are required to force the steel tape to agree with the previously measured distance of 100.00 ft or 30.000 m.
- Repeat the process while switching crew personnel. (Acceptable tolerance is 2 lbs.)
- Record the *normal tension* results (at least two) in the field book—as described in the classroom.
- Include the standard conditions for the use of steel tapes in your field notes:

STANDARD CONDITIONS FOR THE USE OF STEEL TAPES

English System	Metric System
Temperature = 68°F	Temperature = 20°C
Tension = 10 lbs	Tension = 50 N (11.2 lbs)
Tape is fully supported	Tape is fully supported

(For this project, you can assume that the temperature is standard, 68°F or 20°C.)

Discussion   If the class results are summarized (e.g., on the chalkboard), it will be clear that not all survey crews obtained the same average value for *normal tension.*

Discuss the reasons for the tension measurement discrepancies and agree on a "working" value for normal tension for subsequent class projects.

Project 3   Field Measurements with a Steel Tape

Description   The students will measure the sides of a five-sided closed field traverse using techniques designed to permit a precision closure ratio of 1:5000. See Table 2-2. The traverse angles will be obtained from Project 5.

Equipment   Steel tape, two plumb bobs, hand level, range pole or plumb bob string target, and chaining pins or other devices to mark position on the ground.

Alternatively Projects 3 and 5 can be combined, using EDM-equipped theodolites and reflecting prisms. The traverse courses can be measured using an EDM instrument and a prism (pole-mounted or tribrach-mounted)—each station will be occupied with a theodolite-equiped EDM instrument, and each pair of traverse courses can be measured at each setup; traverse computations will use the mean distances thus determined and the mean angles obtained from each setup. **Reference:** Chapters 4 and 5.

Purpose   To permit students to develop some experience in measuring with a steel tape and plumb bobs in the first stage of a traverse closure exercise (see also Project 5).

Procedure

- Each course of the traverse will be measured twice—forward *(direct)* and then immediately back *(reverse)*—with the two measurements agreeing to within 0.03 ft or 0.008 m. If the two measurements do not agree, they will be repeated until they do and before the next course of the traverse is measured.
- When measuring on a slope, the high-end surveyor will hold the tape directly on the mark, and the low-end surveyor will have to use a plumb bob to keep the tape horizontal.
- The low-end surveyor will use the hand level to keep the tape approximately horizontal by sighting the high-end surveyor and noting how much lower she or he is in comparison. The plumb bob will then be set to that height differential. Use chaining pins or other markers to temporarily mark intermediate measuring points on the ground—use scratch marks or concrete nails on paved surfaces.

- If a range pole is first set behind the far station, the rear surveyor can keep the tape properly aligned by sighting at the range pole and directing the forward surveyor on line.
- Book the results as shown below, and then repeat the process until all five sides have been measured and booked. When booked erroneous measurements are to be discarded, strike out (use a straightedge)—don't erase.
- If the temperature is something other than standard, correct the mean distance for temperature (C_T); that is, $C_T = .00000645(T - 68)L_{ft}$ or $C_T = .0000116 (T - 20)L_m$.

Reference   Chapter 2.

Sample field notes for Project 3. See also Figure 2-14.

No. PROJECT #3
TRAVERSE DISTANCES

No. ....
Date MARCH 29, 2000   Page 10

COURSE	DIRECT	REVERSE	MEAN	MEAN (C_T)
111–112	164.96	164.94	164.95	164.97
112–113	88.41	88.43	88.42	88.43
113–114	121.69	121.69	121.69	121.70
114–115	115.80	115.78	115.79	115.80
115–111	68.36	68.34	68.35	68.36

BROWN–NOTES
FIELDING–TAPE
SIMPSON–TAPE
TEMP.=83°F

TRAVERSE

Project 4   Differential Leveling

Description   The students will use the techniques of differential leveling to determine the elevations of temporary benchmark (TBM) #33 and of the intermediate stations identified by the instructor (if any).

Equipment   Survey level, rod, and rod level (if available)

Purpose   To give students experience in the use of levels and rods and in properly recording all measurements in the field book.

Procedure
- Start at the closest municipal or college benchmark (BM) (description given by the instructor), and take a backsight (**BS**) reading in order to establish a height of instrument (**HI**).

- Insert the description of the BM (and all subsequent TPs), in detail, under **Description** in the field notes.
- Establish a turning point (TP #1) generally in the direction of the defined terminal point (TBM #33) by taking a foresight **(FS)** on TP #1.
- When you have calculated the elevation of TP #1, move the level to a convenient location, and set it up again. Take a **BS** reading on TP #1, and calculate the new **HI.**
- The rod readings taken on any required intermediate points (on the way to or from the terminal point) will be booked in the Intermediate Sight **(IS)** column—unless some of those intermediate points are also being used as turning points (TPs) (e.g., see TP#4).
- If you can't "see" the terminal point (TBM #33) from the new instrument location, establish additional turning points (TP #2, TP #3, etc.), repeating the above procedures until you can take a reading on the terminal point.
- After you have taken a reading **(FS)** on the terminal point (TBM #33) and calculated its elevation, move the level slightly, and set it up again. Now, take a BS on the terminal point (TBM #33), and prepare to close the level loop back to the starting benchmark.
- Repeat the leveling procedure until you have surveyed back to the original BM. If you use the original TPs on the way back, book them by their original numbers—you do not have to describe them again. If you use new TPs on the way back, describe each TP in detail under Description, and assign it a new number.
- If the final elevation of the starting BM differs by more than 0.04 ft or 0.013 m from the starting elevation (after the calculations have been checked for mistakes by performing an "arithmetic check"—also known as a "page check"), **repeat the project.** Your instructor may give you a different closure allowance, depending on the distance leveled and/or the type of terrain surveyed.

Note
- Keep BS and FS distances from the instrument roughly equal.
- "Wave" the rod (or use a rod level) to permit a vertical reading.
- Eliminate parallax for each reading.
- Use only solid (steel, concrete, or wood) and well-defined features for TPs. If you cannot **precisely** describe a **TP**, do not use it !
- Perform an *arithmetic check* on the notes before assessing closure accuracy.

Reference   Chapter 3.

Sample field notes for Project 4.

No.... PROJECT #4 ....
..... DIFFERENTIAL LEVELING ....

No. ....
Date .. MARCH 1, 2000 .... Page ...... 11 .....

STA	BS	HI	IS	FS	ELEV	DESCRIPTION
						BROWN—INST.
						SMITH—ROD
						TEMP.=65°F
BM #21	0.54	182.31			181.77	BM. BRONZE PLATE ON E. WALL OF S.E.
						STAIRWELL OF PHASE 1 BLDG., ABOUT
						1 m ABOVE THE GROUND.
TP #1	0.95	175.04		8.22	174.09	N. LUG ON TOP FLANGE OF HYD.@
						E/SIDE OF BUS SHELTER
TP #2	0.80	168.76		7.08	167.96	SPIKE IN S/SIDE OF HP @ 237 FINCH
						AVE.
TP #3	0.55	160.20		9.11	159.65	SPIKE IN S/SIDE OF HP @ 245 FINCH
						AVE.
111			4.22			TRAVERSE STATION I.B.
112			4.71			TRAVERSE STATION I.B.
113			2.03			TRAVERSE STATION I.B.
114			1.22			TRAVERSE STATION I.B.
TP #4	3.77	163.45		0.52	159.68	TOP OF I.B. @ STA. 115
TBM #33				1.18	162.27	BRASS CAP ON CONC. MON.-CONTROL
						STATION 1102
TBM #33	1.23	163.50			162.27	
TP #4	2.71	162.39		3.82	159.68	
TP #3	8.88	168.53		2.74	159.65	
TP #5	11.86	177.38		3.01	165.52	TOP OF N.E. CORNER OF CONCRETE
						STEP @ 233 FINCH AVE.
TP #1	10.61	184.72		3.27	174.11	
BM #21				2.94	181.78	(e=+0.01)
ΣBS = 41.90				ΣFS = 41.89		
	ΣBS,	41.90	- ΣFS,	41.89 =	0.01	181.77 + .01 = 181.78, CHECK

After the arithmetic check has been successfully applied, compute the elevations for the intermediate readings—I.S.

Project 5 Traverse Angle Measurements and Closure Computations

Description   The students will measure the angles of a five-sided field traverse (see also Project 3) using techniques consistent with the desired precision ratio of 1/5000.

Equipment   Transit or theodolite and a target device (range pole or plumb bob string target).

Purpose   To introduce students to the techniques of setting up a theodolite over a point, turning and doubling interior angles, and checking the precision of the work by calculating the precision ratio. (For traverse computation purposes, assume a direction for one of the courses; for example, the direction of 115–111 in the illustrative data can be assumed to be 339°39′40″ or N 20°20′20″ W—or any other values suggested by the instructor.)

Procedure

- Using the same traverse stations as were used for Project 3, measure each of the five angles (direct and double).
- Read all angles from left to right. Begin the first (of two) angles at 0°00′00″ ("direct"), and begin the second angle ("double") with the value of the first angle reading. See Section 4-4.
- Transit the telescope between the direct and double readings.
- Divide the double angle by 2 to obtain the "mean" angle, if the mean angle differs by more than 30″ (or other value as given by your instructor) from the direct angle, **repeat the procedure.**
- When all the mean angles have been booked, add the angles to determine the geometric closure.
- If the geometric closure exceeds 01′ (30″ $\sqrt{N}$), find the error. See Traverse Specifications—Table 8-2, Third Order, Class II.
- Combine the results from Projects 3 and 5 to determine the precision closure of the field traverse (1/5000 or better is acceptable), using an assumed direction for one of the sides (see above).

Project 6   Topographic Survey

Topographic field surveys can be accomplished in several ways:

- Stadia with a manual plot of the tie-ins and contours.
- Cross sctions and tie-ins with a manual plot of the tie-ins, cross sections, and contours.
- EDM with a manual plot of the tie-ins and contours.
- Total Station with a computer-generated plot on a digital plotter.

Purpose   Each type of topographic survey shown in this section is designed to give students experience in collecting field data (details and elevations) using a variety of specified surveying equipment and surveying procedures. The objectives of these different approaches to topographic surveying are the same—that is, the production of a scaled map or plan showing all relevant details and height information (contours and spot elevations) of the area surveyed. Time constraints will normally limit most programs to incorporating just one or two of these approaches.

Sample field notes for Project 5. See also Figure 4–20.

No. __PROJECT #5__

    __TRAVERSE ANGLES__

No. _____

Date __MAY 3, 2000__   Page __15__

STATION	DIRECT	DOUBLE	MEAN
111	102°28'00"	204°56'28"	102°28'14"
112	102°10'40"	204°21'00"	102°10'30"
113	104°42'00"	209°23'48"	104°41'54"
114	113°05'00"	226°09'00"	113°04'30"
115	118°34'00"	237°07'44"	118°33'52"
		Σ =	539°116'180"
		=	539°59'00"
		ERROR =	−01'
ADJUST EACH MEAN ANGLE BY +12" (60/5)			
111	101°28'26"		
112	102°10'42"		
113	104°42'06"		
114	113°04'42"		
115	118°34'04"		
Σ = 538°118'120" = 540°00'00" (CLOSED)			

POND

112

111

TRAVERSE 113

115 114

SMITH—INSTRUMENT

BROWN—TARGET

JONES—TARGET

TEMP. = 77°F

N

Stadia Topographic Survey

Description   The students will use **stadia** techniques to determine the horizontal position and elevation of selected topographic features on the campus and prepare a contoured plan plotted at a scale of 1" = 40 ft or 1:500 metric (or other scale as given by the instructor). See Figure 7-11 for sample field notes. See Section 7-8 for stadia field practice.

Equipment   Theodolite and leveling rod.

Procedure

- Set a theodolite up on a control station—as indicated by your instructor.
- Measure the **hi** with the rod (from the top of the monument to the optical center of the theodolite). Enter the value in the notes as shown in Figure 7-11.
- Backsight on another control station @ 0°00'00". Describe in the field book.
- Use the elevation of the theodolite station as determined in Project 4 or as given by your instructor.
- Use **stadia** techniques to determine the elevation and position of the topographic features required.
- Prepare a sketch (in the field book) of the topographic features being surveyed (before the survey commences), and number each feature reading directly on the sketch—see typical notes in Figure 7-11.

- Obtain the horizontal angle (**HCR**), the vertical angle (**VCR**), and the **rod interval** for each feature.
- Record the **VCR** at the value of the **hi** on the rod unless that value is obscured (in which case, sight any point on the rod).
- To obtain the rod interval, first sight roughly on the rod on the value of the **hi**, and then move the lower stadia hair onto an even foot or meter (or decimeter). Read the upper stadia hair, and mentally subtract the even lower hair reading to obtain the rod interval.
- After the rod interval has been booked, move the main crosshair back onto the **hi** value on the rod, and wave "OK" to the rod holder—who can then move to the next feature.
- Read and book the **HCR** and the **VCR**, and put the station number in the **"Station"** column and on the sketch at the appropriate location.

Cross Sections and Tie-Ins Topographic Survey

Description   Using the techniques of right-angled tie-ins and cross sections (both referenced to a baseline), the students will locate the positions and elevations of selected features on the designated area of the campus. A sketched area, as shown on Figure 7-11, could be used as a sample area.

See Figure 7-2 for typical topographic field notes and Figures 3-21 and 3-22 in Section 3-9 for cross-section techniques.

Equipment   Cloth or fiberglass tape, steel tape, and two plumb bobs; right-angle prism optional.

Procedure

- Establish your own baseline using wood stakes or pavement nails, or, for example, use a curb line, as is shown in Figure 7-11, as the survey baseline.
- 0 + 00 will be the point of intersection of your baseline with some other line, or point—as defined by your instructor.
- Measure the baseline stations (e.g., 50 ft or 20 m) precisely with a steel tape, and mark them clearly on the ground.
- Determine the baseline stations of all features left and right of the baseline by estimating 90° (swung-arm technique) or by using a right-angled prism.
- When you have booked the baseline stations of all the features in a 50-ft or 20-m interval (the steel tape can be left lying on the ground on the baseline), determine and book the offset (o/s) distances left and right of the baseline to each feature using a cloth tape. Tie in all detail to the closest 0.10 ft or 0.03 m.
- Do not begin the measurements until the sketches have been made for the survey area.
- Elevations will be determined using a level and a rod. The level will be set up in a convenient location where a benchmark (**BM**) and a considerable number of intermediate sights (**IS**) can be "seen."

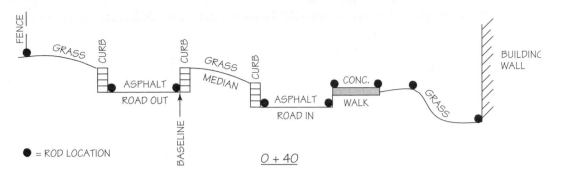

FENCE

GRASS CURB

ASPHALT
ROAD OUT

CURB

GRASS
MEDIAN

CURB

ASPHALT
ROAD IN

CONC.
WALK

GRASS

BUILDINC
WALL

● = ROD LOCATION

BASELINE

0 + 40

Typical cross section for campus roadway—showing the rod reading locations needed to properly define this topographic surface.

- The rod will be held on the baseline at each station and at all points where the ground slope changes (e.g., top/bottom of curb, edge of walk, top of slope, bottom of slope, limit of survey). See the typical cross section above.
- When all the data (that can be "seen") have been taken at a station, the rod holder then moves to the next (50-ft or 20-m) station and repeats the process.
- When the rod can no longer be seen, the instrument operator will call for the establishment of a turning point (**TP**), and the instrument will be moved closer to the next stage of work. In addition to cross sections at the even 20-m intervals, it will be necessary to take full or partial sections between the even 20-m stations if the lay of the land changes significantly.

EDM Topographic Survey

Description Using electronic distance measurement instruments (EDMI) and optical or electronic theodolites, the students will locate the positions and elevations of all topographic detail and a sufficient number of additional elevations to enable a representative contour drawing of the selected areas.

Equipment Theodolite, EDMI, and one or more pole-mounted reflecting prisms.

Procedure
- Set the theodolite at a control station (N.E. and elevation known), and backsight on another known control station.
- Set an appropriate reference angle (or azimuth) on the horizontal circle (e.g., $0°00'00''$ or some assigned azimuth).
- Set the height of the reflecting prism (hr) on the pole equal to the height of the optical center of the theodolite/EDMI (hi); if the EDMI is not coaxial with the theodolite, set the height of the target (target/prism assembly) equal to the optical center of the instrument (see left illustration in Figure 5-6).
- Prepare a sketch of the area to be surveyed.

LEGEND

⊖ HYD	HYDRANT	
○ MH	MANHOLE	
● LP	LIGHT POLE	
۞ DECIDUOUS TREE		
✳ CONIFEROUS TREE		
⊟ CB	CATCH BASIN	
△ TRAFFIC SIGN		

SMITH – NOTES
BROWN – TAPE
GREEN – TAPE
TEMP. = 63°F

BASELINE (SPLIT)

CURB   CURB   CURB

1+60.1 ← 47.9 → ⊖

N   13.5   25.0'   12.0' 25.0' 5.0'

ROAD   GRASS MEDIAN ISLAND   ROAD   CONCRETE SIDEWALK

△← 28.2-0+90.9

CHAIN LINK FENCE

△← 28.2-0+67.9

CONC. VALVE CHAMBER

8.0'   12.0

0+53.1 ← 53.1 →

← 61.0 →   0.5' DIA.

△← 30.1-0+34.1   ← 58.4 →   1.0'DIA.

0+12.1 ●

CONC. S.W.

CURB   0+00

FINCH AVE. EAST

- Begin taking readings on the appropriate points, entering the data in the field notes (see below) and entering the "shot" number in the appropriate spot on the accompanying field-note sketch. Keep shot numbers sequential, perhaps beginning with 1000.

- When all field shots (horizontal and vertical angles and horizontal distances) have been taken, sight the reference backsight control station again; verify that the height of the prism is unchanged. Take the vertical angles to the prism target or to the center of the prism (if the EDMI is coaxial with the theodolite).

- Reduce the field notes to determine station elevations and course distances—if required.

- Plot the topographic features and elevations at 1″ = 40′ or 1:500 metric—or at other scales as given by your instructor.

- Draw contours over the surveyed areas. See Section 7-12.

STA.	B.S.	H.I.	I.S.	F.S.	ELEV.	DESCRIPTION
BM#3	8.21	318.34			310.13	S.W. CORNER OF CONC. VALVE CHAMBER
						@ 0+53.1
0+00			3.34		315.00	₵, ON ASPH.
			0.03		318.31	75.0' LT, ON ASPH.
			7.35		310.99	50.0' RT, ON ASPH.
0+50			6.95		311.39	₵, ON ASPH.
			7.00		311.34	25' LT, BOT. CURB
			0.3		318.0	38.5' LT, @ FENCE, ON GRASS
			7.5		310.8	6' RT, ₵ OF ISLAND, ON GRASS
			8.32		310.02	12' RT, BOT. CURB
			8.41		309.93	37.0' RT, BOT. CURB
			8.91		309.43	37.0' RT, TOP OF CONC. WALK
			9.01		309.33	42.0' RT, TOP OF CONC. WALK
			9.3		309.0	46.9' RT, TOP OF HILL, ON GRASS
			11.7		306.6	56.6' RT, @ BUILDING WALL, ON GRASS

Total Station Survey

Description   Using a Total Station and one or more pole-mounted reflecting prisms, the students will tie in all topographic features and any additional ground shots (including *break lines*) that are required to accurately define the terrain. See Section 5-10.

Equipment   Total Station and one, or more, pole-mounted reflecting prisms.

Procedure

- Set the Total Station over a known control point (N.E. and elevation known). Turn on the instrument, and index the circles (by transiting the telescope and revolving the instrument 360°—on many Total Stations). Some newer Total Stations do not require this operation.
- *Alternately the station can be set in any convenient location and its position determined using the on-board resection program—after sighting the required number of visible control stations.*
- Set the program menu to the type of survey (topography) being performed and to the required instrument settings. Select the type of field data to be stored (e.g., N, E, and Z). Set temperature and pressure setting—if required.
- Check configuration settings [e.g., tilt correction, coordinate format, zenith vertical angle, angle resolution (5″), c + r correction (no.), units (ft/m, degree, mm Hg), auto power off (say, 20′)].

STA	HCR	H.DIST.	V. DIST.	ELEV.
	⌐ @ C. M. #112,	hi = 5.61	= hr	247.63
111	0°00'00"			
1000	64°08'20"	58.2	–7.1	240.5
1001	61°30'40"	77.5	–7.1	240.5
1002	71°49'20"	94.9	–7.2	240.4
1003	90°15'30"	95.7	–7.0	240.6
1004	101°33'50"	82.3	–7.0	240.6
1005	127°51'50"	86.3	–7.1	240.5
1006	142°20'20"	87.7	–7.2	240.4
1007	154°41'30"	72.7	–7.0	240.6
1008	141°26'20"	55.3	–7.0	240.6
1009	124°01'10"	53.1	–6.9	240.7
1010	103°36'50"	50.6	–7.1	240.5
1011	81°10'50"	53.8	–7.1	240.5
1012	50°49'20"	47.6	–7.6	240.0
1013	127°03'40"	24.0	–8.3	239.3
1014	161°52'30"	40.6	–9.1	238.5
1015	218°07'30"	50.7	+3.2	250.8

(Drawing in grid area shows: POND with points 1000–1011, SWALE with points 1012–1014, TRAVERSE with stations 111, 112, LP, and north arrow N.)

BROWN – ⌐
SMITH – PRISM
TEMP. = 73°F

- Identify the instrument station from the menu. Insert the date, station number coordinates, elevation, and hi. Alternately it may be possible to upload all control station data prior to going out to the field—in that case, just scan through the data, and select the appropriate instrument station and backsight station(s). Enter the height of instrument (hi), and store or record all the data.

- Backsight to one or more known control point(s) (point number, north and east coordinates, and elevation known). Set the horizontal circle to 0°00′00″ or to some assigned reference azimuth for the backsight reference direction. Store or record the data.

- Set the initial point number in the instrument, and set for automatic point number incrementation. Set the height of the reflecting prism (hr) equal to the instrument hi.

- Begin taking intermediate sights—the first reading point could be numbered 1000. Provide an attribute code (consistent with the software code library) for each reading. Some software programs enable attribute codes to automatically provide for feature "stringing" (e.g., curb1, edge of water1, fence3), whereas other software programs require the surveyor to prefix the code with a character (Z), which turns on the stringing command. See Section 5-10-7 and Figure 5-27(a) and (b). Most Total Stations have an automatic mode for topographic surveys, where one button-push will measure and store all the point data as well as the code and attribute data. The Code and attribute data of the previous point are presented to the surveyor as a default setting—if the code and attribute data are the same for a series of readings, the surveyor only has to press "enter" and not repeat entering all that identical data.

- Put all, or some, selected point numbers on the field sketch. This will be of assistance later in the editing process if mistakes have occurred in the numbering or with the coding.

- When all required points have been surveyed, check back into the control station originally backsighted to ensure that the instrument orientation is still valid.

- Transfer the field data to a computer in a properly labeled file.

- After opening the data-processing program, import the field data file, and begin the editing process and the graphics generation process (this is automatic for many programs).

- Create the TIN and contours.

- Either finish the drawing with the working program or create a *dxf* file for transfer to a CAD program, and then finish the drawing.

- Prepare a plot file, and then plot the data (to a scale assigned by your instructor) on the lab digital plotter.

TYPICAL CODE LIBRARY

Control		Utilities	
SCM	Seneca concrete monument	HP	Hydro pole
CM	Concrete monument	LP	Lamp pole
SIB	Standard iron bar	BP	Bell pole
IB	Iron bar	GS	Gas valve
RIB	Round iron bar	WV	Water valve
NL	Nail	CABLE	Cable
STA	Station		
TBM	Temporary benchmark		

Municipal		Topographic	
CL	Centerline	GND	Ground
RD	Road	TB	Top of bank
EA	Edge of asphalt	BB	Bottom of bank
BC	Beginning of curve	DIT	Ditch
EC	End of curve	FL	Fence line
PC	Point on curve	POST	Post
CURB	Curb	GATE	Gate
CB	Catch basin	BUSH	Bush
DCB	Double catch basin	HEDGE	Hedge
MH	Manhole	BLD	Building
STM	Storm manhole	RWALL	Retaining wall
SAN	Sanitary manhole	POND	Pond
INV	Invert	STEP	Steps
SW	Sidewalk	CTREE	Coniferous tree
HYD	Hydrant	DTREE	Deciduous tree
RR	Railroad		

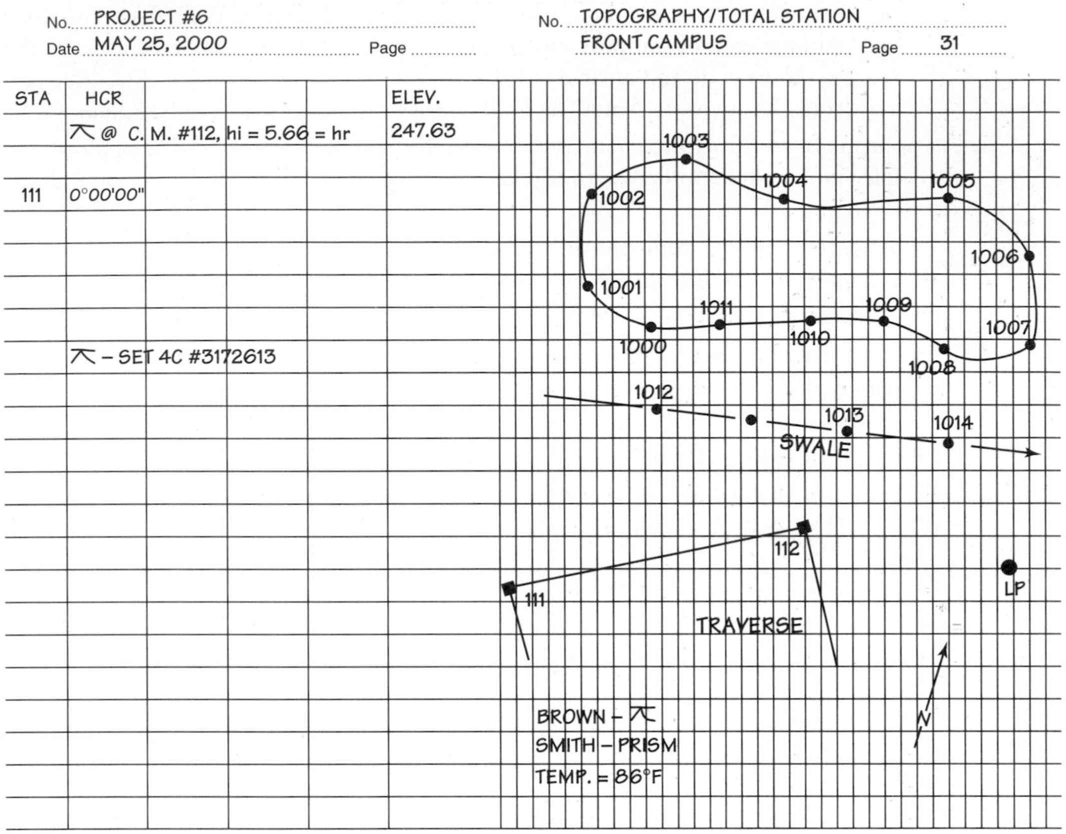

STA	HCR			ELEV.
	⅄ @ C. M. #112, hi = 5.66 = hr			247.63
111	0°00'00"			
	⅄ – SET 4C #3172613			

1003
1002
1004
1005
1001
1006
1011 1009
1000 1010 1007
1008
1012
1013 1014
SWALE
112
111
LP
TRAVERSE
BROWN – ⅄
SMITH – PRISM
TEMP. = 86°F
N

Project 7 Building Layout

Description The students will lay out the corners of a building and reference the corners with batter boards.

Equipment Theodolite, steel tape, plumb bobs, wood stakes, light lumber for batter boards, clamps, keel or felt pen, level, and rod. (A theodolite/EDMI and prism could replace the theodolite and steel tape.)

Purpose To give students experience in laying out the corners of a building according to dimensions taken from a building site plan and in constructing batter boards, referencing both the line and grade of the building walls and floor.

Procedure
- After the front and side lines have been defined by your instructor and after the building dimensions have been given, set stakes X and Y on the front property line, as shown in the sketch below.
- Set up the theodolite at X, sight on Y, turn 90° (double), and place stakes at A and B.

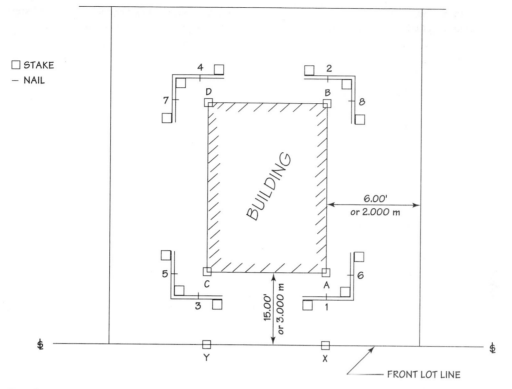

STAKE
NAIL

4

2

D

B

7

8

6.00'
or 2.000 m

BUILDING

5

6

C

A

15.00'
or 3.000 m

3

1

Y

X

FRONT LOT LINE

Transfer this sketch to your field notes.

- Set up the theodolite at *Y*, sight on *X*, turn 90° (double), and place stakes at *C* and *D*.
- Measure the building diagonals to check the accuracy of the layout; adjust and re-measure if necessary.
- After the building corners have been set, offset the batter boards a safe distance (e.g., 6 ft or 2 m), and set the batter boards at the first-floor elevation—as given by your instructor.
- After the batter boards have been set, place *line* nails on the top of the batter boards as fellows.

    (a) Set up on *A*, sight *B*, place nail 2, transit the telescope, and set nail 1.
    (b) From setup on *A*, sight *C*, place nail 5, transit the telescope, and place nail 6.
    (c) Set up on *D* and place nails 3, 4, 7, and 8 in a similar fashion.

Project 8   Horizontal Curve

Description   Given the centerline alignment of two intersecting tangents (including a station reference stake), the students will calculate and lay out a horizontal curve.

Equipment   Theodolite, steel tape, plumb bobs, wood stakes, and range pole or string target. (A theodolite/EDMI and prism could replace the theodolite and steel tape.)

Purpose   To give students experience in laying out a circular curve at specified station intervals after first calculating all the necessary layout measurements from the given radius and the measured location of the PI and the Δ field angle.

Procedure
- Intersect the two tangents to create the PI.
- Measure the station of the PI.
- Measure (and double) the tangent deflection angle (Δ).
- After receiving the radius value from your instructor, compute T and L, and then compute the station of the BC and EC. See Section 10-3.
- Compute the deflections for even stations—at 50-ft or 20-m intervals. See Section 10-4. Compute the equivalent chords. See Section 10-5.
- Set the BC and EC by measuring from the PI along each tangent.
- From the BC, sight the PI, and turn the curve deflection angle (Δ/2) to check the location of the EC. If the line of sight does not fall on the EC, check the calculations and measurements for the BC and EC locations, and make any necessary adjustments.
- Using the calculated deflection angles and appropriate chord lengths, stake out the curve.
- Measure from the last even station stake to the EC to verify the accuracy of the layout.
- Walk the curve, looking for any anomalies (e.g., two stations staked at the same deflection angle) The symmetry of the curve is such that even minor mistakes are obvious in a visual check.

Project 9   Pipeline Layout

Description   The students will establish an offset line and construct batter boards for line and grade control of a proposed storm sewer from MH 1 to MH 2—stakes marking those points will be given for each crew in the field.

Equipment   Theodolite, steel tape, wood stakes, and light lumber and "C" clamps for the batter boards. (A theodolite/EDMI and prism could replace the theodolite and steel tape.)

Purpose   To give students experience in laying out offset line and grade stakes for a proposed pipeline. The students will learn how to compute a grade sheet and construct batter boards and how to visually check the accuracy of their work by sighting across the constructed batter boards.

Procedure
- Set up at the MH 1 stake, and sight the MH 2 stake.
- Turn off 90°, measure the offset distance (e.g., 10 ft or 3 m), and establish MH 1 on offset.

- Set up at the MH 2 stake, sight the MH 1 stake, and establish MH 2 on offset.
- Give the MH 1 offset stake a station of $0 + 00$, measure out to establish grade stakes at the even stations (50 ft or 20 m); finally, check the distance from the last even station to the MH 2 stake to check that the overall distance is accurate.
- Using the closest benchmark (BM), determine the elevations of the tops of the offset grade stakes—close back to the benchmark within the tolerance given by your instructor.
- Assume that the invert of MH 1 is 7.97 ft or 2.430 m below the top of the MH 1 grade stake (or other assumed value given by your instructor).
- Compute the invert elevations at each even station, and then complete a grade sheet similar to those shown in Table 3-3 and Figure 13-7—selecting a convenient height for the grade rod.
- Using the "stake to batter board" distances in the grade sheet, use the supplied light lumber and "C" clamps to construct batter boards similar to those shown in Figure 13-6. Use a small carpenters' level to keep the cross pieces horizontal. Check to see that all cross pieces line up in one visual line—a successful visual check is a check on all the work.

Appendix E

Answers to Selected Problems

CHAPTER 2

2-2(a). 2647.26 ft, 806.88 m
2-2(c). 2502.06 ft, 762.63 m   **2-3.** 54.6 ft
2-6 56.867 m   **2-9.** 582.75 ft
2-12. 4621.97 ft   **2-15.** 98.806 m
2-18. 813.42 ft   **2-21.** 176.231 m
2-23. 176.94 ft   **2-27.** $C_s = -0.006$ m
2-29. 72.53 ft

CHAPTER 3

3-1(a). 0.003 m   **3-1(b).** 0.03 ft
3-1(f). 1.080 m   **3-2(a)ii.** 1.73 ft
3-2(b)iii. 0.987 m   **3-3.** 22.96 mi
3-18(a). $B = 185.556$ m
3-18(b). Leveling error = 0.004 m

CHAPTER 5

5-1. -0.030 m   **5-3(a).** 1878.622 m
5-3(b). 228.71 m   **5-5.** H = 386.504 m,
elev. $B = 139.077$ m

CHAPTER 6

6-1 124°40'   **6-3(a).** S 35°33' W
6-3(e). N 88°07' W   **6-4(a).** 344°42'
6-4(e). 303°47'   **6-12(d).** $E = 0.80$ ft,
precision = 1/3100   **6-15.** A = 7.66 acres
6-19. $A = 5.27$ hectares (ha)
6-20. $AD = 1851.44$ ft
6-21. $CD = 852.597$ m, brg.
DE = S 74°30'23" W.   **6-25.** $A = 2430$ m^2

CHAPTER 7

7-3(a). $H = 263.4$ ft
7-3(b). Elev. $M = 481.9$ ft   **7-5(a).** 112.5 m
7-5(b). 241.83 m   **7-7.** Point 4, $H = 255$ ft,
elev. = 565.0 ft; point 9, $H = 410$ ft, elev. =
582.4. ft; point 10, $H = 351$ ft, elev. = 586.1 ft

CHAPTER 8

8-1. Grid bearing AB = S 79°29'00" W,
$AB = 290.722$ m   **8-2.** $B = 186°21'09.1"$
8-4. Geodetic bearing = S 74°35'18.2" W
8-5. $B = 186°21'01.3"$

CHAPTER 10

10-2. $T = 44.85$ ft, $L = 89.58$ ft   **10-4.** BC at
15 + 43.25 ft, EC at 16 + 32.83 ft
10-6. BC   5 + 829.183   0°00'00"
              5 + 840   1°01'59"
              5 + 860   2°56'35"
              5 + 880   4°51'11"
       EC   5 + 896.116   6°23'31"
10-12. A to BC = 565.07 ft, B to EC = 408.89 ft
10-13. $R = 29.958$ m   **10-14.** $T_1 = 226.52$ ft,
$T_2 = 272.24$ ft   **10-16.** Summit @ 20 + 07.14,
elev. = 722.48 ft
10-17. BVC   0 + 180   151.263
                0 + 200   151.841
                0 + 250   153.091
                0 + 300   154.063
                0 + 350   154.757

PVI	0 + 360	154.863
	0 + 400	155.134
High Pt.	0 + 450	155.273
	0 + 500	155.134
EVC	0 + 540	154.863

10-18. T.S. = 9 + 85.68, S.C. = 11 + 35.68,
C.S. = 11 + 94.85, S.T. = 13 + 44.85

10-23. T.S.	1 + 195.597	0°00.0′
	1 + 200	0°00.71′
	1 + 220	0°21.83′
	1 + 240	1°12.28′
	1 + 260	2°32.06′
S.C.	1 + 266.620	3°04.93′ (θ_s)

CHAPTER 12

12-1. At 4 + 00, cut 0′10 7/8″   **12-2.** At 0 + 60, "on grade"   **12-4.** At 4 + 50, CL elev. = 508.20 ft   **12-5.** At 4 + 50, curb elev. = 508.46 ft   **12-6.** At 4 + 50, "on grade"
12-7(a). L = 54.98 ft   **12-7(b).** Slope at 1.11%
12.7(c) and 12.7(d).

Station	Curb Elev.	Stake Elev.	Cut	Fill
A	505.02	504.71		0′3 3/4″
B	505.22	506.22	1′0″	
C	505.44	506.37	0′11 1/8″	
D	505.63	506.71	1′1″	

CHAPTER 13

13-1. At 1 + 50, cut 7.58 ft; for grade rod of 14 ft, stake to batter board distance of 6′5″
13-2. At 0 + 80, cut 2.534 m; for a grade rod of 4 m, stake to batter board distance of 1.466 m
13-3. At 1 + 00, 495.60   **13-4.** At 1 + 00, cut 8.01 ft   **13-5.** GR = 14 ft; at 1 + 00, 5′11 7/8″   **13-7.** First leg, 0 + 40 = 183.740 m
13-8. First leg, 0 + 40, cut 3.093 m
13-9. First leg, GR = 5 m; at 0 + 40, cut 1.907
13-10. At lot #13, sewer invert opposite #13 = 496.85 + (32 × 0.01) = 497.17
springline elevation = 497.17 + (1.25/2) = 497.80
60 ft of sewer connection pipe   @2% = +1.20
minimum invert elevation of connection   = 499.00

CHAPTER 16

16-1. Trapezoidal technique, 289 yd^2; Simpson's 1/3 rule, 290 yd^2 **16-2.** A = 334 yd^2
16-3. V = 401 m^3 **16-4.** V = 60.7 yd^3
16-5. V = 2639 yd^3 **16-6.** V = 88.6 yd^3

Appendix F

Examples of Emerging Technology

This appendix contains examples of emerging technology in computerized surveying data systems (see Figure 5-37). The science of Geomatics includes all forms of data acquisition—ranging from field surveying techniques (stressed in this text) to remotely sensed techniques such as aerial photography and satellite imagery. Appendix F includes illustrations of digital (softcopy) photogrammetry (see page 19) and real time and precise GPS measurements (Chapter 9).

The author believes that these two technologies, together with motorized theodolite Total Station technology (Chapter 5), constitute the platform from which most future developments in computerized surveying, mapping, and data analysis technologies will be built in the new millennium.

FIGURE F.1   An older SOCET SET Windows NT workstation. The operator is using an active viewing system—the StereoGraphics® CrystalEyes® product—in which there is an infrared emitter on top of the stereo monitor. The operator wears active eye wear, in which the LCD shutters are synchronized with the left and right images as they are displayed in turn on the screen. (Courtesy of LH Systems, San Diego, CA)

FIGURE F.2 SOCET SET Unix workstation. The host computer is a Sun Ultra 60®, the operating system is Solaris 2.6, and the viewing system is ZScreen. This photograph also shows the LH Systems 3D Hand Controller to advantage—this is a device for XYZ control of the floating mark in the stereo model. The XY motion is just like a mouse, then there is a thumbwheel for Z and a number of buttons for image operations, changing the feature code, etc. (Courtesy of LH Systems, San Diego, CA)

FIGURE F.3 DSW300 scanner with Sun Ultra 60® host computer. This high precision photogrammetric photo and film scanner has four elements: (1) movable xy cross carriage stage with flat film platen; (2) fixed array CCD (Charge-Coupled Device) camera and image optics; (3) Xenon light source and color scanning software; and (4) computer hardware, including storage. (Courtesy of LH Systems, San Diego, CA)

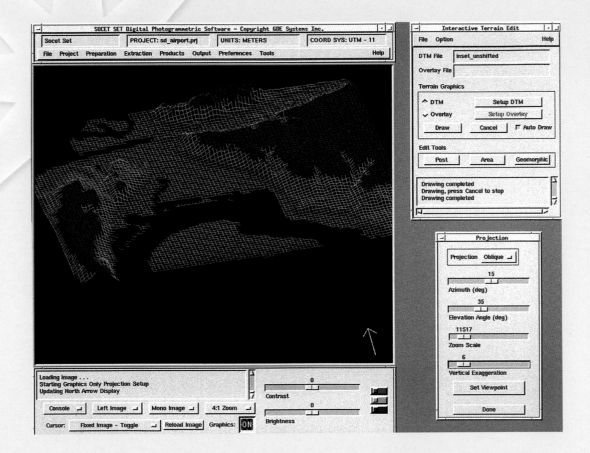

FIGURE F.4 Computer screen printout, developed using SOCET® software, showing a typical oblique projection of a Digital Terrain Model (DTM). (Courtesy of LH Systems, San Diego, CA)

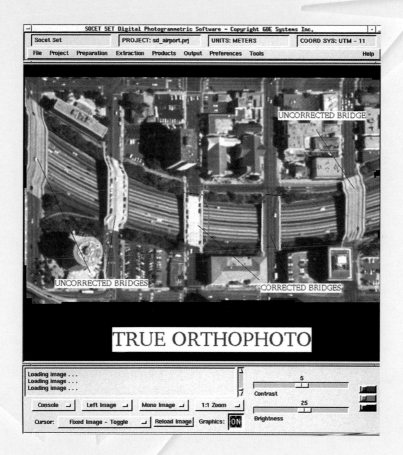

FIGURE F.5 Computer screen printout, developed using SOCET® software, showing a partially corrected orthophoto. (Courtesy of LH Systems, San Diego, CA)

FIGURE F.6 Trimble dual frequency GPS Total Station 4800, shown with the Trimble TSC1 data logger attached to the PowereLiTE™ GPS pole. The GPS receiver and antenna are mounted atop the pole; for those who wish to perform real-time differential (Real Time Kinematic—RTK) GPS surveying, the RTK radio modem and radio antenna are also included in the package atop the pole. The complete system, including the pole and attached TSC1 data logger, weighs just 8.5 lbs. Initialization can be accomplished while moving (on-the-fly [OTF]) or in static mode in less than one minute. (Courtesy of Trimble, Sunnyvale, CA)

FIGURE F.7 Trimble TSC1™ data collector, featuring their Survey Controller™ software. This instrument, used attached to the GPS pole, is designed to perform RTK and post-processed surveys in all kinds of weather conditions. The Survey Controller™ software performs all GPS measurement control, displays the status of the satellite receiver and base communications radio link, permits the layout of a pre-defined horizontal and vertical layout, uses the geoid model for real-time GPS derived orthometric heights, shows maps for reviewing the survey project, shows

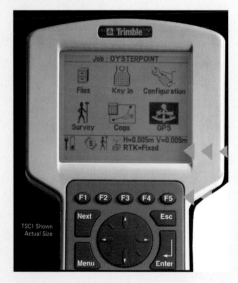

field configuration of data radios, and supports fast initialization with the newer receivers. The data logger comes with 2 MB of internal data storage along with PCMCIA cards, which allow unlimited data storage. (Courtesy of Trimble, Sunnyvale, CA)

FIGURE F.8   Trimble TRIMTALK™ 450s multichannel, UHF radio modem. This modem is compatible with any differential GPS system and can be operated in any weather. Used as a base station, the radio modem is mounted on a tripod and can broadcast up to 10 km line-of-sight under optimal conditions. Path and terrain obstructions can reduce the effective range to 3–5 km. Up to two additional units can be networked to extend range and provide seamless coverage. (Courtesy of Trimble, Sunnyvale, CA)

Index

F

4-foot mark, 509
Field notes, 13
    for angles by direction, 106
    for angles by repetition, 115
    for closed traverse, 192
    for control points, 274
    for cross sections (highway format), 76
    for cross sections (municipal format), 75
    for fencing measurements, 524
    for GPS field log, 327
    for leveling, 71
    for open traverse, 191
    for removal of sewer pipe, 525
    for pile driving, 526
    for prepared coordinates for layout, 297
    for profile, 73
    for sodding measurements, 523
    for stadia surveys, 242
    for station visibility diagram, 325
    for taping, 45, 46, 47
    for three-wire leveling, 81
    for topography, single baseline, 226
    for topography, split baseline, 226, 227
Fill, 335, 419
Final surveys, 541
Forced centering, 103, 136
Foresight, 65
Free net, 271
Free station, (resectioning), 135, 169, 515
Freeway, 431
Front-end loader, 481

G

General arrangement plan, 490
Geodetic datum, 50
Geodetic Reference System, 1980 (GRS 80)
    280, 235
Geodetic surveying, 2
Geodimeter, 18
Geographic information system, (GIS), 184
Geographic meridian, 193
Geoid, 337, 339
Geoid height (h), 336
Geoid undulation, (N), 336

Geomatics, 2
Geometric Dilution of Precision, (GDOP)
    320, 324
Geometry (coordinate) review, 551
Global Positioning System (GPS), 2, 19, 94,
    130, 223, 264, 430
    accuracy standards, 268, 306
    Active Control Station (ACS), 322
    Anti-Spoofing (A-S), 313
    applications, 332
    background, 303
    carrier phase, 313, 316
    Coarse Acquisitions (CA) code, 312
    code phase, 312, 313
    Continually Operating Receiver (COR),
        321
    cycle slip, 317
    differential positioning, 313, 318
    errors, 320
    field procedures, 328
    geoid, 337
    geoid height (h), 336
    geoid undulation (N), 336
    Geometric Dilution of Precision (GDOP),
        320, 324
    initial ambiguity resolution, 317
    L-band frequencies, 307, 312
    planning, 322
    Precision code (P), 312
    pseudorange, 314
    rapid static technique, 330
    real time kinematic technique (RTK), 330,
        341
    receivers, 306
    relative positioning, 312, 320
    reoccupation technique, 328
    satellite signals, 312
    Selective Availability (SA), 312, 320
    stop and go kinematic technique, 330
    traditional kinematic technique, 331
    traditional static technique, 328
    vertical positioning, 335
    visibility diagram, 323, 327
GLONASS, 311
Gon, 10
Grad (*See* Gon)